TREATMENT OF OFFENDERS WITH MENTAL DISORDERS

TREATMENT OF OFFENDERS WITH MENTAL DISORDERS

Edited by

ROBERT M. WETTSTEIN

THE GUILFORD PRESS
New York   London

To Stacey, Zachary, and Emma,

for play deferred

© 1998 The Guilford Press
A Division of Guilford Publications, Inc.
72 Spring Street, New York, NY 10012
http://www.guilford.com

Printed in the United States of America

This book is printed on acid-free paper.

Last digit is print number: 9 8 7 6 5 4 3 2

Library of Congress Cataloging-in-Publication Data

Treatment of offenders with mental disorders / edited by Robert M.
Wettstein.
    p. cm.
   Includes bibliographical references and index.
   ISBN 1-57230-272-2 (hc.)   ISBN 1-57230-552-5 (pbk.)
  1. Criminals—Mental health services. 2. Prisoners—Mental
health services. 3. Forensic psychiatry. I. Wettstein, Robert M.
RC451.4.P68T74   1998
362.239′086′927—dc21   97-42397
                                               CIP

CONTRIBUTORS

Jack Arbuthnot, PhD, Ohio University, Athens, OH

Howard E. Barbaree, PhD, Clarke Institute of Psychiatry, Toronto, Ontario, Canada

Fred Cohen, JD, State University of New York Albany, Albany, NY

Joel Dvoskin, PhD, Private Practice, Tucson, AZ

Louis Fulton, MD, St. Clair Hospital, Baraboo, WI

William Gardner, PhD, University of Wisconsin Madison, Madison, WI

Don Gordon, PhD, Ohio University, Athens, OH

Janice L. Graeber, MS, University of Wisconsin Madison, Madison, WI

Patricia Griffin, PhD, Wyndmoor, PA

Linda S. Grossman, PhD, University of Illinois Chicago, Chicago, IL

Thomas L. Hafemeister, PhD, JD, University of Nebraska, Lincoln, NE

Kirk Heilbrun, PhD, Allegheny University of the Health Sciences, Philadelphia, PA

Gregory Jurkovic, PhD, Georgia State University, Atlanta, GA

Susan J. Machkovitz, PhD, University of Wisconsin Madison, Madison, WI

Gary J. Maier, MD, Mendota Mental Health Institute, Madison, WI

William L. Marshall, PhD, Queen's University, Kingston, Ontario, Canada

Jeffrey L. Metzner, MD, University of Colorado, Denver, CO

Raymond F. Patterson, MD, Department of Public Safety and Correctional Services, State of Maryland; University of Maryland, Baltimore, MD

Robert M. Wettstein, MD, University of Pittsburgh, Pittsburgh, PA

ACKNOWLEDGMENTS

Many people participated in the development and completion of this volume, and I am grateful to every one of them. I am especially appreciative to the contributors themselves, who tolerated many requests to rework and update their lengthy chapters. Their efforts were much greater than what is usually asked of chapter authors in edited volumes.

The reader may not readily appreciate the contributions of the many people who helped bring this work to completion. Credit for the idea for the book, and its initial development, goes to James Cavanaugh, Jr., who evenutally passed the project on to me. He properly recognized the need for such a book many years ago. Each chapter draft was peer reviewed by colleagues knowledgeable in that particular specialty, and the able assistance of these reviewers should be recognized. They are Michael Arthur, William Davidson, Naomi Goldstein, Gary J. Maier, Jeffrey Metzner, Stephen Morse, Robert Pary, Robert Phillips, Vernon Quinsey, Stephen Rachlin, Loren Roth, Stuart Silver, and Renata Wack.

Finally, my thanks go to Seymour Weingarten, of The Guilford Press, who was amazingly patient and supportive during the time it took to complete this volume.

CONTENTS

ix

I

ADMINISTRATION OF TREATMENT PROGRAMS FOR OFFENDERS WITH MENTAL DISORDERS

Joel A. Dvoskin
Raymond F. Patterson

INTRODUCTION

This chapter addresses in a broad, yet practical manner the administrative factors crucial in the treatment of offenders with mental illness. In most respects, treatment of this population is no different from that of people diagnosed with mental illness who have not been referred from the criminal justice system. Thus, all of the usual mental health, psychiatric, and hospital administrative concerns[1] are equally applicable in providing services to forensic populations.[2] In addition, however, there are a myriad of particular administrative considerations required by the various statutes under which a person may come into contact with the public mental health system, as well as those required by the settings in which the treatment occurs.

This chapter is organized around where the services are provided, rather than the clinical or legal status of the people served, for it is the setting itself which has the largest impact upon the lives of the patients.

I

Whether people receive services in a maximum security hospital or in an outpatient clinic while living at home, regardless of legal status, *where* they live is often the single most salient feature of their lives. From an administrative point of view, location is even more important, and virtually all of the issues explored in this chapter are specific to the treatment setting. In addition to the patient's clinical status, treatment setting may be affected by many factors including fiscal considerations, culture, legal status, age, gender, and politics.

The first section of this chapter describes some general philosophical and political issues that define the environment and context in which services are delivered. The second section moves on to specific and practical administrative considerations offered to assist forensic mental health administrators in using their limited resources to the best possible advantage in serving both their clients/patients[3] and the community, and to recipients of these services and their families, who deserve to understand the forces that can so profoundly affect their lives.

CONTEXT: POLITICS AND PHILOSOPHY

The Dual Mandate

The dilemma facing every forensic administrator is the difficult dual mandate society imposes with regard to the treatment and custody of offenders with mental illness.[4] On one hand, politicians, courts, and the press have made clear their desire to have these "criminally insane" individuals removed from the community and thus incapacitated from harming presumably innocent citizens[5] in the community. On the other hand, the courts have made it clear that long-term restrictions on a person's liberty place several heavy burdens on the state, not the least of which is the provision of adequate psychiatric treatment.[6]

At first blush, these two mandates seem quite compatible, and embodied by maximum security hospitals. Maximum security hospitalization is expensive, however, and constitutionally limited in duration. States are allowed to hold insanity acquittees in maximum security only for as long as they remain dangerous.[7] The ability of clinicians to make accurate, long-term predictions about the dangerousness of individuals upon release has been repeatedly criticized and is, at best, unproven.[8] This inability to make predictions is compounded by fiscal constraints that limit the number of forensic inpatient beds and thus the number of people who can be served in this most restrictive level of care without creating overcrowded conditions that endanger staff and patients.[9] Further, as the mental health disciplines have improved their ability to provide treatment for people with serious and persistent mental illness, there has been an increasing acknowledgment of the incapacitating effect of years of institutionalization.[10] In other words, unnecessarily long periods of maximum security hospitalization could actually *reduce* a person's ability to safely return to the community. Thus, the best treatment may require progressive movement to less structured, more independent settings where a person can learn or relearn the life skills necessary for a safe return to eventual freedom. Indeed, most clinicians believe that the best way to ensure an eventual safe return to freedom is to allow graduated decreases in structure and increases in freedom and responsibility.[11]

These clinical and fiscal pressures to move patients to less secure settings are directly opposed by public safety advocates, who demand that the system "fix" these patients in the hospital *before* they are released.[12] Clinicians respond that to properly treat them, it may well be clinically appropriate to progressively expose them to increased freedom.[13] Finally, the stakes in this conflict of interests are raised astronomically by "spectacular failures"—those rare persons who return to the community to commit highly publicized, violent acts.[14] The fact that these incidents are rare does nothing to diminish their effect on public perceptions about the dangerousness of people with mental illness, especially those with prior histories of violent crime. Such incidents may also have a demonstrable effect as the impetus for legislative change, an effect graphically illustrated after the insanity acquittal of John W. Hinckley, Jr.[15]

The "fix 'em or forget 'em" philosophy has found graphic expression in states, such as Washington and Kansas, which have passed "sexually violent predator" legislation. Aimed primarily at convicted sex offenders who are completing their sentences, these laws allow states to indefinitely extend incarceration beyond completion of the sentence by "pathologizing" the tendency to commit such crimes, calling such tendencies mental illness, and invoking civil commitment processes to prevent postsentence return to freedom. A complete discussion of these laws is beyond the scope of this chapter,[16] but their potential negative impact upon forensic mental health services is significant. By attributing sex crimes to mental illness, people with actual mental illnesses will be further unfairly stigmatized, treatment beds may be wasted on people who are inappropriate for such treatment settings, and the chances that sex crimes perpetrators could gain inappropriate access to an insanity defense increases. This is not to suggest that long-term, even permanent confinement of certain sex offenders is not desirable, but such a goal is much better served by longer sentences than by civil commitment.[17] Finally, if civil commitment is utilized for such persons, their confinement and treatment does not need to occur in hospitals, which often have a variety of expensive requirements (e.g., 24-hour nursing coverage) that have nothing to do with the treatment that sex offenders may receive during their confinement. Rather, such confinement can occur in non-hospital settings, such as special treatment prisons, at dramatically lower expense to state governments.

In its extreme form, this tension between the public's demand for a complete guarantee of nondangerousness and the clinical desirability of a gradual return to freedom can result in a class of people who have been committed by courts to forensic hospitals, who seem to be gaining no benefit from treatment in a psychiatric hospital, whose psychotic illnesses, if they ever existed, have long since disappeared,[18] and yet whose prior violent acts—whether or not the person was found criminally responsible—are perceived as so heinous as to permanently preclude release. Given the established inability of clinicians to accurately predict long-term dangerousness, clinicians are of course also unable to accurately predict who will *not* pose a danger if released. Thus, in the case of a man who has killed and mutilated the bodies of a number of young boys, the public asks, "How can you even think of releasing this person when you cannot *assure* that he is no longer dangerous?"[19] More to the point, state officials will be precluded from doing so, whether through the courts, political influence, or public pressure mounted by the media.[20]

One way of examining what we do know and what we can predict is to give prediction of dangerousness a risk–benefit analysis. Arguably, there are four kinds of data about an individual patient that are of value in making release decisions:

1. *Severity of risk.* Prior acts, especially the offense that led to the current hospitalization or incarceration, tend to define the potential costs of failure to predict accurately. Therefore, the risk of inappropriately releasing a murderer is seen as greater than it would be in the case of a simple assault.

2. *Likelihood of risk.* It is this area in which mental health professionals have been most severely and rightly criticized, because the evidence clearly suggests that long-term predictions about individual dangerousness are more likely to be wrong than right.[21] Although these criticisms are justified with regard to absolute predictions, the case may be overstated with regard to relative predictions. That is, a person who has committed 25 similar assaults is far more likely to do so again than is a person who has committed such an act only once.

3. *Changes in the person.* Demonstrable changes, especially in response to treatment, can alter both the potential severity and the likelihood of a harm occurring.[22] This information may lessen (or increase) the perceived risk, but evidence of improvement needs to be more impressive as the severity of the offense increases. These changes can be attitudinal (e.g., "insight into one's mental illness," or a willingness to take medication and participate in other forms of treatment), physical (as in the case of a

person who has become nonambulatory and terminally ill), or rehabilitative (demonstrated new ability to manage one's behavior, resolve disputes, etc.). Perhaps most important are the general course of hospital treatment and successful adaptations to progressively less structured situations.

4. *Conditions.* Because violent behavior is an interaction between a person and his/her situation, the specific conditions under which the harm is more or less likely to occur have important implications not only for prediction, but also for managing the risk, or the conditions under which the proposed release is to be accomplished and supervised. These conditions can involve an almost unlimited number of aspects of the person's life, from housing to relationships to employment.

After gathering data within each of these four categories, administrators must adopt a decision-making process that will stand up to retrospective and, at times, hostile scrutiny in the event of a bad outcome. Throughout the nation, one principle has become consistently accepted in creating such processes: It is never enough for one clinician to make a release decision. The process must allow for multiple, independent reviews of each prospective releasee.[23] In many states, the process is culminated by an independent decision-making authority, such as a court or Psychiatric Security Review Board (PSRB), but even if this process is internal to the agency it is imperative that the final decision be made by someone who is not directly involved in the person's treatment. Multiple case reviews have a variety of advantages, but the most important is the most obvious: It is evidence of caution. Forensic administrators have found a willingness, albeit a grudging one, among the public to accept the fact that some risk is unavoidable, but a lack of caution is not; nor is premature release in the interest of the patient. Premature release, or failure to attend the obvious risk factors, is likely to cause the releasee to lose a great deal more freedom (in the event of another violent act) than is a more cautious release process.

On the other hand, there is no evidence that time in a hospital by itself reduces risk. It is imperative that the time be spent teaching the person how to manage his/her symptoms, identify and avoid high-risk situations, and acquire the skills necessary to survive in the community. A more thorough discussion of the role of treatment planning in reducing the risk of violence appears in the second section. Thus, a person with more severe offenses, a greater number of offenses, and thus a high likelihood of repetition will need to demonstrate a higher degree of clinical improvement prior to release, and upon release should receive a greater degree of scrutiny, supervision, and support than those with less serious offenses.[24]

Management of risk has been the subject of programmatic and research attention. In a retrospective look at published data on inmates released from Maryland's Patuxent Institution, Steadman interpreted the data as suggesting that the crucial factors in determining recidivism are the support and scrutiny devoted to released offenders in the community.[25] Several states have addressed similar issues in the provision of services to insanity acquittees released to the community, through intensive community mental health service packages, research efforts, or both. Some noteworthy examples are the PSRBs in Oregon[26] and Connecticut,[27] California's Conditional Release Program (CONREP) of outpatient programming for offenders with mental disorders,[28] comprehensive forensic outpatient services in Maryland[29] and Florida,[30] and New York's 7-year follow-up of insanity acquittees released to the community.[31]

Whereas the necessity of a nonjudicial decision panel such as the PSRB or even court review is not clear, a review of these various release decision-making processes reveals some important principles to be considered in safely returning insanity acquittees to freedom[32]:

1. *Discharge planning.* Release must be preceded by the preparation of a comprehensive release plan. This plan should involve not only the hospital from which the person is to be released, but also the agencies that will supervise treatment in the community. Each acquittee must be involved in the discharge planning process, as his/her willingness to participate in treatment is almost universally believed to be an important indicator of likely success.

2. *Independent review of release decisions.* Historically, forensic hospitals in some states (e.g., New York until 1980[33]) were able to release insanity acquittees as a purely clinical decision. Increasingly, the clinical team is seen as providing information and recommendations to more independent reviewers, such as courts, PSRBs, and the like.

3. *Outpatient monitoring.* The plan must include some ability to monitor the person's attendance at treatment activities and perhaps other observable behaviors which are related to their risk. These may include monitoring of urine testing for drug use, living situation, maintenance of employment, and the like. One excellent way to accomplish this monitoring is through some type of intensive case management strategy which allows for very small caseloads (such as 10 clients per case manager). Case management teams should have the capacity to respond to crises on a 24-hour basis and the "power to convene" the various individuals and agencies that provide services to the individual.

4. *Periodic or regular reevaluation.* Regular participation in treatment affords officials the opportunity to monitor the person's mental status, and to reduce the possibility that his/her condition will "tailspin" into a dangerous exacerbation of his/her mental illness. In the absence of regular treatment participation, periodic reevaluation visits are essential. It is also important to note that the length of the interval between these evaluations

must be guided by the person's history of violent behavior; that is, how long has it taken the person to "tailspin" in the past? Finally, if there is a history of certain illegal drug use (especially cocaine and other stimulants), the intervals may need to be quite short and accompanied by drug screening, as these drugs can change mental status for the worse quite suddenly.

Advocacy

Like all public human services, the context of forensic mental health services is affected in fundamental ways by finances. Adequate mental health treatment of offenders in secure settings can be expected to be more costly than psychiatric treatment in nonsecure hospitals or in the community. One obvious reason for this increased cost is the need to establish a secure physical plant with a secure perimeter, electronic surveillance, various communications systems, and the like. It is also likely that for offenders with mental illness who are released to the community, the public will demand increased scrutiny, supervision, and accountability. At the same time, good clinical practice will require increased support systems and intensified case management for clients whose prior histories include violent crimes.[34] These more intensive services require additional staff, and are thus more costly than the treatment ordinarily afforded to most other persons diagnosed with serious mental illness in the community. In the absence of effective advocacy, it is unfortunately likely that the additional security costs mentioned above would be taken directly out of the funding that might otherwise be available for treatment.

Generally, there are four powerful factors influencing funding of forensic treatment services: (1) concerns about public safety; (2) fear of litigation; (3) advocacy by forensic administrators; and (4) nongovernmental advocacy groups.

The public pressure mounted in the media by public safety advocates, victims and their families, and politicians advocating for public safety can sometimes result in increased funding for programs solely on the basis of their contribution to public safety. Unfortunately, this type of pressure alone tends to respond exclusively to the retributive instincts of the public[35] and can increase punitive programs at the expense of treatment and rehabilitation.

A second influence on funding decision making is litigation, which can push legislative bodies toward increasing funding for either treatment or public safety activities. For example, in right-to-treatment[36] or conditions of confinement[37] litigation, the state may be forced, via settlement or court order, to improve conditions, increase active treatment, improve quality assurance, and the like. On the other hand, the fear of wrongful death actions or other tort litigation brought by victims of released patients[38] may prompt states to fund increased scrutiny of releasees or to increase the capacity or security of forensic facilities to allow for longer lengths of stay.

The third factor more effectively balances these competing interests of treatment and public safety. In many states, the public mental health agencies, and specifically their forensic divisions, have battled against a long history of inadequate resources and punitive political philosophy to press for improved treatment, better living conditions for patients, enhanced security (both perimeter and internal), and community support systems upon release for forensic patients. They do so in the belief that balance between treatment and security, between support and scrutiny, and between the dignity of each individual patient and the public's right to be safe is the best way to make communities safer.

To be sure, the history of forensic institutions in the United States, up until recently, could be described as a shameful and embarrassing tribute to the human ability to mistreat each other.[39] Fortunately, litigation[40] in a number of states has led to dramatic changes in forensic inpatient treatment. However, even in recent years the efforts of forensic administrators to increase the quality of treatment have been hampered as forensic services compete with other nonforensic agency priorities such as services to children and families or other populations that have strong nongovernmental advocacy groups.

These advocacy groups were, for many years, almost silent on the subject of persons with mental illness in criminal justice settings. For many years, mental health advocacy groups largely ignored criminal justice populations, and prisoners' rights groups only occasionally focused on the special issues involving mental illness. Fortunately, this trend has changed dramatically during the past decade, a change which bodes well for the future of services to offenders with mental illness. In recent years, several advocacy groups that had previously focused predominantly on civil patients began to focus their efforts on the often controversial issues of advocacy for forensic patients. Specifically, the National Alliance for the Mentally Ill (NAMI) and the National Mental Health Association (NMHA), organizations with strong records of advocacy for people with mental illness and their families, developed specific projects and subcommittees to advance issues specific to offenders with mental illness. NAMI created a forensic network involving the strong and effective voices of concerned family members, as well as mental health professionals frustrated with the current system. Other organizations, such as the National Coalition for Mental and Substance Abuse Health Services in the Criminal Justice System, have been created to specifically address the intersection of the two large systems.

Accreditation agencies such as the Joint Commission on Accreditation of Healthcare Organizations (JCAHO) have incorporated practice standards with a specific focus on forensic issues. These issues have included training, communications/collaboration, privacy of information, and the interface between care and custody.[41]

Quality Assurance Standards

As various states have begun moving toward a quality of services for forensic patients commensurate with that afforded civil populations, the expectations of the advocacy bar and the patients themselves have risen accordingly. Thus, as additional resources are made available, expectations for the level and quality of forensic mental health services rise. The Americans with Disabilities Act (ADA)[42] is also likely to increase expectations, although the exact contours of this legislation are not yet clear.[43]

Despite the fact that forensic clinicians and administrators will be held accountable to any standards that are ultimately adopted, they have been at the forefront of efforts to develop such standards at levels that clearly exceed Constitutional requirements. One example is the American Association of Correctional Psychology, which in 1980 published standards for the provision of psychological services to correctional patients. These standards were purposely ambitious and designed to encourage states to improve the quality of such services, rather than merely to reify the level and quality of services that existed at the time.[44] In 1989, the American Psychiatric Association published its own set of guidelines for correctional mental health services, an exceptionally clear and useful document that any clinician or mental health administrator working in jails or prisons should read.[45]

For more than a decade, the State Mental Health Forensic Directors, a division of the National Association of State Mental Health Program Directors, has worked closely with the JCAHO to assure the appropriateness of existing standards for forensic hospitals and to develop new standards where necessary.[46]

The decision to seek accreditation is not without significant risk for forensic facilities. Criticism of forensic facilities for not seeking accredited status is rare or nonexistent, except in litigation citing constitutional deficiencies. The relative lack of reimbursement[47] (e.g., Medicaid, Medicare, etc.) for forensic patients removes the fiscal incentive to improve care and conditions, and many states have been unwilling to provide resources needed to achieve accreditation in the absence of such a fiscal incentive. Once sought, failure to become accredited or the subsequent loss of accreditation can prove to be both politically and professionally embarrassing. Finally, such a failure can have a devastating effect on staff morale and could even encourage litigation.

Nevertheless, many forensic administrators and state mental health agencies have found seeking accreditation a risk work taking. With strong leadership, managers can use accreditation as a rallying point to improve staff morale and erode what may have been a longstanding acceptance of old-fashioned or even sloppy administrative and clinical practices. It also allows staff an opportunity to demonstrate publicly, before an impartial national organization, the quality of its services to patients. Recruiting efforts, traditionally made difficult by inconvenient locations and dual stigma against mental illness and criminality, can be enhanced dramatically by accreditation. Finally, medical schools are much more likely to be willing to develop affiliations with accredited facilities, a consideration which has implications in a variety of ways, including recruitment, retention, and professional education of medical staff.

Programs as a Function of Legal Status

Traditionally, terms such as "mentally disordered offender" have referred to individuals in one or more of the following legal statuses: not guilty by reason of insanity (NGRI); incompetent to stand trial (IST); jail or prison inmates diagnosed with serious mental illness or in psychiatric crisis; and in some states, mentally disordered sex offenders (MDSO). Many forensic hospitals also include civilly committed patients (civil transfers) whose violence was unmanageable within nonsecure civil hospitals. During the past decade, however, forensic administrators have begun to creatively expand the scope of their responsibilities. This trend has extended forensic mental health services into the community, where more preventive programs have been designed to serve previously underserved populations and consultative outreach has been extended to criminal justice agencies. In this new context, forensic services have become more broadly defined as the area of overlap between publicly funded mental health services and the criminal justice system.

Although this expanded view of forensic services is still relatively young, the list of new and innovative programs is impressive. In Florida, the Department of Human Services funded and developed guidelines for comprehensive community forensic programs.[48] One of these programs, in Palm Beach County, used special forensic case managers to address the needs of patients of virtually all forensic legal statuses, including contacts prior to release from jail or forensic hospitals. The case managers reported a dramatic decrease in the arrest rates of their clients following assignment to their caseloads.[49] California has developed an extensive system of contracted community-based services, including intensive case management, for judicially committed forensic patients.[50]

A number of states, including Tennessee,[51] Virginia,[52] Maryland,[53] and Florida[54] have developed training and funding mechanisms to promote community-based forensic evaluations. Several jurisdictions, including Maryland and the District of Columbia, have developed screening and evaluation services in their courts and detention facilities. These community-based evaluation programs have resulted in better cost containment by decreased utilization of hospital bed days and resulted in the availability of forensic expertise at the local level. This has further resulted in more appropriate forensic referrals and improved relationships with the courts. Originally conceived as more cost efficient,[55] the contact between community mental health providers and forensic patients has also resulted in increased familiarity with and acceptance of these previously stigmatized (and often excluded) clients by community health providers.[56]

In New York, the Bureau of Forensic Sciences of the State Office of Mental Health (OMH) created a division devoted exclusively to community forensic issues. This division collaborates with other state and local agencies to address a number of issues, among them the following:

• In collaboration with the State's Commission of Correction and other agencies, a comprehensive, statewide suicide prevention program for local jails and police lockups has been developed. This program trains officers to identify high-risk inmates and facilitates the development of interagency policies and procedures for their management. Data since 1984 indicate a significant decrease in suicides within jails and lockups and suggest a marked increase in collaboration between local mental health and criminal justice systems.[57]

• In collaboration with the State Bureau for Municipal Police, a sophisticated training curriculum and program to teach police officers how to recognize and deal with mental illness and emotional crises in the community were created. The program includes joint planning efforts involving local police and mental health agency executives and the development of interagency procedures for handling law enforcement situations involving persons with mental illness or in psychiatric crisis.

• Multiple advocacy and linkage programs have been demonstrated and implemented to divert persons with mental illness from inappropriate incarceration. These programs adapt case management and generic mental health service models to identify clients, propose release plans, and then utilize interagency protocols to access existing probation and/or alternatives to incarceration programs. Each program works with the criminal justice alternatives that are available within their community. Complementing these efforts is a statewide training program for local mental health staff in the area of criminal justice interventions.

• A long-term relationship with the New York State Division of Parole has resulted in a comprehensive system of discharge planning and service linkages for persons with mental illness leaving state prisons. This system includes (1) procedures that guide OMH "prerelease coordinators" and parole staff in the state correctional facilities in discharge planning; (2) service linkages mechanisms to community-based mental health providers prior to release; (3) intensive case management services for parolees with serious mental illness; (4) programs in large, urban areas specifically funded to service, monitor, and link parolees with mental illness to needed services; and (5) inservice and basic recruit mental health training curricula for parole officers. Expansion of this program is being considered in the areas of prerelease programming for inmates with mental illness, allocation of housing resources in the community, prescreening for Medicaid eligibility, and Social Security entitlement (SSI/SDI) eligibility determination before release.

Other states have moved toward similar community forensic initiatives. For example, in Maryland, a presentence psychiatric evaluation program enables judges to order community evaluations of convicted individuals who may have mental health needs. This program has decreased inappropriate referrals by courts to mental health facilities and to private mental health practitioners. This has also facilitated effective communication between the courts and the state mental health system to assure that recommended services are in fact available and will be provided. In the District of Columbia, the Forensic Services Administration developed a 120-bed mental health program in the DC Jail with liaisons to the Lorton Prison and the St. Elizabeths Hospital Forensic Service. Additionally, a court-based clinic for forensic screening of pretrial defendants as well as a preparole team with liaison to the Division of Parole contributed to integrating services for both pretrial and posttrial individuals.

Services and Locations

The universe of mental health services for offenders can be broadly placed into the following categories: screening, evaluation, psychiatric treatment, rehabilitation, housing, custody, consultation, case management, and special treatments. Similarly, there are a limited number of settings in which forensic mental health services generally occur, including forensic hospitals, civil psychiatric hospitals, outpatient or community mental health clinics, and jails (including police lockups) and prisons, in addition to centers for persons with developmental disabilities and juveniles (both juvenile justice and children's psychiatric facilities).

Historically, psychiatric treatment of offenders, for better or worse, was not substantially different from that afforded nonforensic patients—generally, psychotropic medication and various forms of psychotherapy—though these services generally took place within secure hospital settings. Yet, there were some very meaningful exceptions. Certainly, the goals of treatment were more likely to be related to the legal status of the patient. Also, the treatment tended to be of much longer duration, as "mentally disordered offenders" remained hospitalized for long periods of time and at the discretion of the courts or treatment agencies. Finally, the violent acts that frequently led to the person's criminal justice status, and the public's fear of persons with that status, typically led to a presumption that violence is a psychiatric symptom, even though the violent behavior may have preceded any mental illness and may in fact have had little relationship to it.

Fortunately, the treatment provided to persons with serious mental illness has undergone a great deal of change in the past decade, as consumers, clinicians, and families have begun to question the "chronicity" of chronic schizophrenia. Although medication remains a cornerstone of treatment, many of the most exciting changes have occurred in nonbiological treatment, especially skill building and psychiatric rehabilitation.

Psychiatric rehabilitation represents a recognition of the limits of traditional psychiatric treatment and is largely the result of the psychosocial rehabilitation movement spearheaded by service recipients themselves.[58] When large numbers of patients were returned to communities during the periods of rapid deinstitutionalization of the 1950s, '60s, and '70s, it became increasingly apparent that institutional treatment had eroded already weak skills needed for independent living and that, absent those skills, traditional psychiatric treatment was unlikely to result in a greatly improved quality of life.[59] As a result, educational models were developed or borrowed from mental retardation treatment settings and adapted to fit the needs of people with serious mental illness. To some extent, forensic systems have lagged behind in embracing these ideas, in large part due to the long lengths of stay that continue to characterize many forensic settings.

However, the belief that psychiatric rehabilitation is ill suited to maximum security settings is wrong. For example, MacKain and Streveler described a large program to teach social and independent living skills to inmates with serious mental illness in a California prison.[60] Similarly, in New York, mental health programs within hospitals and prisons have successfully adapted psychiatric rehabilitation principles within secure settings.

Both to patients and the public, the most important service provided to offenders with mental illness is housing, and by extension, promotion of the safety of the community. The public has always seemed to demand that the "criminally insane" [sic] be isolated from the community, and it is their involuntary hospitalization to which patients most often object. It is important in administering mental health services to offenders that managers realize that the hospital represents a great deal more than the activities that occur within its walls; it is the act of hospitalization itself that may have the most telling effect on the lives of forensic clients.[61] Because forensic hospitals are frequently geographically isolated, hospitalized patients are likely to have little interaction with family,[62] even when those family members want to remain supportive. Even in the most progressive institutions, time and resource constraints require a great deal of regimentation, which many patients find dehumanizing to varying degrees. Ironically, the worst thing about life in a forensic hospital, according to many patients, is the company they are forced to keep. Patients are as likely as the communities from which they come to fear neighbors who have histories of violence.

Summary

The context in which forensic mental health services are delivered is a demanding one. On one hand, limited resources, legal requirements, and a constant flow of new cases continually force administrators to release people with histories of mental illness and serious violence. At the same time, however, the public (through its political and media representatives) demands that none of these people commit new violent crimes after they are released. As this pressure for perfection has heightened, forensic administrators have almost universally moved toward a strategy of *managing risk* after release through various mechanisms of ongoing assessment, supervision, support, and treatment in the community. When something does go wrong, which is of course inevitable, the combination of multi-tiered release decision making and careful case management after release is simply the best that can be done. Whereas public reaction to a bad outcome is never good, it is likely to be infinitely worse if there is not sufficient evidence that caution has been exercised.

PRACTICAL CONSIDERATIONS

There are several administrative issues that are in some way unique to settings that provide services to offenders with mental disorders, and include not only issues of administering services within treatment settings, but also administering forensic *systems* that often transcend those treatment settings.

Managing Facilities

Clinical Issues: Treatment Planning and Implementation

Traditionally, a weakness of the forensic services system has been an overreliance on institutional behavior in assessing the risk of future violence in different settings. The idea that compliant behavior in a structured setting predicts nonviolent survival in the community is, to say the least, counterintuitive. Equally illogical is the notion that a person who behaves violently in a crowded, artificial, social milieu of forced, congregate living would also get in fights if left alone in the community setting (such as an adult care home or a single-room-occupancy hotel). As noted in the first section of this chapter, even for repetitively violent people, the situations in which violence occurs are crucial in assessing risk, *and even more crucial in reducing risk upon their eventual release.*

Given the highly structured, artificial environment in which they work with patients, how then are hospital clinicians to effect risk reduction? To answer this question, one must first turn to the treatment plan itself.

It is important for clinicians to aim treatment at specific risks faced by individual patients. For nonforensic hospitals, these risks can range widely: homelessness, eviction, job loss, divorce, victimization by others, poverty, and the like. For forensic facilities, the most important risk to be avoided is the perpetration of violence. Unfortunately, however, this notion of the treatment plan as primarily focused on risk reduction is not yet a matter of common practice.

Traditionally, treatment plans have been based upon diagnoses and symptoms. Diagnoses by necessity look for robust conceptual categories and tend to minimize individual differences and styles. Symptoms, on the other hand, may be quite individualized but are generally limited to what is observable while the person is observed by clinicians, in this case during the day shift at (usually) large state psychiatric hospitals.

The treatment plan must be seen as a risk reduction plan, and one aimed at the most important risks and the factors that cause those risks to be high. We recommend the following steps to maximize the salutary effects of treatment upon the risk of violence:

1. *History of violence.* The team must first take a broad look at the role violence has played in the person's life. Each act of violence should be explored. The team should assess the circumstances in which the violence occurred, the relationship to the victim(s), the outcome of the violent episode, the clinical status of the perpetrator at the time, and perhaps most often neglected, the *meaning* of the violence in the person's emotional and cognitive life.

2. *Identifying and avoiding risky situations.* Assuming that the person has some motivation to reduce his/her level of violence[63] (including the wish to leave the hospital), the team should then proceed to teach the person the skills needed to identify and avoid the highest risk situations, *within and outside of the hospital,* in the future. Remember to focus on the aspects of situations that are most cogent to the violence. This process is almost completely analogous to relapse prevention treatment for substance abuse

and addiction, and must involve the active participation of the person (such as through a formal, signed treatment contract).[64]

3. *Skill acquisition.* Of course, some situations prove unavoidable. It is thus important to help the person identify the skill deficits that have prevented him/her from successfully resolving risky situations in the past. These skills may involve managing symptoms (via medication, cognitive strategies, etc.), social skills (e.g., negotiation, conflict resolution, assertiveness, etc.), or concrete life management skills such as those needed to retain housing or employment.

4. *Crisis resolution.* Despite a person's best efforts to avoid risky situations and to use new or recovered skills to safely manage such situations, it is essential to understand the inevitability that these strategies will not always succeed. Emotional or psychiatric crises may still occur, and the person may still find themselves in high-risk situations where their skills are not working. Rehearsing such situations requires clear and simple ideas about when and how to access help in a crisis. Thorough knowledge of mental health system resources (e.g., mobile crisis teams) and criminal justice resources (e.g., predicting the likely police response to requests for assistance) can be of tremendous value in such situations.

This approach rests on the fundamental truth that violence prevention, especially in the community, cannot be accomplished solely or predominantly by coercion.[65] It is not the things that clinicians do for people (or *to* them) that will reduce the risk of violence. Rather, it is what people learn about their own violence and how to avoid it that ultimately serves them and the safety of the community best.

Quality Assurance and Risk Management

As noted above, many forensic administrators have found accreditation a risk worth taking. This section will briefly discuss some strategies for moving a hospital into position to seek accreditation. Generally, such an undertaking can occur in one of two ways: as a conscious, long-term investment or in response to outside pressure. In the first category fall those states who, during times of relative stability and reasonably adequate resources, decided to raise expectations by seeking accreditation. This approach, although preferred, is not entirely without risk. Staff, especially management staff, may fear that taking on a major new challenge in the absence of dramatic increases in resources sets the stage for failure. Further, when things are going well, governments are often hesitant to entertain increases in resources in the absence of strong external pressures. Nevertheless, one value of this strategy is that by raising expectations, one can create the tension necessary for resources to increase.

The second strategy is to take one's chances and wait for external pressure. The most predictable form of this pressure is litigation.[66] Further, in response to criticism, predominantly from then-Senator Lowell Weicker (R-CT), the Department of Justice in the 1980s dramatically expanded its investigations into civil rights violations of institutionalized populations.[67] These investigations often resulted in highly publicized, adverse findings that were devastating to staff morale, and whose negative effects and subsequent litigation in some cases persisted for years. Whereas lawsuits and Justice Department investigations have also resulted in increased staffing, administrators involved are nevertheless virtually unanimous in their unhappiness with this method of gaining resources. This is not to say that accreditation alone will guarantee freedom from adverse scrutiny by courts or the Justice Department, but in a number of cases[68] courts have found JCAHO accreditation to be presumptive of constitutionally adequate treatment.

In selling accreditation to the hospital management team, it is helpful to stress quality assurance as a risk management tool. When release decisions go through a well-documented process with multiple levels of scrutiny, it is far easier to defend the reasonableness of the decision not only to the media, but also in subsequent litigation.[69] Similarly, the quality of medical records will determine the quality of testimony in support of release and other treatment decisions, as litigation frequently takes years to reach trial and memories will have faded. Extensive incident review also helps administrators to discipline and even remove abusive, dangerous, or offensive staff.[70] Finally, forensic hospital staff frequently have a great deal of justifiable pride in their own performance. When confronted with their apparent "second-rate" status as nonaccredited facilities, they can be motivated to join a process that will certify their competence before a recognized, independent agency.

One common obstacle to accreditation can be found in staff complaints of "paper treatment." This criticism is particularly ironic in forensic settings, given the high priority placed on proper paperwork and documentation. More importantly, the criticism is unfair. Whereas documentation is clearly a cornerstone of the accreditation process, the process also covers a wide array of specific and observable conditions that matter very much to the staff and patients of a hospital. The most obvious of these are fire prevention and other aspects of physical plant safety. Further, the consultative and educational aspects of the survey process invariably provide staff with valuable new knowledge about staff and patient safety and the treatment process.

Hospital accreditation is not the only form of independent certification of competence available to the forensic system; clinicians may also seek such status. Board certification in psychiatry, licensure in psychology or social work, and specialty certification in forensic psychiatry and psychology all are based upon standardized requirements in training, experience, practice, and documentation. Staff who achieve these levels of professional stature often demonstrate better morale and an enhanced sense of professional ethics and practice, and inspire their colleagues to seek licensure or board certification themselves.

Recruitment and Retention of Staff

The stigma of "criminally insane patients," and the resultant unwillingness of communities to accept facilities that house them, has historically resulted in the frequent placement of forensic facilities far from urban centers. Salaries in the public sector may not be competitive for psychiatrists, nurses, psychologists, and other clinicians. Many forensic inpatient programs are located in old, poorly maintained buildings that were designed for other purposes or as maximum security prisons, leading to unpleasant environments with inadequate office and program space. Finally, the stigmatized and stereotypical view of public sector forensic psychiatrists is of foreign medical graduates who will keep their jobs only until they learn enough English to make more money somewhere else, or of American psychiatrists who have broken legal or ethical tenets in other settings and have been deemed fit for no "better" classes of patients.

These are ugly myths, but they exist and present enormous recruiting difficulties for forensic administrators. Worse, they are cumulative and interactive. Ultimately, they can damn a program to mediocrity or inadequacy, as no program is ever better than its personnel. The extent to which forensic programs have improved over time is largely the extent to which they have found ways to deal with these difficulties in recruitment and retention of high-quality and appropriately trained staff. The following are but a few of the successful methods that states have created or borrowed:

- *Environmental improvements.* By spending money on rehabilitating buildings and increasing cleaning and maintenance staff (which generally *are* recruitable), forensic hospitals have been able to remove one of the major obstacles to creating a decent quality of work life for existing staff, and the promise of one for recruits.
- *Salary increases.* Many states have documented their inability to recruit staff for specific locations and have been able to secure geographical cost-of-living differentials, higher initial salaries within the existing range, higher salary ranges, and bonuses. In Pennsylvania, the largest forensic facility was able to obtain permission to contract for medical services at much higher salaries than the civil service system would have otherwise allowed. In Massachusetts, the entire clinical program of a forensic facility was turned over to contractors, again with dramatically higher clinical salaries than were available to the rest of the state system. In the District

of Columbia, while under the federal system, clinical work in forensic settings carried a salary bonus and earlier retirement eligibility, which were major factors in recruitment and retention of a highly respected and well-integrated forensic staff.

• *Academic affiliations.* Many mental health professionals of all disciplines value the chance to obtain respect and credibility through gaining academic appointments. In some cases, this has even been accomplished through institutions far from the university or medical school in question. The presence of students, interns, residents, and fellows is generally stimulating to experienced professionals and serves the added benefit of bringing new information into facilities. Staff also enjoy the ability to spend time with their colleagues who function predominantly in the academic world. More concretely, it is also possible to use university affiliations to legally and ethically increase the salaries of some staff by allowing them to earn money teaching. Finally, and ultimately most importantly, these affiliations provide a training ground for young clinicians who learn respect for the needs of forensic patients, the staff who meet those needs, and the rewards for doing so. Ultimately, such training programs are the best source for recruitment of clinicians.

• *Recruiting at national conferences.* Recruitment efforts aimed at out-of-work clinicians can sometimes be successful, but they may often yield clinicians with good reasons for being out of work. On the other hand, for leadership positions especially, the most likely people to provide help are those who are currently employed in other states and active in their respective national organizations. These individuals may not apply for advertised jobs in another state, yet they may be recruitable. National conferences such as that of the American Psychiatric and Psychological Associations are ideal places to recruit good staff. Recruiting is a tiring and frustrating task; it takes a complete commitment of one's energy at conferences. However, there is no better place to find a number of good, young candidates all in the same place than at national conferences. Additionally, recruiters should not spend all of their time in the placement office. Many of the best candidates, as noted before, are not out of work and can be found at scholarly presentations. It is enormously seductive to be actively recruited, and few people will ever have that pleasure in their life; there is great pleasure in knowing that they are needed and that they have been selected from the thousands of people at the conference. Finally, prospective employers should plan to fail much more often than they succeed. As of yet, there are simply not enough good candidates with the desire to work in forensic settings.

There is one other important aspect to the use of out-of-state travel as a recruiting tool. One of the consistent fears expressed by young mental health professionals when asked about working in forensic settings is that they will be "swallowed up." They fear that they will lose the intellectual and professional stimulation to which they had become accustomed in graduate and professional schools. Two of the best ways to put these appropriate fears to rest are the aforementioned affiliations with medical schools and the promise of some reasonable amount of state-sponsored travel to professional conferences. Other recruitment tools include provision of a varied forensic experience, with opportunities to work in community forensic programs as a complement to their inpatient responsibilities. Consultation/liaison opportunities to courts and attorneys, training in academic and community settings, and opportunities to participate in program development may be seen as stimulating by prospective staff and are effective additional recruitment strategies.

Recruitment can also be a problem in regard to "line staff." These are the people who generally staff 24-hour posts, and include not only nurses but psychiatric technicians, therapy aids/assistants, and the like. Many prospective candidates for these jobs may believe that the sole mission of forensic facilities is to provide permanent custody and housing. In fact, the reality is that the great majority of patients in forensic facilities, whether they be hospital based or corrections based, will ultimately return to the community. This reality demands greater expertise and commitment to both quality of care and community safety issues. Ideally, line staff in forensic facilities should be expected to have more preservice experience, education, or training than their counterparts in civil hospitals, and should receive higher salaries commensurate with these requirements. Earlier retirement eligibility has facilitated the recruitment and retention of staff in many forensic settings, and in addition can reduce the likelihood that aging staff may be injured by young, physically fit, and violent patients.

Capital Planning

Several years ago, one of us (J.A.D.) had the opportunity to tour a new forensic hospital which had been built after an expensive and exhaustive architectural effort to achieve "the state of the art," yet the results were frightening and operationally devastating. In brief, the facility was built in a way which guaranteed that whenever it was less than fully staffed, virtually no staff would be able to interact with patients due to the large numbers of required post positions to open and close electronically controlled access points throughout the facility. Elevators required operation from a central control officer who was visibly upset, distressed by the continuous buzzing of the elevator call buttons. A sophisticated electronic entry system was routinely bypassed by staff because it was "too much trouble."

The message here was obvious: Architects should not build buildings without input from the users. Experienced forensic clinicians, from treatment assistants to nurses to psychiatrists, know that the most important aspect of security is knowing one's patients. Exaggerated security measures within the building, especially those that prevent interaction between staff and patients, convey to both patients and staff the message that the patients are dangerous and should be sequestered. Both groups will, of course, live up (or down) to these expectations.

On the other hand, even older forensic hospitals with terribly inadequate security systems often operate smoothly because staff have learned to work around the building's defects by understanding and supervising patients. It is extremely important to understand the term "staff" to mean *all* treatment and support staff, including "professional," "paraprofessional," "line," "direct care," and "custody/security." An interdisciplinary team approach to the care, treatment, and custody of forensic patients is essential.

Before building a new facility or renovating an old one, the following steps are essential:

1. Talk to the staff who are currently working with the patients who will live there. Find out what *they* want in the new building. Generally, weight should be given to opinions in inverse proportion to salary, as the generally lower paid treatment assistants, nurses, and perimeter security staff are the personnel who are on site 24 hours a day and who have hands-on familiarity with patients and equipment.

2. It is highly advisable to talk to current patients in the existing building. Their knowledge of the building's strengths and weaknesses will prove extensive and practical. Further, their candor is often as impressive as it is surprising.

3. Administrators should visit other facilities in several states with a small delegation, including representation of direct care staff, perimeter security staff, and the like. These visits should include frank discussions of what the staff of these facilities like *and* dislike about their own buildings.

4. The Director or Superintendent of the new facility should be an ongoing and integral part of the capital planning process. This may require selection and hiring of this person several years in advance of the building's completion.[71] The architectural decisions made early in a project will largely define the operating principles of the hospital. Therefore, the most knowledgeable and invested people should have ample opportunity to contribute to the design prior to these decisions being made.

In renovations of existing facilities, the presence of construction teams means frequent, unimpeded ingress and egress as well as the existence of a variety of potentially dangerous tools being introduced within a secure perimeter. Although the forensic administrator will have negotiated rules for attending to such security issues as part of the construction contract, these rules may be new and foreign to construction crews. As a result, constant vigilance is required to assure adherence to the agreed-upon conditions. It is quite helpful in this regard to provide a security briefing to the construction workers, stressing the importance of security measures to their own safety. In addition, one staff member should be delegated to oversee the construction process as all or part of his/her duties and to serve as the single point of liaison to the construction supervisor.

An equally important concern is the impact of construction upon space currently required for patient housing or programming. As exercise yards or dormitories can be unusable for months, alternative arrangements must be made to ensure that adequate programming is available and to avoid or minimize overcrowding in living areas.

Perimeter Security

Discussions of security hardware must begin with an analysis of what risk the perimeter protects against. All too often, administrators fall in love with "bells and whistles," some of which can actually decrease security if indiscriminately or inappropriately applied. In one New York facility, for example, a bank of some 30 television monitors created a nightmare for staff, who found the array dizzying to watch. In fact, subsequent reviews and consultations revealed that a much smaller number of cameras and monitors would be much more effective. Although the appropriate modifications were eventually made, they were costly, slow, and should not have been necessary.

Security consultants are available who know a tremendous amount about securing perimeters of military installations, industrial research and development operations, nuclear reactors, and prisons. The latter group are most convenient, as every state has a prison system, usually with a capital and architectural staff who can consult with mental health administrators in their own state at no expense. These consultants will be able to provide perimeter security expertise. The perimeter must not only be secure from escape from within, but it must also be resistant to accidental or purposeful violation from without.

Generally, modern perimeter security systems include two barriers, usually fences. The main purpose of the inner fence is to define the so-called "no man's land," into which patients are not to go. Either the inner fence and/or the space between the fences must have one (or preferably two) electronic alarm systems which alert security staff to the fact that "no man's land" has been violated. It is important to avoid the use of easily accessible razor ribbon or concertina wire on the inside of the inner fence, as self-destructive or psychotic patients may use it to deliberately inflict self-harm.

The outer fence has two purposes. First, it prevents the facility from being entered from the outside. More important is its role in delaying for as long as possible anyone attempting to leave. Once "no man's land" has been violated and an alarm sounded, it is important that the potential escapee not be able to leave the perimeter quickly, before the patrol arrives. For this reason, the outer fence (and often the ground between the fences) is often made unclimbable by the use of fine (unclimbable) mesh, arched fencing, and/or razor ribbon or concertina wire (on the inside and top of the outer fence, where neither the public nor nonescaping patients can easily touch it).

Two approaches are commonly used to protect the perimeter while simultaneously dealing with predictable public hesitancy about the presence of a secure facility. The first approach is to understate the secure nature of the facility. This approach precludes the use of man-barrier razor ribbon, which is perhaps the most dramatic and potentially offensive symbol and tool of a secure perimeter. Instead, less offensive arched fences, frequently with unclimbable mesh, can be used in conjunction with "invisible" alarm systems such as motion detectors mounted on the chain link fences or underground seismic detection systems.

In the alternative approach to security, every effort is made to visually sell the facility as a "fortress" from which the community has nothing to fear. Facilities that select this approach generally use all the razor ribbon they can afford. Sophisticated microwave detection systems and frequent mobile patrols are also both effective and symbolically impressive.

The decision as to which approach to apply tends to be idiosyncratic to the community in which the facility is located. Few generalizations apply. Small towns in which the facility is impossible to ignore are as likely to require the "invisible" approach as they are the "fortress." Similarly, large cities in which it would be easy to "hide" forensic facilities are no more likely to favor the "invisible" approach. Some factors that appear to play a role are the facility's history (or that of its predecessor, if new), the presence of nearby prisons, the local economy (and its need for the newly created jobs), the community's general attitude toward corrections (law and order versus human services), and the posture taken by local politicians toward the very existence of the facility. Whatever the eventual outcome, the process should therefore include discussion and visits with local politicians, community groups, family and support groups, and impacted others to address their concerns in a realistic manner.

Small Forensic Units

In addition to the above concerns, a few special perimeter security considerations come into play in the administration of small forensic units that are part of larger state hospitals. Each of these concerns relates to the fact that the large civil facility cannot be treated as a secure facility. In brief, some obvious reasons for this include potential stigmatization of civil patients and violations of their right to a least restrictive setting (or at least reasonably nonrestrictive conditions of confinement[72]), staff and union objections to being scrutinized upon entry and exit, resistance of family members to visiting within a secure facility, and the security problems caused by constant movement in and out of the facility that is required to facilitate off-campus programming and community reintegration.

There is thus an immediate, built-in complexity to running these smaller forensic units; that is, the unit must maintain a secure perimeter within a campus that is anything but secure. To make matters worse, it will likely be financially impossible to duplicate all of a larger institution's services in the forensic unit. Pharmacy and food service, for example, are services typically provided by preparation outside of the secured area, moved via carts into the secure perimeter, consumed by secure patients, with dirty utensils returned to the nonsecure area. Further, the staff who tend to perform these functions, such as food service workers, are often in lower paying positions with high turnover, decreasing the likelihood that staff will have been employed long enough to gain a high level of trust.

The dangers presented by these seemingly innocuous food carts are predominantly related to the introduction of contraband weapons and drugs into the secured facility. Despite the relative infrequency with which such contraband is likely to be introduced, the potential for tragedy is great. The expectation of forensic staff is thus one of perfection. Even one street weapon coming in is unacceptable. Of course, the concern for the introduction of contraband into the secure area is not limited to dietary or housekeeping staff and services, but includes any and all persons, packages, and vehicles (from carts to trucks) that enter and exit the facility.

Whether in prison or in forensic hospitals, the rights of captives will be limited by the security needs of the institution.[73] Particularly in forensic hospitals, patient rights are reflected not only in law, but in clinical practice and accreditation/certification standards as well. Such privacy rights as the right to receive mail, visitors, and telephone calls must be evaluated within the context of a safe and secure therapeutic milieu.[74] Although the act of balancing privacy rights against the needs of the institution can be complicated, it is always a good idea to carefully document the clinical or security necessity of each limitation of a right, either in facility policy (if general) or in the individual patient's chart.

The safest way to ensure the safety and security of small forensic units is to exaggerate the perimeter security so that staff and patients feel safe enough to avoid an overly restrictive and oppressive environment *within* the unit. Adequate attention to the perimeter will convince staff and patients alike that they are safe. This safety is a necessity if one is to create a therapeutically appropriate environment in which treatment can take place.

To achieve this sense of perimeter security in a small forensic unit, a number of specific strategies will be helpful. First, it is important to have the same staff working the forensic unit day in and day out, both on the ward and as perimeter safety officers.[75] In addition to knowing the building's idiosyncrasies and the procedures on the unit, these staff will also begin to take pride in attention to small details which are essential to security. One way to achieve this goal and to maximize the staff's pride is to create positions for line staff and perimeter safety officers that are at a slightly higher pay grade than the corresponding positions on civil units or facilities. Such pay incentives not only promote pride as "specialized" and high-intensity services, but they also aid in recruitment efforts. A second strategy is to educate staff, both within the secure unit and on the facility's civil side, as to the ways in which the perimeter is protected. Security procedures should be few enough that they can be adhered to rigidly, to avoid the assumption that because a unit is small its policies are necessarily weak and overly flexible. To avoid or minimize the traditional polarity or "us versus them" regarding "security" and "clinical" staff, mutually respectful cross-training for all staff is essential.

In addition to these perimeter security concerns in small forensic units, there are some programmatic issues that relate simply and directly to size. Often, such units have only one ward. In the likely event that two patients develop a problematic aggressive or sexual relationship, the staff does not have the simple option of moving them apart. Similarly, when patients require specialized programs in such units, there is not an adequate "critical mass" of staff necessary to provide for the variety of clinical specialties necessary to meet the varied special needs of the patients. There may be no easy solution to this problem within a unit. In that case, it is important to understand that the resulting additional transportation or consultant expenses must be included in the annual budget.

Unions

Like many of the factors discussed in this chapter, labor unions have an enormous potential to help or to hinder in the provision of services to offenders with mental disorders. By negotiating for higher salaries and earlier retirements, the unions can assist tremendously in recruiting new staff and retaining on-board staff. On the other hand, in some states unions have made it much more difficult to terminate staff with whom the management of the facility is dissatisfied.[76] In states with strong labor unions, especially those with large mental health systems, there are usually a cadre of specialists in labor relations within the central office of the mental health authority. Generally they, or statewide agencies, assume the major responsibility for contract negotiation. The concern here is that there be adequate input from the program experts to avoid well-meaning but destructive contractual changes.

Rather than focus on contract negotiations, forensic directors are more likely to be concerned with day-to-day aspects of labor–management relations. The problematic aspects of labor relations, such as disputing terminations, will always exist. What may not exist is a constructive relationship with the unions, one in which they are constantly invested and challenged with improving the work life of their members and hence the running of the hospital. It is rare that a change that greatly benefits employees will not also benefit the patients. Generally such changes improve either the safety of the facility, which obviously benefits patients, or employee morale, which can have a dramatic and positive effect on patient care. To create such a relationship, hospital directors must look for issues in which the union's involvement will be real and welcome, issues in which both the facility and the unions have convergent interests. For example, time and attendance abuses among employees result in increased mandatory overtime.[77] Employees required to work double shifts with no warning become angry, fatigued, and even physically ill, resulting in more call-ins and mandatory overtime. Unions that are responsive to their members will search for creative ways to avoid the time and attendance abuses that start this destructive cycle. Successes in areas such as this, even small successes, can build a "safety net" of trust which will make the necessary disputes less destructive later on.

Similarly, labor and management should collaborate in planning for facility training, some of which may be funded by labor–management funds contained in the union contract. For example, Maryland's forensic hospital includes in its annual budget funds for training off-site for each independent unit, including staff at all levels and across all three shifts. The unions were a part of the planning for this training, and faculty include all levels of staff responsible for care and security.

Staffing Levels

There has been little in the way of empirical investigation of staffing levels or staff to patient ratios in psychiatric hospitals of any kind, whether public or private, forensic or nonforensic. In 1989, however, under the auspices of the Association of State Mental Health Forensic Directors (ASMHFD), Way et al. completed a national survey of all 50 states and the District of Columbia.[78] This survey included information about staffing and census for every public forensic hospital in the United States. The results revealed a national mean of 1.3 direct patient care staff for each patient, with a range from 0.35 to 4.0 direct care staff per patient. These data represent existing staff levels around the country and do not represent recommended or optimal levels of staffing. Several states have done their own staffing guidelines, but the national literature is almost nonexistent. Based on our review of programs around the country, however, the following is one example of a reasonable level of direct patient care staff for a 24-bed ward in a maximum security psychiatric hospital serving adults:

1	Treatment team leader
1	Psychiatrist
1	PhD clinical psychologist
1	Master's-level social worker (two in predischarge unit)
5	Registered nurses (one 24-hour post)
2	Clinical nurses (patient education, primary therapy duties, etc.)
20	Treatment/security assistants (four 24-hour posts)
2.5	Treatment/security supervisors
4	Activities therapists (occupational, recreational, rehabilitative, etc.; four 10-hour posts, 7 days per week)
1	Teacher

38.5 Total (direct care staff-to-patient ratio of 1.6:1)[79]

The above list ignores any number of special considerations, including the treatment philosophy of the ward, the average length of stay of its patients, and the availability of centralized activity and rehabilitation staff during the day. These considerations will affect the desired staffing levels, as well as the mix of professions on the ward. For example, a ward with more medical problems among its patients would likely require more nurses and fewer treatment assistants; a prerelease ward might opt for an additional social worker while giving up an activities therapist.

Several other considerations should be mentioned in regard to staffing. As noted above, forced overtime is an unmanageable and expensive burden to many programs, damaging morale as well as patient care. Some overtime is unavoidable, but excessive staffing on day shifts creates predictable call-ins due to illness. When hiring new staff, it is sensible to include evening and weekend work as part of the original expectations of the employee, not only among line staff but among the higher paid clinical disciplines as well.

Many facilities have successfully reduced overtime by the creation of "overtime pools." This practice takes advantage of careful data gathering, which often reveal that overtime is a quite predictable phenomenon during certain days of the week or shifts. For example, if an average of two patients per night are placed on one-to-one status during the night shift, it is wasteful to staff this function with overtime, which typically costs 50% more than straight time. In this example, a hospital would simply create two posts on the night shift for this purpose. The same practice has saved many hospitals money by reducing overtime that would otherwise be needed to transport patients to off-site medical or court appointments. Obviously, the most cost-effective use of staffing resources, which always seem in short supply, requires accurate and detailed data and the attention of hospital administrators. Finally, if central office staff wants facilities to creatively reduce overtime in this manner, they must find ways to allow the facilities to keep a fair share of the savings, to fund these additional post positions.

Transportation

Some security risks do not occur within the perimeter. Transportation services for persons under the custody requirements of the forensic mental health or criminal justice systems requires consideration of the individual's health care status, custody and restraint procedures, provision of services off-site, and potential interaction with members of the community. Transporting patients can have a massive effect on the facility's budget, primarily due to the use of overtime for security or nursing personnel.

Unfortunately, it is necessary to move patients outside of the perimeter on a surprisingly frequent basis. These trips include movement to and from courts, jails, prisons, hospitals, and outpatient clinics. Despite one-to-one or two-to-one coverage, these trips still present forensic staff with a difficult challenge to maintain custody of patients. The staff of general hospitals and medical clinics are not likely to know much about security procedures and may have a distinct antipathy toward them. Many will insist that restraint devices such as handcuffs be removed before they will treat the patient. Even in two-to-one coverage, one staff member or the other will occasionally be unavailable, for example, while using the restroom.

As a result, forensic administrators have come to view trips as a significant security liability. To mitigate the risks involved, we recommend several steps:

1. Despite any wish to avoid correctional appearance, it may be necessary to use metal handcuffs during the transportation of especially dangerous patients.
2. All staff accompanying the patient on trips must have basic training in the procedures involved in such trips.
3. Staff must be given adequate communication capability, generally via radio or cellular phone.

4. A clinical determination of security level must be made by the treatment team and communicated to the transportation staff prior to the beginning of any trip.

5. If possible, at least one person accompanying the patient should know the patient ahead of time, such as through ordinary duty on the patient's housing unit.

6. Administrators should take the time to explain their security requirements to the hospitals or clinics to which they will be transporting patients on a regular basis, in addition to becoming familiar with the physical layout of the hospital, clinic, or other destination.

7. It is desirable to dress the individual in clothing which will allow for easy identification in the event that he/she is able to break free of supervision and needs to be chased.

8. Depending on staff assessment of escape risk, it is often not advisable to notify the person ahead of time as to the time and location of his/her off-site visit. Such notification could allow the person to plan an escape with the help of outside confederates.

9. Cooperative relationships must be maintained with state and local police agencies so that, in the event of an escape, the response is quick and well coordinated.

Although these steps will not eliminate the risk presented by such trips outside of the hospital's perimeter, they will significantly reduce the likelihood of escape or injury.

Systemic Considerations

Budgets

One of the most important aspects of an administrator's job is to "sell" budget proposals to regulatory agencies (e.g., the Governor's Budget Office) and legislative bodies. It is unlikely that budget increases for forensic services will result from the kind of advocacy that can be anticipated with regard to children's services or other, more sympathetic groups. Nevertheless, there are aspects of services to offenders with mental disorders that are compelling in their own way, and lead to successful strategies for budgetary growth. The most important of these is to stress the public safety aspects of forensic mental health services.

As helping professionals, forensic administrators frequently feel a need to exaggerate distinctions between mental health as a human service and police or correctional work as public safety activities. Such distinctions are unfair to police and correctional agencies, who frequently and appropriately view their own jobs as human service enterprises. Further, these distinctions tend to alienate a potential source of support in seeking resources. As one example, in a Northern Virginia community several years ago, a community mental health agency began working hand in hand with police in a mobile crisis effort that had mental health workers operating out of police cruisers. The results were so positive that the local criminal justice agencies joined together to successfully lobby the local government for dramatic increases in the scope and funding of the program.[80]

It is not news when mental health officials solicit mental health funds. On the other hand, when sheriffs, police chiefs, and correctional administrators lobby for another agency to receive additional monies, the novelty tends to get instant attention. Additionally, liberal politicians, who traditionally support human service funding, and their conservative counterparts, who tend to support public safety initiatives, can often find philosophical agreement in this dual approach to the mission of forensic services.

The strategy outlined above should not be construed as pandering to public paranoia about offenders with mental disorders. To the contrary, in educating the public about our acceptance of our responsibility to help protect the community's safety, we are also helping to create a more receptive environment to our patients upon their eventual release. By seeking to market our ability to serve and to monitor our patients in the community, we can decrease police and public fear that offenders with mental disorders will be returning to a community without support or supervision.

In summary, the successful and creative forensic administrators will serve their dual mandate best by stressing the public safety aspects of the job as prominently as the human service ones. In addition, they should create allies and advocates among judges, police, sheriffs, and correctional agencies whose support will be politically powerful.

Planning

All state mental health agencies prepare annual plans. The benefits of planning seem obvious, as it enables programs to participate and ready themselves for expected short- and long-term changes in their fiscal, political, or service environments. Planning is, however, a double-edged sword. The destructive potential of planning poorly done can be significant, and its pitfalls are several. First, there is an unfortunate tendency for the *process* of planning to take on the appearance of a goal. The plan becomes a destination, rather than the vehicle to get there. A second pitfall is that one plan is usually presented to regulatory actors both within and without the agency, with the tacit or explicit expectation that the plan will be carried out exactly as written. But an exaggerated wish to hold managers accountable to their plans can result in rigidity and a loss of creativity throughout the system. A third pitfall has to do with the conflicting purposes of planning. On one hand, a realistic, reachable numerical target will allow managers to be held to reasonable goals. On the other hand, if the plan is meant to drive performance, to stretch staff capabilities, and to *improve* services, goals must be slightly more ambitious than projected performance. Finally, if managers use two numbers, which seems like a sensible solution at first blush, they will be accused by regulatory agencies of holding themselves accountable to "funny" numbers, whereas staff will whine endlessly about obviously impossible goals.

Despite these pitfalls, however, planning done well can improve staff morale, increase resources, bring agencies together, and extend the tenure of commissioners. Best of all, it is easier to do well than poorly. Here, then, are some suggestions about planning services to offenders with mental disorders:

1. Planning is the job of management. Use agency planning professionals as resources to assist you in fine tuning your process, but forensic administrators should plan their own services.

2. Planning must invest the stakeholders in the plan. Depending on the area of service, these stakeholders might include facility directors, unions, line staff, family members, affected state and local agencies, judges, prosecutors, and a host of others. Perhaps most importantly, the patients and clients who will ultimately receive services should have real and meaningful input into the decisions that will so profoundly affect their lives.

3. When investing in stakeholders, administrators should not pretend to be giving up their own authority. Stakeholders deserve to be heard, but it serves no purpose to pretend that they are calling the shots if you are not prepared to live with their decisions.

4. Keep your plan short enough to remember. If you cannot remember what you are trying to accomplish, neither will your staff.

5. Plans should be robust enough to withstand creativity in responding to unanticipated problems, but specific enough so that everyone will know what is expected of them. Successful plans will set realistic but progressive goals and compliance thresholds that inspire staff to improve. They reflect knowledge of the current state of affairs, a desired endpoint, a pathway and timeframe to get there, and a mechanism to evaluate performance. Perhaps most importantly, consequences, whether rewards or sanctions, must be clearly identified in the plan and applied as promised.

6. Finally, public officials should be skeptical of plans in which every goal was reached. Such an outcome is far more likely to indicate a weak plan than a strong staff. The planning process should *move* the system in

a positive direction. Thresholds for success should be realistic but ambitious.

"Dumping"

By its nature, forensic administration requires that services to offenders with mental disorders involve two or more agencies. Often, the agency primarily responsible for the person will provide them with housing. In addition to being expensive, housing a person often creates in the public's mind a responsibility for any future crimes the person might commit. Thus, there is often an incentive for giving responsibility for a person to another agency, especially with regard to those individuals who are most difficult to manage and/or those deemed to be at highest risk for future violence. In most states, offenders with mental disorders are seen as the least desirable population to serve. This disparaging characterization of patients is of course a predictable and unfortunate consequence when agencies feel that patients have been "dumped" on them by an irresponsible and unfeeling sister agency.

There are several reasons for the perception that offenders, even those with severe mental illness, require or deserve minimum service. Mental health and criminal justice agencies may not have similar goals for the management of individuals in their custody. Either mental illness or a known history of violent crime can cause a person difficulty in gaining acceptance into community-based human service programs, especially housing, but the combination of these two characteristics can pose an extraordinary hurdle. Further, when services, such as housing and employment, are supplied by multiple agencies, funding can be quite difficult to coordinate. Programs may operate under significantly different sets of regulations and with different measures of success.

The good news in the above scenario is that it is easy to be thought of as a "hero" by the other agencies involved. The agency that embraces treatment of offenders with mental illness can become powerful in a hurry. Receiving a "dumped" patient is frustrating and disempowering, but an affirmative decision to take on a "tough case" is quite a different matter. It is different in terms of staff morale; staff can begin to take enormous pride in being able to handle what other agencies cannot. In terms of planning, even though the forensic administrator may get more tough cases, he/she has seized control of the supply. Finally, when budget season rolls around, the willingness to take on tough cases, especially if they were successfully managed, can sometimes result in a wish among executive or legislative branches of government to expand such a valuable capacity for service.

For example, in many states, prison transfers are a chronic source of bad feeling between the Department of Corrections and the Department of Mental Health when the latter provides psychiatric hospitalization of inmates. By fighting about each tough case, there is bad morale among staff of both agencies, and someone always loses the never-ending fight for the "front door" to the hospital. If, however, the Department of Mental Health cedes control of the admissions process to the Department of Corrections, it can also begin to immediately set limits: "There are 200 beds here, and we will gladly admit and assess anyone you feel needs hospitalization. Of course, when the census reaches 201, you will have to take someone back." In return, the Department of Mental Health negotiates control of its "back door" (i.e., discharges). The problem of limited resources remains in this example, but now both agencies have power, control, and responsibility.

No interagency relationship will ever be free of problems, and this model is not perfect. There will always be areas of conflict between the people responsible for meeting the treatment needs of individual inmates and those responsible for keeping the prison safe, even when they work for the same organization. There are simply times when what is best for the individual is unacceptably dangerous for the group. Rather than pretending that these conflicts will not occur, it is better to build them into the service delivery system. Each conflict should be focused on the specific treatment or custody issue raised, thus avoiding the personalized charges of irresponsibility that are so common to correctional mental health.

One of the most common areas of intersystem conflict in correctional mental health occurs when mental health staff inform correctional administrators that an inmate "is not mentally ill, but a management problem." Such a response creates anger and distrust on the part of wardens, as they are painfully aware that diagnosis of a mental illness neither precludes nor guarantees that a person will pose a management problem; they are largely independent traits. Instead, mental health staff should be encouraged to respond with a positive statement, accepting responsibility for helping to meet the crisis while simultaneously reinforcing the warden's respect for their clinical expertise: "Of course we will help you out. Let me talk to the inmate and see what services seem to make the most sense." All that has been agreed to is a willingness to help.

In many states, such as Maryland, the maximum security hospital is operated by the mental health system, whereas outpatient and residential mental health services are provided by the prison.[81] Other models place responsibility for all mental health services within either the department of corrections (e.g., Ohio) or of Mental Health (e.g., New York). Though much is made of the question of auspice, it is far more important to look at the resources available and the way they are used in judging the adequacy of a prison mental health system. Whatever model is chosen, what is important is not each detail of the agreement, but the fact that each agency is clear about its rights and responsibilities with the negotiated agreement.

Another likely area for interagency conflict involves the treatment of offenders with diagnoses of both mental illness and mental retardation. Mental retardation (MR) systems have dramatically reduced their residential census as care has moved into the community. As a result, institutional care is generally reserved for the most severe cases of retardation. An offender whose IQ is 60 is likely to be seen, not surprisingly, as unsuited for the programs offered in MR institutions. This reality can be extremely frustrating to mental health administrators, who recognize the ineffectiveness of their programming for an individual with mental retardation.

On one hand, mental retardation programs, especially behavioral treatment and special education programs, can be essential if an offender is to progress. On the other hand, MR facilities seldom have adequate psychiatric expertise to manage severe psychotic illnesses.

The answer to this dilemma lies in an objective assessment of the two disorders and each individual's treatment needs, which will vary over time. Mental retardation is a generally static condition, whereas mental illness is subject to episodic variations that can be quickly responsive to treatment. Thus, in periods of acute psychiatric exacerbation, it is indeed the mental health authority who ought to take primary responsibility for treating dually diagnosed offenders. However, when the patient has been psychiatrically stabilized, the focus of responsibility should usually shift back to mental retardation experts. Again, it is essential that a clear interagency agreement, which includes objective and independent conflict resolution, be in place.

Prison mental health is not the only area where "dumping" is a danger. Local jails and police lockups also have prevalence rates of mental illness that far exceed the general population.[82] Unlike state prisons, where there is usually only one mental health provider agency, local sheriffs may have to deal with many different community mental health agencies and general hospitals. Further, the typically short lengths of stay in jails make it more difficult to get to know the detainee's service needs and history. The impact of these difficulties is particularly evident when there has been a bad outcome, such as a suicide in a jail or escape from the mental hospital, but is more consistently reflected by frequent rearrest and/or rehospitalization among mentally ill misdemeanants. Frequently, individuals are unsuccessful because of poor or incomplete aftercare and discharge planning.

Treatment of the "Misfit"

Despite our best efforts, in every setting there are people who repeatedly experience "treatment failures," patients who attract the passionate efforts of each new clinician and the cynicism of experienced line staff who have watched as these patients seem to chew up and spit out clinical optimism. Worse, these patients often account for frequent and severe injuries to themselves, other patients, and staff members. Although there are no good answers for these dilemmas, there are a number of ways in which the destructive potential of such situations can be minimized.

Much of the damage caused by these patients is directly attributable to staff fears of being "manipulated" by patients. It is ironic, to say the least, to think that a prisoner or forensic patient who is locked in a sideroom, perhaps in restraints, has succeeded in manipulating much of anything. To paraphrase Professor Hans Toch, when we put a person in (what is for them) an intolerable situation, we should not be surprised when they behave in the only way we have made it possible for them to get out of it.[83] In reviewing the care of these difficult individuals, the following suggestions will be useful:

1. The safety of these individuals, and the rest of the institution, is best served by the creation of a specific management plan for each. The management plan will include clinical as well as "custodial" interventions. Ideally, treatment teams should consider behavioral programs, especially cognitive-behavioral or social learning programs, that will teach the person how to manage his/her own behavior, thus reducing the amount of coercion necessary to keep the person safe.

2. More coercion does not always increase safety. For some patients, their fears of staff may be the direct cause of their violent behavior. For example, staff should be given explicit permission to "do nothing" when in their judgment waiting is the safest response.

3. Treatment team meetings for these patients must include staff from all shifts to reduce the cross-shift "splitting" common in such cases.

4. Where multiple agencies are involved in serving the person, regular meetings should include representatives from each provider, preferably with authority to make commitments for the agency.

Public Information

No matter how proactive and creative a state has been in conceptualizing its forensic service system, its plans will topple if crises are handled poorly. One of the most crucial elements of managing crises is dealing with the media. Many state mental health agencies employ a full-time public information officer who is responsible for maintaining relationships with the press and the electronic media. Nevertheless, when a patient escapes or dies under suspicious circumstances, when there is a riot or hostage situation, or when a former patient engages in serious violence, the forensic or facility director will undoubtedly be answering the phone, in some cases at a time when the public information officer is unavailable.

The most important step to take in dealing with a crisis involving the media is, not surprisingly, accomplished long before the crisis. To avoid the feeling of panic that inevitably ensues when one is unprepared for an interview, every public official should acquire the skills which will help to inform the public on issues about which it has a right to know while simultaneously protecting patients, staff, and the agency from the inadvertent divulging of appropriately confidential information. The official must also seek to respond in a manner which will not cause undue public alarm, embarrassment to the agency, or termination of that official's employment. Finally, it must be remembered that "no comment" has come to be viewed by the public as an admission of guilt. To avoid these traps, the spokesperson must be personally prepared and well informed both as to content and as to rules for making information public.

When the phone rings following a crisis, the following suggestions will be helpful:

1. Make sure to gather all the facts before making public comment. There is nothing wrong with truthfully limiting comments to "under investigation," especially when presented in the context of fairness to staff. Never speculate about causes, conclusions, or likely remedial actions in the absence of reliable information.

2. When in doubt, err on the side of confidentiality of patients, families, and staff. On the other hand, make it clear to reporters that you are giving them everything to which they are entitled.

3. If possible, buy some time. Ask to call the reporter back in 10 minutes or an hour. Use the time to gather thoughts into focused and clear comments which will be appropriate for public exposure.

4. Ask reporters about deadlines, and try to get back to them in time to meet their deadlines. They will appreciate your consideration and bend over backwards to treat you fairly.

5. Even in a crisis, it may be possible to "teach" the reporter about the requirements of the law, or good clinical practices that support the decision which is being called into question. For example, if a person was released pursuant to a careful and rigorous process, it is essential that the press understand the process that led to the decision, even if the decision turned out to be a bad one.

CONCLUSIONS
AND FUTURE CONSIDERATIONS

The role of forensic administrators, to provide treatment while protecting the public, has not changed, but the world in which forensic systems operate has changed remarkably. As a result, the settings and the strategies will continue to change at a rapid pace. As state mental health systems continue their move toward community-based treatment, the role of forensic systems will continue to expand. Forensic inpatient units and facilities will occupy an increasing proportion of state inpatient census, and a significant number of former patients released to the community will undoubtedly continue to have interactions with criminal justice agencies for some time to come.

As forensic systems become more important, there will be an ever-increasing need to manage forensic systems with safety, efficiency, and good psychiatric care. Discharge planning must be well documented and cautious. It is ironic but true that the dream of communities accepting and treating their mentally ill citizens is to a large extent dependent upon the forensic system's ability to safely manage those few patients who pose the highest degree of risk to public safety.

Similarly, the growing number of people with serious mental illness who will live and receive treatment in their communities will require creative new programming at the areas of interface between the mental health and criminal justice systems. Boundaries will seldom be clear when dealing with these areas of interface, such as police contact with mentally ill citizens, alternatives to incarceration for persons with mental disabilities, suicide prevention and crisis intervention in local jails and police lockups, and treatment of mentally ill parolees.

As the availability of more sophisticated mechanical devices for industry has benefited society, the availability of weaponry in our urban areas has promoted a rapid decline in public safety. To an unprecedented degree, forensic administrators must consider access to weapons, especially firearms, when preparing and approving release plans.

Improved technology for data management will enhance our ability to "track" high-risk patients. However, this enhanced capacity is likely to bring with it significantly higher expectations from a public that is increasingly unwilling to accept bad outcomes.

Forensic mental health is facing a period of unprecedented opportunity. Whereas the changes facing forensic systems will arise from judicial and legislative mandates, it is the executive branch of government, the mental health departments and their forensic administrators, who must provide knowledge of the past, a firm and cautious hand on the present, and an innovative and creative vision of the future if forensic mental health is to take its rightful place at the forefront of the public mental health system.

ACKNOWLEDGMENTS

We wish to acknowledge the following for their creative contributions to earlier drafts of this chapter: Michael Perlin, Judy Cox, Hank Steadman, Lisa Callahan, Paul Hillengas, Melissa Warren, John Petrila, Renate Wack, Robert Phillips, Hal Smith, and Beverly Wise.

NOTES

1. See, for example, Lion, J. R., Adler, W. N., & Webb, W. L. (1988). *Modern hospital psychiatry.* New York: Norton.
2. See section on "Programs as a Function of Legal Status." Generally, this term will be used to include those individuals receiving mental health services or with serious mental illness who are under the jurisdiction of criminal justice agencies or those whose mental health commitment was through criminal procedures such as insanity acquittal or a finding of incompetence to stand trial.
3. Throughout this chapter, terms such as patient, client, consumer, service recipient, and offender will be used to refer to those individuals, diagnosed with mental illness, who receive mental health services within forensic or criminal justice systems. We have made every effort to avoid using such terms in a manner that implies disrespect, stereotype, or stigma. Where we have failed, we ask the reader's indulgence.
4. See generally Hafemeister, T. L., & Petrila, J. (1994). Treating the mentally disordered offender: Society's uncertain, conflicted and changing views. *Florida State University Law Review, 21,* 729–871. See also Perlin, M. L. (1994). *The jurisprudence of the insanity defense.* Durham, NC: Carolina Academic Press.
5. New curb for violence. (1980, March 17). Albany (NY) *Times Union*; Locking the barn. (1980, March 15). *New York Post*; Roth, L. H., Aldock, J. D., Briggs, K. K., Dvoskin, J. A., Parry, J. W., Phillips, R. T. M., Silver, S. B., & Weiner, B. A. (1988). Final Report of the NIMH *Ad Hoc* Forensic Advisory Panel. *Mental and Physical Disability Law Reporter, 12,* 77–109; Dvoskin, J. A., & Steadman, H. J. (1994). Using intensive case management to reduce violence by mentally ill persons in the community. *Hospital and Community Psychiatry, 45,* 679–684.
6. Scott v. Plante, 691 F.2d. 634 (3rd Cir. 1982).
7. Foucha v. Louisiana. 112 S.Ct. 1780 (1992).
8. Monahan, J., & Steadman, H. J. (Eds.). (1994). *Violence and mental disorder: Developments in risk assessment.* Chicago: University of Chicago Press; Barefoot v. Estelle, 462 U.S. 880 (1983). (Blackmun, J. dissenting); Heller v. Doe, 113 S.Ct. 2637 (1993); Monahan, J. (1981). *The clinical prediction of violent behavior.* Rockville, MD: U.S. Department of Health and Human Services; Steadman, H. J., & Cocozza, J. (1978). Criminology: Psychiatry, dangerousness, and the repetitively dangerous offender. *Journal of Criminal Law and Criminology, 69,* 226–231.

9. See, for example, Doe v. Gaughan, 808 F.2d (1st Cir. 1986). The (district) court agreed that Bridgewater was crowded and lacked sufficient staff in some areas. It found that in recent years the population of the institution has risen steadily and that the crowding has had a deleterious effect upon Bridgewater's ability to deliver its services. Doe by Roe v. Gaughan, 717 F.Supp. 1477, 1480 (D.Mass. 1985). The court also noted that the reduction in personal space available to each resident, caused by overcrowding, tends to cause increased tension and conflict between residents. Id. at 1481.

10. Action for Mental Health. (1961). *Joint Commission on Mental Illness and Health.* New York: Basic Books. See also Kiesler, C. A., & Sibulkin, A. E. (1987). *Mental hospitalization: Myths and facts about a national crisis.* Newbury Park, CA: Sage.

11. Roth et al., *supra* note 5. See also McGreevey, M. A., Steadman, H. J., Dvoskin, J. A., & Dollard, N. (1991). Managing insanity acquittees in the community: New York State's alternative to a psychiatric security review board. *Hospital and Community Psychiatry, 42,* 512–517.

12. Mental-patient release bill passed. (1980, June 11). *Newsday*; New curbs for violence. (1980, March 17). Albany (NY) *Times Union.*

13. Specter, M. (1987, April 15). Furlough debate intensifies: Treatment, security needs often clash. *Washington Post,* p. A8; Roth et al., *supra* note 5.

14. Curran, W. J., McGarry, A. L., & Shah, S. A. (1986). *Forensic psychiatry and psychology.* Philadelphia: F. A. Davis.

15. Caplan, L. (1984). *The insanity defense and the trial of John W. Hinckley, Jr.* Boston: David R. Godine. See also Perlin, *supra* note 4; Steadman, H. J., McGreevey, M. A., Morrissey, J. P., Callahan, L. A., Robbins, P. C., & Cirincione, C. (1993). *Before and after Hinckley: Evaluating insanity defense reform.* New York: Guilford Press.

16. For an informative debate about Washington's law, see LaFond, J. Q. (1992). Washington's sexually violent predator law: A deliberate misuse of the therapeutic state for social control. *University of Puget Sound Law Review, 15,* 655–708, and Brooks, A. (1992). The constitutionality and morality of civilly committing violent sexual predators. *University of Puget Sound Law Review, 15,* 709–754.

17. See Hendricks v. Kansas, 117 S.Ct. 2072 (1997). See also Zanini, J. P. (1997). The treatment of sex offenders: Considering *Hendricks v. Kansas* for Massachusetts: Can the Commonwealth constitutionally detain dangerous persons who are not mentally ill? *New England Journal of Criminal and Civil Confinement, 23,* 427.

18. In 1992 the Supreme Court, in Foucha v. Louisiana, 112 S. Ct. 1780, precluded states from holding insanity acquittees who are no longer mentally ill, but individual judges are still pressured to find mental illness where most clinicians would not if such a finding is required to keep an obviously dangerous person from returning to the community.

19. See Perlin, *supra* note 4 at 133–138.

20. State drafts stricter regulations for mental patients, furloughs. (1980, March 15). Rochester (NY) *Democrat and Chronicle.*

21. Monahan, J., & Steadman, H. J. (Eds.). (1994). *Violence and mental disorder: Developments in risk assessment.* Chicago: University of Chicago Press.

22. Litwak, T. R., & Schlesinger, L. B. (1987). Assessing and predicting violence: Research, law, and applications. In I. B. Weiner & A. K. Hess (Eds.), *Handbook of forensic psychology* (pp. 205–257). New York: Wiley.

23. Poythress, N. G. (1989). Negligent release litigation: A proposal for procedural reform. *Journal of Psychology and Law, 17,* 595–605.
24. State v. Fields, 390 A.2d 574 (N.J. 1978). Note, however, the U.S. Supreme Court's apparent disregard for this notion in Jones v. U.S. 463 U.S. 354 (1983); Roth et al., *supra* note 5. See also Dvoskin & Steadman, *supra* note 5.
25. Steadman, H. J. (1977). A new look at recidivism among Patuxent inmates. *Bulletin of the American Academy of Psychiatry and the Law, 5,* 200–209.
26. Rogers, J.L., Bloom, J. D., & Manson, S. M. (1986). Oregon's Psychiatric Security Review Board: A comprehensive system for managing insanity acquittees. *Annals of the American Academy of Political and Social Sciences, 484,* 86–99; Bloom, J. D., Williams, M. H., Rogers, J. L., & Barbur, P. (1986). Evaluation and treatment of insanity acquittees in the community. *Bulletin of the American Academy of Psychiatry and the Law, 14,* 231–244.
27. Connecticut General Statutes. Section 17-257a through 17-257w (Enacted July 1985).
28. Armstrong, J., & Saito, C. (1986). *Conditional release programs operations manual.* Sacramento, CA: Forensic Mental Health Association of California, and Forensic Services Branch, California Department of Mental Health.
29. Spodak, M., Silver, S. B., & Wright, C. (1984). Criminality of discharged insanity acquittees: Fifteen year experience in Maryland reviewed. *Bulletin of the American Academy of Psychiatry and the Law, 12,* 373–382.
30. Dvoskin, J. A. (1989). The Palm Beach County, Florida Forensic Mental Health Services Program: A comprehensive, community-based system. In H. J. Steadman, D. W. McCarty, & J. P. Morrissey, *The mentally ill in jail: Planning for essential services* (pp. 178–197). New York: Guilford Press.
31. McGreevey et al., *supra* note 11.
32. See, generally, Wack, R. C. (1993). The ongoing risk assessment in the treatment of forensic patients on conditional release status. *Psychiatric Quarterly, 64,* 275–293. These principles are not limited in applicability to insanity acquittees, though persons found incompetent to stand trial are most often returned not to the free community, but to court for trial. See also Dvoskin & Steadman, *supra* note 5. This article advocates intensive case management as an effective approach to reducing community violence that may be associated with mental illness and lists essential features of such programs, including small caseloads, 24-hour availability, the power to convene various agencies and individual caregivers, and cultural similarity or competence.
33. Steadman et al., *supra* note 15 at 86–101.
34. Dvoskin & Steadman, *supra* note 5.
35. Oliver, C. (1992, August 26). "Wild Man" puts fear in folks on Upper West Side. *New York Post.*
36. For example, Wyatt v. Stickney, 344 F.Supp. 373 (M.D. Ala.1972).
37. For example, Ruiz v. Estelle, 503 F.Supp. 1265 (S.D.Tex.1980).
38. See, for example, Beck, J. C. (1985). *The potentially violent patient and the Tarasoff decision in psychiatric practice.* Washington, DC: American Psychiatric Press; Halleck, N. H., & Petrila, J. (1988). Risk management in forensic services. *International Journal of Law and Psychiatry, 11,* 347–358.
39. Scott v. Plante, 641 F.2d 117 at 128 (3d Cir. 1981), vacated, 457 U.S. 307 (1982). Discussing the Vroom Building, the maximum security forensic wing of New Jersey's Trenton State Hospital, the Court found the following:

There was ample evidence that Scott and the other inmates were exposed for twenty four years to subhuman living conditions, including poor plumbing with leaking pipes covering the floor with inches of water; inoperative sinks and toilets; inadequate ventilation; absence of windows or inoperative windows; inability during seven months of the year to go into the yard for fresh air; inoperative radiators resulting in indoor temperatures below fifty degrees; summer temperatures reaching 105 degrees due to absence of ventilating equipment; for a time availability of showers only once a week; and absence of hot running water in sinks in the cells. As to many of these gross physical deficiencies the testimony was not even disputed.

40. Doe v. Gaughan, 808 F.2d. 871 (1st Cir. 1986); Scott v. Plante, 641 F.2d.117 (3d Cir. 1981).
41. Joint Commission for the Accreditation of Healthcare Organizations (1994). *Accreditation manual for hospitals.* Oakbrook Terrace, IL: Author; Joint Commission for the Accreditation of Healthcare Organizations. (1994). *Mental health accreditation manual.* Oakbrook Terrace, IL: Author.
42. U.S.C.12101 et seq.
43. See generally Perlin, M. L. (1993). The ADA and persons with mental disabilities: Can sanist attitudes be undone? *Journal of Law and Health, 8,* 15–45; and Cornwell, J. K. (1996). Confining mentally disordered "super criminals": A realignment of rights in the nineties. *Houston Law Review, 33,* 651–730.
44. American Association of Correctional Psychology. (1980). *Standards for psychology services in adult jails and prisons.* Beverly Hills, CA: Sage.
45. American Psychiatric Association. (1989). *Psychiatric services in jails and prisons: Report of the Task Force on Psychiatric Services in Jails and Prisons.* Washington, DC: Author.
46. The receptiveness of the JCAHO to this effort is in large part due to the efforts of Marvin Chapman, MD. As Wisconsin's longtime Director of Forensic Services and a surveyor for the JCAHO, Dr. Chapman has lobbied with forensic facilities all over the country to accept the challenge of seeking accreditation while simultaneously helping the JCAHO to make its standards meaningful and realistic in light of the many special features of forensic hospitals. See also Joint Commission for the Accreditation of Healthcare Organizations, *supra* note 41.
47. Whitlock, M (1993) *Forensic services: The next generation or deep space nine?* Unpublished manuscript, Department of Mental Health and Mental Retardation, Vernon State Hospital, TX.
48. Wright, J. J., & Sherwood, A. (1985). *Suggested components of a community forensic mental health program.* Unpublished manuscript, Florida Alcohol, Drug Abuse and Mental Health Program Office, Tallahassee, FL.
49. Dvoskin, *supra* note 30.
50. Armstrong & Saito, *supra* note 28. See also Dvoskin & Steadman, *supra* note 5.
51. Laben, J. K., Kashgarian, M., Nessa, D. B., & Spencer, L. D. (1977). Reform from the inside: Mental health center evaluations of competency to stand trial. *Journal of Clinical Psychology, 5,* 52–62.
52. Melton, G. B., Weithorn, L. A., & Slobogin, C. (1985). *Community mental health centers and the courts: An evaluation of community-based forensic services.* Lincoln, NE: University of Nebraska Press.
53. Wise, B. (1994). *Summary of Maryland community forensic programs.* Unpublished manuscript, Department of Health and Mental Hygiene, Clifton T. Perkins Hospital Center, Jessup, MD.

54. Wright & Sherwood, *supra* note 48.

55. Melton, Weithorn, & Slobogin, *supra* note 52.

56. One clinician was quoted as calling insanity acquittees "the most despised and feared group in society," (p. 982); Scott, D. C., Zonana, H. V., & Getz, M. A. (1989). Monitoring insanity acquittees: Connecticut's Psychiatric Security Review Board. *Hospital and Community Psychiatry, 41,* 980–984.

57. Cox, J. F., Landsberg, G., & Pravati, M. P. (1989). The essential components of a crisis intervention program for local jails: The New York local forensic suicide prevention crisis service model. *Psychiatric Quarterly, 60,* 103–117.

58. Roger, E. S., Anthony, W., & Jansen, M. A. (1988). Psychiatric rehabilitation as the preferred response to the needs of individuals with severe psychiatric disability. *Rehabilitation Psychology, 33,* 5–13.

59. Kiesler & Sibulkin, *supra* note 10.

60. MacKain, S. J., & Streveler, A. (1990). Social and independent living skills for psychiatric patients in a prison setting. *Behavior Modification, 14,* 490–518.

61. Kiesler & Sibulkin, *supra* note 10.

62. Johnson by Johnson v. Brelje, 701 F.2d. 1201 (7th Cir. 1983).

63. If there is no motivation at all to participate in this process, then the goal of treatment becomes simply to inform the person regarding the relative costs and benefits of violence. This task is made easier because they will, by definition, have lost their freedom due to the latest violent act.

64. See Hall, S. M., Wasserman, D. A., & Havassey, B. E. (1991). Relapse prevention. *NIDA Research Monograph, 106,* 275–293. See also Wack, R. C. (1993). The ongoing risk assessment in the treatment of forensic patients on conditional release status. *Psychiatric Quarterly, 64,* 275–293.

65. Dvoskin & Steadman, *supra* note 5.

66. Perlin, M. L., Gould, K. K., & Dorfman, D. A. (1995). Therapeutic jurisprudence and the civil rights of institutionalized mentally disabled persons: Hopeless oxymoron or path to redemption? *Psychology, Public Policy and Law, 1,* 80–119.

67. Hammersley, M. (1988, February 6). State claims U.S. suit is in bad faith. *Buffalo News*. Perlin, M. L. (1989). *Mental disability law: Civil and criminal* (Vol. 2). Charlottesville, VA: Michie.

68. Woe v. Cuomo, 729 F.2d 96 (2d Cir. 1984). See also Cospito v. Heckler, 742 F. 2d. 72 (3rd Cir. 1984), cert. denied 471 U.S. 1131 (1985).

69. Poythress, N. (1987). Avoiding negligent release: A risk management strategy. *Hospital and Community Psychiatry, 38,* 1051–1052.

70. Goodwin v. Shapiro, 545 F. Supp 826 (D.N.J. 1982).

71. Of course, this responsibility may not be a full-time job. The person selected to direct the new facility will be available for other duties prior to the opening of the new facility, often as Deputy or Acting Director of another psychiatric hospital.

72. See Perlin, Gould, & Dorfman, *supra* note 66. Youngberg v. Romeo, 644 F.2d 147 (3d Cir. 1980), vacated 457 U.S. 307 (1982).

73. For a general discussion of the rights of captives, see Cohen, F. (1991). *Law of deprivation of liberty,* Durham, NC. Carolina Academic Press, especially Chapter 4 (dealing with the comparative rights of captives who are in civil or criminal status). This issue is especially complicated when dealing with captives under two different legal statuses at the same time. Cameron v. Tomes, 783 F. Supp. 1511, (D.Mass. 1992), aff'd as mod, 990 F.2d. 14 (1st Cir. 1993).

74. Roth et al., *supra* note 5, at 92–94, 101–102.

75. Similarly, in large facilities with multiple levels of security, the ability to consistently staff units with the same staff members is crucial. Unit-based staff allows each team to define and promote consistency of the milieu and to develop a therapeutic culture among each treatment team.

76. To be fair, unions are likely to argue that management's difficulty in terminating employees stems predominantly from its failure to fairly and appropriately document poor performance, and that the union's contribution is to assure a fair process. It is not our intention to debate the two sides of this old argument, but merely to point out that strong unions can, rightly or wrongly, make it more difficult to terminate staff. See, for example, N.Y. State Association for Retarded Children, Inc. v. Carey, 456 F. Supp. 85 (E.D.N.Y.1978), where the court held that constitutional rights prevail over labor–management contracts or civil service rules.

77. Overtime *per se* can be a valued source of additional income for staff, so it is not wise to count on Union cooperation in reducing all overtime, but mandated overtime is almost universally resented by staff, as it interferes with social and family lives as well as with second jobs.

78. Way, B. B., Dvoskin, J. A., Steadman, H. J., Huguley, H., & Banks, S. (1990). Staffing of forensic inpatient psychiatric services in the United States. *Hospital and Community Psychiatry, 41,* 172–174.

79. This refers only to direct care staff on the unit, across all three shifts and including relief. It assumes the presence of support services staff, including nonpsychiatric (physical) medical, pharmacy, dental, clerical, housecleaning, medical records, food service, and educational services.

80. Dunn, C. S., & Steadman, H. J. (Eds.). (1982) *Mental health services in local jails: Report of a special national workshop. Crime and delinquency issues: A monograph.* Washington, DC: United States Departments of Health and Human Services and Alcohol, Drug Abuse and Mental Health Administration.

81. For a more complete discussion of mental health services in prisons, see Dvoskin, J. A. (1994). The structure of prison mental health services. In R. Rosner (Ed.), *Principals and practice of forensic psychiatry.* New York: Chapman and Hall; and Cohen, F., & Dvoskin, J. A. (1992). Inmates with mental disorders: A guide to law and practice. *Mental and Physical Disability Law Reporter, 16,* 339–346, 462–470.

82. For a more detailed description of mental health services in local jails, see Dvoskin, J. (1990). Jail-based mental health services. In H. J. Steadman (Ed.), *Effectively addressing the mental health needs of jail detainees.* Boulder, CO: National Institute of Corrections.

83. Toch, H. (1984, November 24). Personal communication.

2

LEGAL ASPECTS OF THE TREATMENT OF OFFENDERS WITH MENTAL DISORDERS

Thomas L. Hafemeister

INTRODUCTION

The law reflects the society that generates it with the attitudes of society, accurate or not, often dictating that law.[1] When there are multiple and conflicting attitudes, the law can become a complex matrix attempting to accommodate diverse perspectives. In addition, different perspectives may prevail during different circumstances or times.

This interplay between diverse perspectives is particularly pronounced in the law pertaining to the treatment of offenders with mental disorders, individuals with mental disorders who are either charged with or convicted of committing a crime. This treatment has received close public and legal scrutiny in recent years. However, this scrutiny does not appear to have helped settle related legal issues; if anything, it has led to continuing fluctuations as the law attempts to accommodate these various perspectives. Offenders with mental disorders are often envisioned as individuals who violently, unexpectedly, and without reason attack innocent victims. Furthermore, the system supposedly treating them is seen as neither reducing the likelihood of future danger nor as protecting society from it. For others, however, offenders with mental disorders trigger sympathy as victims of impulses over which they have little control and as caught in a system they do not understand, which fails to respond to their unique needs. This divergence is frequently reflected in the law and may leave treatment professionals uncertain as to what is expected of them, but concerned that they will be subject to legal liability if they make the wrong choice.

EVOLUTION OF THE LAW

Pre-Civil Rights Movement

The treatment of offenders with mental disorders was not always closely scrutinized. Historically, little public attention was given to them, perhaps because systems were in place with broad discretion to quickly and quietly remove a dangerous, "crazy" person from the community, sometimes even before a criminal act occurred.

For example, the criminal justice system could discreetly "sweep up" offenders. Individuals could be taken into custody on the arresting officer's judgment that an individual was disruptive, offensive, or likely to commit a criminal act, and he/she could be charged with a relatively indeterminate crime or a "status offense" such as vagrancy. Criminal suspects were provided relatively few protections during investigations (e.g., law enforcement officials had wide latitude in obtaining confessions). Criminal sanctions could be enhanced for individuals perceived as particularly threatening. Once incarcerated, the focus was assuring secure custody at minimal cost.

The mental health system had a similar ability to cast a wide net. Civil commitment criteria tended to be broad and applied liberally. Once initiated, commitment was difficult to resist, with few procedural protections. Individuals committed had few rights and little input into their treatment. Treatment staff wielded great control over admission and release decisions, with few external checks, and long-term custody was the norm. Emphasis was placed on minimizing any potential danger to the community.

Thus, if society felt frightened or uneasy about a "crazy" person, ready avenues were available for removing that person from society. Because society was effectively insulated from offenders with mental disorders and the offenders had virtually no voice of their own, their treatment received little attention.

Civil Rights Movement

During the 1960s and 1970s attention was given to the rights and interests of individuals who traditionally had been voiceless and powerless, including offenders with mental disorders. This had the effect of diminishing the prior emphasis on protecting society.

On the criminal justice side, punishment for a status offense was ruled unconstitutional. Sanctions were limited to specific forbidden acts, with the likelihood of criminal behavior generally considered an insufficient basis for prosecution. Laws such as vagrancy laws with a broad sweep and the potential for arbitrary and discriminatory enforcement were struck down as unconstitutionally vague. Indigent defendants were guaranteed counsel. Close review was taken of confessions and waivers of rights in general. A series of rights associated with arrest and trial were recognized.[2] A defendant could not be held indefinitely while waiting for trial, even after an initial judicial determination of incompetence to stand trial. Increased scrutiny of a defendant's competence to participate at trial and to assist his/her attorney was mandated. The proportionality of sentences was examined more closely. Many of these rulings enhancing protections for criminal defendants did not address offenders with mental disorders specifically, but they reduced the likelihood that they would be subject to criminal sanctions and limited the criminal justice system's ability to remove offenders from the community.

A series of landmark cases (albeit somewhat later) placed similar restrictions on using the mental health system to remove offenders with mental disorders from the community. Increased attention was given to the negative implications of civil commitment, and narrower and more precise criteria for civil commitment were imposed. Some courts required proof of a recent, overt act demonstrating the need for commitment, thereby preventing commitment in anticipation of dangerous behavior. Greater evidentiary showings that individuals met the commitment criteria were required. The decision-making process shifted from an informal, unrecorded hospital decision to a relatively formal, adversarial hearing generally before a judge. Notice and an opportunity to be heard were mandated, with maximum periods of time established for detaining an individual without a hearing. Numerous procedural rights associated with the hearing itself were also guaranteed.[3] Less restrictive alternatives to involuntary hospitalization sometimes had to be formally considered, with mandatory periodic reviews of commitment decisions and means established for committed individuals to challenge their commitment. Finally, although not widely recognized, some courts did assert that a "right to treatment" accompanied involuntary civil commitment. These changes, at least on their face, had the effect of making involuntary hospitalization more difficult to impose and maintain.

While these developments in the criminal justice and mental health systems were progressing, there was initially little attention given to their impact on offenders, individuals who, although candidates for both systems, were in many ways appropriate for neither. Ultimately, however, the treatment of offenders with mental disorders received closer scrutiny. From the mid-1960s through the 1970s a similar evolution occurred affecting their treatment. During this era judicial decisions relied on four premises that led to a shift away from an emphasis on the security interests of the community and toward a recognition of the individual rights of offenders with mental disorders.

Equal Protection of the Law

Offenders with mental disorders, regardless of their criminal behavior, were found to be entitled generally to the same substantive and procedural rights as similarly situated individuals. For example, in 1966 the U.S. Supreme Court ruled that a prison inmate, upon the completion of his/her prison term, could not be directly placed in a psychiatric facility without being afforded the same procedural protections as any other individual being civilly committed.[4] Whereas the individual's criminal history could be considered in determining the type of care and housing subsequently provided, it was not dispositive with regard to the initial decision on whether the individual was subject to civil commitment. Six years later, the Supreme Court, in rejecting the indefinite commitment to a psychiatric facility of someone found incompetent to stand trial (IST) on criminal charges, noted that criminal inmates, insanity acquittees, and sex offenders had all been found by various courts to be entitled to the same protections against indefinite psychiatric commitment as civil patients.[5]

Disparagement of the Clinician's Skills

A second premise frequently appearing during this era was that clinicians' diagnostic and prognostic skills were generally unreliable, particularly when it came to predicting dangerousness. This premise led to a heightening of the showing required for the involuntary commitment of offenders with mental disorders. For example, the Supreme Court of California extensively reviewed research on the reliability of clinical predictions in determining that a more demanding standard of proof was required for committing sex offenders with mental disorders.[6] The court concluded that clinicians experience considerable difficulty in diagnosing mental illness, even more so when attempting to predict the consequences of such illness.

The Judiciary as the Primary Decision Maker

A third recurring theme was that judges or juries, rather than clinicians, should be primarily responsible for determining whether offenders should enter the mental health system. The courts suggested that clinicians were not sufficiently reliable or unbiased to be entrusted with a decision of such great importance to the freedom of an individual. In addition, courts determined that this was not a clinical decision per se, but rather a societal determination regarding the necessity of removing an individual from the community for the safety of the individual or others. As such, it was appropriate and necessary to assign this responsibility to a body of individuals more fully representing society, that is, judges and juries.

Least Restrictive Alternative

A fourth premise that received some, albeit hesitant, recognition was that the least restrictive treatment alternative (LRA) should be employed. Some courts believed that fairness dictated that LRAs be considered because an order of commitment could greatly curtail the individual's freedom and it carried an implicit promise of treatment. Although this approach received more attention in civil commitment cases, it did carry over to the cases of offenders with mental disorders to some degree. The courts' hesitancy to endorse it with regard to offenders with mental disorders was perhaps because it made a relatively quick return of offenders to the community more likely. During this era there tended to be limited alternatives to institutional confinement for offenders, and, from the community's perspective, those that did exist (e.g., supervised community placement) were virtually indistinguishable from total discharge. Despite a growing recognition of the individual rights of offenders with mental disorders, this approach was likely seen as having the greatest potential for placing the community at risk from them.[7]

Impact

During this era, paralleling a general trend of increased recognition of the rights of the disadvantaged, the rights of offenders with mental disorders received greater attention. This, in turn, contributed to a number of changes in processing them. For example, a number of jurisdictions began to decentralize their forensic services, moving from a maximum security model for the evaluation and treatment of offenders with mental disorders to a mixed-model paradigm providing services in a range of environments. Offenders with mental disorders were more frequently placed in less secure settings and cared for on the same basis as civilly committed psychiatric patients. Evaluations were done increasingly in outpatient settings. In addition, a wide range of procedural protections were instituted to ensure that offenders received a fair hearing on commitment and release decisions.

However, changes during this period focused on selected aspects of the legal system's processing of offenders with mental disorders. Attention was given mainly to the initial steps taken to remove offenders from the community, and, to a lesser extent, the potential for indefinite psychiatric commitment. Little attention was given to the actual care provided the individual. In the era that followed, this issue would assume greater importance. At the same time, courts would ease barriers to the commitment of offenders with mental disorders and become more reluctant to order release.

Premises of the 1980s and 1990s

During the 1980s and 1990s judicial attitudes toward offenders with mental disorders changed, particularly in the federal courts, where many of the rulings of the preceding era originated. To those concerned about a general curtailing of the rights of offenders with mental disorders, this change may be attributed to a general "chilling" of America wherein there is less interest in helping the troubled or disadvantaged. To those arguing for greater protection of society's interests, this change may be perceived as reflecting a general "heating-up" of America, wherein citizens are seen as increasingly vulnerable to and in need of protection from violent and dangerous individuals. Whatever the specific cause, three premises generally have guided judicial opinions of the 1980s and 1990s, some of them radically different from the premises accepted just a short time before.

All Patients Are Not Equal

Led by the United States Supreme Court, the courts retreated from earlier assertions that all psychiatric patients have the same rights. Instead, greater restrictions on the release of offenders with mental disorders are now often permitted, with the need to protect the community taking precedence over the liberty interests of the offender. To justify this the courts have tended to focus on the offender's dangerousness or simply on his/her status as an offender with a mental disorder, whether that status was determined at a prior hearing or by the mere fact of the offender entering a plea for status as an offender with a mental disorder. Conversely, however, when evaluating the treatment to which offenders with mental disorders are entitled, differences have been deemphasized except when a direct link can be established that the treatment provided will affect the security needs of the community. Then, greater disparity tends to be allowed (e.g., offenders with mental disorders may be denied the least restrictive alternative).

Expansion of "Dangerousness"

Courts have almost always taken dangerousness into account in their determinations regarding offenders with mental disorders. However, whereas dangerousness was defined relatively narrowly during the 1960s and 1970s, in the 1980s and 1990s the tendency has been to use an expansive definition. In addition, a wide range of evidence is used to establish its presence; the burden is often placed on offenders to show an absence of dangerousness; trial courts are afforded considerable discretion in making this determination, including disregarding expert testimony; assertions regarding the difficulty of predicting future dangerousness are discounted; and reliance is placed on relatively remote conduct and acts as a substitute for present dangerousness. In addition, courts are less likely to require an individualized evaluation of the dangerousness of the offender and are more likely to accept instead broad-ranging assumptions about offenders with mental disorders as a class. Allowing an expansive consideration of possible dangerousness makes offenders with mental disorders being processed by the mental health system more likely to be found appropriate for commitment to a psychiatric facility and less likely to be released subsequent to treatment. However, the courts' adoption of this premise has been largely limited to commitment and release decisions when the safety of the community is arguably most at risk. When evaluating the treatment provided during commitment, courts have tended not to focus on the relative dangerousness of the offender. This may be due to an implicit assumption that within the therapeutic environment public safety is not endangered and the mental disability of the individual, rather than the offender's dangerousness, should guide treatment decisions.

Reduced Judicial Scrutiny and Informal, Nonadversarial Proceedings

In the 1980s and 1990s many courts issued rulings that restored considerable decision-making authority to mental health professionals and reserved for the judiciary a more residual function as the reviewing body of last resort. Furthermore, courts approved more informal, nonadversarial proceedings for offenders with mental disorders being processed within the mental health system. The rationale often given by the courts is that less formal procedures are permissible because these proceedings are designed to help offenders, not punish them. Courts also note that they have a limited ability to make the necessary diagnoses and prognoses, that mental health professionals are better or adequately equipped to make these determinations, and that assigning the decision-making responsibility primarily to mental health professionals is more likely to ensure the safety of the community. In addition, courts assert that increasing procedural requirements will do little to increase the accuracy of the determinations being made, they impose an undue financial burden on the state, and courts remain available to correct flagrant abuses. However, some exceptions have been noted. When courts conclude that such proceedings do not adequately protect the community and lead to premature releases, they tend to reserve the ultimate decision for the judiciary. Additional procedural protections have also been required upon a determination that the public safety is not endangered and that either the offender is at a distinct disadvantage or his/her treatment is in question.

Impact

During this era, when courts considered commitment and release decisions for offenders with mental disorders, the balance between the individual rights of the offender and the security interests of the community has tended to shift back toward the latter. However, this shift has been accompanied by a greater willingness to scrutinize the nature of the treatment provided the offender. Although courts may be *less* reluctant to involuntarily commit offenders with mental disorders for psychiatric treatment and *more* reluctant to release the individual back into the community, the courts have often recognized that such offenders are entitled to better treatment in the course of their forced stay. This may be due to a belief that improved treatment will optimize the offender's recovery, thereby offsetting the imposition of readier commitment and restricted release. Alternatively, it may be that more efficacious treatment is seen as minimizing the likelihood that offenders with mental disorders will pose a danger upon release. As a result, however, mental health professionals may perceive that their treatment prerogatives are increasingly challenged, that their traditional discretion in making treatment decisions has been circumscribed, and that there is greater uncertainty over what constitutes an appropriate treatment for offenders with mental disorders.

CURRENT LAW

The evolution of these underlying premises led to subtle but significant changes in the law pertaining to the treatment of offenders with mental disorders. The rest of this chapter discusses these changes.

Initial Hearing and Commitment

Burden of Proof Placed on Offenders

Generally, the party assigned the burden of proof must present evidence that is more persuasive than that presented by the opposing party. In a criminal case, the State has the burden to prove (beyond a reasonable doubt) that the defendant committed all the elements of the crime. Earlier courts frequently held that because the State was seeking to limit the freedom of offenders with mental disorders, the State had the burden of proof at hearings where such decisions were made. However, this burden has shifted to the offenders in recent years in a number of contexts.[8]

For example, the burden of proof was often on the prosecution to show that a criminal defendant was sane at the time of the crime. Many states and the federal government, however, have revamped their laws so that insanity (as part of an insanity defense) now has to be asserted and proven by the defendant. Courts have generally upheld this change.[9] Among the reasons given are that assigning the burden of proof to the defendant avoids the anomaly of having the State argue at the criminal trial that the defendant was sane, and then, if it loses, having to argue at a subsequent commitment hearing that the defendant is seriously mentally ill to prevent the offender's release. In addition, insanity is characterized as an exculpatory fact (i.e., a reason for excusing the crime) and not an element of the crime.

Even when the burden is placed on the State, courts exercise considerable discretion in determining whether the defendant was sane at the time of the crime, including disregarding expert testimony to the contrary or considering a relatively broad range of evidence.[10] Some states have even taken the step of abolition the insanity defense and courts have ruled that this abolition does not constitute a denial of a fundamental constitutional right.[11] Placing the burden on the defendant to show incompetence to stand trial and establishing a presumption of competence to stand trial have also been upheld.[12]

Automatic Commitment and Retention

Courts have also upheld statutory schemes requiring immediate hospitalization after a successful insanity defense.[13] A hearing to review the need for hospitalization is typically mandated, generally within 40 to 60 days, although it may be longer. Before that hearing, however, the insanity acquittee may be hospitalized solely because of the insanity verdict, even though there has been no finding that the defendant is currently mentally ill and dangerous as is otherwise required for civil commitment, and even though a considerable period of time may have passed since the criminal act.[14] An initial involuntary period of evaluation for individuals found IST has also been upheld.[15]

In upholding this approach, courts assert that the need to protect the public safety justifies this temporary deprivation of the individual's liberty. This approach is also considered necessary to give mental health professionals an opportunity to more fully explore the defendant's mental health status so they may more accurately predict the defendant's future behavior and dangerousness. Courts distinguish offenders with mental disorders from individuals who in the preceding era were found to be similarly situated, namely, individuals subjected to civil commitment. For insanity acquittees, because automatic commitment occurred only because of the offender's insanity defense, courts conclude that there is less risk of an inappropriate commitment and the defendant's acknowledgment of a criminal act eliminates the possibility that the individual will be committed for "idiosyncratic behavior." The courts also assert that requiring another hearing on the acquittee's mental status immediately after the criminal trial requires an inefficient relitigation of much of this trial.

Extended or Indefinite Commitment

In contrast to a prior emphasis on placing finite time limits on the involuntary hospitalization of offenders with mental disorders,[16] legislatures and courts now generally accede to societal pressures to extend the commitment of an offender with a mental disorder. Earlier cases typically ruled that an offender could be held for mental health treatment only while the individual was being actively treated, with de facto preventive detention to protect society from potential harm not permitted. However, courts have expanded the bases and maximum lengths of time such individuals can be confined for treatment.[17]

For example, legislation that allows courts to commit insanity acquittees indefinitely has been upheld by the U.S. Supreme Court.[18] The Court further ruled that the acquittee could be hospitalized beyond the time the individual could have been incarcerated if convicted of the crime charged. The Court refused to find analogous its holding from the preceding era in *Jackson* that a person found IST could not be hospitalized for an indefinite period of time. Again, the underlying premise was to protect society from the potential dangerousness of the offender. The fact that the offender was being treated and not punished was emphasized, making the corresponding criminal sentence irrelevant. Finally, putting a different twist on a theme used during the preceding era, the Court found that mental health professionals' inability to predict the course of mental illness justified an indeterminate period of commitment.

Similarly, the Minnesota Supreme Court recently upheld a statute that commits repeat sexual offenders found to have a "psychopathic personality" to a secure psychiatric facility for an indeterminate period.[19] The court noted that Minnesota, like other states, has long wrestled with how to deal with the legitimate public concern over the danger posed by predatory sex offenders. The court found a compelling government interest in the protection of the public from persons who have an uncontrollable impulse to sexually assault and concluded that this statute fell within one of the permissible categories when the State may constitutionally deprive an individual of liberty, namely, when a person is mentally ill and dangerous.

The court noted that even though "psychopathic personality" is not currently classified as a mental illness, it does identify a "volitional dysfunction which grossly impairs judgment and behavior," can be systematically assessed, and is not a mere social maladjustment. The court rejected the defendant's argument that treatment for the psychopathic personality never works, but also asserted that even if successful treatment is problematic, as it often is, the State's interest in the safety of others is no less legitimate and compelling, and all that is required is that treatment and periodic review be provided.

Several states and Congress have adopted an approach that limits involuntary treatment to a period of time equal to the maximum term for which an offender found NGRI or IST could have been convicted.[20] Courts have upheld this approach[21] but have also applied it in ways that resulted in indeterminate or relatively lengthy periods of commitment.[22] In their rulings, courts have emphasized that such an approach is necessary to protect society, can be beneficial to offenders with mental disorders as treatment will be provided during this time and confinement can only continue so long as treatment is necessary, and gives mental health professionals an adequate opportunity to effect change in the offender. Similarly, for certain offenders with mental disorders the subsequent imposition of a prison sentence after successful completion of a treatment program has been upheld,[23] as well as indefinite commitment for treatment after serving a substantial portion of a criminal sentence[24] or—in the case of involuntarily committed offenders who are NGRI—in lieu of a criminal sentence over the offender's objection.[25] Furthermore, as discussed in the Addendum to this chapter, the U.S. Supreme Court upheld a state law permitting the indefinite commitment of "sexually violent predators" as they complete their prison sentence, or of those found NGRI, or of those IST.[26]

There has also been considerable interest in the Guilty But Mentally Ill (GBMI) verdict alternative. Although often justified in terms of ensuring both that an individual guilty of a crime be incarcerated, thereby protecting society, and that he/she receive needed treatment, such dispositions may result in extended confinement and far more punishment than treatment.[27] One judge expressed the hope that this law might be revised some day, but noted that "given the current climate of near-hysteria over violent crime and lack of sympathy for persons suffering from mental disabilities—[this] is not terribly likely."[28]

Treatment Decisions

Courts have adopted a somewhat different perspective when assessing the treatment provided offenders with mental disorders while in custody. Unlike placement or release decisions, in this context the interests of the offender are more likely to be recognized. Because the public's safety interests tend to be paramount in commitment and release decisions, the courts may counterbalance this by increasing their scrutiny of the treatment provided the offender. Placement in a secure facility may also reassure courts that potential danger to the public is thereby minimized. Exceptions may occur when the offender is placed in the community or when there is a high risk of escape.

Three aspects of treatment decisions for offenders with mental disorders have received specific attention by the courts: a right to treatment, a right to refuse treatment, and the acceptable parameters of the treatment programs provided.[29] Because courts remain cautious when offenders with mental disorders are in a nonsecure setting, court rulings have tended to differ for nonsentenced offenders frequently placed in a mental health facility from those for sentenced offenders placed within the relatively secure confines of a prison.

Right to Treatment

NONSENTENCED OFFENDERS

In 1966, the federal Court of Appeals for the District of Columbia became the first court to formally recognize a right to treatment for individuals involuntarily hospitalized.[30] However, most current discussions of this right center on *Youngberg v. Romeo,* the U.S. Supreme Court's only opinion to date on this issue.[31]

Although this 1982 opinion established the constitutional rights of an involuntarily hospitalized individual with mental retardation (with a resulting emphasis on habilitation/training rather than treatment), it has been broadly read to provide the basis for a similar recognition of the treatment rights of individuals with a mental illness. This conclusion is reinforced by the Court's simultaneous remand of two lower court opinions addressing treatment issues pertaining to individuals with a mental illness for reconsideration in light of its opinion in *Youngberg.*[32]

In *Youngberg,* the Court was clearly conscious that it was treading new ground and proceeded cautiously. Although it readily recognized a right to safe conditions and freedom from bodily restraint, the Court professed concern over an asserted constitutional right to "minimally adequate habilitation" or training.[33] The Court noted the lack of precision and consistence in the use of the term "habilitation" and disagreement among mental health professionals regarding needed habilitation and training, and their ultimate success. The Court also maintained that the state must be allowed considerable discretion in designing and delivering such services. Thus, the Court refrained from recognizing an explicit constitutional right to habilitation/training. Instead, the Court recast this as a means to an end, namely, that minimally adequate or reasonable training is needed to ensure that the rights to safety and freedom from undue restraint are not jeopardized.

The Court further ruled that even these rights are not absolute, but have to be balanced against "the demands of an organized society." Relevant State interests have to be taken into account. Although it did not explicitly define the particular State interests at stake, the Court did identify the necessity for institutional care; the often unavoidable overcrowding and understaffing of such institutions; the wide range and number of daily decisions, needs, and problems faced by staff; and the necessity that such staff not work with the cloud of potential lawsuits influencing every decision. In addition, the Court was concerned that a lack of uniformity would result from leaving this balancing to the "unguided discretion of a judge or jury." Instead, the Court ruled that these decisions generally should be left to the professionals providing care. The Court held:

> The decision, if made by a professional, is presumptively valid; liability may be imposed only when the decision by the professional is such a substantial departure from accepted professional judgment, practice, or standards as to demonstrate that the person responsible actually did not base the decision on such a judgment.[34]

Despite the U.S. Supreme Court's cautious approach, other courts have been increasingly willing to scrutinize the care provided in state facilities for persons with a mental disability.[35] Generally, the critical question has been whether professional judgment was exercised.

Judicial recognition of a right to treatment for offenders with mental disorders followed a similar track. A series of early opinions by one federal court found a right to "reasonably suitable and adequate" treatment for persons involuntarily committed after being found not guilty by reason of insanity (NGRI)[36] or after being determined to be a sexual psychopath.[37] This court concluded that because commitment could last indefinitely, confinement could only be justified if therapeutic treatment was provided as well. Such individuals were considered indistinguishable from civilly committed individuals and were thus entitled to a relatively expansive right to treatment, including a right to "the least restrictive alternative consistent with the legitimate purposes of a commitment."[38]

Recent judicial opinions, however, have been unwilling to recognize such a broad right to treatment for offenders with mental disorders who have not been convicted of a crime and as a result are often placed in a relatively nonsecure mental health facility. These cases tend to conclude that the potential dangerousness of offenders with mental disorders requires a treatment modality that recognizes the recurring need to protect public safety. These courts generally defer to the judgment of professional staff, distinguish other types of patients, place less emphasis on exploring less restrictive alternatives, and allow budgetary restraints to be taken into account.[39]

In an opinion expressing particularly strong reservations on a right to treatment for offenders with mental disorders, the First Circuit of the U.S. Court of Appeals found that the constitution did not require that all patients in state-run psychiatric facilities receive the same rights or care.[40] Thus, the court upheld distinctions in privileges afforded various groups of patients based on the severity of their illness, their violent propensities, and the type of treatment they were believed to need. This permitted different limitations on mailing privileges, visitations, personal grooming, handling of patient moneys, and storage of patient property. The court placed great emphasis on the need for security and control when working with offenders with mental disorders, recognizing that in light of finite resources the state might expend more on stabilizing and controlling "violent patients" and less on the "usual psychiatric approaches." However, the court did note that the need for greater security could not be a basis for totally denying psychiatric care and adopted the *Youngberg* professional judgment standard for assessing this care.[41] Like other courts, the First Circuit stressed that this standard appropriately minimized judicial interference with the internal operations of state institutions.

Although only a limited right to treatment for nonsentenced offenders with mental disorders has been recognized, ironically, pressure for an enhanced right to treatment may come from a setting where traditionally few individual rights were recognized, namely prisons. Nonsentenced offenders may benefit from the increased recognition of a right to treatment for sentenced offenders (discussed in the following section) because they are typically perceived as entitled to no less treatment than that afforded prison inmates. Indeed, although the "legal hook" differs, the analytical approach used for the two populations appears to be converging.[42] Judges presiding over prison cases have shown a tendency to discuss whether the treatment provided represents a substantial departure from the professional judgment expected in this setting.[43] The limited recognition of a right to treatment for nonsentenced offenders may be a function of the relatively few number of judicial opinions addressing the issue.[44] The enhanced scrutiny of the treatment of sentenced offenders with mental disorders may well be used as a rationale for similarly scrutinizing the treatment provided nonsentenced offenders who, after all, have not been convicted of a crime.

Nevertheless, to the extent that courts perceive that affording nonsentenced offenders with mental disorders an expansive right to treatment places society at risk, they may remain hesitant to closely scrutinize the level of care they are provided. For example, if it is argued that this right to treatment should include (as has been the case for civil patients) ready access to the community (e.g., by emphasizing the use of noninstitutional environments, passes, or off-grounds privileges), courts may give greater weight to the need to protect society and resist this expansion.

SENTENCED OFFENDERS

A right to treatment for offenders with mental disorders convicted and sentenced for a crime has followed a different legal track.[45] Their rights are typically based on those of prison inmates in general, with the Eighth Amendment right to be free from cruel and unusual punishment providing the standard for assessing the treatment provided.[46] In contrast, for nonsentenced offenders (including pretrial detainees), the right to treatment is derived (as for civil patients) from the Fourteenth Amendment right not to be deprived of life, liberty, or property without due process.[47] This includes a right to be free from punishment altogether, a right not accorded prison inmates.[48]

The Eighth Amendment, however, has been found increasingly to also assure at least some mental health treatment to prison inmates. A line of cases establishing a right to psychiatric treatment began with the U.S. Supreme Court's 1976 opinion in *Estelle v. Gamble*.[49] *Estelle* established that the critical issue is whether there has been deliberate indifference to a prisoner's serious medical needs.[50] Although *Estelle* focused on the response of prison officials to an inmate's back problems and the Supreme Court has not yet specifically ruled that "serious medical needs" includes psychiatric needs, while initially reluctant, numerous courts since *Estelle* have made this extension.

Early opinions tended to address the very basic parameters of a right to mental health treatment. In one of the first opinions recognizing the right, the Fourth Circuit found no underlying distinction between a right to medical care for physical illness and one for mental illness.[51] The court held that prison inmates suffering from a mental illness are

> entitled to psychological or psychiatric treatment if a physician or other health care provider, exercising ordinary skill and care at the time of observation, concludes with reasonable medical certainty (1) that the prisoner's symptoms evidence a serious disease or injury; (2) that such disease or injury is curable or may be substantially alleviated; and (3) that the potential for harm to the prisoner by reason of delay or the denial of care would be substantial.[52]

However, the court qualified this by limiting required treatment to that which could be provided on a reasonable cost and time basis, and to that which was a medical necessity and not simply "desirable." The court also appeared to be reluctant to get courts involved in clinical judgments, stating a desire to limit judicial review of treatment decisions. Nevertheless, although the requisite showing of deliberate indifference by staff to the treatment needs of the inmate is intended to be relatively difficult to accomplish, the court clearly felt compelled to ensure that at least some treatment is provided.

The basic analytical model set out by the Fourth Circuit has generally been employed by courts subsequently addressing these issues. At first courts typically adopted those portions that were relatively conservative. These courts focused on whether *any* mental health treatment was present.[53] Furthermore, they were reluctant to grant the same treatment rights to sentenced offenders with mental disorders as those recognized for nonsentenced offenders.[54]

Subsequently, however, courts appear more willing to accept a right to treatment for mentally ill inmates, have broadened its scope, and more closely scrutinize the treatment provided. As a result, this right may soon, if not already, be comparable to that of nonsentenced offenders (and, potentially, civilly committed individuals).[55]

For example, courts may engage in a detailed examination of the day-to-day treatment provided, review the inmate's treatment history, and examine medical or incident records (i.e., not rely solely on expert testimony).[56] Going beyond the mere presence or absence of services, courts may look at the specific types of services provided and consider how well the treatment provided matches general and individual needs of offenders with mental disorders.[57]

Greater attention is being given to whether systems are in place for identifying and monitoring persons with a mental illness, and to their effectiveness in responding to mental health needs. Required systems may include intake procedures (e.g., obtaining and reviewing upon arrival inmates' past psychiatric records); referral procedures (e.g., means for inmates to make their medical needs known to the medical staff); means for ensuring effective communication between security and mental health staff; limiting inappropriate referrals to mental health staff (i.e., "dumping," which takes time away from inmates genuinely needing services); and written rules and procedures regarding the management of inmates with a mental illness (e.g., a policy for handling "unstable" inmates).[58]

There may be an insistence that an environment conducive to treating serious mental illness be provided, including separating mentally ill inmates from the general prison population, extending services to inmates placed in special housing units (cells for inmates who have violated the prison's disciplinary code), limiting the use of "lockdown" as an alternative to mental health care, and providing prompt transfer of inmates in need of services to a more appropriate treatment setting.[59] Staffing requirements often include on-site mental health staff, a greater number of staff (reasonable caseloads), a greater range of expertise, enhanced credentials, and program specific training.[60]

Specific treatment procedures required may include having a system to ensure that inmates take prescribed medications, monitoring inmates on psychotropics (e.g., periodically testing blood levels), not discontinuing medications without face-to-face interviews, not allowing nonmedical staff to override medical decisions of psychiatric staff, providing more intensive programming such as one-on-one counseling and group therapy, limiting delays in responding to requests for services, and providing follow-up services.[61]

These courts have tended not to be swayed by a lack of available funding (and sometimes not even by good faith efforts to obtain needed treatment resources), have shown less deference to prison officials, have expanded the liability of supervising officials, and have been less receptive to arguments asserting a need to maintain prison security.[62]

A federal District Court of Georgia, for example, held that liability could result from a consulting psychiatrist's decision to abruptly take a prison inmate off antipsychotic medication when the inmate shortly thereafter engaged in self-mutilation.[63] After undertaking a detailed review of the psychiatrist's prior contacts with the inmate, the court determined that a jury could find that there had been storm warnings that the psychiatrist had ignored even though there had been no acts of self-mutilation for several preceding months. Similarly, after closely reviewing the prison doctor's contacts with the inmate, the court also ruled that a jury might find the prison doctor liable for failing to contact the psychiatrist after he learned of the inmate's depression and attempts to cut his arm. However, particularly striking is the extreme detail with which the court discussed the treatment provided by a wide range of staff, including nonpsychiatric staff. The court ultimately embarked on an extensive critique of both the criminal justice system for placing people with a severe mental disability in the prison system and the prison system for failing to adequately treat them. This court, like others, indicated that when severe restrictions are placed on the freedom of offenders with mental disorders by imposing prison sentences, these restrictions must be counterbalanced by increasing the level of treatment provided during incarceration.[64]

Another opinion engaging in an extensive evaluation of the specifics of the treatment provided was issued by the First Circuit.[65] Within a few months of transfer to an overcrowded jail, a mentally ill inmate was found dead, his body dismembered. The acts of supervisory (including non-mental health supervisors) as well as treatment personnel were subjected to close scrutiny and found liable. The court noted that all had the ability to prevent the tragedy without relying on the psychiatric judgment of another. A detailed chronology of the inmate's psychiatric history, the decisions made, and the care given were provided. The court ruled that staff were obligated to carefully read an inmate's records, to ensure that psychiatric records were in the files, to review these records within a few days of transfer, and to have in place procedures to screen out psychologically disturbed prisoners. A lack of control over appropriations was not an acceptable excuse. Furthermore, although other courts have ruled that a prisoner does not have the right to be placed in a particular setting as long as his/her mental health needs are adequately addressed,[66] this court found that prison officials can be held liable when they intentionally place a mentally ill prisoner in a dangerous surrounding and fail to identify the inmate's need for psychiatric hospitalization.

A 1995 court-approved consent decree provides an indication of the type of programming that satisfies legal requirements. A federal district court approved an agreement that increased use of a prison's Special Needs Units, providing on-site therapeutic bed space for seriously mentally ill inmates.[67] The agreement required that a treatment plan be developed for each inmate placed on these units, that programming be strengthened, that inmates be evaluated at least once every 6 months for signs of tardive dyskinesia and if detected, necessary medical treatment be provided, and that inmates refusing prescribed psychotropic medications not be placed in administrative custody solely because of such refusals. Doublecelling of inmates with mental health problems with general population inmates was permitted when the placement was first screened by a mental health provider and documented in the inmate's mental health record. Also approved was the use of a psychiatric observation room (typically a room stripped of furnishings to prevent suicide attempts) for inmates who decompensate and who are waiting for admission to a forensic facility when there is a well-documented record showing that the inmate's behavior is so disruptive that the inmate is a danger to self or others.

At the same time, some cases from the mid-1990s suggest that the courts may have reached their limits on the treatment they are willing to assure prison inmates, and are increasingly satisfied with the treatment provided. If it could be established that inmate mental health needs were monitored, a system was in place for receiving requests for treatment or determining that treatment was needed, and means were provided for responding to identified mental health treatment needs, courts were not likely to closely scrutinize the treatment provided unless there was a clear demonstration that inmates incurred actual harm. Much of the case law of the 1980s suggested an almost total failure to monitor and respond to inmate mental health needs and a pervasive lack of mental health treatment within prisons. Since then, much progress has been made and court decisions appear to be reflecting this, placing limits on what is required and strongly indicating that inmates are not entitled to their "treatment of choice."[68] Furthermore, these courts were likely to be impressed by an individual mental health provider's good-faith efforts to provide an appropriate treatment program, particularly if the choice reflected a reasoned approach and adjustments were made as needed in the course of the program (e.g., by responding to inmate complaints).[69]

In addition, when the treatment program has the potential to place the community at risk, courts have been resistant to efforts by offenders with mental disorders to reshape these programs. For example, both a federal court and a state court upheld changes to the eligibility requirements for admission of an offender with a mental disorder to a program for reintegrating individuals into the community.[70] Complaints were filed by individuals who had been sentenced to serve an extended prison term and simultaneously adjudged a "sexually dangerous person" and committed to the Massachusetts Treatment Center for Sexually Dangerous Persons. As patients at the Center, they were entitled to receive mental health treatment and to be released when no longer sexually dangerous, at which point they would be returned to the Department of Corrections to serve the remainder of their criminal sentence. Among other things, the program in question at the Center provided for outside day placement or other short-term release. However, after the escape of two residents from the program, the State adopted new rules that limited enrollment and excluded the plaintiffs. The courts in both cases denied the plaintiffs' claims, noting that they did not have a protected liberty interest in short-term release; that a legitimate distinction could be made between civilly and criminally committed patients; that the revised rules were not punitive (and thus not a potential violation of the Cruel and Unusual Punishment Clause), but rather related to the State's concern for community safety; and that these changes were not a change in their terms of sentence (and thus not a violation of the constitutional prohibition of *ex post facto* laws) because the change was only the revocation of a privilege voluntarily granted.

Relatedly, one group of sentenced offenders with mental disorders whose treatment rights has not been expansively defined or scrutinized is convicted sexual offenders. Courts have generally been unwilling to closely examine their treatment, even though the effect may be to delay their ability to qualify for early release (e.g., parole).[71] Courts may not be displeased by a delay in returning what is viewed as a particularly dangerous, treatment-resistant population to the community.

Treatment Refusals

Unlike the right to treatment, federal courts have been reluctant to recognize a broad right to refuse treatment for offenders with mental disorders.[72]

They have concluded that the State's interests in overriding a treatment refusal can outweigh the offender's interests. However, the federal courts have not ruled that this is solely a question of federal law and the states are free to expand the offender's right to refuse treatment.[73] Indeed, a number of state courts have independently recognized this right, given greater weight to the offender's interests, and added requirements with which treatment providers in these states must comply.

Generally, the question is not whether offenders with mental disorders can voice an objection and have it heard. This has been widely accepted; even the federal courts do not give treatment providers carte blanche to override an offender's objection. Instead, the issues are who can override an objection, when, and how. It should be noted, however, that enhanced procedural protections associated with a right to refuse treatment tend to extend only to psychotropic drugs, ECT, and psychosurgery.[74] These same safeguards have not generally been required for other forms of treatment because they are not considered as intrusive, onerous, or nonreversible.[75]

Like the right to treatment cases, courts addressing a right to refuse treatment have tended to distinguish between a nonsentenced offender typically placed in a mental health facility and a sentenced offender typically placed within a relatively secure prison environment.

NONSENTENCED OFFENDERS

The federal courts have taken a relatively restrictive view of the right of nonsentenced offenders with mental disorders to refuse treatment. For example, the Fourth Circuit sitting *en banc* ruled on an objection to being forcibly administered psychotropic medication by an individual involuntarily committed after being found not competent to stand trial.[76] The court rejected the offender's argument that a judicial determination of incompetence to make medical decisions is required before he could be medicated without consent. Instead, the court emphasized: (1) the limited ability of the judiciary to make treatment decisions, (2) the superior skill of the treatment staff and the necessity of deferring to their professional judgment, and (3) the inappropriateness of an adversarial hearing to resolve such issues. The court stressed that the government has an obligation to attempt to restore such individuals to mental competence so they can be returned to society. Court review was seen as imposing administrative burden and delay that hamstrung the treatment staff's ability to respond to patient needs and inappropriately required the courts to make treatment decisions. Other federal courts have ruled similarly.[77]

In contrast, a Wisconsin Supreme Court decision typifies the various state court opinions that have supplemented federal court requirements.[78] A Wisconsin federal court decision 2 years earlier held that courts contemplate and tacitly approve the administration of psychotropic drugs when they commit individuals for involuntary treatment, and thus these drugs can be administered without further court authorization.[79] The Wisconsin Supreme Court, however, disagreed and asserted that an involuntary commitment is not equivalent to a finding of incompetence to make treatment decisions, that such decisions invoke protected civil rights, and that further court involvement is required before disregarding an objection to treatment.

The court determined that just as an involuntarily committed civil patient can still be competent to make decisions regarding psychotropic medication, so also individuals found IST and insanity acquittees can be competent to make these decisions. The court also concluded that the finding of dangerousness made when these offenders were committed is irrelevant in determining whether to override a patient's objection to treatment. Although a prerequisite for commitment, such a finding was not necessarily related to whether the person was competent to refuse psychotropic drugs. The court stressed the dangers of such drugs, including the potential for substantial side effects and the countertherapeutic effect of forced medication.

The court was also not prepared to defer to the professional judgment of the treating staff regarding such decisions and strongly criticized the federal district court's argument that sufficient safeguards are provided by simply requiring that a physician prescribe the medication. The court concluded that because it is a question requiring an application of the law, a judicial determination is required to decide whether an individual is incompetent to make a treatment objection, and the professional judgment of a treating physician to that effect is not sufficient by itself. A full judicial hearing was needed to protect individual rights and to prevent individuals being declared incompetent for "mere convenience, control or expense," with the burden placed on the state to show that the patient is not competent to make such an objection.[80] However, the court did note that these procedural safeguards could be bypassed during an emergency to prevent serious physical harm to the patient or others.

The decision by the Wisconsin Supreme Court closely resembles a number of other state court opinions that mandate judicial review before overriding an objection to psychotropic medication.[81] State courts have also set out specific procedural requirements besides judicial review that must be satisfied, including that an offender be given advance notice of the proceeding; that he/she be permitted to be present, present evidence, cross-examine witnesses, and be assisted by an advisor who understands the psychiatric issues involved; and that when an objection is overridden, the order be specific both as to the nature of the treatment to be provided and its duration.[82] There have, however, been efforts to streamline this process (e.g., by having the committing court also review subsequent treatment objections rather than assigning it to another court with no knowledge of the offender).[83]

Like the Wisconsin court, state court opinions concerning the right to refuse treatment have generally disregarded the precepts driving judicial decisions concerning the right to treatment of nonsentenced offenders with mental disorders. Why? Unlike a right to treatment that encompasses a wide range of issues and has the potential to embroil the courts in many aspects of mental health treatment, the courts may consider judicial review of a refusal of psychotropic medication relatively easy to provide. Perhaps these courts believe that behavioral outbursts associated with a treatment refusal will occur within the confines of a relatively secure facility and be addressed by treatment providers equipped to handle these outbursts. Also, because staff can administer treatment over objection in an emergency, they may believe that there is little likelihood that the public will be placed at risk by such outbursts or by delays from a more extensive review process. In any case, the interests of offenders with mental disorders have been given greater recognition in this context. It remains to be seen whether state courts will continue to adhere to this perspective if such offenders are placed more frequently in the community.

Neither state nor federal courts generally address a need to protect staff from outbursts by offenders. Attention is rarely given to the limited ability of treatment providers to refuse or remove difficult or dangerous offenders and the limited range of options they have to control their behavior. It may be that courts feel treatment staff are adequately protected by their ability to administer psychotropic medication over objection in an emergency.[84] However, courts do attach limitations to this prerogative[85] and confusion over when this is permitted may slow staff response, thereby placing them at risk. The impact on staff of treatment refusals has received more attention in conjunction with sentenced offenders with mental disorders.

SENTENCED OFFENDERS

Until recently, few judicial opinions addressed whether sentenced offenders with mental disorders, that is, prison inmates, have a right to refuse psychiatric treatment.[86] This may have been a function of the relatively little treatment historically provided. Also, traditionally wide discretion was given prison officials in administering prisons. However, with (1) increased recognition of a right of prisoners to mental health treatment, (2) expansions in the treatment provided and the number of inmates receiving it, and (3) closer judicial scrutiny of this treatment, it was perhaps inevitable that closer attention be given to an asserted right of prisoners to refuse treatment.

On the federal side, the Supreme Court in *Washington v. Harper*[87] ruled that although inmates have a protected constitutional interest in avoiding forced administration of psychotropic drugs, this interest must be balanced against the State's interests in prison safety and security. In balancing these interests, courts are to consider the impact of any ruling on prison resources and the need to ensure the safety of prison staff, other inmates, and the prisoner. The Court emphasized the danger to others from a behavioral outburst in this setting and that "prison authorities are best equipped to make difficult decisions regarding prison administration."[88]

The Court found that the procedure used by the State of Washington to override an inmate's objection to psychotropic medication was sufficient. An inmate could be subjected to involuntary treatment only if the inmate suffered from a mental disorder and was either gravely disabled or posed a likelihood of serious harm to him/herself, others, or their property. The order for medication had to come from a psychiatrist. If the inmate objected, the inmate was entitled to a hearing before a special committee consisting of a psychiatrist, psychologist, and the associate superintendent of the facility, none of whom could be involved in the inmate's current treatment or diagnosis (previous involvement was permissible). The inmate's objection could be overridden on a majority vote if the psychiatrist was in the majority. The inmate had to be given 24 hours' notice of the hearing, during which time the inmate could not be medicated. The inmate also had to be given notice of the diagnosis, its factual basis, and why staff believed medication was necessary. At the hearing, the inmate had the right to attend, present evidence, cross-examine witnesses, and be assisted by a lay advisor who understood the psychiatric issues involved and was not otherwise involved in the case.[89] The inmate had a right to appeal the decision within 24 hours to the superintendent of the facility and also to seek judicial review. If medication was ordered, it could continue beyond 7 days only with periodic staff review.[90]

The Court held that the decision to medicate did not have to be made by a judge or some "outside decisionmaker."[91] Noting limits on the judiciary's ability to make such decisions, the Court suggested the inmate's interests may be better served by allowing medical professionals from the treatment facility to make such decisions. The Court cited the medical staff's greater ability to make the frequent and ongoing clinical observations necessary to assess the inmate's intentions, which are likely to change over time, and to make a medication decision that the inmate would make if competent at the time. The Court emphasized the predominantly medical nature of the necessary inquiry and that judicial hearings could divert scarce prison resources, including money and staff time, from the treatment of inmates. Thus, the Court held, a state can conclude that a judicial hearing will not be as effective, continuous, or probing as administrative review using medical decision makers.

Even before *Harper,* as with nonsentenced offenders, federal courts have generally limited the right of sentenced offenders with mental disorders to object to treatment and, in particular, they have limited the judiciary's role in reviewing a decision to proceed with treatment over objection.[92] They have focused heavily on the dangerousness issue.[93] One court stressed, "Correctional officers and agencies have a duty not only to protect society from dangerous inmates, but must also take whatever procedures are appropriate in protecting inmates from each other and protecting correctional officers from violent inmates."[94] These courts have also noted their own limitations and the importance of deferring to the professional judgment of the treatment staff when assessing the objection to treatment.[95] Federal courts have allowed an order to forcibly administer medication to be relatively open-ended, allowing a significant amount of time to pass between the issuance of the order and the administration of the medication.[96] One federal court dictated a specific placement for an inmate so that if she stopped taking her medication and her condition deteriorated, she could be readily administered medication against her will.[97] Furthermore, federal courts have emphasized that the procedure to override an inmate's objection to medication can be bypassed in an emergency to protect the safety of the inmate or others.[98] Federal courts have ruled that less intrusive alternatives should be considered before overriding an inmate's objection to treatment.[99] But the Supreme Court in *Harper* undercut this position when it concluded that physical restraints or seclusion are not acceptable substitutes for psychotropic drugs, that the absence of ready alternatives is evidence of the reasonableness of a prison regulation, and that prison officials do not have to "set up" and then "shoot down" every conceivable alternative accommodation of the inmate's complaint.

On the state side, although the Supreme Court's opinion in *Harper* carries considerable weight, a separate body of state law concerning an inmate's objection to treatment may still evolve. Earlier state court opinions recognized a right under state law to routine judicial review of a decision to override an inmate's objection to treatment, as well as imposing other limits on efforts to override objections.[100] However, like *Harper* and unlike state court opinions recognizing a right of nonsentenced offenders to refuse treatment, these opinions have placed an emphasis on not jeopardizing institutional security or public safety. Although generally finding that neither is jeopardized by recognizing enhanced procedural protections, when it could be shown that they are jeopardized, these courts were prepared to place limitations on the right to object to treatment.

The general perception that these objections do not represent a threat to public safety may reflect the courts' belief that because an offender resides within a secure facility, there is little potential impact on public safety. This may, however, indicate a failure to consider that ultimately the offender is released back into the community where untreated psychological problems may be manifest, potentially endangering the public. Also, for some diagnoses, the longer treatment is deferred, the more recalcitrant and treatment-resistant the problem may become. Not surprisingly, as the sentenced offender is placed in a situation where he/she can directly interact with the community, for example, as a resident of a halfway house or during probation or parole, the courts have been far more responsive to issues of public safety. As will be discussed in the section on status changes, in these contexts the courts have been less willing to accord an expansive recognition to the rights of offenders with mental disorders.

Both federal and state rulings on the right of inmates to refuse treatment typically give little attention to its potential impact on the treatment provider (as was true for nonsentenced offenders). Courts may assume that the secure nature of the prison environment minimizes threats to the safety of the treatment staff or other inmates, or to the therapeutic relationship.[101] It may also reflect the fact that the interests of the treatment staff are typically not directly represented in such controversies (e.g., the lawsuit typically pits the inmate against the state).

One final issue that has only begun to be explored involves whether an inmate on death row can be administered psychotropic medication over objection so that the inmate can be restored to competence to be executed. Because an individual currently incompetent cannot be executed,[102] ostensibly an inmate can avoid the death penalty indefinitely by refusing psychiatric treatment that would restore competence. A Louisiana court ruled that state prison officials can forcibly medicate an inmate under these circumstances. However, the U.S. Supreme Court in a one-sentence *per curiam* decision vacated and remanded this decision for further consideration in light of *Harper.*[103] Although the U.S. Supreme Court has not addressed the issue further, other state and federal court rulings suggest that the courts will give credence to a right to refuse treatment under these circumstances. They will also, however, be amenable to assertions that the inmate is competent to be executed.[104]

The Treatment Program

There is now a general expectation that some form of treatment will be provided imprisoned or involuntarily committed offenders with mental disorders, regardless of the setting. But are there limits on what can be provided? Although not widely addressed by the courts, four questions are often asked.[105] First, is the treatment program being used more for punishment, with accompanying physical or psychological pain, than for treatment? Second, is it an experimental program with little firm evidence that a successful outcome will result? Third, is the treatment program overly intrusive? Fourth, has the informed consent of the offender to participate in the treatment been obtained?[106]

AVERSIVE THERAPIES

Therapies causing physical or psychological harm, generally referred to as aversive therapies, have particularly drawn the attention and frequent criticism of the courts. They do not receive much current use, in part perhaps because of this criticism, but earlier review of them established instructive criteria for what constitutes acceptable treatment.

These therapies typically attempt to associate an unpleasant event with an undesirable behavior in an effort to reduce the frequency of the undesirable behavior. However, critics ask whether it is ethical for one person to inflict pain on another and whether these programs induce long-term behavioral change. Of greater interest to the courts, however, have been claims that they were used to punish or for administrative convenience and control, rather than to treat.

One of the first attacks on a treatment program of any type for offenders with mental disorders came from the Ninth Circuit U.S. Court of Appeals.[107] With his consent, a prison inmate was sent to a medical facility to receive "shock treatment." He complained that while there, without his consent and not as part of the shock treatment, he was administered a "breath-stopping and paralyzing fright drug" (succinylcholine) during a systematic program of aversive treatment for criminal offenders. The court ruled that if the inmate could prove his claim, it would "raise serious constitutional questions respecting cruel and unusual punishment or impermissible tinkering with the mental processes."[108]

Similarly, the Eighth Circuit ruled that administering a drug (apomorphine) to induce vomiting as part of an aversive therapy program for inmates at a secure medical facility without their prior informed consent constituted prohibited cruel and unusual punishment.[109] The drug was administered after inmates violated a behavioral protocol established by treatment staff. A key factor for the court was whether the program was used for treatment; if used for punishment it was impermissible. The court was concerned about its "painful and debilitating" aspects and testimony that characterized this approach as highly questionable and relatively unsuccessful.

Another federal court issued a similar ruling with regard to nonsentenced offenders with mental disorders.[110] The court found that the involuntary administration of drugs with a painful or frightening effect to an inmate at a hospital for the "criminally insane" may amount to an unwarranted governmental intrusion into the patient's thought processes in violation of his/her constitutional right of privacy. A state court opinion further indicated that the judiciary is likely to be skeptical of and to closely scrutinize aversive therapy.[111] The Minnesota Supreme Court ruled that in assessing treatments for psychological disorders, including aversive therapy, the extent and duration of their impact, the risk of side effects, and the amount of pain induced should be examined.[112] However, the court also noted that its assessment would be weighed against any legitimate and important state interest furthered by using the treatment, suggesting it might be more amenable to a treatment if it furthered security or personal safety interests.

Expanding what constitutes unacceptable harm, a more recent federal court opinion held that a levels system (a behavior modification program) used at a correctional institution was impermissible because it restricted basic privileges and was not reasonably related to a legitimate penological goal.[113] Although this approach might be used acceptably with individual inmates, the court rejected its across-the-board imposition. The court was concerned that the program regulated virtually all aspects of the inmates' lives, found it punitive, experimental, and arbitrary, and rejected its use absent a showing that it was appropriate for a given inmate. The court was unpersuaded that the program promoted institutional security or preserved order and discipline, responding that it might well impede these goals. The program's harmful impact was reinforced by the unusually high levels of stress, tension, and sleep disturbance among inmates, and by widespread reliance on psychotropic drugs. Refusing to defer to the professionals in charge of the program, the court noted that although courts are not the best forum for testing the validity of scientific theories, they are well equipped to determine if a system is punitive.

EXPERIMENTAL TECHNIQUES

Extensive scrutiny of a treatment program may also be triggered by its not being widely used and accepted among mental health professionals. Aversive therapies have been vulnerable in part because they are seen as experimental. Modern law regarding human experimentation developed from the Nuremberg Code, established by an international court that tried 23 German physicians for their experiments on prisoners of war and civilians during World War II. This court ruled that before an individual could be placed in an experimental program, the person's informed consent had to be obtained.

A frequently cited, although rarely followed, opinion on the use of an experimental treatment program was issued by a Michigan trial court.[114]

An individual committed under a Criminal Sexual Psychopath law challenged a proposed experimental psychosurgery. The court was concerned that the treatment was irreversible and often led to the blunting of emotions, memory, affect, and creativity, and ruled that the individual had a First Amendment right to be free from interference with the mental processes.

In a later case, the Michigan Court of Appeals overturned a probation sentence given a defendant convicted of first-degree criminal sexual conduct.[115] As a condition of probation the defendant was to submit to the administration of an experimental drug (Depo Provera) to help control his sexual urges. In justifying this sentence, the trial court cited the necessity of protecting the public. The appellate court, however, ruled that under Michigan law this program was an "unlawful" condition of probation. Focusing on its experimental nature,[116] the court stated that no state or federal appellate court had ever passed upon or approved voluntary or mandatory treatment of sex offenders with this drug. The court rejected its use because it had not been accepted in the medical community as a safe and reliable procedure.[117]

Although not large in number, other courts striking down treatment programs for offenders with mental disorders have also been concerned about their experimental nature.[118] In general, they want evidence that the treatment is used elsewhere on similar individuals in similar circumstances or that it has been approved by the medical community. The small number of cases discussing the use of experimental techniques to treat offenders with mental disorders may reflect a lack of programs available to this population. Alternatively, judicial opinions striking down or greatly restricting treatment programs may have had such a chilling effect that few innovative programs are being attempted.

All facilities that receive federal funding, which includes most psychiatric facilities, are also required to follow federal guidelines governing research and experimentation involving patients.[119] Among their requirements are that an institutional review board (IRB) review such activities. Although state prisons may not receive federal funding and thus may be exempt from these requirements, some states impose similar requirements. For example, California has significantly limited the conduct of biomedical and behavioral research with prisoners.[120] Outside California, however, fewer controls exist on therapeutic interventions and experimentation with sentenced offenders, although increased regulation is occurring. Before any mental health provider embarks on an experimental program with sentenced or nonsentenced offenders with mental disorders, state and federal law should be carefully reviewed to ensure compliance with applicable requirements. In addition, professional codes of ethics may contain provisions relating to experimental programs.

INTRUSIVE TREATMENTS

A program's intrusiveness has generally been a factor in deciding whether a program is impermissibly aversive or experimental. However, it has also been a key element in its own right when courts scrutinize treatment programs for offenders with mental disorders.

For example, the Supreme Court of Minnesota held that involuntary treatment with psychotropic drugs was an intrusive treatment per se, and thus required prior court approval.[121] An earlier opinion identified ECT and psychosurgery as "intrusive" forms of treatment requiring prior judicial approval after determining that they seriously infringe on a committed mental patient's right of privacy.[122] The Minnesota Supreme Court extended this classification to include psychotropic drugs, emphasizing that the potential impact of such treatments can be so severe that treatment decisions involving them cannot be left solely within the discretion of medical personnel. Although the court noted several criteria for determining whether a treatment required prior judicial review, it focused heavily on the intrusiveness of the treatment.[123] The court ruled that a determination of a treatment's intrusiveness should begin with an evaluation of the treatment's probable effects on the patient's body, as well as the risk of adverse side effects and its potential for being permanent, irreversible, and life threatening.

Although other courts have not focused so directly on the intrusiveness of a challenged treatment program, intrusiveness generally assumes a key role in the courts' discussions.[124] Analyses have been relatively the same for both sentenced and nonsentenced offenders with mental disorders. In addition to examining the nature of the intrusion, the intrusiveness of the treatment (particularly potential side effects) is often compared with that of possible alternative programs. Attention is also given to steps that can be taken to ameliorate its adverse effects. When a program is notably intrusive, particularly if its focus appears to be on punishing or controlling behavior for administrative convenience, courts are more likely to disallow or place restrictions on its use. However, they tend to reach such conclusions only when there has been a clear showing of actual or likely harm to an offender.

INFORMED CONSENT

With the exception of treatment programs disallowed because they are considered too aversive, experimental, or intrusive, a treatment program is generally acceptable if an offender with a mental disorder has indicated a willingness to participate in the program. Indeed, even with aversive, experimental, or intrusive treatment programs, participation may be acceptable if the offender consents to the treatment, although the validity of that consent may be examined more closely.[125] However, unless an overriding need for the treatment can be established, for example, during an emergency, the consent of offenders with mental disorders is generally a prerequisite to participation.[126] The critical question then becomes whether participation is truly consensual, especially in an institutional setting.

There are three elements widely viewed as necessary for a legally acceptable consent to participate in a treatment program. First, the individual must possess the requisite capacity to give consent. In other words, the individual's intelligence and mental status must be sufficient to allow the individual to understand to what he/she is consenting. Even patients held involuntarily are now generally presumed competent to make treatment decisions (absent a court order to the contrary). This is, however, only a presumption and treatment providers must determine for each patient whether he/she has sufficient capacity to consent to treatment, even though the specific criteria for determining capacity are often poorly defined.

The second required element is that offenders with mental disorders be fully informed of the risks and benefits of the program and available alternatives. The criteria for this component have also not been clearly established. Judicial discussions have focused on the disclosures a physician must make to a patient prior to providing medical treatment, but these rulings appear to be generally applicable to mental health professionals treating offenders with mental disorders as well. Courts have split between using a "reasonable patient" standard, that is, what a reasonable patient would need to know to make an informed decision, and a "reasonable physician" standard. There is a further split regarding the latter. One view requires the treatment provider to make such disclosure as comports with the prevailing professional standard in the community. The other view ignores the community standard and only requires such disclosures as would be made by a reasonable treatment provider under similar circumstances.

Proponents of the "reasonable physician" standard argue that the treatment provider is best situated to evaluate the risks associated with a treatment procedure and requiring the treatment provider to review with the patient every possible risk interferes with the flexibility needed to decide what treatment is best for the patient.[127] More recently, however, courts have tended to reject this approach in favor of the "reasonable patient" standard.[128] Among the reasons given for this repudiation are that it conflicts with the patient's general right of self-determination; it is difficult to discern professional custom and how it applies to a particular case; it is inappropriate to allow the "whims" of the professional community to dictate the applicable standard; professional custom is irrelevant in determining what to convey, as nonmedical factors, such as a patient's emotional condition, are important in deciding what to convey; this approach gives a treatment provider in tune with the community standards virtually unlimited discretion, which is inconsistent with a patient's right of self-determination; and this approach is unfair to patients who may have problems locating a treatment provider willing to testify against a colleague.

The rationale for recognizing the "reasonable patient" standard is consistent with judicial opinions discussing the treatment rights of offenders with mental disorders in general. When no risk to the community is involved, as would be the case within a secure treatment facility, the offender's interests have been given considerable weight. Courts recognizing the "reasonable patient" standard, although noting that it may be difficult for the treatment provider to determine the scope of the required disclosure,[129] appear to feel that any resulting confusion is not a sufficient basis for diminishing the patient's right of self-determination. In addition, because of the limited number of treatment alternatives available for offenders with mental disorders, requiring relatively extensive discussion with the patient of these alternatives may not place a great burden on the treatment provider, and the lack of data on their effectiveness and risk may raise issues that can only appropriately be decided by the offender.

The third necessary component for informed consent is that the choice be voluntary and not coerced. This may be the most critical element in evaluating the consent of offenders with mental disorders. If given within an institutional context, rather than indicating a true willingness to participate, the offender's consent may reflect a belief that treatment participation is necessary to obtain the approval of the staff or courts and to facilitate release. This may be particularly true for a nonsentenced offender with a mental disorder whose institutional discharge (and greater freedoms within the institution) is generally contingent on demonstrating therapeutic progress, with voluntary participation in a treatment program used to assess progress. Similarly, as an outpatient, the nonsentenced offender is expected to comply with a prescribed treatment program and may be reinstitutionalized for a failure to comply with that program. Such participation may also affect a sentenced offender's ability to qualify for probation, early release, or parole.[130]

Consent may also be motivated by a willingness to accept the uncertain or delayed risks of treatment rather than be subjected to the more concrete and immediate disadvantages of institutional life. Furthermore, treatment staff may subtly or not so subtly place pressures on offenders to accept the treatment program, not because of its benefit to the offender, but for their own administrative convenience. For example, it may be easier to administer a treatment program implemented on a ward-wide basis, or the program may be used to control or subdue otherwise annoying or offensive behavior.

Arguably, institutionalization or the fear of it may make it almost impossible to obtain a truly voluntary informed consent. However, most courts are likely to conclude that treatment is necessary for the offender's well-being and the ultimate safety of the community, and if a treatment is not shown to be aversive, experimental, or highly intrusive, the voluntariness of consent in an institutional context will probably not receive extensive scrutiny. Furthermore, incentives for agreeing to participate in treatment programs have been upheld. For example, it has been held to be permissible to require as a condition of probation that a sexual offender attend a counseling program, even if participation in the program requires the defendant to admit to committing a sexual assault which the defendant denied at trial (i.e., pled not guilty).[131]

Although seldom raised with regard to offenders with mental disorders, individual treatment providers (as opposed to the facility) have generally not been subject to liability for failing to properly obtain the consent of a participant in a treatment program. However, the Supreme Court has ruled that a patient can recover under federal law for a violation of his/her civil rights if the patient can show that he/she was incompetent when signing forms requesting voluntary admission to a psychiatric facility and authorizing treatment.[132] The Court felt that the presence of mental illness can require treatment staff to exercise additional caution in obtaining informed consent. This patient was entitled to an opportunity to prove allegations that he was hallucinating, confused, disoriented, and clearly psychotic at the time the forms were signed. Under federal law, a plaintiff can recover monetary damages from an individual, acting on behalf of the state, responsible for the violation of his/her civil rights. The individual, however, may be indemnified by the state. It should also be noted, however, that this precedent is more likely to be applied when improperly obtained consent results in a restriction on an individual's ability to come and go or results in physical or psychological harm. When there is little harm and perhaps benefit, for example from an inmate's participation in a group treatment program, the likelihood of a lawsuit recovering monetary damages from a treatment provider is relatively small.

Disclosure of Information

Another aspect of the treatment of offenders with mental disorders that is subject to legal scrutiny is the disclosure of clinical conversations, conclusions, or records compiled in the course of treatment.[133] Relevant issues can be divided into two groups.[134] The first centers on disclosures occurring contrary to offenders' expectation of confidentiality, after which sanctions are sought against the clinician with the burden often on the clinician to justify the disclosure. A second group focuses on efforts by offenders with mental disorders to prevent the release of such information, generally during judicial or administrative proceedings, with the burden usually on the offender to establish why release should not occur.

BREACH OF EXPECTATION OF NONDISCLOSURE

Cases addressing sanctions against a treatment provider for breaching an expectation that clinical information will not be disclosed typically involve general clinical practice and have not focused on offenders with mental disorders. However, as litigation involving offenders with mental disorders increases, such issues may be raised more frequently in conjunction with them.

Mental health professionals typically have both a legal and an ethical obligation not to disclose information obtained during treatment. For example, the ethical standards of psychologists make confidentiality a "primary obligation" that they must take "reasonable precautions" to "respect."[135] Furthermore,

> Psychologists disclose confidential information without the consent of the individual only as mandated by law, or where permitted by law for a valid purpose, such as (1) to provide needed professional services to the patient or the individual or organizational client, (2) to obtain appropriate professional consultations, (3) to protect the patient or client or others from harm, or (4) to obtain payment for services, in which instance disclosure is limited to the minimum that is necessary to achieve the purpose.[136]

A treatment provider who violates such ethical principles may be subject to a review hearing and sanctions by a state licensing board, which can include the revocation of the provider's license to practice. Licensing boards often stress the importance of assuring the public and future clients that treatment providers will respect client confidences. These assurances are considered necessary to encourage reticent clients to make needed disclosures during treatment. Although these proceedings are often initiated by a complaint from the individual receiving treatment, a licensing board may consider such matters so important that it will continue an investigation even though the initiating complaint is subsequently withdrawn.[137]

Alternatively, an individual may file a lawsuit seeking to recover damages for an unlawful invasion of privacy resulting from a wrongful disclosure. Although suits successfully establishing liability for a therapist's breach of a client's confidentiality rights are rare, courts have ruled that a client has a protected privacy interest in keeping communications with a treatment provider confidential that outweighs competing reasons for disclosing the information, entitling the client to compensation.[138]

A relatively wide range of information sources is protected from disclosure. This protection has not been limited to the words spoken by the patient, but may extend as well to the spoken words of the provider, clinical records, and the provider's impressions or opinions.[139] To recover, however, generally the client must establish that there was a client–therapist relationship, that the disclosed information arose during treatment, that the invasion of privacy was intentional, that the intrusion would be offensive to a reasonable person, and that the client was harmed.[140]

Certain exceptions to the general rule of confidentiality have been noted. First, if disclosure was made pursuant to a court order, even if the basis for the disclosure is subsequently reversed on appeal, the treatment provider is immune from sanction.[141] Second, if the individual receiving treatment had no expectation of confidentiality (e.g., the disclosure occurred with the client's informed consent or in the presence of a third party who was not involved in the treatment program), there will be no sanction for subsequent disclosures.[142] Third, the provider is not subject to sanction if there was a legal excuse or justification for disclosure, such as attempting to protect others from danger (indeed, the therapist may be sanctioned for failing to do so).[143] This dangerousness exception, however, has been variously construed—sometimes limited to when "life and limb" are in danger, other times ruled to include psychological harm.[144]

The treatment provider often faces competing demands for the information received. For example, within a correctional setting, this information may be desired by a parole board deciding whether to release an inmate or a disciplinary panel determining whether to impose sanctions for an infraction of the prison's disciplinary code.[145] Indications of dangerousness may be sought by the former, and evaluations of competence or responsibility by the latter. The inmate may be quite willing to waive any right to confidentiality if it will make his/her release or exoneration more likely, but if such outcomes are not likely to result, waivers are not likely to be forthcoming.[146] Yet, it may be precisely in such situations that the information is most needed for the protection of others and society in general. Similar predicaments may face a therapist treating a nonsentenced offender with a mental disorder seeking either outpatient placement or release. There is little law that directly addresses how the treatment provider is to resolve the tension between his/her responsibility to keep clinical information confidential and these competing demands for the disclosure of this information, but the tension is likely to increase as society requires greater assurances that it will not be endangered by offenders with mental disorders.

ATTEMPTS BY OFFENDERS WITH MENTAL DISORDERS TO PREVENT DISCLOSURE

As noted, the generally accepted exceptions to the principle of confidentiality include disclosures made pursuant to a court order, during judicial proceedings, or to prevent danger to others. Offenders with mental disorders have tried to stop the release or use of clinical information concerning them despite these exceptions. These efforts have generally failed, with the courts' emphasizing the need to protect society and placing the burden on offenders with mental disorders to justify nondisclosure.[147]

For example, testimony in a criminal trial disclosing information provided a clinician has been permitted to address the details of a crime, information disclosed earlier to avert danger to others, psychiatric reports that do not recount the statements of the client, and statements construed as not intended to be confidential (e.g., when repeated to a third party, when made after confidentiality was waived, when the defendant's mental status was raised as a defense or otherwise placed in issue, or when made outside the clinical relationship).[148] Also, a defendant's right against self-incrimination and the various evidentiary privileges (e.g., physician–patient privilege) have been ruled inapplicable to disclosures made during treatment of offenders with mental disorders in a number of contexts.[149] The waiver of a right to nondisclosure has even been held to apply to information that predated the criminal offense that is the focus of the proceedings, statements made to a defense-retained mental health professional who was not called to testify by the defense, and statements made during a sex offender treatment program after an earlier conviction.[150]

Among the rationale provided for these rulings are that disclosure is not prohibited when there was no expectation that the communications were confidential; fairness and justice require disclosure (e.g., the trier of fact should not be deprived of valuable information once the defendant's mental condition has been asserted as a plea or defense); certain community concerns "trump" confidentiality (e.g., preventing child abuse, protecting potential victims); a restrictive view of confidentiality is appropriate when the safety of the community is imperiled; and confidentiality is designed to facilitate treatment, and if there is no expectation of treatment, disclosure is permitted.[151]

The exceptions to the traditional rules of nondisclosure have also been applied to postconviction proceedings, including commitment hearings of offenders with mental disorders. For example, the U.S. Supreme Court permitted testimony of an examining psychiatrist in a proceeding pursuant to a Sexually Dangerous Persons Act, stating that guarantees against compulsory self-incrimination are not applicable to civil proceedings designed to provide care and treatment and not punishment.[152] State courts have similarly permitted the introduction of confidential information at recommitment hearings, stressing that their purpose is to afford treatment, not punishment, and to ensure proper placement.[153]

One judicial opinion particularly shows the lengths a court supervising offenders with mental disorders will go in breaching traditional notions of confidentiality to protect the safety of the community. The offender had been found IST for first-degree manslaughter and was subsequently civilly committed to a psychiatric hospital.[154] The District Attorney (DA) sought a judicial order requiring the hospital to give the DA 10 days' notice before transferring or releasing the offender so the DA would have an opportunity to challenge the move. The court ruled that because such notice could not be required for a civilly committed patient, it would be impermissible here. However, because the indictment was still pending, the court concluded that the People of New York, acting through the DA, and the court had important interests in monitoring the defendant's condition and location. Thus, the court appointed an independent expert to monitor the defendant's progress, to report to the court and the DA on a regular basis, and to notify them of any significant changes in the defendant's condition or placement. To facilitate this monitoring, the court gave this expert full access to all of the defendant's clinical records and permission to converse fully with the treatment staff, notwithstanding any confidentiality provisions. The court may have felt that it avoided limitations on disclosure by making the expert an extension of the offender, thereby eliminating the need for a waiver of confidentiality, even though there was no indication that the offender was consulted or agreed to this arrangement.

Notwithstanding traditional limits on disclosure, psychiatric reports regarding offenders with mental disorders introduced at judicial hearings may be released to the general public.[155] The privacy expectations of offenders with mental disorders are considered inapplicable when the records are introduced into public court, unless it can be shown that access is sought for improper purposes (e.g., to sensationalize, gratify public spite, promote public scandal). Although a balancing of the interests of the public and the offender is endorsed, a presumption remains favoring public access. Analogous case law has begun to develop ordering forced HIV testing of an inmate and release of the results of the test to staff who have been assaulted by the inmate and placed at risk.[156]

Perhaps not surprisingly, although the offender may find his/her own expectation of nondisclosure disregarded in criminal or postconviction proceedings, the court may be unwilling to similarly disregard the nondisclosure expectation of the victim of the crime (or a witness to the crime) when the offender seeks clinical information regarding the individual (e.g., to build a defense).[157] Emphasis is generally placed on protecting the victim's privacy, which in turn is believed to enhance the willingness of victims to obtain psychotherapy. As a result, the offender must demonstrate a need for the release of the clinical information. Generally, if a valid reason is given why disclosure is needed, the court will conduct an *in camera* review of the information to determine whether it is reasonably necessary or relevant to the proceeding.[158] Broad assertions that the records might produce some evidence helpful to the defense or that the information is needed to attack the credibility of the victim/accuser are not typically sufficient bases for even *in camera* review.[159] Even if the information is found relevant to the proceeding during the *in camera* review, generally the defendant's access to the information and subsequent admission and discussion in open court will be limited.

Changes in Status

Changes that affect the placement of offenders with mental disorders is another area receiving closer legal scrutiny. When a change may affect public safety by placing offenders with mental disorders in closer proximity to the community, the community's interests tend to be given considerable weight. If the status change poses no threat to society, more attention tends to be given to the interests of the offender. Under both scenarios, proposed status changes and treatment provider recommendations are being more closely examined.

Secure Facility to Secure Facility Transfers

One set of status changes receiving attention involves transfers of offenders with mental disorders between secure facilities with significantly different levels of mental health services.[160] For example, if a prison inmate is to be transferred to a predominantly psychiatric facility, the interests of the offender in this decision have been found to be significant and these decisions must be subject to review, with basic procedural protections afforded.

Vitek v. Jones (1980), decided by the U.S. Supreme Court, remains the leading case on transfers over objection of prison inmates to psychiatric facilities during their prison terms.[161] In New York, at the time, transfer could occur as soon as a physician or psychologist found that the inmate suffered from mental illness and could not be given proper treatment in prison. This transfer procedure was ruled illegal because it provided an inmate inadequate notice and opportunity for a hearing on a matter that could have a substantial adverse impact on the inmate and constitute a major change in the nature of confinement.

The Court equated these inmates with individuals facing civil commitment, rejecting arguments that psychiatric hospitalization would have less impact on them because they were already incarcerated, or that a criminal conviction entitled the state to impose psychiatric hospitalization. Little weight was given to potential countervailing interests of the state.[162] Although the Court acknowledged the medical nature of the transfer decision, by mandating a more formal review process the Court apparently was unwilling to defer to the judgment of treatment providers and perceived offenders with mental disorders at a disadvantage in this process, with no countervailing need to protect society justifying this imbalance.

The Court ruled that the state must provide: (1) written notice to the prisoner that a transfer is being considered; (2) a hearing sufficiently after the notice to give the inmate time to prepare, at which the evidence justifying the transfer must be disclosed and opportunity given the prisoner to appear and contest the evidence; (3) legal counsel or independent assistance to the inmate; (4) after review, a written statement by the factfinder of the basis for the decision; and (5) effective and timely notice of these rights. Although a relatively formal adversarial hearing had to be provided, the Court did find that only "an independent decisionmaker," not necessarily a judge, is needed to determine whether there is a sufficient basis for the transfer.

Allowing a nonjudge to review the matter may have been a function of the fact that *Vitek* was decided at a time when courts were still very reluctant to become involved in treatment decisions for offenders with mental disorders. However, subsequent court decisions have assigned judges a more active role in scrutinizing the transfer of sentenced offenders to psychiatric facilities.[163]

The interests of the treatment provider in these transfer decisions continues to receive little attention, with one court noting that staff must adapt their procedures to meet the needs of the inmate.[164] Often overlooked is that if the required transfer machinery is cumbersome and unresponsive, the inmate's psychological deterioration may progress, increasing the risk of harm to the inmate, staff, or other inmates. Also, staff at the psychiatric facility are more likely to receive an inmate in the midst of a crisis with limited insight into the nature of the crisis, making it difficult to formulate an appropriate response. Although emergency transfer following imminently dangerous behavior is typically allowed, waiting until an emergency arises may endanger both the inmate and others. Unfortunately, the mechanism for processing involuntary transfers may impede timely interventions.[165] Furthermore, a failure to provide timely intervention may result in less effective treatment, thereby placing the community (and the offender) at risk when the offender is ultimately released.

Ironically, whereas some prisoners fight their transfer to a psychiatric facility, others seek to force such transfers even though staff conclude they are not in need of treatment. A psychiatric facility may be perceived as less restrictive and a more preferable placement, particularly if the inmate faces restrictive housing at the prison for violating the prison's disciplinary code. The psychiatric facility is likely to house sentenced offenders with mental disorders in dormitories rather than in cells; to limit sanctions for disciplinary infractions because treatment, not punishment, must be provided in this setting; to provide more diversion in the form of regularly scheduled therapeutic activities; and to provide a more pleasant and permissive environment as part of its treatment milieu.

An inmate seeking such a placement may place considerable pressure on staff, who must decide whether transfer is appropriate and for how long. An inappropriate transfer or retention may deny a bed for a prisoner truly in need of this limited housing. On the other hand, if staff inappropriately reject a proposed transfer or prematurely return the inmate to prison, they could be liable for resulting harm. Courts have *not* thus far generally required a formal review when an inmate's demand for transfer is refused or when the inmate objects to being returned to prison.[166]

More Secure to Less Secure Facility Transfers

A different perspective is often adopted when consideration is given to the transfer of an offender with a mental disorder from a more to a less secure facility.[167] The resulting decrease in supervision and control may be seen as increasing the risk to the community by making it easier for the offender to leave the facility without permission. Programming at such facilities may also involve a gradual reintegration of the offender into the community, but relapses and incidents may occur during such efforts. Courts have tended to give greater weight to the community's interests in this context.

A decision by the Supreme Court of Ohio provides a clear example.[168] Found NGRI to a charge of aggravated murder, the offender was committed to a maximum-security treatment facility. After 4 years, the facility sought a judicial order to transfer him to a less secure psychiatric center. The court reasoned that when considering such a transfer, the offender's mental illness was already established and the need for hospitalization conceded. In such proceedings, therefore, both the welfare of the patient *and* the public safety should be considered. In denying this particular application, the court focused on the threat to public safety and broadly defined the range of potential danger. The court noted that the offender had a history of instability caused by using illicit drugs. The facility to which the offender was to be transferred had been experiencing a serious drug abuse problem, allowed patients to move throughout the facility freely and unescorted, and permitted visitors all day, every day. The court concluded that this atmosphere would provide the offender with easy access to drugs, and thus there was a high potential of the offender destabilizing.[169]

Intrafacility Transfers

Another potential status change for offenders with mental disorders involves transfers between secure and nonsecure wards within a psychiatric facility. A secure ward may be provided for patients in need of close supervision because they are deemed dangerous or escape risks. When they no longer meet these criteria, they are moved to a less secure ward where they typically have greater freedom, including off-ward privileges. Although not often considered, courts have generally ruled that if based on therapeutic rather than punitive reasons, decisions on these transfers lie within the discretion of administrative staff and are not subject to judicial review.

For example, in Ohio an NGRI acquittee was initially placed in the Forensic Unit at the psychiatric hospital to which he was committed. At a retention hearing, the hospital proposed transferring him to a less secure ward. Although a lower court rejected the proposal, an Ohio appellate court reversed this ruling, stating that although the lower court had the power to choose the facility where the acquittee was placed, it did not have supervisory powers over the details of his treatment and thus could not dictate the particular unit or ward in which he was placed.[170] The court stressed the judiciary's lack of expertise in making such treatment decisions and the need to defer to professionals trained to make them. Intrahospital transfers, it concluded, were best left to the discretion of the hospital's administrative staff.

This "hands-off" approach may seem incongruous in conjunction with judicial opinions that appear unwilling to defer to professional judgment in treatment cases or when the result is to give offenders with mental disorders greater freedom. Arguably, it is because neither of the paramount concerns typically connected with the cases of offenders with mental disorders are raised here. The interests of the offender are protected, as treatment is to be provided and the individual can be expected to benefit from the transfer. Similarly, the interests of the community are not endangered, as the patient remains within the same facility and can be returned to the secure ward if a risk to the community becomes apparent. However, when the change in status extends beyond a simple change of wards and specifically involves reentry into the community, courts are more likely to interject themselves into the decision-making process.

Most of the case law on intrafacility transfers has arisen over the movement of inmates into segregated prison housing for protective purposes.[171] Here, too, courts generally defer to the judgment of administrative officials if there is no indication that the move was made for punitive purposes. For example, the Seventh Circuit found that such a move is not improper simply because it imposes harsh and restrictive conditions.[172] Instead, the court looked at any threat to the inmate's physical health from the move, the duration and nature of confinement, the existence of feasible alternatives, and management problems posed by the inmate such as that leaving the inmate in the general population would create a "volatile and explosive situation."

A more controversial intrafacility status change is the placement of a mentally ill inmate in punitive segregation after a violation of the prison's disciplinary code. Such a placement is clearly for punitive purposes. Legal challenges to such placements have centered on the failure of prison officials to respond to the mental health needs of the inmate while segregated. For example, the Seventh Circuit found that a staff psychologist acted improperly by refusing to see during most of her stay a 16-year-old resident of a juvenile correctional institution placed in punitive segregation after an attempted escape, making the placement unlawful.[173]

The propriety of such placements and the issue of providing mental health services to inmates in disciplinary segregation have not been fully resolved.[174] Some courts argue that placing a mentally ill inmate into disciplinary segregation tends to exacerbate that individual's psychiatric symptoms and thus should not generally occur, or it should occur only as a last resort to prevent harm to self or others.[175] However, others argue that there is no such universal effect, such placement may benefit the inmate, placement options need to be available, and, at most, because of the vagaries of mental illness, such placements should be evaluated on a case-by-case basis rather than uniformly prohibited.[176] When such placements are employed for an inmate with a serious mental illness, courts generally require that the inmate be evaluated immediately upon placement and be seen frequently by mental health staff, with prolonged stays not permitted.[177]

Closely linked to this issue is whether a psychiatric evaluation should be provided as part of the prison disciplinary process to determine the likely impact on offenders with mental disorders of being placed in punitive segregation. A New York trial court concluded that an evaluation must be provided for any inmate with a well-documented history of serious psychiatric problems, and the hearing officer must take the inmate's mental state at the time of the incident into consideration in reaching a decision (i.e., that the officer consider the equivalent of an insanity defense).[178] Others have argued that such an evaluation should be conducted, but after disposition and before placement to determine the inmate's ability to tolerate disciplinary segregation.[179] A third group, and perhaps the one that comprises the majority to date, has argued that regular monitoring of offenders with mental disorders placed in disciplinary segregation will provide sufficient warning of any deleterious effects from this placement, allow for the removal of the offender from segregation before any serious or permanent harmful effect occurs, and thereby negate the need for an inquiry into the mental health status of the inmate as part of this disciplinary process.[180]

Another possible issue is whether prison officials have a responsibility to make a general inquiry into the inmate's competence to participate in the disciplinary proceeding. The Supreme Court ruled that if an illiterate inmate is involved or the complexity of the issue makes it unlikely that the inmate will be able to adequately participate, prison administrators are

required to provide inmates with counsel or counsel substitute at disciplinary hearings (the inmate can seek the aid of a fellow inmate or receive
assistance from a staff member or a sufficiently competent inmate designated by the staff).[181] Subsequent cases have addressed whether this assistance should be similarly available to inmates with a mental disability. For
example, the Eighth Circuit held that inmates are not so entitled, provided
the hearing officer determined at the disciplinary proceeding that the inmate
was competent to respond to the charges and to adequately represent
him/herself, particularly if the disciplinary charge was not complex.[182]

Interwoven with these issues is the preference of many prison treatment providers that they not be involved in the prison's disciplinary
process. They argue that requiring them to provide psychiatric evaluations
to disciplinary hearings may require predictions beyond their evaluative
capability and put them in a position where they make the ultimate decision
on an inmate's placement. This, in turn, may undercut their ability to
develop a trusting, therapeutic relationship with their clients as the inmate
comes to perceive the therapist as aligned with the disciplinary forces at
the prison. Alternatively, if the therapist is perceived as being able to find
the inmate not responsible for his/her actions and thereby prevent disciplinary segregation, the inmate may intentionally engage in "acting out"
behavior that the inmate believes is likely to lead to an evaluation of
nonresponsibility, but thereby threatening the safety of staff and inmates.[183]

Passes/Privileges

Providing individuals greater access to passes and privileges as they
gradually improve is widely accepted as an integral component of treatment
plans for individuals with a mental disability who have been placed in an
institution. The goal is to gradually integrate the individual back into the
community under circumstances that allow staff to assess the individual's
ability to successfully handle the responsibilities and pressures that may
accompany this increased freedom. However, because this approach dimin-
ishes the institution's control of the individual and provides the individual
greater access to the community, it may also place society at greater risk
from an unanticipated harmful or violent act by the individual.

Because offenders with mental disorders are perceived as potentially
more dangerous, courts have indicated a reluctance to grant them the same
access to passes and privileges accorded civil patients. For example, the
Georgia Court of Appeals upheld a trial court's refusal to grant off-campus
privileges to a committed insanity acquittee.[184] The court made this ruling
even though the unanimous recommendation of the treatment providers was
that off-campus privileges under a gradual release program would further
the acquittee's progress. The court provided little explanation other than

stating that courts retain ultimate discretion to make such decisions.[185] Similarly, a California appellate court upheld a lower court's refusal to issue grounds privileges, even though hospital staff recommended them, ruling that the burden of proof was on the offender to show that he was entitled to a grounds pass and that he would not pose a danger to the public if he was granted grounds privileges.[186]

A Nebraska appellate court noted that although the state had the burden of proof to show the need for continued retention at review hearings, the state did not have the burden of showing that the restrictions of confinement were the least restrictive necessary.[187] Instead, the court found that the courts have the burden to determine what freedom of movement outside the locked facility is consistent with public safety, and this determination is not assigned or delegable to the treatment staff. An Illinois appellate court concluded that an insanity acquittee did not have an independent right to a judicial hearing to request a change in his treatment plan (here, to provide unaccompanied grounds passes). Because it provided a check for the public safety, such a hearing could only occur upon a request by his facility director, even though civil committees had such a right and the offender could independently request a hearing on release, conditional discharge, or transfer.[188]

Finally, a New York court ruled that in determining whether to permit unescorted furlough into the community of an individual found IST for the violent murder of his mother 14 years earlier, the court must take into account the nature of the original crime, any violent criminal history, and the potential danger posed by the offender's unsupervised entrance into the community, particularly when compliance is left totally up to the offender, notwithstanding treatment staff's recommendation of this furlough.[189] The treatment providers' phrased recommendation of "ready to try" unescorted furlough was considered an insufficient guarantee in light of the harm that could be caused "by loosing such a human time bomb ... upon an unsuspecting general public." In addition, even though the issue was not before the court, the court independently noted its concern that the records indicated that the offender was able to move freely about the psychiatric center, which the court suggested was inappropriate for this and other similarly situated violent offenders.

However, the courts have not been totally consistent on this issue, particularly when it can be established that therapeutic progress will be limited as a result. For example, the Minnesota Supreme Court ruled that the issuance of passes was a treatment modality and not a form of discharge.[190] As a result, passes did not have to be approved in advance by a special review board created to evaluate proposed discharges of this group of patients. The pass program had been challenged as creating a significant risk of harm to the public, but the court found that it was an integral component of treatment plans, furthered the goal of enabling safe reentry into the community, helped the treatment team evaluate progress, and provided an incentive and additional recreational and social opportunities, and its denial would eviscerate the discretion needed by the treatment provider. The court concluded that public safety was sufficiently protected by controls over commitment and discharge, and although a certain degree of trial and error was implicit in the pass program, society must accept some of the burden of resulting errors because "further attempts to predict dangerousness result in an exercise in futility."[191]

Unfortunately, the variability of the courts' rulings on the propriety of issuing passes and privileges leaves treatment providers vulnerable to second guessing. For instance, the Ninth Circuit of the U.S. Court of Appeals ruled that the state director of mental health and three hospital administrators were potentially liable for not setting up a separate, more restrictive procedure for granting passes to offenders with mental disorders.[192] Committed to a state hospital, an insanity acquittee lured a fellow patient from her ward and raped and strangled her. The woman's estate alleged gross negligence and reckless indifference to patient safety in approving ground privileges for such patients when an adequate assessment of the risk of violence from the patient was not made. The estate asserted that the facility's criteria for assessing violence were informal and vague, resulting in patients with considerable potential for violence being granted passes; that staff received no training in assessing this potential; that offenders with mental disorders were not given special consideration in decisions to award passes, nor special treatment to reduce their potential for violence; and that despite a history of violence by offenders, staff made no attempt to rectify the problem. The court concluded that if these allegations could be proven, defendants would be liable for damages.[193]

Simultaneously, there have been legislative attempts to ensure the safety of the community by restricting the access of offenders with mental disorders to passes and privileges. For example, Illinois has enacted a statute whereby an NGRI felony acquittee subsequently committed and placed in a secure setting is not to be allowed in the community, given escorted or unescorted off-grounds privileges, or unsupervised on-grounds privileges without prior court approval. Furthermore, the court can attach such conditions as it deems necessary to reasonably assure the offender's satisfactory progress in treatment and the safety of the offender and others.[194]

Outpatient/Conditional Release

Seeking greater control over offenders with mental disorders during their return to society, many states impose an intermediate step between institutional care and outright release. Variously referred to as "outpatient status" or "conditional release" for nonsentenced offenders and "parole" or "probation" for sentenced offenders, the intent is to closely supervise the offender after institutional discharge.[195] These programs provide means to unilaterally revoke community placements and return offenders with mental disorders to an institutional setting when warning signals occur, such as heightened psychiatric symptoms or failure to adhere to a prescribed treatment program.

This approach represents an attempt to balance the interests of the offender and the community. By shortening or replacing institutional stay, the offender is provided a far less restrictive alternative and an opportunity to establish or maintain ties with the community. By requiring compliance with a given treatment program, treatment providers can better gauge the offender's progress, prevent harm if a relapse occurs, and enhance community safety.

Nevertheless, community placement can bring the interests of the community and the offender into direct conflict. Removed from the structure of facility life, offenders with mental disorders may fail to adhere to their treatment program, decompensate, and harm themselves or others. Alternatively, the relatively unpredictable course of mental illness may result in sudden, unexpected deterioration. Because monitoring and supervision is limited during community placement, early intervention is less likely and there is less ability to prevent harmful behavior. As a result, the community may be more at risk. Reflecting their tendency to favor community interests under such circumstances, court decisions on outpatient or conditional release tend to stress the importance of protecting community safety while closely scrutinizing and limiting the use of this option. One judge noted that the community is not to be treated as a "test tube for psychiatric discovery."[196]

At the same time, courts have indicated a pronounced preference for supervised community placement over outright discharge. Courts have concluded that committed offenders with mental disorders can be required to show that they are capable of handling semistructured living situations before receiving complete discharge. This approach allows for a demonstration of their ability to appropriately function in open society while providing for public safety by monitoring the offender's progress and assuring needed services.[197]

Consistently, courts closely scrutinize the use of conditional release and outpatient treatment for offenders with mental disorders.[198] They retain considerable discretion for themselves to review and assess these placements, and courts often actively monitor them. Emphasizing their responsibility to ensure the protection of the community, they often refuse to defer to the judgment of clinicians and stress the fallibility of predictions about the success of these placements. For example, courts have rejected proposals to place offenders with mental disorders on conditional release even though an offender has completed placement prerequisites; the placement plan is relatively detailed and specifically designed to minimize potential danger to the community; or treatment staff, a string of experts, or the State's representative recommend the placement (one court going so far as to assert that courts should be routinely suspicious of recommendations made by treatment staff).[199] Testimony of lay witnesses regarding the potential dangerousness of a community placement may outweigh expert testimony.[200]

Courts tend to focus on the potential danger of offenders with mental disorders when assessing placements.[201] Relatively broad criteria for refusing or revoking such placements are adopted, including expansive definitions of dangerousness (not just present dangerousness, but also future and past dangerousness) and, to a lesser extent, of mental illness.[202] A wide range of evidence may be considered in determining that offenders with mental disorders may be dangerous, the burden shifted to the offender to establish that he/she is *not* dangerous or mentally ill, procedural irregularities overlooked, and placements involving greater public exposure and less supervision scrutinized more closely.[203]

The rationale for upholding the placement of the burden of proof on the offender has been that the state has a significant interest in preventing the premature release of persons whose dangerousness and mental illness have been previously established.[204] Courts have also cited the benefits to offenders with mental disorders of continued treatment during retention, an offender's eligibility for discharge if treatment staff conclude that discharge is appropriate, and the tendency of the mental health system to favor release.[205] Placing the burden on offenders with mental disorders is considered warranted because, unlike for persons being civilly committed, the likelihood of error is diminished because these issues have been previously adjudicated and, with commission of a criminal act proven, the acquittee is not likely to be committed for mere "idiosyncratic behavior."[206] Similarly, an NGRI acquittal has been ruled to carry with it an inference of continuing mental illness.[207]

A relatively high degree of certainty that the community will not be endangered is required before such placements are approved.[208] Even though, arguably, for institutionalization to be available and of value offenders should be both mentally ill and dangerous, the latter is generally the decisive issue. For example, a court may reject the conclusion of examining professionals that the offender's mental illness is in remission and their recommendation of conditional release if there are indications of the potential for violent behavior.[209] Even if conditional release is granted, placements may be accompanied by an extensive set of conditions, the violation of which can lead to reinstitutionalization, and placements can be readily revoked.[210] Courts have recognized judicial authority to attach such conditions even without an explicit legislative enactment to this effect.[211]

Courts generally distinguish outpatient/conditional release proposals for offenders with mental disorders from those for involuntarily hospitalized patients in general and impose different procedural review schemes.[212] Courts point to the prior criminal conduct of the offender as sufficient rationale for this distinction. Also, they tend to view these placements as privileges and not rights, thereby limiting the State's obligation to provide them and the level of procedural review required for placement refusals or revocations, allowing the State to readily refuse or revoke them.[213] Indeed, close supervision, revocation, or denial of a community placement has been asserted to benefit both the community and the offender if the offender is unlikely or unable to adapt to the increased freedoms associated with such placements. Even though treatment staff may consider these placements integral to effective treatment plans, courts consider them more analogous to release/discharge decisions. Even in those jurisdictions that require that the least restrictive alternative be considered when determining whether to grant conditional release, courts proceed differently in civil and criminal commitments. For the latter, the treatment option must be weighed in the context of affording reasonable assurances of public safety, with threats to public safety established by relatively indirect evidence.[214]

Courts are also inclined to assign considerable responsibility to the staff of facilities or agencies where offenders with mental disorders are initially committed to supervise subsequent community placements. Such staff are often familiar with the patient's treatment program and needs, have the ability to smooth the transition, and are familiar to the court and interested parties. Often, however, they are reluctant to accept such responsibilities. Besides questions of liability if harm occurs, associated tracking requirements may require extensive time and effort, there may be limited authority to force the offender to follow directives, and staff may be required to assume a monitoring role that they find unfamiliar, uncomfortable, and antithetical to their usual treatment focus. Nevertheless, this assignment of responsibility has been upheld.[215]

One issue that has not been fully resolved centers on whether an offender's community placement can be revoked when progress or enrollment in a treatment program is blocked because the offender refuses to confess to committing a crime as part of treatment. Such a confession may be considered a requisite predicate for successful treatment, yet the offender may assert his/her innocence of the alleged crime. When the offender has pled guilty to a crime (even though a guilty plea may represent a forced choice by the defendant that a plea is necessary to receive a less severe sentence), courts may revoke community placement for a failure to enroll in or complete a required treatment program. If the offender was convicted after denying guilt, courts may be less likely to revoke a community placement for these reasons.[216]

Release/Discharge

Release or discharge can mark the final severing of the ties binding offenders with mental disorders to the system treating them.[217] Ideally, release will be the culmination of a gradual reintegration of offenders with mental disorders back into the community, with a series of "successes" indicating that offenders can be safely discharged.[218] The legal framework governing offenders with mental disorders, however, is not often crafted with this progression in mind. Indeed, constructing legal criteria for each of the clinical decision points would probably be unwieldy and perhaps impossible, considering the myriad of factors that go into each of these decisions. As a result, legal and clinical criteria for release may not produce the same result.[219] Nonetheless, the legal criteria govern when release occurs.

Offenders with mental disorders will generally want to end custody as soon as possible and they are entitled to periodic hearings on whether they meet the legal criteria for release. If met, ostensibly an offender must be released, regardless of the offender's progress in his/her treatment program. Theoretically, because the offender's mental illness and dangerousness are the bases for the state's custody of the offender, when those elements are no longer present, custody should cease. However, the legal determination may subtly or not so subtly also take into account other factors that attempt to assure public safety.

Numerous judicial opinions discuss the release process. As with conditional release, courts tend to closely scrutinize release proposals for the likelihood of the offender posing a danger to the community. Because release provides even less opportunity to monitor the offender, however, courts have been even more cautious about approving them. In making release decisions, courts allow themselves wide discretion, including the option of ignoring psychiatric testimony that recommends release.[220] Courts often use expansive definitions of mental illness and dangerousness to block the offender's release and consider a wide range of information.[221]

For example, future (rather than current) dangerousness has been held to satisfy the dangerousness criteria.[222] Alternatively, prior criminal acts may suffice, even though a long period of time has passed since they occurred and they are not likely to be repeated.[223] The nature of the previous criminal act may also be taken into account, with release less likely when the crime was heinous, or the court may consider an offender's lengthy criminal and psychiatric history.[224] Because the offender may have been institutionalized since the crime occurred, courts reason that it is unrealistic to expect recent evidence of violent conduct.[225] In addition, careless, noncriminal conduct (e.g., being involved in an auto accident while driving under the influence of alcohol), even when there is no apparent relation to the offender's mental illness, has been cited to satisfy the dangerousness requirement.[226]

A broad range of evidence concerning dangerousness may be admissible at an offender's release hearing. For example, statements made to hospital staff during commitment may be admitted, notwithstanding the right against self-incrimination or a patient–therapist privilege.[227] The need to gather information relevant to the release decision and the protection of the public safety is considered to outweigh any countervailing interests.

Because dangerousness may be difficult to show, courts sometimes use the offender's mental illness to establish dangerousness, even though technically the two criteria are distinct and should be independently established.[228] If the offender's mental illness is in remission or currently controlled by medication, considerable emphasis is then placed on testimony that indicates there is a significant risk that the offender will decompensate and show overt psychotic behavior under circumstances likely to await the offender upon release or when removed from the structured environment of a treatment facility.[229] When such risk is present, courts have been unmoved by arguments that offenders with mental disorders will not benefit further from the treatment being provided and will receive only custodial care, even though arguably treatment is one of the reasons for hospitalization.[230] Emphasis may also be placed on the likelihood that the offender is exhibiting good behavior to enhance the possibility of release.[231]

If their mental illness is in remission, it could also be concluded that offenders with mental disorders do not meet the commitment criterion of being currently mentally ill. However, courts frequently reject this conclusion, even though mental illness is seldom viewed as "cured" and often is seen as in remission.[232] Alternatively, courts may conduct a broad-ranging search for evidence of mental illness, rely upon acts of violence to show that the mental disorder is not in remission, allow the consideration of the offender's psychiatric history, emphasize the relatively short period of time in treatment, focus on fluctuations in the offender's mental status over time, note the lack of change in the offender's mental status since commitment (notwithstanding a current evaluation indicating the absence of mental illness), cite the offender's lack of participation in treatment programs, establish a presumption of continuing mental illness the offender must rebut, require additional psychiatric evaluations or rely on lay testimony, or label the mental illness as relatively incurable.[233] These means allow a court to ignore expert testimony that asserts the absence of the necessary mental illness element.[234]

Other considerations courts take into account in determining whether offenders with mental disorders continue to be mentally ill or dangerous are whether an individual has an appropriate place to go after release, a support network, and insight into his/her illness, and whether the individual can be trusted to adhere to the prescribed treatment plan, including taking medication and abstaining from alcohol or the use of illicit drugs.[235] Such assurances are considered necessary to ensure that offenders with mental disorders will not suffer a relapse after discharge.

A U.S. Supreme Court opinion that might have made release easier to obtain has had limited effect. In *Foucha v. Louisiana* (1992), a statutory scheme was struck down that permitted the continued commitment of an insanity acquittee who was dangerous but no longer mentally ill. However, the decisive concurring opinion by Justice O'Connor emphasized the narrowness of the Court's holding. She asserted that the ruling would not prevent a state from ever confining dangerous insanity acquittees after they regain mental health. Because psychiatric diagnoses are uncertain, she argued that courts should pay particular deference to reasonable legislative judgments about the relationship between dangerous behavior and mental illness. Thus, it might be permissible to confine an insanity acquittee who has regained sanity if "the nature and duration of detention were tailored to reflect pressing public safety concerns related to the acquittee's continuing dangerousness."[236] However, she noted that confinement requires "some medical justification" and must take into consideration the nature of the acquittee's crime, suggesting that an acquittee involved in a nonviolent or relatively minor crime could not be so confined.

Subsequent court rulings have, indeed, applied *Foucha* narrowly. For example, it has been interpreted to require release when offenders with mental disorders are dangerous but cannot be shown to be insane, but not requiring release when they are insane but cannot be shown to be dangerous.[237] Alternatively, it has been ruled that release of a dangerous, but not mentally ill offender is not required if the offender is receiving relevant treatment and the length of commitment does not exceed the maximum term of imprisonment that could have been imposed for the offense charged.[238] Another court ruled that an antisocial personality disorder satisfies the mental illness requirement if the disorder is treatable (*Foucha* ruled that an antisocial personality disorder was insufficient to establish mental illness because it was untreatable).[239]

Furthermore, as noted earlier, there are many means by which a court may conclude that an offender remains mentally ill, including that the offender's mental status has not changed during the course of hospitalization or that his/her mental illness has not been manifested only because institutional care has kept the offender from engaging in drug or alcohol abuse which causes his/her condition to deteriorate.[240] *Foucha* has also been read to apply only when offenders with mental disorders have been institutionalized, not when they are living in the community under conditional discharge or are subject to a mandatory program of outpatient treatment of limited duration.[241] Furthermore, notwithstanding *Foucha,* a series of cases have upheld statutes placing the burden of proof on offenders with mental disorders at release hearings or establishing a presumption of continuing insanity.[242]

Another issue that has arisen is whether the offender's mental status should be evaluated in a medicated or unmedicated state. Courts allowing offenders with mental disorders to be evaluated in a medicated state argue that requiring an offender to prove that he/she is not mentally ill or dangerous without medication is to ask the offender to return to a state that initially triggered the need for commitment, would force the offender to languish indefinitely in custody without meaningful treatment, and ignores the fact that many people with a mental illness function successfully in society with the aid of medication.[243] Other judges, however, assert that offenders with mental disorders may show little insight into the need for medication or may fail to continue taking medication after release; their behavior is likely to drastically alter if medication is discontinued, thereby placing the public's safety at risk. Thus, offenders with mental disorders should be required to show they are not mentally ill and dangerous in an unmedicated state.[244]

Courts have also upheld a series of procedures that make it more difficult for offenders with mental disorders to obtain release in general; for example, placing the burden on offenders to establish that the criteria for release have been met and imposing a presumption of continuing insanity at the release hearing have been upheld.[245] It has also been ruled permissible to require a psychiatric evaluation of offenders with mental disorders prior to release, to refuse the requests of indigent offenders with mental disorders for the appointment of an independent evaluating psychiatrist, to require judicial approval of the treating hospital's release decision, to make release standards more stringent or to impose a different standard for release than for the initial insanity acquittal, to impose a clear and convincing evidentiary standard, to not require that the release proceedings be adversarial in nature, to put in place an independent board to review all release decisions, to open release hearings to the general public, to limit the frequency of release petitions or permit the refiling or late filing of commitment petitions, to permit the state to appeal a release decision, and to require that offenders with mental disorders first complete a mandatory, 1-year period in a local outpatient program.[246]

These procedural devices have been approved even though they might not be acceptable for a committed civil patient. Justification is derived from the need to protect society from the offender's potential dangerousness, as the offender has already committed a criminal act (i.e., to ensure that the offender is ready for release); the need to prevent abuses of the criminal process (e.g., by discouraging false insanity pleas); and the need to conserve the financial resources of the State (e.g., by avoiding duplicative proceedings).[247] Furthermore, courts have suggested that these heightened procedural requirements are necessitated by the inability of treatment providers to make predictions concerning future mental illness and dangerousness and the public's perception that offenders with mental disorders are being released too readily.[248] The opposing interests of offenders with mental disorders are generally given little weight. Any potential stigma from a finding of mental illness is considered to have already attached prior to the release proceeding, and offenders with mental disorders are not considered harmed by continued hospitalization, but rather likely to benefit. One court discounted the likelihood of unnecessary retention because treatment providers have no interest in retaining offenders with mental disorders longer than needed and will actively seek to promote their release.[249] At the same time, if the original crime was neither particularly egregious nor heinous, there will be less pressure to apply these procedural restrictions as rigorously during release decisions.[250]

One judicial opinion contemplating the release of offenders with mental disorders noted the societal pressures placed both upon treatment staff and judges assigned to these cases, especially following particularly violent behavior.[251] It noted that treatment staff attempt to manipulate the process to force the courts to take ultimate responsibility for the release decision, in part because of the difficulty of predicting future behavior of offenders with mental disorders and concerns over possible liability if such predictions prove wrong. Courts typically are no more eager to assume this responsibility.

Postrelease

The treatment provider's responsibility may not end with the release or discharge of offenders with mental disorders. The treatment plan may envision that services will continue after release, the release order may require periodic meetings with treatment providers, or the offenders may independently seek such contacts.[252] These contacts provide an opportunity to assess how well offenders with mental disorders are adjusting to life in the community and to fine-tune treatment. The return to the community, however, is not always smooth; relapses may occur that result in dangerous or injurious behavior. The treatment provider may be able to anticipate and prevent such behavior, but its unpredictability may result in failures to do so. Considerable attention has been given to the legal duty of treatment providers to warn or protect third parties from such behavior.

Although most judicial decisions addressing third party liability involve civil patients,[253] some courts have taken a close look at the actions of treatment providers involved in the release or monitoring of an offender reentering the community who subsequently harms a third party. Further-more, the argument may be made that if the client is an offender with a mental disorder, the therapist has greater reason to anticipate violent behavior and a greater duty to warn or protect potential victims.

Traditionally, treatment providers were not liable for the harm done by their clients to third parties because there was no contractual relationship between the third party and the provider (i.e., the provider was liable only to the person receiving services). However, a number of jurisdictions have imposed a duty of care that extends to third parties that the provider could reasonably foresee might be harmed by the client. The extent of this duty and the range of third parties the courts have concluded it was foreseeable might be harmed have varied. When liability is imposed, the need to protect third parties from serious harm is generally found to outweigh any damage to therapist–client interactions resulting from required breaches of confidentiality.

When addressing potential liability after a released offender harms someone in the community, judges tend to focus on the scope of the therapist's duty of care and the foreseeability that the particular person would be harmed. A Washington court in a case involving the release of an NGRI acquittee ruled that a "therapist has a duty to take reasonable precautions to protect any person who might foreseeably be endangered by his patient's mental problems."[254] Reviewing the record, the court noted that the release order, an order that the outpatient treatment provider received and placed in its records, stated the substantial danger the acquittee posed for the general public and the conditions of release. In addition, the provider's records showed an awareness that the acquittee had missed several appointments, was not taking his medication, and was exhibiting paranoid behavior.[255]

The court concluded that these facts could establish that it was foreseeable that the acquittee would act as he did in shooting and killing a woman who lived across the street from him 5½ months after release.[256] Furthermore, if such acts were foreseeable, then it might be shown that the provider should have taken certain steps when it became aware that the acquittee was violating the conditions of his court-ordered release. However, the court indicated that a relatively high standard for recovery might be imposed in recognition of the difficulty in predicting and preventing such behavior. Thus, a required showing of gross negligence rather than ordinary negligence might be appropriate when evaluating whether the steps taken were deficient.

An Oregon court also addressed the liability of providers treating a released offender.[257] The offender was initially found NGRI following a high-speed automobile chase with police, during which he hit and seriously damaged two cars. Initially committed to a psychiatric hospital, after a first conditional release to a private medical center failed (resulting in rehospi-talization), the offender was subsequently again conditionally released to the center. Seven months later the offender admitted himself to the center's residential program because he was depressed and feared loss of control. He was permitted to leave 3 days later, but the following morning he called and complained of auditory hallucinations. He kept an appointment the next day—during which he reported problems with visual and color distor-tions—but missed his next appointment 2 days later. Two days after the missed appointment, while driving 70 miles per hour in a 35 mile-per-hour zone, he ran two red lights and collided with a car, killing the driver. The decedent's estate sued the medical center for wrongful death. The court ruled that the center, having accepted the offender as a patient, had a duty of reasonable care to control its patients' acts and a breach of this duty could entail liability to persons foreseeably endangered by this breach.

The court determined that there were four key facts in determining whether the offender's acts and the risk to the public were foreseeable and the center's response deficient. The first key fact concerned the amount of contact the center had with the offender. The court acknowledged the difficulty of foreseeing the actions of an individual only observed a few hours per week. Nonetheless, this did not mean that the individual's acts were totally unforeseeable. The court noted that a therapist at the center had recently met with the offender and talked to him on the phone, providing at least a limited opportunity to evaluate the offender's mental condition.

The second key fact concerned the identifiability of the victim. The court indicated that ordinarily, the fact that the offender had not threatened to harm anyone nor threatened to drive so as to injure persons would limit the duty of care to readily identifiable victims. However, in this case, the court noted that the center had a statutory duty to control the offender, not just for the offender's sake, but "for the peace and safety of the general public." Thus, the fact that the decedent had not been identified in advance did not mean that the offender's acts harming the decedent as an unidenti-fied member of the public were unforeseeable.

The third key fact was the impact of prior reckless driving by the offender. Again, the court indicated that ordinarily the fact that the offender had on a prior occasion exhibited reckless driving would not make this collision foreseeable, as "[c]areless or reckless driving habits are hardly limited to psychiatric outpatients." However, the court noted that it was reckless driving that brought the offender to the center, and thus was a significant risk to be considered in deciding to allow the offender to remain in the community and appropriate to consider in determining foreseeability.

The final key fact was the extent to which the offender's mental condition had deteriorated. The court ruled that it was appropriate to take into account the offender's reports to the center that he feared he was losing control, felt out of touch with the outside world, and was suffering auditory hallucinations and visual and color distortions. An additional consideration could be the failure of the center to attempt to take the offender into custody or notify the agency with authority to recommit the offender of these changes. The court concluded that there was sufficient dispute over these facts that it must remand the matter to the trial court to resolve.

Such rulings[258] have drawn sharp reactions.[259] It has been argued that they force treatment providers to make the protection of society their primary concern, with the needs of the patient secondary. Furthermore, it has been predicted that these rulings will lead prudent providers to have offenders with mental disorders taken into custody whenever there is doubt over the offenders' future acts, in turn, limiting the use of outpatient treatment, slowing recovery, and resulting in the treatment provider deciding custody matters rather than an independent court of law. Also, it may require providers to make decisions that they are not adequately trained to exercise, namely protecting society and predicting dangerousness; create a conflict of interests, as providers have to choose between protecting society and treating the patient; and impose on the offender and the therapist the "cost" of protecting society. Finally, it has been asserted that these courts rely inappropriately on the belief that treatment providers can predict dangerousness. These judicial opinions, nevertheless, once again clearly indicate that the courts are seeking, and requiring, greater assurances that the placement of offenders with mental disorders back into the community will not result in the recurrence of violent or harmful behavior by the offenders.

Recognizing perhaps that these judicial opinions may place too great a burden on mental health professionals treating offenders with mental disorders released back into the community, some steps have been taken to shield these professionals from liability. For example, several states have enacted statutes that restrict the liability of therapists to third parties (e.g., to where there has been a specific threat).[260] Similarly, some states grant immunity to institutions or persons that release a patient or prisoner who subsequently injures a third party.[261] Finally, absolute immunity has been afforded to professionals responding to an order of the court or participating in a judicial proceeding when the judge retains ultimate decision-making authority.[262]

In addition to efforts to require treatment providers to play a greater role in monitoring and supervising released offenders with mental disorders, most states require a group widely considered to be analogous to and to overlap with offenders with mental disorders, namely, released sex offenders, to register with the police upon release. This registration may require the individual to provide among other things fingerprints, a photograph, and a place of residence. Courts have upheld the retroactive application of these registration requirements.[263] A number of states also provide for some form of community notification when a convicted sex offender moves into the community. Courts have split on whether these notification provisions could apply to offenders convicted prior to the enactment of these provisions.[264] A number of appellate courts have also upheld statutes that require any person convicted of a sexual offense or institutionalized as a sexually dangerous person to provide, before release, specimens of their blood to a state data bank recording the genetic identity of sexual offenders, with its information made available to law enforcement officials for solving past and future crimes.[265]

In addition, New Jersey, in a particularly detailed statutory scheme, makes extensive community notification mandatory when the individual is classified as a repetitive–compulsive sex offender. The New Jersey Supreme Court found both the registration and the mandatory community notification requirements to be rationally related to legitimate state interests in protecting the public from the risk of recidivist offenders and to outweigh the offender's limited privacy interest in not having his/her home address, appearance, and other information made public.[266]

A range of notifications was created in conjunction with the law, with the extent of the notice determined by the likelihood of the individual committing another sex offense. If the risk is low, only law enforcement officials are informed of the offender's home address and the like. If the risk is moderate, institutions and organizations responsible for caring for and supervising children and women are given notice. If the risk is high, members of the public likely to encounter the offender are notified. Furthermore, the law was allowed to apply retroactively to previously convicted offenders and applies to both convicted offenders and those found NGRI.

Registration is a lifetime requirement unless the individual is offense-free for 15 years after release and can convince a court that he/she is not likely to pose a threat to the safety of others. Registration is required even if the offender has successfully completed a prescribed treatment program. The court did rule that the individual is entitled to notice and judicial review of the classification before release of this information, with counsel provided if needed.

The court noted with approval that the law was limited to repetitive–compulsive sex offenders and characterized the law not as a further punishment of such offenders but as giving the community an opportunity to protect itself. The court argued that statistical and other information made it clear that reoffense was a realistic risk and knowledge of their presence a necessary and realistic protection from this risk. Successful treatment of sex offenders was considered to be rare, with recidivism rates not declining with age. The court also noted that an effort was made to identify those most likely to reoffend (those with repetitive and compulsive characteristics) and to limit the extent of notification based on that criteria.

SUMMARY

The law has struggled with the dilemma of balancing humane treatment for offenders with mental disorders with the need to ensure public safety. In the past, a relatively monolithic approach was adopted, with virtually all treatment and administrative decisions left to treatment providers. This is no longer the case.

Current law regarding the treatment of offenders with mental disorders can best be described as a continuum at either end of which two major conflicting interests are balanced. At one extreme, the law is dominated by society's fears regarding the dangerousness of offenders with mental disorders. Society appears to be unwilling to rely on the implicit promises of the 1960s and 1970s that treatment alone will make offenders with mental disorders nonthreatening and nondisruptive. Instead, the community insists that such individuals be removed from its midst and placed in a setting where the acts that brought them into the criminal justice system cannot be repeated.

However, the premises of the 1960s and 1970s do not appear to have been totally abandoned, albeit applied in a somewhat different context. Although perhaps less willing to grant offenders with mental disorders their freedom, society, as reflected through its laws, continues to believe that treatment can help and should accompany the restrictions on the offender's liberty. Indeed, there may be a rough attempt to balance increased restrictions on the offender's liberty with increased oversight of the treatment provided to ensure that the offender is given an optimal opportunity to recover.

This continuum, however, pays little heed to the treatment providers who are given the responsibility of treating offenders with mental disorders, or to the dilemmas it poses for them. On the one hand, they are obligated to assure the safety of the community. On the other hand, they are required to treat and promote the recovery of the offenders. They are asked to predict which offenders should be allowed into society and which should not, and may themselves be "punished" if they are wrong. Whereas their treatment of offenders with mental disorders receives increasing scrutiny, the range of treatment options available to them may be limited by the community's unwillingness to risk a premature return to society. Also, this tends to be a treatment-resistant population, and finding an effective treatment modality may be extremely difficult.

Despite some fluctuation, the standard of care that professionals are expected to meet while caring for offenders with mental disorders has risen in the last 3 decades. Whereas identifying that standard can be a bewildering prospect for the treatment provider who perceives the law to be inconsistent, it is possible to find a mooring in the "professional judgment" standard that has been increasingly adopted as an overarching principle in scrutinizing the actions of treatment providers.

As a general rule, if the professional can demonstrate that he/she acted according to professional standards, liability will not be imposed. Ascertaining what professional standards apply, however, can be arduous and unsettling. Although beyond the scope of this chapter, the professional judgment standard is where most legal analysis of the appropriateness of a provider's actions begins, tempered by the concerns for rights and public safety discussed throughout this chapter.

ADDENDUM

As this chapter goes to press, the law pertaining to the treatment of offenders with mental disorders continues to evolve. The area that receives perhaps the most attention involves the treatment of sexual offenders, particularly those who are repeat offenders.

Repeat sexual offenders have been a particularly troubling population. Their actions tend to outrage and frighten the community, and mental health providers have found it difficult to develop treatment programs that are effective in controlling their behavior. Indeed, there has been debate over whether such individuals are treatable or even suffer from a mental disorder as mental disorders are typically defined. Nevertheless, public outcry has called for more aggressive and restrictive steps to be taken with regard to this population that will enhance public safety.

Perhaps reflecting the uncertainty over what, if anything, can be done to circumscribe this behavior, unlike other offenders with mental disorders, courts have tended *not* to expansively define or scrutinize the treatment rights of convicted sexual offenders.[1] Courts have ruled that these offenders need not be amenable to treatment to be committed; indeed, there may be specific recognition that no effective treatment has been developed, with emphasis placed instead on providing for the protection of others.[2] Similarly, sexual offenders have been required to attend counseling programs as a condition of probation, even if participation in the program mandates that the individual admit to committing a sexual assault which he/she denied at trial; a refusal to provide this admission has resulted in the individual being returned to prison.[3] A sexual offender may be required to make "reasonable progress" in a treatment program as a condition of community placement following release from prison.[4] Statements made by an individual during a sex offender treatment program that were arguably confidential have been admitted during subsequent criminal prosecutions or at recommitment hearings.[5]

The greatest attention to sexual offenders with a mental disorder, however, has occurred in conjunction with their potential release back into the community.[6] This is probably not surprising, since the release decision is perceived as having the greatest potential to place the public safety at risk.

One option, discussed earlier in this chapter, that has been widely pursued requires sex offenders to register with the police upon their release. Information that must be provided upon registration may include finger-prints, a photograph, a place of residence, and blood specimens from which genetic identities may be drawn and used in subsequent criminal investiga-tions. These registration requirements have generally been upheld.[7] Many states have also provided for some form of community notification when a convicted sex offender moves into a community (generically referred to as "Megan's Law," so-named for a young child who was killed by a released repeat sexual offender).[8] Courts have retained for themselves considerable discretion in determining the registration and notification required.[9]

Another option that a number of states have pursued is to establish procedures for the civil commitment of persons who due to a mental disorder are likely to engage in predatory acts of sexual violence. In 1994 Kansas enacted such procedures, which the U.S. Supreme Court upheld in 1997 in *Kansas v. Hendricks*.[10] Under this law, civil commitment could be imposed on (1) persons presently confined following conviction for a sexually violent offense and scheduled for release, (2) persons charged with a sexually violent offense but found incompetent to stand trial, or (3) persons found not guilty of a sexually violent offense because of insanity or because of a mental disease or defect.

The focus of this lawsuit, Leroy Hendricks, was a prison inmate scheduled for release shortly after the Kansas Act became law. Hendricks had what the Supreme Court described as "a long history of sexually molesting children," had most recently been convicted of taking "indecent liberties" with two 13-year-old boys, had served nearly 10 years of his sentence, and was scheduled for release to a halfway house. Shortly before his scheduled release, the state sought his civil confinement as a sexually violent predator under the new Kansas law. The Supreme Court noted that during the hearing associated with the civil commitment proceedings Hendricks acknowledged that he repeatedly abused children whenever he was not confined, that he could not control the urge to molest children when he got "stressed out," and that the only sure way he could keep from sexually abusing children in the future was to die.

The Court rebuffed a number of the attacks that have been lodged against such procedures.[11] Of particular relevance to this chapter, the Court found that the Kansas definition of the mental disorder required for civil commitment satisfied constitutional requirements. Involuntary hospitalization could be instituted upon a finding that the person suffered from a "mental abnormality" or "personality disorder." Critics of such laws have argued that these criteria are inherently vague and subject to misapplication, at variance with medical standards, and because they do not require a finding of "mental illness" do not constitute a sufficient indication of a mental disorder to justify involuntary hospitalization. Furthermore, critics charge that such provisions relegate individuals to indefinite confinement since treatment programs have generally been unable to change such an individual's mental disorder. Indeed, the preamble to the Kansas Act noted the relative uniqueness of the criteria employed, stating, "In contrast to persons appropriate for civil commitment under the [general involuntary civil commitment statute], sexually violent predators generally have antisocial personality features which are unamenable to existing mental illness treatment modalities."[12]

The Supreme Court, however, ruled that the state did not have to show that Hendricks suffered from a mental illness per se and that legal definitions need not mirror those advanced by the medical profession. The Court found that Kansas merely had to limit involuntary civil confinement to "those who suffer from a volitional impairment rendering them dangerous beyond their control" and that the definitions provided sufficiently narrowed the class of persons eligible for confinement to those who are unable to control their dangerousness. The Court emphasized that Hendricks had conceded that when he became "stressed out" he could not control the urge to molest children. The Court concluded that this admitted lack of volitional control, when coupled with a prediction of future dangerousness, sufficed.

The Court, as it had in the past in the context of other commitments for treatment, found that commitment here did require a finding of dangerousness either to one's self or to others and that this finding required proof of more than a mere predisposition to violence. However, the Court did not require proof of present dangerousness, which might be difficult to establish when the individual has been confined and closely monitored in a prison environment. Instead, a finding of dangerousness could be based on previous instances of violent behavior, which in turn could be used as indicators of future violent tendencies.

Although these procedures are currently in place in only a handful of states, following the Court's approval of them, they are likely to be enacted in a number of others. State courts have similarly upheld commitment pursuant to Sexually Dangerous Persons or Sexually Violent Predators Acts despite both state and federal constitutional challenges.[13] Furthermore, at least one court has ruled that a judge has no duty to warn a defendant when he/she enters a guilty plea to a criminal charge that one of the possible consequences of this plea is that it may later subject him/her to an indefinite term of commitment under such an Act.[14]

Although space precludes its discussion here, considering their general emphasis on protecting society from offenders with mental disorders, it is perhaps not surprising that the courts have been, if anything, more cautious and conservative in permitting the subsequent release of sexual offenders with mental disorders.[15]

ACKNOWLEDGEMENTS

This chapter is an updated and somewhat modified version of an article that originally appeared as Thomas L. Hafemeister & John Petrila, *Treating the Mentally Disordered Offender: Society's Uncertain, Conflicted, and Changing Views,* 21 FLA. ST. U. L. REV. 729–871 (1994).

NOTES

1. The primary focus of this chapter is on judicial opinions as opposed to constitutional provisions, legislative enactments, or executive regulations, although all contribute to the law governing the treatment of offenders with mental disorders. I chose this focus in part because to canvas all of these materials would incorporate more information than I could reasonably present within the space limitations of this chapter and in part because of the pivotal role of the judiciary in shaping this law. Not only does the judiciary generally have the final voice in shaping the law, but courts are also integrally involved in individual treatment decisions for offenders.

2. These rights included the right to be free from unreasonable searches and seizures, the right to be free of compelled self-incrimination, the right to be present at trial, the right to a speedy trial, the right to a jury trial, the right to obtain witnesses, and the right to confront opposing witnesses.

3. These rights included the right to an attorney or other assistance, a privilege against self-incrimination, and the application of traditional rules of evidence, including the exclusion of hearsay.

4. Baxstrom v. Herold, 383 U.S. 107 (1966).

5. Jackson v. Indiana, 406 U.S. 715 (1972).

6. People v. Burnick, 535 P.2d 352 (1975).

7. In a sense, the least restrictive alternative approach was a harbinger of things to come. By comparing treatment alternatives, the courts' attention was focused, at least briefly, on the internal workings of the psychiatric facility and the care provided there. Nevertheless, although cases in the 1960s and 1970s provided

greater recognition of the liberty interests of offenders with mental disorders, once an offender was placed for psychiatric care mental health professionals were generally given wide latitude in making their treatment decisions, even where the least restrictive alternative doctrine was incorporated. As will be discussed, only later would the discretion of clinicians be questioned.

8. Although this discussion focuses on the burden of proof during the initial trial and commitment process, as will be noted later, the burden of proof has been similarly placed on offenders at subsequent release hearings.

9. *See, e.g.,* United States v. Byrd, 834 F.2d 145 (8th Cir. 1987); State v. Moorman, 744 P.2d 679 (Ariz. 1987); People v. Bouchard, 535 N.E.2d 1001 (Ill. App. Ct. 1989); Treece v. State, 532 A.2d 175 (Md. Ct. Spec. App. 1987); People v. Kohl, 527 N.E.2d 1182 (N.Y. 1988); State v. Davis, 361 S.E.2d 724 (N.C. 1987); State v. Marley, 364 S.E.2d 133 (N.C. 1988); State v. Box, 745 P.2d 23 (Wash. 1987).

10. *See, e.g.,* Janezic v. State, 1996 Ala. LEXIS 278 (Ala. Crim. App. 1996); People v. Pace, 33 Cal. Rptr. 2d 352 (Ct. App. 1994); State v. Walls, 445 S.E.2d 515 (W. Va. 1994).

11. *See, e.g.,* State v. Searcy, 798 P.2d 914 (Idaho 1990); State v. Card, 825 P.2d 1081 (Idaho 1991); State v. Cowan, 861 P.2d 884 (Mont. 1993).

12. *See, e.g.,* Medina v. California, 112 S. Ct. 2572 (1992); Commonwealth v. duPont, 681 A.2d 1328 (Pa. 1996). The U.S. Supreme Court, in Cooper v. Oklahoma, 116 S. Ct. 1373 (1996), ruled that a state cannot require a criminal defendant to prove his/her incompetence by clear and convincing evidence, a relatively arduous evidentiary standard, but expressly let stand its earlier ruling in *Medina* which established that a state may presume that a defendant is competent and place the burden on the defendant to prove his or her incompetence by a lesser preponderance of the evidence standard.

13. *See, e.g.,* Jones v. United States, 463 U.S. 354 (1983); Glatz v. Kort, 807 F.2d 1514 (10th Cir. 1986) (for up to 180 days); People v. Catron, 246 Cal. Rptr. 303 (Cal. Ct. App. 1988) (180 days); *In re* Martin B., 525 N.Y.S.2d 469 (N.Y. Sup. Ct. 1987); State v. Huiett, 394 S.E.2d 486 (S.C. 1990). One opinion recommended automatic commitment where the legislature had not instituted such a procedure. *See* Waldrop v. Evans, 681 F. Supp. 840, 862 (M.D. Ga. 1988), *aff'd*, 871 F.2d 1030 (11th Cir. 1989). These rulings stand in contrast to earlier rulings that rejected automatic commitment. *See, e.g.,* Bolton v. Harris, 395 F.2d 642 (D.C. Cir. 1968); Cameron v. Mullen, 387 F.2d 193 (D.C. Cir. 1967); People v. Lally, 224 N.E.2d 87 (N.Y. 1966).

14. A period of months, even years, may pass between the commission of a criminal act and trial.

15. *See, e.g.,* United States v. Shawar, 865 F.2d 856 (7th Cir. 1989); United States v. Waddell, 687 F. Supp. 208 (M.D.N.C. 1988).

16. *See, e.g.,* Jackson v. Indiana, 406 U.S. 715 (1972).

17. Again, whereas the focus of this section is on the initial commitment decision, as I will discuss, this orientation also applies to retention decisions.

18. Jones v. United States, 463 U.S. 354 (1983).

19. *In re* Blodgett, 510 N.W.2d 910 (Minn. 1994). In a case discussed in the Addendum to this chapter, the U.S. Supreme Court similarly upheld a Kansas statute permitting the commitment of individuals likely to engage in "predatory acts of sexual violence" for an indefinite period, even after the individual has completed a period of incarceration for a related crime. Kansas v. Hendricks, 117 S. Ct. 2072 (1997).

20. *See, e.g.*, 18 U.S.C. § 4244(d) (1988).
21. *See, e.g.*, Hickey v. Morris, 722 F.2d 543 (9th Cir. 1983); State v. Hungerford, 267 N.W.2d 258 (Wis. 1978).
22. *See, e.g.*, United States v. Roberts, 915 F.2d 889 (4th Cir. 1990), People v. Colvin, 171 Cal. Rptr. 32 (Cal. Ct. App. 1981); People v. Bolden, 266 Cal. Rptr. 724 (Cal. Ct. App. 1990); Dorman v. State, 457 So. 2d 503 (Fla. Dist. Ct. App. 1984). *But see* People v. Minor, 277 Cal. Rptr. 615 (Cal. Ct. App. 1991); People v. Gunderson, 279 Cal. Rptr. 494 (Cal. Ct. App. 1991); People v. Palmer, 592 N.E.2d 940 (Ill. 1992); People v. Partewski, 622 N.E.2d 69 (Ill. App. Ct. 1993).
23. *See, e.g.*, People v. Taylor, 272 Cal. Rptr. 424 (Cal. Ct. App. 1990).
24. *See, e.g.*, Commonwealth v. Davis, 551 N.E.2d 39 (Mass. 1990).
25. *See, e.g.*, State v. Hass, 566 A.2d 1181 (N.J. Super. Ct. Law Div. 1988).
26. Kansas v. Hendricks, 117 S. Ct. 2072 (1997).
27. *See, e.g.*, Waldrop v. Evans, 681 F. Supp. 840 (M.D. Ga. 1988), *aff'd*, 871 F.2d 1030 (11th Cir. 1989); State v. Neely, 876 P.2d 222 (N.M. 1994).
28. *Neely,* 876 P.2d 222, 227 (Montgomery, C.J., concurring).
29. The focus of this section is on treatment provided the offender while in the custody of the State. Cases discussing this treatment are generally distinct from cases discussing the right of offenders with mental disorders to minimally adequate conditions of confinement (e.g., a right to adequate clothing, food, shelter) and the duty imposed on custodial staff to protect offenders with mental disorders from harm (e.g., prevention of suicide, assault).
30. Rouse v. Cameron, 387 F.2d 241 (D.C. Cir. 1967).
31. Youngberg v. Romeo, 457 U.S. 307 (1982).
32. *See* Rennie v. Klein, 653 F.2d 863 (3rd Cir. 1981), *vacated*, 458 U.S. 1119 (1982); Scott v. Plante, 532 F.2d 939 (3rd Cir. 1976), *vacated*, 458 U.S. 1101 (1982), *on remand*, 691 F.2d 634 (3rd Cir. 1982).
33. Because the Court focused on the constitutional rights of a committed individual with mental retardation, its discussion referred to a right to "habilitation" or training. Sometimes the phrase "right to treatment" has been reserved for committed individuals with a mental illness. Although the types of services that would be required differ, from a legal perspective the right to habilitation and the right to treatment are closely linked and have often been used interchangeably, and will be so used here.
34. *Id.* at 323.
35. *See, e.g.*, United States v. Tennessee, 925 F. Supp. 1292 (W.D. Tenn. 1995); Woe by Woe v. Cuomo, 638 F. Supp. 1506 (E.D.N.Y. 1986), *aff'd in part*, 801 F.2d 627 (2nd Cir. 1986); Sabo v. O'Bannon, 586 F. Supp. 1132 (E.D. Pa. 1984); People v. Gilliland, 769 P.2d 477 (Colo. 1989); Kort v. Carlson, 723 P.2d 143 (Colo. 1986).
36. *See* United States v. Ecker, 543 F.2d 178 (D.C. Cir. 1976); Ashe v. Robinson, 450 F.2d 681 (D.C. Cir. 1971); Rouse v. Cameron, 387 F.2d 241 (D.C. Cir. 1967); Tribby v. Cameron, 379 F.2d 104 (D.C. Cir. 1967).
37. *See* Millard v. Cameron, 373 F.2d 468 (D.C. Cir. 1966).
38. Although relatively few other courts discussed the right to treatment of offenders with mental disorders during this period, at least one other court adopted a relatively similar position. *See* Ohlinger v. Watson, 652 F.2d 775 (9th Cir. 1980). This court was also willing to require individualized treatment and to actively interject itself in the treatment decision-making process, and was unwilling to recognize budgetary restraints on the ability to provide necessary treatment.

39. *See, e.g.,* Thompson v. County of Mediana, Ohio, 29 F.3d 238 (6th Cir. 1994); Knight v. Mills, 836 F.2d 659 (1st Cir. 1987); Partridge v. Two Unknown Police Officers of Houston, 791 F.2d 1182 (5th Cir. 1986); *Woe by Woe,* 638 F. Supp. at 1506; *Kort,* 723 P.2d at 148; *Gilliland,* 769 P.2d at 483; State DHRS v. Schreiber, 561 So. 2d 1236 (Fla. Ct. App. 1990); *In re* G. S., 551 N.E.2d 337 (Ill. Ct. App. 1990); Commonwealth v. Davis, 551 N.E.2d 39 (Mass. 1990); Bahrenfus v. Bachik, 806 P.2d 170 (Ore. Ct. App. 1991).

40. Doe v. Gaughan, 808 F.2d 871 (1st Cir. 1986).

41. In ruling that conditions were acceptable, the court focused on the lack of murders and the minimal number of suicides while housing a dangerous and unmanageable population; the procedures that limited and reviewed the use of restraints; isolated incidents of staff abuse; the use of both standard and innovative treatments; the exercise of professional judgment despite overcrowding; and a failure to show a loss of preexisting self-care skills.

42. This overlap between these two populations can be traced in part to the analysis used for pretrial detainees with a mental disorder, a group that tends to bridge the two populations. While awaiting trial on a criminal charge, these individuals are often detained within an institutional setting (typically a jail) that also houses individuals convicted of crimes carrying a relatively short sentence (e.g., 1 year or less) or awaiting transfer to a prison setting. The U.S. Supreme Court has ruled that the Fourteenth Amendment be used to assess the treatment rights of pretrial detainees (Bell v. Wolfish, 441 U.S. 520 (1979)), while the Eighth Amendment, as discussed in the next section, be used to decide the treatment rights of convicted criminals (Estelle v. Gamble, 429 U.S. 97 (1976). Because they have not been convicted of a crime, the rights of pretrial detainees are considered to be analytically distinct, but because their institutional placement and care is often relatively indistinguishable from convicted criminals, numerous courts have held that pretrial detainees, while protected under the Fourteenth Amendment, are entitled to the same rights as afforded convicted prison inmates under the Eighth Amendment. *See, e.g.,* Hare v. City of Corinth, 74 F.3d 633 (5th Cir. 1996); Thompson v. County of Mediana, Ohio, 29 F.3d 238 (6th Cir. 1994); Belcher v. City of Foley, Ala., 30 F.3d 1390 (11th Cir. 1994). *But see* Shaw by Strain v. Strackhouse, 920 F.2d 1135 (3rd Cir. 1990).

43. *See, e.g.,* White v. Napoleon, 897 F.2d 103, 113 (3d Cir. 1990); Bowring v. Godwin, 551 F.2d 44, 48 (4th Cir. 1977); Farley v. Doe, 840 F. Supp. 356, 357 (E.D. Pa. 1993); Langley v. Coughlin, 715 F. Supp. 522, 538 (S.D.N.Y. 1989); Knop v. Johnson, 667 F. Supp. 512, 528 (W.D. Mich. 1987).

44. There are considerably more opinions addressing the care provided sentenced than nonsentenced offenders. Indeed, the flood of litigation from pro se prison inmates has become a major concern of the courts.

45. Included in this discussion are individuals who receive a prison sentence in conjunction with a finding of a mental disability (e.g., individuals sentenced as sexual offenders with mental disorders, guilty but mentally ill) or individuals for whom mental disorder was not a factor at conviction or sentencing but who exhibit symptoms of a mental disorder requiring treatment during the course of incarceration.

46. Although less discussed and developed, an inmate may also possess a right to mental health treatment under state law. *See* Lewis v. Griffin, 376 S.E.2d 364 (Ga. 1989); Villarreal v. Thompson, 920 P.2d 1108 (Or. App. 1996). *But see* Melville v. State, 793 P.2d 952 (Wash. 1990).

47. *See* Bell v. Wolfish, 441 U.S. 520 (1979).
48. Some courts use an Eighth Amendment standard to assess the treatment provided pretrial detainees, but these courts have indicated that this is a minimal standard, and such detainees may be entitled to more. *See, e.g.*, City of Revere v. Mass. General Hosp., 463 U.S. 239 (1983); Partridge v. Two Unknown Police Officers of Houston, 791 F.2d 1182 (5th Cir. 1986); Elliott v. Cheshire County, 750 F. Supp. 1146 (D.N.H. 1990); Tittle v. Mahan, 566 N.E.2d 1064 (Ind. Ct. App. 1991). In contrast, generally courts refrain from using the Fourteenth Amendment as a guide or a baseline for assessing the mental health care given an inmate, largely holding this line of cases inapplicable.
49. Estelle v. Gamble, 429 U.S. 97 (1976).
50. In Farmer v. Brennan, 114 S. Ct. 1970 (1994), the U.S. Supreme Court addressed how "deliberate indifference" is to be established by requiring a showing that the prison official was "subjectively" aware of a substantial risk of serious harm to an inmate.
51. Bowring v. Godwin, 551 F.2d 44 (4th Cir. 1977).
52. *Id.* at 47.
53. *See, e.g.*, Inmates of Allegheny County Jail v. Pierce, 612 F.2d 754 (3rd Cir. 1979); Ramos v. Lamm, 639 F.2d 559 (10th Cir. 1980); Hoptowit v. Ray, 682 F.2d 1237 (9th Cir. 1982); Wellman v. Faulkner, 715 F.2d 269 (7th Cir. 1983).
54. *See, e.g., Youngberg,* 457 U.S. at 321–22; *Hoptowit,* 682 F.2d at 1255, n.8; Doe v. District of Columbia, 697 F.2d 1115, 1123 (D.C. Cir. 1983); Woe by Woe v. Cuomo, 638 F. Supp. 1506, 1517 (E.D.N.Y. 1986) *aff'd in part,* 801 F.2d 627 (2d Cir. 1986); State v. Christopher, 652 P.2d 1031, 1034 (Ariz. 1982). There was also a reluctance to grant sizable monetary damages. *See, e.g.*, Doe v. District of Columbia, 697 F.2d 1115 (D.C. Cir. 1983).
55. *See, e.g.*, Langley v. Coughlin, 715 F. Supp. 537 (S.D.N.Y. 1989).
56. *See, e.g.*, Torraco v. Maloney, 923 F.2d 231 (1st Cir. 1991); Smith v. Jenkins, 919 F.2d 90 (8th Cir. 1990); Greason v. Kemp, 891 F.2d 829 (11th Cir. 1990); Meriwether v. Faulkner, 821 F.2d 408 (7th Cir.), *cert. denied*, 484 U.S. 935 (1987); Rogers v. Evans, 792 F.2d 1052 (11th Cir. 1986); Arnold *ex rel.* H.B. v. Lewis, 803 F. Supp. 246 (D. Ariz. 1992); Tillery v. Owens, 719 F. Supp. 1256 (W.D. Pa. 1989), *aff'd,* 907 F.2d 418 (3rd Cir. 1990); Waldrop v. Evans, 681 F. Supp. 840 (M.D. Ga. 1988), *aff'd,* 871 F.2d 1030 (11th Cir. 1989); Guglielmoni v. Alexander, 583 F. Supp. 821 (D.C. Conn. 1984).
57. *See, e.g., Greason,* 891 F.2d at 829; *Tillery,* 719 F. Supp. at 1256; *Waldrop,* 681 F. Supp. at 861.
58. *See, e.g., Greason,* 891 F.2d at 835–36; Coleman v. Wilson, 912 F. Supp. 1282 (E.D. Cal. 1995); Casey v. Lewis, 834 F. Supp. 1477 (D. Ariz. 1993); *Arnold,* 803 F. Supp. at 246.
59. *See, e.g.*, Hoptowit v. Ray, 682 F.2d 1237 (9th Cir. 1982); *Coleman,* 912 F. Supp. at 1320; *Casey,* 834 F. Supp. at 1477; *Arnold,* 803 F. Supp. at 246; *Langley,* 715 F. Supp. at 522; *Tillery,* 719 F. Supp. at 1303; Lovell v. Brennan, 566 F. Supp. 672 (D. Me. 1983), *aff'd,* 728 F.2d 560 (1st Cir. 1984).
60. *See, e.g., Smith,* 919 F.2d at 90; *Greason,* 891 F.2d at 829; Ramos v. Lamm, 639 F.2d 559 (10th Cir. 1980); *Coleman,* 912 F. Supp. at 1306; *Tillery,* 719 F. Supp. at 1256.
61. *See, e.g.*, Belcher v. City of Foley, Ala., 30 F.3d 1390 (11th Cir. 1994); *Coleman,* 912 F. Supp. at 1308; *Casey,* 834 F. Supp. at 1477; Arnold *ex rel.* H.B. v. Lewis, 803 F. Supp. 246 (D. Ariz. 1992).

62. *See, e.g.,* Greason v. Kemp, 891 F.2d 829, 836 (11th Cir. 1990); Cortes-Quinones v. Jimenz-Nettleship, 842 F.2d 556 (1st Cir. 1988); Wellman v. Faulkner, 715 F.2d 269 (7th Cir. 1983); Hoptowit v. Ray, 682 F.2d 1237 (9th Cir. 1982); *Ramos,* 639 F.2d at 559; *Coleman,* 912 F. Supp. at 1315; *Casey,* 834 F. Supp. at 1477; *Arnold,* 803 F. Supp. at 246; Tillery v. Owens, 719 F. Supp. 1256 (W.D. Pa. 1989); Waldrop v. Evans, 681 F. Supp. 840 (M.D. Ga. 1988).

63. *Waldrop,* 681 F. Supp. at 840.

64. Courts have thus far left largely unanswered the question of whether prison inmates in general are entitled to recover damages for harm incurred at the hands of a mentally ill inmate. *But see Wellman,* 715 F.2d at 273, n.3; *Tillery,* 719 F. Supp. at 1256. Judicial opinions have tended to focus on the needs and rights of the mentally ill inmate. However, in other contexts, courts have recognized the right of inmates to be protected from other inmates. This could impose liability for failure to control inmates by providing treatment to them.

65. *Cortes-Quinones,* 842 F.2d at 556.

66. *See, e.g.,* Riddle v. Mondragon, 83 F.3d 1197 (10th Cir. 1996); Jackson v. Fair, 846 F.2d 811 (1st Cir. 1988).

67. Austin v. Pennsylvania Dep't of Corrections, 876 F. Supp. 1437 (E.D. Pa. 1995).

68. *See, e.g.,* Gates v. Shinn, 98 F.3d 463 (9th Cir. 1996), *cert. denied,* 117 S. Ct. 2454 (1997); Riddle v. Mondragon, 83 F.3d 1197 (10th Cir. 1996); Thompson v. County of Mediana, Ohio, 29 F.3d 238 (6th Cir. 1994); O'Hara v. Wigginton, 24 F.3d 823 (6th Cir. 1994). However, in cases of severe mental illness, courts may still conclude that a prison setting is incapable of meeting the mental health needs of the inmate. *See, e.g.,* Arnold *ex rel.* H.B. v. Lewis, 803 F. Supp. 246 (D. Ariz. 1992).

69. *See, e.g.,* Lair v. Oglesby, 14 F.3d 15 (8th Cir. 1993).

70. Martel v. Fridovich, 14 F.3d 1 (1st Cir. 1993); Abany v. Fridovich, 862 F. Supp. 615 (D. Mass. 1994).

71. *See, e.g.,* Riddle v. Mondragon, 83 F.3d 1197 (10th Cir. 1996); Langton v. Johnston, 928 F.2d 1206 (1st Cir. 1991); Balla v. Idaho State Bd. of Corrections, 869 F.2d 461 (9th Cir. 1989); Russell v. Eaves, 722 F. Supp. 558 (E.D. Mo. 1989), *dismissed,* 902 F.2d 1574 (8th Cir. 1990).

72. Although this discussion is limited to individuals for whom an initial criminal proceeding has been completed and custody for purposes of treatment imposed, the U.S. Supreme Court ruled in Riggins v. Nevada, 504 U.S. 127 (1992) that pretrial detainees also have a qualified right to refuse the administration of psychotropic medication. *See also* Heffernan v. Norris, 48 F.3d 331 (8th Cir. 1995); State v. Armstrong, 649 So.2d 683 (La. Ct. App. 1994).

73. *See* Mills v. Rogers, 457 U.S. 291 (1982).

74. *See, e.g., In re* Salisbury, 524 N.Y.S.2d 352 (N.Y. Sup. Ct. 1988); Sundby v. Fiedler, 827 F. Supp. 580 (W.D. Wis. 1993).

75. *See, e.g.,* McCormick v. Stalder, 105 F.3d 1059 (5th Cir. 1997), in which prison officials did not act unconstitutionally by forcing an inmate to undergo treatment for tuberculosis. There may, however, be other bases for objecting to less intrusive treatments, such as a violation of freedom of religion rights under the First Amendment. *See, e.g.,* Griffin v. Coughlin, 626 N.Y.S.2d 1011 (App. Div. 1995).

76. United States v. Charters, 863 F.2d 302 (4th Cir. 1988) (en banc).

77. *See, e.g.,* Dautremont v. Broadlawns Hosp., 827 F.2d 291 (8th Cir. 1987). Also, although Washington v. Harper, 494 U.S. 210 (1990), discussed below, only

addressed the right of prisoners to refuse treatment, the U.S. Supreme Court's rejection of the need for automatic judicial review is likely to be construed by other federal courts as applicable to nonsentenced offenders with mental disorders as well. *But see* Enis v. Dep't of Health & Social Services, 962 F. Supp. 1192 (W.D. Wis. 1996) in which a previous judicial finding of NGRI cannot be used in lieu of hearing on competence to make medical decisions.

78. State *ex rel.* Jones v. Gerhardstein, 416 N.W.2d 883 (Wis. 1987).

79. Stensvad v. Reivitz, 601 F. Supp. 128 (W.D. Wis. 1985). *But see Enis,* 962 F. Supp. at 1192, in which the State cannot rely on previous finding of NGRI to show dangerousness for the purpose of administering psychotropic medication over the offender's objection; the State must establish present dangerousness and present need for medication.

80. This court also subsequently rejected an effort to expand the means by which an individual can be shown to be incompetent to make a treatment decision. *See In re* Virgil D., 524 N.W.2d 894 (Wis. 1994).

81. *See, e.g.,* People v. Medina, 799 P.2d 1282 (Cal. 1990), *cert. granted in part,* 112 S. Ct. 336 (1991); Riese v. St. Mary's Hosp. & Medical Ctr., 243 Cal. Rptr. 241 (Ct. App. 1987); *In re* M.P., 510 N.E.2d 645 (Ind. 1987); Williams v. Wilzack, 573 A.2d 809 (Md. 1990); Rogers v. Comm'r of Dep't of Mental Health, 458 N.E.2d 308 (Mass. 1983); Jarvis v. Levine, 418 N.W.2d 139 (Minn. 1988); Opinion of the Justices, 465 A.2d 484 (N.H. 1983); Rivers v. Katz, 495 N.E.2d 337 (N.Y. 1986).

82. *See, e.g.,* People v. Gilliland, 769 P.2d 477 (Colo. 1989); *Williams,* 573 A.2d at 809; *In re* Steen, 437 N.W.2d 101 (Minn. Ct. App. 1989); *In re* Lambert, 437 N.W.2d 106 (Minn. Ct. App. 1989).

83. *See, e.g., Gilliland,* 769 P.2d at 477; Tolley v. Commonwealth, 892 S.W.2d 580 (Ky. 1995).

84. *See, e.g.,* Bee v. Greaves, 744 F.2d 1387, 1395 (10th Cir. 1984).

85. *Id.* at 1287.

86. Earlier cases did challenge entire treatment programs. *See, e.g.,* Knecht v. Gillman, 488 F.2d 1136 (8th Cir. 1973). However, they questioned the program per se, and did not focus on the right of an individual to refuse an otherwise acceptable treatment program. These cases are discussed in the Treatment Program section.

87. Washington v. Harper, 494 U.S. 210 (1990).

88. *Id.* at 223–24.

89. In addition, minutes of the hearing were to be kept and a copy provided to the inmate.

90. A similarly composed committee had to initially review the treatment after 7 days, and the treating psychiatrist had to review the case and prepare a report for the Department of Corrections medical director every 14 days thereafter.

91. The Court also held that if the inmate was provided the assistance of an independent lay advisor who understood the psychiatric issues involved, the inmate did not have to be represented by counsel.

92. *See, e.g.,* Sullivan v. Flannigan, 8 F.3d 591 (7th Cir. 1993); Gilliam v. Martin, 589 F. Supp. 680 (W.D. Okla. 1984); Osgood v. District of Columbia, 567 F. Supp. 1026 (D.D.C. 1983).

93. For example, the finding of dangerousness associated with a determination that the inmate is subject to involuntary hospitalization has been held to satisfy the dangerousness requirement for forced administration of medication. *See* Washington v. Silber, 805 F. Supp. 379 (W.D. Va. 1992).

94. *See, e.g., Gilliam,* 589 F. Supp. at 682.
95. *See, e.g.,* Sullivan, 8 F.3d at 591 (the need for medication is a question the Supreme Court has surrendered to the medical professional); *Silber,* 805 F. Supp. at 379 (it is neither helpful nor possible to judicially micromanage an inmate's psychiatric treatment and staff must be free to respond to fluctuations in the patient's condition).
96. *Sullivan,* 8 F.3d at 591; *Silber,* 805 F. Supp. at 379.
97. *See* Arnold *ex rel.* H.B. v. Lewis, 803 F. Supp. 246 (D. Ariz. 1992).
98. *See, e.g.,* Hogan v. Carter, 85 F.3d 1113 (4th Cir. 1996), *cert. denied,* 117 S. Ct. 408 (1996); Walker v. Shansky, 28 F.3d 666 (7th Cir. 1994); Chambers v. Ingram, 858 F.2d 351 (7th Cir. 1988); Wilson v. Chang, 955 F. Supp. 18 (D.R.I. 1997).
99. *See, e.g.,* Enis v. Dep't of Health & Social Services, 962 F. Supp. 1192 (W.D. Wis. 1996); *Osgood,* 567 F. Supp. at 1031.
100. *See, e.g.,* Large v. Superior Court, 714 P.2d 399 (Ariz. 1986); California Dep't of Corrections v. Office of Admin. Hearings, 61 Cal. Rptr. 2d 903 (Cal. Ct. App. 1997); People v. Delgado, 262 Cal. Rptr. 122 (Ct. App.), *review denied, opinion withdrawn by order of court,* 1989 Cal. LEXIS 2460 (1989); Keyhea v. Rushen, 223 Cal. Rptr. 746 (Ct. App. 1986); People v. Woodall, 257 Cal. Rptr. 601 (Ct. App.), *review denied, opinion withdrawn by order of court,* 1989 Cal. LEXIS 3119 (1989). *But cf.* Harmon v. McNutt, 587 P.2d 537 (Wash. 1978).
101. However, it can be argued that the recognition of this right (1) undercuts the authority of the treatment staff, leading to a lack of confidence in and reliance on the staff by offenders with mental disorders; (2) introduces multiple decisionmakers and slows progress because of the uncertainty and confusion resulting from conflicting treatment decisions; (3) undermines the confidence and morale of the treatment staff, as they become preoccupied with what the judiciary will rule regarding their decisions; and (4) results in decisions being made according to legal rather than clinical criteria.
102. *See, e.g.,* Ford v. Wainwright, 477 U.S. 399 (1986).
103. Perry v. Louisiana, 498 U.S. 38 (1990). On remand, the Louisiana Supreme Court held that the administration of antipsychotic medication to a death row inmate against his will was indeed a constitutional violation. State v. Perry, 610 So. 2d 746 (La. 1992).
104. *See, e.g., In re* Zettlemoyer, 53 F.3d 24 (3rd Cir. 1995) (that inmate was voluntarily taking psychotropic medications at the time does not invalidate his waiver of appeals); Singleton v. Endell, 870 S.W. 2d 742 (Ark. 1994) (argument that administering antipsychotic drugs violates death row inmate's rights not sufficiently pursued; reports of treating physician that defendant's psychosis was in remission supported denial of sanity examination for death row inmate); State v. Perry, 610 So. 2d 746 (La. 1992) (while affirming that the prisoner was not competent for execution, reversed lower court order requiring the state to medicate him with antipsychotic drugs without his consent and stayed execution of death sentence until such time, if ever, inmate regains sanity independent of and without the influence of antipsychotic drugs); Singleton v. State, 437 S.E.2d 53 (S.C. 1993) (forcible administration of medication to facilitate execution a violation of *state* law; improper to vacate death sentence and impose life sentence in its place; though no current cure, always a potential for change; instead issue a temporary stay of execution); State v. Harris, 789 P.2d 60 (Wash. 1990) (evidence supported determination that defendant competent to be executed;

directions provided on proper procedures to follow in making competency determinations).

105. The majority of these cases involve sentenced offenders with mental disorders. In establishing these limits, however, there has been little to indicate that they would not apply equally to nonsentenced offenders.

106. A potential fifth limit, although even less discussed, is that the treatment impermissibly infringes on the religious rights of offenders with mental disorders. *See* Griffin v. Coughlin, 626 N.Y.S.2d 1011 (A.D. 1995).

107. Mackey v. Procunier, 477 F.2d 877 (9th Cir. 1973).

108. *Id.* at 878. A lower court had dismissed the inmate's complaint prior to trial as not stating a constitutional claim. The Court of Appeals' reversal allowed the inmate to go forward in an attempt to prove his allegations.

109. Knecht v. Gillman, 488 F.2d 1136 (8th Cir. 1973).

110. Souder v. McGuire, 423 F. Supp. 830 (M.D. Pa. 1976).

111. Price v. Sheppard, 239 N.W.2d 905 (Minn. 1976).

112. Other factors to be examined included whether the technique is widely accepted among treatment providers or viewed as experimental, the technique's intrusiveness, and the patient's ability to assess the treatment.

113. Canterino v. Wilson, 546 F. Supp. 174 (W.D. Ky. 1982). *See also* Green v. Baron, 879 F.2d 305 (8th Cir. 1989).

114. Kaimowitz v. Dep't of Mental Health, No. 73-19434-AW (1973) (reported at 1(2) Mental & Physical Disability L. Rep. 147 (1976)).

115. People v. Gauntlett, 352 N.W.2d 310 (Mich. App.), *modified*, 353 N.W.2d 463 (Mich. 1984).

116. The court also noted the wide range of adverse reactions produced by the drug, that participation in its use had always been voluntary and in conjunction with psychotherapy, and its originator had been criticized for it.

117. Commentators did attack this opinion as overstating the experimental nature and risks of Depo-Provera.

118. *See, e.g.*, Knecht v. Gilman, 488 F.2d 1136 (8th Cir. 1973); Mackey v. Procunier, 477 F.2d 877, 878 (9th Cir. 1973); Jarvis v. Levine, 418 N.W.2d 139 (Minn. 1988).

119. *See* 45 C.F.R., Part 46 (1992). *See also* Federal Food, Drug and Cosmetic Act, 21 U.S.C. § 355(i) (1988); 21 C.F.R. § 312 (1993) (regulation of use of subjects for clinical trials of drugs). States have instituted similar restrictions. *See Gauntlett,* 352 N.W.2d at 310.

120. *See* Cal. Penal Code §§ 3500–3509.5 (West 1982 & Supp. 1995).

121. *Jarvis,* 418 N.W.2d at 139.

122. Price v. Sheppard, 239 N.W.2d 905 (Minn. 1976).

123. Other criteria were the treatment's experimental nature and acceptance by the medical community, and the patient's ability to competently determine whether the treatment is desirable.

124. *See, e.g.*, Washington v. Harper, 110 S. Ct. 1028, 1039 (1990); Large v. Superior Court, 714 P.2d 399 (Ariz. 1986); State *ex rel.* Jones v. Gerhardstein, 416 N.W.2d 883 (Wis. 1987).

125. *See, e.g,* Knecht v. Gilman, 488 F.2d 1136, 1138–39 (8th Cir. 1973).

126. *See, e.g., Jones,* 416 N.W.2d at 883; Lojuk v. Quandt, 706 F.2d 1456 (7th Cir. 1983).

127. *See, e.g.*, Aiken v. Clary, 396 S.W.2d 668 (Mo. 1965); Largey v. Rothman, 540 A.2d 504 (N.J. 1988).

128. *See, e.g.*, Korman v. Miller, 858 P.2d 1145, 1149 (Alaska 1993) ("the modern trend is to measure the physician's duty of disclosure by what a reasonable patient would need to know"); *Largey*, 540 A.2d at 504 (cites twelve other states that have rejected the "reasonable physician" standard); Canterbury v. Spence, 464 F.2d 772 (D.C. Cir. 1972), *cert. denied*, 409 U.S. 1064 (1972); Bedel v. Univ. of Cincinnati Hosp., 669 N.E.2d 9 (Ohio Ct. App. 1995); Villanueva v. Harrington, 906 P.2d 374 (Wash. Ct. App. 1995).

129. *See Largey*, 540 A.2d at 504.

130. *See, e.g.*, Langton v. Secretary of Public Safety, 636 N.E.2d 299 (Mass. Ct. App. 1994); People v. Gauntlett, 352 N.W.2d 310 (Mich. App.), *modified*, 353 N.W.2d 463 (Mich. 1984); State v. King, 925 P.2d 606 (Wash. 1996). *See also* State v. Smith, 933 S.W.2d 450 (Tenn. 1996) (defendant told he would be indicted if he did not seek counseling).

131. State v. Cavrizales, 528 N.W.2d 29 (Wis. Ct. App. 1995). *See also* Austin v. Pennsylvania Dep't of Corrections, 876 F. Supp. 1437 (E.D. Pa. 1995); Patterson v. Webster, 760 F. Supp. 150 (E.D. Mo. 1991).

132. Zinermon v. Burch, 494 U.S. 113 (1990). To recover under this federal law, however, the patient must show that the treatment provider was a "state actor"—for example, an employee of the state—which will generally not encompass privately employed treatment staff. However, such staff may be subject to liability under a state law claim of false imprisonment. Foshee v. Health Management Associates, 675 So. 2d 957 (Fla. Ct. App. 1996), *rev. denied*, 686 So. 2d 578 (Fla. 1996).

133. This section focuses generally on confidentiality and privilege. A *privilege* typically focuses on specific relationships (e.g., therapist–patient), is relatively narrow in scope, and is generally limited to placing restrictions on the testimony an individual (e.g., a therapist) can provide at trial. In contrast, *confidentiality* generally encompasses all client–clinical staff relationships, all communications and records, and nondisclosure is required across all settings. For both, limits on disclosures are considered necessary to encourage frank and full discussions (e.g., between a therapist and client), without which treatment would be impossible. Although their applications are somewhat different, they are sufficiently similar to permit grouping them together here.

134. A third possible group, which overlaps with both of these groups but will be discussed later, focuses on the obligations of treatment providers to act upon or release information to protect others.

135. American Psychological Association, *Ethical Principles of Psychologists and Code of Conduct*, 47(12) AM. PSYCHOLOGIST 1597, 1606 (1992) (Standard 5.02).

136. *Id.* (Standard 5.05(a)).

137. *See, e.g.*, Mississippi State Board of Psychological Examiners v. Hosford, 508 So. 2d 1049 (Miss. 1987).

138. *See, e.g.*, Renzi v. Morrison, 618 N.E.2d 794 (Ill. App. Ct. 1993) (right to privacy outweighs the need to reach the truth in a judicial proceeding); Leggett v. First Interstate Bank of Oregon, 739 P.2d 1083, 1086 (Or. Ct. App. 1987). The client may also be able to recover punitive damages if it can be shown that the wrong committed was willful and malicious. *See, e.g.*, Doe v. Roe, 400 N.Y.S.2d 668 (Sup. Ct. 1977); *Leggett*, 739 P.2d at 1083. Although even less frequently asserted, when there has been a "publication" (i.e., an unauthorized release to a third party) of confidential information injuring the reputation of the patient, the client may

pursue a legal action based on the tort of defamation. Alternatively, a contractual relationship may be claimed that required the therapist to keep in confidence all disclosures made by the client regarding his/her condition or all discoveries made by the therapist in the course of treatment. *See* RALPH REISNER & CHRISTO-PHER SLOBOGIN, LAW AND THE MENTAL HEALTH SYSTEM: CIVIL AND CRIMINAL ASPECTS, 249–55 (1990 & Supp. 1995). Finally, the State may authorize by statute a cause of action following disclosure, typically when it considers it particularly important that the information be kept confidential. *See, e.g.*, V. v. State, 566 N.Y.S.2d 987 (Ct. Cl. 1991).

139. *See, e.g.*, State v. Brelsford, 587 A.2d 1062 (Conn. App. Ct. 1991); Rocca v. Southern Hills Counselling Center, 671 N.E.2d 913 (Ind. Ct. App. 1996); *Hosford,* 508 So. 2d at 1049. *But see* People v. Doe, 430 N.E.2d 696 (Ill. App. Ct. 1981); Commonwealth v. Clancy, 524 N.E.2d 395 (Mass. 1988).

140. *See, e.g.*, State v. Cole, 295 N.W.2d 29 (Iowa 1980); *Doe,* 400 N.Y.S.2d at 668; *Leggett,* 739 P.2d at 1083. Not all of these limitations, however, may apply when a licensing board reviews a wrongful disclosure complaint.

141. *See, e.g.*, Linch v. Thomas-Davis Med. Centers, 925 P.2d 686 (Ariz. Ct. App. 1996); *Doe,* 400 N.Y.S.2d at 668.

142. *See, e.g.*, *Doe,* 400 N.Y.S.2d at 668. However, the validity of the consent may be questioned if obtained in the course of treatment. *See, e.g.*, Commonwealth v. Wiseman, 249 N.E.2d 610 (Mass. 1969); *Doe,* 400 N.Y.S.2d at 668.

143. *See e.g.*, Menendez v. Superior Court (People), 279 Cal. Rptr. 521 (Cal. Ct. App. 1991); *Rocca,* 671 N.E.2d at 913; MacDonald v. Clinger, 446 N.Y.S.2d 801 (N.Y. App. Div. 1982).

144. *See, e.g.*, Mississippi State Board of Psychological Examiners v. Hosford, 508 So. 2d 1049 (Miss. 1987).

145. *See, e.g.*, Powell v. Coughlin, 953 F.2d 744 (2d Cir. 1991); Oakland Prosecutor v. Dep't of Corrections, 564 N.W.2d 922 (Mich. Ct. App. 1997).

146. However, this is not universally the case, as the stigma from being labeled mentally ill and the subsequent ramifications from receiving such a label may outweigh the inmate's desire for release or exoneration.

147. *See, e.g.*, State v. Cole, 295 N.W.2d 29, 38 (Iowa 1980).

148. *See, e.g.*, United States v. Snelenberger, 24 F.3d 799 (6th Cir. 1994); United States v. Crews, 781 F.2d 826 (10th Cir. 1986); United States v. Schwensow, 942 F. Supp. 402 (E.D. Wis. 1996); People v. Clark, 789 P.2d 127 (Cal. 1990); *In re* Lifschutz, 467 P.2d 557 (Cal. 1970); People v. Clark, 22 Cal. Rptr. 2d 689 (Ct. App. 1993); People v. Superior Ct. (Broderick), 282 Cal. Rptr. 418 (Ct. App. 1991); Menendez v. Superior Ct. (People), 834 P.2d 786 (Cal. 1992); State v. Brelsford, 587 A.2d 1062 (Conn. App. Ct. 1989); State v. Bright, 683 A.2d 1055 (Del. Super. Ct. 1996); Whitehead v. State, 511 N.E.2d 284 (Ind. 1987); State v. Ortiz, 555 So. 2d 623 (La. Ct. App. 1989), *aff'd in part and rev'd in part,* 567 So. 2d 81 (La. 1990); State v. Rainey, 580 A.2d 682 (Me. 1990); State v. Andring, 342 N.W.2d 128 (Minn. 1984); State v. Gullekson, 383 N.W.2d 338 (Minn. Ct. App. 1986); People v. Edney, 350 N.E.2d 400 (N.Y. 1976); State v. Moore, 927 P.2d 1073 (Or. 1996); State v. Valley, 571 A.2d 579 (Vt. 1989). *But see* People v. Howe, 503 N.W.2d 749 (Mich. Ct. App. 1993) (not entitled to confidential information where psychologist was not contacted to provide evaluation of defendant's sanity, but only to respond to defendant's mental health needs); United States v. D.F., 115 F.3d 413 (7th Cir. 1997) (confession inadmissible where

given by a juvenile murder defendant at a governmental mental health facility during a treatment program, where there was a record of a close relationship between staff and law enforcement officials, where staff went to great lengths to gain her trust and to encourage her to talk about her crimes, where privileges were contingent on confessions, and where she was directly questioned about her past crimes). A footnote in a Supreme Court opinion specifically left unresolved issues regarding the admissibility of clinical conversations that initiate a criminal investigation. *See* Minnesota v. Murphy, 465 U.S. 420 (1984).

149. *See, e.g.,* Payne v. Thompson, 853 F. Supp. 932 (E.D. Va. 1994), *affirmed,* 94 F.3d 642 (4th Cir. 1996); Russell v. Eaves, 722 F. Supp. 558 (E.D. Mo. 1989); State v. Thornton, 929 P.2d 676 (Ariz. 1996); *Broderick,* 282 Cal. Rptr. at 418; State v. Manfredi, 569 A.2d 506 (Conn. 1990); Hayes v. State, 667 N.E.2d 222 (Ind. Ct. App. 1996); *Bright,* 683 A.2d at 1060; State v. Rieflin, 558 N.W.2d 149 (Iowa 1996); State v. Prince, 688 So. 2d 643 (La. Ct. App. 1997); *Gullekson,* 383 N.W.2d at 338; *Moore,* 927 P.2d at 1079; State v. Smith, 933 S.W.2d 450 (Tenn. 1996); Lagrone v. State, 942 S.W.2d 602 (Tex. Cr. App. 1997); State v. King, 925 P.2d 606 (Wash. 1996); State v. Warner, 889 P.2d 479 (Wash. 1995); State v. Gleason, 576 A.2d 1246 (Vt. 1990); State v. Foster, 561 A.2d 107 (Vt. 1989).

150. *See, e.g., Thornton,* 929 P.2d at 676; Gray v. District Court, 884 P.2d 286 (Colo. 1994); *Warner,* 889 P.2d at 479.

151. *See, e.g., Snelenberger,* 24 F.3d at 799; *Crews,* 781 F.2d at 826; *Thornton,* 929 P.2d at 682; People v. Clark, 789 P.2d 127 (Cal. 1990); *Broderick,* 282 Cal. Rptr. at 418; *Gray,* 884 P.2d at 286; *Brelsford,* 587 A.2d at 1062; *Bright,* 683 A.2d at 1055; Whitehead v. State, 511 N.E.2d 284 (Ind. 1987); *Ortiz,* 555 So. 2d at 623; *Rieflin,* 558 N.W.2d at 154; *Gullekson,* 383 N.W.2d at 338; *Moore,* 927 P.2d at 1079; *Smith,* 933 S.W.2d at 450; *Lagrone,* 942 S.W.2d at 610–12; *Warner,* 889 P.2d at 479.

152. *See* Allen v. Illinois, 478 U.S. 364 (1986).

153. *See, e.g.,* People v. Sword, 34 Cal. Rptr. 2d 810 (Ct. App. 1994); People v. Henderson, 172 Cal. Rptr. 858 (Ct. App. 1981); State v. Edmundson, 805 P.2d 1289 (Mont. 1990); *King,* 925 P.2d at 606; State v. Hungerford, 267 N.W.2d 258 (Wis. 1978). *But see* Asherman v. Meachum, 932 F.2d 137 (2d Cir. 1991); Pens v. Bail, 902 F.2d 1464 (9th Cir. 1990).

154. People v. Villanueva, 528 N.Y.S.2d 506 (N.Y. Sup. Ct. 1988). In conjunction with the "Jackson" petition the court found there was no substantial probability that the offender would attain the capacity to stand trial in the foreseeable future, thus requiring the State to either institute a civil commitment proceeding with its standard protections or release the defendant.

155. *See* State v. Cribbs, 469 N.W.2d 108 (Neb. 1991). *See generally* People v. Adams, 555 N.E.2d 761 (Ill. App. Ct. 1990), *aff'd,* 581 N.E.2d 637 (Ill. 1991); Detroit News, Inc. v. Recorder's Court Judge, 509 N.W.2d 894 (Mich. Ct. App. 1993); Commonwealth v. Milice, 584 A.2d 997 (Pa. Super. Ct. 1991). *But see In re* Calu, 693 A.2d 911 (N.J. Super. Ct. App. Div. 1997) (*in camera* hearing required where no possibility of unescorted release of NGRI acquittee into the community).

156. *See* Doe v. Burgos, 638 N.E.2d 701 (Ill. App. Ct. 1994).

157. *See, e.g.,* Mainiero v. Jordan, 105 F.3d 361 (7th Cir. 1997); United States *ex rel.* Patosky v. Kozakiewicz, 960 F. Supp. 905 (W.D. Pa. 1997); Dill v. People, 927 P.2d 1315 (Colo. 1996); State v. Bruno, 673 A.2d 1117 (Conn. 1996); State v. Rogers, 674 A.2d 1364 (Conn. Ct. App. 1996); State v. Ortiz, 555 So. 2d 623 (La.

Ct. App. 1989), *aff'd in part and rev'd in part*, 567 So. 2d 81 (La. 1990); Goldsmith v. State, 651 A.2d 866 (Md. 1995); Commonwealth v. McDonough, 511 N.E.2d 551 (Mass. 1987); Commonwealth v. Syrafos, 646 N.E.2d 429 (Mass. Ct. App. 1995); People v. Tessin, 547 N.W.2d 641 (Mich. 1995); State v. Solberg, 564 N.W.2d 775 (Wis. 1997); State v. Munoz, 546 N.W.2d 572 (Wis. Ct. App. 1996); State v. Behnke, 553 N.W.2d 265 (Wis. Ct. App. 1996).

158. *See, e.g.*, Pennsylvania v. Ritchie, 480 U.S. 39 (1987); People v. Webb, 862 P.2d 779 (Cal. 1993); People v. Nandkeshwar, 38 Cal. Rptr. 2d 41 (Ct. App. 1995); *Rogers*, 674 A.2d at 1370; People v. Stanaway, 521 N.W.2d 557 (Mich. 1994) (provides extensive review of case law on point); People v. Brooks, 604 N.Y.S.2d 219 (A.D. 1993); State v. Gonzales, 912 P.2d 297 (N.M. Ct. App. 1996); State v. Ramos, 858 P.2d 94 (N.M. Ct. App. 1993); State v. Speese, 528 N.W.2d 63 (Wis. Ct. App. 1995).

159. *See, e.g.*, *Bruno*, 673 A.2d at 1126–27; *Stanaway*, 521 N.W.2d at 557; *Munoz*, 546 N.W.2d at 572–73; *Behnke*, 553 N.W.2d at 265.

160. If the transfer is between equally secure facilities with similar levels of mental health services, the transfer decision is generally left to the discretion of the administrators of these facilities. *See, e.g.*, Vitek v. Jones, 445 U.S. 480 (1980); Young v. Breeding, 929 F. Supp. 1103 (N.D. Ill. 1996); People v. Lego, 570 N.E.2d 402 (Ill. Ct. App. 1991).

161. Vitek v. Jones, 445 U.S. 480 (1980). *See also* Sandin v. Conner, 115 S. Ct. 2293 (1995) (affirming *Vitek*).

162. The Court's discussion of the State's interest in a truncated transfer procedure was limited to a single sentence.

163. *See, e.g.*, United States v. Watson, 893 F.2d 970 (8th Cir. 1990); United States v. Horne, 955 F. Supp. 1141 (D. Minn. 1997); *In re* Foster, 426 N.W.2d 374 (Iowa 1988); *In re* Moll, 347 N.W.2d 67, 70 (Minn. Ct. App. 1984); Harmon v. McNutt, 587 P.2d 537 (Wash. 1978). *See also Young*, 929 F. Supp. at 1108. In California, as a condition of parole, sentenced offenders may be civilly committed to a psychiatric facility following a judicial hearing (with a right to a jury trial) with inpatient treatment to be provided unless there is reasonable cause to believe the offenders can be safely and effectively treated on an outpatient basis. CAL. PENAL CODE §§ 2960–2981 (West Supp. 1995).

164. *See* Foster, 426 N.W.2d at 374.

165. *See, e.g.*, King v. Breach, 540 A.2d 976 (Pa. Commw. Ct. 1988).

166. *See, e.g.*, Jackson v. Fair, 846 F.2d 811, 818 (1st Cir. 1988). *But see* Dall v. State, 888 P.2d 680 (Utah Ct. App. 1994).

167. Considerable latitude is also typically afforded to decisions to initially place offenders with mental disorders within a secure facility. *See, e.g.*, Zinkerman v. State, No. CV96-0565171, 1997 Conn. Super. LEXIS 1505 (Conn. Super. Ct. 1997). Relatedly, an inmate can be required to undergo a mental health evaluation before transfer to a less restrictive/secure facility. Molesky v. Walter, 931 F. Supp. 1506 (E.D. Wash. 1996).

168. State v. Johnson, 512 N.E.2d 652 (Ohio 1987). *See also* McSwain v. Stricklin, 540 So. 2d 81 (Ala. Civ. App. 1989); State v. Hargis, 889 P.2d 1117 (Idaho Ct. App. 1995); People v. Villanueva, 528 N.Y.S.2d 506 (Sup. Ct. 1988); State v. Lanzy, 569 N.E.2d 468 (Ohio 1991); State v. Green, 683 N.E.2d 23 (Ohio Ct. App. 1996).

169. Furthermore, after concluding that the public safety is endangered, a court may

act *sua sponte* (i.e., on its own motion) to order the transfer of an NGRI acquittee to a more secure psychiatric facility over the offender's objection, that of the offender's treating physician, and that of the facility where the offender is currently placed. *See, e.g.*, State v. Kinman, 671 N.E.2d 1083 (Ohio Ct. App. 1996).

170. State v. Lake, 515 N.E.2d 960 (Ohio App. Ct. 1986). *See also* Bohlmann v. Lindquist, 562 N.W.2d 578 (S.D. 1997).

171. For the leading case on the transfer of prison inmates into segregation in general, see Sandin v. Conner, 115 S. Ct. 2293 (1995) (federal courts should avoid involvement in day-to-day management of prisons with discretion deferred to administrative officials).

172. Meriwether v. Faulkner, 821 F.2d 408 (7th Cir. 1987). *See also* United States v. Perez, 28 F.3d 673 (7th Cir. 1994).

173. Mary & Crystal v. Ramsden, 635 F.2d 590 (7th Cir. 1980).

174. *But see* Newman v. Alabama, 559 F.2d 283 (5th Cir. 1977); O'Brien v. Moriarty, 489 F.2d 941 (1st Cir. 1974); Sostre v. McGinnis, 442 F.2d 178 (2d Cir. 1971).

175. *See, e.g.*, Casey v. Lewis, 834 F. Supp. 1477 (D. Ariz. 1993) (inappropriate to house self-abusive inmates in segregation facilities or to house acutely psychotic inmates for more than 3 days); Arnold *ex rel.* H.B. v. Lewis, 803 F. Supp. 246 (D. Ariz. 1992).

176. *See, e.g.*, Anderson v. County of Kern, 45 F.3d 1310 (9th Cir. 1995).

177. *See, e.g., Anderson,* 45 F.3d at 1310; *Casey,* 834 F. Supp. at 1477; *Arnold,* 803 F. Supp. at 246.

178. *See, e.g.*, New York *ex rel.* Reed v. Scully, 531 N.Y.S.2d 196 (Sup. Ct. 1988).

179. *See* DIANE STEELMAN, THE MENTALLY IMPAIRED IN NEW YORK PRISONS (1987).

180. *See* ME. REV. STAT. ANN. tit. 34-A, § 3032(3)(D) (West 1988 & Supp. 1996).

181. Wolff v. McDonnell, 418 U.S. 539 (1974).

182. Kulow v. Nix, 28 F.3d 855 (8th Cir. 1994).

183. These arguments have been recognized by the Second Circuit, albeit in a slightly different context. *See* Powell v. Coughlin, 953 F.2d 744 (2d Cir. 1991).

184. Senior v. State, 369 S.E.2d 49 (Ga. App. Ct. 1988).

185. *See also* Barichello v. McDonald, 98 F.3d 948 (7th Cir. 1996) (mental health facility's elimination of program allowing IST patients to obtain passes for unsupervised access to facility grounds after the escape of 2 patients who had off-grounds passes was not a constitutional violation); Barna v. Hogan, 964 F. Supp. 52 (D. Conn. 1997) (administrators properly acted within their professional judgment when they revoked, pending individual review, off-grounds privileges of insanity acquittes for 2–3 months following off-grounds incidents involving 2 other patients); O'Neal v. State, 365 S.E.2d 894 (Ga. App. Ct. 1988); *In re* Calu, 693 A.2d 911 (N.J. Super. A.D. 1997); State v. Lanzy, 569 N.E.2d 468 (Ohio 1991).

186. People v. Michael W., 38 Cal. Rptr. 2d 556 (Ct. App. 1995).

187. State v. Morris, 518 N.W.2d 664 (Neb. App. Ct. 1994) (denial of an insanity acquittee's request upheld even though it was contrary to the recommendation of treatment staff, who wanted to determine his readiness for greater freedoms at a later time and to reinforce his steady progress in his treatment program).

188. People v. Owens, 645 N.E.2d 483 (Ill. App. Ct. 1994). *See also* People v. Robin, 638 N.E.2d 666 (Ill. App. Ct. 1994) (treatment staff criticized for failure to

adequately explore all aspects of an insanity acquittee's psychological problems and dangerousness in reviewing request for unsupervised off-grounds passes; appropriate to rely on nontreating staff in rejecting request).

189. *In re* Giardina, 625 N.Y.S.2d 836 (Co. Ct. 1995). *See also* Albert F. v. Stone, 646 N.Y.S.2d 950 (Sup. Ct. 1996) (forensic mental health agency must provide detailed report concerning appropriateness of unescorted furlough privilege).

190. County of Hennepin v. Levine, 345 N.W.2d 217 (Minn. 1984). Although this case dealt with patients who were civilly committed as mentally ill and dangerous to the public, and thus not technically offenders with mental disorders, this group of patients under Minnesota law is distinguished from patients committed simply as mentally ill, and thus because of their special classification as being dangerous are closely analogous to nonsentenced offenders with mental disorders.

191. *See also* Amadon v. State, 565 N.Y.S.2d 677 (Ct. Cl. 1990).

192. Estate of Conners v. O'Connor, 846 F.2d 1205, 1208 (9th Cir. 1988).

193. Like other courts in the 1980s and 1990s, this court was thus quite willing to allow a distinction between offenders with mental disorders and other patients, particularly when the offender's dangerousness to others could be established. *See also* Dep't of Mental Health v. Allen, 427 N.E.2d 2 (Ind. Ct. App. 1981); Tamsen v. Weber, 802 P.2d 1063 (Ariz. Ct. App. 1990); Amadon, 565 N.Y.S.2d at 677.

194. *See* 730 ILL. COMP. STAT. ANN. 5/5-2-4 (West. Supp. 1997).

195. For both offenders with mental disorders and involuntarily hospitalized patients in general, outpatient care and conditional release are increasingly likely to be used.

196. Grass v. Nixon, 926 SW.2d 67 (Mo. Ct. App. 1996).

197. *See, e.g.*, Lialberg v. Steffen, 514 N.W.2d 779 (Minn. 1994).

198. *See, e.g.*, United States v. Ecker, 543 F.2d 178 (D.C. Cir. 1976); State v. Johnson, 753 P.2d 154 (Ariz. 1988); People v. Henderson, 233 Cal. Rptr. 141 (Ct. App. 1986); Brown v. United States, 682 A.2d 1131 (D.C. Ct. App. 1996); People v. Cooper, 547 N.E.2d 449 (Ill. 1989); People v. Butler, 550 N.E.2d 1250 (Ill. App. Ct. 1990); People v. White, 518 N.E.2d 1262 (Ill. App. Ct. 1988); *In re* Martin B., 525 N.Y.S.2d 469 (Sup. Ct. 1987). Courts are also given wide latitude to require a convicted criminal defendant to participate in a treatment program as a condition of probation or community placement. *See, e.g.*, Felce v. Fiedler, 974 F.2d 1484 (7th Cir. 1992); State v. Caffee, 840 P.2d 720 (Or. Ct. App. 1992); State v. Eaton, 919 P.2d 116 (Wash. Ct. App. 1996). A failure to comply with a condition that an individual obtain or participate in mental health services has been held to provide an adequate basis for the revocation of probation and the subsequent imposition of a prison sentence. *See, e.g.*, United States v. Gallo, 20 F.3d 7 (1st Cir. 1994); State v. Villano, 634 A.2d 907 (Conn. Ct. App. 1993); State v. Fife, 771 P.2d 543 (Idaho Ct. App. 1989); Stinchcomb v. State, 562 A.2d 781 (Md. Ct. Spec. App. 1989); State v. Emery, 593 A.2d 77 (Vt. 1991); State v. Foster, 561 A.2d 107 (Vt. 1989); *Eaton*, 919 P.2d at 116; Von Arx v. Schwarz, 517 N.W.2d 540 (Wis. Ct. App. 1994).

199. *See, e.g.*, *Ecker*, 543 F.2d at 178; People v. Sword, 34 Cal. Rptr. 2d 810 (Ct. App. 1994); People v. Henderson, 233 Cal. Rptr. 141 (Cal. Ct. App. 1986); Marsh v. State, 942 S.W.2d 385 (Mo. Ct. App. 1997); *Grass*, 926 S.W.2d at 67.

200. *See, e.g.*, Viswanger v. State, 875 S.W.2d 796 (Tex. Ct. App. 1994).

201. *See, e.g.*, *Ecker*, 543 F.2d at 178; *Henderson*, 233 Cal. Rptr. at 145; Bergstein v. State, 588 A.2d 779 (Md. 1991); *Martin B.*, 525 N.Y.S.2d at 469; State v. Jefferson, 471 N.W.2d 274 (Wis. Ct. App. 1991).

202. *See, e.g.*, People v. Sword, 34 Cal. Rptr. 2d 810 (Ct. App. 1994); *Marsh,* 942 S.W.2d at 385 (mental illness may only be in remission and acquittee lacks insight into his mental illness); McKee v. State, 923 S.W.2d 525 (Mo. Ct. App. 1996) (dangerousness includes an inability to conform conduct to the requirements of law); *Grass,* 926 S.W.2d at 71 (psychiatrists unable to identify cause of mental illness and stressors that trigger violent behavior); *In re* Francis S., 663 N.E.2d 881 (N.Y. 1995); Rios v. Psychiatric Security Review Board, 934 P.2d 399 (Or. 1997) (does not matter that NGRI acquittee's diagnosis now different from when first committed).

203. *See, e.g.*, *Sword,* 34 Cal. Rptr. 2d at 810; People v. Kirkland, 29 Cal. Rptr. 2d 863 (Ct. App. 1994); State v. Miller, 933 P.2d 606 (Hawaii 1997); *In re* Lund, 617 N.E.2d 1013 (Mass. App. Ct. 1993); Syles v. State, 877 S.W.2d 113 (Mo. 1994); State v. Tooley, 875 S.W.2d 110 (Mo. 1994); *McKee,* 923 S.W.2d at 525 (shortness of time since crime); *In re* Jill ZZ, 608 N.Y.S.2d 161 (NY 1994).

204. *See, e.g.*, United States v. Wallace, 845 F.2d 1471 (8th Cir. 1988); Glatz v. Kort, 807 F.2d 1514 (10th Cir. 1986); Hickey v. Morris, 722 F.2d 543 (9th Cir. 1983); Williams v. Wallis, 734 F.2d 1434 (11th Cir. 1984); *Syles,* 877 S.W.2d at 113 (*Foucha* does not invalidate statute placing burden of proof on person seeking conditional release); *Tooley,* 875 S.W.2d at 110; *In re* Hayes, 432 S.E.2d 862 (N.C. Ct. App. 1993); Hearne v. United States, 631 A.2d 52 (D.C. Ct. App. 1993). *But see* State v. Boudreaux, 605 So. 2d 608 (La. 1992); *In re* D.F.R., 945 S.W.2d 210 (Tex. Ct. App. 1997).

205. *See, e.g.*, *Wallace,* 845 F.2d at 1471; *Williams,* 734 F.2d at 1434, 1440.

206. *See, e.g.*, *Wallace,* 845 F.2d at 1471; *Glatz,* 807 F.2d at 1514; Miller, 933 P.2d at 606 (citing string of cases placing burden on offenders with mental disorders).

207. Marsh v. State, 942 S.W.2d 385 (Mo. Ct. App. 1997).

208. *See, e.g.*, People v. Sword, 34 Cal. Rptr. 2d 810 (Ct. App. 1994); Bahrenfus v. Psychiatric Review Board, 862 P.2d 553 (Or. Ct. App. 1993).

209. *See, e.g.*, United States v. Jackson, 19 F.3d 1003 (5th Cir. 1994).

210. *See, e.g.*, Levine v. Torvik, 986 F.2d 1506 (6th Cir. 1993); United States v. Woods, 944 F. Supp. 778 (D. Minn. 1996); Ex Parte Cunningham, 647 So. 2d 103 (Ala. Cr. App. 1994); People v. DeGuzman, 39 Cal. Rptr. 2d 137 (Ct. App. 1995); *In re* Oswald N., 661 N.E.2d 679 (N.Y. 1995); *In re* Gene "DD", 602 N.Y.S.2d 705 (App. Div. 1993).

211. State v. Stark, 550 N.W.2d 467 (Iowa 1996).

212. *See, e.g.*, United States v. Ecker, 543 F.2d 178 (D.C. Cir. 1976); Brown v. United States, 682 A.2d 1131 (D.C. Ct. App. 1996); Bergstein v. State, 588 A.2d 779 (Md. 1991); *Oswald N.,* 661 N.E.2d at 679; *In re* Francis S., 663 N.E.2d 881 (N.Y. 1995); *In re* Martin B., 138 Misc. 2d 685 (N.Y. Co. Ct. 1987).

213. *See, e.g.*, Barnes v. Superior Court, 186 Cal. App. 3d 969, 231 Cal. Rptr. 158 (1986); People v. Catron, 200 Cal. App. 3d 546, 246 Cal. Rptr. 303 (1988); *Martin B.,* 138 Misc. 2d at 695; *Bergstein,* 588 A.2d at 779.

214. *See, e.g.*, Reese v. United States, 614 A.2d 506 (D.C. 1992); Jackson v. United States, 641 A.2d 454 (D.C. Ct. App. 1994).

215. *See, e.g.*, People v. White, 518 N.E.2d 1262 (Ill. Ct. App. 1988). *But see* State v. Gravette, 393 S.E.2d 865 (N.C. 1990).

216. *See, e.g.*, State v. Imlay, 813 P.2d 979 (Mont. 1991); Morstad v. State, 518 N.W.2d 191 (N.D. 1994).

217. Although this section addresses primarily the release of nonsentenced offenders

with mental disorders,sentenced offenders' imprisonment may be shortened by placement on parole. As a condition of parole, sentenced offenders may be required to obtain mental health services, with parole subject to revocation should they fail to adhere to their treatment program. Parolees are typically subject to supervision but entitled to certain due process protections should the state attempt to revoke parole. Because their goals are similar, the law governing parole parallels that for the release or discharge of nonsentenced offenders. For example, parole can be rescinded upon evidence broadly interpreted to indicate that the inmate may pose a danger to society. *See, e.g.*, Powell v. Gomez, 33 F.2d 39 (9th Cir. 1994).

218. For a description of a typical program leading up to discharge, see State v. Perez, 648 So. 2d 1319 (La. 1995).

219. *See, e.g.*, Sikes v. State, 485 S.E.2d 206 (Ga. 1997) (successful completion of involuntary conditional release treatment program does not necessitate release); Dall v. State, 888 P.2d 680, 683 n.5 (Utah Ct. App. 1994).

220. *See, e.g.*, United States v. Jackson, 19 F.3d 1003 (5th Cir. 1994); Turner v. Campagna, 667 N.E.2d 683 (Ill. Ct. App. 1996) (distinguishing from civil commitment).

221. *See, e.g.*, Parrish v. Colorado, 78 F.3d 1473 (10th Cir. 1996); Barnett v. State, 942 S.W.2d 860 (Ark. 1997); Mueller v. Psychiatric Security Review Board, 937 P.2d 1028 (Or. 1997); Osborn v. Psychiatric Security Review Board, 934 P.2d 391 (Or. 1997).

222. *See, e.g.*, People v. Bolden, 266 Cal. Rptr. 724 (Ct. App. 1990).

223. *See, e.g.*, Canidate v. Stricklin, 568 So. 2d 1234 (Ala. Civ. App. 1990); Yiadom v. Kiley, 562 N.E.2d 310 (Ill. App. Ct. 1990); State v. Simants, 517 N.W.2d 361 (Neb. 1991); *In re* Watt, 525 A.2d 421 (Pa. Super. 1987). *But see* Carlisle v. State, 512 So.2d 150 (Ala. Ct. App. 1987).

224. *See, e.g.*, *Carlisle,* 512 So. 2d at 150; State v. Perez, 563 So. 2d 841, 845 (La. 1990); *In re* Francis S., 618 N.Y.S.2d 660 (A.D. 1994).

225. *See, e.g.,* Cooley v. State, 695 So. 2d 1219 (Ala. Crim. App. 1996) (verbal threat sufficient); *In re* Hill, 661 N.E. 2d 1285 (Mass. 1996).

226. See Jackson v. United States, 641 A.2d 454 (D.C. Ct. App. 1994).

227. *See, e.g.*, People v. Henderson, 172 Cal. Rptr. 858 (Ct. App. 1981).

228. *See, e.g.*, *Watt,* 525 A.2d at 421; *Carlisle,* 512 So. 2d at 150.

229. *See, e.g.*, Williams v. Wallis, 734 F.2d 1434 (11th Cir. 1984); McSwain v. Stricklin, 540 So. 2d 81 (Ala. Civ. App. 1989); Carlisle v. State, 512 So. 2d 150 (Ala. Crim. App. 1987); State v. Johnson, 753 P.2d 154 (Ariz. 1988); People v. Sword, 34 Cal. Rptr. 2d 810 (Ct. App. 1994); State v. Foucha, 563 So. 2d 1138 (La. 1990), *rev'd,* 112 S. Ct. 1780 (1992); *In re* Francis S., 618 N.Y.S.2d 660 (A.D. 1994); People *ex rel.* Schreiner v. Tekben, 611 N.Y.S.2d 734 (Sup. Ct. 1994); *In re* Watt, 525 A.2d 421 (Pa. Super. 1987). *But see* State v. Perez, 648 So. 2d 1319 (La. 1995).

230. *See, e.g.*, United States v. Steil, 916 F.2d 485 (8th Cir. 1990); Yiadom v. Kiley, 562 N.E.2d 310 (Ill. App. Ct. 1990); Mental Hygiene Legal Services v. Wack, 551 N.E.2d 95 (N.Y. 1989); *Watt,* 525 A.2d at 421. *But see Carlisle,* 512 So. 2d at 150; People v. Williams, 244 Cal. Rptr. 429 (Ct. App. 1988).

231. *See, e.g.*, *In re* Francis S., 618 N.Y.S.2d 660 (A.D. 1994).

232. *See, e.g.*, United States v. Jackson, 19 F.3d 1003 (5th Cir. 1994); Cooley v. State, 695 So. 2d 1219 (Ala. Crim. App. 1996); *Carlisle,* 512 So. 2d at 150; *Johnson,*

753 P.2d at 157; People v. Sword, 34 Cal. Rptr. 2d 810 (Ct. App. 1989); State v. Perez, 628 So. 2d 241 (La. Ct. App. 1993); Mental Hygiene Legal Services v. Rhodes, 606 N.Y.S.2d 834 (A.D. 1994); Bahrenfus v. Psychiatric Security Review Board, 862 P.2d 553 (Or. Ct. App. 1993); State v. Smith, 482 S.E.2d 687 (W.Va. 1996).

233. *See, e.g.*, Parrish v. Colorado, 78 F.3d 1473 (10th Cir. 1996); United States v. Jackson, 19 F.3d 1003 (5th Cir. 1994); Benham v. Ledbetter, 785 F.2d 1480 (11th Cir. 1986); *Cooley*, 695 So. 2d at 1219; *Sword*, 34 Cal. Rptr. 2d at 810; People v. Coronado, 33 Cal. Rptr. 2d 835 (Ct. App. 1994); People v. Hilton, 902 P.2d 883 (Colo. Ct. App. 1995); Arnold v. State, 328 S.E.2d 572 (Ga. Ct. App. 1985); Loftin v. State, 349 S.E.2d 777 (Ga. Ct. App. 1986); LaDew v. Comm'r of Mental Health, 532 A.2d 1051 (Me. 1987); *In re* Hill, 661 N.E.2d 1285 (Mass. 1996); State v. Simants, 517 N.W.2d 361 (Neb. 1994); People v. Goodman, 619 N.Y.S.2d 501 (Sup. Ct. 1994); Hodgin v. Psychiatric Security Review Board, 873 P.2d 466 (Ore. Ct. App. 1994); Niswanger v. State, 875 S.W.2d 796 (Tex. Ct. App. 1994); State v. Pepin, 883 P.2d 934 (Wash. Ct. App. 1994).

234. *See, e.g.*, United States v. Jackson, 19 F.3d 1003 (5th Cir. 1994).

235. *See, e.g.*, Williams v. Wallis, 734 F.2d 1434, 1437–38, n.4 (11th Cir. 1984); McSwain v. Stricklin, 540 So. 2d 81 (Ala. Civ. App. 1989); Carlisle v. State, 512 So. 2d 150 (Ala. Crim. App. 1987); People v. Bolden, 266 Cal. Rptr. 724 (Cal. Ct. App. 1990); State v. Stark, 550 N.W.2d 467 (Iowa 1996); Jensen v. State, 926 S.W.2d 925 (Mo. Ct. App. 1996); Mental Hygiene Legal Services v. Wack, 551 N.E.2d 95 (N.Y. 1989); State v. Perez, 563 So. 2d 841 (La. 1990); State v. Perez, 628 So. 2d 241 (La. Ct. App. 1993); Bahrenfus v. Psychiatric Security Review Board, 862 P.2d 553 (Or. Ct. App. 1993).

236. Foucha v. Louisiana, 112 S. Ct. 1780, 1789 (O'Connor, J., concurring).

237. *See, e.g.*, People v. Sword, 34 Cal. Rptr. 2d 810 (Ct. App. 1994); People *ex rel.* Schreiner v. Tekben, 611 N.Y.S.2d 734 (Sup. Ct. 1994).

238. State v. Randall, 532 N.W.2d 94 (Wis. 1995). *See also* Commonwealth v. Tate, 675 N.E.2d 772 (Mass. 1997).

239. People v. Parrish, 879 P.2d 453 (Colo. Ct. App. 1994); People v. Jones, 935 P.2d 28, *cert. denied*, 1997 Colo. LEXIS 257 (1997).

240. *See, e.g.*, Nagel v. State, 442 S.E.2d 446 (Ga. 1994); *In re* Henry, 900 P.2d 1360 (Idaho 1995) (condition unchanged for 16 years).

241. *See, e.g.*, People v. Beck, 55 Cal. Rptr. 2d 340 (Cal. Ct. App. 1996); State v. Pepin, 883 P.2d 934 (Wash. Ct. App. 1994).

242. One court that did use *Foucha* to strike down a release provision for insanity acquittees that permitted continued confinement based upon present dangerousness only, explicitly noted that its ruling would have limited effect since that state had subsequently abolished the insanity defense. *In re* Gafford, 903 P.2d 61 (Idaho 1995).

243. *See, e.g.*, Carlisle v. State, 512 So. 2d 150 (Ala. Crim. App. 1987); People v. Williams, 244 Cal. Rptr. 429 (Cal. Ct. App. 1988) (majority opinion).

244. *See, e.g.*, State v. Perez, 648 So. 2d 1319 (La. 1995); Niswonger v. State, 875 S.W.2d 796 (Tex. Ct. App. 1994); State v. Pepin, 883 P.2d 934 (Wash. Ct. App. 1994).

245. *See, e.g.*, Benham v. Ledbetter, 785 F.2d 1480 (11th Cir. 1986); Williams v. Wallis, 734 F.2d 1434 (11th Cir. 1984); Canidate v. Strickland, 568 So. 2d 1234 (Ala. Civ. App. 1990); State v. Johnson, 753 P.2d 154 (Ariz. 1988); People v. Bolden,

266 Cal. Rptr. 724 (Cal. Ct. App. 1990); People v. Chavez, 629 P.2d 1040 (Colo. 1981); People v. Hilton, 902 P.2d 883 (Colo. Ct. App. 1995); Hearne v. United States, 631 A.2d 52 (D.C. Ct. App. 1993); Nagel v. State, 442 S.E.2d 446 (Ga. 1994); Nagel v. State, 427 S.E.2d 490 (Ga. 1993); Loftin v. State, 349 S.E.2d 777 (Ga. Ct. App. 1986); People v. Finkle, 573 N.E.2d 381 (Ill. App. Ct. 1991); LaDew v. Commissioner of Mental Health & Mental Retardation, 532 A.2d 1051 (Me. 1987); Taylor v. Commissioner of Mental Health & Mental Retardation, 481 A.2d 139 (Me. 1984); Styles v. State, 877 S.W.2d 113 (Mo. 1994); State v. Tooley, 875 S.W.2d 110 (Mo. 1994) (discussion of other courts reaching same decision); State v. Seidt, 805 S.W.2d 737 (Mo. Ct. App. 1991); In re Hayes, 432 S.E.2d 862 (N.C. Ct. App. 1993); State v. Pepin, 883 P.2d 934 (Wash. Ct. App. 1994). But see United States v. Bilyk, 29 F.3d 459 (8th Cir. 1994) (inference of continuing mental illness does not last forever); State v. Metz, 645 A.2d 965 (Conn. 1994); People v. Shelton, 667 N.E.2d 562 (Ill. Ct. App. 1996).

246. See, e.g., Benham v. Ledbetter, 785 F.2d 1480 (11th Cir. 1986); Williams, 734 F.2d at 1434; People v. Ellis, 60 Cal. Rptr. 2d 572 (Cal. Ct. App. 1997); People v. Beck, 55 Cal. Rptr. 2d 340 (Cal. Ct. App. 1996); People v. Coronado, 33 Cal. Rptr. 2d 835 (Ct. App. 1994); People v. Superior Court (Woods), 268 Cal. Rptr. 379 (Ct. App. 1990); State v. Metz, 645 A.2d 965 (Conn. 1994); Jackson v. United States, 641 A.2d 454 (D.C. Ct. App. 1994); State v. Gee, 695 P.2d 379 (Idaho 1985); People v. Savage, 659 N.E.2d 439 (Ill. Ct. App. 1995); People v. Finkle, 573 N.E.2d 381 (Ill. App. Ct. 1991); LaDew v. Commissioner of Mental Health & Mental Retardation, 532 A.2d 1051 (Me. 1987); Taylor v. Commissioner of Mental Health & Mental Retardation, 481 A.2d 139 (Me. 1984); Anderson v. Dep't of Health & Mental Hygiene, 528 A.2d 904 (Md. Ct. App. 1987); In re Hill, 661 N.E.2d 1285 (Mass. 1996); State v. Tooley, 875 S.W.2d 110 (Mo. 1994); In re Hayes, 432 S.E.2d 862 (N.C. Ct. App. 1993); Harris v. Oklahoma County District Court, 750 P.2d 1129 (Okla. Crim. App. 1988). But see Turner v. Campagna, 667 N.E.2d 683 (Ill. Ct. App. 1996) (72-month delay in holding hearing impermissible).

247. See, e.g., Benham, 785 F.2d at 1480; Williams, 734 F.2d at 1434; Beck, 55 Cal. Rptr. 2d at 342–46; Woods, 268 Cal. Rptr. at 379; Loftin, 349 S.E.2d at 777; Taylor, 481 A.2d at 151; State v. R.R.E., 470 N.W.2d 283 (Wis. 1991).

248. See, e.g., Benham, 785 F.2d at 1480; Beck, 55 Cal. Rptr. 2d at 343–44; Taylor, 481 A.2d at 139; LaDew, 532 A.2d at 1053; State v. Foucha, 563 So. 2d 1138 (La. 1990), rev'd, 112 S. Ct. 1780 (1992).

249. See Williams, 734 F.2d at 1438.

250. See, e.g., Cook v. Psychiatric Security Review Board, 860 P.2d 855 (Or. Ct. App. 1993).

251. See, e.g., Carlisle v. State, 512 So. 2d 150, 160 (Ala. Crim. App. 1987).

252. See, e.g., Herrod v. State, 552 So.2d 173 (Ala. Crim. App. 1989); Owens v. Taylor, 772 S.W.2d 596 (Ark. 1989).

253. The leading nonoffender case on a treatment provider's duty to warn or protect third parties is Tarasoff v. Regents of University of Cal., 551 P.2d 334 (Cal. 1976). Although in some states courts have refused to impose such a duty or considerably limited its scope, judicial opinions in other states have expanded liability for failing to take adequate steps to warn or protect others. Compare Sellers v. United States, 870 F.2d 1098 (6th Cir. 1989); Morton v. Prescott, 564 So. 2d 913 (Ala. 1990); King v. Smith, 539 So. 2d 262 (Ala. 1989); Baldwin v. Hospital Auth. of

Fulton Cty., 383 S.E.2d 154 (Ga. Ct. App. 1989); Eckhardt v. Kirts, 534 N.E.2d 1339 (Ill. App. Ct. 1989); Wofford v. Eastern State Hosp., 795 P.2d 516 (Okla. 1990); Dunkle v. Food Service East, Inc., 582 A.2d 1342 (Pa. Super. Ct. 1990); Rogers v. South Carolina Dep't of Mental Health, 377 S.E.2d 125 (S.C. Ct. App. 1989) *with* Jablonski v. United States, 712 F.2d 391 (9th Cir. 1983); Hamman v. County of Maricopa, 775 P.2d 1122 (Ariz. 1989); Hedlund v. Superior Ct. of Orange County, 669 P.2d 41 (Cal. 1983); Perreira v. State, 768 P.2d 1198 (Colo. 1989); Naidu v. Laird, 539 A.2d 1064 (Del. 1988); Durflinger v. Artiles, 673 P.2d 86 (Kan. 1983); Evans v. Morehead Clinic, 749 S.W.2d 696 (Ky. Ct. App. 1988); Hutchinson v. Patel, 637 So. 2d 415 (La. 1994); Davis v. Lhim, 335 N.W.2d 481 (Mich. Ct. App. 1983); Estates of Morgan v. Fairfield Family Counseling Center, 673 N.E.2d 1311 (Ohio 1997); Littleton v. Good Samaritan Hosp. & Health Ctr., 529 N.E.2d 449 (Ohio 1988); Schuster v. Altenberg, 424 N.W.2d 159 (Wis. 1988). For a summary of the conflicting case law, see Matt v. Burrell, Inc., 982 S.W.2d 796 (Mo. Ct. App. 1995).

254. Bader v. State, 716 P.2d 925, 928 (Wash. Ct. App. 1986).

255. The offender did keep one appointment 4 days before the incident and showed no impairment at the time.

256. As a potential exonerating factor, the court noted that there was no indication that the provider had any knowledge about the acquittee's victim.

257. Cain v. Rijken, 717 P.2d 140 (Or. 1986).

258. *See also* Semler v. Psychiatric Inst. of Wash., D.C., 538 F.2d 121 (4th Cir. 1976); Tamsen v. Weber, 802 P.2d 1063 (Ariz. Ct. App. 1990); Santa Cruz v. Northwest Dade Community Health Center, Inc., 590 So. 2d 440 (Fla. Ct. App. 1991); Hartford Ins. Co. v. Manor Inn, 642 A.2d 219 (Md. 1994); Lundgren v. Fultz, 354 N.W.2d 25 (Minn. 1984); Davis v. North Carolina Dep't Human Resources, 465 S.E.2d 2 (N.C. Ct. App. 1995); Peck v. Counseling Services of Addison County, Inc., 499 A.2d 422 (Vt. 1985).

259. Paul S. Appelbaum, *The Expansion of Liability for Patients' Violent Acts,* 35 HOSP. & COMMUNITY PSYCHIATRY 13 (1984); Mark J. Mills & Anne M. O'Keefe, *Legal Issues in Outpatient Treatment,* 44(6) J. CLINICAL PSYCHIATRY 33, 38 (1983); Peter C. Sheridan, *Cain v. Rijken: Creation of a Statutory Duty of Care to Protect Others from the Tortious Conduct of Third Parties,* 23 WIL-LAMETTE L. REV. 493 (1987); Barbara A. Weiner, *Legal Issues in Treating Sex Offenders,* 3(4) BEHAV. SCI. & L. 325 (1985).

260. *See* Barry v. Turek, 267 Cal. Rptr. 553 (Ct. App. 1990); Porter v. Maunnangi, 764 S.W.2d 699 (Mo. Ct. App. 1988).

261. *See* VanLuchene v. State, 797 P.2d 932 (Mont. 1990); Fay v. City of Portland, 782 P.2d 182 (Or. Ct. App. 1989); Melville v. State, 793 P.2d 952 (Wash. 1990).

262. *See, e.g.,* Bader, 716 P.2d at 927 (1986); Walker v. State, 806 P.2d 249 (Wash. Ct. App. 1991).

263. *See, e.g.,* State v. Noble, 829 P.2d 1217 (Ariz. 1992); People v. Adams, 581 N.E.2d 637 (Ill. 1991); State v. Costello, 643 A.2d 531 (N.H. 1994). *But see In re* Reed, 663 P.2d 216 (Cal. 1983) (overbroad in its application to defendants convicted only of a misdemeanor).

264. *Compare* State v. Sorrell, 656 So. 2d 1045 (La. Ct. App. 1995) (condition of parole and thus law in effect at time of release governs terms of release); State v. Ward, 869 P.2d 1062 (Wash. 1994) (does not consider punishment, nor does it impose significant additional burdens and thus does not violate *Ex Post Facto*

Clause) *with* State v. Babin, 637 So. 2d 814 (La. Ct. App. 1994) (violation of *ex post facto* provisions).

265. *See, e.g.*, Jones v. Murray, 962 F.2d 302 (4th Cir. 1992); Doe v. Gainer, 642 N.E.2d 114 (Ill. 1994); People v. Calahan, 649 N.E.2d 588 (Ill. App. Ct. 1995); State v. Olivas, 856 P.2d 1076 (Wash. 1993). *See also* People v. McVickers, 840 P.2d 955 (Cal. 1992) (mandatory AIDS blood testing of sexual offenders upheld, with a positive test result to be used to enhance sentences for a subsequent conviction of a sex offense).

266. Doe v. Poritz, 662 A.2d 367 (N.J. 1995). This law was also reviewed in Artway v. Attorney General of New Jersey, 876 F. Supp. 666 (D.N.J. 1995), where the federal District Court of New Jersey found the registration requirement and the making of this information available to law enforcement agencies to be constitutional. It did find the retroactive application of the public notification provisions for Tier 2 and Tier 3 offenders to be unconstitutional.

NOTES TO ADDENDUM

1. *See, e.g.*, Riddle v. Mondragon, 83 F.3d 1197 (10th Cir. 1996).
2. *See, e.g.*, People v. Superior Court (Cain), 57 Cal. Rptr. 2d 296 (Cal. Ct. App. 1996); Hubbart v. Superior Court (People), 58 Cal. Rptr. 2d 268 (Cal. Ct. App. 1996); State v. Post, 541 N.W.2d 115 (Wis. 1995).
3. *See, e.g.*, Austin v. Pennsylvania Dep't of Corrections, 876 F. Supp. 1437 (E.D. Pa. 1995); State v. Cavrizales, 528 N.W.2d 29 (Wis. Ct. App. 1995).
4. *See, e.g.*, State v. Eaton, 919 P.2d 116 (Wash. Ct. App. 1996).
5. *See, e.g.*, State v. Smith, 933 S.W.2d 450 (Tenn. 1996); State v. King, 925 P.2d 606 (Wash. 1996); State v. Warner, 889 P.2d 479 (Wash. 1995).
6. *See, e.g., In re* Goodson, 544 N.W.2d 611 (Wis. Ct. App. 1996) (discussing notice provisions for supervised release and holding that failure to first obtain a supervision plan from the Department of Health and Social Services and the county to which the offender is to be released is grounds for vacating an order of release).
7. *See, e.g.*, Jones v. Murray, 962 F.2d 302 (4th Cir. 1992); Doe v. Gainer, 642 N.E.2d 114 (Ill. 1994); People v. Calahan, 649 N.E.2d 588 (Ill. App. Ct. 1995); State v. Costello, 643 A.2d 531 (N.H. 1994); State v. Olivas, 856 P.2d 1076 (Wash. 1993).
8. *See, e.g.*, Artway v. Attorney General of New Jersey, 876 F. Supp. 666 (D.N.J. 1995); Doe v. Poritz, 662 A.2d 367 (N.J. 1995); State v. Sorrell, 656 So. 2d 1045 (La. Ct. App. 1995), *cert. denied*, 657 So. 2d 1035 (La. 1995); State v. Ward, 869 P.2d 1062 (Wash. 1994); State v. Post, 541 N.W.2d 115 (Wis. 1995).
9. *See, e.g., In re* Registrant G.B., 685 A.2d 1252 (N.J. 1996); *In re* C.A., 679 A.2d 1153 (N.J. 1996).
10. Kansas v. Hendricks, 117 S. Ct. 2072 (1997).
11. Of significant importance to Hendricks, the Court ruled that commitment could be imposed on someone who had previously been convicted and served time for a crime, where that crime provides the primary rationale for imposing commitment. The Court found that this law could be applied retrospectively to individuals whose criminal offenses predated the enactment of the law.
12. Kan. Stat. Ann. § 59-29a01 (1994).
13. Hubbart v. Superior Court (People), 58 Cal. Rptr. 2d 268 (Cal. Ct. App. 1996); *In*

re Linehan, 557 N.W.2d 171 (Minn. 1996); *In re* Young, 857 P.2d 989 (Wash. 1993); *In re* Aqui, 923 P.2d 705 (Wash. Ct. App. 1996); State v. Carpenter, 541 N.W.2d 105 (Wis. 1995); State v. Post, 541 N.W.2d 115 (Wis. 1995). Although the Kansas Supreme Court had struck down the Kansas Act as unconstitutional under federal law, the U.S. Supreme Court opinion in *Hendricks* reversed this holding.

14. *In re* Paschke, 909 P.2d 1328 (Wash. Ct. App. 1996).
15. *See, e.g.*, People v. Ellis, 60 Cal. Rptr. 2d 572 (Cal. Ct. App. 1997); *In re* Hill, 661 N.E.2d 1285 (Mass. 1996).

3

INPATIENT TREATMENT OF OFFENDERS WITH MENTAL DISORDERS

Gary J. Maier
Louis Fulton

INTRODUCTION

More than 20 years ago the principal author (G.J.M.) reviewed the literature describing the treatment of the offenders with mental disorders.[1] In a chapter entitled "Therapy in Prisons" he concluded by saying:

> Corrections do not correct, reformatories do not reform. No matter what kind of program we institute, recidivism remains high. We are aware at the present time that we need to improve the caliber not only of programs but of research tools used to investigate them. There is a growing consciousness of these needs. At the same time programming in institutions does change the quality of life. There is less impersonality and depersonalization, and morale seems to be higher with an active program. What these factors have to do with recidivism has yet to be determined. (Maier, 1976, 130–131)

Today the growth in this subspeciality lies less in the specific treatment approaches to the mentally disordered (neuroleptics are equally effective with patients with schizophrenia in hospitals and prison psychiatric units) and more in refinements in the design of the forensic system in each jurisdiction. Boundary clarifications between the role of security and treatment staff, better design of the inpatient treatment system in security hospitals, and the recognition that a patient's right to treatment must be balanced by his/her right to refuse treatment are the growing edge, and whereas the primary goal of the coordinated multidisciplinary team is the successful treatment of the patient, it is supposed to result in successful rehabilitation in the community. What these new factors have to do with recidivism is still an open question.

In an influential issue of *Behavioral Sciences and the Law,* Rogers (1988) stated that treatability and treatment outcome are two important and interrelated topics. *Treatability* is the assessment of an individual offender's capacity to comply with and respond to treatment. Goals of treatability may vary from total remission of psychiatric symptoms to the more circumscribed objectives of reduced recidivism. In contrast, *treatment outcome* is the evaluation of designated categories of offenders with mental disorders in specific treatment programs. In other words, whereas treatability determines who will be placed into treatment, treatment outcome addresses to what extent these treatment decisions are valid. These distinctions underline a host of questions that future forensic research will need to address, such as the following:

1. What is the effect on court dispositions of treatment recommendations at the pretrial and presentence phases?
2. Are "treatable" and "nontreatable" offenders with mental disorders clinically distinguishable on the basis of prior treatment history, history of criminal offenses, and diagnostic variables?
3. What system issues most affect treatment and recidivism?
4. What is the psychological impact of prison on the average inmate, and on offenders with mental disorders?

With these questions in mind we reviewed the relevant forensic literature and conducted a telephone survey of facilities in five states (California, Colorado, Connecticut, New York, and Wisconsin). From this review it is clear that systems issues are the growing edge of progress in the treatment of offenders with mental disorders. Further, there is general agreement that the inpatient treatment of offenders with mental disorders is receiving increasing attention. There are standards (National Commission on Correctional Health Care, 1996, 1997) that govern the treatment of offenders with mental disorders. Before standards could be developed, however, coherent mental health and criminal justice systems had to be in place so that quality assurance goals could be set. Consider the following issues that the standards must address.

Ethical Issues in Assessment and Treatment

Forensic psychiatry and psychology play a critical role in meeting the treatment needs of these patients (Silver & Gelpi, 1987). However, forensic psychiatry is in the ironic position that the psychiatrists with the greatest expertise often restrict their involvement with offenders with mental disorders to the assessment phase of the criminal process, especially if it involves the insanity defense. For example, fewer than 10% of the members of the American Academy of Psychiatry and the Law (AAPL) actually provide service to jails, prisons, or security hospitals (Harry, Maier, & Miller, 1989). What this means in reality is that the most qualified experts pass the complicated treatment of offenders with mental disorders to less experienced therapists. In medicine, the surgery resident triages the patient in the emergency room. The more complicated the case, the more senior the surgeon who performs the surgery. The reverse happens in forensic psychiatry. The nationally known experts testify at the insanity phase of the trial and then absolve themselves of the responsibility for actually treating the patients that they have determined were insane at the time of the crime. Offenders with mental disorders then are "treated" in a potentially hostile environment by a less renowned forensic psychiatrist. There is more money and glamour in the assessment phase. To ensure this lucrative style of practice, the experts have determined that it is unethical to testify at the insanity phase and then "inherit" the insanity acquittee as a patient. This problem, plus the obvious problems with the insanity defense itself, still plague the treatment phase of offenders with mental disorders (Halpern, 1992).

Staffing Patterns

In spite of these aberrations, some states are in the process of establishing a broad-based treatment approach for offenders with mental disorders. In particular, administrators at Atascadero, the maximum security hospital in the Department of Mental Health in California, made a decision to increase the psychiatrist–patient ratio. In the last 10 years they hired more than 25 psychiatrists and 25 psychologists in a determined effort to provide active treatment for the broad range of mental disorders that they diagnose in offenders in their security hospital. Further, they developed a specialized communication skills training program for line staff, so that the staff will be verbally skilled when relating to offenders with mental disorders. Miller, Maier, and Kaye (1988) developed a similar program for all nursing staff who work in a maximum security hospital. They found that 20% of the line staff's time was taken with physical security procedures, for example, escorting, screen checks, and the like. Nearly 80% of the staff's time was devoted to interactions with or about the patients, for example, charting and cross-shift communication. Good communication skills are an essential part of assessment and documentation.

Staffing patterns are critical and often neglected. Because there are no national forensic staffing standards, the courts have been drawn into the debate by way of class-action suits. Way, Dvoskin, Steadman, Huguley, and Banks (1990) polled forensic inpatient facilities in all 50 states and the District of Columbia. They found that direct care staff–patient ratios ranged from 0.35 to 4 staff per patient, with a mean of 1.3 staff per patient. They found that 20.4% of forensic units were over patient capacity and that it was these facilities that had the lowest staff–patient ratios. They concluded that a poor staffing pattern precluded treatment and forced the hospital into a custodial role.

Security versus Treatment

The "treatability" of the patient also depends on the philosophical position of the facility administration. The relationship between security and treatment staff (and between security and treatment) must be well defined. With the long-standing pressures on the relationship between security values, care and custody, and therapeutic values, treatment must be addressed by the facility (Maier, 1986). Security can have a positive or negative impact on treatment. That both roles are needed in a security hospital is obvious, but that both roles are equally respected and work in a coordinated way toward mutual goals is rare. The use of what Eisler called a "dominator model" rather than a "partnership model" is characteristic of most security institutes. It forces one side to dominate the other (Eisler, 1988).

Prisons, jails, and security hospitals are harsh environments. Older buildings are not air conditioned and are often smelly and poorly designed. Feelings of powerlessness and helplessness can pervade them. The limits of the environment are matched by the limits of spirit. Further, that release is through the court or special review board confronts the psychiatrist with a particular challenge in regard to his/her own identity in the treatment process. In fact, the personal coping mechanisms necessary to survive in a prison environment must be addressed (Maier, Bernstein, & Musholt, 1989) Staff burnout is a significant problem. Waiting for security to transport an inmate or assessing the offender in "the hole" can generate feelings of helplessness and disempowerment that can weigh on the morale of the psychiatrist working with this patient group.

The boundaries that define the differences between a civil hospital, a forensic hospital, and a prison are outlined in Table 3.1. Understanding the principal differences between these institutions, but especially under-

TABLE 3.1. Differences between Institutions Serving Mentally Disordered Persons

	Civil patient	Forensic patient	Inmate/patient
Governing principles	Care Treatment	Care Custody Treatment	Punishment Retribution Deterrence Rehabilitation
Environment (mileu)	Humane	Humane Secure	Humane Secure–spartan
Security	Open/locked Least restrictive	Maximum Medium Minimum	Maximum Medium Minimum Camps
Admission criteria	1. Mentally ill 2. Dangerous	1. Mentally ill but, 2. Not responsible	Convicted
Rights	Right to remain silent Right to treatment Right to refuse treatment Least restrictive	Right to remain silent Right to treatment Right to refuse treatment No least restrictive	Right to remain silent Right to treatment Right to refuse treatment No least restrictive
Release criteria	Asymptomatic Least restrictive	Dangerousness	Time (good time)

standing the boundaries of one's own institution, can help the clinician set realistic expectations for change in the offender and for him/herself (Maier, 1992a). Inmates, whether they are in jails or prisons, have fewer rights than do forensic patients, who have fewer rights than do civilly committed patients. Offenders with mental disorders do not have the right to the least restrictive alternative (LRA) that governs the formation of the therapeutic alliance, the options available for treatment, and the ability to set short-term goals (see Table 3.1).

THE CRIMINAL JUSTICE PROCESS

Because system issues are critical, understanding the criminal justice process is important. All too often, those working in security hospitals miss the forest for the trees and fail to understand the symptoms of offenders with mental disorders as they relate to their legal and social status within the institution. Understanding this system begins with the unspoken assumptions that underpin criminal justice theory. The defendant is (1) innocent until proven guilty, (2) competent unless shown to be incompetent, (3) sane unless proven to be insane, and (4) responsible unless proven to be not responsible.

Unfortunately, these unspoken assumptions seem to allow the court to ignore the psychological aspects of the criminal, because the court assumes that those offenders who are mentally ill will eventually receive treatment. Halleck (1986) pointed out that some courts believe offenders with mental disorders who fall below an arbitrary and shifting "threshold" do not warrant special treatment. The severely mentally ill are routed through an evaluation and treatment process. Those who fall below the threshold as defined in any particular case are treated as though they are healthy, with the expectation that if they get worse they will be treated in corrections. At times the severity of the crime can affect the position of this threshold. Defendants charged with capital crimes receive more attention than do those charged with misdemeanors. It is difficult to draw a clear line, on a scientific or clinical basis, between the seriously mentally disordered and others. Thus, many offenders with mental disorders are not diagnosed or treated at the front end of the system.

To facilitate understanding the movement of offenders with mental disorders through the criminal justice system to the forensic hospital system, we present the "seven C's" of the criminal justice process (see Figure 3.1). The process begins with the commitment of a crime (C1) and the capture of the defendant (C2). Miranda rights and possible evaluation of competence to waive rights are considered at this point (Miller, Maier, & Kaye, 1985, 1986). Charges (C3) are filed, the defendant is arraigned, and the trial process begins (C4). If the defendant appears as though he/she is mentally ill, the court orders an evaluation of competence to stand trial.

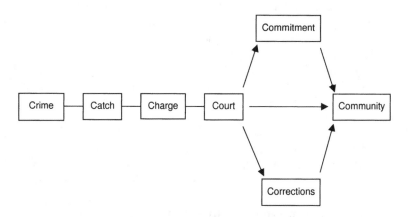

FIGURE 3.1. The "seven C's" of the criminal justice process.

(Sometimes the defendant decompensates after the trial has progressed and an evaluation of competence to proceed will then be ordered.) If the defendant is found to be incompetent to stand trial, he/she is then ordered to a hospital to be treated to competence. Once competent, the trial begins. If the defendant raises the insanity defense, the court orders an evaluation of the defendant's criminal responsibility. If the defendant is found guilty, he/she is sent to corrections (C5). If found not guilty by reason of insanity (NGRI), he/she is committed to the security hospital administered by the state Department of Health and Social Services, such as Atascadero in California (C6). To complete the system, more than 95% of offenders with mental disorders ultimately return to the community (C7).

Consider some of the demographic statistics that describe the pretrial phase of this process. Defendants begin confinement in city and county jails. A 1988 U.S. jail census showed a total population of more than 395,000 and growing (Steadman, 1990). A study by Abram and Teplin (1991) of inmates in the Cook County Jail in Chicago showed that schizophrenia, severe depression, and mania occur up to three times as often among men in urban jails as in the population at large. Most of these prisoners could also be dually diagnosed with substance abuse, and a high percentage had an antisocial personality disorder. They concluded that about 24,000 inmates confined to jails currently suffer from a severe mental disorder.

Once convicted, the defendant moves from jail to prison. In most states, offenders are sent to a classification center and, if found to have mental disorders at that point, they are sent to a specialized forensic facility for treatment administered by the state Department of Corrections, such as Vacaville in California. In theory, they will receive appropriate care.

Roth (1980) estimated that between 15% and 20% of prisoners need treatment for mental illness at some time during their incarceration. This approximates that of the population at large. Halleck (1988) found that many mentally ill in prison were not identified as such and were therefore untreated. He estimated the prevalence of mental illness to be much higher than 20%. A more recent study of Canadian facilities reported that 9% of some 10,000 male inmates were acutely psychotic at any one time. Many offenders with mental disorders were believed to be lost in the system (Deurloo, 1992). Monahan and Steadman (1983) found that 32% of the felons who came to trial were found IST; only 1% of accused felons raised the insanity defense; of these, 26% were found NGRI or guilty but mentally ill (GBMI); and 84% of these felons were committed to a forensic facility with a DSM-III Axis I (American Psychiatric Association, 1980) diagnosis. The literature agrees that the incidence and prevalence of mental illness is high in confined settings, but that the diagnosis and reporting of offenders with mental disorders varies greatly between states. Let us consider how services are provided.

MODELS OF SERVICE DELIVERY

In general, each state provides psychiatric services for those found IST and NGRI in psychiatric facilities in the mental health system and, for those who "become" mentally disordered while in the prison, in prison psychiatric units. Seriously ill offenders with mental disorders are usually transferred to a security hospital in that mental health system for more intensive treatment. Beginning in the 1980s, with the growth of the prison system, states began to develop sophisticated psychiatric hospitals administered by the prison system. According to Harold Carmel (personal communication, February 1992), California has two centralized state hospitals with about 4,700 beds. The facility administered by the mental health system at Atascadero is a single-level, maximum-security facility and has about 900 patients. ISTs are treated in a single program and NGRIs and prison transfers are treated on general purpose wards. Vacaville is the state prison hospital. In 1992, it had about 3,800 offenders with mental disorders. Colorado has a single state facility with about 280 beds for forensic patients; 20 of these are for prison transfers. All levels of security are present in this facility. According to Robert T. M. Phillips (personal communication, January 1992), Connecticut has a maximum security hospital and five free-standing satellite court clinics around the state. The maximum security facility is organized on a "levels of care" system and includes a neurodiagnostic and transitional treatment unit. Civil, criminal, or court cases can be found on any given ward. The regional hospitals maintain medium (locked) and minimum (unlocked) security levels. Consider, then, a general description of the different system "hospitals."

The Forensic Security Hospital

There is wide variation among states in the way psychiatric services are delivered to forensic patients. Way, Dvoskin, and Steadman (1991) surveyed forensic program directors in 1986. On the sample day, there were 5,424 NGRI and 3,204 IST patients. The rates of NGRIs per population varied among states, ranging from 62 per 100,000 in Washington, DC, to zero in a few states. (IST rates ranged from 3.66 in Florida to zero in some). Sixty-nine percent of NGRIs and 71% of ISTs were treated in forensic units; the rest were treated in civil units. Some states treat all of their NGRIs and ISTs on civil units, whereas 1,255 patients designated as "dangerous civil patients" were treated in forensic beds. This study suggested that states with lower-than-average rates of NGRIs had more punitive societal values than the other states.

Most states send IST and NGRI patients to forensic facilities that utilize a three-level security system: maximum, medium, and minimum.

This closely parallels that used in correctional facilities. Persons found to be IST are ordered by the court to forensic facilities, the security consistent with their charge, with the expectation of treatment and timely restoration to competence. Pendleton (1980) described the treatment program for these patients in California. Most of the patients were diagnosed with paranoid schizophrenia. The full range of treatment modalities were utilized, including an innovative program utilizing a simulated mock trial and written examinations. Over 90% of patients were rendered competent within the prescribed time. Similar success rates have been reported by other states.

Correctional facilities have added higher and lower security levels to the standard maximum, medium, and minimum. There are "super-maximum" security prisons, such as the federal prison at Marion, Illinois. At the other end of the spectrum, states are experimenting with electronic home detention. Various security levels can be found either individually in hospitals (or prisons) dedicated to one security level, or two or all three levels can be found in one facility. There are advantages and disadvantages to having multiple security levels at a single facility. Some states with small populations are predominately rural and need a centralized facility in one location to maximize their resources. Large, centralized facilities are often distant from the main population centers, which decreases family input into diagnosis and treatment. An NIMH survey (1987) noted that a number of states lacked specialized facilities for women and children.

Prison Psychiatric Units

Most prisons have a small mental health unit designed to manage acute psychiatric patients. In the event that their clinical resources fail to manage a difficult offender, the patient is transferred either to a secure forensic hospital, or in some states to a maximum-security prison hospital. Patients who are refractory to treatment can be transferred from the prison hospital to a forensic hospital. The optimal prison system would have a small psychiatric unit with well-trained staff in each prison. The hospital milieu compared with the prison differs in several basic areas that affect treatability. The hospital milieu is based on trust, whereas the prisons often create conditions which stress inmates, who then become distrustful. The treatment implications are obvious.

A number of specialty programs have been developed in maximum-security hospitals that offer patients the hope for change, including behavioral modification programs that teach patients how to function in the system. According to Dvoskin (personal communication, January 1992), New York has an accredited, free-standing psychiatric hospital and a unique system of prison mental health units within 15 of the state's largest prisons. The prison units focus on the positive aspects of corrections, education, vocational programs, relief of suffering, and a safe environment. The psychiatric hospital has an admissions ward and wards for sentenced male inmates, those with special needs, and a prerelease ward.

In our opinion, small psychiatric units attached to major prisons with dual management (security and clinical) have the most to offer. Prison and mental health expertise are required at the administrative level to ensure that both security and treatment needs are met. Small units are less entrenched in excessive security. They offer a greater level of trust, better staff communication, and the possibility of specialization. When morale is good they even offer the potential of a rewarding career to the mental health professionals who choose to work in this subspeciality (Maier & Miller, 1987).

MANAGEMENT AND TREATMENT

Hospital System Design

After commitment, a patient is admitted to a high-security admission/assessment unit where he/she will remain for several days to 2 months as assessment progresses. The system design of security hospitals has been given progressive attention. It is not just that those found NGRI often require specialized care; there are a number of NGRI patients who do not want treatment and, because they have the right to refuse treatment, refuse. A growing number are immature, impulse ridden, and behaviorally disturbed. The need to create hospital units to meet the needs of each patient type has become painfully clear.

First, consider an approach to the treatment design based on an analysis of patient personality traits and social skills. Rice and Harris (1988) developed a decision tree to assign patients to appropriate units (see Figure 3.2). In their study utilizing cluster analysis, they grouped newly admitted patients into several categories with common management–treatment goals. The categories assessed were: intellectual and life skills functioning, institutional management problems, psychotic symptomatology, and social withdrawal. These were prioritized with security considerations (institutional management problems) first, level of functioning (life skills and intellectual ability) and interpersonal problems (social withdrawal) second, and psychotic symptomatology last. The decision tree helped identify the high-risk patient, that is; a patient who required special treatment or a special management program. It also helped to identify a subset of patients who were not overtly aggressive, but who had trouble with confined living. These patients were often in a power struggle with the institution. Some were considered "jail-house attorneys," who were themselves litigious and promoted this in their peers (Cleary, 1973; Gilman, 1979).

In summary, the decision tree divided new admissions into one of two

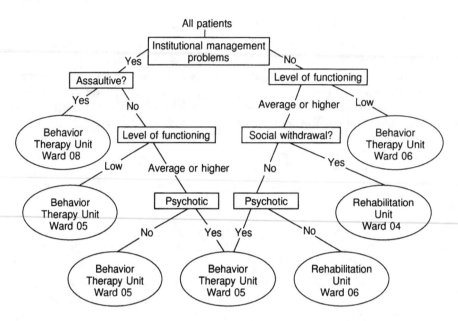

FIGURE 3.2. A decision tree to be used to assign patients to wards. From Rice and Harris (1988). Copyright 1988 by John Wiley & Sons. Reprinted by permission.

broad categories: (1) those who had trouble in the institution because they are dangerous to themselves or others or because they had specific problems with institutional living; and (2) those whose problems stemmed from their mental illness and required specialized treatment for their mental disorder, but without the extra concern that behavior stemming from their mental disorder would purposely disrupt other patients or staff. Figure 3.2 describes the patient needs in the units.

Second, consider the impact that the rights to treatment and to refuse treatment have on patient behavioral control and system design. In particular, the time has come to notify patients of their responsibilities with the same enthusiasm with which we notify them of their rights. When staff inform patients of their rights on admission, verbally and in writing, they should also notify them of their responsibilities verbally and in writing. Sometimes the patient is so disorganized that this information has little meaning. Therefore, when patients become more aware of their clinical circumstances and are ready to move off the admission unit, they should be reinformed of their rights and their responsibilities. They should be informed that one of their rights is the right to treatment and another is the right to refuse treatment.

When they understand that they have the right to treatment and the right to refuse treatment, patients should be introduced to the idea that it is their responsibility to negotiate the form of treatment with staff. If they decide to exercise that right, they will enter into a track of high-intensity staff interaction. In other words, their treatment plan will reflect the fact that unit resources will be applied as much as possible to help them identify and resolve their personal pathologies. They will be involved in organized, treatment-oriented therapy. For example, recreational therapy may focus on team play, which will differ from a "management" program called "gym" designed to work off excessive energy.

If they decide to exercise the right to refuse treatment, they should then be informed of the responsibility that they are taking on themselves when they exercise that right. The "treatment plan" will be renamed a "management plan" and will reflect their noninvolvement in the treatment structures of the unit. Thus, some patients will have a treatment plan and others, a management plan. Whereas every patient on the unit has the right to access what the unit has to offer (small dayroom, large dayroom, yard, gym, etc.) and access to interaction with the staff, the difference between a patient on a treatment plan and a patient on a management plan would be that those involved in treatment would enter a treatment program designed to further their treatment goals; those not involved in treatment would enter a management program designed to help them maintain citizenship on the unit and to learn how to manage their behavior within the policies of the unit and institution.

The difference between treatment and management is critical. *Treatment* is the interactive process in which the staff and the patient develop a therapeutic alliance, based on trust, that will enable him/her to explore feelings and behavior so that the patient will become more responsible for him/herself. Change, often requiring painful exploration resulting in greater self-acceptance, is part of this process. *Management* is a didactic interaction between the patient and staff. It is not necessarily based on trust. It does not require personal change, but only conformity to the rules. Patients who cannot control themselves or are willfully not involved in treatment must still conform their conduct to the unit and institution policies. A trusting relationship is not necessary to manage and control patients who have difficulty in this area.

Whereas the treatment process is often described in hospital policies, it is time that hospitals develop an equally sophisticated description of the management process. Figure 3.3 is a management/treatment decision tree that can identify the needs of the 10–25% of any inpatient population who only want "management." A management plan should include the following patient agreement: (1) to abide by unit policies and procedures; (2) not to disrupt therapy for others; and (3) that noncompliance with unit policies

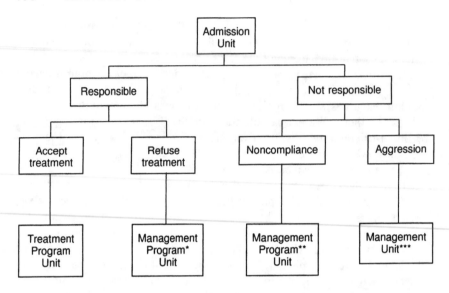

FIGURE 3.3. Program decision tree: Rights/responsibilities. Each unit has patients in treatment and patients being managed in the Management Program. * Refuse treatment. Patients would be on a no-treatment plan of treatment for high-functioning, usually personality-disordered patients. ** Noncompliance. This is for the group of patients who could not decide to participate in treatment but were not aggressive. *** Management Unit. A specialized unit of repetitively aggressive patients.

and procedures will result in the use of sanctions, deterrent or incapacitating, or transfer to a more secure unit or hospital.

Major Mental Disorders

The following sections briefly outline important aspects of the treatment process. We identify them because, from a systems perspective, they highlight particular problems that must be addressed.

Incidence/Prevalence of DSM-IV Diagnoses

Offenders with mental disorders span a broad range of DSM-IV (American Psychiatric Association, 1994a) diagnoses. Axis I disorders make up the majority, such as schizophrenia, bipolar disorder, and substance abuse disorders. Axis II personality disorders that are revealed when the patient's primary Axis I diagnosis is in remission are also common. Whereas antisocial personality disordered (APD) patients are specifically excluded from using the NGRI defense by law in most states, there are significant numbers of offenders with personality disorder, antisocial type, as a secondary diagnosis. The NIMH survey of facilities (Kerr & Roth, 1987) found that the diagnoses of schizophrenia and personality disorders jointly accounted for more than 70% of all diagnoses. Dual and multiple diagnoses are common. Many have a secondary diagnosis of mental retardation. Callahan, Steadman, McGreevey, and Robins (1991) studied the insanity defense in eight states. They found that the defense was raised in 1% of all felony cases, and only 26% of those claiming this defense were successful. Of those pleading NGRI, 55.2% were schizophrenic or had another psychosis or affective disorder. Of those acquitted, 84% had these diagnoses; 65% of acquittees were indicted for violent or potentially violent offenses. Most (81.5%) of those successfully using the NGRI defense had prior psychiatric hospitalizations. Kerr and Roth (1986) compared the demographics of the population of state forensic units with that of federal prisons. They found about twice as many youths under age 17 and more residents aged 65 or older in state forensic units. Youths tried as adults comprised only 1.6% of the population of adult offender psychiatric units, compared with 2.6% in the general prison population.

Axis II Personality Disorders

Offenders with mental disorders with APD as a secondary diagnosis require special attention because they are seen in large numbers in forensic facilities. In DSM-III (American Psychiatric Association, 1980), the diagnosis of APD (principal) could not be made in the presence of schizophrenia or mental retardation. This changed with DSM-III-R, angering some clinicians who believed that "psychopath" is a completely separate entity. The diagnosis then evolved through the various editions of the DSM (Maier, 1990). Widiger (1992), in his report on changes in DSM-IV, discussed the fact that the DSM-III-R criteria were long and complex; a diagnosis required consideration of 30 items. Given the emphasis on past criminal and delinquent acts, he thought it was overdiagnosed in forensic and prison populations.

   Most clinicians believe that APDs are untreatable. There is a significant correlation between the antisocial personality and a previous diagnosis of attention deficit disorder with hyperactivity (Mannuzza, Klein, & Giampino, 1989), and antisocials who abuse drugs and alcohol commit the most serious crimes. The hard criteria can help refine the diagnosis, but even then it is difficult to separate this from the criminal personality (Reid, 1985; Yochelson & Samenow, 1976). The Hare Psychopathy Scale is gaining popularity in assessing these patients (Hare, 1991; Hare, McPherson, & Forth, 1988).

The Suicidal Patient

Pretrial and trial experiences are very traumatic. Defendants are confronted with the impact and magnitude of their crimes and the media increases their notoriety. Often, after the trial, when they have been admitted to a facility, they begin to realize for the first time that they have lost their freedom. High-risk patients who have had their self-esteem damaged are at risk for harming themselves as a reaction to the stress, more than to depression. It is important to consider these patients at risk for physical aggression as a way of coping with stress. Early identification of patients at risk for self-harm or aggression is important; appropriate suicide or aggression precautions should be instituted. In some jails, the suicide rate among inmates 18 to 24 years of age is nearly five times the rate among their peers in the general population. The risk is thought to be greatest with young, first-time offenders during the first few hours or days of incarceration (Kimmel, 1987).

The Difficult Patient

Many patients have difficulty with incarceration and manifest this difficulty not with aggression toward self or others but by passive–aggressive grievances and lawsuits, both socially approved, legal methods. The so-called "jurisgenic disease" (Morowitz, 1981) is well known in the prison system. Lawsuits have resulted in some needed reform in the past, but many simply waste taxpayer resources and are a nuisance aggravation to prison systems. A lawsuit can cause real stress because it singles out an individual (called *targeting*). Many prisoners become jailhouse lawyers because they feel it gives them prestige among their peers. With the criminalization of the mentally ill, more and more experienced jailhouse lawyers are seen in forensic hospital settings, where they teach the techniques to other patients. Miller, Maier, Blancke, and Doren (1986) discussed the utility of looking at litigiousness as a form of resistance to treatment. Chrzanowski (1980) studied problem patients with concealed hostility and found complex dynamics underlying much of their behavior. Feelings of helplessness with regard to authority were associated with litigiousness.

Teaching jailhouse lawyers legitimate ways to use the system to achieve their ends and to respectfully respond in a nonangry way to their legitimate complaints through the use of the grievance process are the most respectable ways of managing them. It is important that patients know that we are practicing good medicine, we cannot be intimidated, and we will not back down in the face of nonlegitimate complaints, even to avoid a lawsuit.

The Politically High-Profile Patient

Forensic patients who have attracted media attention because of the nature of their crimes pose an additional management/treatment problem. When treating such a patient it is equally important to manage the media. The media "treatment plan" must be in place before the patient is admitted. Outside interference is damaging and disruptive to both staff and the patient. Discussions with the staff prior to the patient's arrival are helpful in minimizing countertransference. How and when peers should be prepared is a further problem. As there is essentially no literature in this area, we recommend that facilities with this problem contact another facility that has had experience with a notorious patient (e.g., St. Elizabeths, because of its experience with John Hinckley, Jr.).

The principal author (G.J.M.) was involved in preparing his hospital for the possible admission of Jeffrey Dahmer (Maier, 1991). The process was not only intense, but ultimately destructive to the therapeutic milieu. For instance, while in jail pretrial, Dahmer received thousands of letters, both love letters and hate letters. Senior health officials believed that the pattern would continue if he was found NGRI. Further, they thought that someone might try to kill him with a letter bomb. Because in the mental health system he would have had the patient's right to reasonable access to mail, the simple process of checking his mail each day would have overwhelmed our resources. This issue was only one of many wherein security concerns could have infringed on his "patient" rights. By the start of the trial, administrative anxiety had intensified to such a degree that the initial goal of "normalizing" Mr. Dahmer not only faded, but plans were put in place to fortify the security on his future unit, including replacing all windows with bulletproof glass, lest a sharpshooter with a nightsight "pick him off" when he went to the bathroom. We were greatly relieved that he went to a prison where security issues rightly dominate the attitude toward care—although in this case security measures still proved inadequate.

Prosecuting Assaultive Patients

Some patients in the acute phase of their illness cannot control themselves because they have lost their executive functioning governing behavioral control. The non-goal-directed, aggressive behavior of these patients becomes a management issue. Staff are trained to manage aggressive behavior and often tolerate the injuries that result, but they have the same rights as other citizens. Because patients have numerous protections against system abuse, they should be held responsible, even criminally responsible, when they break the law (Miller & Maier, 1987). When an asymptomatic patient willfully assaults a staff member or peer, he/she should be held legally accountable. It is important to hold patients whose symptoms are in remission responsible for their behavior. They need to know that there are consequences in the real world for unlawful, controllable behavior. Prosecuting such behavior safeguards the integrity and morale of peers and staff alike.

Norko, Zonana, and Phillips (1991) discussed prosecuting willful aggression by patients and proposed guidelines governing the appropriateness of prosecution, along with criteria to include in a hospital policy. According to Norko and colleague it is important to inform patients upon admission of the hospital's policy regarding prosecution of willful aggression. They should know that each aggressive incident will be reviewed and an assessment will be made of the patient's mental status at the time of the aggressive act. They believed that in the event that prosecution is pursued, the complaint should not be filed by the treating staff to avoid a conflict of interest and to try to preserve the therapeutic alliance. Others think that the therapeutic alliance is broken by aggressive behavior and that the responsible way to manage the prosecution is for the staff to participate in the criminal process in an active manner (Maier, 1989). The American Psychiatric Association Task Force (1992), on clinician safety, supported this position, as did Hoge and Gutheil (1987).

Management of Aggression

An episode of aggression consists of a five-phase process: pre-aggression, aggression, control, diagnosis and assessment, and treatment and management (Maier, 1993). Maier, Van Rybroek, Doren, Musholt, and Miller (1988) and Maier, Stava, Morrow, Van Rybroek, and Bauman (1987) developed a model for the assessment, management, and treatment of aggressive behavior that depends on understanding the Tao of aggression, that is, the "how" of aggression. The coordinated use of staff interventions has been shown to break the repetitive, cyclic, and pathological aggression pattern and then provide effective treatment and a safer environment (Fisher, 1994; Monroe, Van Rybroek, & Maier, 1988). The model identifies the importance of a good staffing pattern and the role that specialized training plays in managing aggression. Units which specialize in managing aggressive patients will inevitably be developed (Tardiff, 1996). A unique ambulatory restraint procedure was developed for use in conjunction with this model (Van Rybroek, Kuhlman, Maier, & Kaye, 1987). Preventive aggression devices (PADs) are restraint devices that offer an intermediate approach to control of aggression, short of seclusion or 4/5-point restraint. These devices respect the patient and help the staff reduce negative feelings of fear and anger toward the aggressor (Maier, Van Rybroek, & Mays, 1994).

Most programs employ behavior modification programs to shape the behavior of aggressive patients toward more acceptable goals. These programs commonly utilize a token economy, privilege levels, and the principles of reward and punishment. Henderson (1989) discussed an effective social skills training program used in a British maximum-security prison to manage aggressive offenders. Training revolved around three major skills areas relevant to aggression: assertiveness, self-control, and social anxiety. Crucial to the program was an accurate assessment process utilizing a multimethod approach, followed by an individualized training program (Maier, 1996).

Effective programs are known to cause behavioral changes that generalize in the facility. Some patients, however, are incapable of learning from models that use long-term rewards and punishments. Repetitively aggressive patients often feel hopeless and give up trying to improve. Van Rybroek, Maier, McCormick, and Pollock (1988) developed the *today–tomorrow* behavioral concept. This is one component of their comprehensive model for the management and treatment of the aggressive inpatient. Individual patients earn daily privileges based on reaching targeted goals on the previous day. Patients are rated at the end of each day and night shift and earn different levels of privileges contingent on their behavior. Today's behavior affects tomorrow's privileges. No one can lose privileges for longer than one day, contingent on their behavior. The expectations are individualized for the patient to maximize success. Once the patient learns how to succeed in the system, the behavioral expectations are adjusted upward at a pace tolerable to the patient. A major theme in this approach is that the patient's individual program is directly developed by the line staff. This has been well received by staff and has resulted in an increase in their motivation and commitment to help the patient. Further, and most important, patients who have experienced endless failure are literally hooked into becoming successful because, from the start, the program is developed to ensure that they will succeed before it becomes demanding (Liberman, 1988; Lukoff, Liberman, & Neuchterlein, 1986; Paul & Lentz, 1977).

TREATMENT PROCESS

Patient Issues

There are a number of factors that must be considered before the treatment process begins. As noted at the beginning of this chapter, *treatability* refers to the assessment of the offender's capacity to comply with and respond to treatment. The assessment of treatability is critical in formulating treatment goals (Quinsey & Maquire, 1983). Rogers, Gillis, Dickens, and Webster (1988) showed that the assessment of treatability was a complex process. They noted marked interclinician variability and proposed several questions of crucial importance concerning the accuracy of treatability assessments, whether assessments become "self-fulfilling," whether treatability can be distinguished on the basis of history or other variables, and finally, whether treatment can affect future criminal behavior (Eichelman & Hartwig, 1995).

Fein (1984) concluded that the NGRI acquittal itself actually reduced the treatability of offenders. He believed that acquittal removed responsibility from the offender and therefore lessened the patient's desire to change his/her perceptions and behavior. He considered factors such as diminished capacity to form relationships and inability to mourn as important factors governing treatability. Halleck (1982, 1988) developed a model for asserting patient responsibility to facilitate treatment. The model presumed free will and acknowledged the individual limits of the patients. In the model, the psychiatrist attempts to maximize the patient's performance by holding him/her as responsible as humanely possible for his current and future behavior. When applied flexibly and consistently, he found the approach effective even in the treatment of offenders with personality disorders.

Treatment Planning

Whereas the factors above are important from a systems perspective, the quality of treatment varies directly with the standards of care and the review process that governs the whole process. Treatment in a Joint Commission on Accreditation of Healthcare Organizations (JCAHO) accredited facility utilizing the standard multidisciplinary team format or in a jail or prison accredited by the ACA is the best indicator that the facility is committed to treatment. These formats identify standards for each discipline. Professional organizations such as the National Association of State Forensic Directors (NASFD) and the American Academy of Psychiatry and the Law (AAPL) have made important contributions toward defining standards of care that are beginning to bring quality psychiatric care to all offenders with mental disorders. Quality care can involve recidivism and postdischarge outcome. It is also helpful in diminishing the impact of lawsuits from watchdog groups. The standard treatment approaches include all modalities of traditional therapy, psychopharmacology, and behavioral medicine as they have been modified to meet the needs of offenders with mental disorders. Patients benefit from a well-conceived combination of treatment modalities, and a coordinated treatment approach is more efficacious than any one modality alone.

Psychopharmacological Treatment

NEUROLEPTICS

THE RIGHT TO REFUSE TREATMENT WITH NEUROLEPTICS.   The unstructured use of neuroleptics in the 1960s and '70s led to a number of reforms, regulations, and changes in patients' rights. The *Rogers* decision in Massachusetts in 1979 (*Rogers v. Okin*, 1979) was the first to recognize the patient's right to refuse psychotropic medication. The right to refuse derives from the right to receive treatment, which was driven by realistic concerns regarding the poor treatment offered in some mental health institutions. "Treatment" varied from no treatment at all to the use of aversive behavioral techniques. This led to the codification of laws guaranteeing the rights of patients to receive *effective* treatment. Procedural safeguards and protective rights were initiated. One of the last rights won by patients was the right to refuse psychotropic medication, which then expanded to the right to refuse treatment in general. *Rogers* was the prototypical case. It led to the enactment of laws in most states governing the patient's right to refuse. In general, these laws apply to forensic patients as well as to those civilly committed.

The laws cluster around five variations of two models, one treatment driven and the other, rights driven. Appelbaum (1988) stated that the treatment-driven model had two variations for committed patients. In variation *A,* the physician determined medication regimens regardless of the consent of the patient. In variation *B,* if the patient refused, an independent clinical review resulted that could overturn the patient's refusal. The rights-driven model had three variations. Variation *C* was similar to *B,* but an independent clinical review also determined if the patient continued to be incompetent; if competent, the patient's decision stood. Variation *D* was similar to *A,* except that the problem of the patient's competence was addressed initially at the commitment hearing, and only incompetent persons could be committed. (This is the variation endorsed by the American Psychiatric Association.) Variation *E* required a judicial hearing if the patient refused and the physician believed him/her to be incompetent. The judge determined the competence of the patient, the appropriateness of the medication, and the patient's best interests. Most clinicians believe that variation *E* is not in the patient's best interests, as some jurists are hostile to neuroleptics despite a formidable body of literature that demonstrates that they are effective and safe.

The laws of Massachusetts and other states follow variation *E.* Appelbaum (1988) and other clinicians noted several problems with variation *E* that are serious impediments to effective patient care. For most committed patients, effective treatment is nothing less than neuroleptic medication. After all, patients are committed to receive treatment. The hearings are another burden on the court and hospital personnel, and force judges to act as physicians. Appelbaum noted that whenever judges act in the place of physicians, they think like physicians and rule for medication almost 100% of the time. One wonders what is being accomplished by the right to refuse treatment except that it creates a windfall for lawyers.

Other courts extended the same standards considered above for civilly committed patients to forensic patients. Courts have been divided on whether a patient found IST can be forced to accept medication to be rendered competent. Some courts cling to a commonly held misconception that medications impair or change patients in a fundamental way. They do not allow "chemical competence." Later courts did allow medication, considering the compelling state interest to bring defendants to trial. Several courts have ruled in favor of restoring competence to stand trial initially, and then permitted the defendants to refuse treatment and proceed in a "natural state" through the rest of the trial.

In 1987, the Wisconsin Supreme Court held that a "right to refuse" standard similar to variation E was required, and extended its protection to all involuntary patients (*State* ex rel. *Jones v. Gerhardstein et al.,* 1987). Patients who were committed without a specific court order to treat were allowed to refuse medications. Van Rybroek, Miller, and Maier (1988) studied the impact of this decision on a 165-bed state forensic hospital. Whereas the Massachusetts law required separate hearings for commitment and treatment decisions, the Wisconsin law allowed treatment issues to be decided at the time of the commitment hearing. The law increased the incidence of patient refusal because Wisconsin required affirmative, written consent rather than passive assent. It was expected, therefore, that refusal rates in general would be higher for forensic patients than for civil patients, as they are more legally sophisticated and often have negative feelings toward the facilities.

The study showed that the reasons for refusal were, in order of frequency: denial of illness, assertion of legal rights, complaints about the side effects, the use of medication as leverage to bargain with staff over unrelated issues, confusion about the issue to refuse or consent, and the assertion that the medication had not helped in the past. As expected, there was an increase in the use of seclusion and transfer to more secure units as patients deteriorated while waiting for the court hearing. In the beginning, the average time from petition, to treat, to court order was 5 weeks. Later, this was reduced to 10 days. The delay resulted in an increase of staff time spent managing acutely psychotic patients. As expected, judges ruled for medication in almost 100% of cases.

Whereas we agree that a finding of IST or insanity does not automatically mean that a patient is also incompetent to make treatment decisions, given the above, we conclude that judicial review is unnecessary and counterproductive to the needs of the patient and society. The most acceptable model would be similar to variation *B* or *C,* and would include an independent clinical review board. The board could be composed of peer physicians, or even be multidisciplinary. As recommended by Appelbaum (1988), it would be fair to utilize this board for all patients, including those who accept treatment. The courts do not add clinical safeguards to treatment, but a clinical review board would, which would also decrease malpractice exposure on the part of the prescribing physician.

Federal courts have ruled that medications cannot be used with insanity acquittees for behavioral control alone. Halleck (1986) recommended that neuroleptics be used prudently because of their side effects. He noted that neuroleptics are effective in maintaining a peaceful milieu, but as an effect that is secondary to the management of the patient's primary illness. He believed that facilities dealing with offenders with mental disorders should have sufficient structure to control aggressive behavior without use of neuroleptics for this purpose alone. This is even more important in facilities that lack adequate staffing to monitor for side effects.

In one maximum security prison, 38% of the inmate population were on one or more neuroleptics. These were prescribed on a request basis. The consulting psychiatrists had nonverbally agreed to help the patients sleep, remain calm, relax, manage stress, stop "voices," and self-manage anger by complying with any inmate request for "pills." Whereas the inmates were not able to exchange medication with each other, the demand/request for a specific medication was clear. "Doc, I have nightmares" meant more of a sleeper. "Doc, I'm going to kill someone" meant more neuroleptic. One of us (G.J.M.) brought these practices to the attention of the Chief of Clinical Services, who told G.J.M. that he would look into it. No change in prescribing habits resulted.

TREATMENT WITH NEUROLEPTICS.   Treating the major clinical syndromes of schizophrenia and bioplar disorder with neuroleptics and mood stabilizers is beyond the scope of this chapter. There are many good references that direct the clinician on the standard protocols in using typical neuroleptics and mood stabilizers to bring the symptoms of these major clinical syndromes under control. Perhaps the most recent and comprehensive set of references are contained in the American Psychiatric Association's (1997) *Practice Guideline for the Treatment of Patients with Schizophrenia,* and (1994b) *Practice Guideline for the Treatment of Patients with Bipolar Disorder.* If there is a limit to the method of practice of using neuroleptics and mood stabilizers with major clinical syndromes, it is that clinicians are not patient enough in letting the medications work before they change them.

A standard algorithm given by Lieberman (1996) suggests that oral fluphenazine (20 mg) be given for a period of 6 weeks before there is any change, that it be increased to 40 mg for 4 weeks with no change, and that if there is no clinical response to these doses, the medication should be changed to haloperidol 20 mg for 6 weeks and then increased to haloperidol 40 mg for 4 weeks; finally, if there is no response, molindone can be given up to 300 mg or clozapine can be used up to 900 mg (Lieberman, 1996). Offenders with mental disorders are also in a stressful, paranoia-inducing environment and it may be that medications in those environments take even longer to bring symptoms under control.

ATYPICAL NEUROLEPTICS.   Clozapine, risperidone, olanzapine, and quetiapine are atypical antipsychotic agents that have proven effective for psychotic patients refractory to traditional neuroleptics and those who experience intolerable side effects to conventional neuroleptics, including tardive dyskinesia. Maier (1992b) studied the impact of clozapine on 25 refractory schizophrenic or schizoaffective forensic patients. Besides the refractory criteria, the use of clozapine was based on two forensic criteria: an increase in the safety of the unit and the possibility of the release of the patient in 1 year. Because of side effects, irresponsible behavior (hoarding for suicide attempts), or lack of response, clozapine was discontinued for six (24%) of the patients, but for the remaining 19 (76%), the response was significant. More than half improved. Twenty percent (5) of the patients improved enough that judges were willing to release them. Twenty-eight percent (7) were advanced to a less secure unit or were transferred to a civil facility. Clozapine, risperidone, and olanzapine (Tollefson et al., 1997) are useful in treating the negative symptoms of schizophrenia. These neuroleptics should be made available to offenders with mental disorders in all settings whose symptoms do not respond to traditional neuroleptics. Some states have been remiss in making these medications available to patients in maximum-security settings.

ANTIDEPRESSANTS

Depression is common in forensic facilities once confined patients begin to realize how their crime has affected their lives. First they feel the loss of their freedom. Many then experience the loss of self-esteem that is a result of the public trial. Some feel shame for the embarrassment the incarceration brings to themselves and their families. Before treating the symptoms of sadness, loss of appetite, loss of weight, poor sleep pattern, and low energy level, it is useful to consider the reaction to the above stressors in the same model used to understand and treat grief from any traumatic loss. Normal grief is not a pathological process. Our opinion is that patients should experience these feelings and learn to adjust and work through the various stages (Wortman & Silver, 1989). If the symptoms are intense, supportive psychotherapy is appropriate. Suppressing this process with psychoactive medication can delay the necessary grieving process. As in any grieving process, the patient will sometimes become overwhelmed. This condition can be appropriately treated with antidepressant medications in addition to psychotherapy as indicated.

When depression is a symptom of bipolar disorder or other Axis I disorders unrelated to the stressors of incarceration, symptoms should be treated aggressively with tricyclics or selective serotonin reuptake inhibitors (SSRIs) and psychotherapy. When depression is associated with an Axis II disorder, fluoxetine, an SSRI, is a good choice for an antidepressant. Markovitz, Calabrese, Schultz, and Meltzer (1991) reported on a study using fluoxetine in the treatment of offenders with borderline and schizotypal personality disorders. They hypothesized that symptoms of loss of impulse control arose from serotonergic dysregulation and suggested that fluoxetine would be useful. The results showed that more than half of the patients improved. The use of SSRI antidepressants with aggressive patients is now being considered.

MOOD STABILIZERS

With the advent of valproic acid and divalproex sodium, another valuable mood-stabilizing medication is available (Calabrese, Woyshville, Kimmel, & Rapport, 1993; Jacobsen, 1993). The register shows that this medication is equally effective as lithium in treating the manic phase of biopolar disorder. These medications are also useful in treating patients who have aggressive impulses associated with their major clinical syndromes. This medication is now gaining momentum and clinicians need to become progressively more aware of its usefulness in treating not only the manic phase of bipolar disorder, but in stabilizing mood, especially aggressive impulses in patients with schizophrenia and other disorders. This medication is also worth a trial on patients with Axis II personality disorders.

BENZODIAZEPINES

Because many offenders with mental disorders have an extensive history of substance abuse, benzodiazepines have been abused in these facilities. As a result, the prevailing belief is that they should not be used with these patients. There are effective alternatives for short-term pharmacological management of insomnia. Trazodone has been an effective hypnotic that does not alter sleep architecture. Although polypharmacy is usually frowned on, for patients on high-potency neuroleptics, the addition or partial substitution of a small amount of the highly sedative neuroleptics mesoridazine or chlorprothixene can also be effective.

Treating the Patient with Antisocial Personality Disorder

Patients with APD can evoke strong feelings of fear and anxiety in clinicians who attempt to treat them. Strasburger (1986) discussed the importance of identifying and resolving countertransference feelings. They are normal, necessary, and sometimes useful in the treatment of the patient, as long as they remain in control. Dubin (1989) believed that working through countertransference feelings was the principal problem for the therapist in treating antisocial offenders.

In attempting to treat the APD patient, one needs a theoretical model that can help to understand his/her needs. Kierulff (1988) discussed the personal-responsibility theory of Yochelson and Samenow (1976) with insight provided by deterministic social-responsibility theories. Kierulff believed that it is possible to integrate free will with determinism, and in this process the therapist can create the ability to choose in the APD patient. With appropriate reinforcers and empathy (but not sympathy), patients with APD can develop a sense of responsibility. Field (1986) considered the models of Millon (1981) and Yochelson and Samenow (1976) and proposed an alternative model based on a careful analysis of the specific characteristics of the APD. According to this model, the APD has low frustration tolerance and is high in stimulus-seeking behavior, which is associated with impulsivity. APDs thinking is rigid and compartmentalized; they are unable to process affect. Though they are believed to be fearless, they are truly fearful. Based on these premises, Field proposed a treatment intervention. Contrary to researchers such as Hare, he believed that the APD does have a superego, but it is underdeveloped and distorted. Group therapy and life-skills training are the optimum forum to help the APD develop impulse control while he/she comes to tolerate feelings. However, Hare and colleagues (1988) studied 521 inmates in Canadian facilities and found that the severity and frequency of offenses committed by APDs markedly decreased after the age of 40.

Individual Psychotherapy and the Therapeutic Alliance

Many offenders with mental disorders have committed notorious crimes or crimes they repress and of which they are ashamed. One of the first issues that must be addressed in individual therapy is the patient's defensiveness regarding his/her crime. Many claim amnesia of the event. The patient will have difficulty working with his/her therapist if he/she cannot believe that the information he/she shares will be treated in confidence. In private practice the patient is guaranteed confidentiality, but in an inpatient setting there is mixed agency; the clinician's allegiance lies with both the patient and the state. Gratzer, Gruenberg, Cavanaugh, and Brakel (1995) believe that although trusting relationships between clinicians and offenders with mental disorders are difficult to achieve because of countertransference and dual agency, developing such a relationship is absolutely necessary for success. In his discussion of psychotherapy with criminal patients, Carney (1973) also wrote that confidentiality is an integral part of the trust necessary for psychotherapy. Therefore, clinicians working with offenders with mental disorders should be trained in a therapy model that emphasizes trust and confidence. Clinicians benefit from this as much as the patients do.

At St. Elizabeths Hospital in Washington, DC, confidentiality of patient therapeutic communications is assured by the use of a modified therapist–administrator split (NIMH, 1987). In an effort to preserve most of the patient's confidences, clinicians do not chart the actual content of their therapeutic interactions, nor do they discuss them with others; this includes group therapy. Confidences are not revealed without the patient's consent, with an exception made for imminent dangerousness. Most of the staff at St. Elizabeths are committed to this approach and it has been supported by the courts. This model could be usefully adopted by other jurisdictions. The issue of charting and patients' access to their records is another critical area where trust and confidentiality can be developed (Miller, Morrow, Kaye, & Maier, 1987).

To put this critical issue in clear perspective, consider again that in private practice patients choose their therapists. In security settings, patients and therapists are cast together. A skilled therapist should look on this as a challenge and be able to develop a therapeutic alliance or be able to work effectively without it. Two groups of patients emerge: those who desire treatment and proceed to develop a trusting therapeutic alliance with us, and those the clinician does not trust because they are aggressive or those who distrust us and exercise their right to refuse treatment cordially. Gutheil (1984) described variations of the therapeutic alliance in forensic settings. He discussed problems such as the patient blackmailing the therapist by talking to him/her only in exchange for promises of help. Some patients believe that cooperation with the clinician will mitigate their responsibility for their crimes. For those patients who do develop a trusting relationship, the goals of therapy vary from depth work, which roots out the unconscious causes underpinning the motivation to deviate, to sector therapy, which is designed to help the inmate/patient adjust to institutional living.

Staff Issues

Therapist Issues

Forensic patients are frequently untruthful and good at appearing innocent. They can manipulate an inexperienced therapist and make him/her feel inadequate. Many of the patients have committed serious crimes, the nature of which may negatively effect the personal sensibilities and emotions of the therapist. When clinicians first begin to treat offenders with mental disorders they must learn to adapt to a mistrusting paradigm. If they cannot adapt, they may encounter a crisis in professional identity. These issues should be discussed with newly employed clinicians before their first patient encounters. Group discussions with more senior clinicians should be mandatory. The senior clinician would benefit, too, because over time clinicians can lose empathy for offenders with mental disorders. Supervisors need to be especially understanding and aware of this process.

Gutheil (1984) identified problems encountered by clinicians working in forensics for the first time. One concerned the fear of and anger toward the patient as it related to the patient's dangerousness and/or the repugnant nature of the crime. Another concerned "rescue fantasies" toward patients who are perceived as victims of circumstance. Yet another was the frustration experienced with the legal bureaucracy in forensic systems. These problems may not change with experience and can become part of the clinician's countertransference reaction to the system or institution, or they may be misplaced onto the patient (Poster & Ryan, 1994).

Group Psychotherapy

Group psychotherapy is the mainstay of most treatment programs in security settings because it maximizes the use of resources. Groups can be effective, sometimes more effective than individual therapy, especially for patients who cannot develop an individual therapeutic alliance. A full range of groups are used in forensic facilities: support groups, anger management groups, and substance abuse groups are just a few examples.

The importance of the group therapy approach is unquestioned in the literature. Staff led, it acts as a safe dialogue medium where the two poles of patient–staff can be safely encountered. It is a forum where trust can begin to build. Once trust has been built and the therapy process has had some duration, the dialogue moves to exposure of life histories and criminal experiences, including details of sexual perversion, physical and sexual violence, homosexuality, and accounts of family deprivation. Rappaport (1971), reporting on group therapy in prisons, noted that although groups of violent patients met, they were rarely out of control during therapy. Patients are usually highly defensive and appear more controlled than they really are. Rappaport believed that in a prison setting the therapist must minimize the traditional "objective" analytic approach and be prepared to be encountered as a real person. He recognized the difficulties of this position and noted problems with the therapist being accepted as a group member, as he/she also represents the institution. In a follow-up study of one therapy group, Rappaport found heightened self-awareness, improved ability to communicate ideas and feelings, and increased insight into the origins of patients' behavior. Only one member of the studied group returned to prison.

Stein and Brown (1991) studied the effectiveness of group psychotherapy on a group of NGRIs in Canada. They found the following personality characteristics in the patients, even those not diagnosed with a personality disorder: denial of responsibility, inability to form attachments or transference, inability to trust others, and egocentricity. Stein and Brown believed that because of this, the patients were not able to form cohesive groups in the traditional sense.

Staff Conflict

The most underaddressed issue in the process of assessment and treatment of offenders with mental disorders is the lack of attention given to staff needs. The first concern is effective, appropriate training.

Staff Training

Staff need to be trained in the basic understanding and management of the major mental disorders. They must be trained to work competently and safely in the forensic environment. The job-specific training content is in general adequate for most job descriptions: security staff, aide staff, nursing staff, and the professions. What is still inadequate are programs to assist employees who have skills deficits or personal problems that impede their ability to provide humane care. Most programs have employee assistance programs (EAPs). These have evolved to broader SAFE (staff assistance for employees) programs. This is a peer-assistance group that deals with any staff problem, but especially problems that arise from injury on the job. Programs called "Care for the Caregiver" have been developed (Mendota Mental Health Institute, 1993). Under this program the administration demonstrates that it cares for and is interested in the staff by providing ongoing inservices for them to increase their work skills, self-esteem, and professional development. One inservice is entitled "Managing Your Feelings." It was designed with an understanding that the stress of working in a security environment will bring out emotional problems which negatively impact the quality of care.

Types of Conflict (Maier, 1992a)

STAFF–PATIENT CONFLICT

There are several types of conflict besides patient–patient conflict with which staff need to deal. The front-line staff, particularity nursing aides or psychiatric technicians, are the emotional "shock absorbers" of the entire system. The psychiatrists and psychologists have a more narrowly defined role in dealing with the patients than do the front-line staff, who become involved with patients in every facet of their institutional lives. Patients also are more respectful to the psychiatrists and psychologists than they are to the line staff. Because of this, staff–patient conflict is common and it is critical that the administration recognize and find creative ways to deal effectively with these conflicts (Crowner, Stepcic, Peric, & Czobar, 1994).

STAFF–STAFF CONFLICT

Half of the problems in the institution are caused by the patients, the other half are caused by the staff. Identifying and managing staff–staff conflict is essential. The morale on a unit can be devastated by conflict between just two staff members.

STAFF–ADMINISTRATION CONFLICT

It is important that the administration be responsive to important staff needs such as staffing ratios, understaffing, environmental problems, hygienic conditions, union leverage, injuries, and other complaints as perceived important to the staff. Monthly union management meetings are the norm in states with unions.

Countertransference Issues

Countertransference refers to conscious or unconscious staff feelings toward patients. Some of the feelings patients engender in staff are fear, anger, helplessness, and frustration. These can lead to hate and rage. Staff tend to have significant difficulty in tolerating these feelings; their most common response is to deny them. The danger of denial is that it engenders a false sense of security and impairs the staff's sense of danger. Because the staff work in a structured setting, they have few options when it comes to sharing frustration. Wishnie (1977) noted that repressed staff fear should be suspected when unusual staff behavior patterns such as calling in sick, lateness, excessive seclusion, and the like develop. Sick jokes and disparaging comments about the patients by the staff are ways of releasing or ventilating stress. Such comments are a sign that staff are losing their reserve.

Working through these countertransference issues is important. The process can be facilitated by the development of a countertransference policy. Maier (1986a) developed a countertransference policy and procedure. The policy recognizes that working with offenders with mental disorders will arouse intense feelings in staff. It identifies four forums where staff can discuss these feelings: Staff members are expected to share their feelings toward the patients on admission, at team meetings, in individual supervision, and in a special, structured meeting called "Me-Time" (Maier & Van Rybroek, 1995).

ME-TIME

The best way that administrators can care for the staff is to meet with them privately on a regular basis (Flannery, Fulton, Tausch, & DeLoffi, 1991). Me-time was created as a special environment for 1 hour each day (or 1 hour each week on some units), where the A.M. and P.M. staff meet with clinical administrators and process their countertransference feelings. Throughout the day the staff at all levels acknowledge how they feel about a specific patient during informal discussions with each other. These feelings are then addressed in a confidential manner during me-time. Me-time is governed by few rules: All nursing and clinical staff must attend, and racist and sexist comments are not acceptable. Though staff may first meet me-time with resistance, as they come to trust each other they welcome the experience. Staff are encouraged to express themselves in language that is meaningful and satisfying to them (Maier & Miller, 1993). They may talk about any issue, including peer issues. Staff cannot be protected from the process of their own struggles, but the structure of me-time can provide the safety necessary to ensure that their issues are worked through in a respectful manner. The process has resulted in a cohesive staff and has helped eliminate staff splitting. When the process of me-time cannot change the countertransference for some staff members, the process moves into individual supervision. At times, personal issues may be such that they require a referral to the EAP or even in private counseling.

DISCHARGE PLANNING AND OUTCOME

Release Issues

A planned transition from confinement to the community is critical to the successful rehabilitation of offenders with mental disorders (Wexler, 1991). Roth (1987) believed that this process should be broken down into many small steps. In all hospital systems resources are targeted for patients who are nearing release. For offenders with mental disorders it is critical to begin this effort well in advance of release. This is especially important in the area of work skills, as many patients have no marketable skills, or if they have, their skill level will have waned during the long confinement. Community support programs (CSPs) help offenders with mental disorders make a satisfactory transition to community life. In such a CSP, the offender undergoes a comprehensive vocational assessment and begins appropriate training tailored to his/her needs and abilities. The program can have two tracks: one for high- and one for low-functioning offenders with mental disorders. Many offenders with mental disorders do volunteer work in the community as part of this program. The final step for most is employment in the community.

In the CSP described by Evans, Souma, and Maier (1989), the average length of stay was over 2 years. Initial studies indicated greater success for patients with schizophrenia than for those with personality disorders. Careless acts by the patients, or worse, a high-profile crime, can jeopardize the program. A number of safeguards were included in this program to preserve community support (Miller, Maier, Van Rybroek, & Weidemann, 1989). Careful patient selection is most important. Further, patients had to agree to be closely monitored. When patients were allowed into the community, the city police were notified. Staff met regularly with community leaders who were kept informed about the patients' whereabouts. The community leaders were also encouraged to make recommendations regarding security measures. In a 7-year follow-up study, the recidivism rate for 75 NGRI acquittees was 10%, without one violent crime. Recidivism was defined as revocation, not necessarily the addition of new charges.

Halleck (1986) pointed out that released insanity acquittees committed new crimes at the same rate as did noninsane felons who were imprisoned for similar crimes. This suggested that there are other factors to consider in releasing offenders with mental disorders besides treatment for the mental illness (Wettstein & Mulvey, 1988). He pointed out that many of the offenders with mental disorders had personality pathology underlying their psychosis, particularly paranoid, antisocial, narcissistic, and borderline personality states, and that this pathology was underappreciated during treatment. Halleck also cautioned that patients whose crimes were associated with drug and alcohol abuse are difficult to assess for dangerousness in that these substances are generally not available to the patient while hospitalized, but they are freely available to him/her when released.

Role of the Court

In the majority of states, the release of an NGRI is decided by the committing court. In some states patients can petition the court for release on a periodic (4–6 month) basis. The court takes evidence from the treating facility and, if convinced that the potential acquittee is no longer dangerous, they release the patient. The discharge can be an outright discharge or a conditional release. New York, California, Maryland, and other states have conditional release programs. McGreevy, Steadman, Dvoskin, and Dollard (1991) described New York's system and compared outcome studies with similar programs in other states. The state mental health agency administers the program, which is subject to judicial review and approval. The court determines the level of security and/or hospitalization the acquittee needs. Some states provide for an order of conditions (OC), which defines the conditions to be followed by the patient after release. The conditions last for up to 5 years and can be extended. There are provisions for recommitment through a court hearing. Funding is not provided for outpatient treatment (most states do not fund this); thus, patients must utilize existing services in the community. Studies of one cohort of offenders with mental disorders showed a recidivism (arrest) rate of 22%. Most of the arrests were for minor offenses; 28% of those rearrested were involuntarily hospitalized and 22% were voluntarily hospitalized. Applications for recommitment were filed for 12%. The effectiveness of these programs was due to the fact that a centralized authority was able to coordinate an effective network of mental health services that used a uniform standard of treatment and supervision.

Security Review Boards: Oregon

The security review board model is considered the release mechanism of choice because of the control the board has over the NGRI acquittee as both an inpatient and outpatient. Released acquittees are monitored closely through an extensive conditional release program. The committing judge has no further jurisdiction after the insanity verdict.

Since 1978, Oregon's Psychiatric Security Review Board (PSRB) has had sole authority for managing acquittees. The board consists of a psychiatrist, a psychologist, a lawyer, a lay person, and a person with experience in probation. This centralized board has established uniformity in the supervision and treatment of acquittees and retains the fiscal responsibility for the treatment that they mandate. The board closely monitors patients and can revoke their release when they feel it is necessary. Follow-up data show that this model is effective and the recidivism (rearrest) rate for those under control of the PSRB is much lower than for non-mentally ill felons. Between 1978 and 1980, about 10% of those under the system were rearrested. Forty percent of the patients had their releases revoked by the board. To paraphrase Bloom and Williams (1992), a more recent study of the Oregon system showed that Oregon's trial court judges assigned 67% of the 1,156 insanity acquittees to the Board's jurisdiction after felony offenses, whereas 23% were assigned after having committed misdemeanor offenses. From 1987 to 1989 the number of individuals assigned to the Board's jurisdiction fell, the percentage of misdemeanors in the entry cohorts also fell to an average of 18%. The types of crimes leading to PSRB jurisdiction cut across the entire spectrum of offenses. The leading felony offenses were assault (13%) and burglary (12%). Murder and manslaughter accounted for 6% of the sample. The leading misdemeanor was harassment.

Several important features make this review board model attractive compared with a traditional management system dependent upon trial court judges as the determiners of hospitalization and release of insanity acquittees. These advantages include the centralization of authority in a five-member, multidisciplinary panel, providing the opportunity for a more consistent program in which the Board has specialized knowledge of the patient population and of the resources available to care for patients. Three aspects of the Oregon system are important: First, the insanity acquittee is given a fixed sentence. In other jurisdictions, it is possible for insanity acquittees to be confined in security hospitals for an indeterminate time, as long as they remain mentally ill and are determined to be dangerous. Second, insanity acquittees are eligible for conditional release. The development of programs for the conditional release of insanity acquittees is the single most important advance in this area in the last decade. Third, mental health professionals have authority in the overall system.

Outcome Studies

Outcome studies are necessary to improve the quality of treatment. Further, favorable statistics help to prevent unfavorable public opinion. When a released NGRI commits a violent crime, though this rarely occurs, the public becomes strongly polarized against the forensic mental health system. Further, the NIMH "Final Report" (1987) reported a strong body of data that cast doubt on the ability of forensic clinicians and the court to make long-term predictions about the dangerousness of individual patients upon release. Three kinds of data were considered essential in making release decisions: prior criminal acts, response to treatment, and conditions of release (the more serious the crime, the greater the need for close supervision). Heilbrun et al. (1988) wrote that accurate treatability assessment could also be valuable to legal decisionmakers. So far, however, efforts by clinicians to develop reliable instruments lacked interclinician reliability and suffered from disagreement over definitions and goals.

In a study of 127 NGRIs in Maryland, Silver, Cohen, and Spodak (1989) showed that it was possible to combine actuarial, criminological, and clinical data to determine the likelihood of success after release. Success was inversely related to recidivism, or rearrest rates. Several variables have been especially useful in predicting success. These variables were adjustment in the hospital (need for seclusion, obeying rules, etc.), clinical assessment of patient improvement, the Global Assessment Scale score at release, and level of functioning prior to the offense. These relate to the patient's progress in the hospital. Evaluation of functioning prior to commitment considers the severity of the offense, substance addiction, work history, and several demographic variables, but these variables have not yet been correlated with recidivism. MacCulloch and Bailey (1991) discussed the importance of evaluating other factors that affect the quality of life of the patients. They thought that quality-of-life factors should be evaluated across the whole spectrum of patient treatment, from admission to postdischarge.

Impact of Prison Life

As a final note, we must address an issue full of opinion and prejudicial positions. Traditionally, the punishment imposed by the prison system is thought to *cause* mental illness in many inmates. It is not only that the mentally ill have been criminalized; the harsh circumstances of prison life also break the psychological defenses of the inmate. Consider, then, how these notions must be rethought in light of the following proactive study.

Zamble and Porporino (1988) conducted a sophisticated, proactive study that successfully measured the psychological impact of imprisonment on 133 short-term (5 years), medium-term (5 to 10 years), and long-term (10 years to life) inmates in the Federal Prison System in Ontario, Canada. There were nearly equal cohorts in each sentence group. The factors studied were personal characteristics, demographic variables, and modes of coping first in the prison system and then in society through a 16-month follow-up.

The results in general showed that before conviction most inmates abused alcohol and substances, lived an unstructured lifestyle, and had poor social skills. They bonded weakly to family and friends and tended to be unable to "work through" problems. The regimentation of the prison system was a completely reversed world for them. Nevertheless, they adapted to it. Although the system forced them to change, however, it did not have a lasting psychological impact.

Contrary to the popular notion, the inmates did not suffer general psychological deterioration as a consequence of the prison experience; the assumed harmful effects of the harsh prison milieu could not be found. On the other hand, whereas it was true that maladaptive coping mechanisms were apparent at various points during incarceration, these did not persist when external circumstances changed. Thus, the researchers concluded that prisons do not produce permanent harm to the psychological well-being of inmates. This surprising conclusion was followed by a valuable insight:

Prisons not only do not promote positive change, but more destructively, they require the inmate to "store" certain qualities or skills until release. They place inmates in a psychological "deep freeze." Once incarcerated, their behavioral coping skills remain in their original pattern so that the prisoner is frozen developmentally. The long-term impact is that imprisonment can trap the inmate in a cycle of regular recidivism.

The bottom line demonstrated that prison forces immediate change in inmates, but it has no significant, long-term psychological impact except that it arrests psychological development. It thus perpetuates immature modes of coping with life, which, paradoxically, can result in later increased, rather than decreased, criminal activity. It is this point that criminologists need to address as they rethink the value of punishment as the principal consequence of the criminal justice process and the role prisons play.

GLOSSARY OF TERMS

In reviewing the literature, it is apparent that authorities use both clinical and legal language to describe the assessment and treatment process. Maier (1986c) pointed out the need to clarify and define words that relate to types of interpersonal conflict. Words such as *dangerous, abusive, destructive, disruptive, violent, aggressive, distractive, unsafe, suicidal,* and *assaultive* are often used interchangeably when describing aggressive acts. Similarly, terms that describe assessment and treatment get confused. To clarify these terms we offer the following definitions:

Aggression: divided into two types, physical and verbal. **Physical aggression** refers to any behavior that has or could have resulted in an injury to a person or destruction of property. **Verbal aggression** refers to a spoken threat or physical gesture that evokes fear, whether intended or not, such as intrusion of a person into the personal space or body of another. The common targets of aggression are persons and property. Persons are aggressive. Societies are violent.

Assault: aggressive behavior in a legal context.

Assessment: the process of determining the management tools required to continue to keep a patient who has been out of control, in control. It leads to a management plan.

Classification: a term used in correctional settings to determine the security needs of an inmate. Inmates are classified as maximum, medium, or minimum.

Control: the physical process, augmented by verbal, physical, and chemical restraint, of physically subduing and restraining an aggressive offender with a mental disorder who has lost "control" of him/herself.

Diagnosis: a medical/psychiatric procedure that results in a DSM-IV determination of physical or mental disease. Diagnosis leads to treatment.

Evaluation: a court-ordered, goal-oriented evaluation of an accused for the purpose of determining competence to stand trial or criminal responsibility. An evaluation is conducted by an expert mental health professional, usually a psychiatrist or psychologist. Evaluations are conducted in a jail or hospital, or in the community. A report is generated that includes DSM-IV diagnosis and concludes with an expert opinion about the issue, for example, is or is not competent, and the like.

Management: the plan generated to help a patient continue to maintain self-control. Most professionals are not trained in management techniques.

Treatment: standard medical and psychiatric interventions to prevent, cure, and rehabilitate disease processes. Treatment is based on the development of a therapeutic alliance. When we treat under a court order, we recognize that a therapeutic alliance may not exist. In forensics, treatment does not end with remission of symptoms.

Violence: sociological term that refers to aggressive behavior in a social context.

NOTE

1. Offenders with mental disorders are defined as those found incompetent to stand trial (IST) and ordered by the court to receive treatment; individuals found not guilty by reason of insanity (NGRI), and jail or prison inmates with psychiatric disorders. Forensic patients are offenders with mental disorders (Gratzer, Gruenberg, Cavanaugh, & Brakel, 1995). See Glossary of Terms at the end of this chapter.

REFERENCES

Abraham, K. (1989). The effect of co-occurring disorders on criminal careers. *International Journal of Law and Psychiatry, 12,* 133–134.

Abram, K., & Teplin, D. (1991, June 16). *Science News,* p. 372.

American Psychiatric Association. (1980). *Diagnostic and statistical manual of mental disorders* (3rd ed.). Washington, DC: Author.

American Psychiatric Association. (1994a). *Diagnostic and statistical manual of mental disorders* (4th ed.). Washington, DC: Author.

American Psychiatric Association. (1994b). Practice guideline for the treatment of patients with bipolar disorder. *American Journal of Psychiatry, 151* (Suppl.), 1–36.

American Psychiatric Association. (1997). Practice guideline for the treatment of patients with schizophrenia. *American Journal of Psychiatry, 154* (Suppl.), 1–63.

American Psychiatric Association Task Force. (1992). *Clinician safety* [Report no. 33]. [Unpublished report of the American Psychiatric Association Task Force on Clinician Safety]

Appelbaum, P. S. (1988). The right to refuse treatment with antipsychotic medications: Reprospect and prospect. *American Journal of Psychiatry, 145,* 413–419.

Black, T. (1984). Treatment in maximum security settings. In M. Craft & A. Craft (Eds.), *Mentally abnormal offenders.* London: Baillere Tindal.

Bloom, J. D., & Williams, M. H. (1992). Oregon's experience with insanity acquittees. *Psychiatric Annals, 22,* 579–583.

Brooks, A. (1974). *Law, psychiatry and the mental health system.* Boston: Little Brown.

Calabrese, J. R., Woyshville, M. J., Kimmel S. E., & Rapport, D. (1993). Mixed states and rapid cycling and their treatment with divalproex sodium. *Psychiatric Annals, 23,* 70–78.

Callahan, L. A., Steadman, H. J., McGreevy, M. A., & Robins, P. C. (1991). The volume and characteristics of insanity defense pleas: An eight-state study. *Bulletin of the American Academy of Psychiatry and the Law, 19,* 331–338.

Carney, F. L. (1973). Three important factors in psychotherapy with criminal patients. *American Journal of Psychiatry, 27,* 220–231.

Chrzanowski, C. M. (1980). Problem patients or troublemakers? Dynamic and therapeutic considerations. *American Journal of Psychotherapy, 34,* 17–29.

Cleary, M. D. (1973). The writ writer. *American Journal of Psychiatry, 130,* 319–322.

Crowner, M. L., Stepcic, F., Peric, G., & Czobar, P. (1994). Typology of patient–patient assaults detected by videocameras. *American Journal of Psychiatry, 151,* 1669–1672.

Deurloo, B. (1992, January). *The Psychiatric Times* [Letter], p. 43.

Dubin, W. R. (1989). The role of fantasies, countertransference, and psychological defenses in patient violence. *Hospital and Community Psychiatry, 40,* 1280–1283.

Eichelman, B. S., & Hartwig, A. C. (Eds.). (1995). *Patient violence and the clinician* (Clinical Practice #30). Washington, DC: American Psychiatric Press.

Eisler, R. (1988). *The chalice and the blade.* San Francisco: HarperCollins.

Evans, B., Souma, A., & Maier, G. J. (1989). A vocational assessment and training program for individuals in an inpatient forensic mental health center. *Psychosocial Rehabilitation Journal, 13,* 61–69.

Fein, R. A. (1984). How the insanity acquittal retards treatment. *Law and Human Behavior, 8,* 283–292.

Field, G. (1986, December). The psychological deficits of chronic criminality. *Federal Probation,* pp. 117–123.

Fisher, W. A. (1994). The use of seclusion and restraints: A review of the literature. *American Journal of Psychiatry, 151,* 1584–1591.

Flannery, R. B., Fulton, P., Tausch, J., & DeLoffi, A. Y. (1991). A program to help staff cope with psychological sequelae of assaults by patients. *Hospital and Community Psychiatry, 42,* 935–938.

Gilman, A. D. (1977, March). Jailhouse lawyers. *Corrections Magazine,* pp. 63–70.

Gratzer, T. G., Gruenberg, L. F., Cavanaugh, J. L., & Brakel, S. J. (1995). Treatment of mentally disordered offenders. In R. Michaels (Ed.), *Psychiatry* (Vol. 3, 2nd ed.). Philadelphia: Lippincott–Raven

Gutheil, T. G. (1984). Clinical issues in forensic psychiatry. In R. Michaels (Ed.), *Psychiatry* (Vol. 3, pp. 1–13). Philadelphia: Lippincott–Raven.

Halleck, S. L. (1982). The concept of responsibility in psychotherapy. *American Journal of Psychotherapy, 36,* 292–302.

Halleck, S. L. (1986). *The mentally disordered offender.* Rockville, MD: National Institute of Mental Health.

Halleck, S. L. (1988). Which patients are responsible for their illnesses? *American Journal of Psychotherapy, 42,* 338–352.

Halpern, A. L. (1992). Misuse of post-acquittal hospitalization for punitive purposes. *Psychiatric Annals, 22,* 561–565.

Hare, R. D. (1991). *Hare Psychopathy Checklist—Revised manual.* North Tonawanda, NY: Multi-Health Systems.

Hare, R. D., McPherson, L. M., & Forth, A. R. (1988). Male psychopaths and their criminal careers. *Journal of Consulting and Clinical Psychology, 56,* 710–714.

Harry, B., Maier, G. J., & Miller, R. D. (1989). A survey of forensic psychiatrists who work in institutions. *Bulletin of the American Academy of Psychiatry and the Law, 18,* 99–106.

Heilbrun, K., Bennett, W. S., Evans, J. H., Offutt, R. A., Reiff, H. J., & White, A. J. (1988). Assessing treatability in mentally disordered offenders: A conceptual and methodological note. *Behavioral Sciences and the Law, 6,* 479–486.

Henderson, M. (1989). Behavioral approaches to violent crime. *Violence.* West Sussex, England: Wiley.

Hoge, S. K., & Gutheil, T. G. (1987). The prosecution of psychiatric patients for assaults on staff: A preliminary empirical study. *Hospital and Community Psychiatry, 38,* 44–49.

Jacobsen, F. M. (1993). Low-dose valproate: A new treatment for cyclothymia, mild rapid cycling disorders, and premenstrual syndrome. *Journal of Clinical Psychiatry, 54,* 229–234.

Jefferson, J. W., Greist, J. H., Ackerman, D. L., & Carroll, J. A. (1993). *Lithium encyclopedia for clinical practice* (3rd ed.). Washington, DC: American Psychiatric Press.

Kerr, C. A., & Roth, J. A. (1986). Populations, practices, and problems in forensic psychiatric facilities. *Annals of the American Academy of Political and Social Sciences, 484,* 127–143.

Kerr, C. A., & Roth, J. A. (1987). *Survey of facilities and programs for mentally disordered offenders.* Rockville, MD: National Institute of Mental Health.

Kierulff, S. (1988). Sheep in the midst of wolves: Personal-responsibility therapy with criminal personalities. *Professional Psychology: Research and Practice, 4,* 436–440.

Kimmel, W. A. (1987). *Services for the mentally ill inmate: An exploratory inquiry.* Rockville, MD: National Institute of Mental Health.

Liberman, R. P. (1988). *Psychiatric rehabilitation of chronic mental patients.* Washington, DC: American Psychiatric Press.

Lieberman, J. A. (1996). Pharmacotherapy for patients with first-episode, acute, and refractory schizophrenia. *Psychiatric Annals, 26,* 515–518.

Lukoff, D., Liberman, R. P., & Neuchterlein, K. H. (1986). Symptom monitoring in the rehabilitation of schizophrenic patients. *Schizophrenia Bulletin, 12,* 578–602.

MacCulloch, M., & Bailey, J. (1991). Issues in the provision and evaluation of forensic services. *Journal of Forensic Psychiatry, 2,* 247–265.

Maier, G. J. (1976). Therapy in prisons. In J. R. Lion & D. J. Madden (Eds.), *Rage, hate, assault and other forms of violence.* New York: Spectrum.

Maier, G. J. (1986a). Relationship security: The dynamics of keepers and kept. *Journal of Forensic Sciences, 31,* 603–608.

Maier, G. J. (1986b). *Mendota Mental Health Institute policy manual.* Madison, WI: Author.

Maier, G. J. (1988c, November). Terminology of violence [Letter]. *Psychiatric News,* p. 2.

Maier, G. J. (1989). The successful prosecution of a not guilty by reason of insanity patient for the willful assault of a hospital staff. *Psychiatric Residents' Newsletter, 9,* 1–2.

Maier, G. J. (1990). Psychopathic disorders: Beyond countertransference. *Current Opinion in Psychiatry, 3,* 766–769.

Maier, G. J. (1991). Afterword. In R. W. Jaeger & M. W. Balousek (Eds.), *Massacre in Milwaukee.* Oregon, WI: Waubesa Press.

Maier, G. J. (1992a). Managing conflict in institutional settings. *Directions in Psychiatry, 20,* 1–8.

Maier, G. J. (1992b). The impact of Clozapine on 25 forensic patients. *Bulletin of the American Academy of Psychiatry and the Law, 20,* 297–307.

Maier, G. J. (1993). Management approaches for the repetitively aggressive patient. In W. H. Sledge & A. Tasman (Eds.), *Clinical challenges in psychiatry* (pp. 181–213). Washington, DC: American Psychiatric Press.

Maier, G. J. (1996). Training security staff in aggression management. In J. R. Lion, W. R. Dubin, & D. E. Futrell (Eds.), *Creating a secure workplace: Effective policies and practices in health care.* Chicago: American Hospital Publishing.

Maier, G. J., Bernstein, M., & Musholt, E. A. (1989). Personal coping mechanisms for clinicians who work in security settings: Toward transformation. *Journal of Prison and Jail Health, 8,* 29–39.

Maier, G. J., & Miller, R. D. (1987). Models of mental health service delivery to correctional institutions. *Journal of Forensic Science, 32,* 225–232.

Maier, G. J., & Miller, R. D. (1993). Toward the therapeutic use of obscene language: A legal and clinical review. *Bulletin of the American Academy of Psychiatry and the Law, 21,* 227–243.

Maier, G. J., Morrow, B., & Miller, R. K. (1989). Security safeguards in community rehabilitation of forensic patients. *Hospital and Community Psychiatry, 40,* 529–531.

Maier, G. J., Stava, L., Morrow, B., Van Rybroek, G., & Bauman, K. (1987). A model for understanding and managing cycles of aggression among psychiatric inpatients. *Hospital and Community Psychiatry, 38,* 520–524.

Maier, G. J., & Van Rybroek, G. J. (1995). Managing countertransference reactions to aggressive patients. In B. S. Eichelman & A. Hartwig (Eds.), *Patient violence and the clinician* (pp. 73–104). Washington, DC: American Psychiatric Press.

Maier, G. J., Van Rybroek, G. J., & Mays, D. V. (1994). Staff injuries and ambulatory restraints. *Journal of Psychosocial Nursing, 32,* 23–29.

Maier, G. J., Van Rybroek, G. J., Doren, D., Musholt, E. A., & Miller, R. D. (1988). A comprehensive model for understanding and managing aggressive inpatients. *American Journal of Continuing Education in Nursing,* pp. 11–18.

Mannuzza, S., Klein, R., & Giampino, T. (1989). Hyperactive boys almost grown up. *Archives of General Psychiatry, 16,* 1073–1079.

Markovitz, P. J., Calabrese, M. D., Schulz, S. C., & Meltzer, H. Y. (1991). Fluoxetine in the treatment of borderline and schizotypal personality disorders. *American Journal of Psychiatry, 148,* 1064–1067.

McGreevy, M. A., Steadman, H. J., Dvoskin, J. A., & Dollard, D. (1991). New York State's system of managing insanity acquittees in the community. *Hospital and Community Psychiatry, 42,* 512–517.

Mendota Mental Health Institute. (1993). *Policy manual.* Madison, WI: Author.

Miller, R. D., Bernstein, M. R., Van Rybroek, G. J., & Maier, G. J. (1989). The impact of the right to refuse treatment in a forensic patient population: Six-month review. *Bulletin of the American Adacemy of Psychiatry and the Law, 17,* 107–119.

Miller, R. D., & Maier, G. J. (1987). Factors affecting the decision to prosecute mental patients for criminal behavior. *Hospital and Community Psychiatry, 38,* 50–55.

Miller, R. D., Maier, G. J., Blancke, F. W., & Doren, D. M. (1986). Litigiousness as a resistance to therapy. *Journal of Law and Psychiatry, 61,* 109–123.

Miller, R. D., Maier, G. J., & Kaye, M. S. (1985). Miranda comes to the hospital: The right to remain silent in civil commitment. *American Journal of Psychiatry, 142,* 1074–1077.

Miller, R. D., Maier, G. J., & Kaye, M. S. (1986). The right to remain silent during psychiatric evaluation in civil and criminal cases: A national survey and an analysis. *International Journal of Law and Psychiatry, 9,* 77–94.

Miller, R. D., Maier, G. J., & Kaye, M. D. (1988). Orienting the staff to a new maximum security forensic facility. *Hospital and Community Psychiatry, 39,* 780–781.

Miller, R. K., Maier, G. J., Van Rybroek, G. J., & Weidemann, J. (1989). Treating patients "doing time": A forensic perspective. *Hospital and Community Psychiatry, 40,* 960–962.

Miller, R. D., Morrow, B., Kaye, M. S., & Maier, G. J. (1987). Patient access to medical records in a forensic center: A Review of the literature and a controlled study. *Hospital and Community Psychiatry, 38,* 1081–1085.

Millon, T. (1981). *Disorders of personality.* New York: Wiley.

Monahan, J., & Steadman, H. (1983). *Mentally disordered offenders.* New York: Plenum Press.

Monroe, C. M., Van Rybroek, G. J., & Maier, G. J. (1988). Decompressing aggressive inpatients: Breaking the aggression cycle to enhance positive outcome. *Behavioral Sciences and the Law, 6,* 543–557.

Morowitz, H. J. (1981, June). Jurisgenic disease. *Hospital Practice, 16,* 170–171.

National Commission on Correctional Health Care. (1996). *Standards for health services in jails.* Chicago: Author.

National Commission on Correctional Health Care. (1997). *Standards for health services in prisons.* Chicago: Author.

National Institute of Mental Health. (1988, January–February). *Final report, National Institute of Mental Health ad hoc forensic advisory panel,* p. 13.

Norko, M. A., Zonana, H. V., & Phillips, R. T. (1991). Prosecuting assaultive psychiatric inpatients. *Hospital and Community Psychiatry, 42,* 193–194.

Paul, G. L., & Lentz, R. J. (1977). *Psychosocial treatment of chronic mental patients: Milieu versus social-learning programs.* Cambridge, MA: Harvard University Press.

Pendleton, L. (1980). Treatment of persons found incompetent to stand trial. *American Journal of Psychiatry, 137,* 1098–1100.

Poster, E. C., & Ryan, J. (1994). A multiregional study of nurses' beliefs and attitudes about work safety and patient assult. *Hospital and Community Psychiatry, 45,* 1104–1108.

Quinsey, V. L., & Maquire, A. (1983). Offenders remanded for a psychiatric examination: Perceived treatability and disposition. *International Journal of Law and Psychiatry, 6,* 193–205.

Rappaport, R.G. (1971). Group psychotherapy in prison. *International Journal of Group Psychotherapy, 21,* 265–274.

Reid, W. H. (1985). The antisocial personality: A review. *Hospital and Community Psychiatry, 36,* 831–837.

Rice, M., & Harris, G. (1988). An empirical approach to the classification and treatment of maximum security psychiatric patients. *Behavioral Sciences and the Law, 6,* 497–513.

Rogers v. Okin, 478 F. Supp. 1342 (D. Mass. 1979).

Rogers, R. (1988). Treatability and treatment outcome. *Behavioral Sciences and the Law, 6,* 441–442.

Rogers, R., Gillis, J. R., Dickens, S. E., & Webster, C. D. (1988). Treatment recommendations for mentally disordered offenders: More than roulette? *Behavioral Science and the Law, 6,* 487–495.

Roth, L. H. (1980). Correctional psychiatry. In W. Curran, C. Peety, & A. L. McGarry (Eds.), *Modern legal medicine, psychiatry, and forensic science* (pp. 677–719). Philadelphia: Davis.

Roth, L. H. (1987). Treating violent persons in prisons, jails, and security hospitals. In L. H. Roth (Ed.), *Clinical treatment of the violent person* (pp. 207–234). New York: Guilford Press.

Silver, S. B., Cohen, M. I., & Spodak, M. K. (1989). Follow-up after release of insanity acquttees, mentally disordered offenders, and convicted felons. *Bulletin of the American Academy of Psychiatry and the Law, 17,* 387–400.

Silver, S. B., & Gelpi, J. A. (1987). The forensic hospital. In *Modern hospital psychiatry.* New York: Norton.

State *ex rel.* Jones v. Gerhardstein et al., 141 Wis.2d 710, 416 N.W.2d 883 (1987).

Steadman, H. J. (1990). *Jail diversion for the mentally ill: Breaking through the barriers.* Grant from National Institute of Corrections, U.S. Department of Justice, Washington, D.C.

Stein, E., & Brown, J. D. (1991). Group therapy in a forensic setting. *Canadian Journal of Psychiatry, 36,* 718–722.

Strasburger, L. H. (1986). The treatment of antisocial syndromes: The therapist's feelings. In W. H. Reid et al. (Eds.), *Unmasking the psychopath* (pp. 191–207). New York: Norton.

Tardiff, K. (1996). *Concise guide to assessment and management of violent patients* (2nd ed.). Washington, DC: American Psychiatric Press.

Tollefson, G. D., Beasley, C. M., Jr., Tran, P. V., Street, J. S., Krueger, J. A., Tamura, R. N., Graffeo, K. A., & Thieme, M. E. (1997). Olanzapine versus haloperidol in the treatment of schizophrenia and schizoaffective and schizophreniform disoders: Results of an international collaborative trial. *American Journal of Psychiatry, 154,* 457–465.

Van Rybroek, G. J., Kuhlman, T. L., Maier, G. J., & Kaye, M. S. (1987). Preventive aggression devices (PADS): Ambulatory restraints as an alternative to seclusion. *Journal of Clinical Psychiatry, 48,* 401–405.

Van Rybroek, G. J., Maier, G. J., McCormick, D. J., & Pollock, D. E. (1988).

Today–tomorrow behavioral programming: Realistic reinforcement for repetitively aggressive inpatients. *American Journal of Continuing Education in Nursing,* pp. 1–11.

Van Rybroek, G. J., Miller, R. D., & Maier, G. J. (1988). Keeping up with the Jones decision: A committed patient's right to refuse medication. *Wisconsin Bar Bulletin, 61,* 11–13, 61–63.

Way, B. B., Dvoskin, J. A., & Steadman, H. J. (1991). Forensic psychiatric inpatients served in the United States: Regional and system differences. *Bulletin of the American Academy of Psychiatry and the Law, 19,* 405–412.

Way, M. A., Dvoskin, J. A., Steadman, H. J., Huguley, M. A., & Banks, S. (1990). Staffing of forensic inpatient services in the United States. *Hospital and Community Psychiatry, 41,* 172–174.

Wettstein, R. M., & Mulvey, E. P. (1988). Disposition of insanity acquittees in Illinois. *Bulletin of the American Academy of Psychiatry and the Law, 16,* 11–24.

Wexler, D. B. (1991). Health care compliance principles and the insanity acquittee conditional release process. *Criminal Law Bulletin, 27,* 18–41.

Widiger, T. A. (1992). Antisocial personality disorder. *Hospital and Community Psychiatry, 43,* 6–8.

Wishnie, H. (1977). *The impulsive personality.* New York: Plenum Press.

Wortman, C. & Silver, R. (1989). The myths of coping with loss. *Journal of Consulting and Clinical Psychology, 57,* 349–357.

Yochelson, S., & Samenow, S. (1976). *The criminal personality* (Vols. 1–2). Northvale, NJ: Jason Aronson.

Zamble, E., & Porporino, F. J. (1988). *Coping, behavior, and adaptation in prison inmates.* New York: Springer-Verlag.

4

COMMUNITY-BASED FORENSIC TREATMENT

Kirk Heilbrun
Patricia A. Griffin

INTRODUCTION

Historically, there has been relatively little attention paid to the community-based treatment of offenders with mental disorders. During recent years, however, there has been a trend toward treating such individuals in the community as well as in high-security, geographically remote institutions, roughly paralleling the deinstitutionalization movement for civilly committed patients over the past three decades. As community-based forensic treatment (CBFT) programs increase in number, it is important to determine what is known about them and those they treat, what broader principles apply to this specialized form of treatment, how we might improve the research that adds to this knowledge, and what implications may be drawn from the current literature. These areas will be addressed in this chapter, which expands our earlier discussion (Heilbrun & Griffin, 1993).

Issues of Definition

The phrase *mentally disordered offender* has been used to describe four categories of individual: (1) incompetent to stand trial (IST), (2) not guilty by reason of insanity (NGRI), (3) mentally disordered sex offender, and (4) mentally ill (jail or prison) inmate (Steadman, Monahan, Hartstone, Davis, & Robbins, 1982). Other definitions have included these categories, both preadjudication (e.g., "to be evaluated for trial competency") and postadjudication, and have also included other populations in the criminal justice/mental health systems (e.g., "defective delinquent") (Kerr & Roth, 1986). As different chapters in this book will address the treatment of sexual offenders (Barbaree & Marshall, Chapter 6, this volume) and offenders with mental disorders in jails and prisons (Metzner, Cohen, Grossman, & Wettstein, Chapter 5, this volume), our focus will be on the community treatment of individuals who are NGRI or on parole or probation. Initially, we had planned to include the legal category of IST individuals as well. However, because of the absence of programmatic information or empirical data on the treatment of such individuals in nonjail community settings, we did not include them in this chapter. We will consider only adults, as the treatment of juvenile offenders is addressed in another chapter (Gordon, Jurkovic, & Arbuthnot, Chapter 8, this volume).

The next issue involves the definition of *community-based*. Forensic services have traditionally been delivered in maximum-security hospitals, often geographically remote from the patient's community (Melton, Weithorn, & Slobogin, 1985). A less restrictive alternative involves the establishment of forensic centers within regional civil hospitals (see, e.g., Petrila, 1982). The least restrictive, and most recent, model involves the delivery of forensic services within the community. Facilities delivering such services might include jails, halfway houses, outpatient clinics, crisis stabilization units, and inpatient psychiatric facilities. This chapter will focus on the community-based service delivery model. It will not include jails, however, as they are discussed in another chapter in this book.

Treatment services will not exclude any of the forms of mental health treatment commonly delivered to mental health patients. Psychotropic medication, case management, psychotherapy, vocational training, and other forms of treatment will all be included. We will also consider treatments geared toward specific deficits: anger management, for example, or behavioral or psychosocial interventions.

Sources of Information

Several sources of information have been used in preparing this chapter. The first is the existing literature on the CBFT of our population groups (NGRIs and offenders with mental disorders on parole or probation). We have characterized each source as either *descriptive* or *evaluative*. In a descriptive report, an author provided an account (not necessarily quantitative) of the "who, what, when, where, or why" of a treatment program.

An evaluative account used control groups and/or inferential statistics to provide some measure of intervention effectiveness. Published articles were identified through the following computerized databases: PSYCHINFO, PSYCHALERT, Criminal Justice Periodical Index, Sociological Abstracts, MEDLINE, and EMBASE.

Second, we contacted researchers and clinicians in the field, whom we asked to identify relevant articles and presentations. A number of individuals involved in as clinicians, researchers, or administrators reviewed a draft of this chapter and provided us with useful feedback.

Finally, we incorporated our own perspectives. Our collective experience with CBFT includes clinical practice, hospital and state government department-level administration, research, and consultation in a number of states. This experience proved useful as we tried to transform an uneven but emerging literature into a coherent chapter that would be useful to clinicians, administrators, policy makers, and researchers.

COMMUNITY-BASED PROGRAMS FOR NGRI PATIENTS

There has been a good deal written about the treatment of NGRI patients in nonjail community settings. The descriptive and evaluative literature on community treatment of NGRI patients has come primarily from Illinois, Oregon, and Maryland, but we have also included material from California, Connecticut, Florida, New York, and Oklahoma. These studies are summarized in Table 4.1.

Illinois

Descriptive data from Illinois have been provided on treatment done through the Isaac Ray Center in Chicago (Rogers & Cavanaugh, 1981). Two primary groups of potentially violent patients were treated: those on probation for violent crimes and those acquitted by reason of insanity and subsequently released from institutions. The Center offered a three-phase intervention model that included assessment, treatment, and follow-up. In its first 2 years of operation, the Isaac Ray Center accepted 54 patients and refused 27. All patients who were accepted had committed crimes of violence, with 61% charged with murder or attempted murder. A total of 87% had a primary diagnosis of schizophrenia or affective disorder. The Center's treatment was eclectic and problem oriented, with both biological and psychosocial interventions employed. Consistent with the focus of other forensic treatment programs, the goals for treatment generally included (1) a reduction of potential for future violent behavior, (2) remission of psychopathology, and (3) development of healthy and responsible inter-

TABLE 4.1. Studies of Not Guilty by Reason of Insanity Patients

Study	Sample	Program	Descriptive studies Goals/findings
Rogers & Cavanaugh (1981)	NGRI acquittees Violent crime probationers (N = 54)	Isaac Ray Center	1. Reduce future violence 2. Remit psychopathology 3. Develop healthy, responsible interpersonal relations
Cavanaugh & Wasyliw (1985)	NGRI acquittees (N = 44)	Isaac Ray Center	1. 25% of patients rehospitalized over a 2-year period 2. 5% of patients rearrested over a 2-year period
Bloom & Bloom (1981)	NGRI acquittees	PSRB	1. Hospitalize and conditionally release 2. Revoke conditional release
Rogers & Bloom (1982)	NGRI acquittees (N = 440)	PSRB	Of persons committed to PSRB in first 3 years of operation: 1. 91% were male 2. Mean age was 30.8 years 3. 67% were psychotic 4. 47% were acquitted of crimes of serious violence
Rogers, Bloom, & Manson (1984)	NGRI acquittees (N = 295)	PSRB/DTP	1. 13% charged with new crimes while on conditional release from 1978–1982 2. Rehospitalization while on conditional release at DTP: 78% (1980), 62% (1981), 31% (1982), and 20% (1983)
Bloom, Williams, et al. (1986)	NGRI acquittees	PSRB/DTP	1. Teach social and living skills 2. Develop vocational interests 3. Maintain psychological health
Goldmeier et al. (1977, 1980)	NGRI acquittees	Residential treatment program (Hamilton House)	1. Goals included medication management, vocational training, and promoting involvement with outpatient treatment 2. Rearrest rate over 22-month period was 15% 3. Rehospitalization rate over same period was 40.5% 4. Cost per patient during 1977–1978 was $27.38
Silver (1983)	NGRI acquittees	Residential treatment program	1. Track rearrest on conditional release (24%) 2. Track rehospitalized on conditional release (11%)

continued

171

TABLE 4.1. (cont.)

Evaluative studies

Study	N	Comparison group?	Measures	Variables	Findings
Norwood et al. (1992)	30	Yes		1. Rearrest 2. Recommitment 3. Contact with CMHCs	During average follow-up period of 960.5 days, outcome measures were obtained for three groups; released at first court review, recommended for release by hospital, and AWOL. Outcomes: 1. Rearrest (33% vs. 19% vs. 80%) 2. Rehospitalization (33% vs. 38% vs. 20%) 3. CMHC contact (44% vs. 81% vs. 20%)
McGreevy et al. (1991)	331	Yes		1. Rearrest 2. Recommitment	During average follow-up period of 3.8 years in the community: 1. 22% of cohort were rearrested (64% misdemeanors, 92% Class D felonies or less) 2. 12% had applications for recommitment filed, and 5% were rehospitalized
Rogers et al. (1983)	44	No	SADS SADS-C SCL-90	1. Criminal recidivism 2. Rehospitalization 3. Self-reported versus other-observed psychopathology	1. One patient rearrested for misdemeanor 2. 23% rehospitalized 3. Moderate correlations between self-reported and other-observed symptoms
Rogers & Wettstein (1984)	39	Yes	SADS-C Shipley—Hartford	Rehospitalization	1. 18% rehospitalized 2. Males, murder acquittees, and lower functioning patients more likely to be rehospitalized
Cavanaugh et al. (1984)	44	No	SADS SCL-90 MMPI	1. Psychiatric symptoms 2. Psychosocial stress and interpersonal needs 3. Rehospitalization 4. Criminal offenses	1. General improvement across measures over five ratings 2. 25% required rehospitalization 3. No occurrence of crime against person
Cavanaugh & Wasyliw (1985)	44	No	SADS SCL-90 MMPI	1. Psychiatric symptoms 2. Rehospitalization 3. Rearrest	1. Overall level of clinical adjustment in the beginning was negatively correlated with rehospitalization probability 2. Failure to take medication also predicted rehospitalization 3. Age, race, sex, marital status, and MMPI results were not predictive
Bloom et al. (1982)	226	Yes		1. Hospital record diagnosis 2. Rehospitalization 3. Criminal offense 4. Subsequent offense	1. Diagnosis did not distinguish released from nonreleased groups 2. Crime seriousness moderately related to length of hospital stay 3. About 1/3 rehospitalized, 5% rearrested from conditional release

Study	N		Instrument	Outcome measures	Findings
Rogers et al. (1984)	295	Yes		1. Rearrests 2. Reconvictions	1. 13% rearrested on conditional release 2. 5% reconvicted on conditional release
Bloom, Rogers, et al. (1986)	123	Yes		Lifetime police contacts	1. Correlation ($r = .28$) between arrests before and after PSRB jurisdiction 2. 42% rearrested after PSRB discharge 3. Police contact: .78/patient/yr before PSRB; .20/patient/yr during PSRB; 54/patient/yr after PSRB
Bloom, Williams, et al. (1986)	161	Yes	DSM-III	Accepted versus not accepted for treatment at Portland DTP	1. No differences in demographics, crime seriousness, or Axis I diagnoses 2. Greater frequency of antisocial personality disorder diagnosis in rejected group 3. Most frequent reasons for revoking conditional release were deteriorating mental condition and noncompliance with supervision
Spodak et al. (1984)	86	No		1. Rearrest 2. Reconviction	1. 56% arrested over 15-year period 2. 30% convicted over 15-year period
Lamb et al. (1988a)	79	No		1. Rearrest 2. Rehospitalization 3. Revocation of conditional release	1. 16% arrested over 5-year period 2. 34% hospitalized in nonforensic hospitals 3. 48% had conditional release revoked at least once
Cohen et al. (1988)	127	Yes	1. Specially developed inventory 2. GAS	1. Revocation of conditional release 2. Rearrest	1. For NGRI subjects, predictors of successful completion of conditional release included marriage, working, less severe offense, better functioning prior to hospital, rated as improved by hospital staff, and GAS score of 50+ at time of release 2. For NGRI subjects, predictors of no rearrest while on conditional release included no heroin addiction, adjusted well to hospital, seen by clinical staff as improved at time of hospital discharge, GAS score of 50+ on release, had functioned well prior to arrest for acquitted crime, and being only or youngest child in family

Note. CMHC, community mental health center; DSM-III, *Diagnostic and Statistical Manual of Mental Disorders*, third edition (American Psychiatric Association, 1980); DTP, Day Treatment Program; GAS, Global Assessment Scale; MMPI, Minnesota Multiphasic Personality Inventory; PSRB, Psychiatric Security Review Board; SADS, Schedule for Affective Disorders and Schizophrenia; SCL-90, Symptom Checklist 90.

personal relationships. Court orders mandating treatment and regular communication with the courts were part of the program. Follow-up was made
over a period of 1 to 2 years, during which clinical services were gradually
reduced. Brief hospitalizations were employed, particularly upon reemer-
gence of symptomatology similar to that seen during previous episodes of
violent behavior. This is a strategy often used in forensic work, with
symptoms previously related to violent behavior viewed as highly relevant
by staff. Eleven of the Isaac Ray patients accepted for treatment were
subsequently rehospitalized.

A more detailed description of the adjustment of patients treated at the
Isaac Ray Center has also been offered (Cavanaugh & Wasyliw, 1985). In
this study, the investigators tracked all of the NGRI outpatients in treatment
during a 2-year period from July 1981 to June 1983. There were 44 such
individuals, who represented an estimated 85% of the NGRI acquittees
discharged to outpatient treatment in Cook County during this period.
Results indicated that 79% of patients were diagnosed as having schizophrenia or affective disorder, with approximately half in remission at the
time of the first testing. Rehospitalization was needed for 25% of the
patients during the study period, a rate generally consistent with that
reported by other investigators (see Table 4.1). Demographic variables (age,
race, sex, and marital status) were not predictive of rehospitalization, nor
were Minnesota Multiphasic Personality Inventory (MMPI) scales. The
Schedule for Affective Disorders and Schizophrenia—Change version
(SADS-C) and Symptom Checklist 90 (SCL-90) reflected gradual clinical
improvement over time, with overall level of adjustment negatively correlated with probability of rehospitalization. Failure to comply with medication requirements was another major factor contributing to rehospitalization. There were only two rearrests during the 19-month outcome period:
one for shoplifting, another for contempt of court for refusing to comply
with a court order for outpatient treatment.

In a related study utilizing these data, Rogers, Harris, and Wasyliw
(1983) concluded that it was important to use multiple sources of data over
specific periods of time in assessing the treatment progress of NGRI
acquittees. This was important because of the variability in other-observed
versus self-reported symptoms, but also because a small subgroup of
patients at high risk for decompensation were identified more readily
through the use of multiple sources of information. In this study, the level
of disturbance and risk for decompensation for the more severely impaired
patients would have been underestimated by relying exclusively on self-
report. The particular importance of third party information in forensic
assessment has been addressed (Heilbrun, 1988; Heilbrun, Rosenfeld,
Warren, & Collins, 1994; Melton, Petrila, Poythress, & Slobogin, 1997).
Rogers and colleagues' (1983) study suggests that third party information

may be important in planning and assessing the effectiveness of forensic *treatment* as well.

In another Illinois study (Rogers & Wettstein, 1984), the investigators tried to distinguish patients who were not rehospitalized from those who were. Gender and criminal charge were important, with males and homicide acquittees more likely to be rehospitalized. General level of functioning and number of symptoms were also found to distinguish these groups. Generally, the greater the degree of initial psychopathology and the lower the general level of functioning, the greater was the likelihood of rehospitalization.

Further information on the adjustment of NGRI acquittees in treatment at the Isaac Ray Center was provided in another study (Cavanaugh, Wasyliw, & Rogers, 1984), in which the investigators followed 44 patients over a 2-year period. Using a repeated-measures design, they obtained self-report (SCL-90) and clinician ratings (SADS, Global Assessment Scale [GAS]) of symptoms, and ratings of psychosocial stress and interpersonal needs, at five intervals. A general trend of improvement was observed across measures over the five ratings. However, 25% of the sample required rehospitalization during the study period. There was no instance of violent recidivism, although the vast majority of the patients had been acquitted of violent offenses.

Oregon

CBFT services in Oregon are delivered to NGRIs under the supervision of the Psychiatric Security Review Board (PSRB). The PSRB was created by the Oregon legislature in 1977 to supervise Oregon defendants found "not responsible due to mental illness," with the general goal of bolstering disposition-phase procedures so that individual rights and community needs both would be protected. The Board was composed of a psychiatrist and a licensed psychologist with experience in the criminal justice system, a representative from probation and parole, a lawyer experienced in criminal practice, and a member from the general public. All members were appointed by the Governor to 4-year terms. The PSRB, whose jurisdiction over an acquittee was as long as the maximum sentence that could have been imposed following a conviction, had the authority to commit to a maximum-security hospital, to grant a conditional release and set the terms of such a release, or to release unconditionally. The PSRB received monthly reports on each patient it supervised. If an individual on conditional release gave evidence of "substantial danger to himself or others because of mental disease or defect," and was "in need of immediate care, custody, or treatment," then conditional release could be revoked. This information could be provided to the PSRB at any time by a treatment facility director, police officer, or any person responsible for the acquittee's supervision. This is explicitly a "public safety" model, with the prevention of violent behavior a primary goal (Bloom & Bloom, 1981; Rogers, Bloom, & Manson, 1986). With the assurance that they will promptly learn about violations of release conditions or deterioration in a person's mental health, the Board did not need to be convinced that a patient was "rehabilitated" before it granted a conditional release. Rather, when the patient was stabilized and a realistic plan for release was formulated, then the patient could be granted a conditional release (Rogers & Bloom, 1985).

The characteristics of the 440 persons committed to the PSRB during its first 3 years have been described (Rogers & Bloom, 1982). Those committed ranged in age from 17 to 74 years, with a mean of 30.8; the vast majority (91%) were male. A wide range of crimes was represented, with 19% of individuals acquitted of misdemeanors and 47% acquitted of serious violent crimes.

The PSRB is not a program, but rather an administrative umbrella under which all insanity acquittees in Oregon are managed and treated (Bloom & Williams, 1994). However, there is a description of one CBFT program that treated clients under PSRB jurisdiction (Bloom, Williams, Rogers, & Barbur, 1986). This program, located in Portland, Oregon, delivered services to PSRB clients through a large community hospital-day treatment program (DTP). Group as well as individual therapy sessions were utilized; long-term goals for patients included teaching relevant social skills and time-management strategies, developing vocational skills and avocational interests, and maintaining psychological health. Clients attended 9-week modules that began with basic skills training in meal preparation, nutrition, medication management, and familiarization with community resources. They progressed to intermediate-level training in communication, assertiveness, sex education, stress management, coping strategies, and anger identification and resolution. It was not clear whether any special treatment was provided according to legal status.

As with the Isaac Ray Center, the DTP could initially accept or reject patients referred by the PSRB. Differences between those accepted and those not accepted generally involved the latter group being perceived as less motivated for treatment, more acutely ill, more dangerous, and more frequently diagnosed as antisocial or borderline personality. Patients could also be dropped from this treatment program for a variety of reasons, with the mean period of treatment for those successfully completing the program being 63 months, but the mean for those dropped only 9 months. Patients were often dropped from the program after a relatively short time; therefore, this is consistent with the observation of community treatment providers that patients who have difficulty adjusting to the conditional release often manifest these difficulties after a short time.

Evaluative data from Oregon on the community-based treatment of insanity acquittees are also available. Oregon researchers could use records from the PSRB, which maintained jurisdiction over insanity acquittees who continued to suffer from mental disease or defect and to present a substantial danger. The PSRB monitored the ongoing adjustment of patients on conditional release, and much of the Oregon research appears to reflect a useful collaboration between researchers and the PSRB. Such collaboration, utilizing high-quality data for both scientific and applied purposes, should serve as a model for other jurisdictions.

One Oregon study (Bloom, Rogers, & Manson, 1982) compared insanity acquittees who had been conditionally released by the judge following their acquittal ($N = 36$), conditionally released by the PSRB following hospitalization ($N = 90$), and not conditionally released ($N = 100$) from 1978 to 1980. Diagnosis (taken from hospital records and coded according to primary diagnosis only) did not distinguish released patients from those remaining hospitalized, nor did seriousness of crime. Crime severity did distinguish the group "released by judge following acquittal" from that "released by PSRB following hospitalization," however, with a much higher percentage of misdemeanors in the "judge-released" group (47%) than in the "PSRB-released" (11%) or "not released" (24%) groups. Crime seriousness was moderately related to length of hospitalization for felony acquittees prior to release ($r = .30$). There was no difference between the conditional release performance of acquittees released by their judge and those released by the PSRB. Gender, offense, severity of offense, and diagnosis were unrelated to success on conditional release, with "success" defined as no rehospitalization or violation of conditions. The "unsuccessful" group was younger (29 vs. 34 years old), suggesting that the "young adult chronic" population described elsewhere (Lamb, 1976; Sheets, Prevost, & Reihman, 1982) may have been performing poorly on conditional release. Nearly one third (32%) of the released patients were rehospitalized for violating their conditional release plan or experiencing a deterioration in mental condition. A total of 5% of patients were arrested while on conditional release; offenses included four misdemeanors and two felonies (aggravated robbery, burglary). All charges were dismissed in favor of continued PSRB jurisdiction.

A later study (Rogers, Bloom, & Manson, 1984), which included more subjects ($N = 295$) and a longer study period (1978–1982), cited an arrest rate higher than 5% for patients on conditional release under PSRB jurisdiction. Thirteen percent were charged with new offenses, roughly half of which were felonies, and 5% were reconvicted. Even though subsequent crime was relatively rare, a high percentage of PSRB clients had their conditional release revoked within 1 year of entering community-based treatment. Revocation rates were 78% (1980), 62% (1981), 31% (1982), and 20% (1983). It seemed that conditional release was working well, with rehospitalization in many cases apparently preventing possible criminal recidivism. The authors also noted that the number of insanity acquittees at Oregon State Hospital, after climbing rapidly during the 1970s, peaked during 1979 and declined by about 20% the next year (the third year of PSRB operation). This decline in census was attributed to the increased use of conditional release by judges as an alternative to hospitalization, and the conditional release or discharge by the PSRB of a number of acquittees who were initially hospitalized. The latter was of particular interest to legislators who needed to determine the impact of the PSRB upon other components of the forensic mental health system.

In another Oregon study (Bloom, Rogers, Manson, & Williams, 1986), researchers examined the lifetime police contacts (arrests *and* subarrest encounters) of patients ($N = 123$) released from PSRB jurisdiction from 1978 to 1980. A *subarrest contact* was an encounter with police that was recorded, but did not result in an arrest. One valuable (and apparently unique) aspect of this study is the information about police contacts that would not be reflected on an adult arrest record. These included subarrest contacts as a juvenile for various forms of public drunkenness and for "public behaviors consistent with mental illness" (p. 194). There was a significant correlation between the numbers of arrests before PSRB jurisdiction and after it ($r = .28$), indicating that previous criminality affected the risk of future criminality for those under PSRB supervision. There was also an association between younger age and postdischarge arrests; both arrest history and age have previously been reported to be associated with criminal violence (see, e.g., Monahan, 1981). A total of 42% of patients were rearrested following discharge from PSRB jurisdiction. A comparison of persons eventually released after PSRB jurisdiction because it expired with those released as no longer presenting a substantial danger indicated that the "expiration" group had a significantly higher arrest rate prior to NGRI acquittal and significantly more arrests (although not for more severe crimes) during the conditional release period. The two groups did not differ in post-jurisdiction arrest rates.

The evaluative component of an Oregon study already cited (Bloom, Williams, et al., 1986) involved a comparison of those accepted for treatment ($N = 110$) at a day treatment program in Portland with those not accepted ($N = 51$). These groups did not differ on demographic characteristics, crime seriousness, or DSM-III (American Psychiatric Association, 1980) Axis I diagnosis. The rejected group had a significantly greater frequency of antisocial personality disorder diagnoses. Even the treated group, however, frequently had substance abuse (50%) and personality disorder (40%) diagnoses. Within the treated group, a comparison of those remaining in treatment for the duration of the study period ($N = 21$) with those revoked from conditional release ($N = 46$) indicated that the revoked group was involved in more crises, with a greater percentage requiring staff home visits, crisis intervention services, and hospitalization. There was also a difference in living situation: The revoked group spent 41% of their time living in sheltered housing and 55% in independent living, as compared with the successful group, who spent only 13% of their time living in sheltered housing and 86% of their time living independently. This might suggest that "independent living" (particularly with supportive family) favorably affected the likelihood of continuing in treatment and complying with conditional release requirements. It might also mean that better adjusted patients, with more personal and family resources, were less likely to show a deterioration in mental condition and were thus better risks for succeeding on conditional release.

A number of reasons in this study were offered for revoking clients' conditional release: deteriorating mental condition (74%), noncompliance with supervision (74%), noncompliance with treatment (65%), troublesome behavior (59%), elopement (39%), new crime (24%), noncompliance with medication (24%), substance abuse (24%), and other (4%). Although the authors did not describe how these reasons clustered, the average of 3.9 reasons per revocation and the respective frequencies of each reason suggested an overlapping pattern involving deterioration in mental condition in conjunction with other reasons, such as noncompliance with supervision and treatment or troublesome behavior.

Maryland

Descriptive treatment information on NGRI acquittees has also come from Maryland. Insanity acquittees released from the state forensic hospital, Clifton T. Perkins, were required under Maryland law to undergo a 5-year conditional release period. A residential treatment program, Hamilton House, was located on the grounds of the state hospital, Clifton T. Perkins, and was funded for its first 3 years of existence by a National Institute of Mental Health grant. A total of 27 Hamilton House residents, formerly patients at Perkins, were followed over a 22-month period. Four individuals (15%) were rearrested during this time, although none of the arrests were for offenses as serious as the original crimes for which the men were acquitted by reason of insanity, and none of the rearrests occurred while the residents were in Hamilton House. By contrast, 11 of the 27 residents (40.5%) were rehospitalized during this period. The total cost of Hamilton House during this 1977–1978 period was $155,255, or $27.38 per patient per day (Goldmeier, Sauer, & White, 1977; Goldmeier, White, Ulrich, & Klein, 1980).

Another Maryland study (Silver, 1983) indicated that 43% of NGRI acquittees who were conditionally released went to a halfway house. Of the 65 acquittees involved in court-mandated outpatient treatment, 24% were rearrested (primarily for misdemeanors) and 11% were rehospitalized.

Evaluative data from Maryland (Spodak, Silver, & Wright, 1984) were obtained by following NGRI acquittees over a 15-year period after their release from hospitalization. A total of 86 acquittees were studied. Of these, 56% were arrested, and 30% convicted, for new criminal offenses.

A later Maryland study with a larger sample developed a model for predicting the success of insanity acquittees conditionally released to community-based treatment (Cohen, Spodak, Silver, & Williams, 1988; Silver, Cohen, & Spodak, 1989). The investigators performed a longitudinal investigation of 127 male insanity acquittees who had been released from Clifton T. Perkins Hospital Center between 1967 and 1978. All patients charged with felonies, discharged from the hospital on conditional release, and had been living in the community for periods ranging from 7 to 17 years, with an average of 10.8 years. Acquitted offenses included murder (30%), assault (31%), and rape (8%). A control group of convicted subjects ($N = 127$) was also obtained, as was a third group of prisoners with mental disorders ($N = 135$) treated at Perkins between 1969 and 1981. Using discriminant analysis, the authors found that NGRI acquittees who successfully completed conditional release were more likely to have been married, working at the time of the offense, arrested for less severe offenses, functioned "well" or "very well" prior to hospitalization, adjusted well to hospitalization, assessed by hospital clinical staff as considerably improved, and had a GAS (Endicott, Spitzer, Fleiss, & Cohen, 1976) score of 50 or higher upon release. Predictors were also developed for rearrest. NGRI acquittees who were not arrested during their conditional release period were less likely to be heroin addicts, had adjusted well to the hospital, had been assessed by clinical staff as considerably improved at the time of discharge, had a GAS score at release of 50 or higher, had functioned "well" or "very well" prior to arrest for the acquitted offense, and were only children or the youngest child in their families. The rates for successfully completing conditional release (49%) and avoiding arrest (46%) were given, but it was not clear from the article whether these were representative of the overall NGRI population in Maryland during this period.

Connecticut

Descriptive information on the functioning of a Psychiatric Security Review Board in Connecticut has been provided, following that state's 1985 implementation of a PSRB (Scott, Zonana, & Getz, 1990). In addition to describing the nature of the hearings and the number of acquittees ($N =$

173) between 1986 and 1989, the authors discussed the necessary balance between public safety and individual treatment, and the reluctance of some clinicians to provide treatment for this population. The PSRB has apparently obtained widespread acceptance in Connecticut, despite the initial skepticism of state attorneys and public defenders.

Florida

The description of a broader, community-based forensic services program in Palm Beach County, Florida (Dvoskin, 1989) made it clear that the successful integration of assessment and treatment services to insanity acquittees and individuals on parole and probation requires complex administrative coordination as well as specialized service delivery. This chapter provides a useful description of essential community forensic services and evaluation of the strengths and weaknesses of a "model" community forensic program.

California

Follow-up data have been reported on NGRI acquittees conditionally released to outpatient treatment in California (Lamb, Weinberger, & Gross, 1988a). A total of 79 individuals, acquitted by reason of insanity in Los Angeles County between July 1, 1979 and December 31, 1980, were studied. This period was selected because the Conditional Release Program (CONREP), the court-mandated community outpatient treatment program in California, was begun in 1976 and was thus well established by 1979. CONREP provided funding for 18 statewide community outpatient treatment programs for judicially committed patients, including those found NGRI. There were 79 NGRI acquittees followed in this study. The median age was 33 years; 89% were male. The charges of which they had been acquitted were mostly crimes against persons (67%), and almost all (99%) were felonies. The median length of forensic hospitalization prior to beginning court-mandated community outpatient treatment was 20 months. A total of 38 acquittees (48%) had their conditional release revoked at least once during the 5-year follow-up period of community-based treatment. Rearrests were noted for 16% of acquittees during this period (13% for violent crimes), and hospitalization in non-forensic facilities for 34%. The authors suggested that unsuccessful outcomes could have been prevented with greater structure and supervision. This is consistent with our views and those of others (e.g., Rogers et al., 1984): structure, monitoring, and (if necessary) rehospitalization can reduce the risk of criminal recidivism for NGRI acquittees in the community.

Further evidence on the rates of arrest and rehospitalization following hospital discharge of NGRI acquittees in California has been presented (Wiederanders, 1991; Wiederanders & Choate, 1994) by comparing 191 acquittees placed on conditional release with 44 individuals released from hospitalization with no aftercare following expiration of commitment terms. The conditionally released group had a significantly lower community-period arrest rate than did the unconditionally released group. Survival rate analyses, with dependent variables of time until arrest and time until revocation, indicated that revocations made during the first 8 months following discharge reduced the likelihood of arrest within the conditionally released group.

New York

There are also follow-up data available on the outcomes of NGRI acquittees ($N = 331$) released to the community in New York state between 1980 and 1987 (McGreevy, Steadman, Dvoskin, & Dollard, 1991). The follow-up period averaged 3.8 years, with 63% of the cohort followed for more than 3 years. During this period, a total of 22% of the NGRI acquittees were rearrested; the majority (64%) of the arrests were for misdemeanors, and the great majority (92%) were for Class D felonies or less. Some 11% of the group were arrested more than once, with the "most recent arrest" typically minor (34% misdemeanors, 76% for D felonies or less). A smaller percentage of individuals were rehospitalized (5%), although petitions for recommitment were filed on 12% of the sample. The following "key features" of a successful conditional release program were described: (1) centralized responsibility, (2) a uniform system of treatment and supervision, and (3) a network of community services.

Oklahoma

Community outcomes for insanity acquittees in Oklahoma have been provided (Norwood, Nicholson, Enyart, & Hickey, 1992). Rates of rearrest, rehospitalization, and contact with community mental health centers (CMHCs) were cited for three groups of released NGRI acquittees treated between May 1979 and November 1983: (1) those released at first court review ($N = 9$), (2) those released following recommendation by the hospital ($N = 16$), and (3) those who were AWOL ($N = 5$). The numbers of individuals rearrested during the follow-up period (averaging 960.5 days) were noticeably different between the groups (33% vs. 19% vs. 80%, respectively), although statistical comparisons would not have been meaningful because of the low numbers. Rehospitalization rates were less discrepant (33% vs. 38% vs. 20%, respectively), but the number of individuals contacting CMHC showed clear differences (44% vs. 81% vs. 20%, respectively).

Summary

Descriptions of CBFT programs for NGRI acquittees emphasize both the treatment of psychopathology and the management of aggressive behavior. To meet both goals, programs may refuse to accept "high risk" patients, who are generally regarded as more antisocial individuals. Empirical accounts of factors distinguishing between "successful" and "unsuccessful" acquittees on conditional release use rearrest and rehospitalization as outcome criteria. Factors predicting successful outcome in both areas include better functioning before hospitalization, rated as improved by hospital clinical staff, and a GAS score of 50 or higher at the beginning of CBFT. Rearrest rates on conditional release ranged from 2% to 16%, with higher rates (42–56%) seen on long-term follow-up after conditional release is terminated. Rehospitalization rates while on conditional release were both higher and more variable, ranging from 11% to 78%, with most estimates between 11% and 40%. Higher rates of rehospitalization were associated with lower rates of rearrest when clear external control, such as a PSRB, was utilized. The Oregon model appeared exemplary from several perspectives, including public safety orientation, appropriate external control, and facilitation of research and evaluation.

OFFENDERS WITH MENTAL DISORDERS ON PAROLE OR PROBATION

Much of the focus thus far has been on CBFT programs treating individuals with severe mental disorders (e.g., schizophrenia, major affective disorders, organic mental disorders with psychotic features, and mental retardation). The legal category of NGRI is associated with a high proportion of such disorders. However, parole and probation are larger categories, with a weaker association with mental disorder. In discussing the treatment of parolees and probationers in the community, we have tried to include only individuals with comparably severe disorders or individuals with substance abuse disorders. Without this limitation, the reference group would be so large and heterogeneous that the discussion would not be meaningful in the context of this chapter. Descriptive and evaluative studies are summarized in Table 4.2.

Program Descriptions

Several descriptive accounts of CBFT programs for individuals on parole or probation are available. The Linkoping (Sweden) Center for Social and Forensic Psychiatry (Ojesjo, 1981) included outpatient treatment and reha-

TABLE 4.2. Studies of Offenders with Mental Disorders on Parole or Probation

Descriptive studies

Study	Sample	Program	Goals/findings
Bluegrass (1977)	1 outpatient clinic	United Kingdom	Both assessment and treatment services performed
Ojesjo (1981)	1 outpatient	Linkoping, Sweden	1. Treatment services delivered in collaboration with university psychiatry department 2. Clinical–legal evaluations done for the courts 3. Research and training also emphasized
Schottenfeld (1989)	1 outpatient	New Haven, CT (United States)	1. Evaluation of 110 patients per month alcohol/drug treatment 2. 59% of those treated are on probation or charged with criminal offenses 3. Potential problems resulting from involuntary nature of treatment are described, and recommendations for management given
Ben-Arie, Swartz, & George (1986)	1 outpatient clinic	South Africa	1. Clients treated for alcohol abuse and followed 7–9 years posttreatment were abstinent from drinking at 40% rate
Community Systems and Services, Inc. (1985)	67 community forensic programs	Florida (United States)	1. Reduce admissions to state forensic hospitals 2. Increase consistency in forensic evaluations performed in community 3. Provide continuity of care to patients returning from state forensic hospitals
Reid & Solomon (1981)	1 residential program (PORT)	Rochester, MN (United States)	1. Residential treatment provided to men on parole and probation 2. 75% of clients successfully completed program and returned to community 3. During 6 years postdischarge, 35% had no arrests, 40% "mild encounters" with law, and 25% "moderate to severe" encounters
Reid & Solomon (1981)	1 residential program (Portland House)	Minneapolis, MN (United States)	1. Residential treatment provided to men on parole and probation 2. Program is completed by 50% of accepted offenders 3. Rearrest rate for completing group is 10% over 6-year

Evaluative studies

Study	N	Comparison group?	Variables	Findings
Kloss (1978)	106	Yes	1. Rearrest 2. Rehospitalization	1. Intensive, goal-oriented, training-based community treatment is more expensive than probation, but more effective in reducing rearrest and rehospitalization in severely mentally disordered offenders
Gallant, Faulkner, Stoy, Bishop, & Langdon (1967)	19	Yes	1. Treatment attendance 2. Posttreatment drinking abstinence 3. Posttreatment employment	Comparing compulsory and voluntary groups of parolees treated for alcohol abuse: 1. Treatment attendance was more consistent for compulsory group 2. Abstinence from drinking higher in this group 1 year posttreatment 3. Employment rate higher in this group 1 year posttreatment

Note. PORT, Probationed Offenders Rehabilitation and Training.

bilitation services performed in collaboration with the psychiatry department at a university hospital. Research and training were also emphasized. Given heavy service demands and limited staffing, the program staff were constantly balancing competing demands. Such balancing of demands is a constant theme for most CBFT programs.

Descriptive accounts of CBFT programs in Great Britain emphasized that treatment was provided to individuals who committed a variety of offenses, including sex offenses (Craft, 1974), and that both assessment and treatment may be provided by a single program (Bluegrass, 1977). In addition to evaluations for juvenile and adult courts, the program described by Bluegrass (Midlands Centre for Forensic Psychiatry) also provided assessment services for patients referred by psychiatrists, general practitioners, and prisons. It has also been noted that it is important to be able to compel treatment in the community (Gunn, 1979). Having this issue unresolved presented a significant impediment to the effective delivery of CBFT services in Great Britain.

Others (Kunjudrishnan & Bradford, 1985) have described the process of diverting mentally ill offenders in Canada from the criminal justice system to the mental health system. Such diversion is described at different stages of the criminal justice process. In support of diversion, Kunjudrishnan and Bradford commented that there were provisions in both the Canadian Criminal Code and the Mental Health Act to ensure adequate treatment for mentally ill offenders without compromising community safety.

Two residential rehabilitation programs for individuals on parole or probation in Minnesota have been described (Reid & Solomon, 1981). The first (Probationed Offenders Rehabilitation and Training, or PORT) was a program housed in a dormitory on the grounds of a state hospital within walking distance of schools, a college, vocational schools, and downtown Rochester, Minnesota. The program had strong community ties from its inception in 1969; included on its Board of Directors were law enforcement and correctional officers, mental health professionals, educators, and lay persons. Initial grant support evolved into state support for over half the budget, with the remainder coming from local matching funds and the offender's monthly $150 room and board fee. Costs per inmate year were described as being under $5,800 for the main center, and slightly more for two group homes. Individuals referred generally lacked employment and money management skills, most were school dropouts, and approximately 40% had learning disabilities. Well over 50% were severe drug abusers. Treatment was facilitated by a written contract, often used in CBFT, that was clear, easily monitored, and addressed the goals for each individual. Reality oriented, confrontational group meetings with peers were mandatory. The program was described as less costly than other residential alternatives. About 75% of the adult clients successfully completed the program and returned to the community. Post-discharge follow-up indicated that 35% had no arrests, 40% had "mild encounters" with law, and 25% had "moderate to severe" encounters (Tyce, Olson, & Amdahl, 1980).

A second residential program in Minnesota described by the same authors (Reid & Solomon, 1981) was Portland House. Founded in Minneapolis in 1973 under the auspices of local Lutheran Social Services, it was largely supported by $30 per diem payments from each client. Fewer than 20 young adult males (ages 18–30) lived in a large house in a residential neighborhood, with community educational and vocational resources readily available. There were 4–5 full-time nonmedical staff, several resident counselors, and trained volunteers. Broadly considered, the goals of this program involved (1) reversing antisocial behavior and (2) establishing relations with the community in terms of employment, social interaction, interpersonal relationships, and improved self-esteem. Clients participated in regular group and individual therapy, took a money management course, maintained family ties, and worked with other residents. The length of the program was a minimum of 5 months. About 50% of the accepted offenders completed the Portland House program. The authors noted that more serious offenders (e.g., manslaughter, sexual offenses) were more likely to complete the program. Of the 50% who did successfully complete the program, the rate of postdischarge arrest over a 1- to 6-year period was 10%.

One descriptive study of a program treating substance abusers (Schottenfeld, 1989) described the Alcohol and Drug Treatment Unit, a free-standing, satellite clinic of a regional CMHC affiliated with the Yale University Psychiatry Department. Approximately 110 patients were evaluated per month; half of them were retained for extended evaluation. Some 26% were referred by probation officers, 24% for outstanding DWI charges, 9% for other "pending legal difficulties," and the remaining 41% were self-referred. The author described the potential difficulties that can arise when treatment is coerced. These include difficulties in the development of the therapeutic alliance (the lack of freedom to choose conditions of treatment and relative powerlessness of the client) and specific problems for the clinician (how to assess suspiciousness and defensiveness, how to insist on reasonable expectations without exacerbating the client's feeling of powerlessness, and how to manage the therapist's reactions evoked by involuntary clients). Recommended safeguards included: (1) time limits for involuntary treatment, (2) continuing education and consultation with colleagues, (3) direct payment to the clinician, and (4) advance notification of what will be divulged to whom and for what reason.

Program Outcome

We now discuss evaluative research on CBFT programs treating individuals on parole or probation. It should be noted that some of the Oregon, Illinois, and California studies described under the earlier section on NGRI patients would also fit in this section. The Isaac Ray Center, for example, treated probationers and parolees as well as insanity acquittees; the Portland Day Treatment Program treated some patients who were not under the jurisdiction of the PSRB. Ellsworth House, in San Mateo, California, treated NGRI clients as well as those under parole or probation (Lamb & Goertzel, 1974).

Beyond these, however, we located only one further evaluative study focusing specifically on mentally ill individuals on parole or probation. A study involving the "complex offender project" in Dane County, Wisconsin tested the hypothesis that deviant behavior could be altered via training of more acceptable and socially constructive ways of behaving (Kloss, 1978). "Complex offenders" (defined as persons with psychological problems as well as a history of legal involvement) treated through this project were randomly selected as subjects for this study if they met the following criteria: (1) on probation, with no pending charges, (2) ages 18–30, (3) having at least one previous conviction, and (4) having a poor employment record. A total of 106 individuals (mean age of 21, 15% female, 14% minority group members) were seen three times weekly for 20 months. Comparisons between treatment and control groups supported the conclusion that this form of intensive, goal-oriented, training-based community treatment of offenders with mental disorders was an effective approach to treatment with this population. Although such an approach was more costly than probation, it was still less expensive than incarceration.

Compulsory Treatment for Substance Abuse

Treatment for mental illness or substance abuse is often a mandatory condition of parole or probation. Thus, an important question is whether compulsory treatment for alcohol or drug abuse is more effective than voluntary treatment. Compulsory treatment of alcohol abuse in drunken drivers, for example, has yielded claims of improvement in one-half (Argeriou & Manohar, 1977; Ben-Arie, George, & Hirschowitz, 1983) to two-thirds (McGrath, O'Brien, & Liftik, 1977; Rosenberg & Liftik, 1976) of the individuals treated in this fashion. However, follow-up studies such as those just cited have generally used outcome studies of insufficient duration to judge the longer-term impact of such programs. In a follow-up study with a 7- to 9-year posttreatment outcome duration, some 40% of clients were either completely or largely abstinent (Ben-Arie, Swartz, & George, 1986).

Other evaluative research has focused on the issue of compulsory substance abuse treatment of individuals on parole or probation. One small comparative study on this issue (Gallant, Faulkner, Stoy, Bishop, & Langdon, 1967) contrasted the treatment of alcoholic individuals who had served a sentence of 1 year or longer for a major offense associated with an alcohol problem. Subjects were 19 males paroled from Louisiana State Penitentiary, randomly assigned to compulsory or voluntary treatment conditions. Compulsory treatment involved mandatory visits to the New Orleans Alcoholism Clinic for a minimum of 6 months, with the possibility of an extension for another 6 months. Voluntary subjects were only required to keep the first appointment at the clinic, although they were encouraged to continue. Results strongly supported the efficacy of compulsory treatment: Attendance was more frequent, abstinence from drinking was much higher, and more subjects were "abstinent and working" at 1 year in the compulsory group.

The issue of compulsory treatment has also been described as "constructive coercion," in which something of value to the client is made contingent upon treatment success. In a review of early studies on the effect of legal coercion on the treatment of alcoholism, Ward (1979) concluded that most of the studies found that coercion was effective. However, this conclusion is probably not warranted due to flaws in the design of the research being reviewed. In a later study controlling for 10 sociodemographic variables, other investigators (Dunham & Maus, 1982) reported that problem drinkers coerced into outpatient treatment by the courts were more likely than voluntary referrals to have successful treatment outcomes. Consistent with this, Salmon (1982) found that legal coercion facilitated success for longer-term addicts, as measured by the criteria of arrest and abstinence, and Collins and Allison (1983) reported that drug abusers who were legally coerced into treatment performed as well as voluntary clients on a number of outcome measures.

Others, however, have not found such a favorable effect of coercion upon treatment outcome. One group of investigators (Harford, Ungerer, & Kinsella, 1976), for example, did not find that legal pressure improved either retention rate or program completion probability. In another study (Simpson, 1984), it was reported that higher rates of preadmission arrests and incarcerations were related to poorer posttreatment outcomes.

The impact of coercion upon retention in treatment is clearer, however. Several investigators (Collins & Allison, 1983; Steer, 1983) have reported that drug abusers coerced into treatment remained longer than voluntary clients; the most successful were those who were closely monitored (e.g., clients involved in Treatment Alternatives to Street Crime). Others (Kofoed, Kania, Walsh, & Atkinson, 1986) reported a positive relationship between coercion and retention in the treatment of individuals with co-occurring (substance abuse and mental illness) disorders.

Summary

CBFT programs treating individuals in this category may be either outpatient clinics or residential ("halfway house") facilities. The clinics tended to offer both assessment and treatment services to individuals in a variety of legal categories including pretrial, parole, probation, and sometimes insanity acquittee. Certain clinics offering substance abuse treatment also accepted self-referred (voluntary) clients, underscoring the heterogeneity of the client population for such programs.

As may be seen from studies described in this section, facilities providing residential treatment reported rates of successful completion ranging from 50 to 75%, with posttreatment arrest rates typically reported as one form of outcome measure. Both clinics and residential programs shared the necessity of treating individuals on an involuntary basis. The evidence on whether such coercion favorably affected the outcome of substance abuse treatment appears mixed, but it is quite clear that coercion improved in-treatment retention with substance abusers.

ISSUES IN TREATMENT

Thus far, we have focused primarily on descriptive and evaluative aspects of CBFT programs treating patients who are NGRI, IST, or offenders with mental disorders on parole or probation. Some of the issues raised in these areas relate more broadly to CBFT than we have thus far discussed. Therefore, we devote a separate section of this chapter to the discussion of the broader issues in CBFT. We begin with general principles relevant to CBFT. We also discuss some of the related legal issues in this area. From there, we move to more specific areas, including coercion and consent, confidentiality, the applicability of outpatient commitment concepts, and the need to address treatability and violence risk as part of the overall assessment of the patient. Finally, we turn to broader "systems issues." This discussion leads into our next section, in which we summarize and illustrate a proposed set of principles for CBFT.

General Principles

A broad description of proposed goals to guide the interactions of the mental health and criminal justice systems were provided in a symposium with 50 prominent professionals concerned with the interactions between these systems. The goals included (1) improvement of communications between the systems through enhancement of mutual understanding and respect, (2) promotion and attention to the needs of the clients, and (3) improving the functioning of the systems through increased accountability, use of empirical data in decision making, better use of professionals, and improvement of the informational base (Hafemeister, 1991).

Certain "core planning principles" in designing conditional release systems for insanity acquittees have been proposed (Griffin, Steadman, & Heilbrun, 1991). Such planning principles might apply to the community treatment of individuals who are IST or on parole or probation as well as to those who have been released to the community as insanity acquittees. These principles are as follows:

1. There must be an explicit balance between individual rights, the need for treatment, and public safety.
2. Conditional release should not be considered in isolation from the full NGRI and community mental health systems.
3. Know the range of treatment and supervision needs of NGRI acquittees who will be served by the system.
4. Identify and prioritize the critical components for change, so that unexpected legislative action does not eliminate crucial components of the system.

Similar emphasis on the importance of balancing clinical, judicial, and community concerns in the follow-up care of insanity acquittees in Maryland has been provided by Silver and Tellefsen (1991). They noted that it is a major challenge to develop a forensic mental health system that yields consistent practice throughout the state. Three models include a centralized system (easier to manage, but costly), a system embedded in CMHCs (less duplicative, but requiring major and ongoing educational support), and a private practice model (flexible, but administratively challenging).

Further stress on the importance of conditional release as a means of balancing between the broad goals of protecting society and providing treatment in the least restrictive environment has been made (Bloom, Williams, & Bigelow, 1991). This review also highlights development of community programs based on treatment models for chronically mentally ill, adding that monitored community treatment programs appear cost effective when compared with hospital-based programs. Critical considerations include (1) the diminished importance of the long-term prediction of violent behavior, as graduated release with ongoing monitoring can function as a "demonstration model," (2) the availability of monitored community treatment for the chronically mentally ill, and (3) the costs of hospitalization versus those of community treatment. Community care was estimated to cost about 14% of the hospital stay it replaced, as the annual cost of a community slot was $4,841 and the annual cost of hospital bed was $33,948 (Bigelow, Bloom, & Williams, 1990).

The feasibility of implementing community-based forensic services was assessed in a survey of 288 administrators of state hospitals and CMHCs (Schutte, Malouff, Lucore, & Shern, 1988). Respondents estimated that 38% of currently hospitalized IST defendants could be treated in local jails, and 35% (it was not clear whether this was additional or inclusive) could be treated in outpatient community facilities. The authors also found respondents indicating that the presence of certain community resources could produce an earlier discharge for NGRI clients. These resources included transitional residences and enhanced systems for compliance monitoring and case management.

Using their own outcome data as a guide, Lamb, Weinberger, and Gross (1988b) discussed the necessary clinical philosophy and procedures for implementing a successful court-mandated outpatient treatment program for insanity acquittees. They described the following important components: (1) a clearly articulated treatment philosophy with a reality-based approach, (2) close liaison with the court, (3) access to both the criminal justice and mental health systems for developing a comprehensive data base on each patient, (4) an emphasis on structure and supervision, with treatment staff who are comfortable with using authority and setting limits, (5) a recognition of the importance of neuroleptic medication, and (6) a focus on the problems of daily living and an incorporation of the principles of case management.

A number of recurring issues may be observed in these discussions. The first involves having a clearly articulated treatment philosophy with an explicit balance between individual rights and public safety, with treatment serving to address both. Next, the issue of treating individuals in the contexts of both the criminal justice and the mental health systems emerges, along with the danger inherent in isolation from either. To facilitate this sometimes difficult integration, it is important to stress communication between courts, case managers or probation/parole officers, and clinicians. Having at least one person designated to serve as a liaison between the different systems is important to facilitate such communication. The process of identifying client needs and delivering treatment and monitoring services based on these needs seems to yield the following as preferred treatment modalities: medication, structure, a focus on activities in daily living, and a direct approach to avoidance of further criminal activities, with monitoring performed under the umbrella of case management.

Legal Contours

Certain legal contours of providing outpatient treatment to forensic patients are relevant (see, e.g., Weiner, 1985). Such issues include confidentiality and the duty to warn, child abuse reporting statutes, and malpractice. On the issue of confidentiality and duty to protect, the *Tarasoff* (1976) standard requires that when a therapist determines (or should determine, pursuant to the standards of the profession) that a patient presents a danger to another, then that therapist has an obligation to use reasonable care in protecting the victim. This duty may include providing a direct warning to the potential victim. Whereas some states in the United States have rejected such a duty to protect, the standard in many states appears to require a therapist to take some action to protect a potential victim when a specific individual is identified (Monahan & Walker, 1994). In these states, therefore, it is clear that the limits of confidentiality should be made clear to the patient at the outset of therapy; such limits on confidentiality should also be noted because many state statutes explicitly provide for the sharing of treatment information relevant to any threat to public safety with courts and probation/parole when treating NGRI acquittees or individuals on parole or probation.

Other treatment and policy-relevant guidelines for avoiding *Tarasoff* liability have been summarized recently (Monahan, 1993). In particular, therapists should be aware of the child abuse reporting requirements in their particular jurisdiction, and communicate these requirements as well to the patient at the beginning of treatment. Finally, malpractice in the area of forensic treatment may be somewhat difficult to establish because of the relative lack of empirical evidence on the long-term effects of different kinds of treatment of offenders with mental disorders. Nonetheless, the nature and quality of treatment should at least be consistent with that described in the clinical and research literature (Weiner, 1985).

Further, there has been explicit discussion of the role of law (particularly the substantive rules, legal procedures, and roles of lawyers) as a therapeutic agent for offenders with mental disorders within the framework of "therapeutic jurisprudence" (Wexler, 1990; Wexler & Winick, 1996). It is suggested, for example, that offenders with mental disorders or who are impulsive in the community who have a duty to act (e.g., take medication) or refrain from acting (e.g., avoid alcohol consumption) may be prosecuted under reckless endangerment statutes for breaching such a duty. Even when no longer on outpatient or conditional release status, and thus without a direct legal obligation to take medication, the duty may be "derivable indirectly through one's status-imposed duty to prevent harm to family members" (Wexler, 1990, p. 51).

Coercion and Consent

By definition, individuals being treated in CBFT programs are not voluntary. There is a set of conditions, ultimately enforced by the court of jurisdiction, specifying certain parameters of treatment and other aspects of daily life. There is mixed evidence on whether this kind of coercion improves symptom-related outcome, but it is clearer that it increases treatment compliance. It is also a necessary component of CBFT for public safety reasons; individuals who do not comply with treatment or other specified conditions are judged to present an increased risk to public safety, and may be removed from the community for that reason alone.

The overt acknowledgement and utilization of coercion may also result in the law being reshaped by healthcare compliance principles described in non-forensic contexts (Meichenbaum & Turk, 1987). For example, the nature of the insanity acquittee conditional release hearing and the judge's behavior at that hearing might be altered to accommodate the following principles of treatment adherence: (1) adequate instruction about treatment regimen, (2) the development of a behavioral contract, (3) a public commitment to adhere to this contract, and (4) the involvement of the family (Wexler, 1991).

The role of coercion in mental health care has generally been poorly understood and not studied systematically (Dennis & Monahan, 1996; Lidz & Hoge, 1993). Fortunately, this has changed since the late 1980s as a result of the programmatic research on coercion performed by the MacArthur Research Network on Mental Health and Law. Empirical data are now available on the coercive aspects of interactions between patients and mental health staff in psychiatric emergency rooms (Lidz, Mulvey, Arnold, Bennett, & Kirsch, 1993; Lidz et al., 1997) and mental hospitals (Hoge et al., 1993), and approaches to measuring patients' perceptions of coercion during admission to mental hospitals have been developed (Gardner et al., 1993). A logical next step, which remains to be taken, is to apply these approaches to measuring the perceptions of coercion experienced by insanity acquittees and individuals on parole or probation. Questions of how coercion (in a more extreme degree) is perceived, and its impact, remain to be addressed.

Confidentiality

Communication is a critical component for successful CBFT treatment. The sharing of relevant, accurate information regarding the client's treatment needs and risk factors, with direct implications for community management and treatment, should be the beginning assumption regarding confidentiality. This is in contrast with more traditional ethical canons of psychiatry, psychology, and social work regarding therapeutic confidentiality, where the assumption is that confidence is not violated without the client's consent except in situations in which imminent, foreseeable harm to self or an identifiable other appears likely.

Two points can be made in this regard. First, effective CBFT serves both public protection and individual therapeutic needs. The failure to acknowledge the former can have devastating consequences for the victim, the larger society, and the CBFT program itself. Communication with the discharging hospital, the case manager, and the court should facilitate addressing both needs. Without such communication regarding client behavior, treatment progress, and risk, it is far less likely that either need will be served adequately.

The second point is that limited confidentiality can be addressed directly prior to beginning treatment. If the "treatment contract" explicitly calls for regular communication between specified parties and the client is informed of this, there is less risk of a misunderstanding of this component of CBFT.

Discussing the sharing of information with the families of civilly committed patients, Petrila and Sadoff (1992) emphasized the importance of rethinking the traditional clinical reluctance to provide information about patients to families who will house them. They argued that sharing such information should not be discouraged on ethical or legal grounds. A similar kind of argument can be made even more strongly for providing information to CBFT providers.

The responsibility for communicating risk-relevant information with NGRI clients on conditional release, or individuals on parole or probation, should not fall on a single individual. The case manager (for NGRIs) and the probation/parole officer (for individuals on probation or parole) may have primary responsibility for communicating such information. However, it is important that others (e.g., therapists, housing supervisors, family members) share the responsibility for communicating relevant information, and that a specific avenue for such communication be developed early in the community placement. There can be less tension around this expectation if there is a shared agreement between the individual and all associated with his adjustment that (1) the primary goal should be responsible, nonviolent behavior while in the community, and (2) it is the responsibility of all involved, particularly the individual him- or herself, to take the necessary action (including sharing of risk-relevant information) to prevent the recurrence of criminal or violent behavior.

Outpatient Commitment

Outpatient commitment is relevant to CBFT in that most forensic patients treated in the community will be under court jurisdiction or correctional supervision. Indeed, forensic patients are typically more likely than civil (i.e., non-criminal) patients to be under such jurisdiction. However, it is still worthwhile to review what has been written about continued court control in civil cases, where outpatient commitment is primarily applied (Harris & Watkins, 1987; Meloy, Haroun, & Schiller, 1990; Swartz et al., 1995).

The arguments for and against the use of outpatient commitment have been cogently summarized (Mulvey, Geller, & Roth, 1987). Broadly speaking, the arguments against outpatient commitment claim that it undermines the therapeutic relationship, minimizes incentives for compliance, deprives the patient of the right to refuse treatment, has a broad range of activities to be monitored, lowers the standard for state intervention, and that benevolent coercion is generally futile. By contrast, the arguments for the use of outpatient commitment involve the state's obligation to provide "positive liberty" rather than simple noninterference, the likelihood of more effective treatment through broad-based intervention, and the possibility of initiating a positive cycle of community involvement. Mulvey et al. adopted a reasoned middle ground, arguing for the use of outpatient commitment while providing careful limits on eligibility, length of commitment, type of clinical intervention, and procedure. This proposal comes as close as possible to balancing treatment needs with civil liberties. Arguably, the balance should shift somewhat toward greater public safety and away from individual liberties in applying such a model with criminal forensic populations. A treatment intervention approach using "paternalistic, benevolent coercion that was respectful of autonomy and liberty," such as that described by Geller (1986), might serve as a useful (although perhaps insufficiently restrictive) beginning model for CBFT.

Outpatient commitment was perceived as successful by public defenders and psychiatrists in a review of 13 years of experience with its use in Washington, DC (Band et al., 1984). Indications (continued compliance with psychotropic medication) and contraindications (a questionable living situation) of success were noted, with continuity between inpatient and outpatient services described as extremely important. Others, however, sounded a more cautious note on outpatient commitment. It is seldom used even in states that permit it, and it may be necessary for the public, mental health professionals, and the judiciary to change their views of outpatient commitment before it can be used more often (Miller & Fiddleman, 1984). Its use in Tennessee since 1981 has resulted in a reduced rate of hospital readmission for those under outpatient commitment. However, a carefully controlled empirical analysis did not lead to the conclusion that this reduced rate was causally related to outpatient commitment (Bursten, 1986). We should note that conditional release, a variation of outpatient commitment, is currently an integral part of the NGRI post-hospitalization treatment process described in this chapter. If CBFT staff can realistically assure committing courts that patients treated in their programs will present a low risk to public safety, at least during the treatment process, then it seems possible that outpatient commitment/conditional release will be used increasingly with less dangerous patients as an *alternative* to treatment in maximum security hospitals.

Treatability

There are two questions relevant to treatability that need to be addressed by CBFT programs in treating forensic patients: (1) whether the prospective patient will comply with the conditions of treatment, and (2) whether he/she will benefit from treatment, both in terms of symptomatic remission and avoidance of aggressive and other criminal behavior. Research on the treatability of offenders with mental disorders suggests that there is limited clinician–clinician agreement in addressing such questions (Heilbrun et al., 1988; Quinsey & Maguire, 1983; Rogers, Gillis, Dickens, & Webster, 1988; Rogers & Webster, 1989).

It is thus appropriate to recommend that CBFT clinicians use a "demonstration model," relying upon treatment history and currently observed treatment response, in addressing these two questions. Some information relevant to both is available from hospital or prison records of prospective CBFT patients. Has the individual been compliant with taking prescribed medication? Does she indicate a willingness to continue with prescribed medication in the community? Have medical and non-medical therapies been effective in limiting aggressive behavior and stabilizing psychotic symptoms in an institutional setting? Have risk factors for aggression been reduced sufficiently through treatment or monitoring so that the risk to public safety is minimized? Affirmation in all these areas should be regarded as a "necessary but not sufficient" indication of treatability in the community. The remaining task is to construct a treatment plan and *carefully monitor compliance* in the community so that symptom exacerbation and increased risk of aggression (discussed in the next section) can be identified early and acted upon to reduce the risk of criminal recidivism.

Violence Risk

There are a number of points within the criminal justice system at which the assessment of an individual's risk of future violent behavior is relevant (Campbell, 1995). These include bail determination, sentencing, hospital commitment as either IST or NGRI transfer from jail to hospital or prison to hospital, and the return to the correctional setting. Risk assessment in the CBFT context should be conceptualized as conditional. More specifically, given the parameters of the conditional release plan or the conditions of probation, what is the risk of violent behavior? Have the risk factors which, if operative, would elevate such a risk been properly identified and incorporated into the monitoring plan? If so, then the risk assessment is less a prediction than an assessment of compliance with conditions. Some conditions may be more important because of their stronger relationship to aggression toward others (e.g., psychotropic medication and abstinence from drug and alcohol use; see, e.g., Swanson, Holzer, Ganju, & Jono, 1990). The risk assessment becomes more difficult if the major risk factors have not all been identified. However, it is a reasonable beginning assumption that the compliance with the conditions of the plan is the first step in limiting risk of aggression toward others. CBFT clinicians must add to these conditions if they become aware of additional risk factors not identified in and monitored by the plan. However, the great majority of the risk assessment done in the CBFT context should involve assessing compliance with existing conditions rather than making predictions.

A number of studies on risk assessment have been published since the mid-1980s of some relevance to NGRI acquittees and individuals on parole and probation (Monahan, 1996). A systematic program of research on risk factors for aggression in those with mental disorders *without* criminal involvement has been undertaken by the MacArthur Research Network on Mental Health and Law (Monahan & Steadman, 1994). Some of the risk factors identified, such as psychopathy (Hart, Hare, & Forth, 1994), impulsiveness (Barratt, 1994), anger (Novaco, 1994), threat/control override delusions (Link & Stueve, 1994), and social networks (Estroff & Zimmer, 1994) appear particularly promising for individuals with mental disorders involved in the criminal justice system, as well as for those who are not. The results of this program of research may have immediate implications for risk assessment research and practice with offenders with mental disorders.

Systems Issues

An example of a CBFT *system* with both clear strengths and weaknesses has been described for Dade County (metropolitan Miami), Florida (Community Systems and Services, Inc., 1985). This system included a Mental Health Administrator's Office that monitored and developed aftercare plans for mentally ill individuals in the criminal justice system (primarily as IST or NGRI) and reported directly to the courts. It also included a regional hospital with an outpatient forensic evaluation team and an inpatient psychiatric unit that accepted patients with charges pending. A forensic halfway house that received both state and local funding was located in Dade County as well, as was a maximum-security, state-funded forensic hospital. The strengths of this system included the Mental Health Administrator's Office having an experienced, knowledgeable staff with ready access to courts and the availability of the hospital's forensic evaluation team and inpatient forensic beds. Weaknesses were described in several areas. In jail services, these weaknesses included inadequate resources for mental health and trial competence screening, and the need to upgrade the special jail sections used for assessment and treatment of forensic clients.

For outpatient services, weaknesses included poor follow-up and monitoring after jail release, an insufficient number of transitional residential beds, inadequate inpatient or Crisis Stabilization Unit space for clients being treated for restoration of trial competence, and inadequate community services for females and misdemeanants. Finally, in the area of funding, there was a problem with the limited funding to purchase services (Community Systems and Services, Inc., 1985). This analysis clearly outlined the need for a balanced integration of treatment services on a continuum from jail to maximum-security hospital, medium-security regional hospital, and finally, to outpatient CBFT facilities. It also underscored the need for further development of outpatient forensic. services, which were the least adequate. Even in this reatively sophisticated CBFT system, outpatient services were described as insufficient.

The concept of outreach as it applies to CBFT is illustrated by a program in Dane County, Wisconsin. Records of the chronically mentally ill patients in the area were maintained by Crisis Intervention Services, which could then recommend action in the event that a problem arose. The general goal was to avoid rehospitalization whenever possible. Outreach was facilitated by the use of the Mobile County Treatment Unit, which took treatment services to those who could not (or would not) attend them centrally. The Unit assisted with social activities, evaluated and dispensed medication when necessary, and contacted patients directly to encourage them to keep appointments (Johnson, McKeown, & James, 1984). The important point here is that service delivery may be facilitated by flexible and innovative measures designed to address fundamental problems with transportation and reluctance to attend treatment that can be observed with some CBFT clients.

INTEGRATION OF ISSUES IN TREATMENT: PRINCIPLES OF COMMUNITY-BASED FORENSIC TREATMENT

1. *Communication is essential for success. Such communication must encompass individuals within both the mental health and criminal justice systems.* In particular, it must include institution to community, and case manager or probation/parole officer to court, therapist, and living supervisor or family member. The role of the case manager or probation officer in coordinating such communication is very important. Without such an individual's willingness and ability to obtain and communicate relevant information in a timely fashion, it is inevitable that some CBFT clients will present a greater risk for violating the conditions of community living, and possibly breaking the law as well.

2. *There must be an explicit balance between individual rights, the need for treatment, and public safety.* This balance must be operationalized and clearly articulated to clients prior to their entering into community-based treatment. The recommended model for CBFT is oriented explicitly toward public safety. In part, this is a recognition of political reality. Funding for CBFT programs providing community services to individuals involved in criminal behavior who also have mental problems is unlikely to be obtained solely on the basis of treatment needs. Rather, the argument that such programs are likely to deter criminal behavior and the documentation of this experience in other communities is more likely to be persuasive. However, a program that does not balance public protection with respect for human dignity and the delivery of needed services does no more than serve a monitoring function. It is important to have this balance carefully considered, operationalized, and clearly articulated to staff, clients, and others who have contact with the program.

3. *Be aware of the range of supervision and treatment needs of clients who will be served in the community.* These needs have been discussed at some length in this chapter and are familiar to professionals who work with clients at the interface of the criminal justice and mental health systems. CBFT programs should be designed to ensure that treatments such as psychotropic medication, substance abuse groups such as AA and NA, and skills building in interpersonal, aggression control, and vocational areas are delivered as needed. The ongoing availability of housing, as well as disability income for those who cannot work and have no other means of support, is also crucial. However, it remains important for programs to gather empirical information on the type of deficits, treatments administered, adjustment in the community, and rates of rearrest or rehospitalization for the clients they serve.

4. *Use a "demonstration model" in assessing risk of aggression toward others and treatability in the community.* A CBFT treatment plan should demonstrate a logical connection between the risk factors for target behavior classes such as aggression, the pattern of clinical symptoms, and the interventions delivered. The judgments concerning risk and treatment outcome are not always facilitated by the availability of empirical data on large groups of CBFT clients, so it is usually necessary to rely on historical information and theoretical and logical "fit" on a case-by-case basis.

5. *Clarify the legal requirements in areas such as confidentiality and duty to protect, specific reporting demands (e.g., child abuse), and malpractice.* A priori legal consultation is an essential ingredient for any CBFT program. Emergency response procedures for "critical incidents" (such as threats of violence, criminal behavior, or refusal to take prescribed medication) should be specified before such incidents occur. Ready access to legal advice should also be available to clinicians who work with these

clients, given the kind of questions that can require immediate legal consultation.

6. *Set, practice, and monitor sound "risk management" procedures.* Such procedures should include an awareness of risk assessment and the law of the jurisdiction, obtaining recent records, questioning patients and relevant others directly about violent acts and thoughts, and communication of such information to responsible decision-makers. It should also include special handling of difficult cases, consultation from colleagues, and follow-up on lack of compliance with treatment. Documenting the source, content, and date of significant information on risk as well as the content, rationale, and date of actions taken to prevent violence is important. Finally, the development of feasible guidelines for handling risk, subjecting these guidelines to clinical and legal review, educating staff in their use, and auditing their compliance are all encouraged. Tampering with the record or making public statements of responsibility after a violent incident are strongly discouraged, however (Monahan, 1993).

7. *Practice principles promoting health care compliance* (Meichenbaum & Turk, 1987). Develop a contract with CBFT clients before treatment begins. Clients should be provided with clear information regarding the conditions to which they must adhere and the consequences for violating these conditions. Frequent components of such a contract include medication compliance, attendance at scheduled sessions with therapists and case managers, abstinence from alcohol and drug use (and blood or urine screening, if indicated, to monitor compliance), refraining from weapons possession, housing (including where the person will live, applicable rent and how it will be paid, and adherence to housing rules), and the consequence for violating conditions. More specific conditions that can be included as needed include: no contact with the victim, employment, specialized forms of treatment and monitoring, and transportation. Agreement with this contract involves making a public commitment to the CBFT program. The family should be involved if they are available and willing.

DISCUSSION

Considered in its entirety, the discussion in this chapter gives the impression that there are large gaps in the availability of programs and delivery of services. This is probably accurate, although there are undoubtedly some CBFT programs that are neither described in the literature nor known to us through professional contacts. An important next step is a survey to determine whether and to what extent such programs exist, with descriptive and evaluative research to follow. However, to the extent that our discussion does reflect what is presently occurring in CBFT, we can draw several conclusions.

First, it appears that forensic patients treated in jail-based CBFT programs are not categorized by legal status, whereas those treated in non-jail programs are so categorized with greater frequency. In this sense, there is an important difference between jail and non-jail programs. Jail programs, with primary goals of security, management of disruptive behavior, and crisis intervention, have little need to consider legal status to meet these goals. Outpatient programs, by contrast, must depend more upon their relationship with outside agencies (e.g., courts, probation officers, hospitals) to meet their security needs; such outside agencies generally must consider legal status as a part of their jurisdiction over the patient. Nonjail CBFT programs more often tend to treat patients in specific legal categories (especially NGRI), whereas jail programs treat patients with a broader range of legal categories. It would thus appear appropriate that CBFT programs consider legal status explicitly, whereas jail programs do not. This is particularly important for the purpose of ongoing monitoring of forensic patients in the community; explicit consideration of legal status facilitates awareness of and access to the proper reporting authority, which is in turn an important component of CBFT.

The concept of a PSRB must be seriously considered to improve the uniformity and accuracy of decisions regarding the return of forensic patients from the hospital to the community, and their behavior in the community on conditional release. The review board presents a number of potential advantages. Patients under jurisdiction can be plainly identified and records kept centrally. Conditions of release are clearer, particularly if the board has the authority to set these conditions. Communication with treatment facilities should be easier, and follow-up generally more efficient, when done by a board designed for that purpose. Hearings can be scheduled with less difficulty when there is no crowded court docket with which to contend. An immediate response can be obtained when it is needed. Finally, such a board can facilitate research, which in turn can provide specific program direction and broader knowledge that should improve the quality and effectiveness of CBFT services. The PSRB apparently worked well in Oregon with NGRI patients. The jurisdiction of such a board could, with sufficient planning, be expanded to include IST patients under outpatient commitment and offenders with mental disorders on parole or probation.

It is quite clear that forensic patients are a difficult group to treat. (For a further discussion of treatability and treatment goals with forensic patients, see, e.g., Heilbrun et al., 1988; Menzies & Webster, 1988; Quinsey, 1988; Rice & Harris, 1988; Rogers et al., 1988; Rogers & Webster, 1989.) A subgroup of these patients appear to present a number of clinical characteristics of "the young chronic" patient (Bachrach, 1982; Sheets et al., 1982), for whom treatment is rarely a resounding success. Such characteristics may include multiple deficits such as psychosis, antisocial thinking, substance abuse, and skills deficits across a broad range of areas. Clinicians should be prepared to provide interventions in these various areas as needed. It can be very helpful to incorporate third party observations into the ongoing assessment of treatment progress, using the required monitoring as one source of such information. This in turn requires a good working relationship with case managers, probation officers, and other individuals who play an important part in the monitoring process.

Moreover, treatment goals should explicitly incorporate legal as well as clinical standards. For example, the "avoidance of future antisocial behavior that could lead to arrest" should always be considered as a high priority. Treatment interventions can then be made more directly, without the assumption that the ongoing remission of symptoms of mental illness will ensure responsible behavior. There is apparently a strong tendency for the general public (including policymakers and legislators) to equate "further crime" with "treatment failure" when patients have a criminal history. Rather than resist this, it can be useful for clinicians and agencies to provide treatment within a "public safety" model, emphasizing the destructiveness of further criminality for both the individual and the larger community. As part of this "public safety" model, however, it must be recognized that a certain percentage of patients will need to be rehospitalized. Rehospitalization should not be regarded as a failure, but rather as an important further step in a lengthy treatment process. Prompt rehospitalization may also prevent criminal recidivism in some cases, and may indeed indicate that a CBFT program is working well.

Initial selection is also useful; there are simply some patients who present such a poor risk for favorable treatment response or such a high risk for aggression that they should not be accepted into a community-based program. The enhancement of our capacity to assess treatability is greatly needed, and must be accomplished through further research with this population. A related implication is that clinicians must be prepared to acknowledge when treatment in the community is not effective, and advocate rehospitalization or report further criminal behavior under an agreement made between the program and the patient prior to beginning the treatment.

Administrators and policymakers involved with CBFT should be prepared to explicitly balance individual rights, the need for treatment, and public safety. Just as clinicians must be prepared to work within a "public safety" model, so must those who make and administer policy be willing to consider the treatment needs of the individual patients as well as the larger implications for the community. The importance of other recommendations cited previously (Griffin et al., 1991) is underscored here: (1) conditional release should be considered in the context of the full NGRI and community mental health systems, and (2) identify, prioritize, and empirically describe the critical components of a CBFT system, so that unexpected legislative behavior does not eliminate crucial components of the system.

We can clearly and easily conclude that the demand for CBFT far exceeds the supply. What is more difficult to determine is how new CBFT programs will be created. The ingredients of individual initiative and mental health/criminal justice collaboration appear essential. However, a broader view of the context of CBFT must consider the influences of the systems in which the program functions, the operations of the program itself, and the individual needs of staff and patients. From this perspective, it is easy to see why collaboration is essential.

The final conclusion involves the role to be played by research in developing, shaping, and refining CBFT. Much of the research performed in this area is methodologically weak and must be strengthened. University affiliation, one of the forms of collaboration just mentioned, could help to increase the quality and quantity of research performed on CBFT. The utility of good CBFT data, whether used for scholarly research or program evaluation, would be enormous. Legislative, judicial, and public support for CBFT programs are vital. Without such support, a program could very quickly suffer a quick death from a disastrous case, or a gradual fade into funding oblivion because of unmet expectations. Good data can help to educate the needed support groups and set realistic treatment goals. Collecting such data can also provide staff with the occasionally needed diversion from treatment. Finally, publishing such data can provide a form of communication that is also needed by other programs in different stages of development.

ACKNOWLEDGMENTS

A number of individuals gave generously of their time and thoughts to this chapter. We are grateful to Joseph Bloom, Joel Dvoskin, James Cavanaugh, Georg Hoyer, Leif Ojesjo, Norman Poythress, Richard Rogers, Saleem Shah, Stuart Silver, Carolyn Stimel, and Robert Wettstein. We particularly thank Henry J. Steadman for his superb conceptual and technical advice.

REFERENCES

American Psychiatric Association. (1980). *Diagnostic and statistical manual of mental disorders* (3rd ed.). Washington, DC: Author.

Argeriou, M., & Manohar, V. (1977). Treating the problem drinking driver: Some notes on the time required to achieve impact. *British Journal of Addiction, 72,* 331–338.

Bachrach, L. L. (1982). Young adult chronic patients: An analytical review of the literature. *Hospital and Community Psychiatry, 33,* 189–197.

Band, D., Peele, R., Heine, A., Goldfrank, J., Wiant, W., DeVeau, L., & Zanni, G. (1984, October). *Outpatient commitment: A thirteen year experience.* Paper presented at the annual meeting of the American Academy of Psychiatry and Law, Nassau, Bahamas.

Barratt, E. (1994). Impulsiveness and aggression. In J. Monahan & H. Steadman (Eds.), *Violence and mental disorder: Developments in risk assessment* (pp. 61–79). Chicago: University of Chicago Press.

Ben-Arie, O., George, G. C. W., & Hirschowitz, J. (1983). Compulsory treatment of 50 alcoholic drunken drivers: A follow-up study. *South African Medical Journal, 63,* 241–243.

Ben-Arie, O., Swartz, L., & George, G. C. W. (1986). The compulsory treatment of alcoholic drunken drivers referred by the courts: A 7 to 9 years outcome study. *International Journal of Law and Psychiatry, 8,* 229–235.

Bigelow, D. A., Bloom, J. D., & Williams, M. H. (1990). Costs of managing insanity acquittees under a psychiatric security review board system. *Hospital and Community Psychiatry, 41,* 613–614.

Bloom, J. L., & Bloom, J. D. (1981). Disposition of insanity defenses in Oregon. *Bulletin of the American Academy of Psychiatry and the Law, 9,* 93–100.

Bloom, J. D., Rogers, J., & Manson, S. (1982). After Oregon's insanity defense: A comparison of conditional release and hospitalization. *International Journal of Law and Psychiatry, 5,* 391–402.

Bloom, J. D., Rogers, J., Manson, S., & Williams, M. (1986). Lifetime police contacts of discharged Psychiatric Security Review Board clients. *International Journal of Law and Psychiatry, 8,* 189–202.

Bloom, J. D., & Williams, M. H. (1994). *Management and treatment of insanity acquittees.* Washington, DC: American Psychiatric Press.

Bloom, J. D., Williams, M. H., & Bigelow, D. A. (1991). Monitored conditional release of persons found Not Guilty by Reason of Insanity. *American Journal of Psychiatry, 148,* 444–448.

Bloom, J. D., Williams, M., Rogers, J., & Barbur, P. (1986). Evaluation and treatment of insanity acquittees in the community. *Bulletin of the American Academy of Psychiatry and the Law, 14,* 231–244.

Bluegrass, R. (1977). Current developments in forensic psychiatry in the United Kingdom. *Psychiatric Journal of the University of Ottawa, 11,* 53–62.

Bursten, B. (1986). Posthospital mandatory outpatient treatment. *American Journal of Psychiatry, 143,* 1255–1258.

California Department of Mental Health. (1985). *Conditional release program for the judicially committed.d Sacramento, CA: Author.*

Campbell, J. C. (Ed.). (1995). *Assessing dangerousness.* Thousand Oaks, CA: Sage.

Cavanaugh, J., & Wasyliw, O. (1985). Adjustment of the Not Guilty by Reason of Insanity (NGRI) outpatient: An initial report. *Journal of Forensic Sciences, 30,* 24–30.

Cavanaugh, J., Wasyliw, O., & Rogers, R. (1984, October). *The NGRI outpatient: A two-year study.* Paper presented at the annual meeting of the American Academy of Psychiatry and the Law, Nassau, Bahamas.

Cohen, M. I., Spodak, M. K., Silver, S. B., & Williams, K. (1988). Predicting outcome of insanity acquittees released to the community. *Behavioral Sciences and the Law, 6,* 515–530.

Collins, J. J., & Allison, M. (1983). Legal coercion and treatment for drug abuse. *Hospital and Community Psychiatry, 34,* 1145–1149.

Community Systems and Services, Inc. (1985). *Assessment of Florida's forensic mental health services and their supporting law, regulations, policies, and procedures.* McLean, VA: Author.

Craft, M. (1974). A description of a new community forensic psychiatry service for doctors. *Medicine, Science and the Law, 14,* 268–272.

Dennis, D. L., & Monahan, J. (Eds.). (1996). *Coercion and aggressive community treatment.* New York: Plenum.

Dunham, R. G., & Maus, A. L. (1982). Reluctant referrals: The effectiveness of legal coercion in outpatient treatment for problem drinkers. *Journal of Drug Issues, 12,* 5–20.

Dvoskin, J. (1989). The Palm Beach County, Florida, forensic mental health services program: A comprehensive community-based system. In H. J. Steadman, D. W. McCarty, & J. P. Morrissey, *The mentally ill in jail: Planning for essential services* (pp. 178–197). New York: Guilford Press.

Edwards, H., & Coner, A. (1983). Intermediate care program for mentally ill detainees: Development and implementation. *Psychiatric Annals, 13,* 716–722.

Endicott, J., Spitzer, R., Fleiss, J., & Cohen, J. (1976). The global assessment scale. *Archives of General Psychiatry, 33,* 766–771.

Freeman, A. (1978). Planning community treatment for sex offenders. *Community Mental Health Journal, 14,* 147–152.

Gallant, D. M., Faulkner, M., Stoy, B., Bishop, M. P., & Langdon, D. (1967). Enforced clinic treatment of paroled criminal alcoholics. *Quarterly Journal of Studies on Alcohol, 29,* 77–83.

Gardner, W., Hoge, S. K., Bennett, M., Roth, L., Lidz, C. W., Monahan, J., & Mulvey, E. (1993). Two scales for measuring patients' perceptions of coercion during mental hospital admission. *Behavioral Sciences and the Law, 11,* 307–321.

Geller, J. (1986). Rights, wrongs, and the dilemma of coerced community treatment. *American Journal of Psychiatry, 143,* 1259–1264.

Gibbs, J. (1982). On "demons" and "gaols": A summary and review of investigations concerning the psychological problems of jail prisoners. In C. Dunn & H. Steadman (Eds.), *Mental health services in local jails: Report of a special national workshop* (pp. 14–33). Rockville, MD: National Institute of Mental Health.

Goldmeier, J., Sauer, R., & White, E. (1977). A halfway house for mentally ill offenders. *American Journal of Psychiatry, 34,* 45–49.

Goldmeier, J., White, E. V., Ulrich, C., & Klein, G. A. (1980). Community intervention with the mentally ill offender: A residential program. *Bulletin of the American Academy of Psychiatry and the Law, 8,* 72–81.

Griffin, P. A., Steadman, H. J., & Heilbrun, K. (1991). Designing conditional release systems for insanity acquittees. *Journal of Mental Health Administration, 18,* 231–241.

Gunn, J. (1971). Forensic psychiatry and psychopathic patients. *British Journal of Hospital Medicine, 6,* 260–264.

Gunn, J. (1979). The law and the mentally abnormal offender in England and Wales. *International Journal of Law and Psychiatry, 2,* 199–214.

Hafemeister, T. L. (1991). Goals to guide the interactions of the mental health and justice systems. *Journal of Mental Health Administration, 18,* 178–197.

Harford, R. J., Ungerer, M. A., & Kinsella, J. K. (1976). Effects of legal pressure on prognosis for treatment of drug dependence. *American Journal of Psychiatry, 133,* 1399–1404.

Harris, G. A., & Watkins, D. (1987). *Counseling the involuntary and resistant client.* Laurel, MD: American Correctional Association.

Hart, S., Hare, R., & Forth, A. (1994). Psychopathy as a risk marker for violence: Development and validation of a screening version of the Revised Psychopathy Checklist. In J. Monahan & H. Steadman (Eds.), *Violence and mental disorder: Developments in risk assessment* (pp. 81–98). Chicago: University of Chicago Press.

Heilbrun, K. (1988, March). *Third party information in forensic assessment: Much needed, sometimes collected, poorly guided.* Paper presented at the mid-winter meeting of the American Psychology–Law Society/Division 41, Miami, FL.

Heilbrun, K., Bennett, S., Evans, J., Offutt, R., Reiff, H., & White, A. (1988). Assessing treatability in mentally disordered offenders: A conceptual and methodological note. *Behavioral Sciences and the Law, 6,* 479–486.

Heilbrun, K., & Griffin, P. (1993). Community-based forensic treatment of insanity acquittees. *International Journal of Law and Psychiatry, 16,* 133–150.

Heilbrun, K., Rosenfeld, B., Warren, J., & Collins, S. (1994). The use of third party information in forensic assessments. *Bulletin of the American Academy of Psychiatry and the Law, 22,* 399–406.

Hoge, S. K., Lidz, C., Mulvey, E., Roth, L., Bennett, N., Siminoff, A., Arnold, R., & Monahan, J. (1993). Patient, family, and staff perceptions of coercion in mental hospital admission: An exploratory study. *Behavioral Sciences and the Law, 11,* 281–293.

Johnson, J., Mckeown, K., & James, R. (Eds.). (1984). *Removing the chronically mentally ill from jail: Case studies of collaboration between local criminal justice and mental health systems.* Washington, DC: National Coalition for Jail Reform.

Kerr, C., & Roth, J. (1986). Populations, practices, and problems in forensic psychiatric facilities. *Annals of the American Academy of Political and Social Science, 484,* 127–143.

Kloss, J. (1978). The impact of comprehensive community treatment: An assessment of the Complex Offender Project. *Offender Rehabilitation, 3,* 81–108.

Kofoed, L., Kania, J., Walsh, T., & Atkinson, R. M. (1986). Outpatient treatment of patients with substance abuse and coexisting disorders. *American Journal of Psychiatry, 143,* 867–872.

Kunjukrishnan, R., & Bradford, J. M. (1985). Interface between the criminal justice system and the mental health system in Canada. *Psychiatric Journal of the University of Ottawa, 10,* 24–33.

Laben, J., & Spencer, L. (1976). Decentralization of forensic services. *Community Mental Health Journal, 12,* 405–414.

Lamb, H. (1976). *Community survival for long term patients.* San Francisco: Jossey-Bass.

Lamb, R., & Goertzel, V. (1974). Ellsworth House: A community alternative to jail. *American Journal of Psychiatry, 131,* 64–68.

Lamb, H., Weinberger, L., & Gross, B. (1988a). Court-mandated community outpatient treatment for persons found Not Guilty by Reason of Insanity: A five-year follow-up. *American Journal of Psychiatry, 145,* 450–456.

Lamb, H., Weinberger, L., & Gross, B. (1988b). Court-mandated outpatient treatment for insanity acquittees: Clinical philosophy and implementation. *Hospital and Community Psychiatry, 39,* 1080–1084.

Lidz, C. W., & Hoge, S. K. (1993). Introduction to coercion in mental health care. *Behavioral Sciences and the Law, 11,* 237-238.

Lidz, C. W., Mulvey, E., Arnold, R., Bennett, N., & Kirsch, B. (1993). Coercive interactions in a psychiatric emergency room. *Behavioral Sciences and the Law, 11,* 269–280.

Lidz, C. W., Mulvey, E. P., Hoge, S. K., Kirsch, B. L., Monahan, J., Bennett, N. S., Eisenberg, M., Gardner, W., & Roth, L. H. (1997). The validity of mental patients' accounts of coercion-related behaviors in the hospital admission process. *Law and Human Behavior, 21,* 361–376.

Link, B., & Stueve, A. (1994). Psychotic symptoms and the violent/illegal behavior of mental patients compared to community controls. In J. Monahan & H. Steadman (Eds.), *Violence and mental disorder: Developments in risk assessment* (pp. 137–159). Chicago: University of Chicago Press.

McGrath, J., O'Brien, J., & Liftik, J. (1977). Coercive treatment for alcoholic "Driving under the influence of liquor" offenders. *British Journal of Addiction, 72,* 223–229.

McGreevy, M. A., Steadman, H. J., Dvoskin, J. A., & Dollard, N. (1991). New York State's system of managing insanity acquittees in the community. *Hospital and Community Psychiatry, 42,* 512–517.

Meichenbaum, D., & Turk, D. (1987). *Facilitating treatment adherence: A practitioner's guidebook.* New York: Plenum Press.

Meloy, J. R., Haroun, A., & Schiller, E. F. (1990). *Clinical guidelines for involuntary outpatient commitment.* Sarasota, FL: Professional Resource Exchange.

Melton, G., Petrila, J., Poythress, N. G., & Slobogin, C. (1997). *Psychological evaluations for the courts: A handbook for mental health professionals and lawyers* (2nd ed.). New York: Guilford Press.

Melton, G., Weithorn, L., & Slobogin, C. (1985). *Community mental health centers and the courts: An evaluation of community-based forensic services.* Lincoln: University of Nebraska Press.

Menzies, R. J., & Webster, C. D. (1988). Fixing forensic patients: Psychiatric recommendations for treatment in pretrial settings. *Behavioral Sciences and the Law, 6,* 453–478.

Miller, R., & Fiddleman, P. (1984). Outpatient commitment: Treatment in the least restrictive environment? *Hospital and Community Psychiatry, 35,* 147–151.

Monahan, J. (1981). *Predicting violent behavior: An assessment of clinical techniques.* Beverly Hills, CA: Sage.

Monahan, J. (1992). Mental disorder and violent behavior: Attitudes and evidence. *American Psychologist, 47,* 511–521.

Monahan, J. (1993). Limiting therapist exposure to Tarasoff liability: Guidelines for risk containment. *American Psychologist, 48,* 242–250.

Monahan, J. (1996). Violence prediction: The past twenty and the next twenty years. *Criminal Justice and Behavior, 23,* 107–120.

Monahan, J., & Steadman, H. (Eds.). (1994). *Violence and mental disorder: Developments in risk assessment.* Chicago: University of Chicago Press.

Monahan, J., & Walker, L. (1994). *Social science in law: Cases and materials* (3rd ed.). Westbury, NY: Foundation Press.

Mulvey, E., Geller, J., & Roth, L. (1987). The promise and peril of involuntary outpatient commitment. *American Psychologist, 42,* 571–584.

Norwood, S., Nicholson, R. A., Enyart, C., & Hickey, M. L. (1992). Insanity acquittal in Oklahoma: Recommendations for program planning and social policy. *Forensic Reports, 5,* 5–28.

Novaco, R. (1994). Anger as a risk factor for violence among the mentally disordered. In J. Monahan & H. Steadman (Eds.), *Violence and mental disorder: Developments in risk assessment* (pp. 21–59). Chicago: University of Chicago Press.

Ojesjo, L. (1981). Developing forensic psychiatry services for the 80s: The Linkoping experiment. *International Journal of Law and Psychiatry, 4,* 213–218.

Petrila, J. (1982). The insanity defense and other mental health dispositions in Missouri. *International Journal of Law and Psychiatry, 5,* 81–101.

Petrila, J. P., & Sadoff, R.L. (1992). Confidentiality and the family as caregiver. *Hospital and Community Psychiatry, 43,* 136–139.

Quinsey, V. L. (1988). Assessments of the treatability of forensic patients. *Behavioral Sciences and the Law, 6,* 443–452.

Quinsey, V. L., & Maguire, A. (1983). Offenders remanded for a psychiatric examination: Perceived treatability and disposition. *International Journal of Law and Psychiatry, 6,* 193–205.

Reid, W. H., & Solomon, G. F. (1981). Community-based offender programs. In W. H. Reid (Ed.), *The treatment of antisocial syndromes* (pp. 76–94). New York: Van Nostrand Reinhold.

Rice, M. E., & Harris, G. T. (1988). An empirical approach to the classification and treatment of maximum security psychiatric patients. *Behavioral Sciences and the Law, 6,* 497–514.

Rogers, J., & Bloom, J. D. (1982). Characteristics of persons committed to Oregon's Psychiatric Security Review Board. *Bulletin of the American Academy of Psychiatry and the Law, 10,* 155–164.

Rogers, J., & Bloom, J. D. (1985). The insanity sentence: Oregon's Psychiatric Security Review Board. *Behavioral Sciences and the Law, 3,* 69–84.

Rogers, J., Bloom, J. D., & Manson, S. (1984). Oregon's new insanity defense system: A review of the first five years, 1978 to 1982. *Bulletin of the American Academy of Psychiatry and the Law, 12,* 383–402.

Rogers, J., Bloom, J. D., & Manson, S. (1986). Oregon's Psychiatric Security Review Board: A comprehensive system for managing insanity acquittees. *Annals of the American Academy of Political and Social Science, 484,* 86–99.

Rogers, R., & Cavanaugh, J. (1981). A treatment program for potentially violent offender patients. *International Journal of Offender Therapy and Comparative Criminology, 25,* 53–59.

Rogers, R., Gillis, J. R., Dickens, S. E., & Webster, C. D. (1988). Treatment recommendations for mentally disordered offenders: More than roulette? *Behavioral Sciences and the Law, 6,* 487–496.

Rogers, R., Harris, M., & Wasyliw, O. (1983). Observed and self-reported psychopathology in NGRI acquittees in court-mandated outpatient treatment. *International Journal of Offender Therapy and Comparative Criminology, 27,* 143–149.

Rogers, R., & Webster, C. (1989). Assessing treatability in mentally disordered offenders. *Law and Human Behavior, 13,* 19–29.

Rogers, R., & Wettstein, R. (1984). Relapse of NGRI outpatients: An empirical study.

International Journal of Offender Therapy and Comparative Criminology, 28, 227–235.

Rosenberg, C. M., & Liftik, J. (1976). Use of coercion in the outpatient treatment of alcoholism. *Journal of Studies on Alcohol, 37,* 58–65.

Salmon, R. W. (1982). The role of coercion in rehabilitation of drug abusers. *Journal of Offender Counseling, Services, and Rehabilitation, 6,* 59–70.

Schottenfeld, R. S. (1989). Involuntary treatment of substance abuse disorders: Impediments to success. *Psychiatry, 52,* 164–176.

Schutte, N. S., Malouff, J. M., Lucore, P., & Shern, D. (1988). Incompetency and insanity: Feasibility of community evaluation and treatment. *Community Mental Health Journal, 24,* 156–163.

Scott, D., Zonana, H., & Getz, M. (1990). Monitoring insanity acquittees: Connecticut's Psychiatric Security Review Board. *Hospital and Community Psychiatry, 41,* 980–984.

Sheets, J., Prevost, J., & Reihman, J. (1982). Young adult chronic patients: Three hypothesized subgroups. *Hospital and Community Psychiatry, 33,* 197–203.

Silver, S. B. (1983). *Treatment and aftercare of insanity acquittees in Maryland.* Testimony before the Subcommittee on Criminal Law of the Committee on the Judiciary, United States Senate (Serial No. J-97-122, pp. 374–383). Washington, DC: U.S. Government Printing Office.

Silver, S. B., & Tellefsen, C. (1991). Administrative issues in the follow-up treatment of insanity acquittees. *Journal of Mental Health Administration, 18,* 242–252.

Silver, S. B., Cohen, M., & Spodak, M. (1989). Follow-up after release of insanity acquittees, mentally disordered offenders, and convicted felons. *Bulletin of the American Academy of Psychiatry and the Law, 17,* 387–400.

Simpson, D. D. (1984). National treatment system evaluation based on the Drug Abuse Reporting Program (DARP) followup research. In *Drug abuse treatment evaluation: Strategies, progress, and prospects* (National Institute on Drug Abuse Research Monograph No. 51, pp. 29–41). Rockville, MD: National Institute on Drug Abuse.

Spodak, M., Silver, S.B., & Wright, C. (1984). Criminality of discharged insanity acquittees: Fifteen year experience in Maryland reviewed. *Bulletin of the American Academy of Psychiatry and the Law, 12,* 373–382.

Steadman, H., Monahan, J., Hartstone, E., Davis, S., & Robbins, C. (1982). Mentally disordered offenders: A national survey of patients and facilities. *Law and Human Behavior, 6,* 31–38.

Steer, R. A. (1983). Retention in drug-free counseling. *International Journal of the Addictions, 18,* 1109–1114.

Swanson, J., Holzer, C., Ganju, V., & Jono, R. (1990). Violence and psychiatric disorder in the community: Evidence from the Epidemiologic Catchment Area Surveys. *Hospital and Community Psychiatry, 41,* 761–770.

Swartz, M. S., Burns, B. J., Hiday, V. A., George, L. K., Swanson, J., & Wagner, H. R. (1995). New directions in research on involuntary outpatient commitment. *Hospital and Community Psychiatry, 46,* 381–385.

Tarasoff v. Regents of University of California, 551 P.2d 334 (Cal. 1976).

Tyce, F. A., Olson, R. O., & Amdahl, R. (1980). Probationed offenders: Rehabilitation and training. In J. Masserman (Ed.), *Current psychiatric therapies* (pp. 151–157). New York: Grune & Stratton.

Ward, D. A. (1979). The use of legal coercion in the treatment of alcoholism: A methodological review. *Journal of Drug Issues, 9,* 387–398.

Weiner, B. J. (1985). Legal issues raised in treating sex offenders. *Behavioral Sciences and the Law, 3,* 325–340.

Wexler, D. B. (1990). Inducing therapeutic compliance through the criminal law. *Law and Psychology Review, 44,* 43–57.

Wexler, D. B. (1991). Health care compliance principles and the insanity acquittee conditional release process. *Criminal Law Bulletin, 27,* 18–41.

Wexler, D. B., & Winick, B. (Eds.). (1996). *Law in a therapeutic key: Developments in therapeutic jurisprudence.* Durham, NC: Carolina Academic Press.

Wiederanders, M. (1991). Recidivism of disordered offenders who were conditionally vs. unconditionally released. *Behavioral Sciences and the Law, 10,* 141–148.

Wiederanders, M., & Choate, P. (1994). Beyond recidivism: Measuring community adjustments of conditionally released insanity acquitters. *Psychological Assessment, 6,* 61–66.

5

TREATMENT IN JAILS AND PRISONS

Jeffrey L. Metzner
Fred Cohen
Linda S. Grossman
Robert M. Wettstein

INTRODUCTION

The correctional population of the United States increased more than two and one-half times from 1980 through 1993. During 1993, approximately 2.6% of the U.S. population, 4.9 million adults, were on parole, probation, or in jails, which represented an increase of 3 million people since 1980 (U.S. Department of Justice, 1995a). The increased number of persons incarcerated in jails or prisons appears to be predominantly related to increased return of conditional release violators, stricter laws concerning drug offenses, and an increased probability of incarceration following arrest (Gilliard & Beck, 1994). Not surprisingly, studies and clinical experience indicate that 8–19% of prisoners have significant psychiatric or functional disabilities and another 15–20% will require some form of psychiatric intervention during their incarceration (Metzner, 1993).

Correctional systems have experienced significant difficulties in identifying and providing treatment to prisoners with mental illnesses. Efforts to establish adequate mental health systems in prisons were accelerated during the 1970s as a result of successful class action lawsuits. At least one part of the prison system in 21 states included a certified class action suit involving the issue of providing adequate mental health services for inmates during 1988 (Metzner, Fryer, & Usery, 1990).

In this chapter we provide a discussion concerning the legal basis for mandated mental health care, review relevant national guidelines and standards for providing such services, and discuss essential characteristics of a mental health system designed to meet constitutional standards. Special populations that include the developmentally disabled and sex offenders are beyond the scope of this chapter. We briefly review issues pertinent to special needs of women within correctional facilities and prisoners with substance abuse problems. Finally, we present a discussion regarding the role of the mental health professional in providing consultation and training to correctional facilities.

This chapter will describe the general principles applicable to mental health systems within jails and prisons with the recognition that appropriate judgment and flexibility should be exercised in applying these principles to a specific correctional setting. We attempt to summarize, when pertinent, differences between jail and prison mental health systems. We generally describe the incarcerated person within a jail or prison within this chapter as an "inmate," although such a person within a jail setting is generally referred to as a "pretrial detainee" unless the person has been convicted and sentenced.

JAIL AND PRISON DEMOGRAPHICS

Local jails, facilities administered by city or county officials, hold inmates beyond arraignment, generally for more than 48 hours but less than a year. Local jails held an estimated 492,442 adults, or about 1 in every 398 adult U.S. residents, on June 30, 1994. The total U.S. jail census during June, 1994, represented a 119% increase compared with 1983. Since 1983, the inmate population in local jails has nearly doubled on a per capita basis, from 96 to 188 per 100,000 residents (Perkins, Stephan, & Beck, 1995).

Male inmates made up 90% of the local jail inmate population in June, 1994. The majority of the local jail inmates were black or Hispanic: White non-Hispanics made up 39% of the jail population; black non-Hispanics, 44%; Hispanics, 15%; and other races, 2%. The largest source of growth among inmates in local jails between 1983 and 1989 was drug law violators (28,800 to 91,000). In 1993, the average cost of keeping one jail inmate incarcerated for a year was $14,667 (Perkins et al., 1995).

Prisons are correctional facilities in which persons convicted of major crimes or felonies serve their sentences, which are usually in excess of 1 year. In 1991, 34% of sentenced U.S. inmates had a prison term of over 10 years but less than life. Six percent of U.S. inmates had a life sentence or were sentenced to death (Lynch, Smith, Graziadei, & Pittayathikhun, 1994). Six states (Alaska, Connecticut, Delaware, Hawaii, Rhode Island, and Vermont) and one commonwealth (Puerto Rico) have combined jail and prison systems.

The total number of prisoners under the jurisdiction of federal or state correctional authorities was 1,053,738 at the end of 1994. This represented a 141% increase as compared with the 1983 U.S. prison census (Beck & Gilliard, 1995). The rate of incarceration in state and federal prisons more than doubled between 1980 and 1994, from 139 to 387 sentenced inmates per 100,000 U.S. residents (Beck et al., 1993). The rate of incarceration in state and federal prisons was 4,094 per 100,000 black male adults in the U.S. population compared with 502 per 100,000 white male adults (Snell, 1995). The percentage of Hispanic prison inmates from 1980 to 1993 nearly doubled (7.7% to 14.3%) and the percentage of black inmates increased from 46.5% to 50.8% (Beck et al., 1993). The number of female inmates in state and federal prisons increased by 274% during the years between 1983 and 1994. Females accounted for 6% of all sentenced prisoners during 1994 (Beck et al., 1993; Snell, 1995).

The growth in the number of state inmates was greatest among violent offenders, which increased by 221,200 between 1980 and 1993. One third of the increase in the state prison populations since 1980 was attributed to the increasing numbers of sentenced drug offenders (from 19,000 in 1980 to 172,300 in 1992). Sixty percent of all sentenced inmates in the federal prison system were drug offenders during 1992. More probation and parole violators also entered prison during 1992 as compared with 1980 (Beck et al., 1993; Snell, 1995). The average cost of keeping a state prison inmate incarcerated for a year during 1990 was $15,604 (Stephan, 1990), although many consider that a low estimate. For example, the average cost of incarcerating an offender in Pennsylvania was nearly $22,000 per year during 1995 (DeWitt, 1995).

LEGAL BASIS FOR MANDATED MENTAL HEALTH CARE

The federal constitutional obligation to provide mental health care under certain conditions results from a combination of judicial interpretation of the Eighth Amendment, the Due Process Clause of the Fourteenth Amendment, and the substantive due process boundary setting which is now known as the *DeShaney* principle (*DeShaney v. Winnebago County Department of Social Services,* 1989).

The Eighth Amendment prohibits cruel and unusual punishment, and, in the landmark decision of *Estelle v. Gamble* (1976), the Supreme Court found this amendment sufficiently elastic to encompass certain claims to medical care by state prisoners. The limiting conditions of *Estelle*—that the medical condition be serious and that responsible state officials are deliberately indifferent to it—have spawned volumes of interpretative decisions. The essence of *Estelle,* however, remains classically simple and easy to grasp.

Once government deprives a person of liberty, that person is unable to obtain the basic needs for human survival without help from his/her captors. Those needs include food, shelter, clothing, and medical care. Without access to medical care, the courts hold, a person in captivity will suffer needlessly and in some cases die when death was preventable.

Estelle itself dealt with a Texas prisoner's claim of inadequate medical care for a back injury everyone agreed he sustained. Indeed, it was not argued that the injury was minor; rather, the argument was over the level of care provided. In answer to this claim for damages, the Court held that responsible officials must be *deliberately indifferent* to the *serious* medical needs of inmates before Eighth Amendment liability might apply. This was the first time the Supreme Court ever used this term to describe a culpable mental state, and not until 1994 did the Court attempt to provide a definition (Cohen, 1993).

Persons who are convicted of crimes and held in captivity trace their health-related claims to the Eighth Amendment, whereas those who are in captivity awaiting trial (i.e., pretrial detainees) trace their similar claims to the Due Process Clause of the Fourteenth Amendment. In *Bell v. Wolfish* (1979), the U.S. Supreme Court held that whereas prison inmates could not be subjected to cruel and unusual punishment, persons awaiting trial could not be punished at all. Government gains the right to inflict punishment only after a valid conviction. Parenthetically, having ruled in this fashion, it is clear that the Court did not equate penal confinement per se with impermissible punishment.

Bell v. Wolfish ultimately stands for the proposition that the denial of health care to pretrial detainees may result in the infliction of needless suffering or death, and the due process clause mandates appropriate medical or mental health intervention incident to the captivity. Whereas the constitutional source varies between inmates and detainees, case law research discloses that the courts deal virtually identically with both claims.

An occasional decision draws a distinction, and when that is done, it is to decide that an action or inaction relating to a detainee is punishment unless it reasonably relates to a legitimate government objective (*Grabowski v. Jackson Co. Public Defenders Office et al.,* 1995). This test, one of reasonableness, presumably creates a somewhat greater duty of care on health care providers toward detainees than the rather easily met test of deliberate indifference. This, however, is very much a minority view.

The status of pretrial detainee and convicted prisoner are not the only relevant legal statuses inmates may occupy within the criminal justice process. A person is likely to be an arrestee before becoming a detainee. In some jurisdictions a person, typically one who is publicly intoxicated and incapacitated as a result, may be held in protective custody at a police station or jail (see, e.g., *Ringuette v. City of Fall River,* 1995). Whether there are subtle differences in the duty of care owed such inmates will not be addressed here; what is of interest is the fact that all of these inmates are within the confines of the *DeShaney* principle.

In *DeShaney v. Winnebago County Department of Social Services* (1989), the U.S. Supreme Court was confronted with a claim for damages brought by the mother of a brain-damaged child who had been repeatedly beaten by his father. The essence of the legal claim was that the social services agency being sued knew of the child's plight and did nothing effective to intervene and protect the child. Whereas this claim is based on the asserted constitutional obligation of government to protect its citizens, the consequences of the holding reach directly into the parallel claim of government's obligation to provide health care.

A federal court nicely summarized *DeShaney* recently, stating, "DeShaney signaled that a state has a duty to provide necessary services to, and to protect from injury, certain classes of persons in custody, on the broad rationale that such persons—once they enter into a 'special relationship' with the state—are rendered incapable of providing for and protecting themselves" (*Ringuette v. City of Fall River,* 1995, p. 267).

The *Ringuette* decision applied this logic to a person held by the police in civil protective custody because of his substance abuse-related incapacitation. The plaintiff suffered permanent loss of the use of his left arm and leg resulting from compartmental syndrome caused by being allowed to lie in the same position for a sustained period. A person held involuntarily, albeit in protective custody, as in *Ringuette* is entitled to the same affirmative care as an arrestee, a detainee, or a convicted prisoner. On the other hand, persons not in involuntary confinement are owed no duty of protection or access to health care services.

Thus, the *DeShaney* principle must be linked with *Estelle* to create, first, the boundaries of mandated care and, second, the dimensions of that care. Whereas *DeShaney* is, indeed, a duty-to-protect case and *Estelle* is a physical injury/medical care case, there is no doubt that precisely the same principles apply to inmates with serious mental disorders (see *Bowring v. Godwin,* 1977).

Correctional health care is firmly planted in constitutional obligation and in some sense is an aspect of the more expansive claims of a judicially enforceable "right to treatment." Such claims are made, for example, by the civilly confined mentally ill and retarded, substance abusers, and juveniles. The claims of detainees and prisoners are, however, distinguishable from the civilly committed but do bear a certain relationship to those raised by juveniles.

A detainee or prisoner has not been confined because of a mental condition, a disability, or some prediction of dangerousness. They are confined because of a criminal charge or conviction. Thus, the health care owed them is an incident, and not the basis, of their captivity. When mandated care either is absent, improper, or inadequate, the remedy is not release. It is money damages or some form of systemic, future-oriented relief fashioned from a consent decree or other form of judgment issue by a court. A civilly committed person, on the other hand, may argue to "treat me or release me!" That is, the basis for this confinement is a need for care and, it is argued, when that care is absent the very basis for the confinement is eroded (see, e.g., *Youngberg v. Romeo,* 1982; Hafemeister & Petrilla, 1994).

In addition to the differences in remedy there are differences in the way courts approach questions regarding the level or quality of care afforded the penal inmate and the civil inmate. In *Youngberg v. Romeo,* among other things, the U.S. Supreme Court held that the affirmative right to care owed the institutionalized and severely retarded Nicholas Romeo was to be evaluated by the professional judgment standard.

That is, a decision by a professional "is presumptively valid unless it is such a substantial departure from professional judgment, practice, or standards as to demonstrate that the person responsible actually did not base the decision on such a judgment" (*Youngberg v. Romeo,* 1982). The question for us is whether this standard is the one to apply to health care in the prison and jail setting.

As Stefan (1992) pointed out, although the professional judgment standard seems particularly inappropriate in the penal captivity setting, it has been used on occasion. She argued that the relationship between a prison or jail employee and a prisoner or pretrial detainee bears no resemblance to a professional–client relationship. In effect, when the highly deferential professional judgment standard of review is used, Stefan argued that this is simply a code for the courts' unwillingness to intervene.

Although this issue could be explored in greater depth, it is important to contrast the professional judgment standard with the deliberate indifference standard—or mental element—which *Estelle* held is specifically applicable to prison health care services. As will be developed, the professional judgment standard should not be merged with deliberate indifference because to do so is, in effect, to state that there can be no deliberate indifference, if professional judgment was exercised. Professional judgment is more at home on the questions of whether or not an inmate's complaint relates to a disease and, if so, whether or not it is serious.

Deliberate Indifference

Once it is determined that a penal inmate suffers with a serious physical or mental problem, then there is no liability for the absence or poor quality of care unless the system and its functionaries are guilty of deliberate indifference. As indicated earlier, *Estelle* is the first decision in the history of the Supreme Court to use this term, and the Court did not bother to define it.

Estelle did, however, labor to explain what deliberate indifference was not: "An inadvertent failure to provide adequate medical care cannot be said to constitute 'an unnecessary and wanton infliction of pain' or to be 'repugnant to the conscience of mankind.' Thus, a complaint that a physician has been negligent in diagnosing or treating a medical condition does not state a valid claim of medical mistreatment under the Eighth Amendment. Medical malpractice does not become a constitutional violation merely because the victim is a prisoner" (*Estelle v. Gamble*).

Obviously, the *Estelle* disclaimer-type approach does not provide a very clear idea of what affirmatively establishes deliberate indifference. On the other hand, it does clarify that it is a more culpable state than malpractice (or negligence) and that the gratuitous infliction or prolongation of pain is a central concept. *Estelle* has spawned countless decisions struggling to define and apply the concept.

Farmer v. Brennan (1994) dealt with a transsexual federal prisoner who alleged that he was raped while in confinement and that prison officials violated his Eighth Amendment right to personal security by being deliberately indifferent to the risks associated with this inmate's rather obvious condition. Justice Souter, writing for the Court, reaffirmed that prison officials have a clear duty to protect prisoners from violence at the hands of other prisoners and that the challenged act or omission is to be governed by the deliberate indifference standard first born in the area of health care obligation (*Farmer v. Brennan*). *Deliberate indifference* was described by Justice Souter as a mental state positioned somewhere between negligence at one end and purpose or intent at the other. The mental state between these two extremes is recklessness; that is, a high degree of risk creation followed by conduct that seemingly ignores the risk (*Farmer v. Brennan*).

Having settled on recklessness as the closest analogue to deliberate indifference, the Court still had to choose between a "mild" or "hot" version of recklessness. The essential difference between these two extremes is the extent to which a corrections official must actually know and disregard a risk or whether recklessness might be based on a more objective standard that, in turn, places a certain duty of inquiry on the official. The Court adopted a subjective or "actually knew" approach to recklessness.

The *Farmer* definition of deliberate indifference does apply to medical and mental health cases. Perhaps more importantly, what difference might this test make for inmate claims to unconstitutional mental health care? Minimally, the rhetoric will change somewhat, and within the federal judicial system the courts should now be at least more consistent in their terminology.

Whereas *Farmer* rather plainly states that corrections officials have no particular duty of inquiry, it also states that knowledge of a risk is to be determined from the facts, including inferences to be drawn from circumstantial evidence. Thus, in a *Farmer* situation officials knew they had in their custody, in a male prison, a full-breasted, rouged, off-the-shoulder-dressed inmate. It is clear that even a remotely competent corrections official should infer that such an inmate would face an obvious risk of sexual attack or exploitation under such circumstances.

Thus, there need not always, or even regularly, be actual knowledge that an inmate falls into the general class of those with mental disorders, to say nothing of those with serious disorders. However, it is unclear whether general knowledge that perhaps 10% of incoming male inmates may have serious mental disorders places a duty of inquiry on prison officials. This uncertainty also raises issues regarding whether mental health screening is legally required for newly admitted inmates under *Farmer.*

For example, the case law on custodial suicide before *Farmer* was very difficult from the claimants' perspective. Whereas state laws may often be more relaxed, requiring only a negligence standard for liability, "without some actual or potential knowledge of an individual's potential for committing suicide, custodians simply have no [constitutional] liability. . . . The distressing aspect of modern case law is the premium it appears to place on ignorance; a premium that is antitherapeutic and may be life threatening" (Cohen, 1992, pp. 1, 9).

Therefore, to the extent that legal decisions regarding mental health care decisions might begin to parallel the custodial suicide cases, this could be viewed as a loosening of the obligation to provide care. This result is by no means certain and it is too early to know if *Farmer* will contribute to such a result.

As will be described later, intake screening as a means of detecting mental disorder among incoming inmates is viewed generally as one of the most basic aspects of a constitutionally acceptable mental health system (Cohen, 1988). *Farmer* does allow room for an argument that intake screening is not a constitutional requirement and deliberate indifference exists only when, for example, the acting out, aggressive type of inmate with a mental disorder presents him/herself; or when a medical/mental record accompanies the inmate, making it clear that there is a relevant history that cannot now be ignored.

Such an argument can, and undoubtedly will, be made but if it prevails it would be the worst of pyrrhic victories. Calculated ignorance in the face of an opportunity to avoid the violence, deterioration, institutional tension, and use of force often associated with inmates with mental disorders is a self-destructive, inhumane, and ultimately costly policy. It is the worst policy for staff and antitherapeutic in the most basic sense for inmates. Early detection and intervention is clearly the most therapeutic approach and no prison or jail system should view *Farmer* as an invitation to moderate or eliminate intake screening for mental health problems and to simply do classification for security purposes.

Serious Mental Illness

Unless a physical or mental disorder or need is serious, no constitutional liability attaches. In other words, deliberate indifference is not triggered unless a claimant first crosses the threshold of seriousness.

One Federal Court of Appeals recently described "serious medical need" as follows:

> A "serious medical need" exists if the failure to treat a prisoner's condition could result in further significant injury or the 'unnecessary and wanton infliction of pain'. . . . Either result is not the type of "routine discomfort [that] is 'part of the penalty that criminal offenders pay for their offenses against society.' " . . . The existence of an injury that a doctor or patient would find important and worthy of comment or treatment; the presence of a medical condition that significantly affects an individual's daily activities; or the existence of chronic and substantial pain are examples of indications that a prisoner has a "serious" need for medical treatment (*McGuckin v. Smith,* 1992).

This description of "serious" by the Ninth Circuit Court of Appeals, although flawed, is more detailed and more useful than the more standard approach taken by federal courts using the "obviousness" test. That test provides that a "medical need is serious if it is one that has been diagnosed by a physician as mandating treatment, or one that is so obvious that even a lay person would easily recognize the necessity for a doctor's attention. . . . The 'seriousness' of an inmate's needs may also be determined by reference to the effect of the delay of treatment" (*Gaudreault v. Municipality of Salem, Mass.,* 1990).

The "obviousness" test is seriously flawed in several respects. First, doctors frequently diagnose minor ailments as calling for minimal care. Thus, medical involvement by itself is not determinative of seriousness. Second, in the exercise of professional judgment clinicians may disagree and a correctional decisionmaker is entitled to select from among such differing opinions. Third, the "obviousness" test does not mention pain and avoidable, gratuitous suffering as a key ingredient of the *Estelle v. Gamble* (1976) Eighth Amendment formulation. Fourth, the obvious-to-a-layman factor has not become more clear by virtue of its repetition. A broken bone protruding through the skin is one type of obviousness, but serious mental illness is quite another matter. Disruptive or violent conduct may be a manifestation of illness or orneriness. Quiet, seemingly introspective behavior may be just that or it may be evidence of decompensation. Depressions may be mild or basically disabling.

In arriving at a judgment of "seriousness" or determining even whether there is a mental disorder, the possibility of secondary gain in the jail and prison setting often colors the perceptions and reactions of mental health professionals as well as security staff. Inmates may seek hospitalization due to the perception of "easy time" or to establish mental illness as a predicate for an incompetence finding or an insanity defense (obviously more critical in jail), or to be locked down and avoid something bothersome or threatening in the general jail or prison population. Thus, the appearance of objectivity by a clinician may mask a basic distrust for the inmate.

There simply is no definitional clarity on what is a serious disorder for the purposes of mandated medical or mental health care. What pose as definitions tend to be descriptions. Whether an illness is serious will likely be the subject of a battle of expert witnesses. And it is here that the *Youngberg*-created principle of professional judgment likely will hold sway. Thus, the judgment of a mental health professional as to the existence of disease or seriousness usually may be relied on by prison officials. Where there exists more than one such professional judgment, the prison official who elects one over the other is hardly likely to display deliberate indifference.

At times, the seriousness battle may actually be a battle over whether or not there is a recognizable mental disorder or disease. There are conflicting views on whether certain dysfunctional states qualify as mental disorders. This is so, for example, with regard to whether a dysthymic disorder or transsexualism are mental disorders (*Farmer v. Carlson*, 1988). Only if the condition is accepted as a mental disorder does the seriousness question arise, and thereafter the battle is waged over the modalities of treatment.

Alcoholism, drug addiction (see, e.g., *Pace v. Fauver,* 1979; *Norris v. Frame,* 1978) and sexual psychopathy (Group for the Advancement of Psychiatry, 1977) are not *by themselves* viewed as medical or psychiatric disorders for the purpose of constitutionally mandated treatment. Obviously, these conditions may be attended to by medical personnel just as they may be addressed by educators or moralists.

However, an inmate who suffers a medical crisis such as delirium tremens must be given proper medical care for such painful and possibly life-threatening consequences of the addiction or dependence. It is the underlying condition itself that the courts rather consistently hold is not a disease for these purposes.

At another level of analysis, there are a host of syndromes ranging from compulsive gambling to battered spouse syndrome that have been raised as a defense to various crimes. Putting aside the obvious confusion between an effort to explain the cause of an offense and the appropriateness of a defense, these and similar syndromes will not satisfy the disease component of Eighth Amendment jurisprudence.

Finally, six general criteria distilled from the case law may provide some guidance on the questions of serious disease:

1. The diagnostic test relied upon is one of medical or psychiatric necessity.
2. Minor aches, pains, or distress will not establish such necessity.
3. A desire to achieve rehabilitation from alcohol or drug abuse, or to lose weight to simply look or feel better, will not suffice.
4. A diagnosis based on professional judgment and resting on some acceptable diagnostic tool (e.g., DSM-IV [American Psychiatric Association, 1994]) is presumptively valid.
5. By the same token, a decision by a mental health professional that mental illness is not present also is presumptively valid.
6. Whereas behavioral and emotional problems alone do not qualify as serious mental illness, acute depression, paranoid schizophrenia, and organic brain damage do qualify (Cohen, 1988).

With regard to the last point, it is actually the clinicians' choice of the diagnostic terminology which moves these cases from no care to discretionary care or to mandated care. Unfortunately, diagnosis in the custodial setting has often reflected issues relevant to availability of resources, security concerns, and a judgment about the inmate's possible pursuit of secondary gain in contrast to an objective diagnosis based on signs and symptoms.

The Access Concept

Once it is determined that an inmate has a serious mental disorder—and certainly many DSM-IV Axis I diagnoses would suffice—then a host of legal issues and mandates come into play. This is not the occasion for that detailed review. However, it is appropriate here to suggest that in assessing the constitutional efficacy of a prison or jail mental health system, there are three essential factors:

1. Adequate physical resources in terms of beds, treatment and program space, and the like.
2. Adequate human resources in terms of an appropriate number of properly trained or experienced personnel who may identify and treat the seriously mentally ill.
3. Access; that is, an inmate must be able to obtain admission to these physical and human resources within a reasonable time.

Access is the dynamic concept here, whereas physical and human resources are the material or objective aspects of a prison mental health care program. Hypothetically, a system could have a psychiatrist and bed for each inmate who is seriously mentally ill. However, without knowledge of their existence and a way to reach the service within a time frame that is relevant to the condition—a crisis and a chronic condition involve different time frames—there is a fundamental denial of appropriate care.

The access issue, then, pervades the entire correctional mental health system. The courts are reluctant to impose inflexible time frames, preferring instead the generalities of "reasonable" and "timely." The various standards which have been promulgated in this area, although in no sense binding on the courts, do offer some concrete guidance. The most important time frames relate to intake screening and evaluation, inmate orientation, response to a crisis or other emergency, access to diagnosis and appropriate care after the initial reception process, and transfer to a hospital or residential treatment program.

It is essential that pertinent clinicians and administrators specify time frames in the above areas and then monitor compliance. Failure in either aspect is an invitation to a lawsuit and significant increased risk of needless suffering.

Prison Litigation Reform Act

Many of the advances in correctional mental health care are attributable to class action law suits demonstrating systemic failures in basic care. Injunctions and consent decrees have been instituted; court-appointed monitors and Masters oversee compliance, which at times is contentious, and at other times well coordinated.

On April 26, 1996, President Clinton signed into law the Prison Litigation Reform Act (PLRA; 18 U.S.C. § 3626 [1996] *et seq.*), which has the potential to unsettle existing court orders and make it difficult to resolve future prison condition litigation. PLRA, for example, allows defendants to dissolve consent decrees if there is no finding on the record—and there never will be—of unconstitutional conditions. In negotiating consent decrees, defendants uniformly insist on a paragraph stating: "Without admitting any constitutional violation, we agree to . . ."

PLRA severely limits attorney fees and fees paid to Masters. It places a 2-year limit on prospective relief in general, and severely limits preliminary relief as well as inmates' ability to file suit. PLRA, however, does not alter any of the substantive rights discussed here. It is exclusively aimed at procedures and remedies. Thus, inmates' rights to mental health care survive, and whereas Congress has attempted to cripple the process of amicable resolution of this form of civil litigation, suits for damages will no doubt continue.

NATIONAL GUIDELINES AND STANDARDS

In addition to the legal norms distilled from case law, many standards and/or guidelines for correctional health care programs have been published by national organizations such as the American Bar Association (1985), American Nurses Association (1985), American Public Health Association (Dubler, 1986), American Psychiatric Association (APA, 1989), American Correctional Association (1990), National Institute of Corrections (Anno, 1991a), and National Commission on Correctional Health Care (1996, 1997). These guidelines and standards provide a useful framework for establishing mental health systems that adequately address the issue of adequate access to treatment. Standards and guidelines vary based on the nature of the correctional facility (i.e., lockup, size of jail or prison) and specific interest or expertise within the organization promulgating such recommendations. The standards are generally admissible in a lawsuit challenging mental health care and, although relevant, they clearly are not determinative of constitutional obligations.

Steadman, McCarty, and Morrissey (1989) described in a useful fashion the planning process for providing essential services for the mentally ill in jail. Implementing such services has often been complicated by physical plant deficiencies and the rapidly increasing jail population. Miller (1978) reported that about one half of the 3,300 jails in the United States had a designated capacity of fewer than 10 inmates, with another 25% having between 10 and 20 beds. The 130 jails with populations in excess of 250 represent only 4% of all jails, but hold nearly half (45%) of the men and women in custody (Steadman et al., 1989). The nation's 25 largest jail jurisdictions during 1994 accounted for 30% of all jail inmates (Perkins et al., 1995). The large jails that exist in cities such as New York City, Chicago, New Orleans, and Los Angeles have system issues more related to prison correctional mental health systems than to small-jail mental health systems.

Although diversity is clearly present, there is more uniformity among correctional mental health systems within state prisons. There is a clear trend that State Departments of Corrections (DOC) are attempting to establish correctional health care programs consistent with some national set of guidelines (Metzner et al., 1990).

The National Commission on Correctional Health Care (NCCHC) evolved from a program within the American Medical Association that published its first correctional health care standards during 1979. Similar to the NCCHC standards, the standards for health services in correctional institutions developed by the American Public Health Association (Dubler, 1986) focus on general health care issues, although they do contain principles specific to mental health services. The guidelines developed by a task force within the American Psychiatric Association (APA, 1989), which assumed compliance with the standards published by the NCCHC, provide increased specificity concerning correctional mental health services. This section summarizes pertinent guidelines and standards from the American Public Health Association (APHA), NCCHC, and APA due to their wide circulation and usefulness.

Every prison and jail system should develop and implement policies and procedures regarding their mental health services. The legal principles previously discussed and the standards noted above should serve as a framework for the necessary and essential contents for such policies and procedures.

Basic Principles

Policies and procedures provide important guidelines for the health care staff and serve as an excellent training tool for orienting new mental health care staff members to the facility. Such policies and procedures should be developed by health care administrators with input from clinicians. A policy is a facility's official position on a particular issue related to an organization's purpose. The procedure describes in detail how the policy is carried out (NCCHC 1996, 1997). Such policies and procedures should include, but are not limited to, descriptions of the following characteristics of the mental health system (Metzner, 1993):

1. Mission and goal.
2. Administrative structure.
3. Staffing (i.e., job descriptions and required credentials).

4. Reliable and valid methods for identifying inmates with severe mental illnesses.
5. Treatment programs available.
6. Involuntary treatment, including the use of seclusion, restraints, forced medications, and involuntary hospitalization.
7. Other medical–legal issues, including informed consent and the right to refuse treatment.
8. Limits of confidentiality during diagnostic and treatment sessions with pertinent exceptions.
9. Mental health record requirements.
10. Quality assurance/improvement plan.
11. Training of mental health staff regarding correctional and security issues.
12. Formal training of correctional staff regarding mental health issues.
13. Human subjects research.

Review of both the NCCHC standards (1996, 1997) and the APA guidelines (1989) will be of particular assistance in the development of these policies and procedures because they provide a helpful outline for such a task. Many of these principles have characteristics common to noncorrectional mental health systems. We summarize pertinent aspects of these basic principles with an emphasis on issues specific to a correctional system.

Mission and Goals

A mission and goal statement should be developed that clearly distinguishes mental health services, which have a different philosophy and purpose, from correctional services. Correctional services vary somewhat depending on the setting (i.e., jail in contrast to a prison) but generally include security, classification, and inmate management functions. Prisons also have correctional services pertinent to rehabilitation and the parole board. The effectiveness of correctional services is often measured by recidivism rates. Mental health services generally emphasize the importance of identifying and treating inmates with serious mental illness, although a variety of other treatment services are usually available in varying degrees (i.e., crisis intervention, substance abuse treatment, sex offender treatment) depending on the type of correctional setting.

It is a well-accepted principle that clinicians should not be involved in providing both mental health treatment and forensic or correctional services to the same inmate, to avoid a conflict of roles (Greenburg & Shuman, 1997; Strasburger, Gutheil, & Brodsky, 1997). For example, a treating clinician should attempt to avoid examining an inmate for the purpose of producing a parole board evaluation report, due to the potential for blurring of the clinician's role. Similar problems may occur when psychological testing is routinely administered to inmates in a diagnostic reception unit for correctional classification purposes in contrast to the use of such testing as part of the intake mental health screening process (see later section on identification of inmates with mental illness). A conflict of roles for the mental health staff may be perceived by the inmates or actually created, which could be detrimental to the therapeutic alliance with an inmate.

The APHA (Dubler, 1986) standards require that mental health professionals who participate in administrative decisionmaking processes such as parole decisions should not provide direct therapeutic services to those inmates, to decrease the existence of role conflicts for clinicians. The NCCHC (1996, 1997) standards recommend that correctional health care personnel be prohibited by written policy and procedures from participating in the collection of forensic information because their position as neutral, caring, health care professionals is compromised when they are asked to collect information about inmates that may be used against the latter. For similar reasons, participation in executions undermines the credibility of health professionals with their patients and imposes a serious ethical dilemma on such professionals (Bonnie, 1990; Heilbrun, Radelet, & Dvoskin, 1992). Where state laws and regulations require that such acts be performed by health care professionals, the services of outside providers should be obtained (NCCHC, 1997).

The APA guidelines (1989) stated that the fundamental policy goal should be to provide the same level of mental health services to patients in the criminal justice process as that available in an average community. The APA guidelines recognized that the priorities of the provision of care must start with the most severely impaired patients and those with the most severely dangerous and disruptive symptomatology. The purpose of mental health treatment may also vary according to the setting. For example, treatment within a prison setting may enable inmates to make use of rehabilitative opportunities offered to inmates within the prison. Providing consultation with other health care providers and correctional administration and staff is also emphasized as a program goal.

Cohen and Dvoskin (1992a) described the following three reasons for providing mental health treatment within a correctional setting:

1. To reduce the disabling effects of serious mental illness to maximize each inmate's ability to electively participate in correctional programs.
2. To decrease the needless extremes of human suffering caused by mental illness.
3. To help keep the prison safe for staff, inmates, volunteers and visitors.

Administrative Structure

The administrative structure of correctional mental health services is a complex subject due to the diversity of correctional settings. The importance of having a designated health authority on site who is responsible for health care services pursuant to a written agreement, contract, or job description is emphasized by the NCCHC (1996, 1997). The health authorities' responsibilities include arranging for all levels of health care and providing quality, accessible health services to all inmates. The health authority may be a health administrator, governmental agency (e.g., health department or community mental health center [CMHC]), or for-profit health corporation. When this authority is other than a physician, medical judgment rests with the designated licensed responsible physician (NCCHC, 1996, 1997). The frequency per week that the designated health authority is on site depends on the specific characteristics of the correctional setting, such as the average daily inmate count and demographics of the prison population.

The APA Task Force report emphasized that the effective delivery of mental health services in correctional settings requires a balance between security and treatment needs. To achieve the proper balance between security and treatment needs, the director of mental health services or designee should have direct access to the warden, sheriff, or chief administrator with regard to all administrative decisions affecting mental health care issues (APA, 1989; Weinberger & Sreenivasan, 1994). Mental health care services should be discussed at least quarterly at documented administrative meetings between the health authority, official legally responsible for the correctional institution, and other members of the health care and correctional staffs as appropriate. At least monthly mental health staff meetings should be held to review administrative procedural issues, and a statistical report of health services that includes mental health treatment should be provided at least monthly (NCCHC, 1997). Staff should be so organized that there are clear lines of authority, responsibility, and accountability (Dubler, 1986). These standards also emphasize that decisions and actions regarding health care services provided to inmates are the sole responsibility of the health care personnel and should not be compromised for security reasons.

Anno (1991b) reviewed the results of a 1989 NCCHC survey to determine the organizational structure of health services within 50 state departments of correction. Administrative structures ranged from the traditional, decentralized model to a totally centralized system, with variations between these models. For example, some systems had a full-time person at the central office who was responsible for various aspects of health services statewide, but line supervision of health care professionals remained with superintendents in individual institutions. The major problem with such an organizational structure is the dependence on the interest, goodwill, and skill of the wardens for the health care services program. There were also variations in the health care system concerning the integration of mental health care within the medical care system. Anno also described the cost effectiveness of having a health care system organized under a central health care authority, which protects the clinical autonomy of the health providers, enhances continuity of care, and facilitates quality improvements. In 1988, Goldstrom, Manderscheid, and Rudolph (1992) performed a facility-based prison survey of mental health services provided to inmates in state adult correctional facilities that demonstrated that state DOCs differ significantly in their configuration of mental health services.

The specific model to be used by a DOC mental health service is determined by a variety of factors, including the size and location of the correctional system and the working relationship between the state DOC with the State Department of Mental Health. Differences usually exist in the administrative structure of jail mental health services for similar reasons.

Controversy exists concerning whether mental health services and general health care services should have separate directors who both work for a centralized health care authority, or whether mental health care services should report administratively to the medical director of general health care services. There is a trend toward increasing coordination and integration of mental health services with the correctional medical care delivery system. The force behind this trend appears to be litigation, which focuses on inadequate medical care services including psychiatric care, and increasing correctional health costs (Metzner et al., 1990; Metzner, 1993).

Coordination of medical and psychiatric care is an important component of a cost-effective system. According to a national survey conducted by the NCCHC during 1989, the average expenditure for health services in prisons per inmate per year in 47 states reporting was $1,906, whereas the median expenditure was $1,665 (Anno, 1991c). The cost data in this study were not broken down by program area (e.g., medical, dental, mental health care). Between 1982 and 1989, the average per-prisoner expenditure for health care by the states responding to a national survey increased by 103% (McDonald, 1995).

There are a variety of emerging strategies to manage costs and care within correctional settings. These efforts are based on principles of managed health care, use of mandatory copayment by prisoners for health care services, and the emergence of management contracts for correctional health service by outside vendors based on a capitation model (McDonald, 1995).

Staffing

The effectiveness and ultimately the legality of a correctional mental health system is closely related to staffing considerations. Guidelines and standards developed by the APHA (Dubler, 1986), APA (1989), and NCCHC (1996, 1997) emphasize that staffing levels should ensure that sufficient qualified mental health personnel are available to provide access to evaluation and treatment consistent with contemporary standards of care. The training and competence required should be at least equal to community standards as defined by licensure, certification, or registration requirements. Goldstrom et al. (1992) reported the results of a 1988 nationwide survey that found that approximately 40% of staff providing mental health services at the state prisons had less than a master's degree. Psychiatrists accounted for 7% of all providers, psychologists 30%, social workers 9%, and psychiatric nurses 3%.

The staff should undergo continuing education and training as required for professional growth and prevention of burnout. The use of part-time consultants can decrease the negative aspects of institutionalization, such as less creative thinking and decreased use of common sense impacting full-time staff. The national guidelines and standards are clear in prohibiting the use of inmates as mental health personnel either in clerical roles or in providing patient care (Metzner, 1993). It is critical that inmates not have access to mental health files.

A CMHC model, using a multidisciplinary approach, can provide cost-effective treatment (APA, 1989; Cohen & Dvoskin, 1992b; Greene, 1988). A balance between security and treatment needs can be achieved by establishing a cooperative relationship between mental health services staff and the correctional staff. The adoption of a psychiatric liaison model, which includes regular meetings between mental health staff and correctional officers, especially in administrative and disciplinary segregation units, is useful for case finding, primary prevention, and monitoring treatment progress.

Training for the correctional officers should be provided to cover pertinent issues, including identifying inmates with mental illness and preventing suicide. Cooperative relationships between correctional and mental health staff will result in the correctional staff becoming more receptive to input concerning improving general environmental conditions. Correctional staff generally welcome management suggestions regarding difficult inmates, which also helps improve the overall correctional environment. Such training should be more detailed and intensive for security staff who regularly interact with inmates with serious mental illnesses (e.g., correctional staff working in a residential treatment unit).

PREVALENCE RATES

The true prevalence of psychiatric disorders among jail and prison inmates is unknown. Various estimates have been calculated based upon available research data, which are subject to many methodological limitations. Random samples of inmates have rarely been studied, and nonrandomized sampling techniques produce biased results. Studies of inmates referred for evaluation or treatment once in custody, based upon known histories of mental health treatment or suspected mental disorders, result in higher prevalence rates than studies of the entire jail or prison. Some studies rely upon retrospective document reviews without contemporaneous interviews; others use research instruments that assess psychiatric symptoms or functional impairment rather than psychiatric disorders per se. Until relatively recently, precise operational definitions of mental disorder, or standardized assessment procedures using such operational definitions, have not been available. Many studies involve small inmate samples, which precludes statistically significant case finding, or are conducted in different countries, which precludes generalization. Studies of inmates in a single facility may not provide data representative of the entire correctional system in a jurisdiction. Studies of correctional samples often fail to compare prevalence rates with those in the general population, and then to control for demographic differences. Finally, the most seriously ill inmates are usually excluded from research participation, given limitations in their ability to provide research informed consent; thus, prevalence rates for these disorders will be underestimated.

Generally, rates of serious mental disorders are greater for inmates in jail than in prison. By the time an inmate has been convicted of a criminal offense and incarcerated in a prison, many severely mentally ill inmates will have already been hospitalized or treated on a pretrial basis, diverted to the mental health system, adjudicated NGRI, had their charges dismissed, or placed on probation. In either jails or prisons, substance abuse and personality disorders constitute the majority of psychiatric disorders and are disproportionately higher than rates of these disorders in the general population.

Less research has been conducted in prisons than in jails. James, Gregory, Jones, and Rundell (1980) interviewed mostly male, Oklahoma prisoners and diagnosed 5% with schizophrenia, 35% with a personality disorder, and 25% with a primary diagnosis of substance abuse. Steadman, Fabisian, Dvoskin, and Holohean (1987) found that 8% of the New York State prison population had severe psychiatric and/or functional disabilities, and 16% had significant psychiatric and/or functional disabilities. A study in a Maryland, all-male prison found that 19.5% had "definite psychiatric problems" excluding personality disorders and substance abuse, with 9.5

% diagnosed as having a "major thought or schizophrenic disorder" (Swetz, Salive, Stough, & Brewer, 1989). Of this sample, 24% had received inpatient psychiatric treatment prior to their present incarceration. Using the Diagnostic Interview Schedule (DIS; Robins et al., 1981) for males in the Quebec, Canada prison system, Cote and Hodgins (1990) found lifetime rates of serious mental disorders that far exceeded those in the general population: schizophrenia seven times higher, bipolar disorder six times higher, and major depression twice as high. Substantial comorbidity was also detected, with many coexisting diagnoses of substance abuse/dependence and personality disorders. In a randomized sample of male prisoners in two prisons in Edmonton (Alberta, Canada), Bland, Newman, Dyck, and Orn (1990) found overall lifetime prevalence rates for any mental disorder to be twice that of a community sample; whereas mood and substance use disorders were found at two times expected rates, antisocial personality disorders were found at nearly seven times expected rates.

Regarding jails, a nationwide mail survey of 1,391 jails in the United States found that 7.2% of inmates were thought to have serious mental illness by the jail officials who provided the data (Torrey et al., 1992). Serious mental illness was defined as "schizophrenia, manic–depressive illness and related conditions." A well-regarded, large-scale study of male, urban jail detainees using the DIS found that 9% had schizophrenia or major depression during their lifetimes, whereas 6% had an episode within 2 weeks of their arrest (Teplin, 1990). The prevalence rates of schizophrenia, mania, and major depression were two to three times higher than in the general community population. Nearly 35% had a current mental disorder other than antisocial personality disorder (Teplin, 1994). Table 5.1 presents a summary of research on the prevalence of persons in jails with mental disorders.

IDENTIFICATION OF INMATES
WITH MENTAL ILLNESS

The APA Task Force guidelines (1989) described three separate processes leading to identification of inmates requiring psychiatric treatment. These include the receiving mental health screening, intake mental health screening, and mental health evaluation.

Receiving Mental Health Screening

The receiving mental health screening consists of observation and structured inquiry designed to assure that the newly arriving prisoner at the correctional facility, who may require mental health evaluation, is appro-

TABLE 5.1. The Prevalence of Mentally Disordered Persons in Jails: A Summary of the Research

Study	Description of sample	Findings
Bolton (1976)	$N = 1,084$ from jails and juvenile detention centers from five counties; gender unknown	Adults: 6.7% psychotic 9.3% nonpsychotic disorder Juveniles: 2.9% psychotic 20.6% nonpsychotic disorder
Petrich (1976a)	$N = 539$ referred for evaluation; 80% male; 42% felons	49% psychotic 10% depression 27% antisocial 43% drug/alcohol
Petrich (1976b)	$N = 122$ referred for evaluation; 84% male; 80% felons	29% schizophrenia 12% depression 6% mania 43% antisocial 70% drug/alcohol
Piotrowski, Lasacco, & Guze (1976)	$N = 50$ selected from those referred for evaluation; 86% male	22% schizophrenia 10% bipolar 4% OBS
Swank & Winer (1976)	$N = 445$ referred for evaluation; gender not stated; 41% felons	26% psychosis 35% personality disorder 3% neurosis
Kal (1977)	N unknown, randomly selected	DSM-II diagnosis: 50% females, 63% males
Schuckit, Herrman, & Schuckit (1977)	$N = 199$ randomly selected; 100% male; no felony convictions; no current drug charge	3% affective disorder 16% antisocial 27% drug/alcohol 48% any diagnosis
Nielsen (1979)	N unknown; % of those referred for evaluation	24% psychosis 47% narcissistic personality 4% OBS
Monahan & McDonough (1980)	$N = 632$ referred for evaluation; 82% male; 55.5% misdemeanants	32% schizophrenia 22% personality disorder
Whitmer (1980)	$N = 500$ "in need of treatment"; gender not stated; 50% felons (approx.)	Averaged three prior psychiatric hospitalizations
Morgan (1981, 1982)	N unknown; sheriff's perceptions of mental illness	Estimates from 4% to 50%
Lamb & Grant (1982)	$N = 102$ randomly selected from those referred for evaluation; 100% male; 53% felons; drug/alcohol excluded	75% schizophrenia 22% affective disorders 2% adjustment disorders 2% OBS
Lamb & Grant (1983)	$N = 101$ randomly selected from those referred for evaluation; 100% female; 37% felons drug/alcohol excluded	59% schizophrenia 35% affective disorders 5% adjustment disorders 2% dysthymia 2% antisocial

(cont.)

TABLE 5.1 *(cont.)*

Study	Description of sample	Findings
Nizny (1984)	$N = 50$ volunteers; 74% male	26% psychosis 34% drug/alcohol 8% personality disorder 16% neurosis 4% OBS
Virginia DMH (1984)	$N = 171$ from 8 jails, identified as mentally ill by staff; 94% male	40% schizophrenia 47% affective disorders 21% mania 75% mentally ill
Glaser (1985)	$N = 50$ referred for evaluation; gender unknown; Australian sample	48% schizophrenia 16% affective disorders 16% personality 8% OBS
Guy, Platt, Zwerling, & Bullock (1985)	$N = 486$ randomly selected; 100% male; 96 given diagnostic interview	12% schizophrenia 4% affective disorder 9% personality disorder 5% dysthymia 37% drug/alcohol 66% psychiatric problem
Washington & Diamond (1985)	$N = 115$ female adults from Bolton 1976 study	7.0% schizophrenia 6.1% depression 0.9% manic–depression 22.6% personality 4.3% neurosis
Turner & Tofler (1986)	$N = 708$; 100% female; evidence of disorder; British sample	18% psychiatric history 37% drug/alcohol

Study	Description of sample	*Life*	*Current*	
Teplin (1990)	$N = 627$ randomly selected; 100% male	5.7% 2.5% 3.7% 9.5%	3.9% 1.4% 2.7% 6.4%	major depression manic episode schizophrenia any severe

Study	Description of sample	Findings
Torrey et al. (1992)	Nationwide survey of 1,391 jails	7.2% "appeared to have serious mental illness"

Study	Description of sample	*Life*	*Current*	
Teplin (1994)	N = 728 randomly selected; 100% male	6.4% 3.8% 8.9% 32.4% 51.1%	4.1% 3.0% 6.1% 15.3% 19.1%	major affective disorder schizophrenia any severe drug abuse/dependency alcohol abuse/dependency

Study	Description of sample	*Life*	*6-month*	
Teplin, Abram, & McClelland (1996)	$N = 1,272$ randomly selected; 100% female	16.9% 2.6% 2.4% 32.3% 63.6% 33.5%	13.7% 2.2% 1.8% 23.9% 52.4% 22.3%	major depression manic episode schizophrenia alcohol abuse/dependency drug abuse/dependency PTSD

Note. From Teplin and Voit (1996). Copyright 1996 by Carolina Academic Press. Reprinted by permission. DMH, Department of Mental Health; OBS, organic brain syndrome; PTSD, posttraumatic stress disorder.

priately referred and placed in the proper living environment. This initial screening process occurs immediately upon admission to the correctional facility and is usually performed by trained correctional staff or qualified health care personnel.

A form should be developed for the receiving mental health screening that documents that pertinent records accompanying the inmate are reviewed and the inmate has answered a series of structured questions designed to identify significant psychiatric disturbances (e.g., disorganized thinking, bizarre behavior, hallucinations, suicidal and homicidal ideation). Positive findings result in immediate referral for a comprehensive mental health evaluation performed by an appropriately trained clinician.

Intake Mental Health Screening

Appropriately trained health care staff perform the second screening process designed to identify inmates with mental illness as part of the comprehensive medical evaluation provided to every inmate upon entering a correctional system. This screening includes obtaining histories of past psychiatric treatment, substance abuse, and psychotropic medication use, and performing a mental status examination. This screening, due to reasons of cost effectiveness, is often performed by a nonpsychiatric physician, nurse practitioner, or physician assistant as part of the admitting physical examination of the inmate. Depending on the nature of the correctional facility, this screening is generally performed within 7 to 14 days after the arrival of the inmate to the correctional institution

Mental Health Evaluation

The third identification procedure is provided by appropriately trained mental health clinicians in response to referral either from screening processes, other staff, or by self-referral. These assessments are more comprehensive than either screening process and should follow the format of a standard, comprehensive mental health examination.

Other Screening and Evaluation Models

NCCHC (1996, 1997) standards also require receiving screening, similar to the receiving mental health screening recommended by the APA Task Force report, to be performed by qualified health care personnel for all inmates immediately upon their arrival at the prison or jail. The NCCHC standards additionally require a postadmission mental health evaluation of all inmates by qualified mental health care personnel within 14 calendar days of admission to a prison and recommend a similar process to occur within a jail setting. This postadmission mental health evaluation should include the following:

1. A structured interview by a mental health worker in which inquiries into the following items are made:

    a. History of psychiatric hospitalization and outpatient treatment.
    b. Current psychotropic medications.
    c. Suicidal ideation and history of suicidal behavior.
    d. Drug usage.
    e. Alcohol usage.
    f. History of sex offenses.
    g. History of violent behavior.
    h. History of victimization due to criminal violence.
    i. Special education placement.
    j. History of cerebral trauma or seizures.
    k. Emotional response to incarceration.

2. Testing of intelligence to screen for mental retardation. The standards specifically recommend the use of group tests of intelligence or brief intelligence screening instruments that should be followed, when appropriate, by a comprehensive, individually administered instrument such as the Wechsler Adult Intelligence Scale—Revised (WAIS-R; Wechsler, 1981).

Qualified mental health personnel are defined to include physicians, psychiatrists, dentists, psychologists, nurses, physician assistants, psychiatric social workers, and others who by virtue of their education, credentials, and experience are permitted by law to evaluate and care for the mental health needs of patients.

Psychological evaluations were historically used in prisons predominantly for correctional classification purposes before the development of adequate correctional health care systems. Such evaluations were generally performed by psychologists working at a reception and diagnostic center that served as an entry point into the correctional system. The development of adequate prison mental health systems resulted in mental health screening and evaluation by health care professionals occurring in the reception and diagnostic centers for purposes of appropriate referral for mental health treatment in contrast to reasons related to correctional classification (Metzner, Miller, & Kleinsasser, 1994).

Beyond testing of intelligence, neuropsychological screening is sometimes useful, especially in prisons, given inmates' high prevalence of head injury. Neuropsychological screening data can be useful for inmate management, medical treatment, educational placement, work assignments, and psychotherapy (Iverson, Franzen, Demarest, & Hammond, 1993). Whereas comprehensive neuropsychological evaluation is typically not feasible in the correctional setting, screening batteries can be readily developed and used by psychologists and psychiatrists without specialized training in neuropsychology.

Discussion

There are many models that can be used to develop an adequate health screening and evaluation process. The model adopted has important implications for the mental health system related to needs assessment issues and management of limited resources. Variations in these models involve whether all inmates receive mental health screening and evaluation as part of the admission process, the credentials and training required for personnel providing mental health screening and evaluations, the use of psychological testing as part of the assessment process, and whether the assessment results are used only for health care purposes or also for correctional classification reasons (i.e., determining security levels; Metzner et al., 1994).

Virtually all DOCs provide reception mental health screening or prompt intake mental health screening to all newly admitted inmates. Most of these DOCs use health care professionals (not necessarily mental health staff) to provide reception mental health screening. According to one survey, 42 DOCs provide some combination of intake mental health screening and mental health evaluations for all newly admitted inmates (Metzner et al., 1994). Twenty-six percent of DOCs have exceeded the recommendations of the APA Task Force by providing all three types of screening/evaluations for all newly admitted inmates in the prison system. The routine use of standard psychological tests to all newly admitted inmates appears to be a common practice within DOCs (Metzner et al., 1994).

APA Task Force guidelines should be followed regarding mental health screening and evaluation to effectively use limited resources within the mental health system. Specifically, mental health evaluations (in contrast to the two types of mental health screening procedures) are not required for *all* newly admitted inmates. Whereas it is clear that standard psychological tests can be helpful in selected cases for a variety of clinical reasons, the comprehensive use of such tests seem to have limited value.

TREATMENT PROGRAMS

The guidelines developed by the APA Task Force (1989) defined mental health treatment as the use of a variety of mental health therapies, biological as well as psychological, to alleviate symptoms of mental disorders that significantly interfere with the inmate's ability to function in the particular criminal justice environment. It is not unreasonable to expand this definition to include the use of such modalities to alleviate symptoms of mental disorder associated with present distress or with a significantly increased risk of suffering death, pain, or disability. Treatment, which should be multidisciplinary and eclectic in nature, is to be provided consistent with generally accepted mental health practices and institutional requirements. A comprehensive system includes the following components (APA, 1989; Cohen & Dvoskin, 1992b; Dubler, 1986; Metzner, 1993):

1. Crisis intervention program, with infirmary beds for short-term treatment (usually less than 10 days) available.
2. Acute care program.
3. A chronic care program or special needs unit (housing unit within the correctional setting for inmates with chronic mental illness who do not require inpatient treatment but do require a therapeutic milieu due to their inability to function adequately within the general population).
4. Outpatient treatment services.
5. Consultation services (consulting with the prison's management team and/or providing training of correctional officers and program staff).
6. Discharge/transfer planning, including services for inmates in need of further treatment at the time of transfer to another institution or discharged to the community.

It is estimated that 4–9% of the corrrectional population meets the criteria for mental retardation (Santamour, 1989). Habilitative programs for developmentally disabled offenders are important programs within a correctional setting but are beyond the scope of this chapter (see Gardner, Graeber, & Machkovitz, Chapter 7, this volume). Issues pertinent to the treatment of sex offenders are covered by Barbaree and Marshall in Chapter 6. Substance abuse treatment is generally often provided within a correctional setting as either part of the mental health program or as part of a correctional rehabilitation program.

Treatment in jails predominantly involves crisis intervention services, which include transfer to special housing units, use of psychotropic medications, special observation, and brief psychotherapy. Treatment generally emphasizes prescription of psychotropic medications due to the short-term nature of most jail confinements. Some verbal therapies may become part of the treatment regimen for those inmates whose pretrial confinements or sentences may be of longer term (APA, 1989). The essential mental health services for a jail population include access to inpatient psychiatric beds, 7 day-a-week mental health coverage, availability of a full range of psychotropic medications prescribed and monitored by a psychiatrist, appropriate nursing coverage in any medical or mental health area, and procedures developed and monitored by psychiatrists to ensure that psychotropic medications are distributed by qualified medical personnel whenever possible (APA, 1989). Many jails do not provide a comprehensive system of correctional mental health care due to their small size and brief duration of stay.

Prison mental health systems should provide a comprehensive system of mental health care as previously summarized. This need appears to be recognized by many correctional facilities, as evidenced by a 1993 American Correctional Association Task Force on Offenders with Special Needs report, which summarized 202 programs from several provinces in Canada and 39 states in the United States (Task Force on Offenders with Special Needs, 1993). There were a variety of adult programs (both in-house and community-based correctional programs) that included services for offenders with mental illness, emotional disturbance, mental retardation, substance abuse problems, and sex-offending behavior. The importance of a chronic care program for inmates with serious mental illnesses has become increasingly recognized as an essential component of such a system (Metzner et al., 1990).

Specialized Programs for the Seriously Mentally Ill

The correctional mental health literature contains few descriptions of chronic care programs, often referred to as a "residential treatment unit," "intermediate care program," "protective environment," or "special needs unit." Inmates appropriate for these units generally have been diagnosed as suffering from a serious mental disorder and have difficulty coping in a general population environment due to their mental disorder (Mortimer, 1993). See Table 5.2 for a summary of admission criteria for such units, developed by the Ohio Department of Corrections and Rehabilitation (Aungst, 1995).

Such units are often designed to house 30 to 50 inmates per housing unit to staff the unit in a cost-effective fashion. Essential elements of these units include adequate office space (preferably unit staff offices or offices immediately adjacent to the unit); storage rooms for charts, office and program supplies, and equipment; wall-mounted TV and video equipment; blackboard and audiovisual materials; and adequate numbers of individual and group rooms for programming activities. Important recreational and vocational activities require both indoor and outdoor recreational space and ample dayroom space. The availability of an art therapy or music therapy

TABLE 5.2. Residential Treatment Unit (RTU)

Definition: A housing unit within the prison for inmates with mental illness who do not then need inpatient treatment, but who do require the therapeutic milieu and the full range of services and variable security available in the RTU.

Admission criteria	Prioritization of admissions
1. Inmate has a serious mental illness, a substantial disorder of thought or mood that significantly impairs judgment, behavior, capacity to recognize reality or cope with the ordinary demands of life within the prison environment and is manifested by substantial pain or disability. Serious mental illness requires a mental health diagnosis, prognosis, and treatment, as appropriate by mental health staff. *and*	Inmates in any segregation status Inmates in crisis beds Inmates returning from the inpatient psychiatric hospital unit upon discharge recommendation of inpatient treatment team Inmates who are candidates for forced medication Inmates with history of decompensation when off medications and housed in general population units.
2. Mental illness causes impairment in behavior and/or functioning. This may have been manifested as a history of recurrent decompensation of the inmate when housed in the general population. *and*	
3. Inmate's mental illness is unable to be stabilized in a less restrictive setting (outpatient).	

room can be a very useful asset. An ability to provide meals on the unit is often essential. Janitors' closets and adequate shower facilities should not be ignored.

The nurses' area and the correctional officers' station should be designed to have adequate observation of inmates. Other important areas within the unit include a treatment room to conduct sick call, space for crash carts, medication carts, and a medication room. Cells designed for close observation and restraints should be close to the nursing and correctional officers' stations. Important environmental conditions include central air conditioning or the ability to maintain reasonable room temperature, adequate ventilation, and acoustics to minimize noise level in the treatment and housing areas.

See Table 5.3 (Aungst, 1995) for a description of recommended physical plant standards for chronic care units.

TABLE 5.3. Residential Treatment Unit (RTU) Minimum Physical Plant Standards

General standards

1. RTU separated from the general population and administrative segregation units.
2. Ability to maintain reasonable room temperature; adequate ventilation.
3. Acoustics to minimize noise level in treatment/housing areas.
4. Access to outdoor recreation space.
5. If tiered, upper tiers adequately fenced/screened.
6. The statewide correctional system needs at least one RTU that is handicap accessible.
7. All areas of RTU designed to optimize visibility by correctional staff.

Individual housing

1. Primarily single cell with individual bathroom facilities.
2. Cells permit good visibility by correctional staff.
3. Furniture in all cells "safe."
4. If cells have windows, other inmates cannot access windows.
5. Ability to pass medications/food through door on some cells.
6. Some cells able to accommodate "crisis intervention."

Crisis intervention housing (crisis beds of RTU)

1. Security sink/toilets.
2. Cells as "suicide proof" as possible.
3. Good visibility by correctional staff.
4. Ability to implement restraint procedures.

Note. This table was developed with significant input from Jane Haddad, PsyD.

There are a variety of ways to adequately staff a chronic care unit that depend on the size of the unit. A psychiatrist, nursing staff, activity therapists, clerk, and other mental health professionals (e.g., psychologists and social workers) are needed to provide the necessary treatment services. For example, a typical intermediate care unit in the New York Department of Corrections serves 60 inmates and is staffed by 0.5 full-time equivalent (FTE) psychiatrist and 3 to 5 other full-time mental health specialists (e.g., psychologist, nurse, social worker, occupational/recreational therapist; Condelli, Dvoskin, & Holanchock, 1994). A good working relationship between the mental health staff and correctional health officers on these units is vital. It is preferable that the mental health director of this unit have significant input regarding the selection of correctional officers assigned to this unit. The correctional officer's rotation on such a unit should be for at least 6 months to facilitate development of a treatment team concept.

Condelli and colleagues (1994) published one of the few studies that attempted to assess outcomes related to specially designed programs for inmates with serious mental illness. Programs included milieu therapy, individual group therapy, psychotropic medications, recreational therapy, task and skills training, educational instruction, vocational instruction, and crisis intervention. Their results indicate significant reductions in very serious rule infractions, suicide attempts, correctional discipline, and use of crisis intervention, seclusion, and hospitalization for inmates living in an intermediate care program within the New York DOC.

Treatment Modalities

Psychotropic Medication

The use of psychotropic medications is an important treatment modality within correctional health care systems. Use of such medications should be consistent with medication practice outside of the correctional setting, with some additional precautions or special problems particular to the correctional setting. Treatment planning meetings help to coordinate the mental health care provided to inmates, especially when multiple health care professionals are simultaneously involved in the treatment process.

All classes of psychotropic medication should be available to the correctional population, although correctional health care systems often limit the use of sedative–hypnotics, benzodiazepines, and stimulants due to the potential for abuse (Diamond, Brooner, Lowe, & Savage, 1981). Psychotropic medication dispensing should occur using unit dosing rather than stock bottles of tablets or capsules. Licensed health care professionals rather than corrections officers or inmates should dispense psychotropic medication to inmates, though correctional staff should receive basic training concerning such medications and be attentive to problems with compliance. The newer and more expensive psychotropic medications appear to be cost effective with regard to efficacy and increased patient compliance. However, there remains some resistance to the use of some of the newer psychotropic medications in health care systems that are capitated based upon short-term financial considerations.

Given that behavior control is a necessary goal in jails and prisons, inmates are sometimes inappropriately medicated, either by excessive medication dose or by polypharmacy, in the absence of a psychiatric evaluation (Kaufman, 1980) or for nonclinical reasons (Sommers & Baskin, 1991). Lithium, beta blockers, carbamazepine, and clozapine have been used with variable success in managing aggression or violence (Corrigan, Yudofsky, & Silver, 1993; Tardiff, 1992; Wistedt, Helldin, Omerov, & Palmstierna, 1994). Medications should be prescribed only in the context of an adequate clinical examination; appropriate documentation should appear in the inmate's health care record justifying the use of the medication.

Some psychotropic medications such as lithium carbonate, clozapine, medroxyprogesterone (in oral or injectible form for compulsive sex offenders acting out in the institution), and anticonvulsants should be prescribed only when laboratory facilities are available for assessing blood levels of the medication or potential side effects. The institution should have a policy and procedure to ensure adverse drug effect monitoring for populations at risk (e.g. routine and repeated Abnormal Involuntary Movement Scale [AIMS] testing for tardive dyskinesia and tardive dystonia).

Individual Psychotherapy

Due to limited resources, use of individual outpatient psychotherapy is often restricted to crisis intervention, except for supportive psychotherapy for inmates with serious mental illnesses, whether preexisting or of new onset in custody. Inmates with borderline personality disorder are at risk for developing brief psychotic episodes, suicidality, self-mutilation, or violence to others, necessitating crisis intervention that is frequently followed by a more structured and longer term treatment. Inmates with prior histories of victimization resulting in posttraumatic stress disorder or dissociative disorders may also obtain benefit from long-term psychotherapy when resources are available to provide such treatment. Often a psychoeducational approach is useful to inmates, wherein the clinician provides relevant information to the inmate about how to best adapt to institutional living given the inmate's particular psychological capacities and deficits. Assisting inmates to develop better coping strategies is likely to result in improved adjustment to incarceration (Negy, Woods, & Carlson, 1997). Symptomatic relief can also be obtained through means other than mental health treatment, such as support by other inmates and correctional staff, school, recreation activities, family visits, and work. Pervasive issues among inmates such as denial and externalization of responsibility, inability to form interpersonal attachments or to trust others, and egocentricity complicate attempts to conduct individual psychotherapy in a correctional setting.

Group Psychotherapy

Group psychotherapy is the least costly form of mental health treatment within a correctional setting, given resource limitations for mental health care. Groups offer inmates the opportunity to realize that they are not unique in having emotional problems during incarceration, while diluting the stress of an individual psychotherapy. Clearly, many inmates have impaired interpersonal skills that may underlie their criminal behavior and incarceration. These social skill deficits may make some inmates more, or at times less, appropriate for group therapy, depending upon the nature of the group therapy being offered. Special problems for group therapy in prisons involve the prevalence of inmates with severe and primitive personality structures and defenses (i.e., splitting, projection, denial), inmate distrust of staff and other inmates, taboos against talking about emotional closeness, difficulty in assuring confidentiality of group sessions, attendance and scheduling due to institutional restrictions, and disruption of groups by threats or the potential for actual violence (Stein & Brown, 1991).

Acute Hospitalization

Access to psychiatric hospitalization for acute or emergency psychiatric care should be available when needed (Dvoskin, 1994). Such emergency hospitalization is needed to stabilize the inmate, permitting subsequent return of the inmate to the correctional facility. Inpatient hospitalization is accomplished through transfer to an outside psychiatric hospital or unit or to a psychiatric hospital unit contained within the jail or prison.

Therapy Issues

Therapy issues often focus on themes concerning the inmate experience. Power and control are dominant social–psychological issues within a correctional environment. Fear, rage, helplessness, apathy or emotional withdrawal, and loss of self-esteem are common emotional responses while in custody (McCorkle, 1993). Institutional rules and practices regarding strip searches, noncontact visits, yard time, shower time, and administrative or disciplinary segregation are often made for security purposes, but their implementation may reflect control issue dynamics between correctional staff and inmates. The mental health clinician often is sought as an ally by both inmates and correctional staff in these power struggles, especially within administrative segregation units. An understanding of the institutional organization and the inmate's social system will facilitate a reasonable response by the mental health professional. Acknowledging a limited ability to change the system when responding to these struggles will often enhance the mental health clinician's credibility (Metzner, 1993; Roth, 1986).

For both inmates and staff, overcrowding increases the stress of institutional life and compounds the endemic problems of prisons and jails, including poor living conditions with extremes of noise and temperature, lack of meaningful work, boredom, loss of control, lack of privacy, violence, sexual or financial exploitation and intimidation, and weakening of the inmate's usual affectional ties, which are all common therapy issues (Roth, 1986; Toch, 1992; Toch & Adams, 1989). Many inmates are even unable to tolerate having a cellmate, whether due to their primitive emotional or realistic fears for their safety and that of the cellmate. However, incarceration is not necessarily deleterious to all inmates, as many benefit from the highly structured and predictable living circumstances (Bukstel & Kilmann, 1980).

Treatment Planning

A treatment plan, a series of written statements specifying the particular course of therapy and roles of the qualified health care personnel in carrying it out, should be developed for inmates receiving mental health services. It is typically multidisciplinary and based on an assessment of the patient's needs, including a statement of short- and long-term goals as well as the methods by which these goals will be pursued (NCCHC, 1996, 1997). Kennedy (1992) wrote a useful book concerning fundamentals of psychiatric treatment planning.

The APA Task Force (1989) guidelines emphasized discharge and transfer planning, which includes all procedures through which inmates who need mental health care at the time of a transfer to another institution or discharge to the community are assured continuity of care. Case management services, an integral part of discharge and transfer planning, include the following:

1. Appointments arranged with mental health agencies for all mentally ill inmates or a specific subgroup such as those receiving psychotropic medications.
2. Referrals arranged for inmates with a variety of mental health problems.
3. Notification of reception centers at state prisons.
4. Arrangements made with hometown pharmacies to have prescriptions renewed.

Substance Abuse Treatment

The percentage of prison inmates reporting any drug use in the month before the offense leading to their incarceration declined from 56% in 1986 to 50% in 1991, although the percentage of inmates using cocaine or crack during the same time period increased from 20% in 1986 to 25% in 1991 (Timrots & Byrne, 1995). The 1991 Bureau of Justice Statistics survey of state prison inmates indicated that 18% of the inmates committed their offense under the influence of alcohol only, 17% were under the influence of drugs only, and another 14% committed their offense under the influence of both drugs and alcohol (Harlow, 1994). A 1986 national survey of state

prison inmates found that 36% of all inmates repor
major drugs, including heroin, cocaine, and phenc·
Fifty-eight percent of all jail inmates in 198
used drugs regularly, that is, one or more a w(
Twenty-nine percent of jail inmates during 1989
only during the time of offense and another 12(
drugs and alcohol during the time of their offense ,
convicted inmates serving time in jail, 44% had used dru₉ᵤ
before their current offense, 30% daily or almost daily, and 27% weiᵤ
the influence when they committed their current offense (Harlow, 1991).

During 1993, the drug-use forecasting (DUF) program of the U.S. Department of Justice's National Institute of Justice studied drug use by arrestees for serious offenses through urinalysis of samples collected voluntarily and anonymously from arrestees in booking facilities in 23 cities. The percentage of male arrestees testing positive for any drug at the time of arrest ranged from 54% to 81%. A similar study during 1988 demonstrated that the range for female arrestees was from 45% to 83% (Anno, 1991a; National Institute of Justice, 1990). The prevalence of alcohol use was not reported in these studies.

The proportion of drug offenders in state prisons increased from 9% in 1986 to 21% in 1991. The proportion of drug offenders in local jails increased from 9% in 1983 to 21% in 1989. Women were more likely to be incarcerated in a state prison for a drug offense than were men (33% vs. 21%). Blacks were more likely to be serving time for drug offense than whites (25% vs. 12%) but less than Hispanic inmates (33%; U.S. Department of Justice, 1995b).

Lipton, Falkin, and Wexler (1992) reported that 39 states use preliminary substance abuse assessment procedures with newly sentenced inmates; 44 states allow Narcotics Anonymous (NA), Cocaine Anonymous (CA), or Alcoholics Anonymous (AA) self-help group meetings once or twice a week; 44 states have some form of short-term (35–50 hours) drug education programming; 39 states have some form of individual counseling available for drug users in which a counselor or therapist meets with an individual inmate occasionally during the week; 36 states have group counseling in which small groups of inmates meet once or twice weekly with a therapist; and 30 states have some type of intensive residential program, often based on the therapeutic community model.

Brown (1992) described five types of program models available for drug abusers in correctional settings. These include incarceration (1) without specialized services, (2) with drug education and drug abuse counseling, (3) with residential units dedicated to drug abuse treatment, (4) with client-initiated or client-maintained services, and (5) with specialized services that do not directly target users' drug abuse problems.

pite the wide variety of treatment options available, treatment
ces for drug-dependent jail and prison inmates have not kept pace
the demand for services. Peters and May (1992) reported that only
% of 1,737 responding jails in the United States reported that they
offered drug treatment services other than detoxification. Only 12,894
inmates (7%) of an average daily population of 192,461 from their sample
were enrolled in drug treatment programs within a jail setting. The General
Accounting Office estimated that state prisons provided services to just
over 20% of the 75% of state prison inmates who may have substance abuse
problems (U. S. General Accounting Office, 1991). Among state prison
inmates who used drugs during the month before their offense, 31% had
been in a treatment program before entering prison and 25% had been in
such a program once or twice. Almost half of these inmates participated in
drug treatment after receiving their current sentence. This treatment ranged
from intensive inpatient programs to self-help groups. After admission,
22% of all inmates had participated in group counseling and 8% had been
in self-help counseling groups (Beck et al., 1993).

Other Issues

Many inmates seek mental health treatment as a result of requirements
established by the prison classification committee or parole board as a
condition for consideration of transfer and release. Inmates incarcerated for
sexual offenses, who account for over 30% of the population in some
prisons, often overwhelm mental health systems with requests for treatment
because of parole board requirements (Metzner, 1993). This type of treatment is generally referred to as correctional rehabilitative treatment although it is often provided by mental health services staff, whether internal
to the institution or on contract by an outside vendor. The effectiveness of
correctional rehabilitation treatment in general is controversial, despite
studies indicating that effectiveness is dependent upon what is delivered to
whom in particular settings (Andrews et al., 1990; Gendreau, 1996).
Unfortunately, treatment programs for sex offenders, which are not constitutionally mandated, often dissipate limited mental health resources
(Dvoskin, 1991).

Inmates with personality disorders, including antisocial personality
disorder, may benefit from time-limited crisis intervention therapy, which
should be characterized by a straightforward, consistent, here-and-now
approach. Generally, it is an injudicious use of typically limited resources
to attempt to effect significant personality change within a correctional
setting. Correctional settings are likely to have a variety of difficult-to-
manage, threatening, disruptive individuals who consume substantial staff
resources; it may be unclear whether such individuals should be managed

by clinical staff or corrections (Goldstein, 1983). However, the role of correctional mental health staff in the direct treatment of the "normal offender" should not limit the importance that mental health clinicians should attach to promoting "normalization" of the correctional environment, helping decrease, whenever possible, its harshness, and helping increase its opportunity for individual growth (Metzner, 1993; Roth, 1986).

Inmates sent to disciplinary isolation units present a unique set of problems. Isolation may provide an opportunity for the inmate to regain self-control and be removed from an intolerable, external stressor. Nevertheless, serious decompensation or regression can occur in such situations and such inmates should not be neglected (Goldstein, 1983; Grassian & Friedman, 1986; Kaufman, 1980).

INFORMED CONSENT AND INVOLUNTARY TREATMENT

The principles of informed consent remain applicable to inmates in correctional settings although the inherently coercive setting of a correctional facility requires particular sensitivity to the element of "voluntariness." Clinicians should offer to discuss with their patient the nature, purpose, risk, and benefits of various treatment options.

Involuntary treatment, which includes forcible administration of psychotropic medication (see "Involuntary Medication" section), seclusion, and restraints, should be governed by rules, regulations, and laws applicable to the specific jurisdiction. Inmates generally have a right to refuse evaluation and treatment without disciplinary action or punishment. The health care staff should not participate in the nonmedical restraint of inmates except for monitoring their health status (APA, 1989; Dubler, 1986; NCCHC, 1996, 1997).

Transfer

Given the constitutional right to mental health services, can the correctional authority transfer the prisoner to another institution to receive them? In *Vitek v. Jones* (1980) the Supreme Court addressed the question of whether the Due Process Clause of the Fourteenth Amendment entitles a prisoner to certain procedural protections with which to resist a proposed transfer for treatment from a state prison to a state mental hospital.

Four years earlier, the Supreme Court held that a prisoner has no right to procedures by which to resist a prison-to-prison transfer, even to conditions far less favorable. *Meachum v. Fano* (1976) held that as long as any given prison met minimally acceptable conditions of confinement, an inmate did not have sufficient legal autonomy to challenge a state's decision on the place of confinement. In *Meachum* there was no claim of a lost right to mandated care or rehabilitation, nor any claim that invasive procedures awaited the transferee. The inmate claimed a grievous loss in the increased distance from visiting family, loss of work opportunities, even the prospect of danger in adjusting to the "turf" of a new prison. In *Sandin v. Connor* (1995) the Supreme Court abandoned the "grievous loss" and state-created liberty approach previously followed in favor of an analysis that a liberty interests exists only if a prison condition creates an "atypical and significant hardship."

Would *Vitek* then be governed by *Meachum*, or is there something *qualitatively* different about a prison-to-mental hospital transfer? The Court concluded that a prisoner has a reasonable expectation of not being transferred to a mental hospital, absent a finding of mental illness and that adequate treatment was not available in the sending facility. In addition, the stigma of being labeled mentally ill, and the prospect of being subjected to what was termed "mandatory behavior modification" programs, created a liberty interest in the inmate and, thus, the need for a procedural format to resist. It should be added that the *Sandin v. Connor* decision leaves *Vitek* intact.

Vitek, of course, required that a transfer hearing be held only when an inmate resists, and, when held, such hearing need only be of the administrative variety. *Vitek* provides an opportunity to resist, an opportunity that few inmates appear to exercise.

Indeed, the practical problem is exactly the opposite of that confronted in *Vitek*: How may desperately ill inmates gain access to the hospital care they need, given the relatively limited bed space available? In many states delays in hospital transfers can extend for weeks and even months.

Vitek, does, of course, extend some autonomy to the prisoner although, as noted, it hits at the wrong side of the problem. In addition, and perhaps inadvertently, the Court's assertion that the stigma of mental illness creates the basis for a protected liberty interest actually nourishes the stigma. It is one thing to say that a protesting inmate simply has sufficient legal identity or autonomy to resist enforced, and possibly invasive, care or simply to resist moving to a qualitatively different place of confinement. If we are to view mental illness as illness, then it is not the Court's finest moment to say to the inmate "You have a procedural opportunity to avoid being stigmatized on your way to needed care" (Cohen, 1988).

Involuntary Medication

Whereas *Vitek* dealt with the physical location of treatment, *Washington v. Harper* (1990) dealt with an inmate's right to refuse unwanted antipsychotic drugs. Harper was an inmate in the Washington prison who, for 6 years, had consented to the administration of antipsychotic medication. He then said he would rather die than take the medication, but Washington officials were determined to forcibly medicate him.

First, the Court recognized that an inmate has a protected, liberty interest in avoiding the unwanted administration of antipsychotic drugs. However, even if an inmate is competent—that is, understands the nature and consequences of his/her decision—the state is also accorded an interest in pursuing the prisoner's medical interests, and overriding his/her protest with the use of forced medication. Thus, the prisoner does not have an absolute right to resist this form of treatment and the state does not have an unconditional right to impose it. Dilemmas such as this tend to be resolved legally by procedural and burden of proof requirements. To forcibly medicate, the state must establish that a mental disorder exists, that the treatment is in the prisoner's medical interests (and not simply prison security inserts); that the drug is administered under the direction of a licensed psychiatrist; and an administrative hearing, not a judicial proceeding, may suffice to meet due process.

Although the Court abjured the possibility that prison security is, or could be, of paramount concern here, the reality is quite to the contrary. It is the violent, acting-out inmate with a mental disorder who is the prime candidate for forced medication. And whereas the medication may defuse the inmate, it also contributes a great deal to prison security and management.

The majority acknowledged the risks of negative side effects, although not with the vigor of the dissenters. Those risks were not enough to allow a competent inmate to refuse or to require judicial proceedings. If a doctor weighs the risks and monitors the inmate, a majority was satisfied. In *Sullivan v. Flannigan* (1993) it was held that an inmate has no right to a drug-free interlude prior to a *Harper* hearing. The inmate sought to persuade the panel that he could function without medication. The court's ruling means that a doctor may choose to medicate an unwilling inmate for his/her entire term.

Inmates who are noncompliant with their medication—either refusing or simply lapsing—are frequently involved in prison disciplinary proceedings. Often, the refusal or lapse relates to a failure of prison personnel to educate the inmate about the disorder and the consequences of taking or not taking the medication. A drug education program should be in place, inducements to continue on medication should be required before even contemplating force, and involuntary medication should only be utilized in an appropriate treatment setting (i.e., hospital or residential treatment unit) after *Harper* procedures, at a minimum, are employed.

A *Vitek* transfer hearing might actually be used to reach a forcible medication decision, and in some jurisdictions that is the case. When transfer and medication are decided in a single proceeding, the right to administer the drug should be severely time limited—10 days perhaps—until there is an independent review by the psychiatrist at the receiving facility.

The Legal Framework of Treatment

There are three questions consistently asked about correctional health care services:

1. Does the inmate have a right to choose the modality of care?
2. Does the inmate have the right to insist on a preferred caregiver either by name, training, or experience?
3. Is there a right to treatment at a particular location or in a particular setting?

The basic answer, with only a few twists, to each question is *no*. As long as the modality of treatment is within the range of treatment options for that diagnosis, even if it is a technique employed only by a "respectable minority" of caregivers, it will be legally acceptable.

As for selecting a particular person or, say, a psychiatrist who follows a particular school of thought, there is simply no such right held by the inmate. Courts review whether or not the particular caregiver is trained or licensed to perform a particular function—for example, psychologists cannot prescribe psychotropic medication—but they rarely go further.

As to where care is given, as long as the setting, wherever located, is appropriate for the function, courts have little to say about the geography of care. The *Vitek* principle, as discussed, is an exception, albeit a procedural one. Certainly it is true that a crisis/observation room has to be physically suited for the task to be performed (e.g., ready observation, no breakable fixtures or opportunities for hanging), but beyond those sorts of things the courts have little to say.

Here, as noted earlier, the access concept is central. That is, where a crisis bed or cell is located is less important than how quickly it may be accessed and, then, how physically suited it is to the task.

SUICIDE PREVENTION PROGRAMS

Suicide is the third leading cause of death in prisons, behind natural causes and AIDS. The National Center on Institutions and Alternatives reported that the rate of suicide in prisons throughout the country, based on data gathered from 1984 to 1993 was 20.6 deaths per 100,000 inmates, or more than 1½ times greater than that in the general population. The rate of prison suicide is lower than that of jail suicide, which was reported during 1988 to be 9 times greater than that in the general population (Hayes, 1988; Hayes, 1995a). The annual rate of suicide in the general population within the United States was reported in 1991 to be 12 per 100,000 (U.S. Bureau of the Census, 1991).The vast majority of suicides in custody occur by hanging, and when the inmate is housed alone or at night while the cellmate is asleep. In jails, half or more of suicides occur within the first month of incarceration (Marcus & Alcabes, 1993; DuRand, Burtka, Federman, Haycox, & Smith, 1995).

Nonlethal forms of self-injury are also common in correctional settings. Such behavior is frequently dismissed by correctional staff as manipulative in design, and punished by segregation or isolation (Hayes, 1995a). Such response, however, may be counterproductive. Clinicians may be able to distinguish those inmates with suicidal intent from those who are self-mutilators (Fulwiler, Forbes, Santangelo, & Folstein, 1997). Even with manipulative inmates, intervention that fails to modify such behavior by providing close supervision, social support, and access to psychosocial resources may lead to escalating self-destructiveness (Hayes, 1995a).

Hayes reported that the majority of Departments of Correction have not comprehensively adopted the suicide prevention standards advocated by the NCCHC and the American Correctional Association. The standards include the following essential elements of a suicide prevention program (NCCHC, 1996, 1997):

1. Identification.
2. Staff training.
3. Assessment of an inmate's level of suicide risk by a qualified mental health professional.
4. Monitoring of an inmate who has been identified as potentially suicidal.
5. Appropriate housing of a suicidal inmate.
6. Referral of potentially suicidal inmates to mental health care providers or facilities.
7. Communication between health care and correctional personnel regarding the status of suicidal inmates.
8. Intervention regarding how to handle a suicide in progress.
9. Notification and reporting to appropriate authorities and family members of attempted or completed suicides.
10. Administrative review if a suicide occurs.

Such elements should be adequately defined through appropriate policies and procedures (Hayes, 1995b).

The use of inmates to function as observation aides for suicide watch remains controversial. Only a handful of jurisdictions throughout the country use inmate observation aides to observe suicidal inmates, with most of these jurisdictions using aides to supplement staff observation at 15-minute intervals (Morris, Steadman, & Veysey, 1997). West Virginia and the Federal Bureau of Prisons are reported to be the only prison systems that authorize the use of inmate observation aides in place of any staff supervision of suicidal inmates (Hayes, 1995a). Ethical and legal concerns provide the focus for the controversy for the use of inmate aides.

The use of closed-circuit television (CCTV) is a commonly used form of observation for inmates who are on a suicide watch. CCTV can be an effective supplement for regular checks of inmates by correctional and health care staff. However, the use of CCTV should not replace direct staff observations for a variety of reasons, including the therapeutic importance of direct contact between the inmate and staff and technical limitations involving the use of CCTV.

RESEARCH

Human subjects research within a correctional setting requires policies and procedures consistent with established ethical, medical, legal, and regulatory standards for human research. The Code of Federal Regulations allows, under appropriate circumstances and with pertinent external reviews and approvals, for the participation of prisoners in studies of the possible causes, effects, and processes of incarceration; studies on conditions particularly affecting prisoners as a group; and research designed with reasonable probability to improve the health and well being of the subject (NCCHC, 1996, 1997; U.S. Department of Health and Human Services, 1983). In addition, state law, as well as institutional or department policy, may govern the conduct of research in jails and prisons.

CONFIDENTIALITY

APHA (Dubler, 1986), NCCHC (1996, 1997), and APA (1989) standards or guidelines all discuss the need for specific, written policies and procedures regarding confidentiality for evaluation, treatment, and health record keeping. Exceptions to confidentiality are recognized by these organizations and include when the inmate is suicidal, homicidal, or assaultive or presents a clear and present risk of escape or the creation of internal disorder or riot.

Other circumstances that may lead to a lack of confidentiality concerning health care issues often depend on the nature of the institution and specific jurisdiction. For example, psychological testing conducted at reception or intake is often used for classification purposes and recorded in the inmate's institutional record, making it easily accessible to non-health care professionals. Also, parole boards in some states have access to an inmate's health care record without obtaining consent from the inmate. Correctional officers often need to be informed when an inmate is receiving psychotropic medication, or require specific information regarding the reasons for transfer of an inmate to a special unit for observation or treatment.

It is important that the clinician be familiar with state laws, rules, and regulations pertinent to the issue of confidentiality. Retention and release of substance abuse records are governed not only by federal law but also by state law in many states. Pertinent aspects concerning policies and procedures regarding confidentiality should be clearly explained to the inmate as part of the informed consent process when evaluation or treatment services are provided. Such explanations should occur whether the services are provided on an individual or group basis (Roback, Moore, Bloch, & Shelton, 1996). In general, because of the frequent exceptions to maintaining confidentiality, it is recommended that the inmate be informed that there are many occasions when confidentiality will not be maintained, but the clinician will use his/her judgment regarding the nature of the information to be released (Metzner, 1993).

Mental health records stored in the prison should be kept under secure conditions separate from custody records, and access to such records should be controlled by the health authority consistent with the applicable local, state, and federal law (NCCHC, 1996, 1997). Institutions should have written policies and procedures regarding inmate access to their own health, mental health, and institutional records.

QUALITY ASSURANCE

A quality assurance (QA) plan should be developed to monitor and evaluate the system's achievements of its goals and compliance with procedures as described in the policies and procedures manual. Regular chart reviews, monitoring of the use of seclusion and/or restraints, suicides, and other relevant areas are important components of the QA program. Fromberg (1988) described a 10-step monitoring evaluation process that had been designed for use in all QA activities by the Joint Commission on Accreditation of Healthcare Organization (JCAHO). A quality assurance committee should meet at least quarterly to monitor the quality of health services provided.

NCCHC (1996, 1997) standards require a comprehensive quality improvement (QI) program involving a multidisciplinary quality improvement committee of health care providers who meet frequently with correctional administrators on a regular basis to design QI monitoring activities and to review the results. The JCAHO (1992) provided a useful publication for providing guidance to organizations transitioning from QA to QI programs.

MANAGEMENT INFORMATION SYSTEMS

Little has been reported in the medical literature about computerized management information systems within correctional health care. Correctional systems are increasingly developing management information systems that provide information concerning medication prescriptions, psychiatric diagnosis, level of functional impairments, nature of the mental health intervention provided, and routine demographic data. A systemwide management information system allows the capacity to efficiently generate evaluation reports on facilities and programs and establish routine monitors for utilization review and patient care monitoring. Many quality improvement activities are greatly facilitated by the use of a management information system (Metzner, 1992).

It is important to have a system designed to gather, manipulate, and analyze data to effectively manage large, correctional mental health care systems. The most efficient management information system is one that is computerized and designed to provide pertinent information in a "user-friendly" manner (McDonald, 1995). Such a system allows for ongoing needs assessment studies, better management of operations, long-term planning, and clinical research, and can be useful in providing needed information to support budget requests.

OTHER SPECIFIC TREATMENT POPULATIONS

Violence as a Public Health Problem

The National Commission on Correctional Health Care (NCCHC) endorsed the Centers for Disease Control and Prevention (CDC) initiative to treat violence as a major public health problem. This position was in response to the recognition that interpersonal violence (i.e., homicide, rape, robbery, aggravated assault, abuse and neglect of young and old people) has grown to epidemic proportions. In 1990 the homicide rate in the United States was more than 11 times that of Japan and 9 times that of England (NCCHC, 1995).

The NCCHC recommends that correctional health services incorporate violence risk assessment into receiving screening of all inmates during intake, all inmate health assessments, and mental health evaluations. It is also recommended by the NCCHC that prevention and treatment programs be developed for inmates with histories of expressive violence (i.e., violence which grows out of some kind of interpersonal altercation in which one person intends harm on another). Training for both health care professionals and correctional officers concerning expressive violence and non-physical methods of prevention and controlling disruptive behaviors stemming from expressive violence is emphasized (NCCHC, 1995).

Female Inmates

Female inmates generally, and female inmates with mental disorders in particular, have been less well studied than have male inmates (Fletcher, Shaver, & Moon, 1993; Sommers, 1995). In the past, facilities and services for female inmates have been inferior to those provided to male inmates (Goldstein, 1983). Certainly there are fewer facilities for women than men, given their smaller numbers; this creates problems when a transfer to another facility is desirable for administrative reasons.

One study of pretrial women detainees in an urban jail revealed that lifetime prevalence rates for all mental disorders in women detainees was higher than for those in the general population, except for schizophrenia and panic disorder (Teplin, Abram, & McClelland, 1996). Substance abuse or dependence, primarily heroin and cocaine, were the most prevalent disorders, with over one half of detainees meeting DSM-III-R diagnostic criteria within the previous 6 months. A study involving women prisoners also revealed disproportionately high rates of substance abuse and dependence and personality disorders (antisocial, borderline), compared with women in the general community population (Jordan, Schlenger, Fairbank, & Caddell, 1996). An estimated 41% of women in prison reported that they had been sexually or physically abused, and 39% of all female inmates reported that they had used drugs daily during the month before their offense (Snell, 1994). Women in prison were more likely than their male counterparts to have had at least one member in their immediate family who had been incarcerated. Incarcerated women are more likely than men to be prescribed psychotropic medications (Sommers & Baskin, 1991). Results of various studies have documented the need for developing treatment programs or female inmates, especially concerning issues related to sexual abuse, affective disorders, and substance abuse (Birecree, Bloom, Williams, & Dolan, 1992; Daniel, Robins, Reid, & Wilfley, 1988).

Ackerman (1987) described many topics of concern pertinent to women incarcerated in jail. These issues, though not noted by frequency, include the following:

1. Grief and distress they have caused their relatives.
2. Restrictive telephone hours and visiting.
3. Fear of job loss or future job placement difficulties.

4. Distress over attempting to remain drug-free.
5. Fear of contracting AIDS.
6. Depressive dysphoria.
7. Dislike and fear of correctional officers.
8. Fear of "going crazy."
9. Dislike of jail food and clothing.
10. Fear of sexual advances or violent assault.
11. Inattention to chronic health problems
12. Explaining to their children why they are incarcerated.
13. Lack of physical contact with their children and families.
14. Divorce or custody proceedings against them while incarcerated.
15. Fear of former friends once again getting them into trouble with the law.
16. Fear of being sent to prison.
17. Unfairness of the bond system.

Black Inmates

Mauer and Huling (1995) reported that almost one in three (30.2%) black males in the age group 20 to 29 was in prison or jail, on probation, or on parole at any given day during 1994, compared with 6.7% of similarly aged white and 12.3% of Hispanic men. The total number of young black men estimated to be under the control of the criminal justice system during 1994, 787,692, was greater than the total number of black men of all ages enrolled in college, namely 436,000 as of 1986. Black inmates represented 44% of the jail population during June 1994 (Perkins et al., 1995) and 50.8% of the prison population during 1993 (Beck et al., 1993), which compares with 12.1% of the general population being black (Daphne, 1992). Almost 5% (134,416) of black women in the age group 20 to 29 was under criminal justice control on any given day in 1994. There is increasing evidence that the set of policies and practices contained within the phrase "War on Drugs" has disproportionately affected blacks and other minorities (Mauer & Huling, 1995). Further research and education are required concerning special issues relevant to the treatment of black inmates with mental illness within the criminal justice system; data from one state's prison system revealed that minority inmates were less likely to receive mental health treatment than were white inmates (Steadman, Holohean, & Dvoskin, 1991).

Older and Physically Disabled Inmates

The numbers of older inmates in prison have substantially increased. In 1989, the nation's prisons held 30,500 inmates 50 years or older; by 1993 that number had risen to almost 50,500 (Bragg, 1995). The increase in the older age population is a result of longer prison sentences authorized by statute and ordered by trial courts, "three-strikes" sentencing laws, the abolition of parole in some states, and new laws that require inmates to serve all or most of their sentences. Prison mental health systems need to develop appropriate services for this growing population, including special units or even facilities for a geriatric inmate population. One study, for example, found older, male inmates to have a 1-month prevalence rate of major depression at 50 times that of community samples (Koenig, Johnson, Bellard, Denker, & Fenlon, 1995).

CONCLUSION

There has been an explosion in the numbers of people incarcerated during the past two decades in the United States. A significant number of these inmates require mental health treatment during their stay in either a jail or prison, and increasing numbers of mental health professionals are needed to staff these facilities. Successful class action suits and the development of national guidelines and standards concerning correctional mental health care have accelerated the development of more adequate mental health systems within jails and prisons. Courts have identified the need for correctional systems to provide inmates with reasonable access to adequate mental health systems.

REFERENCES

Ackerman, H. P. (1987). *Therapy with women in jail: A manual for the mental health worker.* Dayton, OH: American Correctional Health Services Association.

American Bar Association. (1985). *Criminal justice mental health standards.* Washington, DC: Author.

American Correctional Association. (1990). *Standards for adult correctional institutions* (3rd ed.). College Park, MD: Author.

American Nurses Association. (1985). *Standards of nursing practices in correctional facilities.* Kansas City, MO: Author.

American Psychiatric Association. (1987). *Diagnostic and statistical manual of mental disorders* (3rd ed., rev.). Washington, DC: Author.

American Psychiatric Association. (1989). *Psychiatric services in jails and prisons* (Task Force Report No. 29). Washington, DC: Author.

American Psychiatric Association. (1994). *Diagnostic and statistical manual of mental disorders* (4th ed.). Washington, DC: Author.

Andrews, D. A., Zinger, I., Hoge, R. D., Bonta, J., Gendreau, P., & Cullen, F. T. (1990). Does correctional treatment work? *Criminology, 28,* 369–404.

Anno, B. J. (1991a). *Prison health care: Guidelines for the management of an adequate delivery system.* Washington, DC: U.S. Department of Justice, National Institute of Corrections.

Anno, B. J. (1991b). Organizational structure of prison health care: Results of a national survey. *Journal of Prison and Jail Health, 10,* 59–74.

Anno, B. J. (1991c). The cost of correctional health care: Results of a national survey. *Journal of Prison and Jail Health, 2,* 105–134.

Aungst, S. (1995). Residential treatment unit: Minimum physical plant standards. Unpublished data, Ohio Department of Rehabilitation and Correction.

Beck, A. J., & Gilliard, D. K. (1995). Prisoners in 1994. *Bureau of Justice Statistics,* NCJ-151654, 1–21.

Beck, A., Gilliard, D., Greenfeld, A., Harlow, C., Hester, T., Jankowski, L., Snell, T., Stephan, J., & Morton, D. (1993). Survey of state prison inmates, 1991. *Bureau of Justice Statistics,* NCJ-136949, 1–33.

Bell v. Wolfish, 441 U.S. 520 (1979).

Birecree, E., Bloom, J. D., Williams, M., & Dolan, M. (1992). *Mental health needs of women in Oregon's prison: A preliminary report.* Paper presented at the 23rd annual meeting of the American Academy of Psychiatry and the Law, Boston, MA.

Bland, R. C., Newman, S. C., Dyck, R. J., & Orn, H. (1990). Prevalence of psychiatric disorders and suicide attempts in a prison population. *Canadian Journal of Psychiatry, 35,* 407–413.

Bolton, A. (1976). *A study of the need for and availability of mental health services for mentally disordered jail inmates and juvenile detention facilities.* Boston: Arthur Bolton Associates.

Bonnie, R. J. (1990). Dilemmas in administering the death penalty: Conscientious abstention, professional ethics and the needs of the legal system. *Law and Human Behavior, 14,* 67–90.

Bowring v. Godwin, 551 F.2d 44, 47 (4th Cir. 1977).

Bragg, R. (1995, November 1). Where Alabama inmates fade into old age. *The New York Times,* p. A1.

Brown, B. S. (1992). Program models. In C. G. Leukefeld & F. M. Tims (Eds.), *Drug abuse treatment in prisons and jails* (pp. 31–37). Washington, DC: U.S. Department of Health and Human Services.

Bukstel, L. H., & Kilmann, P. R. (1980). Psychological effects of imprisonment. *Psychological Bulletin, 88,* 469–493.

Byrne, C. (1995). *Fact sheet: Drug data summary.* Rockville, MD: Office of National Drug Control Policy, Drugs and Crime Clearinghouse.

Cohen, F. (1988). *Legal issues and the mentally disordered prisoner.* Washington, DC: U.S. Department of Justice, National Institute of Corrections.

Cohen, F. (1992). *Liability for custodial suicide: The information base requirements. Jail Suicide Update, 4,* 1–11.

Cohen, F. (1993). Captives' legal right to mental health care. *Law and Psychology Review, 17,* 1–39.

Cohen, F., & Dvoskin, J. (1992a). Inmates with mental disorders: A guide to law and practice. *Mental and Physical Disability Law Reporter, 16,* 339–346.

Cohen, F., & Dvoskin, J. (1992b). Inmates with mental disorders: A guide to law and practice. *Mental and Physical Disability Law Reporter, 16,* 462–470.

Condelli, W. S., Dvoskin, J. A., & Holanchock, H. (1994). Intermediate care programs for inmates with psychiatric disorders. *Bulletin of the American Academy of Psychiatry and the Law, 22,* 63–70.

Corrigan, P. W., Yudofsky, S. C., & Silver, J. M. (1993). Pharmacological and behavioral treatments for aggressive psychiatric inpatients. *Hospital and Community Psychiatry, 44,* 125–133.

Cote, G., & Hodgins, S. (1990). Co-occurring mental disorders among criminal offenders. *Bulletin of the American Academy of Psychiatry and the Law, 18,* 271–281.

Daniel, A. E., Robins, A. J., Reid, J. C., & Wilfley, D. E. (1988). Lifetime and six month's prevalence of psychiatric disorders among sentenced female offenders. *Bulletin of the American Academy of Psychiatry and the Law, 16,* 333–342.

Daphne, D. (Ed.) (1992). *Britannica of the year.* Chicago: Encyclopedia Britannica.

DeShaney v. Winnebago County Department of Social Services, 489 U.S. 189 (1989).

DeWitt, K. (1995, December 25). Crowded jails spur new look at punishment. *The New York Times,* pp. A1, A8.

Diamond, R. J., Brooner, R. K., Lowe, D., & Savage, C. (1981). The use of minor tranquilizers with jail inmates. *Hospital and Community Psychiatry, 32,* 40–43.

Dubler, N. N. (Ed.). (1986). *Standards for health services in correctional facilities* (2nd ed.). Washington, DC: American Public Health Association.

DuRand, C. J., Burtka, G. J., Federman, E. J., Haycox, J. A., & Smith, J. W. (1995). A quarter century of suicide in a major urban jail: Implications for community psychiatry. *American Journal of Psychiatry, 152,* 1077–1080.

Dvoskin, J. A. (1991). Allocating treatment resources for sex offenders. *Hospital and Community Psychiatry, 41,* 229.

Dvoskin, J. A. (1994). The structure of correctional mental health services. In R. Rosner (Ed.), *Principles and practice of forensic psychiatry* (pp. 380–387). New York: Chapman and Hall.

Estelle v. Gamble, 429 U.S. 97 (1976).

Farmer v. Brennan, 511 U.S. 825 (1994).

Farmer v. Carlson, 685 F. Supp. 1335,1339 (M.D.Pa. 1988).

Fletcher, B. R., Shaver, L. D., & Moon, D. G. (Eds.). (1993). *Women prisoners: A forgotten population.* Westport, CT: Praeger.

Fromberg, R. N. (1988). *The Joint Commission guide to quality assurance.* Oakbrook Terrace, IL: Joint Commission on Accreditation of Healthcare Organizations.

Fulwiler, C., Forbes, C., Santangelo, S. L., & Folstein, M. (1997). Self-mutilation and suicide attempt: Distinguishing features in prisoners. *Journal of the American Academy of Psychiatry and the Law, 25,* 69–77.

Gaudreault v. Municipality of Salem, 923 F.2d 203,208 (1st Cir. 1990), cert. denied 111 S. Ct. 2266 (1991).

Gendreau, P. (1996). Offender rehabilitation: What we know and what needs to be done. *Criminal Justice and Behavior, 23,* 144–161.

Gilliard, D. K., & Beck, A. J. (1994). Prisoners in 1993. *Bureau of Justice Statistics Bulletin,* NCJ-147036, 1–11.

Glaser, W. F. (1985). Admissions to a prison psychiatric unit. *Australian and New Zealand Journal of Psychiatry, 19,* 45–52.

Goldstein, N. (1983). Psychiatry in prisons. *Psychiatric Clinics of North America, 6,* 751–765.

Goldstrom, I. D., Manderscheid, R. W., & Rudolph, L. A. (1992). Mental health services in state correctional facilities. In R. Manderscheid & M. Sonnenschein (Eds.), *Mental health, United States, 1992* (pp. 231–254). Washington, DC: U.S. Government Printing Office.

Grabowski v. Jackson Co. Public Defenders Office et al., 47 F.3d 1386, 1397 (5th Cir. 1995).

Grassian, S., & Friedman, N. (1986). Effects of sensory deprivation in psychiatric seclusion and solitary confinement. *International Journal of Law and Psychiatry, 8,* 49–65.

Greenberg, S. A., & Shuman, D. W. (1997). Irreconcilable conflict between therapeutic and forensic roles. *Professional Psychology: Research and Practice, 28,* 50–57.

Greene, R. T. (1988). A comprehensive mental health care system for prison inmates: retrospective look at New York's ten year experience. *International Journal of Law and Psychiatry, 11,* 381–389.

Group for the Advancement of Psychiatry. (1977). *Psychiatry and sex psychopathy legislation: The 30s to the 80s.* New York: Mental Health Materials Center.

Guy, E., Platt, J. J., Zwerling, I., & Bullock, S. (1985). Mental health status of prisoners in an urban jail. *Criminal Justice and Behavior,12,* 29–53.

Hafemeister, T. L., & Petrilla, J. (1994). Treating the mentally disordered offender: Society's uncertain, conflicted, and changing views. *Florida State University Law Review, 21,* 729–871.

Harlow, C. W. (1991). Drugs and jail inmates, 1989. *Bureau of Justice Statistics,* NCJ-130-836, 1–12.

Harlow, C. W. (1994). Comparing federal and state prison inmates, 1991. *Bureau of Justice Statistics,* NCJ-145864, 1–26.

Hayes, L. M. (1988). *National study of jail suicides: Seven years later.* Alexandria, VA: National Center on Institutions and Alternatives.

Hayes, L. M. (1995a). Prison suicide: An overview and guide to prevention. Jail suicide/mental health update. *National Center on Institutions and Alternatives, 6,* 1–16.

Hayes, L. M. (1995b). *Prison suicide: An overview and guide to prevention.* Washington, DC: National Institute of Corrections, U.S. Department of Justice.

Heilbrun, K., Radelet, M. L., & Dvoskin, J. (1992). The debate on treating individuals incompetent for execution. *American Journal of Psychiatry, 149,* 596–605.

Innes, C. A. (1988). *Profile of state inmates.* Bureau of Justice Statistics Special Report. Washington, DC: U.S. Department of Justice.

Iverson, G. L., Franzen, M. D., Demarest, D. S., & Hammond, J. A. (1993). Neuropsychological screening in correctional settings. *Criminal Justice and Behavior, 20,* 347–358.

James, J. F., Gregory, D., Jones, R. K., & Rundell, O. H. (1980). Psychiatric morbidity in prisons. *Hospital and Community Psychiatry, 31,* 674–677.

Joint Commission on Accreditation of Healthcare Organizations. (1992). *The transition from QA to QI: Performance-based evaluation of mental health organizations.* Oakbrook Terrace, IL: Joint Commission on Accreditation of Healthcare Organizations.

Jordan B. K., Schlenger, W. E., Fairbank, J. A., & Caddell, J. M. (1996). Prevalence of psychiatric disorders among incarcerated women: II. Convicted felons entering prison. *Archives of General Psychiatry, 53,* 513–519.

Kal, E. F. (1977). Mental health in jail. *American Journal of Psychiatry, 134,* 463.

Kaufman, E. (1980). The violation of psychiatric standards of care in prisons. *American Journal of Psychiatry, 137,* 566–570.

Kennedy, J. A. (1992). *Fundamentals of psychiatric treatment planning.* Washington, DC: American Psychiatric Press.

Koenig, H. G., Johnson, S., Bellard, J., Denker, M., & Fenlon, R. (1995). Depression and anxiety disorder among older male inmates at a Federal correctional facility. *Psychiatric Services, 46,* 399–401.

Lamb, H. R., & Grant, R. W. (1982). The mentally ill in an urban county jail. *Archives of General Psychiatry, 39,* 17–22.

Lamb, H. R., & Grant, R. W. (1983). Mentally ill women in a county jail. *Archives of General Psychiatry, 40,* 363–368.

Lipton, D. S., Falkin, G. P., & Wexler, H. K. (1992). Correctional drug abuse treatment in the United States: An overview. In C. G. Leukefeld & F. M. Tims (Eds.), *Drug abuse treatment in prisons and jails* (pp. 8–30). Washington, DC: U.S. Department of Health and Human Services.

Lynch, J. P., Smith, S. K., Graziadei, H. A., & Pittayathikhun, T. (1994). Profile of inmates in the United States and in England and Wales, 1991. *Bureau of Justice Statistics,* NCJ-144863, 1–23.

Marcus, P., & Alcabes, P. (1993). Characteristics of suicides by inmates in an urban jail. *Hospital and Community Psychiatry, 44,* 256–261.

Mauer, M., & Huling, T. (1995). *Young black Americans and the criminal justice system: Five years later.* Washington, DC: The Sentencing Project.

McCorkle, R. C. (1993). Fear of victimization and symptoms of psychopathology among prison inmates. *Journal of Offender Rehabilitation, 19,* 27–41.

McDonald, D. C. (1995). *Managing prison health care and costs.* Washington, DC: U.S. Department of Justice.

McGuckin v. Smith, 974 F.2d 1050, 1059–60 (9th Cir. 1992).

Meachum v. Fano, 427 U.S. 215, 96 S.Ct. 2532.

Metzner, J. L. (1992). A survey of university/prison collaboration and computerized tracking systems in prisons. *Hospital and Community Psychiatry, 43,* 713–716.

Metzner, J. L. (1993). Guidelines for psychiatric services in prisons. *Criminal Behavior and Mental Health, 3,* 252–267.

Metzner, J. L., Fryer, G. E., & Usery, D. (1990). Prison mental health services: Results of a national survey of standards, resources, administrative structure, and litigation. *Journal of Forensic Sciences, 35,* 433–438.

Metzner, J. L., Miller, R. D., & Kleinsasser, D. (1994). Mental health screening and evaluation within prisons. *Bulletin of the American Academy of Psychiatry and the Law, 22,* 451–457.

Miller, E. (1978). *Jail management.* Lexington, MA: Lexington Books.

Monahan, J., & McDonough, L. B. (1980). Delivering community mental health services to a county jail population. *Bulletin of the American Academy of Psychiatry and the Law, 8,* 28–32.

Morgan, C. (1981). Developing mental health services for local jails. *Criminal Justice and Behavior, 8,* 259–273.

Morgan, C. (1982). Service delivery models: A summary of examples. In C. Dunn & H. Steadman (Eds.), *Mental health services in local jails: Report of a special national workshop. Crime and delinquency issues: A monograph series* (DHHS Pub. No. ADM 82-1181). Washington, DC: U.S. Government Printing Office.

Morris, S. M., Steadman, H. J., & Veysey, B. M. (1997). Mental health services in United States jails: A survey of innovative practices. *Criminal Justice and Behavior, 24,* 3–19.

Mortimer, D. B. (1993). The psychiatrist's role in the special management unit. *International Journal of Offender Therapy and Comparative Criminology, 37,* 117–130.

National Commission on Correctional Health Care. (1995). Position statement: Correctional health care and the prevention of violence. *Journal of Correctional Health Care, 2,* 71–74.

National Commission on Correctional Health Care. (1996). *Standards for health services in jails.* Chicago: Author.

National Commission on Correctional Health Care. (1997). *Standards for health services in prisons.* Chicago: Author.

National Institute of Justice. (1990). *1989 drug use forecasting annual report.* Washington, DC: U.S. Department of Justice.

Negy, C., Woods, D. J., & Carlson, R. (1997). The relationship between female inmates' coping and adjustment in a minimum-security prison. *Criminal Justice and Behavior, 24,* 224–233.

Nielsen, E. D. (1979). Community mental health services in the community jail. *Community Mental Health Journal, 15,* 27–32.

Nizny, M. M. (1984, February). Mental health in an Ohio jail community. *Ohio State Medical Journal, 80,* 95–99.

Norris v. Frame, 585 F.2d 1183 (3d.Cir. 1978).

Pace v. Fauver, 479 F.Supp. 456 (Dist NJ, 1979), *off'd* 649 F.2d 860 (3d Cir. 1981).

Perkins, C., Stephan, J. J., & Beck, A. J. (1995). Jail inmates 1993–1994. *Bureau of Justice Statistics,* NCJ-151651, 1–22.

Peters, R. H., & May, R. (1992). Drug treatment services in jails. In C. P. Leukefeld & F. M. Tims (Eds.), *Drug abuse treatment in prisons and jails* (pp. 38–50). Washington, DC: U.S. Department of Health and Human Services.

Petrich, J. (1976a). Psychiatric treatment in jail: An experiment in healthcare delivery. *Hospital and Community Psychiatry, 27,* 413–415.

Petrich, J. (1976b). Rate of psychiatric morbidity in a metropolitan county jail population. *American Journal of Psychiatry, 133,* 1439–1444.

Piotrowski, K. W., Lasacco, D., & Guze, S. B. (1976). Psychiatric disorders and crime: A study of pretrial psychiatric examinations. *Diseases of the Nervous System, 3,* 309–311.

Prison Litigation Reform Act (PLRA), 18 U.S.C. § 3626 (1996) *et seq.*

Ringuette v. City of Fall River, 1995 WL 335159 (D.Mass).

Roback, H., Moore, R. F., Bloch, F. S., & Shelton, M. (1996). Confidentiality in group psychotherapy: Empirical findings and the law. *International Journal of Group Psychotherapy, 46,* 117–135.

Robins, L. N., Helzer, J. E., Croughlan, J., et al. (1981). National Institute of Mental Health Diagnostic Interview Schedule: Its history, characteristics, and validity. *Archives of General Psychiatry, 38,* 381–389.

Roth, L. H. (1986). Correctional psychiatry. In W. J. Curran, A. L. McGarry, & S. A. Shah (Eds.), *Forensic psychiatry and psychology: Perspectives and standards for interdisciplinary practice* (pp. 429–468). Philadelphia: Davis.

Sandin v. Connor, 115 S. Ct. 2293 (1995).

Santamour, M. B. (1989). *The mentally retarded offender and corrections.* Washington, DC: Saint Mary's Press.

Schuckit, M. A., Herrman, G., & Schuckit, J. J. (1977). The importance of psychiatric illness in newly arrested prisoners. *Journal of Nervous and Mental Disease, 165,* 118–125.

Snell, T. (1994). *Women in prisons.* Washington, DC: U.S. Department of Justice.

Snell, T. L. (1995). Correctional populations in the United States, 1992. *Bureau of Justice Statistics,* NCJ-146413, 1–182.

Sommers, E. K. (1995). *Voices from within: Women who have broken the law.* Toronto: University of Toronto Press.

Sommers, I., & Baskin, D. R. (1991). Assessing the appropriateness of the prescription of psychiatric medications in prison. *Journal of Nervous and Mental Disease, 179,* 267–273.

Steadman, H. J., Fabisiak, S., Dvoskin, J., & Holohean, E. J. (1987). A survey of mental disability among state prison inmates. *Hospital and Community Psychiatry, 38,* 1086–1090.

Steadman, H. J., Holohean, E. J., Dvoskin, J. (1991). Estimating mental health needs and service utilization among prison inmates. *Bulletin of the American Academy of Psychiatry and the Law, 19,* 297–307.

Steadman, H. J., McCarty, D. W., & Morrissey, J. P. (1989). *The mentally ill in jail: Planning for essential services.* New York: Guilford Press.

Stefan, S. (1992). Leaving civil rights to the "experts": From deference to abdication under the professional judgment standard. *Yale Law Journal, 639,* 704–707.

Stein, E., & Brown, J. D. (1991). Group therapy in a forensic setting. *Canadian Journal of Psychiatry, 36,* 718–722.

Stephan, J. (1990). Census of state and federal facilities, 1990. *Bureau of Justice Statistics,* NCJ-137003, 1–32.

Strasburger, L. H., Gutheil, T. G., & Brodsky, A. (1997). On wearing two hats: Role conflict in serving as both psychotherapist and expert witness. *American Journal of Psychiatry, 154,* 448–456.

Sullivan v. Flannigan, 8 F.3d 591 (7th Cir. 1993).

Swank, G. E., & Winer, D. (1976). Occurrence of psychiatric disorder in a county jail population. *American Journal of Psychiatry, 133,* 1331–1333.

Swetz, A., Salive, M. E., Stough, T., & Brewer, T. F. (1989). The prevalence of mental illness in a state correctional institution for men. *Journal of Prison and Jail Health, 8,* 3–15.

Tardiff, K. (1992). The current state of psychiatry in the treatment of violent patients. *Archives of General Psychiatry, 49,* 493–499.

Task Force on Offenders with Special Needs. (1993). *Report of the task force on offenders with special needs.* Lanham, MD: American Correctional Association.

Teplin, L. A. (1990). The prevalence of severe mental disorder among male urban jail detainees: Comparison with the epidemiologic catchment area program. *American Journal of Public Health, 80,* 663–669.

Teplin, L. A. (1994). Psychiatric and substance abuse disorders among male urban jail detainees. *American Journal of Public Health, 84,* 290–293.

Teplin, L. A., Abram, K. M., & McClelland, G. M. (1996). Prevalence of psychiatric disorders among incarcerated women: I. Pretrial jail detainees. *Archives of General Psychiatry, 53,* 505–512.

Teplin, L. A., & Voit, E. S. (1996). Criminalizing the seriously mentally ill: Putting the problem in perspective. In B. D. Sales & S. A. Shah (Eds.), *Mental health and law: Research, policy and services* (pp. 283–317). Durham, NC: Carolina Academic Press.

Timrots, A., & Byrne, C. (1995). Drug use trends. *Fact Sheet,* NCJ-153518, 1–6.

Toch, H. (1992). *Living in prison: The ecology of survival.* Washington, DC: American Psychological Association.

Toch, H., & Adams, K. (1989). *Coping: Maladaptation in prisons.* New Brunswick, NJ: Transaction Publishers.

Torrey, E. F., Stieber, J., Ezekiel, J., Wolfe, S. M., Sharfstein, J., Noble, J. H., & Flynn,

L. M. (1992). *Criminalizing the seriously mentally ill: The abuse of jails as mental hospitals.* Washington, DC: Public Citizen's Health Research Group.

Turner, T. H., & Tofler, D. S. (1986). Indicators of psychiatric disorder among women admitted to prison. *British Medical Journal, 292,* 651–653.

United States Bureau of the Census (1991). *Statistical abstract of the United States* (111th ed.). Washington, DC: U.S. Government Printing Office.

United States General Accounting Office. (1991). *Drug treatment: State prisons face challenges in providing services* (Pub. No. GAO/HRD-91-128). Washington, DC: U.S. Government Printing Office.

United States Department of Health and Human Services. (1983). *The code of federal regulations* (45 CPR 46, rev. March 6, 1983). Washington, DC: U.S. Department of Health and Human Services.

United States Department of Justice. (1995a). Executive summary: Correctional populations in the United States. *Bureau of Justice Statistics,* NCJ-153849, 1–2.

United States Department of Justice. (1995b). Drugs and crime facts, 1994. *Bureau of Justice Statistics,* NCJ-154043, 1–37.

Virginia Department of Mental Health. (1984). *The mentally ill in Virginia's jails: Final report of the Joint Task Force.* Richmond, VA: Virginia Department of Mental Health and Mental Retardation and the Virginia Department of Corrections.

Vitek v. Jones, 445 U.S. 480 (1980).

Washington v. Harper, 110 S.Ct. 1028 (1990).

Washington, P., & Diamond, R. J. (1985). Prevalence of mental illness among women incarcerated in five California county jails. *Research in Community and Mental Health, 5,* 33–41.

Wechsler, D. (1981). *Manual for the Wechsler Adult Intelligence Scale—Revised.* Cleveland: Psychological Corp.

Weinberger, L. E., & Sreenivasan, S. (1994). Ethical and professional conflicts in correctional psychology. *Professional Psychology: Research and Practice, 25,* 161–167.

Whitmer, G. E. (1980). From hospitals to jails: the fate of California's deinstitutionalized mentally ill. *American Journal of Orthopsychiatry, 50,* 65–75.

Wistedt, B., Helldin, L., Omerov, M., & Palmstierna, T. (1994). Pharmacotherapy for aggressive and violent behavior: A view of practical management from clinicians. *Criminal Behavior and Mental Health, 4,* 328–340.

Youngberg v. Romeo, 457 U.S. 307 (1982).

6

TREATMENT
OF THE SEXUAL OFFENDER

Howard E. Barbaree
William L. Marshall

INTRODUCTION

This chapter is a review of extant treatment programs for sexual offenders. In this review, we concentrate on issues directed toward the treatment of the more dangerous sexual offenders. These include men who have raped or sexually assaulted adult women and men who have molested or sexually assaulted children. We do not consider the treatment of men who have committed less intrusive offenses or who exhibit nuisance sexual deviations such as exhibitionism, voyeurism, or making obscene telephone calls, nor do we consider the treatment of sexual deviations that rarely come to clinical attention, such as frotteurism.

Additionally, there are three subgroups of the sexual offender population that deserve special attention, but more than can be given in this chapter. Juvenile offenders are a special subgroup because antihormonal treatments may be contraindicated before physical maturity, and use of explicit and violent stimulus material during plethysmographic assessments may be harmful or counterproductive. However, for the juvenile offender, the remaining elements of treatment described here are seen by some authors to be crucial (Kahn & Lafond, 1988; Ryan, Lane, Davis, & Isaac, 1987; Saunders & Awad, 1988). Mentally handicapped offenders may not benefit from the cognitive aspects of therapy, and may require more direct supervision to prevent reoffense, although the other elements of treatment described here are crucial (Griffiths, Hindsburger, & Christian, 1985). Finally, female sex offenders have been receiving increasing attention recently, but this chapter will focus on male offenders and will therefore use the masculine pronoun "he" when referring to the offenders. Where germane, these special exceptions will be mentioned, but dealing comprehensively with the treatment of these special groups is beyond the scope of this chapter.

For this chapter, rapists are men who have committed sexual assaults against women above the age of consent. These men are most often in their late teens, their 20s, or early 30s; they have a varied criminal background including such crimes as breaking, and entering, theft, and physical assault, and they usually begin their criminal careers at an early age (Amir, 1971; Christie, Marshall, & Lanthier, 1977; Cohen, Garafalo, Boucher, & Seghorn, 1971; Gebhard, Gagnon, Pomeroy, & Christenson, 1965).

For this chapter, child molesters are men who have been convicted of a sexual assault against a child. The upper age of the "child" category of victim varies across jurisdictions and research studies, depending on the legal age of consent. Usually the definition of a child molester also requires that the offender be at least 5 years older than the victim. Among incarcerated sexual offenders, child molesters are likely to be older than rapists. They do not show the same diversity of nonsexual offenses in their criminal history, compared with rapists, and they are not likely to have begun their criminal careers as early as did the rapists (Baxter, Marshall, Barbaree, Davidson, & Malcolm, 1984). Beyond these generalizations, child molesters are more heterogeneous than rapists in many respects. For example, in terms of scholastic achievement (Bard et al., 1987) and intelligence (Marshall, Barbaree & Christophe, 1986), the distribution of scores of child molesters has a greater variance than that of rapists due primarily to the existence of a large group of individuals at the lower end of each scale. Indeed, this low-IQ subgroup among the child molesters requires special consideration in the planning of treatment and in the assessment of dangerousness (Barbaree & Marshall, 1988; Marshall et al., 1986).

Child molesters have been categorized according to the nature of their offending. It is usual to distinguish between incest offenders who have offended against their own children (primarily their own daughters and stepdaughters) and nonfamilial child molesters, who molest children with whom they have no familial or legal relationship. Child molestation by stepfathers is most often included in the incest category, as is the molestation perpetrated by a common-law husband of the victim's mother. Nonfamilial child molesters have been subdivided according to the gender of their victims, and it has become accepted to refer to these subgroups as heterosexual and homosexual child molesters, but this may be a misnomer. We have found that classifying men who molest boys according to their relative laboratory arousal to adult male and female stimuli results in heterosexuals outnumbering homosexuals by a ratio of 2:1 (Marshall, Barbaree, & Butt, 1988).

Sexual murderers are very rarely seen in treatment programs for sexual offenders. Although these offenses attract a great deal of media and public attention (Quinsey, 1984), they are extremely rare (Swigert, Farrell, & Yoels, 1976). Among a sample of rapists and child molesters, the amount of force used in the commission of offenses varied from subterfuge and verbal threats to severe physical assault (Christie et al., 1977; Marshall & Christie, 1981). In the extreme, the assaults may result in the death of the victims and in this regard, sexual murder may be seen as an extension of the processes and dimensions relevant to less severe sexual assaults. Some writers, however, have regarded sexual murder to be a category apart from other sexual assaults (Quinsey, 1984), and these offenses might be better understood when factors relating to hostility and aggression are given greater consideration (Megargee, 1984), although in at least some cases the murder might be aimed at silencing the victim. Unfortunately, until very recently, the scientific literature on sexual murderers is restricted to clinical impressions and psychoanalytic case histories (Brittain, 1970; Howell, 1972; Revitch, 1965; Thornton & Pray, 1975; Williams, 1964), and the bulk of descriptions of the treatment of sexual offenders does not differentiate murderers from others. Recently, Grubin (1994) has made a more systematic study of sexual murderers. He studied 142 rapists incarcerated in English prisons, 21 of whom had murdered their victims. The sexual murderers were significantly more socially isolated, had fewer peer relations as children, were more likely to live alone, and reported fewer adult sexual relationships compared with the nonmurderers.

When convicted, rapists and child molesters often face prison terms ranging from several months to several years, depending upon the jurisdiction, the number of previous offenses, and the severity of the current sexual assault. Sex offender statutes for those with mental disorders (Weiner, 1985) in the United States and dangerous offender legislation in Canada have provided for indefinite sentences for many sexual offenders. The vast majority of sex offenders in most jurisdictions do not receive treatment, although some are treated in the prison setting or in a secure mental hospital. Less frequently, they are treated in a community-based setting while on probation or parole. Often, treatment is part of a release plan and precedes parole or release to the community. The offender's willingness to involve himself in treatment is typically a consequence of pressure brought to bear on him by the correctional or mental health system. Often, he feels added pressure from his family. To a man entering treatment, its outcome seems to have a bearing on his chances for parole or release. Similarly, when a man enters a community-based treatment setting with criminal charges pending, involvement in treatment may influence whether or not he will be sentenced to a jail term rather than probation, the length of a jail term, or in some cases the avoidance of prosecution altogether.

TREATMENT EVALUATION

Evaluation of treatment efficacy for sexual offenders is enormously difficult. Reviews of this literature may give the impression that treatment is not successful (Furby, Weinrott, & Blackshaw, 1989) or they may be cautiously optimistic (Marshall & Barbaree, 1990). In this circumstance, controversy over the available data is evident (Marshall, Jones, Ward, Johnston, & Barbaree, 1991). Before describing the treatment programs, we consider a number of the more salient methodological difficulties in evaluating treatment efficacy in this area.

Because the primary objective in treating sexual offenders is to prevent further offending, the most important criterion measure of treatment success is reduced rates of reoffense, but reoffense rate can be an elusive measure. It is well known that the rate of reoffense as indicated by police records of charges and convictions is an underestimate of the actual rate of reoffense (Furby et al., 1989; Quinsey, 1983). Arrests and convictions are a product of factors such as the offender's luck or skill at avoiding being caught, the quality of the case against the offender, and the inclinations of the victims to report the matter. It is possible to get information concerning additional reoffenses that have not been recorded by the police, and estimates of recidivism based on these unofficial sources have been up to 2.5 times higher than those derived from the official records (Marshall & Barbaree, 1988). By getting unofficial reports of reoffense, the base rate can be increased, thereby making a statistically significant treatment effect more likely, if a treatment effect is really present.

Another point concerning the outcome measure relates to its accuracy. Some studies (e.g., Abel, Barlow, Blanchard, & Guild, 1977) rely on the self-reports of their patients as to whether or not they have reoffended. We (Marshall & Barbaree, 1988) reported that our attempts to secure self-reports of reoffenses from our former patients were not successful. The majority of former patients did not respond to our written and oral requests for information, and the self-reports we did receive were inaccurate (Marshall & Barbaree, 1988). Therefore, outcome data must be based on some verifiable measure of reoffense. Abel and his associates have relied on these data; their procedures guaranteeing confidentiality appears to increase the likelihood that such reports will be more accurate.

A number of variables besides treatment influence outcome (Prentky, Knight, & Lee, 1997). In a review of the recidivism literature on sex offenders, Furby et al. (1989) found rates of reoffense among untreated offenders to be remarkably different across different studies with rates of 10% to 29% among nonfamilial child molesters who offended against females, and rates of 13% to 40% among men who molested boys. Sturup (1972) showed that recidivism rates for sexual offenders varied considerably, depending on whether the patient was a first or a repeat offender. Meyer and Romero (1980), for example, showed that sex offenders with a low prior rate of arrests for sex crimes (zero to 0.3 per year) had a far lower subsequent recidivism rate (7.9%) than did offenders whose prior arrest rates were high (0.31 to 1.39 per year); 26.2% of the latter group reoffended. Some of the variability between studies can be attributed to differing lengths of the follow-up period. Gibbens, Soothill, and Way (1981) showed that, for child molesters, the longer the follow-up period, the greater the number of reoffenses. Marshall and Barbaree (1988) reported reoffense rates of 12.5%, 38.5%, and 64.3% for groups of men who had been in the community for periods of 0 to 2 years, 2 to 4 years, and 4 to 10 years, respectively. Barbaree and Marshall (1989) demonstrated that two features of the child molester are related to reoffense. First, the offenders who showed deviant sexual arousal and had committed the more severe previous offenses, including the use of force, having a large number of victims, and having intercourse with their victims were more likely to reoffend. Second, the offenders who were of low IQ and socioeconomic status had a larger number of reoffenses. Rice and her associates (Rice, Harris, & Quinsey, 1990; Rice, Quinsey, & Harris 1991) reported that deviant sexual arousal is predictive of sexual reoffenses in both child molesters and rapists. In addition, they found that psychopathy was predictive of reoffense among rapists and that child molesters who reoffended were more likely to have committed previous sex offenses, were more likely to have been admitted to correctional facilities, were more likely to have been diagnosed as personality disordered, and were more likely never to have married. The vast majority of studies of treatment outcome do not compare the treated subjects with a comparison group. Instead, the rate of failure among the treated men is usually compared with some hypothetical rate of failure among sex offenders in general. Given the large number of variables that can influence outcome, this method of treatment evaluation is clearly inadequate. To complete an adequate treatment evaluation it is essential to compare reoffenses among treated offenders with the reoffenses among a group of untreated offenders who are equivalent to the treated group in all important respects except the treatment variable.

Of course, the ideal design for a treatment outcome study would include a comparison between a treated and untreated group, with random assignment of subjects to groups. However, there is only one such research program reported in the literature (Marques, Day, Nelson, & West, 1994). Because of the nature of the offenses these men commit, it has been argued that, in most clinical settings, a randomized, controlled, treatment–outcome study is ethically unacceptable; randomly assigning a dangerous offender, who might accept treatment, to a long-term involvement in a no-treatment experimental condition seems difficult to justify. For the clinical investigator proposing such a study, ethical, practical, and political problems are nearly insurmountable. These problems are too numerous and complex to discuss completely in this chapter, but we will mention the most salient. First, in most areas of clinical science, the standard of ethical acceptability of treatment research is informed consent; if a patient has been fully informed of the potential benefits and risks of both the treatment and the withholding of treatment and agrees to accept the risks, then the study may be judged to be ethical. However, in withholding treatment from the sexual offender, potential victims are at risk who have not been informed and who have not given consent. Some ethics review committees may solve this problem by including representation from, say, a sexual assault crisis center, so that potential victims might be represented, but the outcome of the committee's deliberations is not certain. Second, if such a study were to be done in an institution, with men being released on parole, the parole board would likely release treated men before untreated men, confounding the treatment study. Third, if the study were to be done in a community setting, referral sources would send their clients elsewhere, where they would be assured of treatment. Finally, should a man commit a serious sexual assault after being denied treatment by a research protocol, a wide variety of individuals and groups might be seen to share responsibility and blame with the offender, including the ethics review committee, the funding agency, and the sponsoring institution. Marques et al. (1994) reported findings from a randomized, controlled experiment currently in progress in which the authors avoided ethical difficulties because they drew their small treatment sample from a very large pool of treatment volunteers, in a context in which no other treatment program was available. We describe important findings from this study later in this chapter.

Therefore, all completed treatment studies reported to date have involved compromises to the standards for internal validity typically demanded of a treatment outcome study. It is clear that a comparison group is required to assess the effectiveness of treatment, but studies have varied as to how the comparison group has been formed. If the comparison group cannot be a randomly assigned group, the next best thing would be an untreated group who would accept treatment, but for whom treatment is unavailable for one reason or another. It is critical that the untreated sample is properly matched with the treated sample. As described above, there are many variables that can affect the rate of recidivism, and it is important that the untreated group be matched very carefully with the treated group on the following variables. All too often, reports of treatment programs and studies of untreated men fail to specify demographic, offense history, and other characteristics of their populations and simply describe them as "sex offenders." To adequately evaluate treatment outcome research in this area, it is essential to be able to characterize the treated and untreated samples and to be able to show that the samples do not differ prior to treatment on any important demographic or offense-history variable.

In considering the effectiveness of treatment, Foa and Emmelkamp (1983) described various indices of success or failure. They noted that the real value of a program is not only revealed by the success of those who complete treatment, but also by the number of patients who refuse to enter the program or who drop out once they have commenced therapy. Obviously there is not much value to a program which, although its rate of success is high for those patients who complete treatment, is unable to secure the full cooperation of most of its potential clients.

The most frequent reason for a child molester to refuse treatment is that he denies having committed the offenses. Many studies report a highly selective process at intake, accepting only men who are deemed most suitable for the program. For example, in a treatment program described by Brancale, Vnocolo, and Prendergast (1972), only 30% of incarcerated offenders were suggested as treatment candidates, and of these, only 66% were finally accepted. Of these, only 25% were repeat offenders, making their sample unlike the general population of child molesters. Selection of patients not only occurs at the entry point but also at release. As an example, Cabeen and Coleman (1961) reported that in their program, only patients who were judged to "no longer be a menace" were released from the program. In the treatment program described by Brancale et al. (1972), only 46% of the treated men were finally judged as fit to be released. This filtering process is fatal to program evaluation or to a proper estimate of treatment effectiveness, especially when comparisons of recidivism are made between those selected for treatment and an unselected, untreated group. Unfortunately for the interests of program evaluation, judgments regarding suitability for treatment are usually synonymous with estimates of likely success upon release. Selection processes, then, typically distort the comparison with untreated patients and incorrectly lead to favorable conclusions concerning the supposed benefits of treatment. Because most of the treatment programs reviewed here have exclusion criteria that are often quite extensive, reservations must be expressed about their outcome data.

Wolfe's (1984) explicit selection processes excluded patients who were physically violent, psychotic or "grossly inadequate," or who had problems of addiction, an extensive nonsexual criminal history, poor motivational levels, and counterproductive attitudes. Most experienced clinicians would expect the group of sex offenders who can meet the strict entry requirements to be at low risk to reoffend even in the absence of treatment. Similarly, the Sexual Abuse Clinic in Portland, Oregon (Maletzky, 1987) rejected from treatment all those patients who were determined to be at a high risk to reoffend within the community. These patients were referred to an inpatient unit and were not, therefore, included in Maletzky's program. Again, we anticipate that such an exclusion criterion would markedly lower the subsequent untreated recidivism rate of those who are accepted into treatment.

A further variable that we must considered in evaluating these treatment programs is the dropout rate during the program. Many reports of treatment evaluation in this area have reported outcome only for men who have completed the program. It may be that those who dropout are more likely to fail than those who complete treatment, so these dropouts have to be taken into consideration in an appropriate evaluation of the program. In other areas of treatment evaluation, such as in the treatment of alcoholism (Nathan & Lansky, 1978) and in most areas of behavior therapy (Foa & Emmelkamp, 1983), dropouts are considered to be treatment failures. Abel, Mittleman, Becker, Rathner, and Rouleau (1988) reported a very high rate of dropout from their treatment program. Almost 35% of the patients entering his program withdrew. Of these, 13% were terminated by the therapists because their behavior during treatment was too disruptive, or because they became psychotic, or because their alcoholism became too problematic. Of the rest, 10.4% were jailed before treatment was over, 50.7% refused to continue but did not say why, and 23.9% did not return and could not be contacted thereafter. As part of the voluntary consent procedure, the patients in Abel's program were repeatedly told that they may withdraw from treatment at any time at no cost to them, and they were constantly reassured of the absolute confidentiality of all that happened in treatment.

One last remark is unrelated to methodological criticisms, but is important in an evaluation of the effectiveness of treatment for sex offending. The length of treatment varies considerably across programs, with some offering 2 years or more of treatment. Most treatment programs depend on a long period of intense involvement between offender and treatment staff. Such long-term therapy is not only very expensive, it also markedly limits the number of patients who can be treated in any one period. As sex offending is such a widespread crime with such severe costs to the victims, we cannot afford to have such expensive forms of treatment. Long, drawn-out programs limit the number of offenders who can participate and this in turn encourages careful selection of those patients most likely to benefit. This operates against the treatment of the most dangerous of offenders. If society's response to sexual assault is to be based even in part on a clinical treatment model, programs have to be developed that offer access to a large number of offenders at a reasonable cost.

THE TREATMENT PROGRAMS

Although there are quite a number of descriptions of treatment programs in the literature, the majority of programs have not been formally evaluated. Moreover, the majority have not been described in the readily available literature. Knopp (1984), for instance, identified 197 service programs for sex offenders in the United States, very few of which were known outside their own communities. Even where evaluations have been reported, in most cases it is clear that program evaluations have been considered less important than the delivery of clinical services. Although this is understandable, it inevitably leads to methodological problems that render the evaluations less than adequate.

All treatment programs, whether they make this explicit or not, are predicated on certain assumptions regarding what feature of the offender must be changed (i.e., what it is that is assumed to maintain the aberrant behavior) to reduce or eliminate future offending. Reports should, therefore, distinguish the "within-treatment" goals from "long-term outcome" goals, and an assessment of each of these goals should be described. As an illustration of this, let us consider the often-mentioned notion that marked insecurities about their masculinity leads to the sexually assaultive behavior of rapists (Russell, 1975). The within-treatment goal here would presumably be to enhance the man's confidence regarding his masculinity. In the program evaluation, reports of an appropriate assessment of the within-treatment goal need to be provided to demonstrate that the intervention produced the anticipated benefits. Subsequent follow-up data would then allow the researcher to determine if, indeed, a change in masculine self-confidence is functionally related to the cessation of the offensive behaviors. Unfortunately, within-treatment goals are rarely identified, much less measured. Therefore, when treatment seems to have been successful, we are simply left with changes in the offensive behavior with no basis for inferring just what it was that produced these changes.

Furthermore, clinical assessments are often routine parts of the intake process for many treatment programs. Ideally, these assessments should focus on the behavioral, organic, and cognitive excesses and deficits thought to characterize the offender (subtype) and understood to have led to the offensive behavior. Unfortunately, however, clinical assessments are frequently not related to the goals of treatment or to the theoretical basis of the particular mode of therapy used.

Organic Treatments

The aim of the organic treatments is to reduce sexual urges so that deviant sexuality will be eliminated (Bradford, 1985). However, it has not been clear just what assumptions underlie these procedures. Critics (e.g., Quinsey & Marshall, 1983) have suggested that the use of these procedures requires us to assume that sexual offenders engage in their deviant behavior because they have excessive sexual drive.

There is little convincing evidence to support this notion. On the contrary, the data and authoritative opinion runs counter to this assumption. For example, Record (1977) found that sex offenders were more prudish, censorial, and sexually inadequate than were non-sex offenders, and that nonoffenders displayed greater sexual curiosity, higher general and specific sexual excitement, and stronger libido. Sex offenders were also found by Record to have had their first sexual experience at a later age than either non-sexual offenders or nonoffenders. Christie et al. (1977) reported that pedophiles and rapists preferred a significantly lower rate of sexual activity than did non-sex offenders, and Marshall (1988) found that the majority of sexual offenders reported masturbatory frequencies that did not differ from those of normal males. Similarly, males suffering from Kleinfelter's Syndrome, who are often also paraphiliac and particularly pedophiliac, had sexual drive levels within normal limits (Bancroft, 1983; Raboch, Mellan, & Starka, 1979). Along this same vein, Schmidt and Schorsch (1981) claimed that rapists do not have an enhanced sex drive.

Contrary to the notion that sex offenders are motivated by high sex drive, the majority of modern authors on this subject point to a complex of other factors that underlie the commission of sexual crimes. Several authors (Cohen et al., 1971; Cohen, Seghorn, & Calamus, 1969; Ellis & Brancale, 1956; Gebhard et al., 1965; Glueck, 1956) have claimed that the commission of sexual offenses is a function of the offender's sexual attitudes, particularly their feelings of sexual inadequacy, rather than high drive states. Still others point to sexual preferences for deviant sexual activity or partners as being the motivation for these crimes (e.g., Abel et al., 1977; Freund & Blanchard, 1981), which implicates misdirected rather than excessive drive in sexual crimes.

Associated with this assumption of the proponents of organic treatments relating to high sex drive is the related belief that such high libido is mediated by higher than normal levels of circulating sex steroids. However, the evidence does not support this notion. Whereas Kleinfelter patients display normal intensities of sexual drive, they frequently are found to have lower than normal testosterone levels (Bancroft, 1983, Raboch et al., 1979). Similarly, Rada, Laws, and Kellner (1976) found that only a small percentage of rapists had higher than normal levels of plasma testosterone. Although the individuals with high levels were among the most brutally violent offenders, it is not clear whether the testosterone led to the sexual or aggressive aspects of their offense.

Further, the proponents of organic treatments point to a strong relationship between levels of circulating hormones and the level of sexual activity. For example, Money et al. (1975) provided anecdotal evidence that medroxyprogesterone acetate (MPA), which serves to reduce the level of plasma testosterone, could reduce the frequency of ejaculation, erection, and erotic behavior in males. Pinta (1978) described changes in one patient's drive and fantasies that were linearly related to the dosage of administered MPA. Similarly, Rubin, Henson, Falvo, and High (1979) reported that plasma testosterone concentrations in normals were positively and significantly related to the magnitude and speed of the erectile response. However, the data are not consistent on this point. Rubin et al. found a significant inverse relationship between testosterone levels and the frequency of orgasm, an observation that confirmed the earlier results of Kraemer et al. (1976).

It is clear that sexual behavior is not controlled as much by biological drive as by experiential factors (Hardy, 1964; Whalen, 1966). As one moves along the phylogenetic scale from rats to primates to humans, the influence on sexual activity of the sex steroids seems to be less and less dramatic, and the influence of sexual experience seems more profound. Stone (1927) demonstrated that, after castration, rats displayed progressively less sexual activity over time, with 45% of them no longer copulating after 2 months. However, male cats that are sexually experienced before castration continue to show quite high levels of sexual activity compared with those who have no such prior experiences (Rosenblatt & Aronson, 1958). Dogs castrated after sexual experience continue to copulate for as long as 2 years after the operation (Morgan, 1965). Much earlier, Clark (1945) reported that a prepuberally castrated male chimpanzee engaged in vigorous sexual activity during adulthood.

The effects of castration in reducing sexual activity in humans is not certain. Heim (1981) followed 39 human castrates in West Germany. Sexual potency did not seem to be eliminated as a result of castration. Thirty-six percent of the men from whom Heim obtained data still engaged in sexual intercourse (20% as frequently as one to three times per month), and 19% still masturbated. Some 70% had sexual thoughts at least occasionally, and although this is a bit higher than rates reported by others, nevertheless independent researchers have found that somewhere between 30% and 40%

of castrates fail to show reductions in sexual potency after the operation (Cornu, 1973; Langeluddeke, 1963). For our purposes it is interesting to note that among Heim's patients, the rapists showed the greatest tendency to continue sexual activity after the operation. Seventy-three percent of the rapists continued to engage in some form of sexual behavior, whereas 32% of the pedophiles and 17% of the homosexuals remained sexually active. Finally, 89% of those castrates who considered their sexual drive to be reduced still engaged in at least occasional sexual behaviors. This is consistent with Ford and Beach's (1951) claim that the effects of castration are dependent on the subject's attitudes rather than on his changed hormonal state. In addition, there is evidence that the body adjusts to castration by releasing androgen from the adrenal gland to compensate for the loss of testicular production (Egle & Altwein, 1975). Thus, when castration does reduces sexual activity, it does so by complex processes that involve both the physiological and psychological effects of the procedure.

Further, it may be that when higher than normal levels of sexual activity are found in human males, this is more usually due to nonsexual motives than to somatic factors (Morgenthaler, 1974; Stoller, 1975). According to Schiavi and White (1976), their comprehensive review of the literature indicated that the level of sexual activity is related not only to plasma testosterone but also to situational factors. Indeed, Laschet (1973) in her account of the use of antiandrogens made this point quite clearly when she said that therapeutic failure of the organic treatments is observed in pedophilia when deviant sexual behaviors become independent of testosterone levels.

Clearly the assumptions we have noted, insofar as they form the basis of the use of physical treatment procedures, are questionable. However, organic treatments may still be effective even though the rationale frequently offered for their use may be questionable. For example, if organic therapy can dampen sexual urges and suppress sexual behavior in men despite their initial level of hormonal activity, these methods may form the basis of an effective treatment. Laschet (1973) pointed out that reductions in effective plasma testosterone may be achieved by one of four methods: (1) inhibition of the gonadotropic function of the pituitary by the administration of medroxyprogesterone acetate (MPA); (2) inhibition by antiandrogens (cyproterone acetate; CPA) of the androgenic action at the target organs; (3) physical castration, which involves surgical removal of the main production centers (i.e., the testicles); or (4) surgical destruction of those brain centers thought to mediate sexual behavior. As the latter two procedures are unlikely to be adopted for routine use, we will not review them here but refer the reader to Bradford's (1985, 1990) reviews and that of Quinsey and Marshall (1983).

CPA is a synthetic steroid, structurally similar to progesterone, and its main actions are to block the receptors at the sites of androgen uptake and to block the hypothalamic function that in turn releases pituitary gonado-tropins. MPA increases the metabolism of testosterone in the liver and inhibits the pituitary release of luteinizing hormone, which stimulates the testes to produce testosterone. The objectives of pharmacotherapy are straightforward and they include reduced libido, reduced sexual arousal, reduced sexual behavior, reduced fantasy, and a reduction in the frequency of deviant sexual behavior. Bradford (1985) made the additional claim that the hormonal treatment of sex offenders "is a pharmacological method of reducing sexual drive, as well as the direction of the drive" (p. 360). One case study reported by Bradford and Pawlak (1987) indicated that a patient treated with CPA showed reductions in deviant arousal but a maintenance of socially acceptable arousal. However, the majority of findings and authoritative opinion does not support this claim. Laschet (1973) was very clear in saying that "antiandrogens cannot alter the direction of sexual deviation; they can only reduce or inhibit the sexual reaction" (p. 317). Bancroft, Tennent, Loucas, and Cass (1974) evaluated hormonal interven-tions using penile response measures, and their results indicated that drug interventions do not change men's deviant sexual interests. They found that both CPA and ethinyl estradiol reduced sexual interest and activity, as well as subjective deviant urges, but neither had any effect on penile indices of deviant interests; that is, their patients continued to display preferences for deviant sexual acts and partners even after treatment had reduced their overall sexual urges to low levels.

Numerous studies have evaluated the effects of pharmacotherapy on recidivism in sexual offenders. Laschet (1973) reported on treatment of 66 sexual offenders with CPA for a minimum of 6 months and a maximum of 57 months without interruption. In her report she declared, but offered no detailed supporting information, that the exhibitionists, the largest group of treated offenders, were quickly and completely rehabilitated by CPA. A subsequent, more detailed report (Laschet & Laschet, 1975) of this research helped clarify the findings and seemed to suggest a more conservative estimate of the benefits for the exhibitionists. Of these 24 patients, only five were clearly free of deviant behavior after the cessation of treatment. Of the other 39 sexual offenders (who were mostly child molesters), no data were provided as to outcome but Laschet (1973) indicated that therapeutic failure was observed in pedophiles despite the inhibition of libido and potency.

Reviews of the literature on the effectiveness of CPA by Bradford (1985) and Ortmann (1980) led both reviewers to optimistic conclusions regarding the benefits of CPA in the treatment of sexual offenders. How-ever, neither reviewer was at all critical of methodology, particularly the bases for estimating recidivism, nor did they take account of whether treatment withdrawal affected reoffending. For the most part, evaluations of both MPA and CPA have been based on either official recidivism or on self-reports. As noted earlier, these measures leave much to be desired.

MPA was first reported as a treatment for sexual offenders by Money (1970). Since then a number of reports have become available. For example, Berlin and Meinecke (1981) followed up 20 patients treated with MPA at Johns Hopkins in Maryland and found that three had repeated their offenses while still taking their medication, and that cessation of treatment led to rapid relapse into deviant behaviors. Gagne (1981) claimed that MPA reduced sexual fantasies and deviant urges but did not report reoffense rates.

If offenders need to be medicated for long periods of time, then side effects are a possible drawback of the procedure. The long-term side effects of the continued administration of hormonal agents are not known, but it has been reported that CPA produces gynecomastia in 20% of patients (Mothes, Lehnert, Samini, & Ufer, 1971). Bancroft et al. (1974) had one patient who became severely depressed. However, other studies report either no side effects (Cooper, 1981) or minimal side effects (Laschet & Laschet, 1975). In a careful review of the literature, Lomis and Baker (1981) concluded that "little is known about the psychological effects or the long-term physical effects [of MPA] in human males" (p. 19).

Organically based treatments need to be evaluated in terms of the relapse rates after the withdrawal of treatment and their long-term side effects. If the effects of these drugs are merely to dampen sexual desire, sexual offenders either need to remain on hormonal treatments permanently or they need additional psychologically based procedures to redirect their sexual aims. Langevin et al. (1979) found that administering MPA alone produced such high dropout rates that a proper evaluation of its effect was not possible and, indeed, this seems to be a common problem with hormonal intervention. Dropout rates in the hormonal treatment of sex offenders vary from 30% (Walker & Meyer, 1980) to 100% (Langevin et al., 1979). At Johns Hopkins Hospital, Berlin and Meinecke (1981) reported that 9 of 20 patients treated with MPA dropped out of treatment; of 13 child molesters, five withdrew from treatment and four of these relapsed. An additional four child molesters who completed treatment also relapsed, and only two patients of the total group were clear successes.

Supplementing MPA with training in assertiveness increased the number of patients in Langevin et al.'s (1979) study who remained for the full course of treatment. However, despite the fact that this combined program produced noticeable decreases in the clients' self-reported arousal levels, measures of their erectile response indicated that the patients remained deviant in their sexual preferences. Even more damaging to the supposed value of hormonal interventions is Langevin et al.'s finding that a placebo procedure produced identical reductions in self-reported arousal.

With uncertain beneficial effects, problematic side effects, and high dropout rates, pharmacotherapy in the treatment of the sexual offender is not a panacea (Gijs & Gooren, 1996; Prentky, 1997). The drugs CPA and MPA, when they are effective in reducing sexual behavior and recidivism, do not effect the kind of changes that are desirable in sexual aggressors, such as changed attitudes and beliefs, redirected sexual interests, and the like, which are thought to offer hope for long-term resolution to these problems. These treatments are further disadvantaged by high dropout rates and side effects (Lomis & Baker, 1981). Withdrawal of the drug, with no additional psychological treatment, is associated with high relapse rates. Bradford and Pawlak (1993) have reported that CPA reduced phallometrically assessed deviant sexual arousal but did not reduce appropriate sexual responses. However, the majority of studies seem to indicate that these interventions do not redirect sexual desires away from deviant acts toward more acceptable sexual behaviors.

There has been some recent attention focused on the use of drugs which affect the serotonergic pathways of the central nervous system, rather than on the production of sex hormones (Gijs & Gooren, 1996; Greenberg & Bradford, 1997). Fedoroff (1988) and Pearson, Marshall, Barbaree, and Southmayd (1992) reported reductions in paraphiliac urges and behaviors in single case studies. Fedoroff (1993) has reviewed the literature on the use of serotonergic drugs and reports that these medications may reduce deviant sexual interests without impairing nondeviant interests. It is too early to say whether or not these drugs offer widespread benefits to sex offender treatment.

These methods may have a place in the treatment of those few sex offenders in whom sexual drive is excessively high, due to excessive levels of sex steroids. In these cases, antiandrogens may dampen sexual urges until psychological methods can instill a more permanent state of self-control and redirect sexual preferences. The clinician may find use of these drugs to be helpful when cognitive-behavioral treatments have not been effective, or when they are of limited usefulness, as with developmentally handicapped offenders. The cautious clinician may use the drugs in very high-risk cases. Finally, it may be appropriate to prescribe these drugs when the patient requests them.

Nonbehavioral Psychotherapy

Categorizing procedures as "nonbehavioral psychotherapy" does not do justice to the disparate range of orientations and procedures subsumed therein, and we cannot, therefore, do more than comment on a number of these programs. Even within a particular orientation, there are a multitude of program-specific variations that make generalizations and interprogram comparisons difficult, if not impossible. Within these approaches a variety of procedures are advocated, and in some instances these procedures are common across various approaches. However, when procedures are similar they are often employed for different purposes. Role-playing, for example, is sometimes used to reveal to the patient his own hidden motivations, whereas in other programs it is intended to provide practice in developing interactional skills. Thus it is impossible even to make comparative evaluations of specific procedures.

Castell and Yalom (1972) described a treatment program that used a one-on-one clinical approach following the psychodynamic model of psychopathology. Within this model, sex offenses are assumed to result from unresolved, unconscious conflicts concerning castration anxiety that are manifest in the offender's fears that he is not enough of a "man" (Cohen et al., 1971). Of course, just what these conflicts might be is not initially apparent to the offender, as they are unconscious, and it rests on the therapist to interpret these conflicts. Treatment attempts to show the offender what these unconscious conflicts are and how they cause him to commit his sex crime. When this produces "insight" (i.e., when the patient comes to accept the therapist's interpretations), the patient is judged to be cured.

Individually administered psychodynamic psychotherapy of this kind is very expensive, taking as it does several years to produce changes that satisfy the therapist, and for this and other reasons many programs treat offenders within groups. In his survey of 62 treatment facilities throughout the United States and Canada, Hults (1981) found that 52% of the programs used a group therapy format. The majority of these programs employed a therapist-directed strategy and generally had 8 to 15 offenders meet with one or two professionals as leaders. Discussion centered on practical issues such as whether the men were at risk to reoffend, what factors contributed to their prior offending, and how they could change to reduce potential recidivism. Attitudes toward others, particularly women and children, were generally given central importance, and frequently anxieties about sex or about interactions with others were considered crucial. Many group-therapy approaches assume that deviant sexuality results from stress, so that the open discussion of the sources of stress and helpful suggestions from the group as to how to deal with these stressful situations are thought to reduce the likelihood of future offending.

Peters, Pedigo, Steg, and McKenna (1968) described an analytically oriented group program located within a hospital and dealing with 167 sexual offenders. This program emphasized the importance of intrapsychic determinants of antisocial personality as the basis for sex offending. Group meetings lasted from 75 to 90 minutes, with men staying in treatment over a period of 26.2 weeks, on average. Of these patients, 92 received treatment, whereas the remaining 75 were exposed to the general hospital supervision process. Reoffense was the basis for assessing treatment. In the initial report of outcome, the repeat rate for a sex crime was quite low: 8% in the untreated subjects and a mere 1% in the treatment group. Later reports on this program (Peters & Roether, 1972; Roether & Peters, 1972) were far less encouraging. Peters and Roether (1972) reported 3.2% recidivism in the untreated patients and 7.7% in the treated offenders, and Roether and Peters (1972) reported a 20% failure rate after 1 year for treated subjects. Finally, Peters (1980) indicated that the failure rate over 10-year follow-up for offenders treated in this program was 13.6%, whereas for untreated offenders it was only 1.2%.

Employing a multimodal group treatment approach, Pacht and his colleagues (Pacht, Halleck, & Ehrmann, 1962) treated 475 sexual offenders within a prison setting and reported that only 9% reoffended on a sex crime. The basis for judging recidivism was parole violation, with a distinction made between violations as a result of sexual offenses and violations for other reasons. Again, longer term follow-up (2 years) revealed disappointing results, with 25% of the treated subjects reoffending within this period (Pacht & Roberts, 1968).

Brancale et al. (1972) outlined a group program for offenders in a correctional facility that appeared to focus largely on social ineptitude, although the details are rather vague. More recent reports (Witt, 1981) revealed an increasing behavioral emphasis to this program. Despite poor specification of outcome measures, Brancale et al. (1972) claimed that treated sexual deviants showed very few relapses. However, a subsequent outcome evaluation of 324 patients treated in this program revealed a 9.3% relapse rate over a follow-up period that extended from 0 to 10 years (Prendergast, 1978). No comparison group was followed.

Saylor (1979) described a comprehensive, 22-month group treatment program offered at Western State Hospital in Fort Steilacoom, Washington. This program is interesting because it was primarily a self-help program in which the group was led by a patient elected by his peers. Participation in this peer group involved at least 25 hours each week. Patients, in addition, had very little privacy outside the group, as it was believed that privacy led to withdrawal, which was seen as disadvantageous. This report did not make clear how long the average stay was in the hospital, but it was followed by at least 3 months of work release and at least 18 months of outpatient group therapy after release into the community. This extended program was evaluated on 402 patients released for up to 12 years. The resultant reoffense rate was 22.1% (Saylor, 1979). Again, no comparison group was studied.

The sex offender program at the Connecticut Correctional Institution

(Groth, 1983) employed group therapy based on self-help and mutual-aid concepts. The goals of this program included an expansion of sexual knowledge, an understanding of the dynamics of sexual assault, a personalization of the victims, resocialization, and an identification of the factors which led the man to offend. Patients also participated in a "restitution group" wherein they provide personal information, meant to be relevant to the prevention of sex crimes, to various community-based workers, such as police and parole officers, child care workers, and victim counselors. An evaluation of this program indicated that of 72 offenders released between 1979 and 1982, only six subsequently committed a sexual crime (8.3% recidivism), whereas a further six were convicted of a nonsexual offense. Of those who refused treatment, 15.5% committed a sexual offense after release and 13.1% committed a nonsexual crime. Refusing to accept treatment necessarily makes the untreated offenders different from those who received treatment, confounding the treatment–no treatment comparison.

The programs discussed thus far have all treated mixed groups of offenders, although in most cases patients have been rapists and child molesters. Cabeen and Coleman (1961) outlined a group-therapy program that was applied primarily to child molesters in a prison setting. Group therapy meetings were 90 minutes in duration, held once per week. On average, offenders attended over a 34-week period. The authors provided follow-up evaluations over a 6-month to 3-year period, and reported a low reoffense rate; only 3.8% of 79 released offenders repeated their crimes within this period.

Taken together, these reports do not adequately assess the effects of psychotherapy. These studies have not taken care to ensure that comparison groups were equivalent before treatment, and they used official records only as the source of outcome data; no within-treatment measures of change were offered. In addition, these studies did not specify the therapeutic components in the interventions they offered. Thus, the evidence concerning the efficacy of any form of group psychotherapy seems, at best, to justify further, carefully conducted research.

Marshall and Williams (1975) compared nonbehavioral psychotherapy with behavior therapy. Group psychotherapy was provided by a psychiatrist trained in these methods who had several years of experience in treating rapists and child molesters. The orientation of this psychotherapy component was eclectic, although it combined confrontation with psychodynamic interpretations of the offenders' behaviors and attitudes. The behavioral treatment with which the group psychotherapy was compared involved aversive therapy to reduce deviant sexuality, orgasmic reconditioning to increase appropriate sexual interest, social skill training, self-esteem enhancement procedures, and anxiety-reduction techniques. This program was similar to, but less extensive than those described by Marshall, Earls, Segal, and Darke (1983) and by Marshall and Barbaree (1988). In addition to these treatments, all subjects received sex education.

All subjects were exposed to both treatments in a crossover design, with 3 months of each form of therapy, and an independent experimenter employed behavioral assessment procedures to evaluate the effects of the alternative treatments. These assessments were, however, limited to an appraisal of "within-treatment" goals, as long-term outcome could not differentiate between components due to the crossover design. A subsequent evaluation of long-term outcome, however, was favorable (Davidson, 1984).

It was clear in a series of two replications that not only was the behavioral program superior, but group psychotherapy actually made the patients worse on many measures, including the measures of sexual preference. Just why this happened, or how the psychotherapy procedures achieved this outcome, is not at all clear. The measures used to evaluate treatment, although mutually agreed upon, did fit more harmoniously with the behavioral approach and may, on that account, be considered to be biased.

Results like those reported by Marshall and Williams (1975) support what appears to be a move away from an exclusive reliance on nonbehavioral psychotherapy approaches. As we noted, the program at the Adult Diagnostic and Treatment Center at Avenell, New Jersey (Brancale et al., 1972; Witt, 1981) has shifted toward an emphasis on behavioral procedures; although group therapy components remain even these have important behavioral features. Indeed, Knopp's (1984) introductory remarks to her comprehensive survey of available programs emphasized this recent shift, stressing in particular the value of the assessment procedures introduced by behaviorally oriented researchers and clinicians. To some extent, the same seems to hold true in reverse; that is, behavioral programs are incorporating more elements of traditional psychotherapy by using confrontation of denial and minimization in a group setting (Barbaree, 1991).

Comprehensive Cognitive-Behavioral Therapy

As we mentioned earlier, treatment methodologies are based on assumptions about the nature of the factors which lead to sexual crimes. During the past 25 years however, researchers and clinicians from varied backgrounds have come to recognize that sexual crimes do not result from the operation of a single variable or through a simple, unidirectional sequence of events. Instead, theorists now point to a myriad of historical, socioeconomic, cognitive, behavioral, physiological, and social variables and their interactions as underlying the commission of these crimes. As a consequence, our own treatment program for child sexual abusers evolved from a strictly behavioral program that focused on sexual preferences (Marshall, 1973), to a program that focused on social and personal management skills as well as sexual preferences (Marshall et al., 1983), to a comprehensive cognitive-behavioral program (Marshall & Barbaree, 1988). This latter program has extended the focus of therapy to cognitive variables, such as perceptual distortions, dysfunctional attitudes and beliefs, and faulty knowledge. Other cognitive-behavioral programs have developed along similar lines (Abel, Becker, & Skinner, 1980; Abel, Blanchard, & Becker, 1978; Quinsey, Chaplin, Maguire, & Upfold, 1987), so that the description of our program can be taken as illustrative of this approach.

A Cognitive-Behavioral Model of Sexual Offending

We present a conceptual framework in Figure 6.1 that is meant to formalize and articulate the processes thought to give rise to sexually assaultive behavior. Whereas the organic treatments and the nonbehavioral psychotherapies were based on biological and psychoanalytic models respectively, the model presented here is a social learning model and it forms the basis for the treatments offered under the rubric of cognitive-behavioral treatments. It also gives a formal rational for relapse prevention. Tables 6.1–6.3 provide possible specific instances of each element in the model. The list

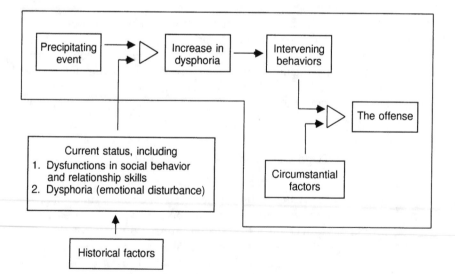

FIGURE 6.1. The cognitive-behavioral chain leading to offense.

TABLE 6.1. Historical Precursors to Sexual Aggression

Precursor	Rapists	Child molesters
Familial chaos	86%	49%
Maternal absence/neglect	41	29
Parental marital discord	59	45
Paternal absence/neglect	59	54
Physically abused as child	45	7
Prior arrest for nonsexual offense	44	15
Sexual victimization		
Prior to age 12	5	56
Between ages 12 and 18	11	6
Limited education (< grade 9 completed)	44	26

Note. Adapted from Pithers, Kashima, Cumming, Beal, and Buell (1988). Copyright 1988 by New York Academy of Sciences. Adapted by permission.

in the table is adapted from a list of precursors to sexual offending provided by Pithers, Kashima, Cumming, Beal, and Buell (1988) and a percentage is presented in tables that indicates the proportion of a sample of rapists and child molesters who reported each precursor. We have ourselves added several items to the lists.

TABLE 6.2. Current Status Precursors to Sexual Aggression

Precursor	Rapists	Child molesters
Dysfunctions in social behavior and relationship skills		
Social skills deficit	59%	50%
Assertiveness skills deficit	42	23
Sexual knowledge deficit	45	52
Emotionally inhibited/overcontrolled	58	51
Interpersonal dependence	30	48
Personality disorder	61	35
Cognitive impairment	9	10
Dysphoria (emotional disturbance)		
Anxiety, generalized	27	46
Anxiety, social	25	39
Anxiety, sexual	39	58
Depression	3	38
Anger, generalized and global	88	32
Anger toward women	77	26
Boredom	45	28
Low self-esteem	56	61

Note. Adapted from Pithers, Kashima, Cumming, Beal, and Buell (1988). Copyright 1988 by New York Academy of Sciences. Adapted by permission.

**TABLE 6.3. Intervening Behavior as Precursors
to Sexual Aggression**

Precursor	Rapists	Child molesters
Paraphiliac behavior		
Cognitive distortions	72%	65%
Deviant sexual fantasies	17	51
Planning of sexual offense	28	73
Pornography use	2	7
Driving car alone without destination	17	1
Masturbation to deviant themes*	—	—
Nonparaphiliac behaviors (disinhibiting behaviors)		
Alcohol use/abuse	42	23
Criminal thinking*		
Provoking conflict*		

Note. Adapted from Pithers, Kashima, Cumming, Beal, and Buell (1988). Copyright 1988 by New York Academy of Sciences. Adapted by permission.
*Added by present authors to original Pithers et al. list.

Starting from the lower left side of the figure, the model recognizes that certain events in the history of the individual make sexual aggression more likely to occur by determining the nature or psychological makeup of the individual at the time of the offense. Rapists and child molesters are often the products of large families living in a disturbed home environment, as indicated by high rates of family psychiatric histories, criminal histories, and substance abuse (Bard et al., 1987). Offenders report having been both sexually (Seghorn, Prentky, & Boucher, 1987) and nonsexually abused as children, and that they were neglected (Bard et al., 1987). A small but significant proportion report having been the victim of some kind of sexual deviation in the childhood home, including sodomy or child pornography, or having grown up in a home where either promiscuity or unusual sexual practices occurred (Bard et al., 1987).

With this kind of background, it is not surprising to find that the psychological difficulties experienced by sexual offenders are not restricted to the direction of their sexual motives. In the model presented here, we divided the psychological disturbances thought to be characteristic of sex offenders at the time of their offense into two broad categories: (1) dysfunctions in social behavior and relationship skills (McFall, 1990; Stermac, Segal, & Gillis, 1990), and (2) dysphoria or emotional disturbance (Langevin, Paitich, Freeman, Mann, & Handy, 1978).

In a study of incarcerated sex offenders, Christie et al. (1977) found that 57% of child molesters and 44% of rapists had received psychiatric attention for other problems such as anxiety, depression, and psychotic episodes. The psychiatric disturbance was described as being severe "at one time or another" in the case of 26% of the child molesters and 32% of the rapists. It is not known whether these difficulties were present at the time of the offense, although no doubt these difficulties were brought on, at least in part, by the stress of institutional life as experienced by sexual offenders. Similarly, in a study of 300 incarcerated sexual offenders, including less dangerous offenders than we consider here, Brancale, Ellis, and Doorbar (1952) found that only 14% were diagnosed as being psychologically "normal"; almost 65% were found to be neurotic, 8% borderline psychotic, 2% frankly psychotic, 5% organically brain damaged, 3% psychopathic, and 4% mentally deficient.

Although it is not known what statistics would result if modern diagnostic criteria (e.g., DSM-IV; American Psychiatric Association, 1994) were to be systematically applied to the population, some educated guesses are possible from our own experiences and from observations reported by other researchers. It is quite clear that apart from the paraphilias, serious Axis I mental disorders are infrequently observed in sex offenders. Abel, Mittleman, and Becker (1985) reported that serious, diagnosable mental disorders were found in less than 25% of sex offenders seen in an outpatient treatment setting. Laws (1981, cited in Knopp, 1984) reported that no more than 10% of incarcerated offenders exhibited serious mental disorders. Some studies of incarcerated sexual offenders using standardized psychological tests have indicated a high rate of clinical symptoms. For example, Hall, Maiuro, Vitaliano, and Proctor (1986) examined the Minnesota Multiphasic Personality Inventory (MMPI) profiles of 406 institutionalized child molesters and found elevated means on all of the clinical scales. Sixty-five percent of the sample had a T score over 70 on the Psychopathic Deviate scale. Similarly, approximately 50% of the sample had elevated scores on both the Schizophrenia scale and the Depression scale. Other reviews of the literature (Quinsey, 1984, 1986) pointed out that both child molesters and rapists show a peak on the Psychopathic Deviate scale (Langevin, 1983; Panton, 1979), but that this pattern of results is not different from that obtained by other groups of incarcerated offenders.

In summary, although serious, diagnosable mental disorders are not frequently encountered among sex offenders, a significant degree of psychopathology is present. The role of this disturbance in their offenses is not at present understood; the psychological disturbance may have preceded and contributed to the offense, or it might be a consequence of the arrest and incarceration. However, it is more likely that some level of psychological disturbance of many incarcerated sexual offenders was a contributing factor in their offense, and that this disturbance was exacerbated by the judicial process and the stresses of incarceration.

Deficits in social skills among sex offenders are widely recognized.

Reflecting the common acceptance of these deficits, social skills training is one of the most often prescribed treatments for sex offenders (McFall, 1990). However, the nature of these deficits and the way in which these deficits contribute to the commission of sexual offenses is not well understood. Reviews in the past two decades of the literature on social skills assessment and training of sex offenders point to serious conceptual and methodological problems (Earls & Quinsey, 1985; Stermac et al., 1990), and it is still too early to say that social skills deficits are characteristic of sex offenders (Stermac & Quinsey, 1986; Stermac et al., 1990). McFall (1990) argued that the conceptual and methodological weaknesses in the literature have presented an inadequate test of the hypothesis. In response to this, he proposed an information-processing model of social skills particularly designed to specify the social deficits that lead to sexual aggression. The model specifies three stages of social information processing. *Decoding skills* involve the psychological processes that lead to the reception, perception, and interpretation of incoming social information. *Decision skills* involve the generation of response options, matching these to task demands, selection of the best option, searching for that option in the behavioral repertoire, and evaluating likely outcomes of each option. *Enactment skills* are involved in carrying out the behavior selected in the preceding stage. Recent studies have found particular deficits in decoding abilities among sexual offenders in heterosexual social situations. Lipton, McDonel, and McFall (1987) compared rapists, violent nonrapists, and nonviolent nonrapists on measures of heterosocial cue-reading accuracy in first-date and intimate situations. These investigators found that rapists misconstrued social cues given by women, particularly those cues denoting negative moods on first-date situations. Further, there is evidence that sex offenders are deficient in decision skills in social intervention. Connor (1988) examined the social problem-solving skills of child molesters and reported no deficiencies in the child molester's abilities to recognize the existence of a problem or to generate alternative solutions. However, they chose unacceptable solutions and did not recognize the negative outcomes of the solutions they chose. Finally, a number of studies have supported the idea of enactment or deficits among sex offenders. Compared with community control subjects and rapists, child molesters have been found to be less effectively assertive (Segal & Marshall, 1985; Overholser & Beck, 1986).

Related to social misperception, cognitions that contribute to crimes among child molesters have been termed *cognitive distortions* (Abel, Becker, & Cunningham-Rathner, 1984) and focus on mistaken beliefs about childhood sexuality and about the nature of sexual interactions between an adult and a child. They can be understood to represent one of the following misperceptions: Children are not harmed by sexual interactions with an adult; children benefit (in terms of sex education or in terms of affectional attention) through sexual interactions with an adult; children are capable of consenting to sexual interactions with an adult and often desire this (offenders frequently see the child as having been sexually provocative); and an adult male's sexual interactions with a child can be justified or rationalized in some way (i.e., it is not his fault). For example, Stermac and Segal (1987) examined the judgments of offenders and nonoffenders in response to descriptions of adult–child sexual interactions. Child molesters pointed to the benefit of abuse for the child, attributed more blame to the victim, and tended to minimize the effects of sexual assault on children. Also, offenders considered current punishment for offenders to be too severe.

For rapists, there also seems to be a set of attitudes and beliefs that support their rape behavior. Koss and Dinero (1988) administered an anonymous questionnaire to a national probability sample of almost 3,000 undergraduate men in U.S. colleges and universities. The questions differentiated men according to the level of aggression in their sexual interactions with women, ranging from nonaggressive, to forced fondling and kissing, to rape. Three measures of attitudes relating to sexual aggression seemed to differentiate these groups of men, including hostility to women (Check & Malamuth, 1985), acceptance of interpersonal violence (Burt, 1980), and rape myth acceptance (Burt, 1980). Items representative of the hostility measure included, "I feel upset even by slight criticism by a woman," and "It is safer not to trust women." The interpersonal violence items included, "Being roughed up is sexually stimulating to many women," and the rape myths scale included items such as, "Any healthy woman can resist a rape if she really wants to." Assessing these attitudes among offenders is difficult, and should not be done only using these self-report questionnaires, as the questions and their intent are transparent and offenders will attempt to "fake good." However, these attitudes will often become evident in interview or in group treatment sessions.

Besides providing a set of very practical and constructive techniques for use in managing sexual offenders, the movement to relapse prevention in general, and the writings of Bill Pithers in particular (Pithers, 1990; Pithers, Beal, Armstrong, & Petty, 1989) have contributed a conceptual advance in the treatment of the sexual offender. Previously, a number of researchers pointed to offenders' behavioral excesses or deficits interacting with situational factors, particularly those immediately preceding the offense, as being important in sexual assault (Craig, 1990; Marshall & Barbaree, 1984, 1990). Also, some experimental research pointed to situational manipulations that increased sexual arousal to deviant cues, including alcohol intoxication (Barbaree, Marshall, Yates, & Lightfoot, 1983; Briddell et al., 1978), anger (Yates, Barbaree, & Marshall, 1984), and victim blame (Sundberg, Barbaree, & Marshall, 1991). In addition, numerous authors have pointed to the role of antecedent anger in contributing to sexual assault (e.g., Groth, Burgess, & Holmstrom, 1977).

Authors who espouse a relapse prevention approach to the treatment of the sexual offender (e.g., Pithers, 1990) refer to cognitive-behavioral chains. It is widely recognized that sexual offenses are not isolated events independent of other aspects of the offender's current life. Instead, they are the terminal event in a long sequence of events (Nelson & Jackson, 1989). In Figure 6.1, elements of the cognitive-behavioral chain are contained inside the black border. The chain is a sequence of events, thoughts, emotional responses, and behaviors that precede the offense. For offenders who report more than one offense, the offense chain's preceding different offenses often bear considerable similarity, and as a consequence, the chain is often referred to an "offense cycle." There is recognition that the details of offense cycles are idiosyncratic and vary from offender to offender.

Pithers, Marques, Gibat, and Marlatt (1983) were the first to describe the concept of an offense chain. They described the chain as involving four stages. First, the offender has certain lifestyle, personality, and circumstantial factors that serve as a background to his offense behavior. Second, the offender becomes dysphoric as a result of feelings of deprivation or loss, or in response to conflict or stress. As a result of this dysphoria, the offender allows himself to enter a high-risk situation that may include a potential and vulnerable victim. In the third stage, the offender "lapses," by which is meant he engages in behavior that approximates a sexual assault, such as fantasizing about children. In the fourth stage, a relapse occurs in which the offender assaults a child. Pithers et al. (1983) introduced three cognitive–emotional mechanisms seen to operate in the transitions from stage to stage of the chain. First, seemingly irrelevant decisions were choices the offender had made that could be described superficially as innocent and not directed toward sexual assault, but that had the effect of allowing for increased opportunity for contact with a potential victim. Second, offenders were seen to respond to the immediate, powerful reinforcement or gratification of sexual assault without responding to the longer term negative effects of the assault. Third, these authors described an abstinence violation effect as a negative emotional reaction to a lapse or relapse. These convince the offender that he is unable to control his own urges, leading to increases in the dysphoria that initially began the chain.

Ward, Louden, Hudson, and Marshall (1995) elaborated the concept of the offense chain further by providing a descriptive model of the offense chain for child molesters, based on an empirical study of 26 incarcerated child molesters before their involvement in treatment. The study indicated that there are no fewer than eight or nine distinct stages in the offense cycle. In their study, Ward et al. describes the offense as being followed by a stage in which the offender evaluates his relationship and behavior with the child. If there was a positive evaluation, then the offender would express the expectation that he would likely commit such offenses in the future. If there was a negative evaluation, then the offender would make a renewed commitment to resist future urges to child sexual assault.

The behavioral chain begins with a precipitating event. Not surprisingly, given the dysfunctional social behavior among these men, the precipitating event is often an interpersonal conflict that causes an increase in emotional disturbance. The offender's inability to resolve the interpersonal conflict leaves him vulnerable to continuing interpersonal conflict and leaves him feeling angry and frustrated. In response to this increased dysphoria, the offender engages in behaviors that are both an expression of the emotional disturbance he feels and designed in part to relieve his dysphoria. We subdivided the intervening behaviors into two categories: paraphiliac and nonparaphiliac. *Paraphiliac behaviors* are deviant behaviors that serve to reduce the tension and frustration, or negative emotional state he is feeling. *Nonparaphiliac* behaviors are often expressions of anger or disturbed social behaviors that denote anger and involve continuing interpersonal conflict. These nonparaphiliac behaviors also include behaviors that serve to disinhibit deviant sexual behavior, such as alcohol abuse, which disrupts normal control over sexual misbehavior. Alcohol intoxication is frequently implicated in the commission of sexual offenses. On the basis of rapists' and victims' self-reports, it is estimated that between 30% and 80% of rapists are intoxicated at the time of their offense (Christie, Marshall, & Lanthier, 1979; Gebhard et al., 1965; Johnson, Gibson, & Linden, 1978; Scully & Marolla, 1984; Wormith, 1983). Moreover, between one third (Groth, 1979) and over three quarters (77%) (Wormith, 1983) of child molesters report having been intoxicated at the time of the offense. However, it is not known whether or not offender self-report of intoxication is exaggerated to reduce their culpability in the offense (Quinsey, 1984).

Paraphiliac behaviors are deviant behaviors that serve to reduce the tension and frustration the offender experiences. In the state of increased tension and dysphoria, offenders may engage in sexual fantasy with deviant themes, they may become aroused to deviant themes culminating in masturbation, and they may use pornography as part of their fantasy and masturbation. These offenders then engage in cognitive distortions that justify and normalize their own paraphiliac behaviors to themselves. As the chain progresses, the offender's fantasy evolves into a plan for an offense. In this circumstance, with the disturbed offender involved in continuing interpersonal conflict and engaging in sexually deviant approximations to offending, the terminal offense becomes more likely. When the offender is presented with the opportunity, he offends, thereby temporarily reducing his tension and frustration.

The model applies in a flexible way to each offender. Not all offenders would be described as having all components of the model. For example, for some offenders, paraphiliac behaviors are absent, and the offense seems impulsive, with no planning. For others, the paraphiliac behavior seems predominant, with no apparent precipitating event, and the paraphiliac behavior seems to be relatively autonomous. However, the model offers a framework for (1) understanding the offending in each individual offender, (2) the assessment of behavioral deficits and excesses which lead to the offense in each individual, and (3) targeting behavior in treatment that will reduce the likelihood of his committing the offense in the future.

Pretreatment Assessment

A pretreatment assessment of the sex offender serves three major functions. First, it helps the clinician make judgments concerning the likelihood of the man reoffending. Second, it assists the clinician in making recommendations for parole, release, and sentencing, and the need for treatment of both sexual and nonsexual problems. Third, it assists in operationally defining treatment targets, and assessment of these targeted variables provides a pretreatment baseline level against which to judge improvement brought about by treatment.

Results of the comprehensive assessment are almost always communicated outside the treatment clinic, and the information and recommendations in the assessments contribute to various decisions in the criminal justice system. The offender's lawyer may request an assessment to assist in making an appropriate plea and in arguing the offender's case both in terms of the criminal charges and with respect to sentencing. The court may consider a comprehensive assessment in determining an appropriate sentence or conditions of probation. Further, child protective agencies may request an assessment to guide them in child custody and access actions. Finally, assessments of incarcerated offenders assist parole boards in making decisions regarding release into the community. Because of the nature of the offensive behaviors and their legal implications, and because the clinician is usually in frequent communication with agents external to the clinic, there are important limitations to the confidentiality that usually accompanies a therapeutic relationship. Kelly (1987) clearly articulated the conflict facing the therapist for the sexual offender between the need for confidentiality in a therapeutic relationship and the therapist's "duty to report" and "duty to warn."

Within the context of treatment, the assessment assists in making important decisions concerning the offender. As we noted, a significant segment of the sex offender population has other psychological, behavioral, and psychiatric problems that may or may not be related to their offending.

Referrals to other appropriate treatment agencies that can be integrated into the overall program must be arranged and monitored if the primary treatment is to succeed. For example, many sex offenders are also problem drinkers (Christie et al., 1977). When assessments reveal this as an important problem, referral to an appropriate alternative service dealing with problem drinking is useful, as resources are typically too limited to deal with these difficulties within the sex offender program. On the other hand, when assessment consistently reveals severe interpersonal deficits, it may be more appropriate to develop a component within the sex offender program that addresses this issue, because problems of an interpersonal nature are pervasive in this population and are importantly related to both the deviant acts and the cognitions that maintain such offensive behaviors. However, when these problems concern marital relationships, and when these appear to require long-term counseling, it may be most efficient to make a referral to an external agency. In our program, we deal with most of these problem areas, but not in the depth sometimes required and certainly not over an extended period, which is occasionally necessary to allow the offender to fully integrate the changes into his daily life.

Denial and Minimization

Perhaps the most important issue to be addressed in assessment is denial and minimization. Denial and minimization are often the result of the offender lying, but they are also the result of a psychological process involving distortion, mistaken attribution, rationalization, and selective attention and memory. The process serves to reduce the offender's experience of blame and responsibility for his offenses, and it seems to be successful. Wormith (1983) found that only 14% of sexual offenders report themselves as being remorseful for their offense. Denial and minimization are both products of the same self-serving cognitive process, but they are different in two ways. First, denial and minimization represent different degrees of the process; whereas denial is extreme and categorical, minimization is graded. Second, denial usually concerns either the facts in the case or whether or not the offender has a "problem" that needs treatment, whereas minimization concerns the extent of the man's responsibility for the offense, the extent of his past offending, and the degree of harm his victim(s) have suffered.

Scully and Marolla (1984) surveyed a nonrandom sample of 114 volunteer incarcerated rapists, dividing the sample into those men who admitted to the offense for which they had been convicted (41%) and those who denied committing a sexual offense (59%). Both groups presented justifications intended to support their denial or to minimize responsibility for the offense. For example, among the deniers, 31% reasoned that they had not committed an offense because the victim provoked them by being seductive. Thirty-four percent of the deniers and 24% of the admitters argued that their victims meant "yes" even though they said "no." Of the deniers, 69% claimed that their victims eventually relaxed and enjoyed the rape, and the same argument was put forward by 20% of the admitters. Sixty-nine percent of the deniers and 22% of the admitters alluded to the victims' unsavory sexual reputations as excuses for their crimes. Seventy-seven percent of admitters and 84% of deniers excused their behavior by attributing it to alcohol intoxication, whereas 40% of deniers and 33% of admitters explained their crimes by pointing to emotional problems caused by an unhappy childhood or current marital conflict.

A Canadian survey of 205 incarcerated adult sexual offenders (Wormith, 1983) found that one in three offenders denied that they committed a sexual offense. For the adolescent offender, denial is also an important characteristic (Kahn & Lafond, 1988). Denial is generally regarded as an important impediment to successful therapy (Conte, 1985; Langevin & Lang, 1985), and as a consequence, most treatment programs most often exclude offenders who steadfastly deny their offense. When denial and minimization are extreme, the offender concludes that he has no problems and that there is no reason for him to enter treatment. When men persist in this form of denial, our experience is that continuing treatment is futile. Even if the offender admits to an offense, he is very likely to distort the truth by minimizing the frequency, severity, and variety of his criminal sexual behavior. In our experience, it is rare to find an offender who does not at least minimize his offense and its impact on the victim. Therefore, denial of the offense and minimization of the offender's responsibility and the harm he has done is so common among these offenders as to be regarded as a defining characteristic of the population.

These denials and distortions compromise both the accurate assessment and the effective treatment of these men. Therapists depend on the offender's veridical descriptions of events leading to past offenses to determine which behaviors need to be targeted in therapy. In assessing progress in therapy, the therapist depends on faithful accounts of the offender's ongoing fantasies and sexual behaviors. The offender will present his denial at every opportunity, often in a compulsive manner, and his arguments are almost always plausible and convincing. For the inexperienced therapist, denial and minimization provide the greatest danger for errors in management and assessment of the offender. Believing the denial or in other ways reinforcing it will serve to increase the offender's resistance to treatment, and will compromise the validity of the clinician's assessment of the offender.

The assessment of denial and minimization requires a detailed and accurate official version that can be taken from the police reports or court records of victim testimony. The assessment of denial and minimization details the discrepancies between the offender's account of the offenses and the official version. It may be argued that the official version is subject to distortion and inaccuracy. However, the wise clinician regards the official version as a "gold standard," because if she admits to the possibility of the record being inaccurate, therapy becomes a forum for the offender to "launch an appeal," and no therapeutic gains are possible in such an atmosphere.

Barbaree (1991) treated denial and minimization in 15 child molesters and 26 rapists as the first stage in a comprehensive cognitive-behavioral group therapy program in a prison setting. Treatment for denial and minimization involved (1) disclosures made by the participant in which he was required to provide his own version of his offense, followed by (2) descriptions of the official version of his offense (from police reports and victim testimony) given by the group therapist, and (3) responses by the participant to challenges made by members of the group with respect to discrepancies between his version and the official version. At pretreatment, 22 of these offenders denied that they were sex offenders or denied that they had committed a sexual offense. At posttreatment, only three offenders remained in denial. For the remainder of the offenders, the vast majority of whom significantly minimized their offending in important ways, treatment served to decrease the severity and extent of the justifications and rationalizations they expressed concerning their offending.

Sex Offender Subtyping

A comprehensive assessment of sexual offenders must take into account the heterogeneity of this population. Sex offenders are diverse in all aspects of their functioning, including social competence, criminality, sexual deviance, intellectual functioning, and other important variables. There have been a number of attempts to classify sexual offenders according to the behavioral topography of the offense and the inferred motivation of the offensive behavior. Notable among these recent efforts is the work of Knight and Prentky and their associates at the Massachusetts Treatment Center (Knight & Prentky, 1990). These authors devised two separate taxonomies: one for child molesters and one for rapists. These taxonomies are complex, multifactorial arrangements of dichotomous and multilevel variables that represent salient features of the offender groups in question.

In the child molester taxonomy, Knight and Prentky (1990) classified offenders on two separate axes. Axis I classified offenders using two independent, dichotomous decisions, yielding four types, as in a 2 × 2 contingency table. In the first decision, offenders were classified as either high or low in fixation on children. Highly fixated subjects were those whose thoughts and social interactions focused primarily on children. These men would be referred to as pedophiles in the DSM-IV (American Psychiatric Association, 1994) typology. Offenders low in fixation did not show the same focus on children. In the second decision, social competence is judged as high or low, depending on the offender's success in employment, adult relationships, and social responsibilities. Axis II classified offenders according to the nature of their contact with children using a series of independent, dichotomous decisions, yielding six separate types. In the first decision, the offender was classified according to the amount of contact he had with children. Offenders who had a great deal of contact were further subdivided according to the meaning of the contact: interpersonal or narcissistic. Interpersonal contact signified contact with children in a broad range of activities, not simply sexual interactions, and the sexual interactions were not primarily directed toward orgasm. Narcissistic contact was primarily sexual and directed toward orgasm. Offenders who did not have a great deal of contact with children were further subdivided into four subtypes, based on two independent, dichotomous decisions. The first distinguished men who had caused a high degree of physical injury to victims from those who had not. The second distinguished men who had sadistic fantasies or exhibited sadistic behaviors from those who did not.

In the rapist taxonomy, Knight and Prentky (1990) first classified men according to four primary motivations for raping, and according to these motivations, rapists were either opportunistic, pervasively angry, sexually motivated, or vindictive. For the opportunistic rapist, the offense resulted from poor impulse control, and the sexual offense was only one of many instances of unsocialized behaviors. The offense did not involve anger, nor any more violence than was required to counter resistance on the part of the victim, but the offenders were indifferent to the harm they did their victims. The pervasively angry rapist often inflicted serious victim injury, resulting in death in the extreme cases. For these men, anger was generalized and the targets of their anger were not restricted to women, but the anger and violence were independent of their sexual arousal and motivation. The sexually motivated rapists were characterized by predominant sexual fantasies and preoccupations and were subdivided into sadists and nonsadists. For the sadist, the sexual and aggressive motivations were not only not differentiated, but they also were mutually facilitating, with anger increasing sexual arousal, sexual stimuli increasing anger and hostility, and violence an important component of their sexual fantasies. For the nonsadist, nonconsenting sex was an outlet for sexual gratification, but these men would not use violence to accomplish the act. Of all the rapist subtypes, this group was regarded as the least aggressive in both sexual and nonsexual contexts. Finally, the vindictive rapists were men whose anger is focused exclusively on women. Their assaults were characterized by verbal abuse and physical violence and usually resulted in victim harm, and the assaults often included the additional elements of degradation and humiliation. Knight and Prentky (1990) further subdivided the opportunistic, sexual nonsadistic and vindictive rapists into two subgroups according to levels of social competence, with social competence defined as it was for the child molesters, as success in employment and in adult relationships and social responsibilities. This approach to classification hopefully will greatly increase our ability to predict both response to treatment and recidivism among these men (Knight, Rosenberg, & Schneider, 1985).

Deviant Sexual Arousal

The DSM-IV describes the essential feature of the paraphilias as "recurrent intense sexual urges and sexually arousing fantasies generally involving either (1) nonhuman objects, (2) the suffering or humiliation of oneself or one's partner (not merely simulated), or (3) children or other nonconsenting persons" (American Psychiatric Association, 1994, pp. 522–523). Therefore, obviously, a significant number of sex offenders would be diagnosed as "paraphiliacs." According to Abel et al. (1985), 100% of child molesters should be diagnosed as "pedophiles." Among rapists, diagnosis is not as straightforward. The only paraphilia presently listed in the DSM-IV that relates to rape is sexual sadism, but it would only apply to those rapists who appear to gain sexual pleasure from the suffering of their victim. A larger proportion of sex offenders, however, would be diagnosed with antisocial personality disorder. For example, Abel et al. (1985) estimated that approximately 30% of rapists and 12% of child molesters can be so diagnosed.

There is now a large number of studies in the literature that show that sex offenders exhibit a disordered pattern of sexual arousal. Early versions of a behavioral approach to treatment of the sex offender depended heavily on the "sexual preference hypothesis" that holds that men commit sexually aberrant acts because these acts and their associated stimuli are preferred over normative sexual activity and cues. The "sexual preference hypothesis" is not as much a formal, well-articulated theory with clearly identified proponents as it is an assumption held vaguely by many. Nevertheless, the assumption underlies much work in this area (Barbaree, 1990). For example, the diagnostic criteria for the "paraphilias" specified in the DSM-IV (American Psychiatric Association, 1994) are based on the sexual preference hypothesis, even though formal reference to it is not made.

The hypothesis is a two-staged proposition. First, it assumes that deviant cues evoke stronger sexual arousal in offenders than do normative sexual cues. Second, it assumes that the overt behavioral preference these men show for deviant acts is a product of this stronger arousal, perhaps because the gratification (reward) consequent upon acting on this stronger arousal is greater. Accordingly, behavior analyses identify deviant stimulus control of sexual arousal as an early event in the sequence leading to the deviant sexual act. Therefore, so the reasoning goes, if a therapist intervenes early in the sequence to reduce the man's physiological response to deviant cues, further occurrence of the deviant behavior will be prevented.

Based on this rationale, the behavioral assessment and treatment of sex offenders has depended greatly on measures of sexual arousal, and a number of detailed reviews of this methodology are available (Earls & Marshall, 1982; Murphy & Barbaree, 1987; O'Donohue & Letourneau, 1992). Offenders have been tested in the laboratory, where their sexual arousal was monitored through direct measurement of penile erection while they were presented with a wide variety of sexual and nonsexual cues. Of particular interest to this hypothesis are two sets of studies based on this laboratory procedure.

In the first set of studies, (Baxter et al., 1984; Freund, 1967a, 1967b, 1981; Marshall et al., 1986; Marshall et al., 1988; Murphy, Haynes, Stalgaitis, & Flanagan, 1986; Quinsey, Chaplin, & Carrigan, 1979; Quinsey, Steinman, Bergerson, & Holmes, 1975) researchers compared the responses of child molesters, incest offenders, and matched nonoffenders to depictions involving male and female children, adolescents, and adults. Generally, nonoffending males respond with strong arousal to adult females but show decreasing arousal to stimuli depicting persons below age 16 years. As a group, nonfamilial child molesters show stronger arousal to children than they do to adults, and some of these men show exclusive responding to children of a very young age. Incest offenders tend to show a more normal pattern of arousal, with greater arousal to adults than to adolescents or children, but they show less arousal to the adult females than do the nonoffenders. These findings are supportive of the sexual preference hypothesis for the nonfamilial offenders in the sense that laboratory procedures revealed stronger arousal to stimuli depicting persons similar in age and sex to their victims. However, the findings with the incest offenders are not supportive.

In evaluating nonfamilial child molesters, our laboratory assessments focus on two aspects of the stimulus control of sexual arousal: responses to the age and gender of the victim, and responses to force and coercion by the offender. In the age preference test, color pictures of nude females or males ranging in age from 3 to 24 years are projected on a screen in front of the seated subject, whose erectile responses are continuously monitored. Different subgroups of men show different patterns (profiles) of responses over this age continuum. We (Barbaree & Marshall, 1989) completed an analysis in which we sorted the individual patterns of responses of offenders and nonoffenders according to profile shape. We found five distinct profile shapes. An *adult* profile was characterized by strong responses to adults and minimal responding to children. The *teen–adult* profile was similar to the adult profile except that responding to the adolescent targets was stronger. A large group of men showed profiles that we judged to be *nondiscriminating,* as they displayed a moderate degree of response to all age categories. Finally, two profile shapes indicated significant responding to children. In the *child* profile we found the archetypal pedophile profile, with strong responding to prepubescent children and little response to adolescents or adults. The *child–adult* profile exhibited a bimodal shape with strong responses to children and adults but decreased responding to adolescents. Primarily, nonoffenders had adult profiles with smaller numbers displaying the teen–adult and nondiscriminating profile categories. Incest offenders were almost equally divided among the adult and nondiscriminating profile groups. Nonfamilial child molesters were a heterogenous group, with 35% showing a child profile and the remainder approximately equally distributed among the other profile shapes.

Men who showed the child or child–adult profiles were of lower IQ and lower socioeconomic status than the other offenders. Those who revealed a child profile had used more force in the commission of their previous offenses and had a greater number of previous victims. In addition, during laboratory tests of their erectile responses to force and coercion, men in the child category had no inhibition of arousal in response to force and coercion, whereas men in all other profile groups were markedly inhibited by these elements (Barbaree & Marshall, 1989).

In the second groups of studies, researchers compared the responses of rapists and matched nonoffenders to depictions of consenting and nonconsenting sexual interactions. Some studies have found that rapists show equal arousal to these two episodes, whereas nonoffenders show greater arousal to consenting than to rape depictions (Abel et al., 1977; Barbaree, Marshall, & Lanthier, 1979; Quinsey & Chaplin, 1984). However, other studies failed to find significant differences between rapists and nonoffenders in these sexual arousal patterns (Baxter, Barbaree, & Marshall, 1986). The findings with rapists, therefore, do not so clearly support the sexual preference hypothesis as do the data from nonfamilial child molesters.

Recently, Barbaree, Seto, Serin, Amos, and Preston (1994) found that different subgroups of rapists exhibited different patterns of arousal. Using the Massachusetts Treatment Center typology for rapists (MTC:R3; Knight & Prentky, 1990), they divided 80 incarcerated rapists into the nine subgroups in this typology. They tested all subjects in the sexual arousal laboratory and calculated a "rape index" by dividing arousal to rape themes by arousal to consenting themes. Rapists in the MTC "sexual" subtypes showed significantly greater rape indices than did the nonsexual subtypes.

It appeared, then, that deviant sexual arousal, as an intervening behavior, is a problem for some rapists, but is not characteristic of all rapists.

Stages of Treatment

The following discussion focuses on the comprehensive treatment program provided to child sexual abusers that we developed at the Kingston Sexual Behavior Clinic. Our treatment program is divided into four stages: pretreatment, treatment planning, treatment, and posttreatment. In pretreatment, we attempt to change denial and minimization of offending into acceptance of responsibility, and to increase the offenders' appreciation of the harm done to victims of sexual assault. The purpose of the first stage is to maximize the offender's motivation for treatment and the resulting behavior change. In treatment planning, we encourage each offender to develop an account of the cognitive-behavioral chain which led to his offenses in the past. By doing so, he will see the relevance of the behaviors targeted in therapy to his risk for reoffense. In the treatment stage itself, the therapist targets the behavioral excesses or deficits or cognitive dysfunctions that figure prominently in the cognitive-behavioral chain and that in a sense, led to previous offenses. Finally, in posttreatment we assist the offender as he develops and implements a relapse prevention plan. The various components of the therapy are presented in a staged format in Table 6.4.

Pretreatment

The objective of the pretreatment stage is fourfold. First, we attempt to have the offender admit to the offensive behaviors; he is to describe in detail his offensive behavior, including the extent and range of these acts and their frequency. Second, we want the offender to accept responsibility for his abuse. To this end, he must acknowledge the contribution of his own desires, urges, fantasies, and behaviors in his offense and demonstrate some understanding of the personal and situational factors which led to his offending. An important feature of this altered perspective requires the patient to agree to a long-term commitment to change, and he must express a determination to prevent further offending. Third, we aim at having the offender develop empathy and appreciation for his victim(s); he must come to understand the nature and extent of the harm his offensive behavior caused his victim(s), and he must see that the victim did nothing to warrant blame. Finally, we want the patient to fully appreciate the degree of social censure his behavior has and will cause, and we make him fully aware of the severity of the penalties that will follow further offending.

Cognitive therapy has been effective for a number of clinical problems

TABLE 6.4. Stages of Treatment of the Sexual Offender

Pretreatment: Developing motivation for behavior change

1. Denial
2. Minimization
3. Victim blame—Victim empathy

Treatment planning

4. Understanding precursors to offending and the behavior chain leading to offense

Treatment: Achieving behavior change

Deviant sexual behavior

5. Reducing deviant sexual arousal and fantasy
6. Reducing cognitive distortions
7. Addressing issues of their own victimization
8. Enhancing healthy sexuality, including increasing sexual knowledge

Nonsexual contributions to offending

9. Increasing social competence and anger control
10. Decreasing criminal thinking, lifestyle, and behavior
11. Substance abuse treatment (if required)
12. Treatment of mental disorder (if required)

Posttreatment: Preventing the recurrence of sexual offending

13. Developing a relapse prevention plan
    a. Internal self-management
    b. External supervision
14. Relapse prevention
15. Follow-up

(e.g., Beck, Rush, Shaw, & Emery, 1979). The process of therapy involves challenges to the inappropriate cognitions, first by the therapist and then by the patient himself. Challenges to these cognitions illustrate their lack of validity and point to their dysfunctional nature. At the same time, more appropriate cognitions are enumerated and the patient is led to see the advantages of these more socially acceptable ways of thinking. In this process it is crucial that the patient be made aware of the profits that will follow upon changing his thinking. Challenges are made by the therapist in a supportive, nonargumentative manner, and they begin immediately after completion of assessment and continue through several individual treatment meetings. Many of the offenders are then enrolled in a group in which these issues are the focus of discussion. We recognize that cognitive changes occur gradually over a long period of time and over many therapeutic interactions. Therefore, we do not expect the man's admission of his offense or his acceptance of responsibility will be accomplished in a dramatic admission or a "flash" of insight. At the same time, however, we will not accept into the formal aspect of treatment those men who, in spite of our best efforts, steadfastly refuse to admit to any sexually abusive behaviors.

The primary role of the therapist is to confront the offender with the allegations made against him and to challenge his denials. Armed with a detailed account of the allegations of abuse presented by a referring agency or contained in police reports and victim testimony in court, we are in a position to make strong arguments that these accusations could not be made or do not make sense unless the sexual abuse was perpetrated by the offender as described by the victim. In the absence of such detailed allegations, it is difficult to proceed and in these cases we rely on the results of our own assessments to challenge the man's denials. Marshall and colleagues (1986) found that of 12 men who denied any involvement in the sexual molestation of children prior to our assessment, the results of erectile measures of sexual preferences were sufficient to persuade seven of them to admit to their offensive behavior. Abel, Cunningham-Rathner, Becker, and McHugh (1983) reported that as a result of feedback of the psychophysiological assessment, 55% of offenders admit to additional offensive behavior.

In group meetings, both the group leaders and other offenders confront each offender in turn. Often, when an offender holds distorted cognitions concerning his own offensive behavior, he is able to correctly identify and criticize these cognitions in other offenders, and this in turn appears to increase his ability to be self-critical. In this process, the clinician must take care not to alienate the patient, remaining supportive and under-standing despite challenging and even contradicting the client's claims. However, we do not allow the patient to infer that we concur with his denials. Making the point that the victim and offender almost always have different versions of the offense, and that this can be accounted for on the basis of psychological processes such a selective attention and memory, gives the patient a face-saving way to gradually "remember" events or aspects of the offense that he had previously denied. Making a clear separation between the man himself and his behavior allows the therapist to take an accepting posture toward the man in general while at the same time condemning the offensive behavior. That is, the clinician must point to the man's strengths and have him realize how much like other people he is in most respects. Perhaps the most crucial factor encouraging the patient to cooperate is to detail a constructive strategy in which his acceptance of the allegations and his efforts in treatment are part of a long-term solution to his problems (criminal charges, applications for parole, custody and access to children, etc.). We make it clear that the courts, parole board, his family, and society will look more favorably on him after his acceptance of responsibility for the offense(s) and his entry into treatment.

Simply imparting information concerning the sexual abuse of children and the social acceptability of various forms of sexual behavior contributes to changes in sexual cognitions. This information is given over numerous interviews and during the group meetings. For example, the offender may be reluctant to accept total responsibility for the offense as long as he regards the child victim as having been provocative in leading him on. Education concerning the sexuality of children and the moral responsibilities of adults with respect to childhood sexuality has the effect of increasing the offender's acceptance of responsibility.

Our approach to reducing denial and minimization seems to be effective. Whereas we begin with approximately 50% of men in denial, after the pretreatment phase of the program only 10% of men are still in denial, and measures of minimization are significantly reduced (Barbaree, 1991).

Treatment Planning

In a cognitive-behavioral treatment program with relapse prevention, treatment planning is based on the concept of cognitive-behavioral chains. To properly plan treatment for the individual offender, the therapist must first develop a detailed account of the chain of events leading to the offenders' previous offenses. Cognitive-behavioral targets for treatment are then specified on the basis of the chain. For example, for a rapist whose previous offenses involved a pattern precipitated by a conflict with his spouse or girlfriend, leading to his drinking excessively, picking up a woman in a bar, and then raping her, the targets for treatment may include interpersonal problem solving and assertiveness, anger or temper control, attitudes toward women, rape-supportive attitudes and beliefs, and substance abuse. For the child molester whose previous offenses involved a pattern precipitated by unemployment and social isolation leading to his seeking out young children for social interaction, leading to fantasies about sex with children, and deviant sexual arousal, leading to his molesting the children, treatment targets may include deviant sexual arousal, sex education, social skills training, and vocational and recreational counseling.

Treatment

Table 6.4 presents the range of treatment targets usually specified in a comprehensive, cognitive-behavioral program. Treatment targets can be broadly divided into those directly related to deviant sexual behavior and those that contribute to deviant sexuality through their involvement in the cognitive-behavioral chain.

Perhaps the best known treatment target for the sexual offender is deviant sexual arousal. Behavioral approaches to the treatment of sexual offenders have been directed toward the modification of patterns of stimulus control of sexual arousal by decreasing deviant arousal and increasing appropriate arousal. Quinsey and Marshall (1983) critically reviewed a broad range of studies covering various offensive and eccentric sexual behaviors. They concluded that whereas some of the procedures appeared to offer some hope, there was little in the way of clear, convincing evidence of their efficacy. Kelly (1982) reviewed the literature on the treatment of child molesters and identified four controlled group studies and 10 controlled case studies, all of which encouraged optimism in the use of behavioral procedures.

Aversive procedures take various forms but basically they involve pairing the presently desired sexual stimulus (e.g., a child or coercive sex) with some aversive event. In overt aversive procedures, this aversive event has been one of a variety of physical stimuli such as a mild electric shock (Quinsey, Chaplin, & Carrigan, 1980) or a strong, aversive odor (Laws, Meyer, & Holmen, 1978). In covert sensitization (covert aversion), the aversive event has been a negative imaginal event generated by the offender under instructions from the clinician. These negative imaginal cues have included physically aversive images such as thoughts about feces or vomit, or psychologically-aversive images such as being discovered during the commission of deviant acts by a spouse, relatives, or friends (Levin, Barry, Gambaro, Wolfinsohn, & Smith, 1977).

Using a between-groups, crossover design, Quinsey et al. (1980) compared biofeedback with an electrical aversion procedure in the reduction of pedophiliac arousal. Eighteen heterosexual child molesters were exposed to pictures of adult and child female nudes while their erectile responses were monitored. All subjects were provided with feedback from their erectile responses. A blue signal light was activated whenever arousal surpassed a present criterion during presentation of the adult stimuli, whereas a red light was activated whenever arousal surpassed a preset criterion during presentation of the child stimuli. Subjects were required to maximize the time the blue light was on and minimize the time the red light was on. Subjects were allocated to one of two groups. In the aversive procedure (signaled punishment), a mild electric shock was delivered to the subject's arm whenever the red light came on during presentation of the child stimulus. The biofeedback group followed the same procedure without the shock. After a number of treatment sessions, the two groups were crossed over to the alternate treatment procedure. Data analysis was conducted over to the alternate treatment procedure. Data analysis was conducted on each subject individually, comparing pretreatment erectile measures with those taken after the first and after the second treatment procedure. Whereas only 4 of 12 offenders showed significant reductions in deviant arousal after the initial biofeedback procedure, 5 of 6 showed significant reductions as a result of the signaled punishment procedure. After the second treatment procedure, two offenders showed no improvement as a result of biofeedback, whereas 5 of 8 showed improvement after the punishment procedure. This study constitutes the only controlled treatment study that convincingly shows the effectiveness of electrical aversion with child molesters.

As in the case of electrical aversion, only one study allowed a strong inference to be made concerning the effectiveness of covert sensitization. Brownell, Hayes, and Barlow (1977) used a multiple-baseline-across-behaviors design wherein they sequentially targeted each of two deviant behaviors. Brownell et al. (1977) studied five deviants, but the results of only one subjects are, strictly speaking, relevant here. Two of the five had relevant deviant arousal, but only one of these was assessed using objective penile tumescence measures. This man had sadistic masturbatory fantasies and he had committed a rape. In addition, he had developed exhibitionistic fantasies and had been arrested for public masturbation. In treatment, during phase 1 of the design, covert sensitization was used to target arousal to exhibitionistic fantasies. This decreased the patient's arousal to exhibitionism, but left arousal to sadistic fantasies at or near 100% of full erection. During phase 2 of the design, arousal to sadistic fantasies was targeted, and this arousal decreased to near zero. Moreover, deviant arousal remained near zero during a 6-month follow-up. The results from this single subject remain the best evidence for the effectiveness of covert sensitization in the reduction of deviant arousal amongst sex offenders.

Satiation is a behavioral method used to reduce deviant arousal, but which does not depend on the use of aversive procedures. Marshall (1979) used single-case research methods to evaluate this procedure that he earlier described (Marshall & Lippens, 1977). In this procedure, offenders were required to masturbate to ejaculation while verbalizing aloud every variation of their deviant fantasy. Upon ejaculation, and throughout the refractory period, patients were instructed to continue to masturbate to the same fantasies, over several, hour-long sessions. Marshall examined two repetitive child molesters who showed considerable arousal to both children and other deviant stimuli and minimal arousal to adult females. In the first case, Marshall used a multiple-baseline-across-behaviors design, targeting in sequence arousal to female children aged 6 to 8 years, female children aged 11 to 13 years, a footwear fetish, and an underwear fetish. As each category was treated, probes revealed that arousal to those stimuli decreased whereas arousal to the other stimuli remained relatively stable. In the second case, Marshall attempted to reduce pedophiliac arousal by the sequential application of self-esteem training, electrical aversion therapy, and finally, satiation. Pedophiliac arousal was resistant to the first two interventions, whereas satiation rapidly reduced deviant responding. For both of these patients, follow-up data are now available over 10 years after treatment and no relapses have occurred (Marshall, 1979). Satiation has been shown to be an effective method for reducing deviant sexual arousal and enhancing appropriate arousal in adolescent offenders (Hunter & Goodwin, 1992; Hunter & Santos, 1993).

In summary, three methods are in frequent use in attempts to reduce deviant sexual arousal, namely aversion therapy, covert sensitization, and satiation. However, the studies that attest to the effectiveness of these procedures are limited in number, although not in methodological rigor. These studies indicated that the procedures used were responsible for the reductions seen in deviant arousal, and they showed that these reductions in deviant arousal persist over several weeks and months.

We have found that men respond idiosyncratically to treatment procedures, and that a man who fails to respond to one may show beneficial effects of another. Accordingly, we tend to use several in combination. It may be that different procedures influence different aspects of the attraction to deviant acts. For example, aversive therapy might reduce the valence of visual images (e.g., images of children in advertising, television, etc.) that might otherwise elicit arousal in these men, whereas satiation may alter masturbatory images that would otherwise maintain deviant interests. We employ portable smelling salts for the man to use as a self-administered punishment for urges elicited by features in his everyday environment (e.g., the sight of children in playgrounds). Whenever an urge occurs, the man takes a rapid inhalation of the smelling salts and turns his thoughts to other matters. In addition, we have the patient write scripts describing possible offenses followed by distressing consequences. These are written on pocket-sized cards that he carries with him and repeatedly reads. This covert, aversive procedure not only serves to punish urges, but it also clearly delineates the whole sequence of responses involved in his deviant acts, thereby allowing him to recognize at an early point in the sequence that he is on course to offend. This seems to make it easier for him to abort the sequence.

A secondary, but no less important, outcome of this component of therapy involves an attempt to increase socially appropriate sexual arousal. Typically we combine the satiation procedure with orgasmic reconditioning (Marquis, 1970) to achieve this goal. The patient is required to masturbate to orgasm using appropriate images, and then during the refractory period, he is required to verbalize as many elaborations of his deviant fantasies as possible. If he is unable to masturbate to orgasm using appropriate cues, because these do not yet have the necessary potency for him, he is instructed to use deviant cues to initiate arousal, switch to appropriate cues once fully aroused, and then either continue to masturbate to orgasm while imagining the appropriate cues, or switch back-and-forth between appropriate and deviant images as necessary to maintain arousal.

It is important to make the point here that this component of therapy is not exclusively "behavioral," as an important contribution to the eventual change in sexual preferences is the offender's developing understanding of the factors that lead to his offending. Although the treatment here focuses on the reduction in deviant arousal, much discussion during meetings with each man centers on his sexual fantasies and urges and the behavioral sequence that leads from urge or fantasy to offense. During homework assignments, the man learns what factors serve to trigger or encourage deviant fantasies. For example, he many find that deviant fantasies occur when he is distressed or when he is feeling lonely or bored.

Perhaps the best psychological construct under which to subsume these variables is the concept of stress. Stress is a disorganized state brought on by environmental demands with which the person cannot cope (Lazarus, 1966). For potential sex offenders, stress increases the likelihood of offending. The sources of stress are many, including financial, marital, parenting, and vocational problems, and the sources of stress vary from one offender to another. Ineptitude in social and personal management skills produces stress and such deficits also limit the man's capacity to secure long-term, satisfactory, appropriate interpersonal and sexual relations.

It is therefore important to assess and treat sex offenders with regard to a wide range of coping behaviors. During interviews, we evaluate a broad range of coping skills, focusing on the deficits which are idiosyncratic to the particular offender. Subsequent formal assessments further define these problems. For example, social skill deficits and social anxiety are a source of stress for many sex offenders. Standardized, self-report tests of assertion, social self-esteem, and social fears and anxiety clarify the relevance of these issues, at least from the patient's perspective. We also videotape the offender during a conversation with a female confederate during a standard behavioral assertion test and during his attempts at resolution of social/interactive problems. These videotapes are scored later by independent observers.

With regard to the offender's social and personal management skills, the objectives of treatment are varied. First, the offender should acquire the knowledge and skills necessary to practice socially acceptable sexual behaviors with an appropriate partner. Second, the offender should acquire the knowledge and skills necessary to develop satisfying, close, and intimate interpersonal relationships based on mutual respect, trust, and cooperation. Finally, the offender should acquire the knowledge and skills necessary to prevent the occurrence of the circumstances that led to his deviant behavior in the past; these skills might include stress management, controlled drinking, and those that increase satisfaction gained from recreational activities. These skills are acquired during both individual and group meetings, through instruction, behavioral rehearsal, group discussion and feedback, and through a series of exercises practiced at home between treatment sessions.

Posttreatment

In a sense it is inaccurate to call our interventions "treatment," as we do not construe our patients as having a "disorder" that can be "cured." Rather, we see them as having learned certain unacceptable behaviors to obtain rewards and satisfactions that their behavioral repertoire did not adequately enable them to achieve by more consensually acceptable routes. Because these deviant acts have produced strong, immediate rewards in the past and because thoughts of deviant acts have been frequently associated with the enjoyment of strong sexual arousal, we expect deviant tendencies to retain some degree of strength even after the very best treatment program. Therefore, posttreatment management is essential; at least, it is necessary to train patients to be capable of dealing with the threat of relapse, which is a feature of posttreatment course.

Relapse prevention has recently achieved prominence as an important strategic component in the management of the sexual offender. Relapse prevention has been suggested as a way to maintain the behavior change produced in the treatment of individuals suffering from various forms of addictions. Marlatt and Gordon (1980, 1985) outlined a strategy for assisting individuals who have completed treatment to prevent the recurrence of drug-taking behavior. The strategy involves (1) identifying situations in which the individual is at high risk for relapse; (2) teaching the individual to identify these high-risk situations and to avoid them; (3) identifying lapses as behaviors that do not constitute full-fledged relapses (e.g., drinking alcohol), but that constitute approximations to the drug-taking behavior and may be a precursor to a relapse (e.g., frequenting bars); (4) teaching the individual to identify a lapse; and (5) teaching the individual various coping strategies that might use in response to both high-risk situations and lapses to minimize the chances of a relapse.

Pithers et al. (1983) extended the relapse prevention strategy for use with sexual offenders, and this approach has had broad clinical appeal. An edited volume was published describing various aspects of the use of relapse prevention with sexual offenders (Laws, 1989). The principles involved are similar to those used with addicts. First, high-risk situations are identified for each offender (MacDonald & Pithers, 1989; Pithers et al., 1989) and he is taught to identify their occurrence. Second, he is taught to identify lapses, or decisions he makes that lead him closer to a relapse (Jenkins-Hall & Marlatt, 1989). Finally, he is taught to cope with high-risk situations and lapses to prevent the occurrence of a relapse (Carey & McGrath, 1989; Steenman, Nelson, & Viesti Jr., 1989). As yet, no studies of outcome have been reported for relapse prevention, but most clinicians are optimistic that relapse prevention will eventually be shown to be an effective component in therapy.

Pithers (1990) made an important distinction between two critical aspects of relapse prevention. In teaching the offender ways of coping with high-risk situations, we enhance his capacity for internal self-management. A second critical aspect of relapse prevention is providing for an environment that supports the offender's attempts at relapse prevention. Pithers referred to the second aspect as *external supervision.* For example, persons in the offender's environment have been used in the follow-up period in an innovative way by Abel and Rouleau (1987) in what they have termed *surveillance groups.* A list is made of four to five persons who are in regular contact with the offender throughout the days and weeks of follow-up. The therapist meets with each person in the surveillance group to construct a method of reporting "risky" situations (the offender becoming angry, stressed, or bored) or provocative behaviors (the offender driving around in their car, walking past school yards, or being unable to account for long periods of time). Reports are made to the clinic on a regular basis, and when the level of risk increases, the therapist recalls the offender to a clinic meeting. It is hoped that appropriate intervention at this critical time will prevent relapse.

Relapse prevention, it might be argued, is a necessary component to the successful management of the sexual offender. Sexual offenders are known to have a high rate of relapse (Furby et al., 1989) even after treatment (Marshall & Barbaree, 1988). Sexual deviance is thought to have elements in common with the addictions (Herman, 1990), with urges and cravings leading to relapse (Marlatt, 1989). High-risk situations and the offender's ability to cope with these are thought to be related to recidivism of sexual offenders (Marshall & Barbaree, 1984). For these and other reasons, the relapse-prevention model has had almost universal appeal. In fact, it has been embraced with such enthusiasm that some programs of treatment have been described as being based on a relapse prevention model without reference to any other components of treatment. Moreover, in some jurisdictions, changes in the criminal justice system with respect to sexual offenders have been proposed based solely on a relapse prevention model. As a cautionary note, Marshall and Anderson (1996) reviewed the outcome literature and did not find any positive benefits for the addition of relapse prevention to cognitive-behavioral treatment programs.

INTEGRATION OF A CORRECTIONS
AND A TREATMENT MODEL

A natural conflict results when the factors underlying the commission of sexual offenses are understood in terms of a medical or psychopathology model by treatment staff on the one hand, and in terms of a moral–legal or criminal justice model by correctional staff on the other. The treatment staff understand the behavior of the offender in terms of an underlying pathology that has arisen through natural causes (biological, sociological, or psychological). According to this model, the pathology has caused the man to offend through processes he may not understand and over which he has limited control. This model evokes an understanding and sympathy for the offender that is not generally shared by the public-at-large or by professionals in the criminal justice system. Opposed to this view is the legal–moral model held by professionals in the criminal justice system, in which the offender is held accountable for his actions, and rehabilitation is not seen to be complete until the offender comes to accept responsibility for the offenses he committed.

As should be apparent from our earlier discussion of the cognitive objectives of treatment, the assumptions underlying the treatment of sex offenders need not be based on a model of psychopathology without considering issues of morality and personal responsibility. A treatment model can engender the appropriate understanding of the underlying causes of deviance of the offender without exonerating the offender. We endorse the simultaneous application of corrections and treatment models and these two activities should have mutually facilitative effects. If the objectives for the cognitive components of therapy are met in treatment, namely that the man comes to accept responsibility for his criminal behavior, then the man's rehabilitation will be recognized within the framework of the criminal justice system. Similarly, a forceful and clear response by the criminal justice system, including initiating charges, aggressive prosecution, and the consistent and fair sentencing of offenders will enhance the effectiveness of treatment.

Sentencing has a number of objectives relevant to treatment, including punishment, deterrence, rehabilitation, and the safety of the community. Punishment in the "just desserts" or an "eye-for-an-eye" sense, and deterrence are common to all sentences. The early stages of therapy should develop an acceptance on the part of the offender of the fairness of the sentence, as part of his taking responsibility for the offense. The latter two components of sentencing are most relevant to the day-to-day work of the therapist. Treatment that targets and modifies the cognitive-behavioral antecedents to sexual offending is obviously related to rehabilitation; in fact, the concepts of treatment and rehabilitation may be synonymous, and finally, when treatment is successful, safety of the community will be enhanced. Therefore, the outcome of successful therapy is consistent with the objectives of the criminal justice system.

By the same token, the effect of the criminal justice system will often be to enhance the effectiveness of therapy. The interface between the correctional/judicial system and treatment provides important sources of motivation for the offender in treatment. As we noted earlier, most men we see initially deny their offenses and their need for treatment. Most would not attend the clinic without the external pressure they feel in the context of the criminal justice system. When evidence is weak, the police might imply to the offender that if he attends our community clinic, they will not press charges. The offender's lawyer might suggest that if the man has completed the treatment program by the time of sentencing, the sentence might be lighter or at least it will make it easier for the lawyer to plead his case. The child protective agency may threaten to deny the man access to his children, or to take custody of his child, unless he attends the clinic for assessment. Almost all our candidates for treatment come to the clinic because of pressure brought to bear by some aspect of the criminal justice system. In this sense, the criminal justice system and our program are mutually reinforcing. The astute therapist uses important landmarks in the system cycle to motivate the offender, focusing him on his objectives and rewarding him for progress in treatment. For example, using delayed, contingent sentencing, a therapist can encourage a man's defense attorney to delay sentencing as long as possible. During this time, the therapist and the offender accomplish as much progress in treatment as possible. Later, the offender goes to court with a treatment progress report documenting the changes he has accomplished, and the court often bases sentencing, at least in part, on the man's acceptance of responsibility for the offense, his obvious motivation for treatment, and his progress to date. During treatment, then, the offender sees clearly how his progress will put him at an advantage and contribute to his progress through the system. Using a similar logic, while the potential candidate is incarcerated, the therapist introduces treatment as one way to increase his chances with the parole board. In treatment, changes in attitudes, beliefs, and behavior are recognized frequently by the therapist as signifying the man's suitability for a program of release, whereas reversion to distorted thinking, victim blame, and outbursts of temper are specified for the offender by the therapists as indicating his continuing risk and that, consequently, a release at this time would be unwise. Successful therapists ensure that the offender understands the contingency between success in therapy and progress through the system. In support of treatment, the successful criminal justice system rewards progress in therapy, as documented in treatment reports by the clinician, with progress through the system. The progress will not necessarily be an outright release, particularly if the safety of the community remains a concern. Instead, the reward may involve a transfer to a more desirable institution, an escorted pass, or access to additional treatment programs.

During the initial pretreatment phase of treatment of the incarcerated offender, while targeting denial and minimization, if the offender remains steadfastly in denial and after a suitable period of time and effort has been expended, the therapist may remove him from treatment and consequent progress through the system. He leaves treatment with the therapist's instruction to contact the therapist if and when he decides to address the issues that resulted in his removal from treatment.

We argue strongly for the integration of treatment in the criminal justice system with the actions of each facilitating the work of the other. In addition, we argue for the integration of various treatment programs that will contribute to the individual offender's rehabilitation. Currently, most treatment programs are institutionally based (in hospitals or prisons). This means that residents or inmates of that institution have access to the program, whereas other men do not. If a man wants access to the program, he must transfer, or be admitted to the institution in question first, and then be admitted to treatment. Similarly, when the man leaves the institution, he leaves the treatment program. Later access to the treatment program is difficult or impossible unless he transfers back to the institution. For men on parole after treatment, access to the institutional treatment staff with whom he is familiar is very difficult, perhaps impossible.

Whereas there are community-based programs available in some urban centers in North America, for the most part they have no formal links with institutionally based programs. Whereas informal links might allow a man leaving an institution to be seen in a community program, often the philosophical and procedural differences between the two programs make it difficult for effective transitioning to occur from treatment in the institution to follow-up and support in the community program. Ideally, treatment programs sharing philosophy and methodology, if not staff and administration, should be arranged vertically, from maximum-security prison settings through medium security to community settings. Then, from whichever level of security the offender is initially sentenced, he can look forward to a gradual and controlled release that will include treatment and support at each level and at each stage. Continuity of treatment would then be assured and the "management" of the sex offender would be more likely to minimize recidivism.

TREATMENT OUTCOME

Institutional Programs

Three treatment programs have described the application of comprehensive, cognitive-behavioral treatment to institutionalized sex offenders, all of whom were either rapists or child molesters. The first of these to appear in the literature was applied to sex offenders incarcerated in the Kingston Penitentiary in Canada (Marshall & Williams, 1975). In a comparative study, Marshall and Williams showed that a behavioral program that included some, but not all, of the elements described above was far more effective than a more traditional psychotherapy program in meeting the within-treatment goals. That is to say, the behavioral program demonstrably achieved its goals in changing various features of these offenders (rapists and child molesters), whereas psychotherapy did not reach its goals. Both programs (the behavioral and the psychotherapy) were short and intensive, and all patients completed both in a balanced, cross-over design. Some years later, Davidson (1984) reported recidivism data, derived from official police records. Although he used a sophisticated method of calculating recidivism derived from official police records, this particular method (proportion of those at risk who recidivated) does not allow comparison with the usual data that describe the percentage of those treated who have reoffended over specified periods of follow-up. However, Davidson's (1979) earlier report indicated overall recidivism for treated offenders to be 11.5%, suggesting an effective outcome. Davidson (1984) provided comparative recidivism from untreated sex offenders who were incarcerated in the same jails as the treated offenders, but whose period of imprisonment was in the 8 years before the availability of the treatment program. Although this is not an ideal control group in that we do not know whether or not these men would have entered treatment had they had the opportunity, it is certainly as good an approximation as was possible under the circumstances. These data revealed greater effectiveness for the treatment of child molesters, but marginal benefits for the rapists.

Quinsey and his associates have over the years described various aspects of the treatment program offered at the Oak Ridge Mental Health Centre in Ontario (Quinsey, Bergersen, & Steinman, 1976; Quinsey et al., 1980; Whitman & Quinsey, 1981). This Centre is a maximum security hospital serving a population of sex offenders who have been either declared insane, involuntarily certified, or referred by the courts for psychiatric assessment. We would expect such a population to be particularly difficult to treat. Whereas Quinsey's reports showed that the treatment procedures produced the expected changes in the treated behaviors (i.e., sexual preferences and social competence), a long-term follow-up of treated offenders compared with untreated offenders failed to show any beneficial effects of treatment on recidivism (Rice, Harris, & Quinsey, 1991).

The sexual offender unit at Oregon State Hospital (Smith, 1984) was evaluated by Freeman-Longo (1984), and the data were somewhat encouraging. Of those limited number of patients who graduated from this long-term program (only 20 patients were released in the period from 1979 to 1983), none committed a sexual offense during the unspecified follow-up period, although two were returned to prison for theft. Again, no comparative data were provided.

The Sex Offender Treatment and Evaluation Project (Marques et al., 1994) was an experimental program conducted at Atascadero State Hospital that randomly assigned subjects to treatment. The program's study sample involved three matched groups: volunteers who were randomly selected for treatment, volunteers who were randomly selected for no treatment, and the nonvolunteer group that received no treatment. The treatment program was 2 years in duration and involved cognitive-behavioral interventions with relapse prevention. Marques and her colleagues have provided recidivism data on sufficient numbers of subjects over a long enough follow-up period for a meaningful conclusion to be drawn. The data derived from Marques, Day, Nelson, and West (1994) suggested some degree of benefit for treated subjects. Survival analyses demonstrated that treated subjects were at significantly lower risk to reoffend than were nonvolunteers, but the differences between the treated and untreated volunteers did not reach acceptable levels of statistical significance. Moreover, additional analyses revealed some interesting complexities to the findings. Marques (1995) reported that four characteristics of the offenders (prior status as a sex offender with a mental disorder, marital status, employment status, and childhood physical abuse) influenced subsequent recidivism. By controlling for these factors in the statistical analysis, Marques was able to demonstrate a statistically significant difference in the rate of recidivism between the randomly assigned treated and untreated offenders.

Community-Based Programs

We completed an outcome study (Marshall & Barbaree, 1988) in which we compared a treated sample of 68 child molesters with a group of 58 untreated men who attended our clinic for an assessment only. The group of untreated offenders whom we used for comparison admitted their deviant behavior and expressed a desire to enter treatment, but were unable to for circumstantial reasons (e.g., living too far away from the clinic for regular attendance). In all other respects (e.g., IQ, socioeconomic status, offense histories, degree of deviance, etc.), these untreated offenders were equivalent to the treated sample.

We followed these men over an average period of 40 months. Reoffending was determined by three methods. We searched the official police computer records for charges and convictions for the men in both samples. These computer records were compiled by the Royal Canadian Mounted Police (RCMP) and included all charges or convictions these men might have had while in or out of Canada (records from the FBI and Interpol and all police forces in Canada were included). We also contacted Children's

Aid Societies (child protective agencies in Canada) and police officers in the local communities we serve, who searched their files for unofficial evidence of reoffending, including evidence of a nature that did not allow the police to proceed with charges, but that nonetheless convincingly indicated a reoffense. Taken together, the official and unofficial records revealed considerable reoffending among both treated and untreated offenders, but only 45% of the total number of offenses were reflected in the official records.

Statistical comparisons between treated and untreated groups were conducted on two outcome variables: the number of men in each sample who had reoffended (the rate of recidivism), and the number of reoffenses for each man. In the untreated sample, approximately one-third of the men had committed a further offense during follow-up, whereas the rate of reoffense among the treated men was reduced to approximately one man in six; this difference was statistically significant and is of sufficient magnitude to also represent a difference of clinical importance. In terms of the number of reoffenses for each man, the untreated men were found to have committed, on average, approximately one offense per man, whereas for the treated men, the reoffense rate was approximately 0.5 per man, a difference that is statistically significant. Therefore, we concluded on the basis of this preliminary analysis that the comprehensive treatment program was effective in reducing the likelihood of reoffense among child molesters.

Because our data (from the Kingston Sexual Behavior Clinic) were based on the unofficial records, we may assume that we could multiply the child molesters' data from Maletzky (1987) by a factor of 2.4, as his data are based on official records. If we do this, we find that Maletzky seemed to be somewhat more successful than we were with those men who molested female children, but it may be that Maletzky included incest offenders in this group. If we average over our familial and nonfamilial offenders against female children, our recidivism data (when corrected for the source of reoffense information) are approximately the same as Maletzky's (i.e., 12.7% for Maletzky's [1987] and 14% for our program). With respect to men who molest boys, we seemed to be more effective than was Maletzky. Indeed, our data on these offenders was contrary to what we had expected and inconsistent with what many clinicians have told us about their experiences over the years. We held the belief that men who molest boys would be far more difficult to treat than other child molesters. Perhaps these pre-data sentiments caused us to inadvertently put greater effort into treating these men or caused us to evolve a program that was particularly suited to them. Abel et al. (1988) were also more effective in treating the men who had molested boys than they were in changing the men who had molested girls.

If we accept that Abel et al.'s (1988) patients were truthful in their reports, then his program seemed to be as effective with child molesters as were the other outpatient programs. However, as recidivism increases progressively from time of discharge (Gibbens, Soothill, & Way, 1981; Marshall & Barbaree, 1988) and Abel et al. only followed their patients for 1 year, in fact, their data are rather disappointing. This observation becomes even gloomier when we consider that despite having at least 64 incest offenders in their group, Abel et al. did not distinguish the familial from the nonfamilial offenders in describing recidivism. As we noted earlier, incest offenders typically have lower reoffense rates than do nonincestuous child molesters. However, as we also noted earlier, Abel's patients were likely to have been the most severe of offenders and the most likely to reoffend.

We also analyzed the pretreatment data for both treated (Marshall & Barbaree, 1987) and untreated men (Barbaree & Marshall, 1989) to discern factors that might predict subsequent recidivism. Treatment was less successful with those men who had engaged in genital–genital contact with their young victims. Among the untreated offenders there were three factors that predicted reoffending: (1) deviance quotient derived from relative arousal to children and adults at the sexual preference test; (2) socioeconomic status; and (3) genital–genital contact with children. These predictor variables are listed in descending order of their strength of prediction, with the untreated offenders most likely to offend being those with high arousal to children, of low socioeconomic status, who had genital–genital contact with their victim(s). These data indicate that we can predict, with some accuracy, who is likely to reoffend if not treated, who is most likely to benefit from our present treatment program, and what it is we have to work on if we are to improve our current success rate.

In conclusion, the evaluation of treatment of the sex offender using reoffense data is fraught with methodological difficulties. However, these data taken as a whole lead us to be optimistic regarding treatment effects. A recently reported meta-analysis of the sex offender treatment outcome literature by Gordon Hall (1995) found an overall positive effect of treatment on reoffense rates, with cognitive-behavioral therapy identified as a viable treatment approach. As well, the meta-analysis found that community-based programs had more positive effects than did institutional programs.

SUMMARY AND CONCLUSIONS

This chapter critically reviewed a wide range of approaches to the treatment of the sex offender. The discussion pointed to the difficulties in conducting treatment outcome research in this area and offered suggestions as to what might be considered minimum requirements of a treatment outcome study. The study should compare outcome of treated subjects with an appropriate untreated comparison group, matched on important demographic and offense history variables. The study should not select patients, but rather it should offer treatment to all men who seek it. The study should not depend on self-reports of reoffense, but on corroborated evidence. Researchers should note that official recidivism is likely to underestimate the true rate of reoffense.

Applying these criteria to the extant reports of treatment for the sex offender leads to the conclusion that the reports to date are not sufficient to evaluate most treatment programs. A number of guidelines for treatment were nevertheless suggested in the discussion of treatment programs. First, treatment that seeks to modify a single defect or pathology is not likely to succeed. A good example of treatment programs based on a single defect are the organic treatments. A review of the literature pertaining to these programs failed to find clear evidence of effective treatment, either in terms of the effect of treatment on sexual arousal/urges or in terms of the rate of reoffense. Similarly, programs that fail to clearly define the nature of the defect in sex offenders that needs to be changed are not likely to succeed. Good examples of programs that fail to carefully define the within-treatment goals are the nonbehavioral psychotherapies. Sexual crimes derive from a complex interaction of cognitive, physiological, and situational variables. Accordingly, a comprehensive treatment program that targets deficits and excesses important and relevant to the commission of sexual crimes is our best hope to prevent reoffending. We described a comprehensive program for child molesters and presented tentative long-term follow-up data. These data support the continued use and further development of the comprehensive program. Further, comprehensive programs can be readily integrated in the criminal justice and mental health systems, and treatment and corrections can and should be mutually reinforcing.

Finally, society's emerging and evolving response to the problem of sexual assault involves many components. Prevention programs educate victims and potential victims, as well as potential offenders. Increasing public awareness makes it more difficult for offenders to escape detection, apprehension, and at times, severe punishment. Continued political and social pressure will change attitudes and behaviors that have caused and condoned sexual assaults. Changes and improvements in the legal system will bring more offenders to prosecution. However, prevention, education, and political and legal action are not sufficient to solve the problem of the sexual offender. Once sentenced and incarcerated, offenders will someday be released. Their treatment and continued management is a crucial part of any intelligent response to the problem of sexual assault.

REFERENCES

Abel, G. G., Barlow, D. H., Blanchard, E. B., & Guild, D. (1977). The components of rapists' sexual arousal. *Archives of General Psychiatry, 34,* 895–903.

Abel, G. G., Becker, J. V., & Cunningham-Rathner, J. (1984). Complications, consent and cognitions in sex between children and adults. *International Journal of Law and Psychiatry, 7,* 89–103.

Abel, G. G., Becker, J. V., & Skinner, L. J. (1980). Treatment of the violent sexual offender. In L. H. Roth (Ed.), *Clinical treatment of the violent person.* Rockville, MD: National Institute of Mental Health.

Abel, G. G., Blanchard, E. B., & Becker, J. V. (1978). An integrated treatment program for rapists. In R. T. Rada (Ed.), *Clinical aspects of the rapist* (pp. 161–214). New York: Grune & Stratton.

Abel, G. G., Cunningham-Rathner, J., Becker, J. V., & McHugh, J. (1983). *Motivating sex offenders for treatment with feedback of their psychophysiological assessment.* Unpublished manuscript.

Abel, G. G., Mittleman, M. S., & Becker, J. V. (1985). Sex offenders: Results of assessment and recommendations for treatment. In M. H. Ben-Aron, S. J. Hucker, & C. D. Webster (Eds.), *Clinical criminology: The assessment and treatment of criminal behavior* (pp. 207–220). Toronto: M & M Graphics.

Abel, G. G., Mittleman, M. S., Becker, J. V., Rathner, J., & Rouleau, J. L. (1988). Predicting child molesters' response to treatment. *Annals of the New York Academy of Sciences, 528,* 223–234.

Abel, G. G., & Rouleau, J. (1987). *Surveillance groups.* Unpublished manuscript.

American Psychiatric Association. (1994). *Diagnostic and statistical manual of mental disorders* (4th ed.). Washington, DC: Author.

Amir, M. (1971). *Patterns of forcible rape.* Chicago: University of Chicago Press.

Bancroft, J. (1983). *Human sexuality and its problems.* New York: Churchill Livingston.

Bancroft, J., Tennent, T. G., Loucas, K., & Cass, J. (1974). Control of deviant sexual behavior by drugs: Behavioral effects of estrogens and antiandrogens. *British Journal of Psychiatry, 125,* 310–315.

Barbaree, H. E. (1990). Stimulus control of sexual arousal: Its role in sexual assault. In W. L. Marshall, D. R. Laws, & H. E. Barbaree (Eds.), *Handbook of sexual assault: Issues, theories, and treatment of the offender* (pp. 115–142). New York: Plenum Press.

Barbaree, H. E. (1991). Denial and minimization among sex offenders: Assessment and treatment outcome. *Forum on Corrections Research, 3,* 30–33.

Barbaree, H. E. (1997). Evaluating treatment efficacy with sexual offenders: The insensitivity of recidivism studies to treatment effects. *Sexual Abuse: A Journal of Research and Treatment, 9,* 111–128.

Barbaree, H. E., & Marshall, W. L. (1988). Deviant sexual arousal, offense history, and demographic variables as predictors of reoffense among child molesters. *Behavioral Sciences and the Law, 6,* 267–280.

Barbaree, H. E., & Marshall, W. L. (1989). Erectile responses among heterosexual child molesters, father–daughter incest offenders, and matched non-offenders: Five distinct age preference profiles. *Canadian Journal of Behavioural Science, 21,* 70–82.

Barbaree, H. E., Marshall, W. L., & Lanthier, R. D. (1979). Deviant sexual arousal in rapists. *Behaviour Research and Therapy, 17,* 215–222.

Barbaree, H. E., Marshall, W. L., Yates, E., & Lightfoot, L. O. (1983). Alcohol intoxication and deviant sexual arousal in male social drinkers. *Behaviour Research and Therapy, 21,* 365–373.

Barbaree, H. E., Seto, M. C., Serin, R. C., Amos, N. L., & Preston, D. L. (1994). Comparisons between sexual and non-sexual rapist subtypes: Sexual arousal to rape, offense precursors and offense characteristics. *Criminal Justice and Behaviour, 21,* 95–114.

Bard, L. A., Carter, D. L., Cerce, D. D., Knight, R. A., Rosenberg, & Schneider. (1987). A descriptive study of rapists and child molesters: Developmental, clinical, and criminal characteristics. *Behavioral Sciences and the Law, 5,* 203–220.

Baxter, D. J., Barbaree, H. E., & Marshall, W. L. (1986). Sexual responses to consenting and forced sex in a large sample of rapists and nonrapists. *Behaviour Research and Therapy, 24,* 513–520.

Baxter, D. J., Marshall, W. L., Barbaree, H. E., Davidson, P. R., & Malcolm, P. B. (1984). Deviant sexual behavior: Differentiating sex offenders by criminal and personal history, psychometric measures, and sexual response. *Criminal Justice and Behavior, 11,* 477–501.

Beck, A. T., Rush, A. J., Shaw, B. F., & Emery, G. (1979). *Cognitive therapy of depression.* New York: Guilford Press.

Berlin, F. S., & Meinecke, C. F. (1981). Treatment of sex offenders with antiandrogenic medication: Conceptualization, review of treatment modalities and preliminary findings. *American Journal of Psychiatry, 138,* 601–608.

Bradford, J. M. W. (1985). Organic treatments for the male sexual offender. *Behavioral Sciences and the Law, 3,* 355–375.

Bradford, J. M. W. (1990). The antiandrogen and hormonal treatment of sex offenders. In W. L. Marshall, D. R. Laws, & H. E. Barbaree (Eds.), *Handbook of sexual assault: Issues, theories, and treatment of the offender* (pp. 297–310). New York: Plenum Press.

Bradford, J. M. W., & Pawlak, A. (1987). Sadistic homosexual pedophilia: Treatment with cyproterone acetate. A single case study. *Canadian Journal of Psychiatry, 32,* 22–30.

Brancale, R., Ellis, A., & Doorbar, R. R. (1952). Psychiatric and psychological investigations of convicted sex offenders: A summary report. *American Journal of Psychiatry, 109,* 17–19.

Brancale, R., Vnocolo, A., & Prendergast, W. E. (1972). The New Jersey Program for Sex Offenders. In H. L. P. Resnick & M. F. Wolfgang (Eds.), *Sexual behaviors: Social, clinical, and legal aspects* (pp. 331–350). Boston: Little, Brown.

Briddell, D. W., Rimm, D. C., Caddy, G. R., Krawitz, G., Sholis, D., & Wunderline, R. J. (1978). Effects of alcohol and cognitive set on sexual arousal to deviant stimuli. *Journal of Abnormal Psychology, 87,* 418–430.

Brittain, R. P. (1970). The sadistic murderer. *Medicine, Science, and the Law, 10,* 198–207.

Brownell, K. D., Hayes, S. C., & Barlow, D. H. (1977). Patterns of appropriate and deviant sexual arousal: The behavioral treatment of multiple sexual deviations. *Journal of Consulting and Clinical Psychology, 45,* 1144–1155.

Burt, M. R. (1980). Cultural myths and supports for rape. *Journal of Personality and Social Psychology, 38,* 217–230.

Cabeen, C. W., & Coleman, J. C. (1961). Group therapy with sex offenders: Description and evaluation of group therapy program in an institutional setting. *Journal of Clinical Psychology, 17,* 122–129.

Carey, C. H., & McGrath, R. J. (1989). Coping with urges and craving. In D. R. Laws (Ed.), *Relapse prevention with sex offenders* (pp. 188–196). New York: Guilford Press.

Castell, R., & Yalom, I. (1972). Institutional group therapy. In H. L. P. Resnick & M. F. Wolfgang (Eds.), *Sexual behavior: Social, clinical, and legal aspects* (pp. 305–330). Boston: Little, Brown.

Check, J. V. P., & Malamuth, N. M. (1985). An empirical assessment of some feminist hypotheses about rape. Special issue: Women in groups and aggression against women. *International Journal of Women's Studies, 8,* 414–423.

Christie, M. M., Marshall, W. L., & Lanthier, R. D. (1977). *A descriptive study of rapists and pedophiles.* Unpublished manuscript.

Christie, M. M., Marshall, W. L., & Lanthier, R. D. (1979). *A descriptive study of incarcerated rapists and pedophiles* (Report to the Solicitor General of Canada). (Available from William L. Marshall, Queen's University, Kingston, Canada K7L 3N6)

Clark, G. (1945). Prepubertal castration in the male chimpanzee with some effects of replacement therapy. *Growth, 9,* 327–339.

Cohen, M., Seghorn, T., & Calamus, W. (1969). Sociometric study of the sex offender. *Journal of Abnormal Psychology, 74,* 249–255.

Cohen, M. L., Garafalo, R. F., Boucher, R. J., & Seghorn, T. K. (1971). The psychology of rapists. *Seminars in Psychiatry, 3,* 307–327.

Connor, J. (1988). *The development and evaluation of social problem-solving as an assessment procedure, for use in sexually deviant populations.* Unpublished BA (Hons.) thesis, Queen's University, Kingston, Ontario.

Conte, J. R. (1985). Clinical dimensions of adult sexual abuse of children. *Behavioral Sciences and the Law, 3,* 341–354.

Cooper, A. J. (1981). A placebo controlled trial of the antiandrogen cyproterone acetate in deviant hypersexuality. *Comprehensive Psychiatry, 22,* 458–464.

Cornu, F. (1973). *Catamnestic studies on castrated sex delinquents from a forensic–psychiatric viewpoint.* Unpublished manuscript.

Craig, M. (1990). Coercive sexuality in dating relationships: A situational model. *Clinical Psychology Review, 10,* 395–423.

Davidson, P. R. (1979). *Recidivism in sexual aggressors: Who are the bad risks.* Unpublished manuscript.

Davidson, P. R. (1984). [Outcome data for a penitentiary-based treatment program for sex offenders]. Unpublished raw data.

Earls, C. M., & Marshall, W. L. (1982). The current state of technology in the laboratory assessment of sexual arousal patterns. In J. G. Greer & I. R. Stuart (Eds.), *Sexual aggression: Current perspectives on treatment* (pp. 336–363). New York: Von Nostrand Reinhold.

Earls, C. M., & Quinsey, V.L. (1985). What is to be done? Future research on the assessment and behavioral treatment of sex offenders. *Behavioral Sciences and the Law, 3,* 377–390.

Egle, N., & Altwein, J. (1975). Postpubertal castration and prostatic carcinoma. *Urology, 6,* 471–473.

Ellis, A., & Brancale, R. (1956). *The psychology of sex offenders.* Springfield, IL: Thomas.

Fedoroff, J. P. (1988). Buspirone in the treatment of transvestic fetishism. *Journal of Clinical Psychiatry, 48,* 408–409.

Fedoroff, J. P. (1993). Serotonergic drug treatment of deviant sexual interests. *Annals of Sex Research, 6,* 105–121.

Foa, E. B., & Emmelkamp, P. M. G. (1983). *Failures in behavior therapy.* New York: Wiley.

Ford, C., & Beach, F. A. (1951). *Patterns of sexual behavior.* New York: Harper.

Freeman-Longo, R. E. (1984). The Oregon State Hospital Sex Offender Unit: Treatment outcome. In F. H. Knopp (Ed.), *Retraining adult sex offenders: Methods and models* (pp. 185–209). Syracuse, NY: Safer Society Press.

Freund, K. (1967a). Diagnosing homo or heterosexuality and erotic age-preference by means of a psychophysiological test. *Behaviour Research and Therapy, 5,* 209–228.

Freund, K. (1967b). Erotic preference in pedophilia. *Behaviour Research and Therapy, 5,* 339–348.

Freund, K. (1981). Assessment of pedophilia. In M. Cook & K. Howells (Eds.), *Adult sexual interest in children* (pp. 139–179). London: Academic Press.

Freund, K., & Blanchard, R. (1981). Assessment of sexual dysfunction and deviation. In M. Hersen & A. S. Bellack (Eds.), *Behavioral assessment: A practical handbook* (pp. 427–455). New York: Pergamon Press.

Furby, L., Weinrott, M.R., & Blackshaw, L. (1989). Sex offender recidivism: A review. *Psychological Bulletin, 105,* 3–30.

Gagne, P. (1981). Treatment of sex offenders with medroxyprogesterone acetate. *American Journal of Psychiatry, 138,* 644–646.

Gebhard, P., Gagnon, J., Pomeroy, W., & Christenson, C. (1965). *Sex offenders.* New York: Harper and Row.

Gibbens, T. C. N., Soothill, K. L., & Way, C. K. (1981). Sex offenses against young girls: A long-term record study. *Psychological Medicine, 11,* 351–357.

Gijs, L. & Gooren, L. (1996). Hormonal and psychopharmacological interventions in the treatment of paraphilias: An update. *Journal of Sex Research, 33,* 273–290.

Glueck, B. C. (1956). *Final report: Research project for the study and treatment of persons convicted of crimes involving sexual aberrations.* Unpublished manuscript.

Greenberg, D. M., & Bradford, J. M. W. (1997). Treatment of the paraphilic disorders: A review of the selective serotonin reuptake inhibitors. *Sexual Abuse: A Journal of Research and Treatment, 9,* 349–360.

Griffiths, D., Hindsburger, D., & Christian, R. (1985). Treating developmentally handicapped sexual offenders: The York Behavior Management Services treatment program. *Psychiatric Aspects of Mental Retardation Reviews, 4,* 49–52.

Groth, A. N. (1979). *Men who rape: The psychology of the offender.* New York: Plenum Press.

Groth, A. N. (1983). Treatment of the sexual offender in a correctional institution. In J. Greer & I. Stuart (Eds.), *The sexual aggressor: Current perspectives on treatment* (pp. 160–176). New York: Von Nostrand Reinhold.

Groth, A. N., Burgess, A. W., & Holmstrom, L. L. (1977). Rape: Power, anger, and sexuality. *American Journal of Psychiatry, 134,* 1239–1243.

Grubin, D. (1994). Sexual murder. *British Journal of Psychiatry, 165,* 624–629.

Hall, G. C. N. (1995). Sexual recidivism revisited: A meta-analysis of recent treatment studies. *Journal of Consulting and Clinical Psychology, 63,* 802–809.

Hall, G. C. N., Maiuro, R. D., Vitaliano, P. P., & Proctor, W. C. (1986). The utility of the MMPI with men who have sexually assaulted children. *Journal of Consulting and Clinical Psychology, 54,* 493–496.

Hanson, R. K. (1997). How to know what works with sex offenders. *Sexual Abuse: A Journal of Research and Treatment, 9,* 129–145.

Hardy, K. (1964). An appetitional theory of sexual motivation. *Psychological Review, 71,* 1–18.

Heim, N. (1981). Sexual behavior of castrated sex offenders. *Archives of Sexual Behavior, 10,* 11–19.

Herman, J. L. (1990). Sex offenders: A feminist perspective. In W. L. Marshall, D. R. Laws, & H. E. Barbaree (Eds.), *Handbook of sexual assault: Issues, theories, and treatment of the offender* (pp.177–193). New York: Plenum Press.

Howell, L. M. (1972). Clinical and research impressions regarding murder and sexually perverse crimes. *Psychotherapy and Psychosomatics, 21,* 156–159.

Hults, B. (1981). Data on 62 treatment facilities. *Treatment of Sexual Aggressives, 4,* 1–7.

Hunter, J. A., & Goodwin, D. W. (1992). The utility of satiation therapy in the treatment of juvenile sexual offenders: Variations and efficacy. *Annals of Sex Research, 5,* 71–80.

Hunter, J. A., & Santos, D. (1990). The use of specialized cognitive-behavioral therapies in the treatment of juvenile sexual offenders. *International Journal of Offender Therapy and Comparative Criminology, 34,* 234–248.

Jenkins-Hall, K. D., & Marlatt, G. A. (1989). Apparently irrelevant decisions in the relapse process. In D. R. Laws (Ed.), *Relapse prevention with sex offenders* (pp. 207–218). New York: Guilford Press.

Johnson, S. D., Gibson, L., & Linden, R. (1978). Alcohol and rape in Winnipeg, 1966–1975. *Journal of Studies on Alcohol, 39,* 1887–1894.

Kahn, T. J., & Lafond, M. A. (1988). Treatment of the adolescent sexual offender. *Child and Adolescent Social Work Journal, 5,* 135–148.

Kelly, J. R. (1982). Behavioral reorientation of pedophiliacs: Can it be done? *Clinical Psychology Review, 2,* 387–408.

Kelly, R. J. (1987). Limited confidentiality and the pedophile. *Hospital and Community Psychiatry, 38,* 1046–1048.

Knight, R. A., & Prentky, R. A. (1990). Classifying sexual offenders: The development and corroboration of taxonomic models. In W. L. Marshall, D. R. Laws, & H. E. Barbaree (Eds.), *Handbook of sexual assault: Issues, theories, and treatment of the offender* (pp. 23–52). New York: Plenum Press.

Knight, R. A., Rosenberg, R., & Schneider, B. A. (1985). Classification of sexual offenders: Perspectives, methods, and validation. In A. W. Burgess (Ed.), *Rape and sexual assault* (pp. 222–293). New York: Garland.

Knopp, F. H. (1984). *Retraining adult sex offenders: Methods and models.* Syracuse, NY: Safer Society Press.

Koss, M. P., & Dinero, T. E. (1988). Predictors of sexual aggression among a national sample of male college students. In R. A. Prentky & V. L. Quinsey (Eds.), *Human sexual aggression: Current perspectives* (pp. 133–147). New York: The New York Academy of Sciences.

Kraemer, H. C., Becker, H. B., Brodie, H. K. H., Doering, C. H., Moos, R. H., & Hamburg, R. A. (1976). Orgasmic frequency and plasma testosterone levels in normal males. *Archives of Sexual Behavior, 5,* 125–132.

Langeluddeke, A. (1963). *Castration of sexual criminals.* Berlin: De Gruyter.

Langevin, R. (1983). *Sexual strands: Understanding and treating sexual anomalies in men.* London: Erlbaum.

Langevin, R., & Lang, R. A. (1985). Psychological treatment of pedophiles. *Behavioral Sciences and the Law, 3,* 403–419.

Langevin, R., Paitich, D., Freeman, R., Mann, K., & Handy, L. (1978). Personality characteristics and sexual anomalies in males. *Canadian Journal of Behavioural Science, 10*, 222–238.

Langevin, R., Paitich, D., Hucker, S. J., Newman, S., Ramsay, G., Pope, S., Geller, G., & Anderson, C. (1979). The effect of assertiveness training, Provera, and sex of therapist in the treatment of genital exhibitionism. *Journal of Behavior Therapy and Experimental Psychiatry, 10*, 275–282.

Laschet, U. (1973). Anti-androgen in the treatment of sex offenders: Mode of action and therapeutic outcome. In J. Zubin & J. Money (Eds.), *Contemporary sexual behavior: Critical issues in the 1970's.* Baltimore: Johns Hopkins University Press.

Laschet, U., & Laschet, L. (1975). Antiandrogens in the treatment of sexual deviation of men. *Journal of Steroid Biochemistry, 6*, 821–826.

Laws, D. R. (Ed.). (1989). *Relapse prevention with sex offenders.* New York: Guilford Press.

Laws, D. R., Meyer, J., & Holmen, M. L. (1978). Reduction of sadistic sexual arousal by olfactory aversion: A case study. *Behaviour Research and Therapy, 16*, 281–285.

Lazarus, R. S. (1966). *Psychological stress and the coping process.* New York: McGraw-Hill.

Levin, S. M., Barry, S. M., Gambaro, S., Wolfinsohn, L., & Smith, A. (1977). Variations of covert sensitization in the treatment of pedophilic behavior: A case study. *Journal of Consulting and Clinical Psychology, 45*, 896–907.

Lipton, D. N., McDonel, E. C., & McFall, R. M. (1987). Heterosocial perception in rapists. *Journal of Consulting and Clinical Psychology, 55*, 17–21.

Lomis, M. J., & Baker, L. L. (1981). *Medroxyprogesterone acetate in the treatment of sex offenders: A literature review.* Unpublished manuscript.

MacDonald, R. K., & Pithers, W. D. (1989). Self-monitoring to identify high-risk situations. In D. R. Laws (Ed.), *Relapse prevention with sex offenders* (pp. 96–104). New York: Guilford Press.

Maletzky, B. (1987). [Data generated by an outpatient sexual abuse clinic]. Unpublished raw data.

Marlatt, G. A. (1989). Feeding the pig: The problem of immediate gratification. In D. R. Laws (Ed.), *Relapse prevention with sex offenders* (pp. 56–62). New York: Guilford Press.

Marlatt, G. A., & Gordon, J. R. (1980). Determinants of relapse: Implications for the maintenance of behavior change. In P. O. Davidson & S. M. Davidson (Eds.), *Behavioral medicine: Changing health lifestyles* (pp. 410–452). New York: Brunner/Mazel.

Marlatt, G. A. & Gordon, J. R. (Eds.). (1985). *Relapse prevention: Treatment strategies in the treatment of addictive behaviors.* New York: Guilford Press.

Marques, J. K. (1995, September). *Outcome data from California's Sex Offender Treatment and Evaluation Project.* Paper presented at a conference on North American and European Sex Offender Treatment and Research, Utrecht, The Netherlands.

Marques, J. K., Day, D. M., Nelson, C., & West, M. A. (1994). Effects of cognitive-behavioural treatment on sex offender recidivism: Preliminary results of a longitudinal study. *Criminal Justice and Behaviour, 21*, 28–54.

Marques, J. K., Day, D. M., Nelson, C., & West, M. A. (1994). Effects of cognitive-behavioral treatment on sex offender recidivism: Preliminary results of a longitudinal study. *Criminal Justice and Behavior, 21*, 28–54.

Marquis, J. N. (1970). Orgasmic reconditioning: Changing sexual choice through controlling masturbatory fantasies. *Journal of Behavior Therapy and Experimental Psychiatry, 1,* 263–271.

Marshall, W. L. (1973). The modification of sexual fantasies: A combined treatment approach to the reduction of deviant sexual behavior. *Behaviour Research and Therapy, 11,* 557–564.

Marshall, W. L. (1979). Satiation therapy: A procedure for reducing deviant sexual arousal. *Journal of Applied Behavior Analysis, 12,* 377–389.

Marshall, W. L. (1988). The use of sexually explicit stimuli by rapists, child molesters, and nonoffenders. *Journal of Sex Research, 25,* 267–288.

Marshall, W. L., & Anderson, D. (1996). An evaluation of the benefits of relapse prevention programs with sexual offenders. *Sexual Abuse: A Journal of Research and Treatment, 3,* 209–221.

Marshall, W. L., & Barbaree, H. E. (1984). A behavioral view of rape. Special Issue: Empirical approaches to law and psychiatry. *International Journal of Law and Psychiatry, 7,* 51–77.

Marshall, W. L., & Barbaree, H. E. (1987). [Tentative outcome data from a behavioral treatment program for child molesters]. Unpublished raw data.

Marshall, W. L., & Barbaree, H. E. (1988). The long-term evaluation of a behavioral treatment program for child molesters. *Behaviour Research and Therapy, 26,* 499–511.

Marshall, W. L., & Barbaree, H. E. (1990). Outcome of comprehensive cognitive-behavioral treatment programs. In W. L. Marshall, D. R. Laws, & H. E. Barbaree (Eds.), *Handbook of sexual assault: Issues, theories, and treatment of the offender* (pp. 363–385). New York: Plenum Press.

Marshall, W. L., Barbaree, H. E., & Butt, J. (1988). Sexual offenders against male children: Sexual preferences for gender, age of victim, and type of behavior. *Behaviour Research and Therapy, 26,* 383–391.

Marshall, W. L., Barbaree, H. E., & Christophe, D. (1986). Sexual offenders against female children: Sexual preferences for age of victims and type of behavior. *Canadian Journal of Behavioural Science, 18,* 424–439.

Marshall, W. L., & Christie, M. M. (1981). Pedophilia and aggression. *Criminal Justice and Behavior, 8,* 145–158.

Marshall, W. L., Earls, C. M., Segal, Z. V., & Darke, J. L. (1983). A behavioral program for the assessment and treatment of sexual aggressors. In K. Craig & R. McMahon (Eds.), *Advances in clinical behavior therapy* (pp. 148–174). New York: Brunner/Mazel.

Marshall, W. L., Jones, D. R., Ward, T., Johnston, P., & Barbaree, H. E. (1991). Treatcome outcome with sex offenders. *Clinical Psychology Review, 11,* 465–485.

Marshall, W. L., & Lippens, K. (1977). The clinical value of boredom: A procedure for reducing inappropriate sexual interests. *Journal of Nervous and Mental Disease, 165,* 283–287.

Marshall, W. L., & Williams, S. (1975). A behavioral approach to the modification of rape. *Quarterly Bulletin of the British Association for Behavioural Psychotherapy, 4,* 78–78.

McFall, R. M. (1990). The enhancement of social skills. In W. L. Marshall, D. R. Laws, & H. E. Barbaree (Eds.), *Handbook of sexual assault: Issues, theories, and treatment of the offender* (pp. 311–330). New York: Plenum Press.

Megargee, E. I. (1984). Aggression and violence. In H. E. Adams & P. B. Sutker (Eds.), *Comprehensive handbook of psychopathology* (pp. 523–545). New York: Plenum Press.

Meyer, L., & Romero, J. (1980). *A ten-year follow-up of sex offender recidivism.* Philadelphia: Joseph J. Peters Institute.

Miner, M. H. (1997). How can we conduct treatment outcome research? *Sexual Abuse: A Journal of Research and Treatment, 9,* 95–110.

Money, J. (1970). Use of androgen-depleting hormone in the treatment of male sexual offenders. *Journal of Sex Research, 6,* 165–172.

Money, J., Wiedeking, C., Walker, D., Migeon, C., Meyer, W., & Borgaonkar, D. (1975). 47 XYY and 46 XY males with antisocial and/or sex offending behaviours: Antiandrogen therapy plus counselling. *Psychoneuroendrocrinology, 1,* 165–178.

Morgan, C. T. (1965). *Physiological psychology.* New York: McGraw Hill.

Morgenthaler, F. (1974). Die stelung der perfersionen in metapsychologie und technik. *Psyche, 28,* 1077–1098.

Mothes, C., Lehnert, J., Samini, F., & Ufer, J. (1971). *Schering Symposium uber sexual deviationen und Ihre Medikamentose behandlung.* Oxford: Pergamon Press.

Murphy, W., & Barbaree, H. E. (1987). *Assessments of sexual offenders by measures of erectile response: Psychometric properties and decision making.* Rockville, MD: National Institute of Mental Health.

Murphy, W. D., Haynes, M. R., Stalgaitis, S. J., & Flanagan, B. (1986). Differential sexual responding among four groups of sexual offenders against children. *Journal of Psychopathology and Behavioral Assessment, 8,* 339–353.

Nathan, P. E., & Lansky, D. (1978). Common methodological problems in research on the addictions. *Journal of Consulting and Clinical Psychology, 46,* 713–726.

Nelson, C., & Jackson, P. (1989). High-risk recognition: The cognitive-behavioral chain. In D. R. Laws (Ed.), *Relapse prevention with sex offenders* (pp. 167–177). New York: Guilford Press.

O'Donohue, W. & Letourneau, E. (1992). The psychometric properties of the penile tumescence assessment of child molesters. *Journal of Psychopathology and Behavioral Assessment, 14,* 123–174.

Ortmann, J. (1980). The treatment of sexual offenders: Castration and antihormone therapy. *International Journal of Law and Psychiatry, 3,* 443–451.

Overholser, J. C., & Beck, S. (1986). Multimethod assessment of rapists, child molesters, and three control groups on behavioral and psychological measures. *Journal of Consulting and Clinical Psychology, 54,* 682–687.

Pacht, A. R., Halleck, S. L., & Ehrmann, J. C. (1962). Diagnosis and treatment of the sexual offender: A nine year study. *American Journal of Psychiatry, 118,* 802–808.

Pacht, A. R., & Roberts, L. M. (1968). Factors related to parole experiences of sexual offenders: A nine year study. *Journal of Correctional Psychology, 3,*

Panton, J. H. (1979). MMPI profile configurations associated with incestuous and non-incestuous child molesting. *Psychological Reports, 45,* 335–338.

Pearson, H. J., Marshall, W. L., Barbaree, H. E., & Southmayd, S. (1992). Treatment of a compulsive paraphiliac with buspirone. *Annals of Sex Research, 5,* 239–246.

Peters, J. J. (1980). *A ten-year follow-up of sex offender recidivism.* Unpublished manuscript.

Peters, J. J., Pedigo, J. M., Steg, V., & McKenna, J. J. (1968). Group psychotherapy of the sex offender. *Federal Probation, 32,* 41–46.

Peters, J. J., & Roether, H. A. (1972). Psychotherapy for probationed sex offenders. In H. L. P. Resnick, & M. F. Wolfgang (Eds.), *Sexual behaviors: Social, clinical, and legal aspects* (pp.255–256). Boston: Little, Brown.

Pinta, E. R. (1978). Treatment of obsessive homosexual pedophile fantasies with medroxyprogesterone acetate. *Biological Psychiatry, 13,* 369–373.

Pithers, W. D. (1990). Relapse prevention with sexual aggressors: A method for maintaining therapeutic gain and enhancing external supervision. In W. L. Marshall, D. R. Laws, & H. E. Barbaree (Eds.), *Handbook of sexual assault: Issues, theories, and treatment of the offender* (pp. 343–361). New York: Plenum Press.

Pithers, W. D., Beal, L. S., Armstrong, J., & Petty, J. (1989). Identification of risk factors through clinical interviews and analysis of records. In D. R. Laws (Ed.), *Relapse prevention with sex offenders* (pp. 77–87). New York: Guilford Press.

Pithers, W. D., Kashima, K. M., Cumming, G. F., Beal, L. S., & Buell, M. M. (1988). Relapse prevention of sexual aggression. In R. A. Prentky & V. L. Quinsey (Eds.), *Human sexual aggression: Current perspectives* (pp. 244–260). New York: New York Academy of Sciences.

Pithers, W. D., Marques, J. K., Gibat, C. C., & Marlatt, G. A. (1983). Relapse prevention with sexual aggressives: A self-control model of treatment and maintenance of change. In J. G. Greer & I. R. Stuart (Eds.), *The sexual aggressor: Current perspectives on treatment* (pp. 214–239). New York: Von Nostrand Reinhold.

Prendergast, W. E. (1978). *ROARE: Re-education of attitudes (and) repressed emotions*. Avenel, NJ: Adult Diagnostic and Treatment Center Intensive Group Therapy Program.

Prentky, R. A. (1997). Arousal reduction in sexual offenders: A review of antiandrogen interventions. *Sexual Abuse: A Journal of Research and Treatment, 9,* 335–348.

Prentky, R. A., Knight, R. A., & Lee, A. F. S. (1997) Risk factors associated with recidivism among extrafamilial child molesters. *Journal of Consulting and Clinical Psychology, 65,* 141–149.

Quinsey, V. L. (1983). Prediction of recidivism and the evaluation of treatment programs for sex offenders. In S. Simon-James & A. A. Keltner (Eds.), *Sexual aggression and the law*. Burnaby, British Columbia: Criminology Research Center (SFU).

Quinsey, V. L. (1984). Sexual aggression: Studies of offenders against women. In D. Weisstub (Ed.), *Law and mental health: International perspectives* (Vol. 1, pp. 84–121). New York: Pergamon Press.

Quinsey, V. L. (1986). Men who have sex with children. In D. N. Weisstub (Ed.), *Law and mental health: International perspectives* (Vol. 2, pp. 140–172). New York: Pergamon Press.

Quinsey, V. L., Bergersen, S. G., & Steinman, C. M. (1976). Changes in physiological and verbal responses of child molesters during aversion therapy. *Canadian Journal of Behavioural Science, 8,* 202–212.

Quinsey, V. L., & Chaplin, T. C. (1984). Stimulus control of rapists' and non-sex offenders' sexual arousal. *Behavioral Assessment, 6,* 169–176.

Quinsey, V. L., Chaplin, T. C., & Carrigan, W. F. (1979). Sexual preferences among incestuous and nonincestuous child molesters. *Behavior Therapy, 10,* 562–565.

Quinsey, V. L., Chaplin, T. C., & Carrigan, W. F. (1980). Biofeedback and signalled punishment in the modification of inappropriate sexual age preferences. *Behavior Therapy, 11,* 567–576.

Quinsey, V. L., Chaplin, T. C., Maguire, A. M., & Upfold, D. (1987). The behavioral treatment of rapists and child molesters. In E. K. Morris & C. J. Braukmann (Eds.), *Behavioral approaches to crime and delinquency: Application, research, and theory*. New York: Plenum Press.

Quinsey, V. L., & Marshall, W. L. (1983). Procedures for reducing inappropriate sexual arousal: An evaluative review. In J. G. Greer & I. R. Stuart (Eds.), *The sexual aggressor: Current perspectives on treatment* (pp. 267–289). New York: Von Nostrand Reinhold.

Quinsey, V. L., Steinman, C. M., Bergersen, S. G., & Holmes, T. F. (1975). Penile circumference, skin conductance, and ranking responses of child molesters and "normals" to sexual and nonsexual visual stimuli. *Behavior Therapy, 6*, 213–219.

Raboch, J., Mellan, I., & Starka, L. (1979). Klinefelter's syndrome: Sexual development and activity. *Archives of Sexual Behavior, 8*, 333–339.

Rada, R. T., Laws, D. R., & Kellner, R. (1976). Plasma testosterone levels in the rapist. *Psychosomatic Medicine, 38*, 257–268.

Record, S. A. (1977). *Personality, sexual attitudes and behavior of sex offenders.* Unpublished manuscript.

Revitch, E. (1965). Sex murder and the potential sex murderer. *Diseases of the Nervous System, 26*, 626–640.

Rice, M. E., Harris, G. T., & Quinsey, V. L. (1990). A follow-up of rapists assessed at a maximum security psychiatric facility. *Journal of Interpersonal Violence, 4*, 435–448.

Rice, M. E., Harris, G. T., & Quinsey, V. L. (1991). Evaluation of an institution-based treatment program for child molesters. *Canadian Journal of Program Evaluation, 6*, 111–129.

Rice, M. E., Quinsey, V. L., & Harris, G. T. (1991). Sexual recidivism among child molesters released from a maximum security psychiatric institution. *Journal of Consulting and Clinical Psychology, 59*, 381–386.

Roether, H. A., & Peters, J. J. (1972). Cohesiveness and hostility in group psychotherapy. *American Journal of Psychiatry, 128*, 1014–1017.

Rosenblatt, J. S., & Aronson, L. R. (1958). The decline of sexual behavior in male cats after castration with special reference to the role of prior sexual experience. *Behavior, 12*, 258–338.

Rubin, H. B., Henson, D. E., Falvo, R. F., & High, R. W. (1979). The relationship between men's endogenous levels of testosterone and their penile response to erotic stimuli. *Behaviour Research and Therapy, 17*, 305–317.

Russell, D. E. H. (1975). *The politics of rape: The victim's perspective.* New York: Stein & Day.

Ryan, G., Lane, S., Davis, J., & Isaac, C. (1987). Juvenile sex offenders: Development and correction. *Child Abuse and Neglect, 11*, 385–395.

Saunders, E. B., & Awad, G. A. (1988). Assessment, management, and treatment planning for male adolescent sexual offenders. *American Journal of Orthopsychiatry, 58*, 571–579.

Saylor, M. (1979). *A guided self-help approach to treatment of the habitual sexual offender.* Unpublished manuscript.

Schiavi, R. C., & White, D. (1976). Androgens and male sexual function: A review of human studies. *Journal of Sex and Marital Therapy, 2*, 214–226.

Schmidt, G., & Schorsch, E. (1981). Psychosurgery of sexually deviant patients: Review and analysis of new empirical findings. *Archives of Sexual Behavior, 10*, 301–323.

Scully, D., & Marolla, J. (1984). Convicted rapists' vocabulary of motive: Excuses and justifications. *Social Problems, 31*, 530–544.

Segal, Z. V., & Marshall, W. L. (1985). Heterosexual social skills in a population of rapists and child molesters. *Journal of Consulting and Clinical Psychology, 53*, 55–63.

Smith, R. (1984). The Oregon State Hospital Sex Offender Unit: Program description. In F. H. Knopp (Ed.), *Retraining adult sex offenders: Methods and models.* Syracuse, NY: Safer Society Press.

Steenman, H., Nelson, C., & Viesti, C. Jr. (1989). Developing coping strategies for high-risk situations. In D. R. Laws (Ed.), *Relapse prevention with sex offenders* (pp. 178–187). New York: Guilford Press.

Stermac, L. E. & Quinsey, V. L. (1986). Social competence among rapists. *Behavioral Assessment, 8,* 171–185.

Stermac, L. E., & Segal, Z. V. (1987). *Condoning or condemning adult sexual contact with children: A criterion group-based analysis.* Unpublished manuscript.

Stermac, L. E., Segal, Z. V., & Gillis, R. (1990). Social and cultural factors in sexual assault. In W. L. Marshall, D. R. Laws, & H. E. Barbaree (Eds.), *Handbook of sexual assault: Issues, theories, and treatment of the offender* (pp. 143–159). New York: Plenum Press.

Stoller, R. J. (1975). *Perversion: The erotic form of hatred.* New York: Pantheon.

Stone, C. P. (1927). Retention of copulatory ability in male rats after castration. *Journal of Comparative and Physiological Psychology, 7,* 369–387.

Sturup, G. K. (1972). Castration: The total treatment. In H. L. P. Resnick & M. F. Wolfgang (Eds.), *Sexual behaviours: Social, clinical and legal aspects* (pp. 361–382). Boston: Little, Brown.

Sundberg, S. L., Barbaree, H. E., & Marshall, W. L. (1991). Victim blame and the disinhibition of sexual arousal to rape. *Violence and Victims, 6,* 103–120.

Swigert, V. L., Farrell, R. A., & Yoels, W. C. (1976). Sexual homicide: Social, psychological and legal aspects. *Archives of Sexual Behavior, 5,* 391–401.

Thornton, W. E., & Pray, B. J. (1975). The portrait of a murderer. *Diseases of the Nervous System, 36,* 176–178.

Ward, T., Louden, K., Hudson, S. M., & Marshall, W. L. (1995). A descriptive model of the offense chain for child molesters. *Journal of Interpersonal Violence, 10,* 452–472.

Walker, P. A., & Meyer, W. J. (1980). Medroxyprogesterone acetate treatment for pedophilic sex offenders. In T. K. Hayes, T. K. Roberts, & K. S. Solway (Eds.), *Violence and the violent individual* (pp. 353–373). Jamaica, NY: Spectrum Publications.

Weiner, B. A. (1985). Legal issues raised in treating sex offenders. *Behavioral Sciences and the Law, 3,* 325–340.

Whalen, R. (1966). Sexual motivation. *Psychological Review, 73,* 151–163.

Whitman, W. P., & Quinsey, V. L. (1981). Heterosocial skill training for institutionalized rapists and child molesters. *Canadian Journal of Behavioural Science, 13,* 105–114.

Williams, A. H. (1964). The psychopathology and treatment of sexual murderers. In I. Rosen (Ed.), *The pathology and treatment of sexual deviation: A methodological approach.* London: Oxford University Press.

Witt, P. (1981). Treating the repetitive offender. *Treatment of Sexual Aggressives, 4,* 1–3.

Wolfe, R. (1984). Northwest Treatment Associates: A comprehensive, community-based evaluation and treatment program for adult sex offenders. In F. H. Knopp (Ed.), *Retraining adult sex offenders: Methods and models* (pp. 85–101). Syracuse, NY: Safer Society Press.

Wormith, J. (1983). A survey of incarcerated sexual offenders. *Canadian Journal of Criminology, 25,* 379–390.

Yates, E., Barbaree, H. E., & Marshall, W. L. (1984). Anger and deviant sexual arousal. *Behavior Therapy, 15,* 287–294.

7

TREATMENT OF OFFENDERS WITH MENTAL RETARDATION

William I. Gardner
Janice L. Graeber
Susan J. Machkovitz

INTRODUCTION

Over the last two decades there has been increased interest among professionals in the fields of juvenile and criminal justice, mental retardation, and mental health in issues relating to the definition, identification, and treatment of those persons with mental retardation who currently or previously have been involved with the judicial, probation/parole, or correctional systems. In the absence of special consideration in the identification, trial, sentencing, and placement processes as well in the specific settings and types of services provided, the offender with mental retardation most typically is a misfit in the correctional system and seldom is provided an effective therapeutic experience (Conley, Luckasson, & Bouthilet, 1992; McGee & Menolascino, 1992). In fact, it is generally recognized that mere incarceration following a crime is ineffective in reducing the likelihood of future criminal acts. This conclusion is supported by an estimated national recidivism rate of 60% (Santamour, 1986, 1988). During parole, offenders with mental retardation are reported to recidivate more quickly and frequently than do nonretarded parolees (Santamour & West, 1977). In spite of these observations, it is estimated that fewer than 10% of inmates with mental retardation in correctional facilities receive any specialized services (Wolford, 1987).

Historically, the courts only identified the defendant with mental retardation whose cognitive impairment was most obvious. Typically such an offender was committed to a state mental retardation facility. This option in the absence of specialized program for the offender was, and continues to be, unsatisfactory for a number of reasons. In these placements, the offender often victimized less able residents, disrupted the program routine of the facility, presented security risks, and presented training needs that most facilities were unable to meet. Staffing patterns and physical facilities of the public institutions were unsuitable for the offender, as these were designed to provide training and care for more easily managed persons with severe handicaps (Brown & Courtless, 1967, 1971).

Recognition of this misfit by professionals in mental retardation has been articulated for decades as reflected in an early description by Fernald (1922) of offenders placed in mental retardation institutions:

> Many of this class are defiant, abusive, profane, disobedient, destructive, and generally incorrigible. They honestly feel that they are unjustly confined and frequently attack those who are responsible for their custody. They resent any effort to amuse or entertain them. They cannot be discharged because they are not safe persons for community life. It is most unfortunate that this criminal type of defective should complicate the care and training of the ordinary defective—who constitutes the legitimate problem of a school for the feeble-minded! (p. 19)

In fact, Brown and Courtless (1968) described the general misfit of the offender with mental retardation in any traditional system, a depiction that generally remains valid three decades later:

> Mental hospitals claim such an offender is not mentally ill; the traditional institution for the retarded complain that they do not have appropriate facilities for the offender. . . . Correctional institutions would like to remove such persons from their populations on the grounds that programs available in the correctional setting are totally inadequate and in many cases inappropriate for application to retarded persons. (p. 366)

Scope of the Problem

Currently, defendants with mental retardation who go unrecognized in the criminal and juvenile justice systems are routinely incarcerated with no attempt made to address their special needs. Although varying considerably from state to state, it is estimated that inmates who do meet the diagnostic criteria for mental retardation are overrepresented (assuming a 2–3%

prevalence rate in the general population) and comprise from 2% to 10% or more of the general prison population (Baroff, 1996; Denkowski & Denkowski, 1985b; Smith, Algozzine, Schmid, & Hennly, 1990). Of those offenders who do have a mental retardation diagnosis, it is estimated that 88% of the total group is mildly impaired, with most of the remaining 12% demonstrating moderate retardation (Kugel, 1986).

The validity of these prevalence rates has been questioned by a number of writers. Critics have highlighted the wide range of practices across states in the process and procedures used in the diagnosis of mental retardation. Both the clinical skills of persons conducting the diagnostic evaluations as well as the types of assessment instruments used have been subject to question. An unknown percentage of offenders provided the label of mental retardation thus appear to have been inappropriately diagnosed. Spruill and May (1988), in illustration, reported that 4% of the inmates in a state's correctional facilities were classified as demonstrating mental retardation based on an IQ score obtained on admission from a group-administered test (Revised Beta). Later examination of a random sample of these inmates with an individually administered Wechsler Adult Intelligence Scale (WAIS-R) revealed a significantly smaller prevalence rate of 1%.

Most studies have indicated that a disproportionate percentage of incarcerated offenders with a diagnosis of mental retardation are blacks or Hispanics who come from poor and unemployed families. In these instances, the sociocultural factors, including lack of appropriate education, need to be considered in the evaluation process (McGee & Menolascino, 1992).

These apparent misdiagnoses, however, may be offset by an unknown percentage of offenders who do meet the diagnostic criteria of mental retardation but who go unidentified during the arrest, trial, and incarceration process. As noted by a number of writers, potential underidentification may reflect such factors as (1) inadequate testing, (2) inadequate experiences of psychologists and psychiatrists in recognizing mental retardation, (3) defendants' successful attempts to conceal signs of mental retardation due to stigma and possible loss of respect, and (4) inadequate training of criminal justice personnel in recognizing mental retardation (Bonnie, 1992; McAfee & Gural, 1988; Smith & Broughton, 1994). In any event, a consensus of opinion among critics of both practices is that offenders with mental retardation appear to be overrepresented in the prison population. As suggested in the 1991 Report of the President's Committee on Mental Retardation, "the number is not insignificant and presents a challenge to the criminal justice system to assure that these individuals are accorded the same measure of justice as other Americans who commit crimes" (1991, p. 4).

Type of Offense

A number of reports indicate that the majority of offenses by persons with mental retardation involving criminal justice contact are crimes against persons, including those of a sexual nature. This is followed by crimes against property, including arson (Baroff, 1996; Noble & Conley, 1992). The percentage of severe crimes relative both to the total number of crimes committed by this group and to those committed by the nonretarded appears to be low. This observation is reflected in the conclusion of the Illinois Mentally Retarded and Mentally Ill Offender Task Force (1988) that "despite common misconceptions that this population commits the majority of violent felony crimes, in reality the overwhelming majority of offenses committed by persons who are mentally retarded and/or mentally ill are misdemeanors, less serious felonies, and public disturbances" (p. 40).

A Look Ahead

This chapter initially identifies a range of vulnerability factors that place some persons with mental retardation at risk for initial and repeated illegal behaviors. Following this description we discuss the status and limitations of traditional roles assumed by the correctional, mental health, and mental retardation agency programs in addressing this group of individuals. Although deficiencies in components of the criminal justice (law enforcement, judiciary/forensic, corrections, parole, and probation) system are numerous and widespread, we discuss these only as they relate to issues of treatment of the offender with mental retardation (Exum, Turnbull, Martin, & Finn, 1992). This is followed by description of agency treatment programs designed to meet some of the specialized treatment needs of the offender with mental retardation. The chapter closes with suggestions of program components viewed as critical in meeting the specialized treatment needs of the offender with mental retardation.

RISK FACTORS FOR CRIMINAL BEHAVIOR

Three major schools of thought have been offered to explain the disproportionately high percentage of offenders with mental retardation in the criminal and juvenile justice systems. The first and earliest of these suggested an intimate relationship between mental retardation and a proclivity for criminality (Fernald, 1909). The most current version of this position, while rejecting a direct cause and effect relationship, suggests that critical cognitive and related personal characteristics of those with mental retardation may contribute under certain circumstances to an unwitting participation in activities that are illegal (Santamour & West, 1977).

The second view posits a relationship between the social environments in which the majority of offenders with mental retardation reside and an increased likelihood for criminal activities. The social influences, and not mental retardation per se, are viewed as the major contributors to the person's criminal activities (Beier, 1964).

The third and final explanation for the disproportionate presence of offenders with mental retardation in the juvenile and criminal justice systems suggests a correlation between features of the judicial system as they interact with various personal characteristics of those with mental retardation (Brown & Courtless, 1971, 1982). We examine each perspective in this section.

Mental Retardation and Criminality

Nearly a century ago, professionals in the field of mental retardation posited a direct association between limited intelligence and criminal acts. This position was reflected by Clark (1894) in his comments that "crime, imbecility, and insanity are hereditary diseases of the mind. . . . All non organic cases of imbecility show somewhere in the family annals where there has been opium eating, immoral living, drunkenness, insanity, imbecility, or actual crime" (p. 25).

This attitude continued into the early decades of the current century, as it was widely assumed that "feeblemindedness" was a major contributor to delinquency, crime, and a variety of other social ills. In interpreting this early prevalent attitude, we should keep in mind that the concept of "feeblemindedness" and the procedures for identifying persons so labeled were different from definitions and multidimensional assessment procedures currently used in the diagnostic process.

Within this historical context, before the availability of standardized intelligence testing, Fernald (1909) suggested that every "imbecile" was a potential criminal needing only the proper environment and opportunity for developing and manifesting his/her criminal tendencies. Further, in commenting on "defective delinquents," he noted the psychopathic nature of their personality:

> They are morally insensible. As a rule, they are able to carefully differentiate in the abstract between what is right and what is wrong as applied to their personal environment, but in practice their ability to make these distinctions bears no relations to their actions and conduct. They seldom show embarrassment or shame when detected in wrong doing. I have never known an imbecile to exhibit remorse. Correction or punishment is of little effect. They revel in mawkish sentiment. They are susceptible to the emotional phase of religious expression. They are apt to choose intimate companions very much younger than themselves, or persons very much beneath them socially or below them in

the scale of intelligence. They are generally cowardly in the presence of actual physical danger. They are very susceptible to suggestion and are easily led. (p. 733)

Christian (1913) and Lurie, Levy, and Rosenthal (1944) in a similar vein emphasized the lack of internalized standards of social conduct and controls and the impulsive and immediate self-gratification nature of the personality structure. More specifically, "defective delinquents" were described as suspicious, depressed, egocentric, selfish, displaying violent tempers, and being obstinate. Christian (1913) commented:

> Their immediate desires must always be satisfied, and they will go to extremes, regardless of known consequences, in order to obtain the moments desire. . . . They are selfish, vain, cruel, and act upon neither reason or judgment, but principally upon impulses. . . . They are vindictive and revengeful, and are always eager to make a personal attack to right any imagined wrong. . . . They have little or no conception of morals, and will indulge in falsehoods and deceit when the truth would have served better. . . . While they are frequently able to differentiate between right and wrong as an abstract proposition, they seem utterly unable to follow the principles in their conduct when at large. . . . The future holds no great concern for these defectives; each day is a day unto itself. They are self-centered and some of them are immeasurably egotistical. (pp. 280–281)

Even though the thesis that there is a direct relationship between mental retardation and delinquent and criminal actions is no longer viewed as tenable, these early descriptions of the social, emotional, motivational, behavioral, and personality characteristics of the adolescent and adult offender nonetheless do bear high similarity to those offered by current writers (Denkowski & Denkowski, 1984, 1986a). As only a *small minority* of those with mental retardation do actually engage in criminal behavior, contemporary writers implicate factors other than general intellectual impairment as assuming a more influential role in the etiology of criminal behavior in this group (Crocker & Hodgins, 1997). These are in fact those commonly viewed as influential in the development of delinquent and criminal behavior in the general population (Beier, 1964; Brown & Courtless, 1971; Owens, 1982). Crime, as noted by Owens (1982), is committed by those with mental retardation for the same complex reasons present in those with higher cognitive skills, that is, because "they need money, they follow others, they seek peer approval, they are impulsive and use poor judgment, they are unemployed, they have emotional problems, crime is a lifestyle, and in some cases, crime is enjoyable" (p. 28).

A number of cognitive and other personal–social characteristics of some persons with mental retardation do overlap those suggested by Owens (1982) and by Denkowski and Denkowski (1986a). These may be viewed as risk or vulnerability factors for delinquent and criminal actions. Due to cognitive limitations, including reduced vocabularies, related verbal skills, and impaired ability to analyze, some persons with mental retardation may not fully understand or appreciate the consequences of certain of their behaviors. As a result, some may display poor judgment and engage in criminal activities when confronted with various activating conditions (Santamour & West, 1977). Additionally, these persons may not have the social and cognitive skills to attain desired goals, and not knowing how or having the skills to use institutions in society to assist them, may resort to illegal acts in an effort to get their needs met (Brown & Courtless, 1971).

Other writers have described the skill and psychosocial limitations of those with mental retardation and the resulting feelings of loneliness and rejection in those lacking adequate social supports. In these persons, criminal activity may represent acts of frustration against society (Santamour, 1989). Additional vulnerability factors include a heightened suggestibility and susceptibility to persons perceived as having high status, acquiescence in the face of perceived authority, and attempts to avoid stigma. The person with these features may more easily be led into criminal activity by other, more influential persons (Luckasson, 1988; Santamour, 1989).

The increased vulnerability of those with mental retardation to expressing symptoms of the entire range of psychiatric disorders represents another significant personal risk feature that may contribute to both initial delinquent and criminal behaviors (Reiss, 1994; Stark, Menolascino, Albarelli, & Gray, 1988) and the high recidivism rate (Klimecki, Jenkinson, & Wilson, 1994). The dual factors of mental retardation, substance abuse, mental illness, and related neuropsychiatric conditions involving organic brain dysfunction magnify the effects of reduced cognitive skills on impulse control, moral judgment, reality testing, and social reasoning (McGee & Menolascino, 1992), all critical ingredients underlying socially appropriate conduct. In brief illustration, criminal violence may be associated with paranoid delusional thinking, hallucinations, the psychotic disorganization or general excitability in schizophrenia, disinhibitions of acute mania states, emotional lability, impaired judgment associated with substance abuse, and the general dyscontrol produced by various organic impairments of the brain (Martell, 1992; Tardiff, 1992).

In summary, although not providing a complete explanation for the apparent overrepresentation of persons with mental retardation in the offender population, these multiple cognitive and personal–social characteristics represent obvious vulnerability features that combine with a variety of other social influences to comprise an increased proclivity for illegal activities among some persons with mental retardation. These personal vulnerability features all represent potential focus points for treatment programs.

Social Environmental Influences

The effects of these psychological and psychiatric vulnerabilities are magnified in a major way as these interact with the deleterious effects of the social environments in which a significant majority of offenders with mental retardation currently reside or were exposed to during critical developmental years. A number of writers describe the sociopsychological features as including broken homes, improper physical conditions, low moral and ethical standards, unwholesome personal and interpersonal family relationships, and a high percentage of parents and siblings presenting mental retardation and psychiatric difficulties (Day, 1988; Denkowski & Denkowski, 1986a; Kugel, Tembath, & Sagars, 1968; Lurie et al., 1944).

Denkowski and Denkowski (1986a) implicated these social influences in describing the family characteristics of a group of adolescent offenders with mental retardation who, over a 34-month period, had been judicially committed to a community residential program. The majority had either one-parent families or families that contained neither natural mother nor father. An enduring father figure resided with the family in only a small percentage of cases. The majority of households were receiving welfare subsistence. In approximately half of the families, one or more adult members abused alcohol and in nearly one-fifth of the families an adult suffered serious mental health problems. Nearly one-third of the youth were either physically abused or neglected to an extent that child welfare intervention was necessary. In sum, most of these adjudicated youth with mental retardation had come from poor, urban backgrounds and approximately two-thirds "were either victims of abuse/severe neglect and/or were exposed to significant familial violence, mental illness, and alcoholism " (p. 76). As noted in the previous section, these family and broader physical and social environmental influences assume a significant role in the development and perpetuation of the personal incompetencies described. These same environmental and family conditions also characterize a significant percentage of adolescent offenders who do not have a diagnosis of mental retardation.

Effects of the Criminal Justice System

Other writers, in rejecting the thesis of mental retardation as a primary cause of criminal acts, have suggested that the excessive numbers of persons with mental retardation in state correctional facilities represent an artifact of the administration of criminal justice (Brown & Courtless, 1971; Conley et al., 1992; Ellis & Luckasson, 1985; MacEachron, 1979; Marsh, Friel, & Eissler, 1975; Perske, 1991; Santamour & Watson, 1982). These and other writers (Clare & Gudjonsoon, 1995; Everington & Dunn, 1995;

Fulero & Everington, 1995; Smith & Hudson, 1995) emphasize that the majority of persons with mental retardation experience considerable injustice in various stages of the criminal justice process beyond that of any other group of offenders. As a group, offenders with mental retardation relative to nonretarded counterparts:

1. Are more likely to be arrested following illegal acts.
2. May be at a disadvantage in police interrogations due to impaired understanding of caution and legal rights and resulting susceptibility to acquiescence, suggestibility, compliance, and confabulation. As a result they
   a. Are less likely to understand the implications of the Miranda Rights being read to them.
   b. Will often confess quickly and be unduly influenced by friendly suggestions and intimidations.
   c. Often plead guilty more readily.
3. Request pretrial psychological examinations and presentencing testing less frequently.
4. Are more often convicted of the arresting offense than a reduced charge.
5. Use plea bargaining less frequently.
6. Seek appeals of conviction less frequently and make fewer requests for postconviction relief.
7. Are more likely to be sentenced to prison, with probation or other noninstitutional programs used less frequently.
8. Have more difficulty in prison adjusting to the routine, which limits parole opportunities and lengthens period of actual prison stay.
9. Are less likely in prison to participate in rehabilitation programs, as these are not designed to accommodate the learning, motivational, and experiential features of those with mental retardation.
10. Make parole less frequently and thus serves longer prison terms for the same offense.

Summary

Whereas no single position in isolation offers a suitable explanation for the apparent disproportionally high percentage of offenders with mental retardation in the juvenile and criminal justice systems, it is evident that each identifies potentially viable risk factors whose influences are compounded through interaction effects. As an illustration, a young person with minimal social assertion skills and limited cognitive and moral judgment skills who comes from a dysfunctional, poverty-burdened family with no dominant adult model for socially responsible behavior may be guided into criminal activities by more cognitively aware, socially assertive, and goal-directed, delinquent peers. Not being cognitively cognizant of the seriousness of his/her actions, needy of peer group acceptance, and without strong internalized standards of conduct, this young man/woman upon being apprehended after an unsuccessful robbery attempt may readily confess his/her involvement. Not being identified as a person with mental retardation by the law enforcement officials or by the court, he/she may become a victim of the criminal justice system.

STATUS AND LIMITATIONS OF TRADITIONAL AGENCY PROGRAMS

The Correctional System

In the prison setting, in comparison with nonretarded counterparts, inmates with a mental retardation diagnosis are slower to adjust to the prison routine, experience difficulty in understanding what is expected, and, as a result, are guilty of a larger number of rule infractions (Santamour & West, 1977). Results of a study of offenders with mental retardation in a 17- to 19-year age group among the prison population of a large southeastern state provided more details on the relative magnitude and specificity of these rule infractions (Smith et al., 1990). In comparison with a nonretarded group matched on age and sex, and a randomly selected group from the general prison population, it was found that

> the number of disciplinary reports received by the retarded group for hygiene violations, noncompliance with authority, assault of other inmates, and assault of correctional officers [was] significantly higher than for either nonretarded group. Inmates with mental retardation received approximately three times as many disciplinary reports for offenses related to personal hygiene and noncompliant behavior; they were reported for assaulting inmates or correctional personnel more than twice as often as nonretarded inmates. (p. 179)

These increased rule infractions and the resulting loss of good time contribute to longer sentences being served in prison. Studies report that the offender with mental retardation may serve on the average of 2 to 3 years longer than other inmates for the same offense (e.g., Kentucky Legislative Research Commission, 1975). Those with mental retardation also are less likely to receive probation, as this option is more frequently granted to persons with supportive community ties and some history of employment. As offenders with mental retardation typically are undereducated, come from disorganized, low income, and urban families, and have few vocational skills and minimal if any successful work history, they are most often assumed to be poor risks for probation (Denkowski & Denkowski, 1986a). Santamour and Watson (1982), providing additional support for the longer sentence conclusion, reported that 43% of offenders with mental retardation served more than 3 years of their present sentence, whereas only 23.5% of the nonretarded offenders served more than 3 years of their present sentence.

It also is reported that the incarcerated offender with mental retardation frequently is the target of practical jokes and is victimized as a scapegoat or sexual object by more sophisticated inmates (Reichard, Spencer, & Spooner, 1982). As a result of these factors, the offender with mental retardation within the correctional setting requires a disproportionate amount of supervision and staff time. Finally, inmates with mental retardation in the prison setting are reported to be highly impressionable and may acquire criminal behaviors not previously shown. Apparently because of their need to be accepted by the more sophisticated inmates, their maladaptive behaviors are intensified as they assume the values of the prison culture (MacEachron, 1979).

It is evident from these descriptions that the criminal justice system, the central mission of which is to provide secure containment of prisoners and to maintain order, does not address the unique habilitation needs of the offender with mental retardation. The major assumption of this incarceration is that prisoners can learn enough from being locked up and the attendant circumstances to inhibit postrelease criminal behavior. Specifically, the inhibiting effect of the punishment experience is assumed to be sufficiently strong to override other factors that may result in future recurrence of criminal acts. A critical consequence of this assumption is that the prison program seldom assesses or treats the specific and individually unique factors that have and continue to contribute to the criminal behaviors of the significant percentage of offenders with mental retardation. This is supported by the previously mentioned observation that during parole the offender with mental retardation recidivates more quickly and frequently than do nonretarded parolees.

A related assumption of the punishment approach to modifying criminal behavior is that the person does have alternative prosocial behaviors that, after release from incarceration, can be self-selected to serve the same functions as served by the criminal acts, for example, to be accepted by peers, to feel important, to obtain money. This assumption is quite faulty when applied to most offenders with mental retardation, as broad skill deficits represent significant contributions to the person's initial criminal acts, that is, alternative prosocial behaviors cannot be self-chosen, as these are not present in the individual's repertoire. A comprehensive skill development approach to habilitation appears to be necessary for effective behavior change.

The Mental Health Service System

In those instances of offenders with mental retardation who present significant mental health difficulties, adequate mental health services are seldom available. Even when provided community and institutional outpatient and inpatient mental health services, the success rate has been discouraging. Although the mental health treatment programs may address the presumed mental illness contributors to the person's criminal acts, other critical problems influencing the offender's behavior typically go untreated. As a result, the person remains vulnerable to engage in repeated criminal activities due to such factors as deficits in those vocational, educational, social, interpersonal, and personal skills needed for successful independent community functioning (McGee & Menolascino, 1992).

The Mental Retardation Service System

Although the habilitation model of the mental retardation service delivery system holds more promise of success than either the punishment or illness models of the criminal justice and mental health systems, the typical habilitation programs are not sufficiently specialized and diverse to address the specific needs of the offender with mental retardation (Laski, 1992). Further, there is no systematic effort to address those psychosocial vulnerability factors that render many with mental retardation both at risk for criminal activities and relatively helpless when they enter the criminal justice system. More specifically, educational and adult service programs insufficiently address those skills needed to be law-abiding citizens (Exum et al., 1992).

In summary, the usual programs offered by the criminal justice, mental health, and mental retardation systems seldom are satisfactory in meeting the special habilitation needs of the offender with mental retardation.

PROGRAMS DESIGNED FOR THE OFFENDER WITH MENTAL RETARDATION

In considering program alternatives to the traditional ones offered by the mental retardation, mental health, and criminal justice systems, it is obvious that no single program option will meet the needs of all offenders with mental retardation. Although the current mental retardation habilitation model has a central philosophical commitment to community-based rather than institutional-based services, such variables as the chronic nature of the offending behavior as well as the severity and potential dangerousness of the criminal behavior require a continuum of treatment options. These range from specialized diversion programs such as a community first-offender probation program, through specialized programs provided in forensic units of mental health facilities, to those involving maximum-security prison units for a small number of persons who engage in serious crimes representing danger to the well-being of others. Effective results, regardless of the specific agency delivering primary treatment services, require programs designed specifically for offenders with mental retardation that reflect active cooperation among criminal justice, mental health, and mental retardation service delivery systems.

Program location and goals for offenders with short sentences and a limited history of criminal behavior requiring low security differ from those for persons who have repeatedly engaged in illegal acts and/or whose criminal behaviors result in maximum-security and extended sentences. The initial groupings by law entail separate programming for adolescents and adults. Within each, a further separation entails those who either are first offenders or have a limited history of crime and those who are repeaters and who typically have failed in previous treatment programs or have committed violent crimes. The physical location and housing of programs is influenced by the nature of the security needed to contain the offender to ensure program involvement and to minimize risk of danger to self or others. When inpatient forensic units within mental health hospital settings or secure units within correctional facilities are required, specialized housing and habilitation programs that reflect the unique habilitation needs of persons with mental retardation are indicated (Browning, 1976; Conley et al., 1992; Denkowski & Denkowski, 1986a; Hall, 1992; Menolascino, 1974, 1975).

Even though there is an expanding literature that both highlights the inadequacies of past and current approaches to treatment of the offender with mental retardation (e.g., Conley et al., 1992) and provides description of program models designed to deal with these (e.g., Denkowski & Denkowski, 1986a; Hall, 1992; Wood & White, 1992), only minimal sound empirical evaluation of program alternatives has been offered. In view of this current status of programs, remaining sections of the chapter include illustrations of a range of program models designed to meet various special needs of persons with mental retardation charged with or convicted of criminal activity. When available, we present data supporting the efficacy of these. Whereas some are more exemplary than others, there are insufficient empirical data to recommend a specific model or agency as best suited for meeting the needs of all offenders with mental retardation. We follow these descriptions with a concluding discussion of selected features that appear to be critical contributors to successful outcome.

Program for Persons Determined Incompetent to Proceed

Norley (1995) offered a description of a Mentally Retarded Defendant Program (MRDP) provided by the Developmental Services Program of the State of Florida Department of Health and Rehabilitative Services. The program was designed to evaluate and treat persons deemed to be incompetent to proceed to trial due to their mental retardation: 60 male and 10 female adults or juveniles waived to adult court who had been charged with a felony and had been court ordered into a secure setting. One of the primary training components of the MRDP was *competency training* designed to strengthen the person's knowledge of court procedures to the extent that he/she could better assist in his/her defense. The average time for completion of competency training was 5 months, although the persons could remain in the program for up to 2 years. During this period, the persons also received training in daily living skills; communication skills; functional academics; life management; leisure/social skills; and antecedents, behaviors, and consequences of crime. A behavioral program designed to reduce maladaptive behaviors and teach/strengthen skills and appropriate social behaviors was provided. In those cases where the person was determined to be competent to proceed, he/she was discharged to continue the judicial process. If deemed incompetent to proceed within the foreseeable future, the charges could be dropped and a residential placement recommended, depending on the person's need for a secure or nonsecure residential placement.

For those males who were ready to leave the MRDP, found to be incompetent to stand trail, but for whom the courts decided they were in continued need of a secure setting, placement was made in a special program (Seguin Unit) located in a state-operated Developmental Services Institution. This stepdown program provided intensive treatment in social skills, independent living, basic academics, vocational skills, and job training/placement. Training was designed to promote successful community living skills, including employment. The Seguin Unit utilized a token economy and a step-level system of contracts designed to provide the motivational structure for more independent living. Residents next moved into a small step-out program housed in a nonsecure program provided 24-hour supervision. Community involvement was gradually increased as the person demonstrated the personal independence to successfully manage less supervision. In both settings, the courts maintained jurisdiction of movement to less restrictive setting or continued placement at either program.

Community Parole/Probation Model

An exemplary community model for habilitation for offenders with mental retardation provided by the Lancaster County (PA) Office of Special Offenders Services was described by Wood and White (1992). Its primary goal was successful completion of probation or parole. This was accomplished by implementing a habilitation plan specifically designed to meet the needs of each offender. The program was a joint systems model in which the combined resources of the Mental Health/Mental Retardation and criminal justice systems were used.

The project was staffed by case management specialists and probation officers who worked with juvenile and adult offenders. The program, in operation since 1980, accepted only offenders with a diagnosis of mental retardation. An average of 50 adults and 35 juveniles were served yearly. The average IQ for clients served from 1982 to 1989 was 66, with first offenders comprising approximately 70% of clients served. Theft was the most common offense among the juveniles, with theft in association with criminal conspiracy and individual assault most common for the adult offender. Approximately 75% of the adults were unemployed at the time of arrest. Additionally, most of the offenders with mental retardation were arrested with another person, typically as followers in breaking the law, for example, being a lookout for a burglary, carrying a forged check in a bank, attempting to sell stolen merchandise, or driving a vehicle for a "friend." For many, participation in the criminal activity appeared to represent a means of peer acceptance.

The basic program philosophy was that the offender is accountable and responsible for his/her actions and thus has a right to be arrested. This perspective was viewed as a critical starting point in the habilitation process, as the offender with mental retardation too frequently is not held accountable for his/her behavior by family and friends. This practice, labeled as *psychological welfarism* by Gardner (1991), tends to reinforce the attitude that criminal behavior will be tolerated or overlooked. The result of this practice is repeated criminal behavior. To offset this effect, adherence to the terms of the probation after arrest and admission to the offenders program was viewed as fulfilling the debt owed to the court and community for having broken the law. Probation services were viewed as a privilege given to the offender and were continued only to those who earned the right through their own actions to receive these. Responsibility and accountability was stressed in all aspects of the client's life—adhering to probation rules, getting along at home, dealing with problems at work, and maintaining appropriate relationships in the community. Development of daily routines was emphasized in which the participant demonstrated consistent adherence to the daily expectations of being on time, dressing appropriately, and demonstrating an appreciation of the work ethic. Active involvement in the services offered is motivated by the contingency that refusal to abide by the requirements of probation or parole may result in being placed in jail as a violator.

The program acknowledged that the majority of offenders with mental retardation become involved in illegal activities to be accepted by peers, and frequently did so without knowledge or adequate consideration of the consequences for their actions. The program addressed these personal features by providing a variety of experiences of an informational, educational, social, recreational, and vocational development nature (Wood & White, 1992). These included work orientation, social skills training, time management, budgeting and banking skills, and citizenship skills. Clients were assisted in securing employment that was best suited for their skill level and personal interests. Within the program, in recognition of the low self-esteem that is pervasive among offenders with mental retardation, clients were consistently rewarded for positive changes and counseled when difficulties were encountered. As noted, the court was supportive in providing reinforcement or punishment as needed.

Wood and White (1992) reported that the Special Offender Services program maintained a recidivism rate of 5%, compared with an estimated national rate of over 60% (Santamour, 1986). The writers suggested that the success of the model was related to (1) the joint systems approach between criminal justice and mental health/mental retardation, (2) the fact that only offenders with mental retardation were served in the program and that client–staff ratios were kept small, (3) the intensive supervision provided (i.e., daily basis initially, crisis situations dealt with immediately, individualized placement in services), and (4) the program philosophy that the clients must be responsible and accountable for all their behaviors in all aspects of their home, work, and community relationships.

Community Adolescent Repeated Offender Model

Denkowski and Denkowski (1985b, 1986a) suggested that if the adolescent with mental retardation and repeated offenses is placed in the typical community habilitation program providing for those with mental retardation, the person usually fails because of rampant escape/avoidance behaviors. The adolescent simply will not adhere to or participate in the habilitation experiences. When the group home intervention program requires changes inconsistent with the adolescent's lifestyle of interpersonal and personal functioning, the offender will leave such placements to seek out activities and goods to meet their immediate, self-centered needs or else will run away to avoid program requirements or contingencies. The therapeutic or habilitative mission of the community program thus is thwarted by the inability of the program environment to contain the person and to implement contingent consequences for appropriate and inappropriate behaviors. As a result, the person goes without habilitation. In fact, the offender behaviors in such program settings may even be strengthened, as these continue to be functional and thus become increasingly more difficult to change.

To address these program deficiencies, Denkowski and Denkowski (1985a) emphasized the necessity of a secure physical facility to ensure containment during the initial stages of the habilitation program. As the person demonstrated increasingly responsible personal and social behaviors, access to a less restrictive living environment was provided.

These writers described the habilitation program provided a group of male adolescent offenders with mental retardation who had been court-committed due to chronic criminal activities and assessed to be inappropriate for conventional community residential treatment due to the violent and dangerous nature of their behaviors. The program facility consisted of a 15-bed halfway house located in a major urban area and equipped in accordance with federal guidelines for Intermediate Care Facility—Mental Retardation (ICF-MR) facilities. They compared the program outcomes of two groups of adolescents.

The eight adolescents in Group 1 obtained a median WISC-R IQ score of 55 (range, 50–65), ranged in age from 12 years, 2 months to 16 years, 4 months, had significant adaptive behavior deficits, had records of multiple involvements with the juvenile justice system, came from low socioeconomic, urban backgrounds, and presented lengthy histories of aggressive behaviors. This group was provided a program consisting of a token economy in which participants could earn points for various appropriate behaviors (e.g., dressing cleanly, attending training classes, assisting with cleanup). Point deductions or fines were incurred for verbal and physical aggression. The adolescents could purchase a variety of items, activities, and privileges with points earned (e.g., play pool, movies, cigarettes). House rules were provided to facilitate an orderly environment (e.g., smoking in designated areas only, radio volume at designated level). No one was permitted to leave the premises alone, although access to outdoors was available between scheduled activity periods. A timeout room was available for calming whenever an adolescent became so agitated that he posed a threat to the safety of self or others.

The comparison group of adolescents (Group 2), with a median WISC-R IQ score of 58 (range, 41–62) and ages ranging from 14 years, 1 month to 17 years, 2 months, also had recurrent juvenile court intervention, lengthy histories of aggressive behavior, and urban, low socioeconomic status. The program for this group was modified to meet major difficulties encountered during the initial phases of treatment of the adolescents in Group 1, namely, verbal and physical aggression and elopement.

Points in the modified program were earned separately for training and social behaviors. Training points, earned for such behaviors as bathing, room cleanup, and class attendance could be used to purchase backup reinforcers of relatively low value (e.g., extra snacks, time off from training, posters). Social points, earned for the absence of aggressive behaviors at the rate of one per hour, were used to purchase highly desired reinforcers such as special items and off-site activities. The occurrence of aggressive behaviors resulted in deductions from the social point balance.

In addition, any physical aggression automatically resulted in time spent in the timeout room. Further, if verbal aggression were noted as a precursor of physical aggression, placement in timeout followed. A 10-minute timeout duration was used, with a 5-minute period of calmness required for release. As a final modification, the physical plant was redesigned to ensure a fully secure unit to eliminate elopement.

In comparing the initial 90 days of treatment of these two groups, significantly lower levels of physical and verbal aggression were evident for Group 2 (incidents of physical aggression of 51 vs. 185 for Group 1; incidents of verbal aggression of 270 vs. 562 for Group 1). The differential reinforcement–punishment contingencies for appropriate–inappropriate behaviors present in Group 2 resulted in significantly fewer aggressive behaviors. Under this choice contingency, clients apparently were able to demonstrate significantly increased self-control of aggressive impulses. Runaway incidents were reduced from 143 in Group 1 to 3 in Group 2 as a result of the fully secured unit added for Group 2. The writers interpreted these differences to support their experience that

> These youth must surmount some "hump" during treatment before their behavior can be managed with the verbal prompts which largely comprise the behavior control strategies utilized in conventional group homes. During this interim, which lasts from three to five months (for most youth), aggression is extensive, resistance to placement into timeout is strenuous, and runaway occurs readily when wants are thwarted. (Denkowski & Denkowski, 1985a, p. 304)

ICF-MR Center for Intensive Treatment Model

The Center for Intensive Treatment (CIT) is a highly structured, active treatment and habilitative residential program within a secure setting operated by the Office of Mental Retardation and Developmental Disabilities in New York State (Finn, 1995). The CIT serves adult males whose assaultive, aggressive, or criminal behaviors require a highly specialized treatment setting. The majority of persons served are committed to the custody of the Commissioner of the Office of Mental Retardation and Developmental Disabilities by the criminal courts after being found incompetent to stand trail or not criminally responsible for their actions due to mental retardation. The CIT physical environment consists of four houses, each with 9 single bedrooms, and a day-program center. All buildings of the CIT are located within a specially designed 14-foot inward curving, unclimbable fence. Additional perimeter protection renders it a secure facility. A sophisticated lock system provides access throughout buildings by reading a person's door access card, thus controlling movement based on the independence level of each resident.

The objective of the CIT is to teach those skills and motivations needed by residents to make reasonable choices and to live as normal lives as possible within the community. This includes the ability to control one's own behavior and to maintain a law-abiding lifestyle. The program includes functional educational/academic skills training, vocational training through a mentoring program with maintenance staff, physical education/recreation programs, and offense-specific treatment programs. These latter programs address such specific problem areas as sexual offender problems, arson problems, substance abuse problems, anger management problems, and violence problems. These treatment programs address the offending problems specific to each resident with a combination of individual therapy, group therapy, medication, educational experiences, and social learning opportunities.

Mental Retardation Residential Facility
Adult Repeated Offender Model

Day (1983, 1988) described the special treatment setting and program provided 20 male offenders in a British hospital for the mental handicapped. The average age of the group was 21.4 years (range, 16–36 years). The IQ of the group averaged 64.6 (range, 58–81), with 60% diagnosed with mild mental retardation. All 20 were reported as displaying abnormal personality traits indicating a personality disorder. Psychosocial histories indicated poor, urban environment and broken homes characterized by parental neglect and abuse, violence, and criminal behavior. Previous residential placements in a range of mental health, mental retardation, and penal institutions, histories of serious and frequently multiple behavior problems dating from an early age, and a past history of convictions characterized the group. Admission offense included those of a sexual, (40%), property (30%), assault (20%), and arson (10%) nature. Half of the property offenses were committed jointly with nonhandicapped companions.

The offenders were housed in a self-contained, eight-bed unit, with two secure rooms available for use in managing episodes of disruptive behaviors. Security was provided by locked doors, reinforced glass, and close supervision. During the initial 2 months of program placement, the offenders were confined to the unit and could leave only under strict supervision. After this period, the person attended the hospital occupational and training departments and gradually gained more freedom, extending from ground parole to escorted and then unescorted community parole. Home leave was provided as soon as it was deemed advisable by the clinical staff.

The individualized treatment program was developed by a core clinical team including a psychiatrist, a psychologist, a social worker, a nurse, and related staff. The program consisted of personal and practical skill training together with a socialization program based on a token economy. Program objectives included those of increasing self-confidence, improving social, occupational, and education skills, facilitating the internalization of an acceptable code of social behavior, increasing the person's sense of personal responsibility, and improving self-control. The practical skill training program consisted of personal and domestic skills, occupational experiences, basic education, and leisure-skills development. Work experience was provided in a special vocational setting serving the offenders.

An incentive-level system reflecting a controlled, token-economy scheme provided the motivation for program participation and progress. Five levels were present, ranging from the first level, providing minimal spending and no social activities or home leave, to the highest level, consisting of a modest spending allowance, unlimited social activities, full weekend leave, bonus cash, and eligibility for a single room after 6 weeks. Offenders were totally dependent on spending money earned within the program. Each person entered the program at Level 3 and would normally rise or fall one grade at a time. Exceptionally positive or negative behaviors (e.g., severe physical aggression, repeated attempts at elopement) resulted in rise or fall of two or more levels. Changes in grade were decided at a weekly staff meeting attended by both staff and offender.

An additional service included individual and group counseling attended on a voluntary basis. Seventy percent of persons received drug therapy, with various psychopharmacological medications used frequently "to reduce aggressivity and control libido." Other medications including hypnotics, anxiolytics, and antidepressants were used as needed to address clear clinical indications.

Average length of stay was 17.75 months. Eighty-five percent remained in the program for 1 year or longer. Fifty-five percent of the total group of 20 showed a good response to treatment, 30% were provided a fair evaluation, and the remaining 15% were viewed as benefiting poorly from the treatment program. Each of the offenders with a poor rating had lengthy histories of behavior problems and offending activities.

The offenders were followed for an average of 3.3 years after discharge and each was provided a rating of well adjusted, reasonably adjusted, or poorly adjusted. Outcome at 6 months was quite favorable, with 85% assessed as either well or reasonably adjusted. After 1 year this percentage fell to 70% but remained stable through subsequent years of follow-up. There was a notable relationship between outcome at last contact and the type of offense, with 92% of offenders originally charged with crimes against the person (sexual and assault) receiving a positive outcome rating, but only 25% of persons with property offenses (property and arson) receiving a similar positive rating. The author suggested that, for the offender with mental retardation, person offenses are essentially problems of poor self-control, which is responsive to treatment, whereas property offenses reflect overall lifestyle and subcultural influences. On discharge, the property offender is likely to return to an environment that continues to encourage and reinforce such property offenses.

Prison Model

The special treatment programs for offenders with mental retardation offered within the prison systems in South Carolina and Texas provide illustrations of this treatment model. The Habilitation Unit at the Stevenson Correctional Institution in Columbia, South Carolina served both male and female inmates recommended for placement by a multidisciplinary review team (Hall, 1992). The facility was a minimum security one; 96% of inmates were first offenders with an average sentence of 9 years. Special services included special education, life-skills and vocational training, recreation, counseling, and prerelease services. The major objectives were increasing socialization skills, and work-related skills, and interpersonal skills; clarifying values; and resolving emotional conflict. Although no evaluation of the program or the relative contribution of its components has been completed, Hall (1992) reported a significant decrease in the recidivism rate for inmates discharged or paroled from this program.

Pugh (1986) described the Program for Offenders with Mental Retardation of the Texas Department of Corrections. Resulting from a class-action lawsuit, the program served all inmates with mental retardation in units specially designated, equipped, and staffed to provide special services. After identifying an inmate as having a diagnosis of mental retardation, an individual habilitation plan was developed by a treatment team to provide those academic, vocational, and social skills required by the inmates to function independently in the community upon release from the prison setting. In addition, the special program ensured that the offenders with mental retardation were provided adequate living facilities and work conditions, fair discipline, and protection from other prisoners. These services were provided through education (including special education), training in life skills and life skills planning, physical education, vocational education, group and individual counseling, appropriate work assignments, prerelease programming, and transitional services. Each staff working with the offender was provided special training to ensure sensitivity to the inmate's characteristics and needs.

Offenders with Mental Retardation and Mental Disorders

Treatment of the offender with a dual diagnosis of mental retardation and a mental disorder poses additional, specialized treatment concerns. As noted, treatment of symptoms of the mental disorder with psychopharmacological agents may reduce or eliminate the symptoms produced by the disorder, but it does not address the broader psychosocial needs of the offender. An integrated biopsychosocial approach to treatment becomes even more essential due to the implications for the person with repeated criminal activities if treatment is incomplete or ineffective (Gardner & Moffatt, 1990; Gardner & Sovner, 1994).

There is a higher prevalence of both major and minor emotional and behavioral disorders in those with mental retardation than in the general population (Stark et al., 1988). This rate is reported by some to be exceptionally higher among offenders with mental retardation. Wood and White (1992) indicated a rate of 50% for juvenile offenders and 56% among adult offenders served in their special community probation/parole program. Most represented personality and behavioral disturbances. Denkowski and Denkowski (1986a), in describing personal features of young offenders with mental retardation served by a community residential program over a 34-month period, reported a rate of 11% presenting symptoms of "severe emotional disturbance," including diagnoses of schizophrenia, schizoid personality, borderline personality, and reactive psychosis. Additionally, 52% of the group were diagnosed as "conduct disorder, undersocialized, aggressive," resulting in an overall rate of 63% with minor and major mental disorders.

Day (1988) reported that the entire group of 20 offenders with mental retardation served in the residential treatment program described earlier "displayed abnormal personality traits amounting to personality disorder" (p. 638). Of these, 85% had a history of serious and frequent multiple behavior problems dating from early childhood. Thirty percent of the group previously had suffered frank psychiatric illness of sufficient severity to require specialist referral, including psychotic schizophrenic features, emotional lability, anxiety, depressive symptoms, suicidal gestures, and alcohol-related problems.

Although there are no research-based data to recommend any specific, specialized treatment approaches for offenders with mental retardation who present specific mental disorders, descriptive data have been reported. Day (1988), for example, reported that 70% of persons served in the residential treatment program described earlier received drug intervention as part of their treatment. Day commented that "Drugs which reduce aggressivity and control libido have proven extremely helpful in facilitating socialization and rehabilitation programs and are used frequently. Hypnotics, anxiolytics and antidepressants are also prescribed when there are clear clinical indicators" (p. 637). Even though there is general agreement in the treatment of various behavioral and emotional symptoms among persons with mental retardation (including the offender) that such symptomatic treatment should be based on a diagnostic presumption of a specific underlying mental, neurological, or other medically based disorder (Gedye, 1989; Lowry & Sovner, 1991; Kastner, Friedman, O'Brien, & Pond, 1990; Sovner & Hurley, 1986), there is increasing disenchantment with psychopharmacological treatment of isolated symptoms such as aggressive and violent behaviors. As emphasized by Yudofsky, Silver, and Schneider (1987), there is no medication that is approved by the Federal Drug Administration specifically for the treatment of violence or related criminal behavior.

A review of the general mental retardation literature indicates that violence and related conduct difficulties as symptoms can be influenced in frequency of occurrence, nature (impulsive or deliberate), and intensity by a wide range of neurological, mental, and physical disorders or conditions (Gardner & Moffatt, 1990; Gardner & Sovner, 1994). In fact, aggressive and related destructive behaviors are among the most socially disruptive, frequent, and chronic behavioral symptoms presented by those with mental retardation. Most frequently, aggressive and correlated difficulties of conduct occur in clusters or as a component of a syndrome of symptoms rather than as isolated acts (Gardner & Cole, 1993).

These observations, supported by descriptions of aggressive acts among offenders with mental retardation (Denkowski & Denkowski, 1986a; Smith et al., 1990), indicate that, just as with the nonretarded, effective treatment of violence and related offenses against person and property for those with mental retardation must reflect the environmental, interpersonal, and intrapersonal contexts in which the violence occurs. Seldom if ever does medication treatment alone represent adequate treatment of those who engage in violent behaviors of a repetitive nature. As suggested, the medication must address the neurological or mental disorder presumed to underlie or contribute to the violence if a therapeutic effect is to be realized (Conn & Lion, 1984; Corrigan, Yudofsky, & Silver, 1993; Sovner & Hurley, 1986; Tardiff, 1992; Yodofsky et al., 1987). Additionally, as emphasized, habilitation of the offender with mental retardation and psychiatric difficulties requires an integrated biopsychosocial treatment experience. This would be exceedingly difficult to accomplish within typical psychiatric, mental retardation, or correctional programs and thus begs for specially designed treatment efforts.

Although *neuroleptic* or *antipsychotic* medication has been used widely in attempts to manage the aggression and related agitated/disruptive behaviors of those with (Conn & Lion, 1984) and without (Yudofsky et al., 1987) mental retardation, in too many instances its use has been directed toward violence and related symptoms that occurred in the absence of an active psychosis. In these instances, the antipsychotics are being used to produce sedative effects, which may affect the symptoms. If the aggression is chronic, the person commonly develops a tolerance to the sedative effects of the neuroleptics and thus requires increasingly higher doses for continued management. As the side effects of neuroleptics are numerous, such nonspecific use of these medications is not justified (Lowry & Sovner, 1991; Yudofsky et al., 1987).

In illustration of the potential negative effects, Elie, Langlois, and Cooper (1980) in a study of 51 persons with mental retardation demonstrated that the use of the neuroleptic thioridazine resulted in an increase rather than a decrease in aggressive and hostile behaviors. The writers suggested that antipsychotic agents serve to lower seizure threshold and produce an organic dyscontrol of rage and violence. Whereas we are not suggesting that antipsychotic agents should never be used, medical logic does dictate that such treatment should be disorder rather than symptom based. When aggression or other criminal acts are presumed to be the result of or influenced by psychoses, these agents may represent the treatment of choice.

Other medications may be useful in treating aggressive and violent behaviors as well as other socially inappropriate behaviors when these acts are presumed to reflect other mental or neuropsychiatric disorders. Although no empirical literature addresses specifically offenders with mental retardation, other drug studies involving persons with mental retardation with symptoms of violent acts offer some treatment guidance. Lithium carbonate may be useful in controlling aggression related to manic excitement and in treating some persons with nonbipolar disorders. Craft et al. (1987) used lithium in a double-blind trial lasting 4 months in 42 patients described as mentally handicapped and presenting chronic problems of aggression. Subjects ranged in age from 22 to 55 years, with a mean of approximately 33 years. Seventy-three percent of subjects showed a reduction in aggressiveness. It should be noted that at least a 2-month trial was needed, with some positive responders requiring 6 to 8 weeks for therapeutic effects to occur. These rates of improvement are consistent with the 63% responders reported by Spreat, Behar, Reneski, and Miazzo (1989). In a retrospective study of persons with mental retardation and clinically significant aggressive behaviors, these writers reported a significant correlation between positive responders and higher pretreatment levels of hyperactivity and severity of the aggressive acts. Of practical significance, and consistent with previous reports of Sovner and Hurley (1981), a higher serum lithium level (at or above 1.0 mEq/liter) was correlated with a favorable response to this medication.

Ratey, Mikkelsen, and Bushnell (1986) found marked improvement in aggression in a group of persons with severe mental retardation in response to an open trail of the beta blocker propranolol. Polakoff, Forgi, and Ratey (1986) described a case study in which the assaultive behavior of persons with mental retardation was controlled by the daily use of nadolol. Ratey et al. (1992) speculated that this class of medication is successful in reducing the person's presumed excessive autonomic reactivity to environmental demands. This heightened reactivity places the person at elevated risk for aggressive reactions.

Bond, Mandos, and Kurtz (1989) reported the successful use of midazolam, a benzodiazepine derivative, in producing a rapid calming effect on clients displaying acute episodes of severe aggressivity and violence. Although not producing an enduring effect due to its relatively short duration of action, its clinical usefulness in producing sedative, anxiolytic, and amnesic effects recommends it for possible use in acute episodes requiring immediate crisis management.

Ratey, Sovner, Parks, and Rogentine (1991) reported the successful use of buspirone, an antianxiety agent, in reducing aggression in a group of adults with moderate mental retardation and a diagnosis of an anxiety disorder. It was speculated that this agent was successful in reducing aggression by impacting on the frustration tolerance, irritability, and impulsivity features of these adults, all of which are risk factors in aggressive reactions. The authors concluded, "While it appears that buspirone may be helpful in reducing aggression and anxiety, it may clinically be most useful for aggression in the low-dosage range" (p. 161).

Although none of these studies specifically addresses the offender with mental retardation, results do suggest potential usefulness with offenders who present mental, neurological, and behavioral difficulties similar to those presented in these clinical studies. Table 7.1 provides a summary of psychiatric disorders and related psychopharmacological agents reported to be useful in reducing aggressive behaviors.

Yudofsky et al. (1987) advised, in conclusion:

> In treating aggression, the clinician, where possible, should diagnose and treat
> underlying disorders with agents specific for those disorders. Thus, if aggression
> is related to active psychoses, antipsychotic agents should be used. In patients

with aggression related to mania, lithium carbonate is the drug of choice in most cases. Where aggression is related to seizure disorders, particularly temporal lobe epilepsy, carbamazepine is indicated. Finally, in those patients whose aggression is secondary to organic brain syndromes . . . we recommend the use of beta blockers. (p. 404)

PROGRAM RECOMMENDATIONS

Treatment programs for the offender with mental retardation, regardless of the group served, the agency providing the program, or its physical location, should address two major sets of factors contributing to the person's criminal behaviors. The initial and most important set consists of those *personal features* most directly involved in the specific criminal acts. This includes such factors as (1) limited understanding of the nature and consequences of one's criminal behavior, (2) limited impulse control under conditions of increased emotional arousal (e.g., intense anger or anxiety arousal), (3) limited internalized inhibitions under conditions of temptation to engage in socially unacceptable acts (e.g., when challenged by peers to engage in a criminal act the person does not become sufficiently anxious and cognitively concerned about potential negative outcome to self-inhibit the criminal behavior), (4) low self-esteem, (5) deficits in internalized

TABLE 7.1. Psychopharmacological Treatment of Aggression

Agent	Indication
Anticonvulsants	Complex seizure disorders Other organic brain disorders
Antidepressants	Mood disorders
Antipsychotics	Psychotic ideation Acute management via sedative side effects
Beta blockers	Organic brain diseases or injuries Irritability not related to psychotic ideation
Buspirone	Anxiety Traumatic brain injury
Lithium	Manic excitement Cyclic affective disorders
Sedatives	Acute management via sedative–hypnotic properties Anxiety associated with personality disorder

Note. Modified from information included in Bond, Mandos, and Kurtyz (1989); Conn and Lion (1984); Corrigan, Yudofsky, and Silver (1993); Martell (1992); Ratey et al. (1992); Ratey, Sovner, Parks, and Rogentine (1991); Sovner and Fogelman (1996); Spreat, Behar, Reneski, and Miazzo (1989); Stanislav, Fabre, Crismon, and Childs (1994); Tardiff (1992); and Young and Hillbrand (1994).

social (moral) standards of conduct, (6) limited skills in postponing immediate self-gratification, (7) limited skills of assertively resisting being unduly influenced by others, (8) limited conflict resolution skills, (9) limited skills in viewing oneself as accountable or responsible for one's own actions, and (10) other personal factors that may be described as reflecting undersocialized personality traits.

In instances of an association between specific criminal acts and various mental disorder symptoms such as the thought, perceptual, and affective difficulties present in schizophrenia, violent outbursts associated with neuropsychiatric conditions, or loss of inhibitions associated with substance abuse, an initial target of treatment must be the underlying psychiatric or related medical disorder. As noted earlier, however, seldom will mere treatment of the mental disorder be sufficient to insure habilitation. The person most typically will continue to reflect the multiple personal deficits described above as present in other offenders with mental retardation (Menolascino, 1974, 1975; Wood & White, 1992).

The second set of factors, although not directly related to specific criminal acts, represent indirect but *major* contributors that render criminal activities more likely in those at risk. Numerous writers have described the pervasive nature of the *community survival skill deficits* in the social, vocational, economic, interpersonal, recreational, educational, and personal care areas. An older adolescent or young adult with mental retardation and without general work and specific vocational skills to obtain and maintain a job may turn to robbery to meet his/her basic needs. Other persons with insufficient knowledge of sexuality and limited social skills to develop and maintain healthy relationships may engage in deviant sexual behavior to meet his/her curiosity and sexual needs (Day, 1988; Denkowski & Denkowski, 1986b; Losada-Paisey & Paisey, 1988).

Habilitation programs for offenders with mental retardation thus must be individualized, multifaceted in nature, and designed to address the person's specific personal, including psychiatric, needs and to improve the overall personal, social, educational, and vocational community survival skill competencies. A well-designed, multileveled, diagnostically based, and community-focused program may well succeed where other institutional-based and -focused (mental health, mental retardation, or correctional) programs have failed. This optimism is justified, however, only when the treatment program is habilitative in nature and designed both to teach these critical personal and community survival skills *and* to provide realistic and community-related motivational/emotional supports to ensure routine use of these skills as replacements for the previously performed criminal acts. The acquisition of the variety of personal and adaptive skills required for independent functioning will be realized only if there is consistence of program implementation that provides immediate and con-

sistent meaningful consequences for both prosocial and inappropriate behaviors.

In developing a treatment plan for the offender with mental retardation,
we offer the following guidelines.

The Treatment Plan Should Be Diagnostically Based

As described throughout the chapter, the offending behaviors of those with
mental retardation reflect the influence of a broad range of environmental
and personal factors. If a meaningful therapeutic effect is to be realized,
the treatment provided must address those arrays of factors that *contribute
directly and indirectly to the offending acts.* As noted above, these vulnerabilities include both *personal features* (e.g., poor impulse control, insufficient internalized standards of social conduct, excessive arousal associated
with neurological impairment, and a weak sense of personal responsibility
or accountability for one's behavior) and *community survival skills deficits*
(e.g., limited vocational skills, limited knowledge of sexual expression and
practices, and limited economic skills). Once identified by means of a
thorough, individualized biomedical and psychosocial diagnostic assessment, the treatment experiences can be individually designed to impact on
these contributing factors.

Criminal behaviors occur in a socioenvironmental context. These
specific conditions associated with the offending behaviors should be
described. As the treatment experiences must change the person if he/she
is to become independent and capable of socially sanctioned behavior even
when exposed in the future to these untoward social influences, it is
valuable to identify the nature of these specific influences. With this
information, the treatment program can teach specific skills of coping with
these specific conditions as replacements for the criminal acts. If, for
example, the offending behavior reflects the undue influence of more
assertive peers, assertiveness training specific to these instigating influences should be provided. Generalization from treatment experiences to
future crime-provoking conditions is best ensured by providing training
under conditions that closely approximate these. General coping strategies
evolve from numerous specific training experiences. As a second example,
if the offending behaviors represent inappropriate sexual behaviors toward
a nonconsenting peer, specific training in competing social–sexual behaviors are indicated.

As suggested by Day (1988), persons with a history of repeated
property offenses frequently return to subcultural influences that continue
to encourage and reinforce a lifestyle that involves such property offenses.
In some instances, the treatment experiences may be unable to change the
person sufficiently to ensure that these instigating conditions for criminal

behaviors will be resisted. Treatment programming can then monitor the person through alternative placement to reduce the likelihood that the person is exposed to these influences.

To emphasize, a comprehensive biopychosocial diagnostic and treatment model should guide the evaluation and treatment planning process. This model reflects a functional rather than an illness perspective (Gardner, 1996; Gardner & Moffatt, 1990; Gardner & Sovner, 1994; Lowry & Sovner, 1991).

The Treatment Plan Should Reflect Habilitation Rather Than Rehabilitation

The rehabilitation model assumed by the mental health and criminal justice service delivery systems is based on the premise that the offender at one time demonstrated the personal features and community survival skills for independent societal functioning. Due to the occurrence of a mental disorder or a shift in personal values, the person engaged in criminal activities. Rehabilitation, either through mental health treatment or incarceration, is therefore provided to restore the person to his/her previous, acceptable level of societal functioning.

With some infrequent exceptions, this model is faulty when applied to offenders with mental retardation. Due to developmental impairments, the offender with mental retardation likely has never attained an adequate level of personal and societal independence. Numerous personal and community-survival skill deficits, environmental limitations involving poverty, lack of vocational training or opportunities, and the like all contribute to a general state of personal and social inadequacy. As noted by McGee and Menolascino (1992), "a disproportionate percentage of defendants with mental retardation are poor, living at the margin, and powerless. They primarily comprise racial minorities, slum dwellers, and school dropouts, as well as chronically unemployed, homeless, illiterate, and politically disenfranchised individuals" (p. 55). The program focus thus of necessity becomes an educative or skill development (habilitation) one to ensure that the person acquires those personal–social and community-survival skills needed to ensure vocational, economic, and social independence and to encourage respect for the code of conduct expected by the community.

Treatment Experiences Should Be Designed to Teach Personal Responsibility for One's Actions

In view of the observation that a person with mental retardation, including the offender, often is not held accountable for his/her own behavior, it is critical that the treatment program be designed to foster an attitude of personal accountability (Gardner, 1991; Gardner & Cole, 1989; Wood & White, 1992). As a result of previous experiences of not being held accountable, this psychological welfarism effect communicates to the person that there will be no differential consequences for appropriate versus inappropriate behaviors (Gardner, 1991). As a result, the person does not develop the social motivational schema needed to engage in socially discriminating responding. Even in those instances in which the person may have alternative prosocial behaviors in his/her repertoire, the offending behaviors may have become more *effective* and *efficient* in gaining desired consequences and thus become predominant modes of behaving, for example, gaining peer acceptance through illegal, gang-related activities. As a result of this lack of differential consequences for appropriate versus inappropriate behaviors, the person is left with the faulty assumption that it is acceptable to engage in such offending behaviors as violence, theft, or property damage or destruction.

To elaborate, without consistent experience with differential consequences provided immediately for appropriate versus inappropriate social behaviors, the normalizing social discrimination process is thwarted in its development. As a result, the person is left without a systematic, experiential basis for developing skills of impulse control. When confronted with stimuli that control aberrant behaviors, the person is not internally prompted by cognitive or emotionally-based stimuli to engage in contrary responses that may mediate or instigate competing prosocial acts. The person thus is under the excessive stimulus control of whatever state of arousal, provocation, or instigating conditions that may occur, for example, anger, thwarting of goal attainment, loss of a desired reinforcer, a sexually provocative object, or persistent urging by peers to engage in illegal acts (Gardner, 1991).

To enhance personal accountability, the habilitation program should:

1. Teach or strengthen specific alternatives to offending behavior when confronted with conditions similar to those in which the behaviors previously occurred. These experiences are next followed by teaching more general problem-solving and coping skills (Goldstein & Glick, 1987).

2. Teach/strengthen internalized standards against which the person can judge contemplated behaviors and which will provide the personal motivation to avoid unacceptable ways of acting. In this program, a number of rules are taught/strengthened and internalized to ensure that the person's social behaviors will be rule governed (Hayes, 1989). This can best be accomplished in a program that (a) has clearly defined and understood rules of social living, (b) places responsibility on the person for respecting the rules, (c) systematically models and labels rule compliance and routinely

reinforces it with valued consequences, and (d) routinely and promptly consequates rule-breaking. As emphasized by a number of programs described earlier, the initial phases of this treatment can best be accomplished in a secure environment. Otherwise the person, due to his/her impulsive nature and difficulty in postponing gratification, will attempt to escape from the therapeutic program. Within a secure environment, the person is informed that he/she has personal control over his/her own behavior and can determine the frequency and kind of consequences produced. To ensure success, each person is taught new social and coping skills relevant to his/her own problem behaviors. The person's behaviors, as suggested, become rule-governed rather than impulse-driven. At this point, increased freedom of movement is provided as the person demonstrates increased independence in respecting socially relevant expectations.

These types of experiences are quite different from the "lockup" experiences of incarceration in a prison or a forensic unit of a mental hospital. The cognitive and motivational–emotional characteristics of the offender with mental retardation frequently have not developed sufficiently to effectively assimilate the lasting effects of incarceration. Again, the internalization of standards of societal conduct and the related cognitive–motivational skills to use these under future conditions will best be accomplished in a program environment that is designed specifically to teach these and related skills of personal or self-management (Gardner & Cole, 1989; Liberman, DeRisi, & Mueser, 1989).

SUMMARY

Some persons with mental retardation are at risk for engaging in criminal behaviors. Early theories suggested a direct link between mental retardation and criminality. Whereas this cause–effect model is not supported by current thinking, some features related to cognitive and adaptive behavior limitations do represent vulnerability or risk factors for delinquent and criminal acts. These consist of personal features most directly involved in specific criminal acts as well as a range of community-survival skill deficits. Included among these personal features is an increased proclivity to experience significant mental health difficulties. Treatment programs should address the constellation of individually specific personal features and community-survival skills deficits. To accomplish meaningful therapeutic results, the treatment program should be diagnostically based, reflect a competency enhancement (habilitation) focus, and place major emphasis on teaching personal responsibility for one's actions.

REFERENCES

Baroff, G. S. (1996). The mentally retarded offender. In J. W. Jacobson & J. A. Mulick (Eds.), *Manual of diagnosis and professional practice in mental retardation* (pp. 311–321). Washington, DC: American Psychological Association.

Beier, D. C. (1964). Behavioral disturbance in the mentally retarded. In H. Stevens & R. Heber (Eds.), *Mental retardation: A review of research* (pp. 453–488). Chicago: University of Chicago Press.

Bond, W. S., Mandos, L. A., & Kurtz, M. B. (1989). Midazolam for aggressivity and violence in three mentally retarded patients. *American Journal of Psychiatry, 146,* 925–926.

Bonnie, R. J. (1992). The competency of defendants with mental retardation to assist in their own defense. In R. W. Conley, R. Luckasson, & G. N. Bouthilet (Eds.), *The criminal justice system and mental retardation* (pp. 97—120). Baltimore: Brookes.

Brown, B., & Courtless, T. (1967). *The mentally retarded offender.* Washington, DC: The President's Commission on Law Enforcement and Administration of Justice.

Brown, B., & Courtless, T. (1968). The mentally retarded offender. In R. C. Allen, E. Z. Ferster, & J. Rubin (Eds.), *Readings in law and psychiatry* (pp. 364–390). Baltimore: Johns Hopkins Press.

Brown, B., & Courtless, T. (1971). *The mentally retarded offender.* Washington, DC: Center on Studies of Crime and Delinquency, National Institute of Mental Health.

Brown, B., & Courtless, T. (1982). *The mentally retarded offender.* Washington, DC: National Institute of Mental Health.

Browning, P. L. (Ed.). (1976). *Rehabilitation and the retarded offender.* Springfield, IL: Charles C Thomas.

Christian, F. L. (1913). The defective delinquent. *Albany Medical Annals, 34,* 280–285.

Clare, I. C. H., & Gudjonsson, G. H. (1995). The vulnerability of suspects with intellectual disabilities during police interviews: A review and experimental study of decision making. *Mental Handicap Research, 8,* 110–128.

Clark, M. (1894). The relation of imbecility to pauperism and crime. *Arena, 10,* 25–26.

Conley, R. W., Luckasson, R., & Bouthilet, G. N. (Eds.). (1992). *The criminal justice system and mental retardation.* Baltimore: Brookes.

Conn, L. M., & Lion, J. R. (1984). Pharmacologic approaches to violence. *Psychiatric Clinics of North America, 7,* 879–886.

Corrigan, P. W., Yudofsky, S. C., & Silver, J. M. (1993). Pharmacological and behavioral treatments for aggressive psychiatric inpatients. *Hospital and Community Psychiatry, 44,* 125–133.

Craft, M., Ismail, I. A., Krishnamurti, D., Mathews, J., Regan, A., Seth, R. V., & North, P. M. (1987). Lithium in the treatment of aggression in mentally handicapped patients: A double-blind trail. *British Journal of Psychiatry, 150,* 685–689.

Crocker, A. G., & Hodgins, S. (1997). The criminality of noninstitutionalized mentally retarded persons: Evidence from a birth cohort followed to age 30. *Criminal Justice and Behavior, 24,* 432–454.

Day, K. (1983). A hospital based psychiatric unit for mentally handicapped adults. *Mental Handicaps, 11,* 140–147.

Day, K. (1988). A hospital-based treatment programme for male mentally handicapped offenders. *British Journal of Psychiatry, 153,* 635–644.

Denkowski, G. C., & Denkowski, K. M. (1984). An in-patient treatment model for MR adolescent offenders. *Hospital and Community Psychiatry, 35,* 279–281.

Denkowski, G. C., & Denkowski, K. M. (1985a). Community-based residential treatment of MR adolescent offenders: Phase I, reduction of aggressive behavior. *Journal of Community Psychology, 13,* 299–305.

Denkowski, G. C., & Denkowski, K. M. (1985b). The mentally retarded offender in the state prison system: Identification, prevalence, adjustment and rehabilitation. *Criminal Justice and Behavior, 12,* 55–70.

Denkowski, G. C., & Denkowksi, K. M. (1986a). Characteristics of the mentally retarded adolescent offender and their implications for residential treatment design. *Behavioral Residential Treatment, 1,* 73–90.

Denkowski, G. C., & Denkowski, K. M. (1986b). Group home designs for initiating community-based treatment with mentally retarded adolescent offenders. *Journal of Behavior Therapy and Experimental Psychiatry, 14,* 141–145.

Elie, R., Langlois, Y., & Cooper, S. F. (1980). Comparison of SCH-12679 and thioridazine in aggressive mental retardates. *Canadian Journal of Psychiatry, 25,* 484–491.

Ellis, J. W., & Luckasson, R. A. (1985). Mentally retarded criminal defendants. *George Washington Law Review, 53,* 414–493.

Everington, C., & Dunn, C. (1995). A second validation study of the Competence Assessment for Standing Trial for Defendents with Mental Retardation (CAST-MR). *Criminal Justice and Behavior, 22,* 44–59.

Exum, J. G., Turnbull, H. R., Martin, R., & Finn, J. W. (1992). Where we need to go: Perspective on the judicial, mental retardation services, law enforcement, and corrections systems. In R. W. Conley, R. Luckasson, & G. N. Bouthilet (Eds.), *The criminal justice system and mental retardation* (pp. 235–244). Baltimore: Brookes.

Fernald, W. E. (1909). The imbecile with criminal instincts. *The American Journal of Insanity, 65,* 732–749.

Fernald, W. E. (1922). *Annual report of the Massachusetts state school for the feebleminded.* Unpublished manuscript. [Available from the Massachusetts Department of Mental Retardation, Boston, MA]

Finn, J. (1995). *Center for intensive treatment.* Unpublished manuscript. [Available from John W. Finn, Bureau of Forensic Services, Office of Mental Retardation and Developmental Disabilities, 44 Holland Avenue, Albany NY 12229-0001]

Fulero, S. M., & Everington, C. (1995). Assessing competency to waive *Miranda* rights in defendants with mental retardation. *Law and Human Behavior, 19,* 533–543.

Gardner, W. I. (1991). Effects of psychological welfarism on durability of behavior disorders in those with mental retardation. *Psychology in Mental Retardation and Developmental Disabilities, 16,* 2–5.

Gardner, W. I. (1996). Nonspecific behavioral symptoms in persons with a dual diagnosis: A psychological model for integrating biomedical and psychosocial diagnoses and interventions. *Psychology in Mental Retardation and Developmental Disabilities, 21,* 6–11.

Gardner, W. I., & Cole, C. L. (1989). Self-management approaches. In E. Cipani (Ed.), *The treatment of severe behavior disorders* (pp. 19–36). Washington, DC: American Association on Mental Retardation.

Gardner, W. I., & Cole, C. L. (1993). Aggression and related conduct disorders: Definition, assessment, and treatment. In J. L. Matson & R. P. Barrett (Eds.), *Psychopathology in the mentally retarded* (2nd ed., pp. 213–252). Boston: Allyn & Bacon.

Gardner, W. I., & Moffatt, C. W. (1990). Aggressive behaviors: Definition, assessment, treatment. *International Review of Psychiatry, 2,* 91–100.

Gardner, W. I., & Sovner, R. (1994). *Self-injurious behaviors: Diagnosis and treatment.* Willow Street, PA: Vida.

Gedye, A. (1989). Episodic rage and aggression attributed to frontal lobe seizures. *Journal of Mental Deficiency Research, 33,* 369–379.

Goldstein, A. P., & Glick, B. (1987). *Aggression replacement training.* Champaign, IL: Research Press.

Hall, J. N. (1992). Correctional services for inmates with mental retardation: Challenge or catastrophe? In R. W. Conley, R. Luckasson, & G. N. Bouthilet (Eds.), *The criminal justice system and mental retardation* (pp. 167–190). Baltimore: Brookes.

Hayes, S. C. (1989). *Rule-governed behavior.* New York: Plenum Press.

Illinois Mentally Retarded and Mentally Ill Offender Task Force. (1988). *Mentally retarded and mentally ill offender task force report.* Springfield, IL: Author.

Kastner, T., Friedman, D. L., O'Brien, D. R., & Pond, W. S. (1990). Health care and mental illness in persons with mental retardation. *Habilitative Mental Healthcare Newsletter, 9,* 17–24.

Kentucky Legislative Research Commission. (1975). *Mentally retarded offenders in adult and juvenile correctional institutions* (Research Report No. 125). Frankfort, KY: Author.

Klimecki, M. R., Jenkinson, J., & Wilson, L. (1994). A study of recidivism among offenders with an intellectual disability. *Australia and New Zealand Journal of Developmental Disabilities, 19,* 209–219.

Kugel, R. B. (1986). *Changing patterns in residential services for the mentally retarded.* Washington, DC: President's Committee on Mental Retardation.

Kugel, R. B., Tembath, J., & Sagars, S. (1968). Some characteristics of patients legally committed to a state institution for the mentally retarded. *Mental Retardation, 6,* 2–8.

Laski, F. J. (1992). Sentencing the offender with mental retardation: Honoring the imperative for immediate punishments and probation. In R. W. Conley, R. Luckasson, & G. N. Bouthilet (Eds.), *The criminal justice system and mental retardation* (pp. 137–152). Baltimore: Brookes.

Liberman, R. P., DeRisi, W. J., & Mueser, K. T. (1989). *Social skills training for psychiatric patients.* New York: Pergamon Press.

Losada-Paisey, G., & Paisey, T. J. (1988). Program evaluation of a comprehensive treatment package for mentally retarded offenders. *Behavioral Residential Treatment, 3,* 247–265.

Lowry, M., & Sovner, R. (1991). The functional significance of problem behavior: A key to effective treatment. *The Habilitative Mental Health Newsletter, 10,* 59–63.

Luckasson, R. (1988). The dually diagnosed client in the criminal justice system. In J. A. Stark, F. J. Menolascino, M. H. Albarelli, & V. C. Gray (Eds.), *Mental retardation and mental health* (pp. 354–360). New York: Springer-Verlag.

Lurie, G. M., Levy, S., & Rosenthal, F. M. (1944). The defective delinquent. *American Journal of Orthopsychiatry, 14,* 95–103.

MacEachron, A. E. (1979). Mentally retarded offenders: Prevalence and characteristics. *American Journal of Mental Deficiency, 84,* 165–176.

Marsh, R. L., Friel, C. M., & Eissler, V. (1975). The adult MR in the criminal justice system. *Mental Retardation, 13,* 21–25.

Martell, D. A. (1992). Estimating the prevalence of organic brain dysfunction in maximum-security forensic psychiatric patients. *Journal of Forensic Sciences, 37,* 878–893.

McAfee, J. K., & Gural, M. (1988). Individuals with mental retardation and the criminal justice system: The view from states' attorneys general. *Mental Retardation, 26,* 5–12.

McGee, J. J., & Menolascino, F. J. (1992). The evaluation of defendants with mental retardation in the criminal justice system. In R. W. Conley, R. Luckasson, & G. N. Bouthilet (Eds.), *The criminal justice system and mental retardation* (pp. 55–77). Baltimore: Brookes.

Menolascino, F. (1974). The mentally retarded offender. *Mental Retardation, 12,* 7–11.

Menolascino, F. J. (1975). A system of services for the mentally retarded offender. *Crime and Delinquency, 21,* 57–64.

Noble, J. H., & Conley, R. W. (1992). Toward an epidemiology of relevant attributes. In R. W. Conley, R. Luckasson, & G. N. Bouthilet (Eds.), *The criminal justice system and mental retardation* (pp. 17–53). Baltimore: Brookes.

Norley, D. (1995). *Program descriptions: The mentally retarded defendant program.* Unpublished manuscript. [Available from author, 529 North Sans Souci Avenue, DeLand, FL 32720]

Owens, C. (1982). The black mentally retarded offender: Concerns and challenges. In A. R. Harvey & T. L. Carr (Eds.), *The black mentally retarded offender* (pp. 27–38). New York: United Church of Christ.

Perske, R. (1991). *Unequal justice.* Nashville: Abingdon Press.

Polakoff, S. A., Forgi, P. J., & Ratey, J. J. (1986). The treatment of impulsive and aggressive behavior with nadolol. *Journal of Clinical Psychopharmacology, 6,* 125–126.

President's Committee on Mental Retardation. (1991). *Report to the President: Citizens with mental retardation and the criminal justice system* (DHHS Publication No. ACF 91-21046). Washington, DC: U.S. Government Printing Office.

Pugh, M. (1986). The mentally retarded offenders program of the Texas Department of Corrections. *Prison Journal, 66,* 39–51.

Ratey, J. J., Mikkelsen, E. J., & Bushnell, S. (1986). Beta blockers in the severely and profoundly mentally retarded. *Journal of Clinical Psychopharmacology, 6,* 103–107.

Ratey, J. J., Sorgi, P., O'Driscoll, G. A., Sands, S., Daehler, M. L., & Fletcher, J. R. (1992). Nadolol to treat aggression and psychiatric symptomatology in chronic psychiatric inpatients: A double-blind, placebo-controlled study. *Journal of Clinical Psychiatry, 53,* 41–46.

Ratey, J., Sovner, R., Parks, A., & Rogentine, K. (1991). Buspirone treatment of aggression and anxiety in mentally retarded patients: A multiple-baseline, placebo lead-in study. *Journal of Clinical Psychiatry, 52,* 159–162.

Reichard, C. L., Spencer, J., & Spooner, F. (1982). The mentally retarded defendant–offender. In M. Santamour (Ed.), *The retarded offender* (pp. 121–139). New York: Praeger.

Reiss, S. (1994). *Handbook of challenging behavior: Mental health aspects of mental retardation.* Worthington, OH: IDS Publishing.

Santamour, M. (1986). The offender with mental retardation. *The Prison Journal, 66,* 3–18.

Santamour, M. (1988). *The mentally retarded offender and corrections.* Laurel, MD: American Correctional Association.

Santamour, M. (1989). *The mentally retarded offender and corrections: An updated prescriptive package.* Washington, DC: St. Mary's Press.

Santamour, M., & Watson, P. (Eds.). (1982). *The retarded offender.* New York: Praeger.

Santamour, M., & West, B. (1977). *The mentally retarded offender and corrections.* Washington, DC: Law Enforcement Assistance Administration, Department of Justice.

Smith, C., Algozzine, B., Schmid, R., & Hennly, T. (1990). Prison adjustment of youthful inmates with mental retardation. *Mental Retardation, 28,* 177–181.

Smith, S. A., & Broughton, S. F. (1994). Competency to stand trial and criminal responsibility: An analysis in South Carolina. *Mental Retardation, 32,* 281–287.

Smith, S. A., & Hudson, R. L. (1995). A quick screening test of competency to stand trial for defendants with mental retardation. *Psychological Reports, 76,* 91–97.

Sovner, R., & Fogelman, S. (1996). Irritability and mental retardation. *Seminars in Clinical Neuropsychiatry, 1,* 105–114.

Sovner, R., & Hurley, A. (1981). The management of chronic behavior disorders in mentally retarded adults with lithium carbonate. *Journal of Nervous and Mental Disorders, 169,* 191–195.

Sovner, R., & Hurley, A. (1986). Managing aggressive behavior: A psychiatric approach. *Psychiatric Aspects of Mental Retardation Reviews, 5,* 16–21.

Spreat, S., Behar, D., Reneski, B., & Miazzo, P. (1989). Lithium carbonate for aggression in mentally retarded persons. *Comprehensive Psychiatry, 30,* 505–511.

Spruill, J., & May, J. (1988). The mentally retarded offender: Prevalence rates based on individual versus group intelligence tests. *Criminal Justice and Behavior, 15,* 484–491.

Stanislav, S. W., Fabre, T., Crismon, M. L., & Childs, A. (1994). Buspirone's efficacy in organic-induced aggression. *Journal of Clinical Psychopharmacology, 14,* 126–130.

Stark, J. A., Menolascino, F. J., Albarelli, M. H., & Gray, V. C. (Eds.). (1988). *Mental retardation and mental health: Classification, diagnosis, treatment, services.* New York: Springer-Verlag.

Tardiff, K. (1992). The current state of psychiatry in the treatment of violent patients. *Archives of General Psychiatry, 49,* 493–499.

Wolford, B. I. (1987). Correctional education: Training and education opportunities for delinquent and criminal offenders. In C. M. Nelson, R. B. Rutherford, Jr., & B. I. Wolford (Eds.), *Special education in the criminal justice system* (pp. 53–82). Columbus, OH: Charles E. Merrill.

Wood, H. R., & White, D. L. (1992). A model for habilation and prevention for offenders with mental retardation. In R. W. Conley, R. Luckasson, & G. W. Bouthilet (Eds.), *The criminal justice system and mental retardation* (pp. 153–166). Baltimore: Brookes.

Young, J. L., & Hillbrand, M. (1994). Carbamazepine lowers aggression: A review. *Bulletin of the American Academy of Psychiatry and the Law, 22,* 53–61.

Yudofsky, S. C., Silver, J. M., & Schneider, S. E. (1987). Pharmacologic treatment of aggression. *Psychiatric Annals, 17,* 397–407.

8

TREATMENT
OF THE JUVENILE OFFENDER

Donald A. Gordon
Gregory Jurkovic
Jack Arbuthnot

INTRODUCTION

Juvenile delinquency is a heterogeneous concept encompassing a range of behaviors from status offenses such as truancy, drinking alcohol, and disobeying parents to felonies such as rape, armed robbery, and homicide. As such, delinquency is a legal rather than a psychological term, as it is the involvement of the legal system (through the filing of a complaint against a juvenile) rather than the mental health system that leads to the label. Delinquents are versatile rather than specialized in their behavior. Adolescents who commit one type of offense also tend to commit other types, and even when delinquents specialize, their delinquent behavior is still more versatile than specialized (Farrington, 1986).

Subgroups of delinquents classified by behavior and/or personality characteristics have been developed and researched without much consistency or support for differential treatment. The four most commonly identified subtypes, as usually labeled, are undersocialized aggression (often psychopathic), socialized aggression, attention deficit, and anxiety–withdrawal dysphoria (Quay, 1987b). Unfortunately, there are few treatment studies that relate outcomes to such subtypes.

In spite of differences among some of the subgroups of delinquents, the majority of delinquents are offered treatment that varies less with their behavioral and psychological characteristics and more with what is locally available. Herein lies a major reason why more serious delinquency is not treated effectively. Institutionalized delinquents are given group milieu therapy and delinquents on probation in the community sometimes receive individual psychotherapy (and occasionally family therapy). The success of these approaches will be reviewed later, with particular attention given to the most promising.

The literature on the treatment of delinquents has expanded dramatically in the past two decades, but the percentage of studies showing clear treatment successes has not expanded proportionately. This fact may account for the increased skepticism toward the treatment/rehabilitative approach by many in the criminal justice system and the resultant juvenile justice policy recommendations to abandon treatment in favor of punishment (Regnery, 1985). This skepticism, plus political pressure favoring a greater emphasis on punishment, has bolstered the antitreatment attitude that is increasingly pervasive (Andrews et al., 1990; Gendreau, 1996; Tolan, Cromwell, & Brasswell, 1986).

Changes in family structure may have contributed to greater numbers of children and adolescents who commit serious offenses across all social classes, adding to public concern over the efficacy of rehabilitation. Economic stresses for many families have led to diminished parental involvement with their children as both parents work more outside the home. Child neglect or abuse resulting from family disruption or stress increases the risk for delinquency by over 50% and for adult criminality by around 40% (Widom, 1992).

The risk factors for children have been amplified by the epidemic rise in divorce rates, which have effectively removed fathers from meaningful socialization of their children, particularly in low-income families, which are especially prone to producing delinquents. It has been estimated that 50% to 70% of children born now will live in a single-parent household during their development, leading to a substantial decline in the quantity and quality of parenting (Bumpass, 1984). For boys, the loss of the male role model is potentially devastating, setting them up for rebellion and a shift in loyalties to their peer groups. With the breakup of families through divorce and an increase in physical and sexual abuse and neglect of children comes an accompanying propensity for violent criminal offenses in these children as they mature (Tarter, Hegedus, Winsten, & Alterman, 1984; Widom, 1992). We are likely to witness substantial increases in serious juvenile offenders in the foreseeable future as marital conflict and violence, family disintegration, and child abuse and neglect all increase.

In this chapter, we discuss the response of the mental health profession to the problems associated with the successful treatment of the juvenile offender. Delinquency is a complex behavior pattern that can be understood on multiple levels (biological, individual, sociofamilial, and community) of analysis. Thus, it should not be surprising that no single approach to treating this problem has proven successful; rather, the current trend is to combine approaches, particularly in the case of the serious juvenile offender. Problematically, eclectic approaches have been neither guided by an overarching theoretical framework nor empirically tested. It is our view that such a framework is sorely needed, and we consider inroads in this area later in the chapter.

As the progress from mild to serious delinquency is well documented, we will highlight treatment approaches that can be implemented earlier in the progression, and we will emphasize their preventive aspects. Because of the small number of well-controlled, successful treatment outcome studies with serious juvenile offenders, any conclusions should be drawn cautiously.

We have divided the approaches into individual, family, and group treatments, and will review them while including some examples of the more promising methods offered for each. We also will critically evaluate residential treatment. Next, we will discuss the relationship between mental health service providers and the juvenile justice system as it affects positive treatment outcomes. Given the fiscally conservative trend in social service funding today, we devote a portion of the chapter to evaluating cost effectiveness of interventions, as changes in the social service system are driven by increasing accountability. Following this we discuss the systemic barriers that have impeded the dissemination of effective interventions, and make suggestions for accelerating the process. Finally, we make specific recommendations for a multisystemic and bidirectional influence perspective to treatment decisions to reduce and prevent the progression from minor misconduct to serious chronic delinquency.

We discuss broader implications for a national policy that addresses the larger causes of serious delinquency, as many believe that we are at a crossroads of thinking and social policy regarding crime and delinquency.

INDIVIDUAL TREATMENT APPROACHES

The individual treatments currently in use with juvenile offenders run the therapeutic gamut: psychodynamic, transactional analysis, gestalt, reality, client-centered, cognitive, and behavioral (Gordon & Arbuthnot, 1987; Lester, 1981). None is typically used singularly; rather, they are often applied eclectically and combined with other interventions (e.g., casework, vocational training, tutoring, group and family therapy, medical treatment, and token economies).

Some form of individual therapy or counseling continues to play a central role in rehabilitative programming for juvenile offenders, in both institutional (e.g., detention facilities, psychiatric hospitals, training schools) and community settings (juvenile courts, child guidance and mental health centers, university-based clinics, private practitioners' offices; Gordon & Arbuthnot, 1987). We argue for much of the rest of this chapter, however, that we should move away from individual psychotherapy as the central treatment modality for delinquents, regardless of the seriousness of their offenses.

Although questions have been raised from a psychological perspective about delinquents' ability to enter into a therapeutic relationship (e.g., Schoenfeld, 1971), an increasing number of psychodynamically oriented clinicians have pointed to the feasibility and need for individual treatment of these youngsters. For example, as early as 1925, August Aichorn illustrated the practical application of psychoanalytic principles to delinquency, identifying those offenders most amenable to therapy (Aichorn, 1925).

Whether aimed at intrapsychic conflict, personality or skill deficits, or irrational and maladaptive thinking, individually oriented interventions with antisocial youths rest on a longstanding assumption that their problem stems, in part at least, from individual pathology or deviance. Thus, even though other treatment approaches differing in their primary level of analysis (e.g., family interaction) may be included in a comprehensive treatment plan, it is assumed that individual issues must be directly negotiated. Interestingly, although family systems therapy developed largely in reaction to this view, many family therapists (Clark, Zalis, & Saccho, 1982; Jurkovic, 1984; Kirschner & Kirschner, 1986) now recognize the importance of evaluating and, if necessary, drawing on traditional practices to address problems on an individual level as an adjunct to family treatment.

Treatment of Serious Offenders

Based on their reviews of reported rehabilitative efforts, including various individual interventions with delinquent youngsters, Martinson (1974), Kassenbaum, Ward, and Wilner (1972), and others essentially concluded that "nothing works" (Goldstein, Sprafkin, Gershaw, & Klein, 1980, p. 10). However, as discussed earlier, when a single approach is applied to a heterogeneous group of offenders, it is not surprising that the overall effect is unimpressive, particularly when evidence of therapeutic integrity is lacking (see Gendreau & Ross, 1987). We agree with Goldstein et al. that closer inspection of the literature reveals that "almost everything works— but only for certain youngsters" (pp. 10–11).

The subgroup that continues to challenge the best efforts of the social service, mental health, and correctional communities is composed of those delinquents variously labelled "psychopathic," "character disordered," and "undersocialized–aggressive" (Hamparian, 1987; McCord, 1982). In comparison to their cohorts in other subgroups (e.g., socialized–subcultural, attention deficit, emotional–withdrawn), these juveniles are more likely to commit violent offenses against people and to display undercontrolled, aggressive behavior (Widom, 1989). Therapists with a psychodynamic, behavioral, and cognitive orientation have been particularly interested in attempting to adapt their methods to the treatment of the characterological or behavioral deficits and excesses (e.g., stimulation seeking, impulsiveness, lack of empathy) of aggressive adolescents.

Psychodynamic Approaches

Many delinquents have difficulty forming attachments to others and articulating their feelings, and act out their conflicts. Thus, Schoenfeld (1971) and others do not view the insight-oriented and relational methods of psychoanalysis and psychodynamic therapies useful with these youngsters, unless their problems are primarily neurotic in nature (cf., Aichorn, 1925). Delinquent adolescents lacking impulse control, judgment, the ability to bind conflict internally, and the capacity for identification and trust have long been met with therapeutic pessimism (Strasburger, 1986; Weiner, 1970).

A major obstacle to successfully treating delinquents is often not their personal qualities, but the qualities of their therapists. Psychodynamic theorists have observed that the action-oriented, manipulative, and sometimes violent nature of these youngsters may engender feelings of rejection and fascination in the clinician, leading him/her to relate to them superficially, "as though they had no inner dynamics" (Strasburger, 1986, p. 192). Strasburger considered the characteristics of therapists who work effectively with this patient population and the countertransference problems (fear of assault or harm, helplessness and guilt, feelings of invalidity, and loss of identity) that they are able to negotiate (Lion, 1981). According to Jones (1984):

> In the treatment of aggressive adolescents, the capable therapist is one who can be a real person, admit his shortcomings and demonstrate honesty and integrity. At the same time, he will provide a strong limit-setting image and will not react with fear and hate of the patient. Working with these patients often demands greater personality development in the therapist than work with other patients. (pp. 373–374)

Psychodynamic therapy of seriously disturbed delinquents also requires that the clinician depart from traditional procedures. Weiner (1970), for example, discussed unconventional techniques for engaging these youngsters in treatment, techniques that fit their behavioral style: (1) developing a narcissistic collusion with them (e.g., expressing interest in the details of their deviant behavior); (2) exercising power in their interest (e.g., persuading a parent to withdraw a restriction); (3) conducting stimulating and variegated treatment sessions (e.g., saying or doing the unexpected such as suddenly inviting them for a soda); and (4) demonstrating a readiness to give help to them (e.g., providing advice on coping with life situations). These relationship-building techniques must be implemented carefully, however, to avoid merely fueling the pathologically collusive nature of the disturbed delinquent's behavioral pattern (see Doren, 1987; Strasburger, 1986; Weiner, 1970).

Recent evidence strongly suggests that the supportive aspects of the therapeutic relationship may be more important than interpretive aspects (Wallerstein, 1989). The goal of developing a relationship with serious juvenile offenders is to induce them to identify with the therapist and thus to begin to experience intrapsychic conflicts and a desire to modify their behavior (Weiner, 1970). These internal changes, along with the self-defeating nature of their delinquent conduct, can then become the focus of therapy. In Weiner's words, "the initial phase of treatment for the psychopathic delinquent can be construed in part as an effort to generate sufficient anxiety to develop him into a neurotically disturbed delinquent, at which point treatment for symptomatic delinquency can be instituted" (p. 337). For instance, it is commonly assumed that familiar and treatable clinical syndromes such as depression underlie the antisocial veneer of seriously delinquent adolescents. Only in the context of a special and valued relationship will these symptoms come to the surface. With many violent and aggressive offenders, however, other primitive personality dynamics, such as those associated with borderline or psychotic disorders, are more evident than neurotic disturbances (Keith, 1984; Masterson, 1972, 1980; Strasburger, 1986).

In his historical review of different individual psychotherapeutic and psychoanalytical approaches to this population, Keith (1984) noted that regardless of the youngster's developmental level, each approach emphasized a common mechanism leading to acting out and violence, that is, the presence of a "sluice" within the ego that must be closed by helping the patient to form healthy identifications, superego controls, and symbolic means of discharging tension. This process, according to psychodynamic therapists, typically requires long-term residential treatment (see Keith, 1984; Strasburger, 1986; Weiner, 1982). In the absence of data showing the efficacy of long-term residential treatment it is difficult to justify such a decision, even if it were affordable.

Behavioral Approaches

Juvenile delinquency has been the target of a wide array of behavioral techniques rooted in conditioning (classical or operant) and social learning models. According to Braukmann and Fixsen (1976), effective behavior therapy of delinquent youngsters involves (1) teaching (through modeling or shaping) new behaviors to broaden their repertoires and provide them with alternative and more adaptive responses to situations that occasion delinquency; (2) establishing behavioral contracts or other contingency management systems to motivate them to learn or change; and (3) implementing these systems through the conditional delivery of consequences.

Behavioral treatment of aggressiveness in adolescence involves the use of techniques for accelerating and decelerating behavior (Varley, 1984). For example, systematic use of positive reinforcement to accelerate desired behaviors, particularly those that are incompatible with aggression, is probably used most extensively (Moss & Rick, 1981). As Varley (1984) noted, positive reinforcement is commonly administered in institutions through token economies or point-level systems (Agee, 1979; Ayllon & Azrin, 1968; Kazdin, 1977; Phillips, Phillips, Fixsen, & Wolf, 1973). On an outpatient basis, home-based point systems, contingent home privileges, and contingency contracting are often used to manipulate controlling contingencies in the youngster's natural environment (Patterson, 1971; Stuart, 1971). Although these outpatient approaches typically employ parents as change agents, other community members (e.g., probation officers) can be trained by the therapist to administer the behavioral program (Fitzgerald, 1974; Fo & O'Donnell, 1975).

Additional techniques that are frequently incorporated into behavior therapy of aggressive adolescents include negative reinforcement, punishment, and extinction (Varley, 1984). The procedures are most useful when combined with positive reinforcement, partly so the client will perceive the therapeutic relationship as supportive.

An important consideration in the application of all behavioral techniques discussed thus far is whether the desired behaviors and skills are within the patient's repertoire. Varley (1984), for example, found that if the behaviors targeted for change are available to aggressive youngsters but are used infrequently or only in certain situations (e.g., peer group), then contingency-applied consequences can readily help them extend their skills to other contexts (e.g., home). Many juvenile offenders, however, have pervasive behavioral deficits and thus require social skills training (Evans & Scheuer, 1987). Such training can be administered individually, although it is typically conducted in groups. Instruction, modeling, rehearsal, role playing, feedback, shaping, and social reinforcement are used to expand the adolescent's repertoire to include a variety of skills (Goldstein et al., 1980). However, without a coordinated approach in which people in the child's natural environment (parents, older siblings, teachers, community members) are prompted to both reinforce these new skills and model them, there is little evidence that the gains persist (see the upcoming section on multisystemic approaches).

Cognitive Approaches

Whereas the focus of the conventional behaviorist is on the environmental contingencies supporting undesirable behaviors and collateral feelings and thoughts, cognitive or rational therapists assign a more important role to mediating cognitions in the treatment of antisocial youngsters. Ellis's (1978) rational–emotive therapy, for example, assumes that the dysfunctional attitudes and behaviors of the delinquent result from irrational belief patterns that must be intellectually disputed (see also Bernard & Joyce, 1984).

Recently, a number of investigations have combined behavioral and cognitive techniques to focus specifically on cognitive processes and skills that mediate self-control (Camp, Blom, Herbert, & Van Doornick, 1977; Meichenbaum, 1977; Novaco, 1979; Williams & Akamatsu, 1978). One treatment package, stress inoculation, is designed to help individuals regulate anger and cope with provocation (Novaco, 1979). Viewing anger as an affective stress reaction with cognitive and behavioral determinants, the intervention program involves three treatment phases: cognitive preparation, skill acquisition, and application training. The components of the first phase include (1) education about anger; (2) identification of conditions that occasion anger; (3) discrimination of adaptive and maladaptive anger; and (4) introduction of anger-management techniques. To facilitate the client's cognitive preparation, an instructional manual and anger diary are used. The former not only acquaints clients with the language of the approach but also engages them in a self-help process and reduces the teaching time during therapy sessions. In the diary, clients record the frequency and intensity of their anger experiences and their coping performance.

During the skill acquisition phase, clients are taught through direct instruction, modeling, and rehearsal how to recognize the determinants and manifestations of anger and alternative coping strategies. Cognitively, clients are helped to change their appraisals and expectations concerning provocation and learn "not to take things personally" (Novaco, 1979, p. 268). Toward this end, a series of self-instructions are taught that correspond to different stages of the provocation experience: preparation ("This could be a rough situation, but I know how to deal with it"); impact and confrontation ("As long as I keep cool, I'm in control of the situation");

coping with arousal ("He probably wants me to get angry, but I'm going to deal with it constructively"); and subsequent reflection ("Don't take it so personally. It's probably not so serious"; Novaco, 1979, p. 269). Relaxation, interpersonal communication, and problem-solving are also taught to provide clients with responses incompatible with anger.

Application training allows clients to practice their newly learned anger-control methods in the face of provocations regulated by the therapist. Imaginal and role-play inductions of anger are used. The provocations are presented sequentially, from the least to the most arousing, based on a hierarchy of anger situations that are personally relevant to the client. In addition to the simulated provocations, clients are encouraged to practice their coping skills in actual provocation situations. In residential treatment, staff can prompt clients in their use. *In vivo* practice is directed by the therapist through information gleaned from the anger diary. Clients are instructed to apply their skills to situations in which they are most likely to succeed before graduating to more arousing situations.

Another cognitive approach that uses behavioral methods has been developed by Yochelson and Samenow (1976, 1977). Based on their experiences with severely delinquent adolescents and "hard-core criminals" at St. Elizabeths Hospital in Washington, DC, they identified some 52 thinking errors associated with criminal behavior. These errors are the foci of intervention in their intensive treatment program, which involves individual and group work, ideally beginning while the client is confined. A major goal is to pair aversive and criminal thoughts by helping individuals to consider how their antisocial thinking and consequent actions led to punitive results for both themselves and others (Varley, 1984).

Potts, Barley, Jones, and Woodhall (1986) illustrated the application of Yochelson and Samenow's methods in their description of the treatment of "Peter," a late adolescent with an extensive history of delinquent behavior. After not responding to the general inpatient treatment program, milieu therapy, and individual and group psychodynamic psychotherapy, his treatment plan was revised to focus more specifically on the antisocial features of his behavior and thinking. A contingency management program was implemented, and Peter was asked to monitor his thinking by keeping a diary with at least two entries per day, reflecting his actions and thoughts, such as thoughts to steal or fight. He also noted in his diary several negative consequences which would result. His diary was critiqued frequently by members of the treatment team, who identified and confronted signs of criminal thinking. During the course of this revised program, Peter's behavior was mostly acceptable. Noting that antisocial patients in confinement often conform to the institutional rules, Potts and colleagues (1986) rationalized that the cognitive intervention, along with psychodynamic change, were necessary to maintain treatment gains.

Generalization of Treatment

Although behavioral therapists have impressively demonstrated the ability to generate desired behaviors in aggressive adolescents, they continue to grapple with how to help these adolescents maintain their gains and generalize these gains to new contexts. Increasing concern by behavior therapists with mediating cognitive and self-regulatory processes stems partly from their recognition that all aspects of the delinquent's environment cannot be controlled or manipulated. Thus, special and innovative techniques are needed to ensure maintenance and generalization of treatment effects, especially when treatment is short-term and newly learned responses are not internalized (Varley, 1984). There is increasing concern about the need for a better understanding of clinical process variables (e.g., therapist–client relationship) mediating effective behavioral work (Patterson, 1985). Interestingly, consideration of these issues has contributed to some rapprochement among behavioral, psychodynamic, and cognitive models of therapy.

Which Method to Use?

Despite the rapid growth of alternative approaches to treating juvenile offenders, some form of individual therapy continues to play a role in rehabilitative programming for these youths, in both community (e.g., juvenile courts, child guidance and mental health centers, university-based clinics, private practitioners' offices) and institutional settings (e.g., detention facilities, psychiatric hospitals, training schools). Whether aimed at intrapsychic conflict, personality or skill deficits, and/or irrational and maladaptive thinking, individually oriented interventions with antisocial youngsters rest on a longstanding assumption that their difficulties stem, in part at least, from individual pathology or deviance.

Interestingly, although family systems therapy developed largely in reaction to such a view of problem behavior, many family therapists (e.g., Clark et al., 1982; Jurkovic & Berger, 1984; Kirschner & Kirschner, 1986) draw on traditional practices to address problems on an individual level as an adjunct to family treatment. Indeed, a growing trend in treating delinquency and developing strong policy recommendations involves use of a multisystemic approach.

To the extent that individually oriented techniques are part of the treatment plan for juvenile offenders, which ones are most useful? Unfortunately, few well-designed studies comparing individual treatments of different subtypes of delinquents are available. Research of particular approaches, however, points to cognitive-behavioral interventions as holding the most promise, particularly for serious offenders, although long-term follow-up studies are needed (Gordon & Arbuthnot, 1987; Kazdin, 1994).

That psychodynamic approaches have not proven helpful underscores reservations voiced by many practitioners of this form of therapy with delinquents, especially when delivered on an outpatient basis. As will be discussed later, their recommendation that these youngsters can benefit most from residential treatment has also not received significant support.

Indications of the efficacy of cognitive-behavioral interventions are interesting from a psychodynamic perspective. Such interventions selectively target behaviors (e.g., poor impulse control, deficient problem-solving skills) that are symptomatic of ego and superego deficits—deficits that are posited by psychodynamic theorists to be central to the problems of serious offenders. Although theoretical differences between cognitive-behavioral and psychodynamic approaches are perhaps reconcilable to some degree, their methods of affecting change differ significantly. Unlike their psychodynamic colleagues, cognitive behaviorists intervene in a highly structured and problem-focused fashion, which most likely accounts for their success.

FAMILY TREATMENT APPROACHES

The Role of the Family
in Serious Juvenile Delinquency

The view that the family is the cause of criminality has surged, faded, and now resurged in the history of the study of criminal behavior. It is now accepted as fact that the roots of adult criminal behavior can be traced to hostility and aggression in childhood, which, along with other antecedents of criminal behavior, are socialized in and controlled by the family (Lorion, Tolan, & Wahler, 1987). Travis Hirschi (1969), in his extensive study of the causes of delinquency, found that the number of children's self-reported delinquent acts was powerfully influenced by their attachment to their parents, communication with the father, and supervision by the mother. Social class and the influence of peer groups, long thought to be predictors of delinquency, pale in comparison to family factors. A variety of thorough investigations have supported these findings (Farrington, 1987; McCord, 1982; Snyder & Patterson, 1987; Towberman, 1994).

Antisocial, aggressive adolescents who are chronic offenders have families that share some common features. The parents of these adolescents tolerate aggression, such as frequent sibling fights. Maternal rejection and a lack of monitoring deviant behaviors also accompanies antisocial delinquency (Loeber & Schmaling, 1985). Single-parent families without adequate social support are prone to produce dysfunctional adolescents for similar reasons. With only one parent in the home, particularly one who is stressed, tired, socially isolated, and often depressed, sibling aggression is likely to be ignored. These mothers are unwilling to perceive conflict as aggressive behavior. Observations of these families reveal a high level of physical violence.

> Older siblings wrenched arms behind backs until the younger screamed with pain; they whipped heads against hard surfaces, pummeled, and kicked. Younger children clearly did not experience this as boyish fun, and the expression of grim purposefulness on the faces of older siblings also precluded playfulness. The noise level alone would have drawn anyone's attention, both for its volume and its quality of pain and alarm, but their mothers would gaze serenely into the middle distance. The observation held for the whole population of aggression-prone children. (Tooley, 1976, p. 38)

Further confirmation of the consistent role of parental behavior in antisocial child behavior was provided by Singer's (1974) study of 30 families with antisocial children. He found a pattern of restrictive rules but overly lax policing, followed by lenient punishment for the minority of deviant acts that were detected. What is compelling is not the finding of a relationship between family function and delinquent behavior, but the remarkable consistency across a variety of investigators with different theoretical perspectives. In a review of family therapy studies with delinquents, Tolan and colleagues (1986) found that three qualities of family systems have been emphasized in studies of family interaction: (1) ineffective parental authority; (2) dysfunctional family communication, especially around conflict resolution; and (3) the function of the delinquent's behavior for the family system.

The most compelling demonstration of the causative role of the family in delinquent behavior comes from the efforts to change family (particularly parent) behavior. Most of the studies (Gordon & Arbuthnot, 1987; Tolan et al., 1986) showed reductions in delinquent behavior such as rearrests, recidivism, and truancy following family therapy. All studies in Tolan et al.'s (1986) review that included measures of family functioning, and those few that included recidivism and family functioning measures, reported improvement. However, weaknesses in experimental design, such as nonrandomly assigned control groups, absence of alternative treatment comparison groups, and selection bias in choosing treated families, limited the strength of a conclusion that family therapy leads to improved family functioning and reduced delinquency.

Behavioral Parent Training

During the 1970s, a number of behaviorally oriented clinicians developed and reported the effects of some parent training procedures, now usually referred to as social learning approaches, used with oppositional and aggressive children. G. R. Patterson (1974) and the Oregon Social Learning

Center developed such procedures, along with films, training manuals, and audiotapes. Behavioral contracting and behavior management training reduced a variety of deviant child behaviors, but there has been little evidence of reduction of recidivism for delinquents. This approach holds promise for arresting escalation to more serious antisocial behavior if implemented before adolescence. A recent review of 26 controlled studies utilizing this approach with antisocial young children demonstrated short-term effectiveness (Serketich & Dumas, 1996). An illustration of the use of the parent training approach combined with school consultation follows:

> Stephen was a 12-year-old boy who fought with his younger siblings, neighborhood boys, and classmates at school. He was suspended from school (where he was a marginal student) five times in 6 months for fighting. His mother was divorced and worked in a tire plant. She habitually ignored the sibling fighting at home, occasionally screaming at and hitting Stephen unpredictably. Stephen was not expected to do chores because he didn't comply with his mother's requests most of the time. He never saw his father, and had no supportive relationship with any other adult. His mother initiated therapy after an ultimatum from Stephen's school. The therapist was a master's level behavioral psychologist, who met with the mother and Stephen at a child-guidance clinic for an initial session, then went out to the home for the next four appointments. She observed Stephen's sibling relationships and the mother's attempts to get Stephen to stop arguing and to pick up his dishes. The therapist encouraged the mother to track Stephen's noncompliance, compliance, and sibling fights between dinner and bedtime. After the second telephone reminder to keep records, the mother began complying. In the fourth session, a contingency management system was set up to reward Stephen for increased compliance, but a week later the mother had failed to notice and award points for Stephen's modest increase in compliance. For the next three sessions (outside of which the therapist consulted with her supervisor and discussed the mother's resistance), the therapist provided support to the mother and discussed the lack of social support she was receiving in her life. With an increased effort to "sell" the mother on the benefits of careful child behavior management, the mother began implementing the contingency management plan, now expanded to include loss of privileges for noncompliance. Over the course of the next four sessions, Stephen's fighting with siblings and neighborhood children was reduced substantially, and the support from his mother, the therapist, and the mother's boyfriend increased proportionately. The mother and the therapist met with the school three times (principal and teachers) and worked out a contract to reduce fighting and increase homework compliance (which included frequent parent–teacher written communication). Therapy was terminated after 15 sessions, at which time Stephen's fighting, homework compliance, and chore compliance were

within the range of normal behavior. A recurrence of school fighting 6 weeks later was controlled after two "booster" sessions with Stephen and his mother, and one session with the teacher and principal.

In the approach detailed with Stephen, the therapist served as a trainer to the mother, supplying her with concrete behavior management procedures. The supportive relationship with the therapist was sufficient in this instance to reduce the mother's noncooperation and motivate her cooperation. The use of the school consultation mobilized another social system impacting Stephen in a coordinated fashion.

Functional Family Therapy

Aside from the Oregon parent training program, which dealt primarily with behavior-disordered predelinquents, the only other systematic research program of family interventions that is also based upon a specific theory of delinquency is the behavioral–systems approach of James Alexander (Alexander & Parsons, 1982). This approach is a blend of parent training methodology that improves family functioning via remediating skill deficits and a systemic approach that sees the delinquent in the scapegoat role in a dysfunctional family system. Unlike the parent training approaches, much focus is on techniques for reducing noncompliance. The early work of Minuchin (Minuchin, Montalvo, Guerney, Rosman, & Schumer, 1967) and Singer (1974) described family interaction patterns that were critical in maintaining delinquent behavior. In these cases, family organization was chaotic and the family was relatively uncooperative and unproductive. Parental behavior was not synchronized, leaving children with unclear, mixed messages. For example, a mother would set a restrictive policy for the daughter's curfew, but would leave monitoring and punishing to the father. The father's disagreement with this policy would then result in permissive, half-hearted monitoring and lenient punishment. Alexander and Parsons (1973) established that families of delinquents communicated in a defensive, disjointed manner, often with one member dominating conversations. These families seemed unable to solve problems or show reciprocity in their behavior or conversations. Therapy improved these communication styles and reduced recidivism. In this approach, described in detail in a training manual (Alexander & Parsons, 1982), therapists assess behavioral sequences to determine interpersonal payoffs or functions, relabel those sequences so as to cause a change in attribution and perspective in the family, and then provide instruction appropriate to the skill deficits of the family (communication, problem solving, contingency contracting, limit setting, reinforcement, etc.).

In a well-designed study comparing various treatment approaches with "soft" delinquents, Alexander and Parsons (1973) found superiority for the family therapy over individual approaches. Recidivism in the behavioral–systems group was significantly lower (20%) than for the other treatments (40–63%; Klein, Alexander, & Parsons, 1977). Furthermore, siblings of the referred delinquents were followed for 2½ years after termination and also showed fewer offenses than controls. According to the authors, these results underscore the validity of changing a dysfunctional system that produces delinquency.

This promising approach was recently replicated with a different sample of delinquents in an economically depressed, rural region. Gordon, Arbuthnot, Gustafson, and McGreen (1988) compared delinquents whose families were treated with Alexander's behavioral-system family therapy in the home to a group of probation-only delinquents. The family therapy group (n = 27) was composed of delinquents averaging two offenses, including felonies and misdemeanors as well as status offenses. The comparison group (n = 28) was largely comprised of status offenders who received only probation services. The training and supervision of the graduate student therapists was longer in duration than in the Alexander and Parsons study (1973), and the intervention procedures were described in detail. Little attrition occurred, partly due to the fact that all sessions occurred in the home, with only one family dropping out of treatment early.

After a 2½-year follow-up period, recidivism (measured by court adjudications) for the treatment group was 11% versus 67% for the controls. These results represent an improvement over those of Alexander and Parsons (1973) in that the recidivism rate of the treated group was one-sixth that of the controls, even with the longer follow-up period and higher risk of the treated group. These differences were attributed to time-unlimited and longer treatment (mean of 16 sessions), increased rapport related to being in the home, and focusing on parental noncompliance during the supervision of therapists. A cost–benefit analysis of the out-of-home placement costs for the two groups showed that costs for the treatment group, including all costs of treatment, were less than for the probation control group. In addition, sibling court contacts for the family therapy group were lower than for the control group.

These delinquents were followed for another 32 months into adulthood, with the family therapy group showing a 9% recidivism rate for criminal offenses versus 41% for the probation-only group (Gordon, Graves, & Arbuthnot, 1995). Demonstration of long-term treatment effects into adulthood is extremely rare, and despite the nonrandom assignment of subjects in this study, the study suggested that changes in the family system may have long-term effects.

Another study applied this functional family therapy model to serious, multiple offenders who had been institutionalized (Barton, Alexander,

Waldron, Turner, & Warburton, 1985). After release, paraprofessionals saw the families in their homes and the youths also received job and school placement services. At a 15-month follow-up, the recidivism rate for this group was 60%, compared with a rate of 93% for a group receiving group-home treatment only.

The replication of this family therapy model in different treatment locations with different populations (status offenders, criminal offenders, first-time and multiple offenders, middle class and lower class) was possible because the therapy was divided into discrete, teachable phases calling for different therapist skills and goals for each phase. A detailed therapist manual described these phases and therapist tasks (Alexander & Parsons, 1982). The phases were also described in a recent replication (Gordon et al., 1995):

> The intervention was divided into three phases: assessment, therapy and education. During the assessment phase, therapists determined which repetitive interaction sequences among family members were maladaptive, and which family members' behaviors needed to change to reduce conflict and promote cohesion. Interpersonal functions, such as contacting and distancing, were identified as providing payoffs for repeated interaction sequences. A reliable assessment instrument was developed for this phase (Roche, Moore, & Gordon, 1987). In the therapy phase, family members' motives underlying their conflictual interactions were relabeled to be benign or positive in an effort to lessen defensiveness and noncompliance. The good relationship skills of the therapists became indispensable during this phase. In the education phase, parenting skill deficits were remediated and family living skills taught in a structured manner (i.e., communication skills, problem solving skills, contingency management and contracting, limit setting, reinforcement). Therapists were careful not to recommend changes which would defeat interpersonal functions (therapy increasing resistance to change. (pp. 65–66)

The final sessions focused on the generalization of the skills the family learned to a variety of naturally occurring situations, with the therapist assigning homework requiring progressively more independence.

A case example of functional family therapy that is fairly typical of our population of low income families with a delinquent follows:

> Larry G was a 16-year-old referred for family therapy by the juvenile court following his third theft, as well as for gang fights after school, as an alternative to institutional placement. Mr. G was physically disabled and stayed home, where he did household chores. Mrs. G worked in a paper plant. They also had a daughter, Heather, 14 years old. Two therapists recently trained in the functional family therapy model met with most of the family weekly in the family's home.

Over three to four sessions, their assessment of the family revealed that communication was defensive, with much blaming and little listening. Members believed the worst of each other's motives and small problems did not get resolved, often escalating into severe conflict after which one person would leave the house. Larry was frequently criticized by both parents, often for his temper. He sought distance from his mother but wanted contact with his father; both parents wanted distance from Larry. They often picked at him until he lost his temper and left to be with his delinquent friends. Heather was her father's favorite, and reliably got both parent's attention by tattling on Larry. Her poor compliance with chores and homework was not noticed by Mr. G and was only sporadically targeted for criticism by Mrs. G. Mr. G loosely monitored the children while Mrs. G was at work, and did not carry out Mrs. G's restrictive policies with either child. The children had no input into rules or consequences, and the parents complained of irresponsible academic, peer, and sibling behavior.

During the therapy phase, covering much of the next five sessions, the family's resistance to changing interaction patterns with each other and to the therapists' suggestions was lessened. (Supervisor requirements were greatest during this phase to provide ideas for handling the resistance and to support the therapists.) The therapists explained how each family member unwittingly got locked into defensive patterns, and how the parents' lack of support for compliance and appropriate behaviors was a result of their own parents' teaching. Larry's motives for acting out with his friends, seen by his parents as lack of respect for them, was portrayed as seeking approval from peers that he was missing at home, and as wanting his parents to be proud of his independence and ability to make decisions that weren't disastrous. Mr. G's distancing of Mrs. G was relabeled as respecting her need for privacy after a tiring day at work. Heather's tattling on Larry was relabeled as her desire for her parents' approval. The presence of conflict was repeatedly tied to poor communication skills and the lack of a specific conflict resolution plan rather than ascribing them to negative personality traits and motives of family members.

The education phase, covering most of five sessions, included teaching and prompting the parents to use reinforcement (verbal, granting privileges) for the children's compliance. Larry also learned stress reduction techniques such as taking a walk outside when he noticed that he was getting angry, telling himself that he was strong enough to withstand provocation by immature peers, and taking several deep breaths while telling himself that he could "keep his cool." Heather agreed to report only on Larry's improved behavior (thereby allowing her to continue to get parental attention). Mr. G relayed these messages to Larry via notes placed on his bedroom door, allowing him to maintain his distance from Larry. Family members practiced active listening and "I" messages during therapy sessions and also with weekly homework assignments (which they completed about 50% of the time). The therapists structured a problem-solving format for the family to follow and led them through several rehearsals. Larry agreed to report to Mr. G when he was going to be late coming home from school (or be grounded the next day) and Mr. G agreed to refrain from criticizing Larry when he brought his friends home. Improved homework and chore compliance led to Larry's being allowed to have friends stay overnight, which increased the supervision he received from his parents. With the decrease in conflict, Mrs. G and Mr. G spent more time discussing improvements and started some family activities, such as trips to a local skating rink and renting movies selected by all. Two follow-up therapy sessions 4 weeks and 3 months after termination revealed minimal conflict and confidence that the family could resolve future problems on their own.

One clear difference between the social learning parent-training approaches and the functional family therapy approach is that the latter devotes a specific phase of treatment to overcoming noncompliance, using specified techniques. Recently, some behaviorists have borrowed a "resistance-reducing" technique from family systems therapy and subjected it to empirical scrutiny. So-called paradoxical instructions alone and in conjunction with reframing (verbal explanation that changes the meaning of a particular situation) had positive effects with noncompliant clients who made little or no progress in behavior therapy (Wolpe & Ascher, 1976). Kolko and Milan (1983) applied this technique in the treatment of families of three delinquents who were routinely truant. Their problem behaviors were reframed in a way to maximize the client's opposition, thus setting them up for the paradoxical intervention in which the symptom was prescribed. One of the delinquents, a 15-year-old boy, was described as having a terrible attitude, not taking his school work seriously, and not assuming responsibility for himself. The reframing procedure involved the therapist interpreting the boy's behavior to both him and his mother as immature, impulsive, and childish. The paradoxical intervention was illustrated in the therapist's statement to the youth:

> "Psychologists sometimes find that children, somewhat younger than you, go through a phase in which they like to misbehave before they are able to become mature young men. This pattern is sort of like a last fling during which the child may get into trouble for a while. It seems that you have not passed through this childish phase yet. It is to be expected that you will be misbehaving and getting into trouble for a while longer than your more mature friends until you grow up like them. We don't want to do anything that might hinder this stage in your development, so we don't want you to try things you might be too young and immature to handle. It seems it would be best for you if you didn't go to school

until you grow through this childish stage; we don't want you to fight the urge
to misbehave since you apparently aren't mature enough to control it." (Kolko
& Milan, 1983, p. 657)

The results of this technique, measured with a multiple baseline
design, indicated significant improvement in the client's attendance and
academic performance, with sustained gains through subsequent reinforcement of the newly appropriate behavior.

In the preceding review of family therapy studies of delinquents, the
approaches were classified according to the model of family therapy
utilized. This classification is subjective in that the investigators chose to
emphasize and conceptualize certain components of their interventions. In
the clinical examples given in this chapter, proponents of other models
could easily reconceptualize the description of the active ingredients to
support their own theoretical orientation. In the absence of reliable coding
systems for therapist behaviors during therapy, we are unfortunately prisoners of the investigator's judgment as to the effective components of
family therapy.

Barriers to Implementing Family Interventions

Integrating different therapeutic perspectives into a coherent, multilevel
approach to delinquency represents a challenging theoretical problem. It is
made even more difficult by the fact that the settings in which services are
provided support an individual responsibility orientation (Gordon & Arbuthnot, 1987). For example, as Bell (1975) noted in reference to the justice
system:

> Our laws and traditional procedures require individual work with the offender,
> as exemplified in probation, institutional placement, or parole. We do not place
> the family on probation, we do not institutionalize the family and consequently,
> it is never on parole. Correctional relations with individuals are written into
> statute. (p. 252)

An additional problem related to the separation of a violent offender
from his/her family in an institution is that the diagnosis of character disorder
is made in the absence of a good developmental history. Potentially treatable
organic and psychotic disorders are thus missed and minimal attempts are
made at meaningful treatment (Lewis, Shanok, Grant, & Ritvo, 1984).

Moreover, whereas juvenile courts routinely mandate treatment for the
individual offender, most do not require family members to attend therapy
sessions, nor are parental figures typically seen as a viable part of the
rehabilitative solution. To the extent that parents are involved, they are

frequently (albeit inadvertently in many cases) blamed for their youngster's difficulties and expected to participate in the treatment process in ways that may not be well established in their behavioral repertoires (such as meeting in a therapist's office on a regular and timely basis). Unfortunately, the kind of outreach efforts (e.g., home and school visits) needed to engage and maintain these families in treatment are frequently resisted by therapists and clinic administrators, who find scheduling and billing for individual appointments on their "turf" more convenient (Gordon & Arbuthnot, 1987). The problems of providing services on an outpatient basis are further compounded in institutional settings. These settings are often located far from the youngster's community, leaving individual and group treatment as the only adjuncts to the institutional milieu (Gordon & Arbuthnot, 1987; Jurkovic, 1984).

Multisystemic and Other Family Therapy Approaches

Among the nonbehavioral family therapy methods, strategic and structural family therapy are the most widely practiced methods among family therapists. Empirical support for their use with juvenile offenders is too meager to report here. Suffice it to say that behavioral–systems methods principally differ from strategic and structural methods in that in the latter (1) it is assumed that the family already possesses most of the necessary skills for healthy functioning and does not require skill training; (2) the methods rely on paradox and reframing to change the family's self-perception and motivation; (3) the emphasis is on short-term intervention (6 to 12 sessions).

Recently, a number of investigators have called for intervention strategies that look beyond the particular individual and even family pattern of juveniles to include all the various levels of analysis, from biology to society, that are relevant to understanding and treating delinquents (Clark et al., 1982; Jurkovic, 1984; Kirschner & Kirschner, 1986). That is, the entire ecological complex of the problem must be systematically considered to avoid treatment strategies that are either too narrowly focused or too broadly and loosely defined to be effective.

Linkages between family, school, and parents' workplaces have been demonstrated to impact the development and treatment of serious delinquent behavior. Bronfenbrenner (1986) reviewed a theoretically convergent but dispersed body of research on social systems that influence the functioning of families. Societal changes that have led to an explosion of single-parent, mother-headed households and stepfamilies have resulted in mothers who have less social support and engage in more unilateral decision-making, which are associated with their children's aggressive acting out. The linkage between parental behavior and peer group influences in child deviance is shown by the increased susceptibility of latchkey children to antisocial peer pressure as a result of weak parental monitoring (Bronfenbrenner, 1986).

School performance and good parent–teacher communication are positively related (Fine & Carlson, 1992). Children's social and academic adjustment is affected by family dysfunction, such as marital conflict (Cummings & Davies, 1994).

Job linkages to family and school processes have been demonstrated in Bronfenbrenner's (1986) review, with research linking increased parental irritability toward children and lower academic achievement by the children when fathers were seen only rarely. Sex of the child predicted whether full-time employment by the mother was harmful (boys) or beneficial (girls) to her children.

Such intersystem connections argue strongly for coordinated interventions that impact several systems (peer group, family, school, and individual) simultaneously. For example, a therapist might improve family communication patterns and involve the adolescents in decision making while concurrently initiating joint parent–teacher conferences to coordinate efforts to improve academic performance and monitor peer relationships. In addition, it could be arranged for the acting out adolescent to get social skills training among nondeviant peers as Feldman, Caplinger, and Wodarski (1983) found effective, followed by individual therapy aimed at developing anger control and stress reduction strategies.

Similar recommendations were made by Mulvey, Arthur, and Reppucci (1993) in their review of prevention and treatment studies. They stressed the need to take a broad-based approach because it is unreasonable to expect a single intervention to have lasting effects, as if it could "innoculate" delinquents against future antisocial behavior. Ongoing provision of services to children identified as at high risk for continuing antisocial behavior in middle and later childhood is more realistic and likely to be effective than the current, one-shot approach during times of crisis. They recommended that these services address the multiple issues of the youth's family, school, and peer relations to have an impact, because behavior must be addressed in its social context.

> Early intervention programs that provide comprehensive care to families, cognitive behavioral curriculae that are coupled with changes in the school environment, and individual interventions that work in the adolescents' home, school, and peer environments all provide more impressive results than myopic programs of similar type. (Mulvey et al., 1993, p. 158)

A recent development along these lines for serious, repeated delinquency is the multisystemic approach described by Henggeler and Borduin

(1990), Henggeler and colleagues (1986), Henggeler, Melton, Smith, and Schoenwald (1993), and Henggeler (1996). Both the juvenile's intra- and extrafamiliar systems are treated concurrently via school consultation, increased parental monitoring, support of peer groups, individual treatment, and development of social support for single-parent families. For antisocial behavior, graduate student therapists taught families to contract, allowing adolescents' input into family decisionmaking in the context of an authoritative parenting style. Keeping contracts resulted in increasingly responsible child and adolescent behavior accompanied by increased freedoms. Parents were taught to set consistent limits, whereas discipline was relabeled a caring parental attitude to diminish hostile communication. For anxious–withdrawn juveniles, therapists encouraged involvement in peer group and community activities while teaching social skills in individual supportive sessions. The therapist consulted any adult with whom the delinquent had close ties to promote conventional and anticriminal behaviors and attitudes. The parents' marital relationship was often the focus briefly, to reduce conflict and increase cooperation. This multisystems approach, compared with typical community mental health services, produced significant reductions in aggression and conduct problems, immaturity, and anxiety while increasing maternal affection for the sample. A 2.4-year follow-up of serious juvenile offenders showed that those who received this multisystemic family preservation approach were less likely to be rearrested than were those who received traditional community services (Henggeler et al., 1993), and that the former was more effective than individual therapy in preventing criminal and violent behavior at a 4-year follow-up (Borduin et al., 1995). This follow-up period, which is lengthy by present standards, is necessary to detect the effects of treatments on recidivism. The promising results of Henggeler's group adds credence to the growing recommendations that multisystemic, coordinated treatment in the delinquent's natural environment is necessary to reduce recidivism. It is encouraging that older, serious offenders can respond to a coordinated intervention approach.

Factors Enhancing Treatment Efficacy

A number of factors mediate the efficacy of family intervention apart from the model used. Therapist skills contribute at least as much to the outcome as does the model (Alexander, Barton, Schiavo, & Parsons, 1976). Relationship skills such as warmth, humor, a nonblaming stance, and integrating feelings and behavior, plus structuring skills such as directiveness, clarity, and specificity positively influenced therapeutic outcomes. Measuring such characteristics in actual therapy sessions has proven difficult, so the development of reliable and efficient therapist coding systems is needed before the contribution to the interaction of model, client, and therapist variables can be studied (Grossman, Gordon, & Moore, 1988). In our own work training graduate students and paraprofessionals (teachers, agency case-workers, probation officers, social workers), certain characteristics predict that someone will be able to make sustained efforts at family interventions and positive change for families. In addition to good interpersonal skills, intelligence and creativity help in overcoming noncompliance and in devising innovative solutions to family problems. A balance of enthusiasm and realism is necessary to keep the therapists motivated to persist in the face of the family's inertia and crises. Maturity and life experience, such as being married or divorced and involvement in raising children, are important not only for credibility with families, but also for empathy and wisdom in selecting parenting techniques to teach. Finally, altruism, as seen in the desire to reduce stress in every family member, ensures that therapists are motivated by more than job requirements or salary.

Another factor mediating effectiveness of various models of family intervention is the location of the intervention sessions. For low-income, multiple-problem families, intervening in the home appears necessary for success (Barton et al., 1985; Gordon et al., 1988; Kinney, Madsen, Fleming, & Haapala, 1976; Michaels & Green, 1979). When interventions occur at a clinic, attrition is so marked that 70% to 85% of referred families fail to receive a sufficient number of sessions for the intervention to have an appreciable effect. Even when juvenile courts order a family's attendance at a community mental health center (CMHC), the modal number of sessions families complete is five, one half to one third the number normally needed for positive effect (Empey & Gordon, 1989). Attrition is high when the intervention is center based because of the stigma involved in being seen at a mental health center, the expense and unreliability of transportation to the center, and the difficulty in getting all family members to the center at the same time. When the intervention is home based, families are more comfortable, assessment of family interaction and environment is more valid, and generalization of skills learned during sessions is more likely to occur. The multisystemic approach of Henggeler, Pickrel, Brondino, and Crouch (1996) discussed earlier found that 98% of families completed a full course of treatment done in the home, versus 78% of families receiving usual community services, who dropped out immediately after referral.

Another factor that enhances effectiveness is support by the juvenile court. Family therapy can be mandated or recommended. In one study, whether the family therapy was court-referred or court-ordered was unrelated to the number of sessions attended at CMHCs. However, when therapists and probation officers communicated frequently about the family's attendance, attendance increased (Empey & Gordon, 1989). Court support for family therapy via diversion (that is, recommending voluntary treatment as an alternative to a court hearing) also appeared to increase families' motivation to attend and, subsequently, the likelihood that a full "dose" of the treatment will be received. Community support also enhanced family therapy completion rates. This support can come from social service agencies, schools, neighbors, relatives, and the media if they perceive that the family interventions available are appropriate and effective.

GROUP TREATMENT APPROACHES

In this section we present an overview of several contemporary group approaches to the treatment and prevention of delinquency, chosen either because of demonstrated effectiveness or promise. The bases for our recommendations are spelled out elsewhere (Arbuthnot, Gordon, & Jurkovic, 1987; Gordon & Arbuthnot, 1987), so we do not attempt a thorough review of the group literature. There are, however, several issues associated with group approaches that need to be addressed to guide the mental health and juvenile justice professional.

The Nature of Group Interventions

Historically, group-oriented interventions have played a major role in the treatment of delinquents, with their greatest initial popularity in the 1950s (Lavin, Trabka, & Kahn, 1984). The early approaches to group treatment were largely based on psychoanalytic or client-centered models, or derivatives thereof, although many group programs were simply didactic in nature. In the 1960s and 1970s, group interventions became more discussion oriented and focused more on present problems rather than on historical antecedents of antisocial behavior (e.g., Glasser's [1965] reality therapy). Although numerous programs continue to be based upon these earlier orientations, many contemporary interventions reflect the growing influence of the cognitive-behavioral and cognitive-developmental models.

Group interactions (in contrast with individual therapy) may contribute to the development of abilities or correction of deviance through the group experience. Yalom (1975) suggested that this experience includes commonality, imitation, education, catharsis, social skills training, interpersonal learning, group cohesion, altruism, and existential factors. The group leader or therapist, among other responsibilities, facilitates group development, defines its purposes, establishes norms and group identity, tests leaders, and develops a psychologically safe and trusting atmosphere. It is essential that group leaders be flexible as to the group's directions and dynamics as members test, grow, and question, but equally essential is the necessity for the leader or facilitator to allow the group to function as a group, to develop cohesion, and thereby (it is assumed), to effect change. To be an effective group leader or facilitator, one must exhibit certain qualities including flexibility, genuineness, honesty, and empathy. The leader must be discriminating about when to provide structure and when to allow the group process to unfold, able to withstand high levels of provocation, and able to monitor interpersonal processes, including one's own. A good sense of humor will not only help the group dynamic, but will also ward off "burnout."

Do Group Approaches Work?

Unfortunately, much of the research on the efficacy of group interventions with juvenile delinquents is not promising (Julian & Kilmann, 1979; Parloff & Dies, 1977; Romig, 1978). There are few outcome studies that examine behaviors, and fewer still that focus on changes external to the group or institution. Among the weaknesses of outcome studies (especially with institutionalized, aggressive delinquents), are that (1) participants are not described specifically beyond general categories such as "delinquent" or "aggressive"; (2) treatment duration is ignored as a variable and attendance rates are not factored into the analyses; (3) "therapist" characteristics are typically ignored (e.g., age, race, sex, training, level of experience, orientation, etc.); (4) description of the treatment program is sketchy or absent and fidelity to the model is rarely monitored; (5) outcome measures, usually short-term recidivism, are psychometrically weak, ignoring effects of time, the inadequacy of official records, and other offenses committed; (6) treatment goals are not individualized as outcome measures (Julian & Kilmann, 1979); (7) design problems exist, such as selective samples, nonrandom assignment, inappropriate or absent control groups, nonblind scoring, and the like; and (8) overreliance upon institutionalized samples is common.

In addition, there are inherent difficulties in the group approach that mitigate against effectiveness. First, most groups are artificial in their composition. That is, they are not the groups to which the juvenile belongs in his/her natural environment. This may not be a serious problem for some therapeutic processes internal to the group itself. However, it is a problem in the transfer and maintenance of group treatment outcomes. Problems that arise from dysfunctional families, peer groups, schools, or neighborhoods cannot be addressed directly in a group composed of institutionalized delinquents from diverse backgrounds, neighborhoods, and cities. Although they may share "common experiences," these can only be addressed indirectly through verbal interactions, and skills for dealing with dysfunctional natural groups cannot be optimally developed and translated into effective action as a result of mere discussion (and perhaps role playing) with similar victims.

The basis for group composition may work against treatment effectiveness. Typically, groups are composed of a certain number of individuals who happen to be available at a common time. Each brings to the group a different history, pattern of offense, etiology, family experience, social environment, ethnicity, personality, cognitive capacity, and style, yet they will be treated together by common methods. If we attempt to make the groups more homogeneous, on what basis will we do this? If we choose the type of offense, we still face differential causes. If we choose a personality typology (Quay, 1987b), we still face differential offenses, intelligence, and family dynamics. Furthermore, even if we are able to make groups homogeneous on certain criteria, there is little reason to expect different youths to respond equally well to one particular type of treatment. In spite of these difficulties, and although the evidence is scant, it appears that homogeneous treatment groups may be more effective (Quay, 1987a).

A final issue concerning group composition is the question of whether groups should be homogeneous or heterogeneous in terms of the participants' antisocial or nonantisocial status. For example, should groups consist only of fellow youths with behavior problems, or would such youths benefit from interaction with and modeling of age mates who are more conventional and prosocial in their behavior?

Feldman (1992; Feldman et al., 1983) claimed that a detailed review of the literature demonstrates that

> treatment programs for antisocial youths must be significantly restructured if they are to achieve maximum success. Put briefly, it is essential to offer treatment in nonstigmatizing environments and in contexts that are comprised of large numbers of prosocial peers. The treatment setting ought to be as similar as possible to the antisocial youth's natural environment and, if feasible, an integral part of it . . . throughout, the subjects should receive maximum exposure to prosocial peers and minimum exposure to antisocial peers. (1992, p. 233)

Supportive of this view, Feldman (1992) claimed, is an interview study by Linden and Hackler (1973) of 13 to 15-year-old working-class boys that showed, among other things, that delinquency is greater for boys with weak ties to parents and/or conventional associates but strong ties to deviant peers. Feldman concluded that such data lead "to the supposition that antisocial youths ought to be treated primarily—and perhaps exclusively— in prosocial environments" (p. 235). This is, of course, one option for treatment. The body of data also could be interpreted to suggest merely that we need to *somehow* provide the missing positive influences of parents and conventional peers, whether it be via positive peer groups or some other developmentally facilitative intervention (e.g., moral reasoning development, as discussed in the next paragraphs).

Feldman's St. Louis project (Feldman et al., 1983) is frequently cited as supportive of the larger claim of the necessity of interventions in heterogeneous groups. This project included several hundred youths ages 7 to 15. Referred youths were characterized by "antisocial motor behaviors, physical contacts, verbalizations, object interference, and distracting others" (Feldman, 1992, p. 236). They were about two-thirds white, and one-third black, and with fathers who were primarily skilled or unskilled workers. Nonreferred youths were recruited from the Jewish Community Centers Association of St. Louis and were not screened for behavior problems.

Some intervention groups were mixtures of referred and nonreferred youths, whereas others were exclusively referred or nonreferred. Treatments included traditional group work, the social learning method, or minimal treatment (see Feldman et al., 1983, pp. 70–75 for descriptions). As Feldman (1992) noted, the relationship between group composition and outcome was rather weak, although most trends were in the expected direction. Treatment method proved not to be a good predictor of positive outcomes. In fact, traditional group work was notably ineffective, and, under some conditions, it was counterproductive. In contrast, the level of experience of the group leader was a strong predictor of outcome.

The greatest deteriorations in behavior were found in groups consisting of referred youths treated in unmixed groups by inexperienced leaders using traditional group work. However, if one excludes this group with such an unfortunate mix of characteristics and excludes the unmixed, "placebo" minimal-treatment group (which showed no change), all of the remaining four unmixed groups showed positive changes. Only two mixed groups (of six) showed positive changes, both of whom were "placebo" groups. Thus, one might well conclude from the St. Louis study that, in contrast to the claim that antisocial youths must be treated in heterogeneous groups, antisocial youths generally do better (or at least not show a worsening in behavior) if (1) treated in homogeneous groups, or (2) not treated at all, or (3) if treated, at least not treated by traditional social work group methods.

Treating Symptoms versus Causes

Most traditional group treatment approaches are left with a logically impossible task: to treat or prevent delinquency by treating not necessarily the "causes" of the antisocial behavior but, rather, the symptoms. To "do something to" individual offenders, or groups of offenders, in the unreal environment of the institution or CMHC does little to address the possible multiplicity of causes of their offenses. What then should we be doing? Weis and Sederstrom (1981), in their compelling monograph for the Office of Juvenile Justice and Delinquency Prevention (OJJDP) on preventing serious delinquency, argued convincingly that

> intervention should be directed toward the social development processes which result in juveniles becoming delinquents or serious delinquents: the focus should be institutional and organizational change of the socializing institutions of family, school, peers, law, and the community. (p. 61)

Whereas we should not be surprised to find sociologists recommending that the causes of delinquency reside within institutions and that, therefore, treatment and prevention programs ought to be addressed properly at those institutions, we can take their argument one step further. What is it about those institutions that has failed the particular individual who has become delinquent? Might we speculate from a psychological perspective that, when faced with an individual offender, the exact causes are irrelevant as long as we can treat the symptom? This reductionist game has led us nowhere for decades.

Rather than dealing with intrapsychic "causes," it may be more profitable to focus on the more immediate deficits related to antisocial behavior—factors that affect behavioral choices, including various skill deficits (social, cognitive, and affective). These developmental deficits are arguably the product of the institutional failures about which Weis and Sederstrom (1981) were concerned. As individual practitioners are often impotent to address these institutions, clinicians may do well to follow the recommendations of Little and Kendall (1979), who suggested that we focus on specific, observable problems common to large numbers of delinquents.

At the same time, we recognize the multiplicity of causes of antisocial behavior, ranging from the highly specific and individualistic, such as biochemical imbalances, to the general and broadly societal, such as lack of job opportunities or racial discrimination. Our effort to prevent delinquency ought to include a variety of weapons, tactics, and strategies, from the micro (e.g., pharmacotherapy or individual psychotherapy) to the macro (institutional change) to the societal (political and policy changes). Certainly, group interventions are not appropriate for dealing with all of the factors that influence antisocial acts. We should utilize them for those factors for which they are best suited.

Types of Group Interventions

Groups seem particularly well suited for interventions that do things *for* youth rather than *to* them. What we can do for delinquents in groups transcends, to a large extent, intrapsychic differences and is largely transferable, thereby avoiding the major limitations of group interventions. Effective group work addresses the developmental skill deficits that are common to most delinquents: poor interpersonal problem solving, impulsivity, poor role-taking and lack of empathy, and poor sociomoral reasoning abilities (Arbuthnot et al., 1987).

Positive Peer Group Interventions

Gottfredson (1982) noted that peer group interventions seem to be based in the observation that youths who engage in delinquent behavior tend to have delinquent friends. It is not clear which is the causal factor, if either. To some theorists (Glueck & Glueck, 1950; Hirschi, 1969) this is simply a further indicator of delinquency—that antisocial youth will associate with other antisocial youth. However, others (Akers, Krohn, Lanza-Kaduce, & Rodesevich, 1979; Sutherland & Cressey, 1974) have argued that this is an indication that antisocial values and attitudes are learned by association with antisocial peers.

Given the latter interpretation, if peer groups can influence members to acquire delinquent orientations or to engage in delinquent acts then, by the same token, peer groups should be able to accomplish the reverse—that is, to promote positive attitudes, values, and behaviors. Historically, a number of programs have been instituted based on the presumed potential for positive influence of the peer group, including peer counseling (Gray & Tindall, 1978; Varenhorst, 1984), sensitivity training (Benne, Bradford, & Lippit, 1964), and various forms of group psychotherapy (e.g., Corsini & Rosenberg, 1955; Hill, 1974).

As Gottfredson (1987) noted, especially strong claims have been made in the more popularized literature for the efficacy of peer group interventions modeled on the Guided Group Interaction (GGI) approach of Bixby, McCorkle, and McCorkle (1951). This model assumes that individuals can be influenced by peer group discussion to comport their behavior to conventional social rules by gaining social rewards for conforming to conventional norms. Trained adult leaders ask questions, create norms of reassurance, repeat ideas expressed by group members, and summarize significant ideas. This process presumably results in group members recognizing deficiencies in their attitudes, values, and behavior.

Various derivatives of this general model emerged in the 1970s—Positive Peer Culture (Vorath & Brendtro, 1974), Peer Group Counseling (Howlett & Boehm, 1975), and Peer Culture Development (National School Resource Network, 1980).

Gottfredson (1987) reviewed the quasi-experimental research on these models, with generally negative conclusions. For example, in the first true experiment involving a GGI-derivative program, Peer Culture Development in a high school setting, the results "lend[ed] no support to any claim of benefit of treatment" and "the effects appear[ed] preponderantly harmful" (p. 708). Although the negative outcomes were not large, there were significant increases in "waywardness," tardiness, and self-reported delinquency, as well as decreases in attachment to parents. This last effect was attributed, at least in part, to a common focus in group discussions on home and parent issues, resulting in "a weakening of parental bonding as a source of restraint" (p. 709).

Gottfredson (1987) further concluded that such approaches should continue only in an experimental setting. He did observe, however, that GGI-type programs in community (nonschool) settings were as effective as incarceration, and were thus cost effective given their significantly lower expense, and probably superior to traditional probation (an effect attributable to the greater supervision supplied by GGI).

Interpersonal Problem Solving and Social Skills

Spivack's research (Mahoney & Arnkoff, 1978; Spivack & Shure, 1974) suggested a consistent link between deficient interpersonal problem-solving skills and the antisocial behavior of both criminal offenders and maladjusted individuals. By using assessment devices such as the Means–Ends Problem-Solving (MEPS) Test (Platt & Spivack, 1975), in which an individual is presented with both the beginning and conclusion to a behavioral episode and is asked to supply the intervening means, Spivack's group showed deficiencies in deviant individuals' solutions in terms of both quantity and realism of the intervening means. Remediation of deficiencies in interpersonal problem solving presumably prove beneficial in reducing antisocial behavior by helping youths to see the connective behavioral choices between given situations and desired goals.

Sarason and his colleagues (Sarason, 1968; Sarason & Ganzer, 1969, 1973) developed an extensive program in the training of social skills for delinquent youth which, although not specifically aimed at the underlying cognitive component of problem solving, no doubt is effective at stimulating some cognitive development. Sarason's program typically included 16 1-hour training sessions that emphasized the development of both alternative actions and consideration of consequences. Sarason's research included both modeling of social skills (combining rehearsals or role plays and critiques) and discussion sessions. Few differences were noted between components. Improvements were noted in institutionalized samples in attitudes, self-concept, and overt behavior. Furthermore, when subjects were classified by Quay's (1987b) subtypes, differential outcomes were achieved, suggesting that the program is likely to be effective for some, but not all, delinquent offenders. Perhaps most importantly, a 3-year follow-up of participants showed lowered recidivism rates compared with control groups and the institution populations as a whole.

Others have found differences favoring role plays of problem solving over mere discussion in terms of reducing antisocial behavior (Scopetta, 1972). Further, including parents in the training of interpersonal and problem-solving skills produced both lower recidivism rates overall and less severe offenses for those who recidivated (Collingwood & Genthner, 1980).

The components of social skills training that reduce antisocial behavior have not been identified; most likely, they vary widely among individuals. Effectiveness in reducing delinquency may be a function not only of the improvements in a targeted social skill, but in accompanying cognitive and affective empathy. This approach may yet show greater promise when combined with other critical cognitive affective and social skills development program.

Controlling Impulsivity

It has long been argued on an intuitive basis that delinquent youths should be expected to demonstrate greater impulsivity in behavioral choices. Empirically, this has not been clearly shown (Arbuthnot et al., 1987), perhaps because of our inabilities to operationalize and validly measure this trait rather than in lack of conceptual validity.

More convincing regarding the role of impulse control in delinquency are interventions with aggressive or otherwise behaviorally disordered youths to teach skills to enable the control of impulsivity. Several researchers (Camp, 1977; Camp & Bash, 1981; Kazdin, 1982; Kendall & Hollon, 1979; Lochman, 1992; Meichenbaum, 1977; Urbain & Kendall, 1980) have devised interventions for helping youth to control impulsive decision making. Most of these use a combination of modeling and cognitive strategies for dealing with problem situations. For example, Camp's program involves learning and saying out loud (and subsequently fading) specific steps in problem solving, such as (1) "What's my problem?"; (2) "What's my plan?"; (3) "Am I using my plan?"; and (4) "How did I do?" Lochman (1992) used a similar cognitive-behavioral approach with aggressive boys, focusing on anger control. A 3-year follow-up showed lower rates of drug and alcohol involvement and higher levels of self-esteem and social problem-solving skills than untreated controls. Unfortunately delinquency rates were unaffected.

Such strategies are effective, no doubt, not only because they train individuals to be more deliberate in their decisions, considering alternatives and evaluating choices, but also may result in some degree of general cognitive development. In a basic sense, impulse control strategies may work because they are an elaborate and repetitive means of getting a youth to interpose a delay between the impulse and subsequent action, perhaps similar to the old "take a deep breath and count to 10" remedy for controlling one's anger. This delay may or may not result in the engagement of more conventional problem-solving skills.

Role-Taking Abilities and Empathy

The work of Piaget and other cognitive-developmental psychologists has long suggested that as a consequence of both biological and social maturation, individuals acquire the ability to decenter, to take more than one perspective regarding a thing or situation simultaneously, and to thereby enable more objective, less egocentric, and more realistic thinking. Should this normal maturational process be limited, the resulting developmental delay would result in individuals who "systematically misread societal expectations, misinterpret the actions and intentions of others, and . . . act in ways which (would be) judged to be callous and disrespectful to the rights of others" (Chandler, 1973, p. 326).

Such deficits in the perspective-taking abilities of youth have been significantly related to delinquency (Arbuthnot et al., 1987). The intervention literature further suggests that programs designed to enhance the development of this ability can reduce recidivism (Chandler, 1973; Little, 1978/1979). Chandler's research, for example, showed that role-taking abilities can be enhanced through experiences that compel alternate role taking. His program consisted of 10 weekly, half-day sessions in which chronically delinquent boys participated in all of the various roles (developing, portraying, acting out, taping, and critiquing such skits) involved in making videotaped productions of situations typically experienced by adolescents. The experience resulted in enhanced role-taking abilities and reduced recidivism at an 18-month follow-up.

An alternative empathy development program combined didactic and experiential training (Avery, Rider, & Haynes-Clements, 1981; Haynes & Avery, 1979; Kaplan, 1986). Participants learned skills in communication, listening, expression, recognition and reflection of feelings, and self-disclosure. Each session addressed different skills and emphasized the value of that skill in improving interpersonal relationships. Didactic sessions included discussions of the value of a skill, its specific components, and participants' reactions. Experiential sessions that followed included modeling of both inaccurate and accurate use of the skill, with each followed by practice (to contrast low and high levels of the skill and its effectiveness). Haynes and Avery (1979) found that adolescents trained in empathy and self-disclosure skills, compared to a matched control group, demonstrated significant increases in levels of empathic understanding (as measured by both written and behavioral measures). These changes were maintained over a 5-month follow-up (Avery, Rider, & Haynes-Clements, 1981).

Sociomoral Reasoning

To some, it is intuitively obvious that delinquent youths are "immoral" in the sense that they have not learned right from wrong and they lack the capacity to choose right behavior over wrong behavior. In spite of its logical appeal and popularity, this assumption is not accurate. In fact, the classic studies of Hartshorne and May (1928), Hartshorne, May, and Maller (1929), and Hartshorne, May, and Shuffleworth (1930) conducted some 60 years ago provided clear evidence that there is no particular relationship between *knowledge* of right and wrong behavior and actual behavior.

There is some indication (Arbuthnot et al., 1987) that whereas delinquents and nondelinquents do not differ in the extent to which they hold conventional and deviant values, those with dominantly conventional value systems show less delinquency. This pattern of relationships suggests that most youths know what is and is not acceptable behavior in the eyes of the larger society, but mere knowledge of the rules has little to do with behavior.

Jurkovic (1980) observed that most theories of delinquency (and we would add, of morality) have focused on the *content* of the delinquent's moral worldview, rather than upon its *structure*. In other words, teaching the rules of morality may or may not affect behavior, depending upon how information is interpreted and integrated into a larger, internally consistent model that the individual uses to view the world and make decisions. For example, theft may be merely a matter of pragmatism, with no necessary awareness of or concern about the owner or the expectations of society.

Numerous cross-sectional studies (Arbuthnot et al., 1987; Blasi, 1980) have shown considerable consistency between stages of moral reasoning and numerous behaviors. Moreover, one finds greater proportions of delinquents at the preconventional stages (1 and 2), and of nondelinquents at the conventional stages (3 and 4). The few delinquents found at Stage 3 are rarely involved in victim-related crimes and, unlike their preconventional peers, they experience guilt and/or self-disapproval over their actions.

The methodology for advancing moral reasoning stages has become quite highly developed (Arbuthnot & Faust, 1981; Hersch, Paolitto, & Reimer, 1979). Typically, one interventionist meets with small groups (e.g., of five or six participants) for weekly or biweekly sessions lasting from 45 to 60 minutes, over a period of several months. The group sessions are carefully planned by the group leader or facilitator and consist largely of guided Socratic discussions of ethical dilemmas, but also incorporate other activities, such as roleplays and simulations. The participants should ideally be at adjacent stages (e.g., Stages 2 and 3), but when working with delinquents, are more often homogeneous (Stage 2). The facilitator structures debate between participants who reason at adjacent stages on particular issues raised by the dilemma (e.g., law, property rights, trust, life, obligation to act), or, if all participants reason at the same stage, on supportive reasons for different behavioral choices, but the nature of the discussions is always directed toward the underlying reasoning and is intended to create sufficient cognitive disequilibrium over time to stimulate advances in reasoning. It is generally acknowledged that presenting participants with "+1" stage reasoning (dilemmas presented that are of the next stage of moral reasoning) is most effective in this regard. Dilemmas are chosen for their interest to the participants as well as for their appropriateness to the groups' age level and the desired stage transition.

That development of higher sociomoral reasoning abilities can result in prosocial behavior changes has been demonstrated by Arbuthnot and Gordon (1986) and Arbuthnot (1992). Their application of sociomoral reasoning development procedures with severely behavior-disordered adolescents resulted not only in significant reductions in problem behaviors, but also in greater reductions for individuals with greater increases in sociomoral reasoning abilities. Furthermore, these changes persisted over a 1-year follow-up. Informal follow-ups of the original samples over a 5-year period revealed no felony or misdemeanor charges against those in the treatment group, but several such charges against members of the matched control groups. Various individuals in the control group were charged with assault, manslaughter, and burglary—including one who admitted to over 120 break-ins in a 1-year period.

The sociomoral reasoning development approach has been utilized successfully with both noninstitutionalized (Arbuthnot & Gordon, 1986) and institutionalized delinquents (Gibbs, Arnold, Ahlborn, & Cheesman, 1984). To date it has not been employed with serious juvenile offenders. However, there is nothing to suggest that it would be inappropriate for such populations. One might expect deeply entrenched preconventional reasoning with low levels of affective empathy in serious offenders. As Gibbs (1997) observed, "We have emphasized the need to transform empathy in antisocial youth from superficial and erratic sentiments or impulses into a stable feeling for other people, one that can inhibit aggression and even prompt altruism" (p. 319). Further, Hoffman (quoted in Gibbs, 1997) related empathy-enhancing inductive teaching to moral education:

> It seems clear that one thing moral education can do is teach people a simple rule of thumb: Look beyond the immediate situation and ask questions such as

"What kind of experience does the person have in various situations beyond the immediate one?," "How will my action affect him or her, not only now but in the future?", and "Are there other people, present or absent, who might be affected by my actions?" If children learn to ask questions, their empathic responses should be less exclusively confined to the here and now. (p. 318)

CONCLUSIONS FROM META-ANALYTIC STUDIES

Several investigators have evaluated large numbers of treatment outcome studies (many of which are not cited in this chapter) to determine which variables are consistently related to larger treatment effect sizes. Garrett's meta-analysis (1985) focused on 111 treatment studies in residential placement. Behavioral approaches produced four times the effect in reducing recidivism in comparison with psychodynamic approaches and two times the recidivism effect of life-skills approaches. Contingency management and cognitive-behavioral methods were the most effective of the behavioral approaches. Comparing individual with family and group therapy showed that family therapy produced an average effect size five to six times greater than either individual or group treatment.

Gottschalk, Davidson, Gensheimer, and Mayer (1987) conducted a meta-analysis of 91 interventions in the community and discovered that interventions with a behavioral focus were more likely to be effective (though modest) than nonbehavioral methods. In general, the more hours put into treatment, the more likely that positive effects occur.

Andrews and colleagues (1990) reviewed 89 treatment studies, evaluating whether appropriateness of the service delivered predicted positive outcomes. Treatments were judged to be appropriate based upon six previous literature reviews from the authors, and typically involved the use of behavioral and social learning principles. Indicators of appropriateness include focusing the interventions on high-risk groups, targeting dynamic risk factors directly related to criminal behavior, and using cognitive-behavioral and social learning methods such as modeling and role playing. (See also Gendreau, 1996, for a detailed discussion of effective treatment strategies.) Studies that met their criteria had a strong mean effect size.

Lipsey (1990) performed a meta-analysis on over 400 interventions with delinquents and found behavioral and skill-oriented interventions to produce the largest effects, especially in community rather than institutional settings. This finding of the clear superiority of community over residential programs is a consistent finding in meta-analytic studies (Andrews et al., 1990; Gendreau & Ross, 1987), with effects on recidivism averaging 10% to 18% and ranging as high as 50%.

These meta-analytic studies show consistency in their general conclusions, while still leaving some unanswered questions regarding type of treatment for specific kinds of delinquents. In general, the most effective treatments (1) are rich in behavioral, cognitive-behavioral, and social learning components; (2) occur with higher risk offenders; (3) are not too brief; (4) occur in the community; and (5) involve people in the juvenile's natural environment.

RESIDENTIAL TREATMENT

Despite the emphasis on deinstitutionalization by the mental health and juvenile justice systems in recent years, placement of delinquents into residential facilities (correctional, institutional, hospital, and group-home settings) continues at a high rate (Quay, 1987a). There is little question that a certain segment of the juvenile offender population needs some form of residential treatment; however, empirically based criteria for identifying this group have not been established. Meta-analytic studies of behavioral residential treatment demonstrated that there is a mild to moderate treatment effect on behavior while in the institution (Quay, 1987a), but that the effect is significantly less compared with similar treatment delivered in the community (Andrews et al., 1990).

Rationale for Residential Treatment

Commission of a violent offense is often tantamount in the juvenile justice system to an automatic consequence of an out-of-home placement, partly because of concern that the youngster's antisocial behavior will continue and represent a threat to the community. However, it is not certain whether prediction of future violence and associated recommendations concerning confinement can be based entirely on previous behavior. Data collected by Hamparian, Schuster, Dinitz, and Conrad (1979), for example, indicated that initial violent offenses are not always followed by more severe acts of violence. Yet, a growing body of literature based upon longitudinal research (Eron, Huesmann, Dubow, Romanoff, & Yarmel, 1987; Gersten, Langer, Eisenberg, Simcha-Fagan, & McCarthy, 1976) suggests that in comparison with most behavioral patterns, aggression (especially in boys) is an enduring characteristic. Thus, current and past behavior may be the only clinically reliable and valid predictor of future violence and aggression (Lochman, 1984).

Whether or not youngsters have acted violently, those who are institutionalized have typically failed in less restrictive, community-based programs and have a long list of court referrals (Quay, 1987a), or these programs have not been available. Out-of-home placement, then, often represents a last resort by the court to control, rehabilitate, and/or punish these adolescents. Indeed, because of the perceived failure of the juvenile justice system to rehabilitate delinquent youngsters, together with public concern over the rising juvenile offense rate, particularly violent offenses, the longstanding role of rehabilitation in juvenile justice is being challenged. Many are now advocating a punishment and offense-based rather than rehabilitative and offender-based model, a publicly and politically popular position that supports confinement of more juvenile offenders (Hamparian, 1987).

Residential treatment may also be recommended by mental health professionals for psychological reasons related to the nature of the juvenile offender's behavioral and personality functioning, as well as to his/her environmental situation. For example, as noted earlier in discussing individually oriented treatment approaches, a therapeutic residential component is commonly seen as necessary in the treatment of violent and aggressive adolescents and other delinquents displaying significant personality deficiencies and psychopathology. According to psychodynamic therapists, the structure of a secure setting not only increases the likelihood of developing a therapeutic relationship, but also it serves to block offenders' typical defenses and acting out, facilitating the expression of internal conflicts that can provide an impetus for change (Keith, 1984; Strasburger, 1986; Weiner, 1982).

Placement of youngsters in residential facilities may also allow for more intensive observation and evaluation of their mental status and behavior. Interestingly, regardless of the reasons for their institutionalization, Lewis, Shanok, and Balla (1979) found that adolescents confined in training schools had more evidence in their histories of severe head and facial injuries, perinatal difficulties, and psychiatric symptomatology than did their nonincarcerated counterparts. These researchers also discovered that within the incarcerated group, the especially violent offenders had more perinatal difficulties, accidents, injuries, and ward admissions than did less violent offenders. In view of these findings, Lewis (1980) called for the "meticulous evaluation of any child accused of serious antisocial acts," including psychiatric interview; mental status examination; a family, social, and medical history; and possibly pediatric, neurological, psychological, and educational assessment. Not only might such an evaluation uncover a variety of potentially treatable problems, but it may also dissuade the clinician from dismissing the serious offender as "simply sociopathic" (Lewis, 1980). Unfortunately, the costs of such extensive evaluations make them unavailable for low-income delinquents and financially strapped state institutions.

A residential placement can also serve to give the delinquent's family a chance to reduce tensions and conflict. Intervening with parent education, family therapy, and/or parental social support can occur at this time and should continue after the delinquent's release back to the family. Care should be taken, however, that the family not "scapegoat" the delinquent while he or she is out of the home.

Many behavior therapists recommend residential treatment for severely disturbed and aggressive teenagers to obtain the necessary environmental control to teach them self-control and other skills (Moss & Rick, 1981; Varley, 1984). Varley (1984) pointed out:

> Outpatient work in the form of behaviorally oriented family therapy counseling, behavioral contracting, and cognitive behavioral programs seem more appropriate to the younger adolescent or school aged child where parents and community agencies have relatively more control over the child and his or her environment. (p. 291)

Type of Placement

In addition to uncertainty about who to place in residential care, systematic and objective decision rules about where to place youngsters are not available. Violent juvenile offenders may be handled through the juvenile justice system, the criminal (adult) justice system, or specialized juvenile justice, mental health, and social service programs (Hamparian, 1987). The result may be placement in an adult or juvenile correctional facility, a state or local psychiatric hospital, or some public or private residential treatment setting.

That various forms of bias may affect placement decisions was suggested by a study of violent, psychiatrically impaired delinquents from a single community: White youngsters were hospitalized, whereas blacks were incarcerated (Lewis, Shanok, Cohen, Kligteld, & Frisone, 1980). In another investigation, Lewis and one of her colleagues (Lewis & Shanok, 1980) found that 59.1% of the boys placed on a secure unit of a correctional school had previous psychiatric placements (hospitals or residential treatment facilities). The authors speculated that many of these youngsters had been transferred from a psychiatric setting because their behavior was too threatening to the staff. Many hospitals will work with only a few violent adolescents at a time, if at all, due to the demands they place upon staff time and energy (Cornwall, Behar, Conrad, Whiteside, & Mark, 1981). With the shrinking number of hospital beds and increasingly stringent criteria for hospitalization, Lewis and Shanok (1980) noted that "correctional facilities are now expected to function as psychiatric treatment centers for disturbed adolescents no longer welcome in therapeutic settings" (p. 953). In short, there are few treatment settings specifically designed to handle violent and disturbed adolescents (Hamparian, 1987).

Type of Treatment

The kind of treatment offered in residential facilities for juvenile offenders is highly variable. Depending upon the setting, it can range from mere custodial care to a sophisticated, multimodal approach. At a minimum, however, institutional treatment attempts to provide a "therapeutic milieu" in which every component of the program has a therapeutic function (Quay, 1987a). Gunderson's (1978) review of the literature revealed that positive therapeutic outcome is related to three qualities of the milieu: (1) distribution of responsibility and decision-making power; (2) clarity in treatment programs, roles, and leadership; and (3) high level of staff–patient interaction.

Other considerations include actively managing aggressive and disruptive behavior to ensure that the institution is physically safe for staff and youngsters. This requires well-trained staff members, fair and consistent controls, and resilience (Agee, 1979; Jones, 1984; Redl, 1959). Agee's (1979) project (Closed Adolescent Treatment Center), which illustrated these characteristics, was a program designed especially for incorrigible, violent adolescents. Her approach drew from behavioral principles such as the use of a point-level system that progressed from maximum external control to self-control. This program required frequent self- and group examination of the quality of relationships, a discipline system, family therapy, recreation, occupational therapy, community reentry programs, sex-offender therapy, a one-to-one relationship with assigned staff, and an education program (Agee & McWilliams, 1984). Agee's approach was tested at Ohio's Paint Creek Youth Center, and, in spite of significant improvements in the behavior of these serious delinquents while in this private institution compared with those sent to a state training school, there were no differences in arrests or self-reported delinquency a year after release. Loss of behavioral gains probably occurred because of weak aftercare plans to reinforce these gains in the community (school and family; Greenwood & Turner, 1993).

Point-level systems or token economies have proved beneficial in many treatment facilities for aggressive adolescents. Although they have been criticized for not generalizing to the natural environment and for serving only administrative control functions, programs such as Agee's and others (Phillips et al., 1973), designed to achieve specific treatment goals, have demonstrated the acquisition, maintenance, and generalization of desired behaviors (Varley, 1984).

Use of a therapeutic team is also now figuring importantly in the management of aggressive youngsters. Consisting of all staff who have contact with the patient, the team makes decisions concerning every phase of management (Jones, 1984). According to Jones, "A truly therapeutic, collaborative decision ... offers therapeutic checks and balances against possible individual countertransference reactions towards the provocative aggressive adolescent" (p. 375).

Although psychotropic medication is usually not used as a major component of the long-term management of aggressive delinquents, it may benefit some patients. Agitation, belligerence, assaultiveness, and irritability in an adolescent may reflect an underlying mental disorder (schizophrenia, major depression, bipolar disorder, attention-deficit/hyperactivity disorder, or organic mental disorder) that may be responsive to pharmacotherapy. Increasing knowledge about the psychobiological mechanisms mediating aggression has led to exploration of various drug treatments, including the use of antipsychotic medication, lithium, anticonvulsant medication, and stimulants (Jones, 1984; Kellner, 1978; Leventhal, 1984). More research is needed on the specific neuroregulatory actions of different medications as well as the interaction between drug therapy and other treatment modalities (Jones, 1984). For example, whereas medications may increase therapeutic accessibility by improving the client's attention, reality testing, memory, and control, psychotherapy may increase anxiety, which counters the biochemical effects of the medication (Klerman, 1975).

Jones (1984) also emphasized the importance of creating and/or maintaining what he referred to as a "psychological taproot" (or source of prosocial bonding) for the adolescent, which is a solid connection with parents or parental surrogates. In many cases this requires intensive therapeutic work with parental figures, which lays the foundation for both residential treatment and aftercare. "When society expects hospitals and psychiatric residential facilities to treat these youngsters without first correcting the social problem of an absent 'psychological taproot,' " according to Jones, "it is dumping social problems into treatment facilities" (p. 363).

Collaboration among the institution, community services, and family is another crucial factor in the successful management of institutionalized delinquents. A case manager may be necessary to serve as the youngster's advocate and to ensure continuity of care (Jones, 1984). Hamparian (1987) reviewed an innovative program developed by the Minnesota Department of Corrections for violent juveniles in which continuous case management played a central role. Another related feature of the program involved contracting with community persons to aid in treating and closely monitoring the adolescents for at least 6 months after discharge from the institution.

The types of psychological therapies used in residential settings include all the different approaches discussed earlier, with heaviest emphasis upon group approaches. Academic education, vocational training, and recreational and athletic activities are also often part of the program (Quay, 1987a). Many settings have experimented with combinations of different approaches. For example, Achievement Place (Phillips, Phillips, Fixsen, & Wolf, 1973), a family-oriented, group-home approach, used behavioral, relational, cognitive, and other procedures to treat juvenile offenders. Potts and colleagues (1986) also illustrated a comprehensive approach to the inpatient treatment of a severely antisocial adolescent integrating psychodynamic, behavioral, and cognitive concepts and methods into other aspects of the program.

There will continue to be an emphasis upon treating repeat offenders in institutional settings for some of the reasons noted above, and because communities often want to "send away" the most troublesome youth. That the status quo is likely to persist is unfortunate, because individual and group therapy are least likely to be effective in these settings. The reliance upon individual and group interventions in institutional settings is not necessarily a criticism of the institutions or the interventionists—after all, we must do *something* with incarcerated youth, and group work seems a worthwhile part of an overall treatment program (Quay, 1987a). This has certain costs, however. Perhaps greatest among these is the illusion that we have done something for these youths during their incarceration that will "fix" them (in the best tradition of the medical model) and set them going in the proper direction upon their release to their families and society. This is costly for several reasons. First, most traditional, residential, group-oriented treatment programs have not been demonstrated to work (Basta & Davidson, 1988; Greenwood & Turner, 1993; Julian & Kilmann, 1979; Parlof & Dies, 1977; Romig, 1978; Sholevar, 1995). Although some show improvement in paper-and-pencil tests of personality and attitudes, or in institutional behaviors (e.g., following rules and procedures), few have shown long-term impacts on meaningful postrelease behaviors such as recidivism, family adjustment, and employment. Second, incarceration allows juvenile court judges to maintain the belief that if youths do not "respond" to whatever community-based programs they are currently funding, there is no need to evaluate and possibly replace such programs with effective alternatives, as one can always send the recalcitrant few to a state institution. Third, incarceration encourages the general public to believe that funding for prison construction programs is money well spent when, in fact, youths sent to such institutions have a greater chance of committing subsequent offenses than do those assigned to alternative treatment programs (Hamparian, Davis, Jacobson, & McGraw, 1985). The consequence is that we not only fail to help the youths involved, but we also increase the monetary and safety costs to the larger community.

In 1993 OJJDP published a comprehensive strategy for dealing with serious, violent, and chronic juvenile offenders. After reviewing relevant statistics, research, and program evaluations, OJJDP concluded that large, congregate-care correctional facilities have not proven to be effective. Instead, they recommended nonresidential, community-based alternatives and small, secure confinement options to incarceration. Their recommendations were to strengthen the family (or family surrogate); support core social institutions such as schools, community organizations, and churches in socializing youths; promote delinquency prevention; intervene immediately, centering on the family; and identify and control the small group of serious, violent, and chronic offenders who do not respond to intervention and community-based treatment. This latter group, when they are a threat to community safety, should be placed in secure, community-based facilities or training schools as a last resort (OJJDP, 1993). Our survey of similar literature, coupled with our clinical and consulting experiences, leads us to the same conclusions.

RELATION OF SERVICE PROVIDERS TO THE JUVENILE COURT

Since its inception, the juvenile justice system has called on the mental health community to help carry out its mission to rehabilitate juvenile offenders. Service providers, however, have found their efforts in this endeavor frustrating and often unsuccessful (Jurkovic, 1984; Lewis, Sacks, Balla, Lewis, & Heald, 1973; Prentice & Kelly, 1966). Part of the problem is that mental health and juvenile justice personnel lack a common technical language and theoretical perspective on delinquency. Additionally, unreliable processing by the juvenile justice system via plea bargaining and undercharging are problematic (Fagan, Hartstone, Rudman, & Hansen, 1984).

Therapy versus the Legal System

Legal needs and controls are frequently in conflict with therapeutic procedures and goals. Perhaps one of the most salient examples of this is the routine practice of mandating therapy for juvenile offenders. Seen by many (Halleck, 1971; Szasz, 1963) as a potentially abusive and oppressive practice, involuntary treatment raises ethical as well as pragmatic questions for the clinician (Lester, 1981). In whose interests, for example, is the therapist working: the juvenile court's or the youngster's? What about the role of the family and society in delinquent misconduct? Should the youngster be helped to adjust to a dysfunctional sociofamilial system? And how can the therapist effectively engage juveniles and their families in therapy against their will?

In response to these and other questions, an increasing number of persons are calling for reforms in juvenile justice (see, e.g., Lemert, 1970; Rosenhelm, 1976; U.S. Department of Justice, 1976). One view is that therapeutic services are particularly needed on a *voluntary* basis at the point of juveniles' initial contact with the court, when they and their families are likely to be in crisis and motivated to seek help, rather than weeks and months later after their hearings (Jurkovic, 1984; Wald, 1976). Involvement in treatment can be presented to the family as diversion from a court hearing. However, for parents who do not respond, their involvement should be required. Another promising change, one already implemented in many parts of the country, is the transformation of the juvenile court into a family court, having jurisdiction over a variety of family-related legal problems (U.S. Department of Justice, 1976).

Currently, therapists are continuing to treat delinquents, many of whom are unmotivated, or "treatment evaders" (Agee, 1979), within and in association with juvenile court settings that may not be conducive to the therapeutic process. At the same time, therapists have also unwittingly contributed to problems in collaborating with juvenile justice personnel and effectively providing clinical services. For instance, they frequently implement their interventions without sufficient concern for the context of the court (Jurkovic, 1984). As family systems theorists have emphasized,

> the contextually relativistic nature of any intervention requires that therapists learn about their interconnectedness with the settings in which they are working. . . . Thus, rather than attribute problems in the court/family (client)/therapy relationship to any one component, it may be more helpful to focus on the relationship itself and on ways of reorganizing it to deal effectively with delinquency. (Jurkovic, 1984, p. 217)

Recommendations for Therapists

Therapists can use a number of strategies at different phases in the treatment process to facilitate their work with delinquents (Jurkovic, 1984). Derived from a family systems perspective, Jurkovic's ideas have implications for the practices of therapists with other orientations as well. In establishing a therapeutic system, for example, it is critical that therapists define their position in relation not only to their clients, but also to the court. In the hierarchy of the juvenile court, clinicians must recognize that their position is subservient to that of the probation officer, a key person whose functions and personal/professional idiosyncrasies should be understood. If therapists conflict with probation officers, untoward triangles often develop in the therapist–court–client relationship. The client stands to lose. Thus, a mutually supportive relationship between therapist and probation officer is important.

Therapists can develop and maintain close ties with court personnel without serving as social control agents or arms of the judiciary even when treatment is mandated (Johnson, 1974; Jurkovic, 1984), but it is critical that therapists, court personnel, and clients clarify their roles in relation to one another, especially concerning information exchange or confidentiality. Two of us and our students, for example, have reached agreements with probation officers and clients to inform the court of their client's attendance at sessions. Other information is shared only after obtaining permission from the family, unless it concerns life-threatening or serious illegal behavior. Even in the latter case, however, family members are told first, if possible, and given the option of informing the court themselves. Families rarely object to the therapists' sharing some information with the probation officer. These and other issues concerning case management (e.g., treatment goals that are in accord with those of the family, the therapist, and the court) are discussed and negotiated as necessary in a joint meeting of the therapist, family members, and probation officers early in the therapy process. Other joint meetings are arranged if problems develop in any aspect of the court–client–therapist relational network.

Although voluntary treatment is preferable and easier to deliver, a court order for therapy may ensure service delivery to many families who otherwise would not seek therapy. Empey and Gordon (1989) found greater attendance at family therapy when it was mandated by the court as part of probation, compared with voluntary attendance. Anglin and Hser (1991) found no differences in the effectiveness of drug treatment whether it was voluntary or coerced. Indeed, considerable outreach on the part of both the court and the therapist is often necessary to prevent premature termination (Clark et al., 1982; Jurkovic, 1984; Stanton & Todd, 1981a, 1981b). Collaboration with the probation officer and other court personnel can greatly expedite this process. If court personnel and probation officers understand the therapist's approach and feel supported by the therapist, they can present the need for treatment to family members in the course of their regular contacts with them. Court personnel and therapists can often develop creative recruitment plans and ideas to counter noncompliance (Jurkovic, 1984). The therapist can also relabel the reasons for therapy to noncompliant family members in empathic ways (e.g., "Perhaps by working with you, I can help get the court off your backs.")

Finally, therapists can strategically capitalize on their relationship with court personnel, as well as many routine court procedures, even those which seem countertherapeutic. Perhaps most fundamental along these lines is that the control and limits exercised by the court help to provide the necessary external structure for conducting therapy with delinquent youngsters. Hearings and conferences called by the court to deal with the adolescent's misbehavior, which often induces a crisis within the family, can also be used strategically. Carefully considered therapeutic input at these points may occasion significant changes in the juvenile and his/her family (Jurkovic, 1984).

COST FACTORS IN TREATMENT DECISIONS

A growing practice among public health, social service, and juvenile justice administrators is to evaluate the cost of various treatment alternatives in making decisions to terminate, change, or continue such programs. For mental health service providers, many of whom were motivated by altruistic and humanitarian concerns when they selected their professions, considering economic factors is anathema. Given the decline in economic prosperity since the 1960s and 1970s, the loss of Law Enforcement Assistance Administration funds, and the increasingly conservative nature of social services funding decisions, a greater number of providers will be expected to show evidence of their effectiveness. When treatment outcomes are quantified, cost–benefit analyses can be done if the treatment costs are known and the cost of the failure of treatment can be estimated. In the delinquency field, these costs are relatively easy to determine because treatment failures usually have immediate and specific costs (i.e., arrest, court and probation costs, out of home placement costs).

Cost Effectiveness of Family Therapy

A small number of investigators have reported on the cost savings of intervening with families of delinquents compared with the costs of regular juvenile justice system processing. Kinney et al. (1976) reported on an intensive, in-home family crisis intervention program (Homebuilders) that prevented out-of-home placement for 90% of children and adolescents at risk during a 16-month period. The program costs, including salaries for therapist, administration, and secretary plus training and travel costs and supplies, were included in the analysis. There was a savings of $2,300 per client compared with what placement would have cost.

Marlowe, Reid, Patterson, and Weinrott (1986) examined the cost differential in institutional placements for a group of 28 delinquents who received behavioral family interventions compared with 27 delinquents referred to community agencies. The family treatment group spent 2,247 fewer days in institutions over a 3-year period than did the comparison group at a savings of almost $135,000, or $4,821 per client. Stratton (1974) used a crisis intervention approach with families of delinquents and compared costs with those of a randomly assigned group who received traditional juvenile court services. There was a savings of $3,956 per client in court, probation, and detention costs for the family crisis intervention group.

In our outcome studies on the effects of behavioral-systems family therapy with delinquents (Gordon, 1988), a conservative cost-effectiveness analysis was performed on out-of-home placement costs. Prior to in-home family interventions, the average annual out-of-home placement costs for the experimental group were $1,387 per client. After family therapy, the annual cost per client was $584. For the probation-only comparison group, the annual cost per client at the start of the same period was $434, but rose to $1,078 by the end of a comparable period of probation. Among the costs not reported were investigation and arrest costs, probation service, and juvenile court hearing costs. Lipsey (1985) calculated these costs for Los Angeles County to be $2,428 per child. Other hidden costs are the extensive paperwork involved with investigations, court hearings, and shifts in funding when children are placed out of the home. Welfare payments and unemployment compensation rise (with associated administration costs) when single parents leave their jobs because of the increased supervision and support needs of acting-out adolescents.

Tate, Repucci, and Mulvey (1995) cited significantly lower costs for effective treatment programs than for correctional incarceration, but they recommended a combination of the two for violent offenders. However, as the public demands more retributive strategies (binding over younger offenders to adult court and longer sentences), less may be spent on the search for effective preventive strategies.

Cautions Regarding Cost-Conscious Decision Making

It is important, however, that the growing emphasis on reducing out-of-home placements and costs not lead to keeping children in abusive or neglecting environments. If protective service agencies and juvenile courts are using competent in-home family intervention programs, the interventions can both assess the risk to children and remediate the situation in most cases. If, on the other hand, the determination of risk is made hastily and superficially, the danger to children increases as well as the long-term costs. Even in the case of unruly adolescents, avoidance of out-of-home placement without effective supportive family services often leads to child abuse, school failure and dropout, or runaways, each of which carries greater long-term costs.

BARRIERS TO DISSEMINATION
OF EFFECTIVE INTERVENTIONS

In light of the general perception among many professionals in the juvenile justice system and the public that nothing works to reduce delinquency, it is tragic that the same ineffective treatment methods predominate. As can be seen in this chapter and the literature reviews of others, there *are* effective interventions, but the spread of these techniques has been slow. As much delinquency is treatable if these techniques are used in the natural environment, the delay in dissemination has been costly. A number of factors account for the failure of the juvenile justice system to benefit from advances of the past two decades.

Most mental health professionals in institutional and community settings were trained primarily in individual therapy, often with a medical-model perspective in which deviance lies within the individual delinquent. Therefore, a group, family, or community-systems approach is not seen as directly relevant to remediating the cause of the disorder. Such a traditional view is perpetuated, as it is held by more senior and powerful staff who make hiring decisions, favoring like-minded individuals.

People who make policy decisions about intervention programs at the state and community levels (judges, political appointees, court administrators) are rarely familiar with the scientific literature that critically evaluates the various treatment approaches. They implement programs that have repeatedly failed in other locations but are conceptually appealing or in vogue (i.e., "scared straight," wilderness experiences, boot camps, individual therapy aimed at giving the delinquent insight into his/her behavior [Lipsey, 1992; Mulvey et al., 1993]). These decisionmakers and the academic researchers who develop and evaluate effective interventions seldom meet, and, as is often the case when there is no communication, they have little respect for each other. There has been, however, an increase in the number of community programs, as states comply with federal deinstitutionalization mandates. Thus, the opportunities are increasing for delinquents to be treated in their natural environments. However, merely being treated in a community setting is not sufficient for successful treatment outcome. Also, some "community" treatments may not be much different than institutional treatment (Coates, 1981).

Community-based programs have been reviewed in terms of effectiveness by Gottschalk and colleagues (1987), with a meta-analysis of some 90 studies involving over 11,000 subjects. Their general conclusion is that "treatments in community settings did not have a large effect on outcomes" (pp. 282–283).

How do ineffective programs survive, much less expand? There are several explanations. Perhaps the most serious is the generally low level of knowledge about intervention programs and program evaluation in most juvenile courts and community advisory committees. Programs are packaged and sold to judges and state officials; political debts may be involved. Once programs are underway—usually with substantial staff and buildings—it is difficult to terminate them, or even to reduce the level of funding to fund more promising programs. Evaluations become anecdotal, and support becomes inexorable.

Another barrier to the spread of effective programs is the lack of standardization of the treatment technique. Most successful interventions defy replication because the interventions are not described in sufficient detail to allow others to implement them in the same way. Therapist manuals to guide the implementation of the technique are largely nonexistent (with the exception of a few, such as Alexander and Parsons [1982]). Methods for ensuring that newly trained therapists are using techniques according to the model are crude (case consultation in which therapists report on their therapy sessions). Reliable therapist coding systems are needed that can measure fidelity to the treatment model. Gordon, Barton, and Jurkovic (1984) have developed session-by-session checklists that guide therapists' behavior and allow them to report on what they did each session.

One method commonly used to disseminate interventions is the workshop format (Gordon & Arbuthnot, 1988). When workshops are presented in a systematic, standardized fashion, relying not upon videotaped or live demonstrations of therapeutic maneuvers, but upon orderly, concrete, didactic presentations, then trainees have a better chance of understanding and remembering the model. Workshop effectiveness is enhanced when trainees read an accompanying text clearly describing the model, and when trainees engage in roleplays dramatizing critical aspects of the technique, getting feedback on their performance. However, even when the workshop is well organized and executed, there is little likelihood that trainees will implement the techniques in their own work settings without ongoing, case-by-case supervision by therapists already knowledgeable in using the technique. In the absence of an on-site supervisor, taped sessions sent to a supervisor who provides trainee feedback and guidance prior to each succeeding therapy session is the most effective method to ensure that trainees learn the techniques. Trainee experience, intelligence, enthusiasm, and interpersonal skills all contribute to the length of the apprenticeship period needed to produce competence.

Finally, administrative support within the trainees' organization is critical to the successful implementation of new treatment techniques (Backer, Liberman, & Kuehnel, 1986). Most administrators fail to appreciate the level of training (including ongoing supervision) needed to improve the competence of their staff and think that simply sending staff to a workshop is sufficient (Gordon & Arbuthnot, 1988).

PREVENTION

Given the extreme difficulty and great cost of treating the most recalcitrant delinquents, early identification and treatment is necessary. Lorion et al. (1987) demonstrated that family functioning is the only psychosocial variable that consistently predicts risk of delinquency. As the family is the dominant force in the development of several forms of adolescent pathology and delinquency, it is crucial that intervention aimed at remediating parenting deficits reaches families at critical periods in the child and family's development.

Because lack of parental attention, supervision, and effective discipline is associated with most forms of serious delinquency, intervention that increases parents' desire and availability to be with their children should reduce children's risk for these disorders. Children's access to their non-custodial parent after divorce (usually fathers) should be dramatically increased. Unfortunately, courts seldom enforce visitation rights, with the result that visitation can be arbitrarily reduced or terminated by the custodial parent. For low-income fathers and their children, the remedies to visitation denial are nonexistent. Mediation between ex-spouses aimed at resolving visitation and child support problems is gaining acceptance and promises to restore contact and financial support between fathers and their children. Mandating divorce education programs is becoming increasingly popular and addresses the importance of parental cooperation and involvement with children without conflict. These programs have been successful at reducing conflict and relitigation and increasing parental sensitivity to their children's needs (Arbuthnot & Gordon, 1997; Arbuthnot, Segal, Gordon, & Schneider, 1994).

Another remedy for the lack of child attention and supervision are Big Brother/Big Sister programs wherein a nurturing adult spends time on a regular basis with at-risk children and adolescents. In rural areas, church and civic groups can provide adults who volunteer for this service. When kinship networks exist, their support of children with diminished parental attention should be sought by agencies.

Early identification of children's problems can occur when teachers and principals insist that parents seek professional help. A promising program in Oregon identified children in the early elementary grades who were at risk for developing chronic delinquency, though they were not so labeled, and explored methods of getting their dysfunctional families into treatment (Drummond, personal communication, June 18, 1989). The use of alternative schools and teaching strategies within public schools (individualized instruction, contingent use of praise and discipline, cooperative peer learning) increases delinquents' academic skill mastery and on-task behavior (Lorion et al., 1987). Schools can also provide social skills training and moral reasoning development programs, either in the curriculum for all students or in specially constituted groups of students in need of these skills. The early identification of children at risk for academic failure and social maladjustment can lead to remediation at school without the parental consent and motivation needed for mental health consultation. Pediatricians can also urge parents to prevent the development of more serious problems by conferring with family therapists and child psychiatrists and psychologists. One of us (D.A.G.) has taken an active outreach approach by contacting a local pediatrician who sees mostly underserved, low-income families. After explaining to the physician the value of family interventions for child behavior disorders, he was invited to see referred clients at the physician's office. After one or two appointments there, the families were then seen in their homes, where three fourths of the families completed a full course of family therapy (averaging 12–14 sessions). Most of these families had refused to go to community mental health centers and would not have received any treatment but for this outreach effort.

Many of the children at risk for serious delinquency come from single-parent families in which the mother is socially isolated and depressed (Dumas & Wahler, 1983; Whitehead, 1993). It is necessary to increase the social support for these mothers to combat their depression and resulting inattention to their children. Outreach efforts to induce mothers to participate in community support networks can involve churches, civic organizations, and schools. By increasing the number of people who track an at-risk child's behavior, coordination of feedback for prosocial and deviant behavior becomes possible. These children and adolescents thus receive an increased amount of adult attention, and hence an opportunity to identify with conventional role models. They also experience more immediate consequences for their behavior.

Another area for prevention that would decrease serious delinquency, including violence, is treatment of family aggression and violence. When parental violence is directed toward children, the odds of future delinquency and adult criminality increases by 40% (Widom, 1992). Although it is widely believed that the intergenerational transmission of violence is well established, Widom's careful review of the literature (1989) indicates the pathway is neither straight nor certain. Within families, there is evidence that children are at risk for behavior problems and delinquency from observing marital discord and aggression, similar to those children who are abused. In this case, family and marital therapy would be the appropriate treatments. In many cases, parental separation and divorce may reduce the children's risk if it decreases the parental aggression the children witness.

Neglect poses an equally serious risk for children's later involvement with delinquency and adult criminality. Nationally, three times as many children are neglected as physically abused, which also increases the odds that they will commit violent crimes as adults (Widom, 1992). Whether the solution to neglect and abuse is out-of-home placement or intensive family intervention and support is currently debated, although recent trends toward family preservation are supported by evidence of cost savings.

Empirical support for prevention programs that reduce either delinquency or behaviors that are precursors to delinquency is building. Yoshikawa's (1994) review of such programs concluded that successful programs intervene educationally during early childhood, provide family support and parent training, and are continuous over many years (as opposed to being a single-dose program). Similar recommendations are echoed by David Farrington (1995) in his review of findings and policy implications from the Cambridge Study in Delinquent Development. Improving school achievement in the early years may be a protective pathway that makes children less susceptible to negative peer group influences. Although two major reviews (Yoshikawa, 1994; Zigler, Taussig, & Black, 1992) of early intervention/prevention programs recommended the strategy of focusing funds on these efforts rather than on later childhood or adolescence, several programs have been successful during middle childhood. These programs reduced antisocial behavior by combining parent training with child social skill training or collaborative classroom teaching practices (Hawkins et al., 1992; Kazdin, Siegel, & Bass, 1992; McCord & Tremblay, 1992; Tremblay et al., 1992).

The longitudinal studies examining later delinquent behavior have embraced an ecological view of child development by treating children in their broad environment rather than with an isolated intervention. The programs involved the parents and taught them childrearing skills and how to network in their communities providing both information and social–emotional support (Farrington, 1994; Zigler et al., 1992). This parental participation may enable them to support the same behavioral goals (academic and social competence) that the programs stress for their children, encouraging continuity once the program ends.

Although there is wide consensus among researchers and clinicians that parental involvement is critical to long-term success with preventing delinquency and reducing serious delinquency, a substantial problem is parental refusal to participate in treatment. The prevalence of conduct disorders and antisocial behaviors is increasing, at a time when existing services and funds are already inadequate. Thus, the parents' refusing to participate are unlikely to be pursued because, in the case of community mental health centers, many willing parents are on the waiting list. Those families seeking treatment for their children represent less than 10% of the population who need mental health services. The stigma attached to mental health services, strongest among lower income families, is undoubtedly a factor.

Creative approaches are needed to increase parent participation among high-risk populations. As mentioned earlier, home-based family interventions are one such creative and promising approach. Another is presenting the parent training as education, not therapy. Videotaped programs of modeled parenting skills have been developed and found to be effective at improving the behavior of conduct-disordered children (Webster-Stratton, 1990), even when they were not accompanied by professionally led group discussion or individual consultation. One of us (D.A.G.) is conducting an evaluation of his computer-assisted, interactive video disk program that teaches parenting skills to parents of adolescents and preadolescents. It addresses the parenting-skill deficits of parents of delinquents. The program shows videotaped scenes of nine common family problems, with three solutions (two poor, one good) to each problem, and is very interactive because parents make many choices and get feedback in response to each choice. The program was developed to be highly engaging and easy to use, and has received high parental satisfaction ratings from low-income parents. Parental knowledge of parenting skills increased, and teen problem behavior decreased substantially, with gains maintained for 6 months, relative to controls (Gordon, Kacir, & Chen, 1997).

CONCLUDING REMARKS

Whereas a variety of interventions are effective for different kinds of juvenile delinquents, coherent, competent, and coordinated treatment approaches are lacking for a majority of such offenders. The failure of many in the criminal justice and mental health communities to appreciate the interdependence of social systems in contributing to serious delinquency is partly responsible for the failure to provide effective treatment. Since the early 1970s, the voting public has believed in and relied upon criminal sanctions and deterrence. This view has prevented the development of a national mandate to provide intensive treatment and allocate resources toward ameliorating the conditions giving rise to serious delinquent pathology. As Currie (1989) observed, professionals (not the public) have reached a turning point in our thinking and social policy toward crime as evidence has mounted that deterrence and sanctions do not work. The conservative political climate, with its neglectful social policies toward the disadvantaged, now has mainstream business people worried that "neglect of the bottom half of society begins to threaten the welfare of the entire nation" ("Human Capital," 1988).

Currie (1989) was appropriately concerned that the reviving interest in early intervention strategies with children and families (likewise, the increased interest in family interventions for delinquents) will create expectations that cannot be met until the larger societal and economic contexts in which the problems arise are confronted. Just as practitioners of individualistic treatment approaches are uneasy about returning the treated delinquent to his/her family, so are family therapists uneasy about returning the treated family to an unsupportive and stressful society.

Recommendations that include changing the way treatment is conducted as well as social policy changes that would serve a preventive function have been offered. We concur strongly with Currie (1989) and Loeber and Farrington (1994) on the need for the following: (1) increasing health and mental health services for high-risk children and youths (this would include pre- and postnatal care as Lewis, 1980, and Lewis et al., 1979, implicated early childhood central nervous system trauma, serious psychiatric problems, malnutrition, and low birth weight, all of which could be detected and treated in the development of delinquency); (2) improving the quality and quantity of early childhood education for more low income families, as these programs have proven to be low cost and effective; (3) increasing family support programs and fostering a profamily economic policy that would reduce the need for parents to chase jobs and move away from their social support networks; (4) improving the treatment and aftercare for incarcerated and adjudicated juveniles, shortening their incarceration (Andrews et al., 1990; Gendreau & Ross, 1987), and ensuring the therapeutic integrity of such programs through establishing a cadre of well-trained interventionists who deliver the treatments as intended. The greatest provision of service should be reserved for the highest risk cases. Family therapy, for example, should be required immediately upon entry into the juvenile justice system for all delinquents with families or foster families, with social skill-oriented group therapy, school intervention in academic remediation, peer group involvement, and cognitive and social skills training added as the seriousness of the offense(s) increases (Ross & Fabiano, 1985).

Implementing these recommendations will require a substantial increase in public spending. Consequently, greater public and political awareness of the interdependency of the various etiological factors leading to serious criminal behavior is necessary. The ways in which these factors connect inextricably to our national social and economic policies must be communicated to our citizens and lawmakers. As professionals in both research and practice who comprehend these complex relationships, we have an obligation to make our voices heard.

NOTE

1. See Alessi, McManus, Grapetine, and Brickman (1984), however, who found that whereas affective disorders are prevalent in serious juvenile offenders, they are not

associated with specific classes of either conduct disorder or criminal activity. They concluded that depression probably does not play a major part in the etiology of serious and repetitive delinquency, although particular depressive features, for example, agitation, may exacerbate violence in youngsters who display a pattern of delinquency.

REFERENCES

Agee, V. C. (1979). *Treatment of the violent incorrigible adolescent.* Lexington, MA: Heath.

Agee, V. C., & McWilliams, B. (1984). The role of group therapy and the therapeutic community: Treating the voluntary juvenile offender. In R. A. Mathias & P. DeMuro (Eds.), *Violent juvenile offenders: An anthology* (pp. 283–296). San Francisco: National Council on Crime and Delinquency.

Aichorn, A. (1925). *Wayward youth.* New York: Viking.

Akers, R. L., Krohn, M. D., Lanza-Kaduce, L., & Rodesevich, M. (1979). Social learning and deviant behavior: A specific test of a general theory. *American Sociological Review, 44,* 636–655.

Alessi, N. E., McManus, M., Grapetine, W. L., & Brickman, A. (1984). The characterization of depressive disorders in serious juvenile offenders. *Journal of Affective Disorders, 6,* 9–17.

Alexander, J. F., Barton, C., Schiavo, R. S., & Parsons, B. V. (1976). Systems behavioral intervention with families of delinquents: Therapist characteristics, family behavior, and outcome. *Journal of Consulting and Clinical Psychology, 44,* 656–664.

Alexander, J. F., & Parsons, B. V. (1973). Short-term behavioral intervention with delinquent families: Impact on family process and recidivism. *Journal of Abnormal Psychology, 81,* 219–225.

Alexander, J. F., & Parsons, B. V. (1982). *Functional family therapy.* Monterey, CA: Brooks Cole.

Andrews, D. A., Zinger, I., Hoge, R. D., Bonta, J., Gendreau, P., & Cullen, F. T. (1990). Does correctional treatment work? A clinically relevant and psychologically informed meta-analysis. *Criminology, 28,* 369–404.

Anglin, M. D., & Hser, Y. (1991). Criminal justice and the drug-abusing offender: Policy issues of coerced treatment. *Behavioral Sciences and the Law, 9,* 243–268.

Arbuthnot, J. (1992). Sociomoral reasoning in behavior-disordered adolescents: Cognitive and behavioral change. In J. McCord & R. E. Tremblay (Eds.), *Preventing antisocial behavior: Interventions from birth through adolescence* (pp. 283–310). New York: Guilford Press.

Arbuthnot, J., & Faust, D. (1981). *Teaching moral reasoning: Theory and practice.* New York: Harper and Row.

Arbuthnot, J., & Gordon, D. A. (1986). Behavioral and cognitive effects of a moral reasoning development intervention for high-risk behavior-disordered adolescents. *Journal of Consulting and Clinical Psychology, 54,* 208–216.

Arbuthnot, J., & Gordon, D. A. (1997). Divorce education for parents and the children. In L. Vandecreek, S. Knapp, & T. L. Jackson (Eds.), *Innovation in clinical practice* (pp. 341–364). Sarasota, FL.: Professional Resource Press.

Arbuthnot, J., Gordon, D. A., & Jurkovic, G. J. (1987). Personality. In H. C. Quay (Ed.), *Handbook of juvenile delinquency* (pp. 139–183). New York: Wiley.

Arbuthnot, J., Segal, D., Gordon, D. A., & Schneider, K. (1994). Court-sponsored divorce education programs: Some guiding thoughts and preliminary data. *Juvenile and Family Court Journal, 45,* 77–84.

Avery, A., Rider, K. C., & Haynes-Clements, L. (1981). Communication skills training for adolescents: A five-month follow-up. *Adolescence, 16,* 289–298.

Ayllon, T., & Azrin, N. H. (1968). *The token economy: A motivational system for therapy and rehabilitation.* New York: Appleton-Century-Crofts.

Backer, T., Liberman, R., & Kuehnel, T. (1986). Dissemination and adoption of innovative psychosocial interventions. *Journal of Consulting and Clinical Psychology, 54,* 111–118.

Barton, C., Alexander, J. F., Waldron, H., Turner, C. W., & Warburton, J. (1985). Generalizing treatment effects of functional family therapy: Three replications. *American Journal of Family Therapy, 13,* 16–26.

Basta, J. M., & Davisdon, W. S. (1988). Treatment of juvenile offenders: Study outcomes since 1980. *Behavioral Sciences and the Law, 6,* 355–384.

Bell, J. E. (1975). *Family therapy.* New York: Aronson.

Benne, K. D., Bradford, L. P., & Lippitt, R. (1964). The laboratory method. In L. P. Bradford, J. R. Gibb, & K. D. Benne (Eds.), *T-Group theory and laboratory method* (pp. 15–44). New York: Wiley.

Berger, M., & Jurkovic, G. J. (1984). *Practicing family therapy diverse settings.* San Francisco: Jossey-Bass.

Bernard, M. E., & Joyce, M. R. (1984). *Rational–emotive therapy with children and adolescents.* New York: Wiley.

Bixby, F., McCorkle, L., & McCorkle, L. W. (1951). Guided group interaction and correctional work. *American Sociological Review, 16,* 455–459.

Blasi, A. (1980). Bridging moral cognition and moral action: A critical review of the literature. *Psychological Bulletin, 88,* 1–45.

Borduin, C. M., Mann, B. J., Cone, L. T., Henggeler, S. W., Fucci, B. R., Blaske, D. M., & Williams, R. A. (1995). Multisystemic treatment of serious juvenile offenders: Long-term prevention of criminality and violence. *Journal of Consulting and Clinical Psychology, 63,* 569–578.

Braukman, C. L., & Fixsen, D. L. (1976). Behavior modification with delinquents. In M. Hersen, R. M. Eisler, & P. M. Miller (Eds.), *Progress in behavior modification* (Vol. 1, pp. 212–234). New York: Academic Press.

Bronfenbrenner, U. (1986). Ecology of the family as a context for human development: Research perspectives. *Developmental Psychology, 22,* 723–742.

Bumpass, L. L. (1984). Children and marital disruption: A replication and update. *Demography, 21,* 71–82.

Camp, B. W. (1977). Verbal mediation in young aggressive boys. *Journal of Abnormal Psychology, 86,* 145–153.

Camp, B., Blom, G., Herbert, F., & Van Doornick, W. (1977). "Think aloud": A program for developing self-control in young aggressive boys. *Journal of Abnormal Child Psychology, 8,* 157–169.

Camp, B. W., & Bash, M. B. (1981). *Think aloud: Increasing social and cognitive skills: A problem-solving program for children.* Champaign, IL: Research Press.

Chandler, M. (1973). Egocentrism and antisocial behavior: The assessment and training of social perspective-taking skills. *Developmental Psychology, 9,* 326–332.

Clark, T., Zalis, T., & Saccho, F. (1982). *Outreach family therapy.* New York: Jason Aronson.

Coates, R. B. (1981). Community-based services for juvenile delinquents: Concepts and implications for practice. *Journal of Social Issues, 37,* 87–101.

Collingwood, T. R., & Genthner, R. W. (1980). Skills training in treatment for juvenile delinquents. *Professional Psychology, 11,* 591–598.

Cornwall, T. P., Behar, L., Conrad, D., Whiteside, R., & Mark, J. (1981). Treatment of the violent adolescent: The role of the psychiatric hospital, I: The milieu. *North Carolina Journal of Mental Health, 9,* 1–12.

Corsini, R. J., & Rosenberg, B. (1955). Mechanisms of group psychotherapy: Process and dynamics. *Journal of Abnormal and Social Psychology, 51,* 406–409.

Cummings, E. M., & Davies, P. (1994). *Children and mental conflict: The impact of family dispute and resolution.* New York: Guilford Press.

Currie, E. (1989). Confronting crime: Looking toward the twenty-first century. *Justice Quarterly, 6,* 5–26.

Doren, D. (1987). *Understanding and treating the psychopath.* New York: Wiley.

Dumas, J. E., & Wahler, R. G. (1983). Predictors of treatment outcome in parent training: Mother insularity and socioeconomic disadvantage. *Behavioral Assessment, 5,* 301–313.

Ellis, A. (1978). *Humanistic psychotherapy: The rational–emotive approach.* New York: McGraw-Hill Paperbacks.

Empey, D., & Gordon, D. A. (1989). Attrition from court-referred family therapy for delinquents. *Juvenile and Family Court Journal, 40,* 45–54.

Eron, L. D., Huesmann, L. R., Dubow, E., Romanoff, R., & Yarmel, P. W. (1987). In D. H. Crowell, I. M. Evans, & C. R. O'Donnell (Eds.), *Childhood aggression and violence* (pp. 249–262). New York: Plenum Press.

Evans, I. M., & Scheuer, A. D. (1987). Analyzing response relationships in childhood aggression: The clinical perspective. In D. H. Crowell, I. M. Evans, & C. R. O'Donnell (Eds.), *Childhood aggression and violence* (pp. 75–94). New York: Plenum Press.

Fagan, J. A., Harstone, E., Rudman, C. J., & Hansen, K. V. (1984). System processing of violent juvenile offenders: An empirical assessment. In R. A. Mathias, P. DeMuro, & S. Allenson (Eds.), *Violent juvenile offenders: An anthology* (pp. 117–136). San Francisco: National Council on Crime and Delinquency.

Farrington, D. P. (1986). Age and crime. In M. Tonry & N. Morris (Eds.), *Crime and justice* (Vol. 7, pp. 29–90). Chicago: University of Chicago Press.

Farrington, D. P. (1987). Epidemiology. In H. C. Quay (Ed.), *Handbook of juvenile delinquency* (pp. 33–61). New York: Wiley.

Farrington, D. P. (1994). Early developmental prevention of juvenile delinquency. *Criminal Behaviour and Mental Health, 4,* 209–227.

Farrington, D. P. (1995). The development of offending and antisocial behavior from childhood: Key findings from the Cambridge Study in Delinquent Development. *Journal of Child Psychology and Psychiatry, 360,* 929–964.

Feldman, R. A. (1992). The St. Louis Experiment: Effective treatment of antisocial youths in prosocial peer groups. In J. McCord & R. E. Tremblay (Eds.), *Preventing antisocial behavior: Interventions from birth through adolescence* (pp. 233–252). New York: Guilford Press.

Feldman, R. A., Caplinger, T. E., & Wodarski, J. S. (1983). *The St. Louis conundrum: The effective treatment of antisocial youths.* Englewood Cliffs, NJ: Prentice Hall.

Fine, M. J., & Carlson, C. (Eds.). (1992). *The handbook of family–school intervention: A systems perspective.* Boston: Allyn & Bacon.

Fitzgerald, T. J. (1974). Contingency contracting with juvenile offenders. *Criminology: An Interdisciplinary Journal, 12,* 241–248.

Fo, W. S., & O'Donnell, C. R. (1975). The buddy system: Effects of community interaction on delinquent offenses. *Behavior Therapy, 6,* 522–524.

Garrett, C. J. (1985). Effects of residential treatment on adjudicated delinquents: A meta-analysis. *Journal of Research in Crime and Delinquency, 22,* 287–308.

Gendreau, P. (1996). Offender rehabilitation: What we know and what needs to be done. *Criminal Justice and Behavior, 23,* 144–161.

Gendreau, P., & Ross, R. R. (1987). Revivication of rehabilitation: Evidence from the 1980's. *Justice Quarterly, 4,* 349–407.

Gersten, J. C., Langer, T. S., Eisenberg, J. G., Simcha-Fagan, O., & McCarhty, E. D. (1976). Stability and change in types of behavioral disturbance of children and adolescents. *Journal of Abnormal Child Psychology, 4,* 111–127.

Gibbs, J. C., Arnold, K. D., Ahlborn, H. H., & Cheesman, F. L. (1984). Facilitation of sociomoral reasoning in delinquents. *Journal of Consulting and Clinical Psychology, 52,* 37–45.

Gibbs, J. C. (1997). Social processes in delinquency: The need to facilitate empathy as well as sociomoral reasoning in delinquents. In W. M. Kurtines & J. L. Gewirtz (Eds.), *Moral development through social interaction* (pp. 301–321). New York: Wiley.

Glasser, W. (1965). *Reality therapy.* New York: Harper & Row.

Glueck, S. E., & Glueck, E. T. (1950). *Unraveling juvenile delinquency.* Cambridge, MA: Harvard University Press.

Goldstein, A. P., Sprafkin, R. P., Gershaw, N. J., & Klein, P. (1980). *Skill-streaming the adolescent: A structured learning approach to teaching prosocial skills.* Champaign, IL: Research Press.

Gordon, D. A.(1988). *A cost–benefit analysis of in-home family therapy vs. probation in treating delinquents.* Unpublished manuscript, Ohio University.

Gordon, D. A., & Arbuthnot, J. (1987). Individual, group and family interventions. In H. C. Quay (Ed.), *Handbook of juvenile delinquency* (pp. 290–324). New York: Wiley.

Gordon, D. A., & Arbuthnot, J. (1988). The use of paraprofessionals to deliver home-based family therapy to juvenile delinquents. *Criminal Justice and Behavior, 15,* 364–378.

Gordon, D. A., Arbuthnot, J., Gustafson, K., & McGreen, P. (1988). Home-based behavioral systems family therapy with disadvantaged juvenile delinquents. *American Journal of Family Therapy, 16,* 243–255.

Gordon, D. A., Barton, C., Jurkovic, G. J. (1984). *Therapist forms for functional family therapy sessions.* Unpublished manuscript.

Gordon, D. A., Graves, K., & Arbuthnot, J. (1995). Prevention of adult criminal behavior using family therapy for disadvantaged juvenile delinquents. *Criminal Justice and Behavior, 22,* 60–73.

Gordon, D. A., Kacir, C., & Chen, P. (1997). *Reducing child problem behavior through interactive video disk parent education.* Unpublished manuscript.

Gottfredson, G. D. (1982). *Role models, bonding, and delinquency: An examination of competing perspectives* (Report No. 331, Center for Social Organization of Schools). Baltimore: Johns Hopkins University (ERIC No. 230 888).

Gottfredson, G. D. (1987). Peer group interventions to reduce the risk of delinquent behavior: A selective review and a new evaluation. *Criminology, 25,* 671–714.

Gottschalk, R., Davidson, W. S. III, Gensheimer, L. K., & Mayer, J. P. (1987). Community based interventions. In H. C. Quay (Ed.), *Handbook of juvenile delinquency* (pp. 266–289). New York: Wiley.

Gray, D. H., & Tindall, J. (1978). *Peer counseling: An in-depth look at training peer helpers.* Muncie, IN: Accelerated Development.

Greenwood, P., & Turner, S. (1993). Evaluation of the Paint Creek Youth Center: A residential program for serious delinquents. *Criminology, 31,* 263–279.

Grossman, K., Gordon, D. A., & Moore, J. (1988). *Relationship between family therapist self-reports with observer and co-therapist measures of family therapy skills.* Unpublished manuscript.

Gunderson, J. (1978). Defining the therapeutic processes in psychiatry milieus. *Psychiatry, 41,* 327–355.

Halleck, S. (1971). *The politics of therapy.* New York: Science House.

Hamparian, D. M. (1987). Control and treatment of juveniles committing violent offenses. In L. H. Roth (Eds.), *Clinical treatment of the violent person* (pp. 156–177). New York: Guilford Press.

Hamparian, D. M., Davis, J., Jacobson, J., & McGraw, R. (1985). *The young criminal years of the violent few.* Washington, DC: U.S. Department of Justice.

Hamparian, D. M., Schuster, R., Dinitz, S., & Conrad, J. R. (1979). *The violent few.* Lexington, MA: Heath.

Hartshorne, H., & May, M. A. (1928). *Studies in the nature of character.* New York: Macmillan.

Hartshorne, H., May, M. A., & Maller, J. B. (1929). *Studies in the nature of character: Vol. II. Studies in self-control.* New York: Macmillan.

Hartshorne, H., May, M. A., & Shuffleworth, F. K. (1930). *Studies in the nature of character: Vol. III. Studies in the organization of character.* New York: Macmillan.

Hawkins, J. D., Catalano, R. F., Morrison, D. M., O'Donnell, J., Abbott, R. D., & Day, L. E. (1992). The Seattle Social Development Project: Effects of the first four years on protective factors and problem behaviors. In J. McCord & R. E. Tremblay (Eds.), *Preventing anti-social behavior: Interventions from birth to adolescence* (pp. 139–161). New York: Guilford Press.

Haynes, L. A., & Avery, A. W. (1979). Training adolescents in self-disclosure and empathy skills. *Journal of Consulting Psychology, 26,* 526–530.

Henggeler, S. W. (1996). Multisystemic therapy: An effective violence prevention approach for serious juvenile offenders. *Journal of Adolescence, 19,* 47–61.

Henggeler, S. W., & Borduin, C. M. (1990). *Family therapy and beyond: A multisystemic approach to treating the behavior problems of children and adolescents.* Pacific Grove, CA: Brooks/Cole.

Henggeler, S. W., Melton, G. R., Smith, L. A., & Schoenwald, S. K. (1993). Family preservation using multisystemic treatment: Long-term follow-up to a clinical trial with serious juvenile offenders. *Journal of Child and Family Studies, 2,* 283–293.

Henggeler, S. W., Pickrel, S. G., Brondino, M. J., & Crouch, J. L. (1996). Eliminating (almost) treatment dropout of substance abusing or dependent delinquents through home-based multisystemic therapy. *American Journal of Psychiatry, 153,* 427–428.

Henggeler, S. W., Rodick, J. D., Borduin, C. M., Hanson, C. L., Watson, S. M., & Urey, J. R. (1986). Multisystemic treament of juvenile offenders: Effects on adolescent behavior and family interaction. *Developmental Psychology, 22,* 132–141.

Hersch, R. H., Paolitto, D. P., & Reimer, J. (1979). *Promoting moral growth: From Piaget to Kohlberg.* New York: Longman.

Hill, W. F. (1974). Systematic group development: SGD therapy. In Alfred Jacobs & Wilford Spradlin (Eds.), *The group as an agent of change.* New York: Behavioral Publications.

Hirschi, T. (1969). *Causes of delinquency.* Berkeley: University of California Press.

Howlett, F. W., & Boehm, R. G. (1975). *School-based delinquency prevention: The Rock Island experience.* Austin, TX: Justice Systems.

Human Capital. (1988, September 19). *Business Week,* p. 103.

Johnson, T. F. (1974). Hooking the involuntary family into treatment: Family therapy in a juvenile court setting. *Family Therapy, 1,* 79–82.

Jones, J. D. (1984). Principles of hospital treatment of the aggressive adolescent. In C. R. Keith (Ed.), *The aggressive adolescent* (pp. 359–402). New York: Free Press.

Julian, A., & Kilmann, P. (1979). Group treatment of juvenile delinquents: Review of the outcome literature. *International Journal of Group Psychotherapy, 29,* 3–37.

Jurkovic, G. J. (1980). The juvenile delinquent as a moral philosopher: A structural-developmental perspective. *Psychological Bulletin, 88,* 709–727.

Jurkovic, G. J. (1984). Juvenile justice system. In M. Berger & G. J. Jurkovic (Eds.), *Practicing family therapy in diverse settings* (pp. 211–246). San Francisco: Jossey-Bass.

Kaplan, P. (1986). *Developing affective empathy and moral reasoning skills in incarcerated delinquent males.* Unpublished doctoral dissertation, Ohio University, Athens, Ohio.

Kassenbaum, G., Ward, D., & Wilner, D. (1972). *Prison treatment and its outcome.* New York: Wiley.

Kazdin, A. E. (1977). *The token economy.* New York: Plenum Press.

Kazdin, A. E. (1982). Current development and research issues in cognitive-behavioral interventions. *School Psychology Review, 11,* 79–82.

Kazdin, A. E. (1994). Psychotherapy for children and adolescents. In A. E. Bergin & S. L. Garfield (Eds.), *Handbook of psychotherapy and behavior change* (pp. 543–594). New York: Wiley.

Kazdin, A. E., Siegel, T., & Bass, D. (1992). Cognitive problem-solving skills training and parent management training in the treatment of antisocial behavior in children. *Journal of Consulting and Clinical Psychology, 9,* 402–417.

Keith, C. R. (1984). Individual psychotherapy and psychoanalysis with the aggressive adolescent: A historical review. In C. R. Keith (Ed.), *The aggressive adolescent: Clinical perspectives* (pp. 191–208). New York: Free Press.

Kellner, R. (1978). Drug treatment of personality disorders and delinquents. In W. H. Reid (Ed.), *The psychopath* (pp. 301–329). New York: Brunner/Mazel.

Kendall, P. C., & Hollon, S. D. (1979). Cognitive-behavioral interventions: Overview and current status. In P. C. Kendall & S. D. Hollon (Eds.), *Cognitive-behavioral interventions: Theory, research, and procedures* (pp. 1–9). New York: Academic Press.

Kinney, J. M., Madsen, B., Fleming, T., & Haapala, D. (1976). Home-builders: Keeping families together. *Journal of Consulting and Clinical Psychology, 45,* 667–673.

Kirschner, D. A., & Kirschner, S. (1986). *Comprehensive family therapy.* New York: Brunner Mazel.

Klein, N. C., Alexander, J. F., & Parsons, B. V. (1977). Impact of family system intervention on recidivism and sibling delinquency: A model of primary prevention and program evaluation. *Journal of Consulting and Clinical Psychology, 45,* 469–474.

Klerman, G. L. (1975). Combining drugs and psychotherapy in the treatment of depression. In M. Greenblatt (Ed.), *Drugs in combination with other therapies* (pp. 67–81). New York: Grune and Stratton.

Kolko, D. J., & Milan, M. A. (1983). Reframing and paradoxical instruction to overcome resistance in the treatment of delinquent youths: A multiple baseline analysis. *Journal of Consulting and Clinical Psychology, 51,* 655–660.

Lavin, G. K., Trabka, S., & Kahn, E. M. (1984). Group therapy with aggressive and delinquent adolescents. In C. R. Keith (Ed.), *The aggressive adolescent: Clinical perspectives* (pp. 240–267). New York: Free Press.

Lemert, E. M. (1970). *Social action and legal change: Revolution within the juvenile court.* Chicago: Aldine.

Lester, D. (1981). *Psychotherapy for offenders.* Jonesboro, TN: Pilgrimage.

Leventhal, B. L. (1984). The neuropharmacology of violent and aggressive behavior in children and adolescents. In C. R. Keith (Ed.), *The aggressive adolescent: Clinical perspectives* (pp. 299–358). New York: Free Press.

Lewis, D. O. (1980). Psychobiological perspectives on delinquency. *Psychiatric Clinics of North America, 3,* 469–481.

Lewis, D. O., Sacks, H. L., Balla, D., Lewis, M., Heald, E. H. (1973). Introducing a child psychiatric service in a juvenile justice setting. *Child Psychiatry and Human Development, 4,* 98–114.

Lewis, D. O., & Shanok, S. S. (1980). The use of a correctional setting for follow-up of psychiatrically disturbed adolescents. *American Journal of Psychiatry, 8,* 953–955.

Lewis, D. O., Shanok, S. S., & Balla, D. A. (1979). Perinatal difficulties, head and face trauma, and child abuse in the medical histories of seriously delinquent children. *American Journal of Psychiatry, 136,* 419–423.

Lewis, D. O., Shanok, S. S., Cohen, R. J., Kligteld, M., & Frisone, G. (1980). Race bias in the diagnosis and disposition of violent adolescents. *American Journal of Psychiatry, 137,* 1211–1216.

Lewis, D. O., Shanok, S. S., Grant, M., & Ritvo, E. (1984). Homicidally aggressive young children: Neuropsychiatric and experiential correlates. In R. A. Mathias, P. DeMuro, & R. S. Allenson (Eds.), *Violent juvenile offenders: An anthology* (pp. 71–82). San Francisco: National Council on Crime and Delinquency.

Linden, E., & Hackler, J. C. (1973). Affective ties and delinquency. *Pacific Sociological Review, 16,* 27–46.

Lion, J. R. (1981). Countertransference and other psychotherapy issues. In W. H. Reid (Ed.), *Treatment of antisocial syndromes* (pp. 30–38). New York: Van Nostrand Reinhold.

Lipsey, M. W. (1985). *Malpractice in program evaluation? The case of delinquency prevention intervention.* Unpublished manuscript.

Lipsey, M. W. (1990). Juvenile delinquency treatment: A meta-analytic inquiry into the variability of effects. In T. D. Cook, H. Cooper, D. S. Cordray, H. Hartmann, L. V. Hedges, R. J. Light, T. A. Louis, & F. Mosteller (Eds.), *Meta-analysis for explanation* (pp. 83–127). New York: Russell Sage Foundation.

Little, V. L. (1978/1979). The relationship of role-taking ability to self-control in institutionalized juvenile offenders (Doctoral dissertation, Virginia Commonwealth University, 1978). *Dissertation Abstracts International, 1979, 39,* 2992B. (University Microfilms No. 78-22, 701)

Little, V. L., & Kendall, P. C. (1979). Cognitive-behavioral interventions with delinquents: Problem-solving, role-taking, and self-control. In P. Kendall & S. Hollon (Eds.), *Cognitive-behavioral interventions: Theory, research and procedures* (pp. 81–115). New York: Academic Press.

Lochman, J. E. (1984). Psychological characteritics and assessment of aggressive adolescents. In C. R. Keith (Ed.), *The aggressive adolescent: Clinical perspectives* (pp. 17–62). New York: Free Press.

Lochman, J. E. (1992). Cognitive-behavioral intervention with aggressive boys: Three-year follow-up and preventive effects. *Journal of Consulting and Clinical Psychology, 60,* 426–432.

Loeber, R., & Schmaling, K. B. (1985). The utility of differentiating between mixed and pure forms of antisocial child behavior. *Journal of Abnormal Child Behavior, 13, 315–336.*

Loeber, R., & Farrington, D. P. (1994). Problems and solutions in longitudinal/experimental treatment studies of child psychopathology and delinquency. *Journal of Consulting and Clinical Psychology, 62,* 887—900.

Lorion, R. P., Tolan, P. H., & Wahler, R. G. (1987). Prevention. In H. C. Quay (Ed.), *Handbook of juvenile delinquency* (pp. 383–416). New York: Wiley.

Mahoney, M. J., & Arnkoff, D. B. (1978). Cognitive and self-control therapies. In S. L. Garfield & A. E. Bergin (Eds.), *Handbook of psychotherapy and behavior change* (2nd ed., pp. 689–722). New York: Wiley.

Marlowe, H., Reid, J. B., Patterson, G. R., & Weinrott, M. (1986). *Treating adolescent multiple offenders: A comparison and follow-up of parent training for families of chronic delinquents.* Unpublished manuscript.

Martinson, R. (1974). What works? *The Public Interest, 35,* 22–54.

Masterson, J. F. (1972). *Treatment of the borderline adolescent: A developmental approach.* New York: Wiley.

Masterson, J. F. (1980). *From borderline adolescent to functioning adult: The test of time.* New York: Brunner/Mazel.

McCord, J., & Tremblay, R. E. (Eds.) (1992). *Preventing antisocial behavior: Interventions from birth through adolescence.* New York: Guilford Press.

McCord, W. M. (1982). *The psychopath and milieu therapy.* New York: Academic Press.

Meichenbaum, D. (1977). *Cognitive-behavior modification: An integrative approach.* New York: Plenum Press.

Michaels, K. W., & Green, R. H. (1979). A child welfare agency project: Therapy for families of status offenders. *Child Welfare, 58,* 216–220.

Minuchin, S., Montalvo, B. G., Guerney, B., Rosman, B. L., & Schumer, F. (1967). *Families of the slums: An exploration of their structure and treatment.* New York: Basic Books.

Moss, G. R., & Rick, G. R. (1981). Overview: Applications of operant technology to behavioral disorders of adolescents. *American Journal of Psychiatry, 138,* 1161–1169.

Mulvey, E. P., Arthur, M. W., & Reppucci, N. D. (1993). The prevention and treatment of juvenile delinquency: A review of the research. *Clinical Psychology Review, 13,* 133–167.

National School Resource Network. (1980). *Peer culture development* (Technical Assistance Bulletin 28). Washington, DC: National School Resource Network.

Novaco, R. W. (1979). The cognitive resolution of anger and stress. In P. C. Kendall & S. D. Hollon (Eds.), *Cognitive-behavioral interventions* (pp. 241–285). New York: Academic Press.

Office of Juvenile Justice and Delinquency Prevention. (1993). *Comprehensive strategy for serious, violent, and chronic juvenile offenders.* Washington, DC: U.S. Department of Justice.

Parloff, M. B., & Dies, R. R. (1977). Group psychotherapy outcome research, 1966–1975. *International Journal of Group Psychotherapy, 27,* 281–319.

Patterson, G. R. (1971). Behavioral inervention procedures in the classroom and in the home. In A. E. Bergin & S. C. Garfield (Eds.), *Handbook of psychotherapy and behavior change* (pp. 751–775). New York: Wiley.

Patterson, G. R. (1974). Interventions for boys with conduct problems: Multiple settings, treatments and criteria. *Journal of Consulting and Clinical Psychology, 42,* 471–481.

Patterson, G. R. (1985). Beyond technology: The next stage in developing an empirical base for training. In L'Abate (Ed.), *Handbook of family psychology and therapy* (Vol. 2, pp. 1344–1379). Homewood, IL: Dorsey Professional Books.

Phillips, E. L., Phillips, E. A., Fixsen, D. L., & Wolf, M. M. (1973). Achievement place: Modification of behaviors of predelinquent boys within a token economy. *Journal of Applied Behavior Analysis, 4,* 45–59.

Platt, J. J., & Spivack, G. (1975). *The MEPS procedure: Manual.* Philadelphia: Department of Mental Health Sciences, Hahnemann Medical College and Hospital.

Potts, L. J., Barley, W. D., Jones, K. A., & Woodhall, P. K. (1986). Comprehensive inpatient treatment of a severely antisocial adolescent. In W. H. Reid, D. Dorr, J. I. Walker, & J. W. Bonner, III (Eds.), *Unmasking the psychopath* (pp. 231–255). New York: Norton.

Prentice, N. M., & Kelly, F. J. (1966). The clinician in the juvenile correctional institution. *Crime and Delinquency, 12,* 49–54.

Quay, H. C. (1987a). Institutional treatment. In H. C. Quay (Ed.), *Handbook of juvenile delinquency* (pp. 244–265). New York: Wiley.

Quay, H. C. (1987b). Patterns of delinquent behavior. In H. C. Quay (Ed.), *Handbook of juvenile delinquency* (pp. 118–138). New York: Wiley.

Redl, F. (1959). The concept of a "therapeutic milieu." *American Journal of Orthopsychiatry, 29,* 721–736.

Regnery, A. S. (1985). Getting away with murder: Why the juvenile justice system needs an overhaul. *Policy Review, 34,* 1–4.

Roche, B. A., Moore, J., & Gordon, D. A. (1987). Assessment of interpersonal functions: Developing measures to aid the functional family therapist. *Journal of Marital and Family Therapy, 13,* 365–373.

Romig, D. A. (1978). *Justice for our children.* Lexington, MA: Lexington Books.

Rosenheim, M. K. (Ed.). (1976). *Pursuing justice for the child.* Chicago: University of Chicago Press.

Ross, R. R., & Fabiano, E. (1985). *Time to think: A cognitive model of delinquency prevention and rehabilitation.* Unpublished manuscript, Institute of Social Science & Arts, Inc., Ottawa, Ontario, Canada.

Sarason, I. G. (1968). Verbal learning, modeling, and juvenile delinquency. *American Psychologist, 23,* 254–266.

Sarason, I. G., & Ganzer, V. J. (1969). Developing appropriate social behaviors of juvenile delinquents. In J. Krumboltz & C. Thoresen (Eds.), *Behavior counseling cases and techniques* (pp. 178–193). New York: Holt, Rinehart & Winston.

Saranson, I. G., & Ganzer, V. J. (1973). Modeling and group discussion in the rehabilitation of juvenile delinquents. *Journal of Counseling Psychology, 20,* 442–449.

Schoenfeld, C. (1971). A psychoanalytic theory of juvenile delinquency. *Crime and Delinquency, 17,* 469–480.

Scopetta, M. A. (1972). A comparison of modeling approaches to the rehabilitation of institutionalized male adolescent offenders implemented by paraprofessionals (Doctoral dissertation, University of Miami, 1972). *Dissertation Abstracts International, 33,* 2822B. (University Microfilms No. 72-31, 901)

Serketich, W. J., & Dumas, J. E. (1996). The effectiveness of behavioral parent training to modify antisocial behavior in children: A meta-analysis. *Behavior Therapy, 27,* 171–186.

Sholevar, G. P. (1995). Residential treatment. In G. P. Sholevar (Ed.), *Conduct disorders in children and adolescents* (pp. 319–340). Washington, DC: American Psychiatric Press.

Singer, M. (1974). Delinquency and family disciplinary configurations. *Archives of General Psychiatry, 31,* 795–798.

Snyder, J., & Patterson, G. R. (1987). Family interaction and delinquent behavior. In H. C. Quay (Ed.), *Handbook of juvenile delinquency* (pp. 216–243). New York: Wiley.

Spivack, G., & Shure, M. B. (1974). *Social adjustment of young children: A cognitive approach to solving real-life problems.* San Francisco: Jossey-Bass.

Stanton, M. D, & Todd, T. C. (1981a). Engaging "resistant" families in treatment: II. *Family Process, 20,* 261–280.

Stanton, M. D., & Todd, T. C. (1981b). Engaging "resistant" families in tretment: III. *Family Process, 20,* 280–293.

Strasburger, L. H. (1986). Treatment of antisocial syndromes: The therapist's feelings. In W. H. Reid, D. Dorr, J. I. Walker, & J. W. Bonner, III (Eds.), *Unmasking the psychopath* (pp. 191–207). New York: Norton.

Stratton, J. G. (1974). Effects of crises intervention counseling on first or second time 601 or misdemeanor 602 juvenile offenders. *Dissertation Abstracts International, 35,* 525–526.

Stuart, R. B. (1971). Behavioral contracting with families of delinquents. *Journal of Behavior Therapy and Experimental Psychiatry, 2,* 1–11.

Sutherland, E. H., & Cressey, D. R. (1974). *Principles of criminlogy.* Philadelphia: Lippincott.

Szasz, T. (1963). *Law, liberty, and psychiatry.* New York: Macmillan.

Tarter, R. E., Hegedus, A. M., Winsten, N. E., & Alterman, A. I. (1984). Neuropsychological, personality, and family characteristics of physically abused delinquents. *Journal of the American Academy of Child Psychiatry, 23,* 668–674.

Tate, D. C., Repucci, N. D., & Mulvey, E. P. (1995). Violent juvenile delinquents: Treatment effectiveness and implications for future action. *American Psychologist, 50,* 777–781.

Tolan, P. H., Cromwell, R. F., & Brasswell, M. (1986). The application of family therapy to juvenile delinquency: A critical review of the literature. *Family Process, 15,* 619–650.

Tooley, K. (1976). Antisocial behavior and social alienation post-divorce: The "man of the house" and his mother. *American Journal of Orthopsychiatry, 46,* 33–42.

Towberman, D. B. (1994). Psychosocial antecedents of chronic delinquency. *Journal of Offender Rehabilitation, 21,* 151–164.

Tremblay, R. E., Vitaro, F., Bertrand, L., LeBlanc, M., Beauchesne, H., Boileau, H., & David, L. (1992). Parent and child training to prevent early onset of delinquency:

The Montreal longitudinal-experiment study. In J. McCord & R. E. Tremblay (Eds.), *Preventing antisocial behavior: Interventions from birth to adolescence* (pp. 47–138). New York: Guilford Press.

Urbain, E. S., & Kendall, P. C. (1980). Review of social-cognitive problem-solving interventions with children. *Psychological Bulletin, 88,* 109–143.

U.S. Department of Justice. (1976). *Task force on juvenile justice and delinquency prevention.* Washington, DC: U.S. Government Printing Office.

Varenhorst, B. B. (1984). Peer counseling: Past promises, current status, and future directions. In S. D. Brown & R. W. Lent (Eds.), *Handbook of counseling psychology* (pp. 716–750). New York: Wiley.

Varley, W. H. (1984). Behavior modification approaches to the aggressive adolescent. In C. R. Keith (Ed.), *The aggressive adolescent: Clinical perspectives* (pp. 268–298). New York: Free Press.

Vorath, H. H., & Brendtro, L. K. (1974). *Positive peer culture.* Chicago: Aldine.

Wald, P. (1976). Pretrial detention for juveniles. In M. K. Rosenheim (Ed.), *Pursuing justice for the child* (pp. 119–137). Chicago: University of Chicago Press.

Wallerstein, R. S. (1989). The psychotherapy research project of the Menninger Foundation: An overview. *Journal of Consulting and Clinical Psychology, 57,* 195–205.

Webster-Stratton, C. (1990). Enhancing the effectiveness of self-administered videotape parent training for families with conduct-problem children. *Journal of Abnormal Child Psychology, 18,* 479–492.

Weiner, I. B. (1970). *Psychological disturbance in adolescence.* New York: Wiley.

Weiner, I. B. (1982). *Child and adolescent psychopathology.* New York: Wiley.

Weis, J. G., & Sederstrom, J. (1981). *The prevention of serious delinquency: What to do?* Washington, DC: U.S. Government Printing Office.

Whitehead, B. D. (1993, April). Dan Quayle was right. *The Atlantic Monthly,* pp. 47–84.

Widom, C. S. (1989). Does violence beget violence? A critical examination of the literature. *Psychological Bulletin, 106,* 3–28.

Widom, C. S. (1992, October). The cycle of violence. *National Institute of Justice: Research in Brief.* Washington, DC: U.S. Department of Justice.

Williams, D. Y., & Akamatsu, T. J. (1978). Cognitive guidance training with juvenile delinquents: Applicability and generalization. *Cognitive Therapy and Research, 2,* 285–288.

Wolpe, J., & Ascher, L. (1976). Outflanking resistance in a severe obsessional neurosis. In H. Eysenck (Ed.), *Case studies in behavior therapy* (pp. 185–206). London: Routledge & Kegan Paul.

Yalom, D. (1975). *The theory and practice of group therapy.* New York: Basic Books.

Yochelson, S., & Samenow, S. (1976). *The criminal personality: A profile for change* (Vol. 1). New York: Aronson.

Yochelson, S., & Samenow, S. (1977). *The criminal personality: The change process* (Vol. 2). New York: Aronson.

Yoshikawa, H. (1994). Prevention as cumulative protection: Effects of early family support and education on chronic delinquency and its risks. *Psychological Bulletin, 11,* 28–54.

Zigler, E., Taussig, C., & Black, K. (1992). Early childhood intervention: A promising preventative for juvenile delinquency. *American Psychologist, 47,* 997–1006.

INDEX